DICTIONARY
OF AMERICAN
PENOLOGY

DICTIONARY OF AMERICAN PENOLOGY

An Introductory Guide

VERGIL L. WILLIAMS

GREENWOOD PRESS
WESTPORT, CONNECTICUT•LONDON, ENGLAND

LIBRARY
The University of Texas
At San Antonio

Library of Congress Cataloging in Publication Data

Williams, Vergil L
  Dictionary of American penology.

  Bibliography: p.
  Includes index.
  1. Corrections—United States—Dictionaries.
2. Prisons—United States—Dictionaries. 3. Criminal
justice, Administration of—United States—Dictionaries.
I. Title.
HV9304.W54   365'.973   77-94751
ISBN 0-313-20327-X

Library of Congress Catalog Card Number: 77-94751
ISBN: 0-313-20327-X

First published in 1979

Greenwood Press, Inc.
51 Riverside Avenue, Westport, Connecticut 06880

Printed in the United States of America

10 9 8 7 6 5 4 3 2 1

To those women in my life
who ignore my faults

Velma Williams
Colleen Jeffries
Pat Pinkston
Darla Youts

and to

Del and Jean Williams

CONTENTS

PREFACE

This reference work is designed for use by several different types of readers: (1) the college student at an undergraduate level; (2) the graduate student specializing in criminal justice; (3) the concerned citizen interested in prison reform; (4) the careerist in corrections; and (5) inmates in penal institutions.

The undergraduate college student will find a broad range of topics to introduce him to the variety of subjects germane to penology. Professors find that students new to a subject have a rather narrow concept of the possibilities inherent in a field of study. This reference work can serve as an introductory guide to these novice students; by turning the pages, they can quickly learn how diverse the issues and numerous the subtopics in the field are. More important, the new student of penology can use this guide to learn the basic facts in the many areas of inquiry. These basics can serve not only as the meat of short reports, but also as the foundation for longer research papers, since each entry offers references to the literature available on the topic.

The graduate student will find that much time is saved with this type of fact file at hand. This guide pulls together information from more than 400 sources into one reference work and allows the serious student to quickly refresh his memory, for no one can be expected to remember all the details of the many areas of penology. The bibliography should be especially helpful to graduate students who would attain depth in a topic.

The concerned citizen interested in prisons and prison reform can use this guide to identify the issues in the field, to get some feel for reforms that are being instituted in various places in the system, and to locate other groups interested in improving prison conditions. The descriptions of the system are useful for this purpose.

The professional in the field will find this work to be a useful fact file identifying prison locations and capacities, outlining key arguments in controversies, and in general, providing a convenient reference for the hundreds of facts needed in the normal course of business.

Inmates in correctional institutions will find the book useful, particularly the addresses of groups that provide personal assistance. In addition, the inmate, as one who is most affected by correctional policies, can benefit by learning how the procedures and processes have evolved.

The focus of the material is on contemporary penology. History is injected only where the author deems it vital to an understanding of present circumstances. The decade of the 1970s has been an exciting time to compile a work on penology because of the major shifts in ideology in the field. In the 1960s there was a surprising amount of concensus among penologists. Prisons authorities would adopt additional therapeutic programs as fast as they could make legislators understand that rehabilitation in the institution would be a bargain. Fewer people, it was held, would be sent to prison as community-based corrections became ever more popular. As more use was made of probation, parole, and options such as work release, the existing prison system would hold fewer inmates.

The 1970s brought an end to the optimism of the previous decade. Community-based corrections did absorb increasing numbers of offenders, but the prisons did not become half deserted as expected. Only the most violent prisoners were incarcerated. Still, the number of violent inmates seemed to grow yearly, and by the latter part of the decade, the system was overcrowded despite massive efforts to expand the use of community-based programs for nondangerous offenders.

Overcrowding became a serious problem. Self-doubt on the part of many penologists became evident as new areas of controversy arose and the old consensus of the 1960s disappeared. Although riots and the threat of riots stem partly from the overcrowding that was not supposed to have occurred, important factions of penologists and interested observers still believed there should be a moratorium on prison construction. Others, seeing the daily pressures caused by overcrowding, fought for new facilities.

The contemporary focus of this work captures the essence of these ideological disputes and presents the issues in an orderly manner, enabling the reader to make intelligent decisions about which faction he is most compatible with. Slightly more than half of the entries are devoted to the ideological disputes in American penology today, custodial and administrative devices important in assuring the day-to-day safety and security of prisons, significant events in the recent history of American penology, and selected therapeutic and rehabilitation approaches directed toward changing the behavior of the offender. A minute number of the entries provide profiles on the most influential personalities in penology today. These profiles are meant to be representative of the hundreds of influential people who might have been selected for inclusion. Those for whom a full profile entry has not been included have not been neglected; they are the authors of the more than 400 separate pieces of literature that have been used as the basis for the entries found herein. Thus, their work and their influence makes this book possible. The reader will find their names mentioned both in the entries and in the bibliography.

Another category of entries, making up some 36 percent of the length of this book, includes those describing federal and state prison systems and a few entries on individual prisons that are discussed separately because of the publicity they have received over the years. The entries on correctional systems provide basic information on their administrative structures, the location and capacity of individual units, facilities for housing male and female adults and juveniles, and in selected cases, the special problems and prospects of the systems. Whether the entry consists of only a terse statement of basic facts or the basics plus a more elaborate discussion of problems and prospects depends solely on whether material on problems and prospects was available in the prison literature, not on any judgment of the relative importance of a system.

These categories of entries make up the alphabetical entries that constitute about 90 percent of the book. The remaining 10 percent is devoted to appendices, bibliography, and the index. The appendices present addresses of organizations, agencies, and correctional systems as well as statistical data. I have attempted to make the bibliography and index more comprehensive than those in the average book to aid in this work's value as a reference. Although dozens of entries are cross-referenced, I felt an extra-large index would be helpful because fads result in different names being used at different times for the same events. A good index can overcome this problem and enable the reader to find material easily.

The prison literature available has shaped the tone and nature of this work, and thus it seems appropriate to comment on the special characteristics of the resource material available. A decade ago, there were many gaps in the literature. Now, there are relatively few areas where at least some quality research is not available. The more than 400 sources cited in this work reflect that good selection of quality research reports. There is, however, a dearth of current material, and there would be none at all except for *Corrections Magazine*. A newcomer among the prison journals, it has already carved out a place for itself by conducting annual prison population surveys and doing similar reporting to keep us up-to-date on recent developments in American prisons. Even the National Criminal Justice Information and Statistics Service, a subdivision of the U.S. Department of Justice, has come to depend on *Corrections Magazine* for many of the tables it publishes in its annual *Sourcebook of Criminal Justice Statistics*. The reader will find that I have used *Corrections Magazine* as a source in some 15 percent of the entries in order to make the information as timely as possible, and I am grateful to the editors for performing this important function.

Vergil L. Williams

ACKNOWLEDGMENTS

It is largely through the assistance of those with whom I am in daily contact that I was able to complete this work. In this respect I am indebted to my wife, Velma, for her patience and understanding in forgoing those holidays that we might have enjoyed. For their help and encouragement, I thank my colleagues Bill Formby, Keith Leenhouts, Bob Sigler, Ortiz Smykla, and John C. Watkins, Jr.

I am especially grateful to my superiors in the University of Alabama hierarchy who have done so much to encourage the growth and development of the Criminal Justice Program at our university. This group includes Howard B. Gundy, E. Roger Sayers, and Richard Thigpen.

In addition, I extend thanks to Moe Furney, Ginger Nunley, Mary Rickles, and my long-time friend Bev Sigler for typing the manuscript.

John Ortiz Smykla wrote the entry on "coed prisons." He is an authority on this emerging field of inquiry.

DICTIONARY
OF AMERICAN
PENOLOGY

A

ABOLITIONISTS. "Abolitionists"—persons or groups interested in prison reform—represent a wide variety of viewpoints and approaches to prison reform. They share one basic belief, that is, that prisons cannot rehabilitate offenders and that, in some cases, prisons should not even try to rehabilitate them. In general, abolitionists contend that prisons, even if well staffed and adequately funded, can harm offenders.

Although the abolitionist philosophy developed only in the 1960s and early 1970s, its basic argument, that prisons cause harm to offenders, was used by various reform groups more than a century ago. Unlike the contemporary abolitionists, however, earlier reformers, such as John Howard, proposed that correctional institutions could be designed and staffed to be more humane and more therapeutic. In contrast, the abolitionists do not believe that institutionalization can be therapeutic under any circumstances. Some, like David Rothenberg of the Fortune Society (*q.v.*), believe that the move to build new therapeutic prisons has aggravated the problems of corrections rather than solving them. Rothenberg describes the new prisons as "pastel fascism."

Jerome Miller is one of the more active and visible representatives of the abolitionist school of thought. Working within the system, he has been able to put his philosophy into practice and has attracted national attention by closing all juvenile institutions in Massachusetts. Miller later attempted to close juvenile institutions in Pennsylvania. Miller believes that those reformers who are fighting to improve conditions within the institutions will ultimately fail. He maintains that fast, massive social change is the only effective means of reform.

The National Council on Crime and Delinquency (NCCD) (*q.v.*) is the largest and most powerful abolitionist group today. The NCCD has advocated community-based corrections since its founding in 1907 as the National Probation Association. Its 1973 policy statement placed the NCCD in the abolitionist group with its declaration that no "non-dangerous" offender should be incarcerated. The NCCD rather narrowly defines "dangerous" offenders as those with persistent records of violence and evidence of mental disturbance. The group estimates that, under their criteria, only 10 to 20 percent of the some 250,000 offenders now incarcerated would qualify for imprisonment. In clarifying its policy position, the NCCD called, in 1973, for a moratorium on the construction of new correctional institutions until a comprehensive correctional plan could be designed to make maximum use of alternatives to incarceration. The NCCD supports its moratorium position by lobbying and lawsuits to block construction of new federal and state prisons. Milton Rector (*q.v.*), as executive director of NCCD, is a leading spokesman for the abolitionist viewpoint.

The Fortune Society, a large ex-offender organization, maintains that 85 percent of incarcerated offenders could safely be released. The organization's official viewpoint is that incarceration is itself the greatest cause of crime in the United States in that it creates a group of alienated people who have been conditioned to violence by the prison subculture. David Rothenberg, the founder of the society, holds that rehabilitation can be accomplished through community-based corrections programs rather than within the confines of a prison.

Former Attorney General Ramsey Clark is a convert to the abolitionist point of view. Clark once promoted improved prison conditions as a mode of reform, as seen in his *Crime in America* (1970), a classic example of the old-style prison reform. At that time, Clark advocated increased expenditures for both state and federal institutions. Clark has now lost faith in the power of prisons to rehabilitiate offenders and favors handling some 80 percent of currently incarcerated offenders in community-based corrections programs. For another type of reform ideology, see PRAGMATISTS.

REFERENCES: Yitzhak Bakal (ed.), *Closing Correctional Institutions: New Strategies for Youth Services,* 1973; Calvert R. Dodge (ed.), *A Nation Without Prisons: Alternatives to Incarceration,* 1975; Norval Morris, *The Future of Imprisonment,* 1974; Milton G. Rector, "The Extravagance of Imprisonment," *Crime and Delinquency,* 1975; Andrew T. Scull, *Decarceration: Community Treatment and the Deviant —A Radical View,* 1977; Michael S. Serrill, "Critics of Corrections Speak Out," *Corrections Magazine,* 1976; Robert Sommer, *The End of Imprisonment,* 1976.

ADMINISTRATIVE REMEDY PROCEDURE. In April 1974, Federal Bureau of Prisons Director Norman A. Carlson (*q.v.*) initiated an additional grievance procedure for inmates (*q.v.*) throughout the federal prison system. The new procedure provides (1) an additional mechanism for internal resolution of problems at the level in direct contact with the offender; (2) continuing review of administrative policies and decisions; and (3) a written record for use in processing a complaint in the event of subsequent review by a court or a higher administrative authority.

This procedure supplements two long-standing vehicles for processing inmate complaints in federal prisons. Mailboxes are provided for inmates who wish to send uncensored letters to public officials; these mailboxes are still in use in the system. A second vehicle, the "cop out," consists of a printed form which the inmate can use to request an interview with a staff member concerning a particular problem. Neither the mailbox nor the cop out procedure provides a time limit for responding to the request or an assurance that the request will be considered.

In filing a grievance under the administrative remedy procedure, the inmate obtains a printed form from a counselor. The counselor will normally try to resolve the grievance at that time, but if it cannot be resolved on the spot, the form is completed by the inmate and a detachable part of the form provides a receipt signed and dated by the counselor. The inmate holding the receipt can expect a reply within fifteen working days. Typically, a complaint is routed from the counselor who receives the written form to the agent—the warden or associate warden—responsible for processing complaints. The warden's office may then send the complaint to a department head; a complaint about the quality of medical care is sent to the head of medical services. Department heads draft replies on the form containing the original complaint. The reply is reviewed by the warden's office before being signed for return to the inmate.

Inmates who are dissatisfied with the written reply to their grievance have the right to appeal the decision to a regional director of the Federal Bureau of Prisons and can expect a reply to the appeal within twenty working days. Final appeals are sent to Washington to Director Carlson's office. Again, a response is filed within twenty days.

The 23,500 inmates in federal prisons filed 1,900 complaints during the first six months of operation of the new grievance system. Initial decisions resulted in the filing of 486 appeals. The majority of the inmates' complaints asked for an explanation of why they had been denied a furlough (*q.v.*) or a transfer to a community corrections center. Many inmates seemed satisfied with the official explanation of the administrative action and did not appeal. Most inmates use the grievance procedure infrequently, but one filed forty-three complaints within a sixty-day period and appealed ten of the decisions. Although such abuses of the procedure consume a great deal of staff time, they do help to reduce the number of frivolous petitions to federal courts and provide a means for separating the grievances made in good faith from the trivia of chronic complainers.

Critics of the procedure are displeased because it does not utilize outsiders or some disinterested third party to obtain impartial review of complaints. However, the Bureau of Prisons feels that it is working well; outsiders would possibly be more impartial, but would almost certainly be less knowledgable about the corrections system. For further discussion of similar material see GRIEVANCE PRO-CEDURES FOR INMATES and OMBUDSMEN IN PRISON.

REFERENCES: J. E. Baker, *The Right to Participate: Inmate Involvement in Prison Administration,* 1974; R. V. Denenberg and Tia Denenberg, "Prison Grievance Procedures: A National Survey of Programs Underway," *Corrections Magazine,* 1975; Virginia McArthur, "Inmate Grievance Mechanisms: A Survey of 209 American Prisons," *Federal Probation,* 1974; Linda R. Singer and J. Michael Keating, *Grievance Mechanisms in American Corrections: The State of the Art,* 1975.

ALABAMA CORRECTIONAL SYSTEM. The three major components of the Alabama correctional system are the State Board of Corrections, which is responsible for the operation of all adult institutions; the State Board of Pardons and Paroles, which provides both probation and parole services for adults; and the Department of Youth Services, which is responsible for operating juvenile training schools, providing consulting services to community-based programs, and establishing certification standards for juvenile probation officers employed by county departments.

All persons aged sixteen or over who are convicted of a felony in Alabama are committed to the State Board of Corrections for execution of their sentences. The adult institutions of the state have a rated capacity of 2,600 inmates but their population reached 5,100 in August 1975. At that time, U.S. District Court Judge Frank M. Johnson banned the acceptance of any more prisoners into the system by issuing a court order enumerating forty-four standards that had to be achieved in order to satisfy the court that inmate living standards were meeting minimum requirements.

The State Board of Corrections estimates that some $200 million will be needed over the next several years to bring the facilities for adult offenders up to the minimum constitutional standards specified in Judge Johnson's court order. While the prison systems of Arkansas, Florida, Louisiana, Mississippi, New York City, and Virginia have also had federal court rulings against them, Judge Johnson's ruling is believed to be the first to provide specific guidelines on services that the prison system must provide for inmates in terms of standards for minimum living space, number of staff members and racial composition of staff members, visiting privileges, classification procedures, personal hygiene, and food service. The court order provided for a committee consisting of thirty-nine citizens to oversee implementation of the standards. The committee was authorized to hire a consultant at the same rate of pay as the state commissioner of corrections. The consultant hired was George Beto, a professor at Sam Houston University in Texas and a former director of the Texas Department of Corrections.

Adult institutions in the state include (1) Draper Correctional Center at Elmore with a rated capacity of 600; (2) G. K. Fountain Correctional Center near Atmore with a rated capacity of 534; (3) Number Four Honor Camp near Montgomery with a normal capacity of 100; (4) Medical and Diagnostic Center near Montgomery with a normal capacity of 440; (5) Frank Lee Youth Center at Deatsville with a normal capacity of 200; (6) State Cattle Ranch at Greensboro with a rated capacity of fifty; and (7) the state's institution for adult female prisoners, the Julia Tutwiler Prison for Women at Wetumpka, with a normal capacity of 250.

The State Board of Corrections and the State Highway Department jointly operate six road camps scattered throughout the state. The average population of each road camp is fifty adult males.

The State Board of Corrections has been experimenting with work release (*q.v.*) centers since opening its first center in April 1972 at Elmore as one way of alleviating the overcrowded adult institutions. The board has since opened additional centers at Alexander City, Atmore, Birmingham, Childersburg, Mobile, and Wetumpka. The centers provide services for a small inmate population ranging from seventeen to fifty adult males; the Wetumpka Center handles thirty-six adult females.

Juvenile institutions in the state are operated under the authority of the Department of Youth Services. The facilities include (1) Chalkville Campus in Birmingham for 108 girls twelve to sixteen years of age; (2) Mount Meigs Campus near Montgomery with space for 250 boys fifteen years of age or older; and (3) Roebuck Campus in Birmingham with space for 240 boys aged twelve to fourteen years. Unlike the adult institutions, the juvenile facilities have not been overcrowded. The three institutions have space for 598 youths, but their average population in 1975 was only 260. The Department of Youth Services plans to convert all three facilities to coeducational status in the near future and to open several diagnostic and evaluation units throughout the state.

The overall prison population in the state is growing. On January 1, 1977, the prison population was 3,096, with 2,300 additional sentenced prisoners in county jails awaiting space in the prison system. By January 1, 1978, the prison system held 3,437, with 2,626 additional prisoners in county jails awaiting space in the prison system. This is a 12 percent increase.

REFERENCES: American Correctional Association, *Directory,* 1975–1976 edition: Steve Gettinger, "Alabama Under Strict Court Order to Upgrade Entire Prison System," *Corrections Magazine,* 1976; Michael Serrill, "Prison Population Rises Again, But at a Slower Rate," *Corrections Magazine,* 1978.

ALASKA CORRECTIONAL SYSTEM. Alaska presents unique challenges to its correctional administrators. As a sparsely populated state, it has a sparsely populated system of institutions scattered over awesome expanses of territory. As a result of particular problems of geography and population, the prisons are in many ways similar to the county jails of other states; all Alaska prisons hold both felons and misdemeanants. Most of the small institutions must house juveniles and females as well as adult males. As of January 1978, the population of the entire system was 689 inmates—a number smaller than the jail count in many single city and county jails in other states. Alaska, along with Vermont, is one of only two states operating without a maximum security prison.

The Alaska Division of Corrections, in operation since the U.S. Bureau of Prisons turned the facilities over to the new state in 1959, operates with some 350 employees and a budget in excess of $10 million. Its McLaughlin Youth Center on the outskirts of Anchorage was opened in 1968. The center has a normal capacity of 120 male and female juveniles ages 13 to 18. Prisons for adults include the Anchorage Correctional Center in Anchorage, which was opened in 1953 with a normal capacity of 90 males ages 18 and above. The nearby Anchorage Correctional Center-Annex was opened in 1973 to hold 123 inmates ages 18 and up. The Eagle River Correctional Center at Eagle River opened in 1974 with a normal capacity of 180 males ages 18 and above. The Fairbanks Correctional Center at Fairbanks was opened in 1967 with room for 90 male and female inmates ages 12 and above. The Juneau Correctional Center at Juneau was opened in 1969 with a normal capacity of 90 male and female offenders ages 12 and above. The Ketchikan Correctional Center at Ketchikan was opened in 1938 with a normal capacity of 36 male and female inmates ages 12 and above. The Palmer Correctional Center at Palmer was opened in 1962 with a normal capacity of 75 males ages 18 and above.

In order to provide detention facilities in the widely spread outlying areas and suitable facilities for inmates with long sentences, the division has a number of contractual arrangements. Thirty-five bush jails and one city jail contract with the division for temporary detention services; long-term inmates are placed in either federal prisons or prisons in other states that are better equipped for this type of inmate. The division is also responsible for the probationers and parolees in the state. As in other states, the minorities (Indians, Aleuts, and Eskimos) make up a disproportionate percentage of the inmate population. These minority group members, the original natives of the state, now constitute 20 percent of the total state population, but some 50 percent of the inmate population.

Unlike many other states, Alaska did not inherit a collection of ancient prisons and long-standing prison conditions. The division is making good use of this unusual opportunity to make a fresh start as is reflected in the architecture and programs of the state's newest facility, Eagle River Correctional Center, completed in 1973. The center houses a maximum of only 180 adult males in a modern setting that makes security measures unobtrusive. Correctional officers in the system are not armed, mail is not censored, nor is there a limit on the number of letters an inmate can receive or send. Visiting periods are frequent, but the long distances often prohibit frequent contact with friends and relatives. Although no conjugal visits are permitted, officials do send some inmates home for short furloughs (*q.v.*). The center utilizes work release (*q.v.*) and education release programs. Correctional officers receive training in transactional analysis (*q.v.*).

The types of rehabilitation programs being established in Alaska are geared to the special problems of the correctional clientele. Although the natives represent a disproportionate share of the prison population, they commit less serious offenses than the Caucasians. Generally, the natives are incarcerated for petty offenses related to alcohol consumption. Alcohol, which was introduced in the region by fur traders, has had a severe impact on the native culture, and until the offense of public drunkenness was abolished in 1972, the prison system was crowded. Although the decriminalization of the condition of alcoholism seems a logical approach, problems do remain. State officials find that if police do not pick up drunks, they freeze to death in the snow or fall into the ocean and drown. Corrections officials realize that treatment programs have not yet been developed. The Division of Corrections has created its own alcohol treatment unit at Palmer Correctional Center in an attempt to alleviate the problem.

Despite the relatively large number of native inmates and the virtually all-Caucasian correctional staff, there is little racial strife in the system. The pay scale for correctional personnel is roughly equivalent to that of the federal system, considering the higher cost of living in the state. The better trained natives attracted into the career field often leave to accept higher paying jobs with other employers, and the system is left with fewer native employees than it would like despite sincere efforts to recruit minorities.

The prison population in Alaska is growing rapidly with a 27 percent increase from 543 on January 1, 1977, to 689 on January 1, 1978.

REFERENCES: American Correctional Association, *Directory, 1975–1976* edition; R. V. Denenberg, "Alaska," *Corrections Magazine,* 1974; Michael Serrill, "Prison Population Rises Again, But at a Slower Rate," *Corrections Magazine,* 1978.

ALCATRAZ. Alcatraz, one of the maximum security prisons in the federal prison system and one of America's most famous penal institutions, was closed, on the order of Attorney General Robert F. Kennedy, in 1963 because of its rundown condition. It was replaced by a new facility at Marion, Illinois.

Alcatraz is located on an outcropping of rock about one mile off San Francisco's Fisherman's Wharf. It received its name in 1769 after being sighted by a Spanish ship and designated "Isla de Los Alcatraces," or "Island of the Pelicans." Because of its ideal location, it became the site of a prison in 1863 when it was used to hold Civil War prisoners. Following the Civil War, it was used for a time to hold Indian prisoners. Beginning in 1909, Alcatraz became a maximum security facility in the new federal prison system.

The island prison was believed to be escape proof because of the difficulty in swimming the mile to San Francisco in the tricky ocean currents. Although a few escapees remain missing, it is believed that they drowned. A number of well-known criminals considered high-escape risks served sentences in Alcatraz. Al Capone spent several years as a federal prisoner in the institution as did George "Machine Gun" Kelly. Robert Stroud, better known as the "Birdman of Alcatraz," spent time in Alcatraz after killing a guard at Leavenworth. Some criminals became notorious while serving sentences at Alcatraz, i.e., Clarence V. Carnes, known as the "Choctaw Kid," participated in an infamous riot at the prison on May 2, 1946. Carnes was the only inmate of the six participating who survived the riot; three of the instigators were killed during the rebellion, and two others were hanged for killing two guards during the incident. Carnes served a total of eighteen years in the prison before being paroled.

In 1973, the National Park Service began conducting public tours of the institution that are scheduled to last through 1978. As a popular part of the Golden Gate National Recreation Area, the facility attracts about 1,500 tourists daily for a 150-minute excursion to the prison. In its first three years, more than a million tourists paid $1.69 million for the popular tour.

REFERENCES: Don DeNevi, *Alcatraz '46: The Anatomy of a Classic Prison Tragedy,* 1974; Ted Needham and Howard Needham, *Alcatraz,* 1976.

AMERICAN CORRECTIONAL ASSOCIATION. This professional organization has an individual membership of 10,000 and thirty-eight affiliated organizations whose membership represents many thousands of persons interested in some aspect of corrections. Its officers and Board of Directors are elected biannually by direct mail vote of its membership. The association is supported primarily by membership dues, with additional income derived from contract consultant services, projects supported by grants from the federal government and private foundations, sale of its publications, convention registration, advertising and exhibits, and contributions. Membership is open to anyone interested in corrections at prices ranging from $5.00 per year for an associate member to $300.00 for a life membership. Associate membership is recommended for volunteers in corrections or for persons not employed in correctional work, who have an interest in corrections. Membership applications should be sent to:

Membership Office
American Correctional Association
4321 Hartwick Road, Suite L-208
College Park, Maryland 20740

Members receive the *American Journal of Correction,* a bimonthly publication containing articles by leaders in corrections, news from affiliated organizations, and information on new developments and techniques in correctional practice. Members may attend a variety of conferences, workshops and institutes conducted by the association. Each August, the association conducts an annual Congress of Correction which offers lectures, seminars, workshops, and exhibits at various locations. Recent dates and locations for the Congress are as follows:

1977	Milwaukee, Wisconsin
1978	Portland, Oregon
1979	Philadelphia, Pennsylvania
1980	San Diego, California

Members also have access to a variety of the association's publications covering all areas of correctional services: the *Manual of Correctional Standards,* a comprehensive guide to prison operation that is widely used by prison administrators; the annual *Directory of Correctional Institutions and Agencies,* which supplies names, addresses, telephone numbers, and basic information about correctional agencies throughout the United States and Canada; and the *Directory,* which is updated and published each fall. Members also have an opportunity to become directly involved in the association's efforts to design model legislation for corrections.

The American Correctional Association was founded in 1870 as the National Prison Association; the name was later changed to the American Prison Association. In 1954, it became the American Correctional Association, a name which better conveys the broad range of its membership's interests, as reflected in the following list of the association's affiliates:

Alabama Council on Crime and Delinquency
American Association of Correctional Psychologists
American Association of Correctional Training Personnel
American Association of Wardens and Superintendents
American Correctional Chaplains' Association
American Correctional Food Service Association
Association for Correctional Research and Statistics
Association of Juvenile Compact Administrators
Association of Paroling Authorities
Association of State Correctional Administrators
Association on Programs for Female Offenders
Central States Corrections Association
Colorado Correctional Association
Correctional Education Association
Correctional Industries Association
Correctional Service Federation—U.S.A.
Federal Probation Officers Association
Florida Council on Crime and Delinquency

International Halfway House Association
Iowa Corrections Association
Kansas Correctional Association
Kentucky Council on Crime and Delinquency, Inc.
Maryland Probation, Parole and Corrections Association
Middle Atlantic States Conference of Correction
Missouri Correction Association
National Association of State Juvenile Delinquency Program
    Administrators
National Association of Training Schools and Juvenile Agencies
National Correctional Recreation Association
National Council on Crime and Delinquency
National Jail Association
National Juvenile Detention Association
Nebraska Correctional Association
Parole and Probation Compact Administrators' Association
Southern States Correctional Association
Texas Corrections Association
The Salvation Army
Volunteers of America
Western Correctional Association

Information about membership in any of the affiliated organizations can be obtained by writing to the American Correctional Association.

REFERENCES: American Correctional Association, *Membership* (pamphlet, no date).

ARCHITECTURE. Correctional philosophy and prison architecture have been ultimately related since the Quakers developed a definitive rationale for imprisonment in 1787. At that time, Dr. Benjamin Rush met with a small group of interested reformers to discuss a new program for the treatment of criminals. Their discussions resulted in a recommendation that criminals serve sentences as their punishment rather than being subjected to capital or corporal punishment as was the established custom. As a result of Rush's recommendations, the Walnut Street Jail in Philadelphia was remodeled in 1790. In remodeling the jail, the architects incorporated this new penal philosophy into the structure by designing cells that would hold convicts for a period of years rather than only until they could be tried and given corporal or capital punishment.

The 1787 reform ideology has made architects and architecture a dominant force in penology since that time. The durability of prisons constructed with concrete and steel produces institutions that ordinarily last for more than a century and lock correctional personnel into a philosophy of corrections shaped by previous generations of reformers. The architectural setting of prisons built decades ago limits and shapes the changes in treatment programming that can be accomplished by contemporary reformers.

One early architect, John Haviland, exerted a lasting influence on the style of prison architecture in America. Haviland designed Eastern Penitentiary (*q.v.*) in Philadelphia. When this institution opened in 1829, its architectural features gave the Quakers their first opportunity to fully test their theories of corrections in a facility designed expressly for that purpose. The Quakers felt that convicts should be completely isolated from each other and from persons outside the prison. These inmates served time as punishment for their crimes in surroundings made fearsome and forbidding. Their isolation from society, the strict discipline of the prison, and the austere surroundings all fostered the Quakers' desire that convicts have ample time to reflect on their crimes and do penance. Haviland designed Eastern State Penitentiary to resemble a medieval castle with massive stone structures enclosed by an imposing wall; this building style has changed very little over the years.

The Quaker ideology of totally isolating each individual inmate from contact with other inmates came to be known as the Pennsylvania System of Prison Discipline (*q.v.*). Following the first attempts to test the idea in the individual cells constructed for that purpose when the Walnut Street Jail was remodeled in 1790, reformers in other states became intrigued by this concept. John Cray, an architect-builder in New York State, designed and built Auburn prison with the help of Elam Lynds, Auburn's first warden, and of convict labor. When Auburn opened in 1817, Lynds and Cray attempted to use the individual isolation approach of the Pennsylvania system by confining inmates in individual cells around the clock. However, the cells at Auburn were much too small to hold convicts for long periods of time, and soon insanity and suicide became a major problem. Inmates were then given work to do in their cells, but even this expedient for relieving the tedium of life in the tiny cells did not prevent an alarming number of suicides.

Lynds and Cray ultimately made some modifications in the isolation approach used in the Pennsylvania system. Inmates were taken out of their cells during the day to work in congregate shops under a strict rule of silence. At night, they were isolated in individual cells. Allowing the convicts to spend a few hours every day away from their cells to work beside other convicts helped the prisoners to maintain their sanity. More significantly for prison architecture, the arrangement produced economic benefits that eventually made the new Auburn system (*q.v.*) the model for American penology. The Auburn inmates made the prison economically self-sufficient by virtue of the efficiency of the congregate shop. Businessmen from the nearby city of Auburn contracted with the prison to obtain the labor for their various manufacturing enterprises. Inmate labor in congregate shops proved much more profitable for the prison than labor performed by individual inmates in cells under the Pennsylvania system. The Pennsylvania and Auburn systems became alternative, competing models of penology, and the relative merits of each system were debated by penologists for decades. Because of its economic efficiency, the Auburn system eventually became the most widely used model of penology in America.

Contemporary prison architecture reflects elements of both the Pennsylvania and Auburn systems. The Quaker concept of long-term incarceration as punishment is reflected in the facilities built to hold inmates over extended periods of time. While modern penologists do not necessarily believe that institutions should look fearsome and forbidding, most penal facilities have this appearance because of their large size, the concrete and steel used to make them escape proof, and the sparseness of their surroundings (lack of funds do not permit expenditures on aesthetic features). The large size is a Quaker contribution to penology inasmuch as they first designed prison facilities to hold prisoners from all over the state rather than from city or county governmental units. Evidence of the Auburn system of penology is still found in most prisons. The congregate shops of prison industries keep a portion of the inmates, who work six days a week, occupied away from their cells for a part of the day. While the rule of silence is not enforced in modern Auburn system prisons, inmate labor is still used to make the prison financially self-sufficient.

One aspect of contemporary prison architecture can be confusing. A particular prison may be classified as maximum security, medium security, or minimum security. These terms refer only to the extent to which architectural features are incorporated to make the prison escape proof; such terms should not be confused with the treatment classifications of individual inmates. Treatment classifications attempt to classify inmates in terms of the propects for their rehabilitation; security grades provide a guide to the amount of security needed to prevent escape. For example, an intelligent inmate can be both an escape risk and an excellent prospect for rehabilitation because of his mental abilities; conversely, a moron may not have sufficient intelligence to effect an escape from any kind of prison but may not be a good prospect for rehabilitation.

The architecture of a maximum security prison normally incorporates the use of "inside" cells. Inside cells are constructed back to back facing the walls that support the roof of the building. The building is surrounded by walls or wire fences. An inmate who manages to break out of an inside cell is still locked inside the building containing the cells; hence, to complete the escape, the escapee must break out of the building and scale a wall or fence under the surveillance of guard towers.

A medium security prison has fewer security safeguards. Cell construction often follows the "outside cell" technique wherein the building walls form the back wall of rows of cells facing an inside corridor. An inmate could gain access to the prison yard by breaking through the back of the cell or through a cell window overlooking the yard, but he would still be confronted with the task of getting past a fence watched from guard towers.

Minimum security institutions do not depend on locked doors or fences to keep inmates from escaping. Inmates who leave these institutions without being authorized to do so are considered "walkaways" and not "escapees." The ultimate force used to prevent walkaways is simply the inmate's knowledge that he will ultimately be captured and will be returned to a less pleasant maximum security type of facility. Minimum security prisons use dormitories instead of cells, or, in some cases, rooms that provide the inmate with some privacy and that are locked only by the inmate for purposes of safeguarding his possessions. For related information, see AUBURN SILENT SYSTEM, NATIONAL CLEARINGHOUSE FOR CRIMINAL JUSTICE PLANNING AND ARCHITECTURE, and PENNSYLVANIA SYSTEM OF PRISON DISCIPLINE.

REFERENCES: Harry Elmer Barnes, *The Evolution of Penology in Pennsylvania: A Study in American Social History,* 1968 (1927); Donald R. Cressey (ed.), *The Prison: Studies in Institutional Organization and Change,* 1966; Howard B. Gill, "Correctional Philosophy and Architecture," in Robert M. Carter and others (eds.), *Correctional Institutions,* 1972; Norman Johnston, *The Human Cage: A Brief History of Prison Architecture,* 1973; William G. Nagel, *The New Red Barn: A Critical Look at the Modern American Prison,* 1973.

ARGOT. The word "argot," officially defined as the specialized vocabulary and idioms of those in the same work or way of life, originates from the French thieves' jargon. Thus, it is appropriate that a significant body of the institutional literature relies heavily on prison argot to identify and define the parameters of male and female inmate subcultures. Academic sociologists, who have conducted much of the research into the nature and meaning of inmate subcultures *(q.v.)*, have identified an array of typologies with which to classify the social relationships of inmates. In constructing these typologies, the researchers identified the social types by using inmate argot rather than neutral labels, probably because they realized that the inmates use the typologies in the normal course of their daily associations.

Donald Clemmer, a staff sociologist at Menard Penitentiary in Chester, Illinois, conducted research on the nature of the male prison subculture during the Depression of the 1930s. The work stemming from that research was published as *The Prison Community* (1940) and became a highly respected treatise on the subject of inmate subculture. *The Prison Community* triggered interest in the subject matter among other academicians and became the standard point of reference for the body of prison subculture literature that is still being formulated. Clemmer commented extensively on the nature and use of prison argot. One of his conclusions was that it was not intended to be a secret language since staff members commonly used it in talking with inmates or with one another, reverting to more traditional language in the presence of outsiders. An appendix in *The Prison Community* provides a rather complete dictionary of argot terms in vogue at the time of his research. Some of those terms have dropped out of usage, but researchers in later years have remarked on the general durability and universality of the argot expressions. The word "rat," for example, as readily connotes an informer in today's correctional institution as it did among Clemmer's research subjects.

Clemmer's techniques of personal observation of inmates, concentration on prison argot because language transmits much of what we know about culture, and illustration of points with direct quotations from inmates were adopted by later researchers. The resulting body of literature is a colorful mix of formal sociological jargon relieved by earthy prison argot quotations to illustrate theoretical constructs.

A more recent researcher into the inmate subculture is Gresham M. Sykes, author of *The Society of Captives* (1971). His work includes an intriguing development of inmate typologies in terms of argot roles. Sykes identifies a social type known as a "Center Man" in the New Jersey State Maximum Security Prison at Trenton, where he conducted his research. A Center Man, known as a Square John in other prisons, rejects the antisocial values of the inmate subculture and attempts to associate with prison staff members. The origin and usage of this one term among the many Sykes studied illustrate the importance of argot in inmate subculture studies.

Inmates, recognizing a recurring pattern of behavior among certain segments of the prison population, originated the term Center Man for the inmate who hung around the control center of the prison in an attempt to engage staff members in conversation. The term obviously has a negative connotation because the value system of the inmate subculture prohibits cooperation and/or communication with staff members on a voluntary basis. An outside observer noting the use of the term is able to understand not only the language of the inmate group, but something about the sub rosa value system as well. A study of the common characteristics of a number of Center Men gives an understanding of how different offenders adjust to prison life, some predictability as to how a particular offender might adapt to the institution routine, and some insight into appropriate strategies for controlling the inmate population.

By grasping the behavior patterns associated with argot roles, it is not difficult to stay abreast of different argot terms encountered in different times and places. When one comes to understand the pattern of behavior associated with Sykes' "Real Man," the inmate who lives up to the tenets of the inmate code of behavior, it is readily apparent that the role expectations of the "Solid Convict" in an Alabama prison are identical.

REFERENCES: Donald Clemmer, *The Prison Community*, 1958; Gresham M. Sykes, *The Society of Captives*, 1971; Vergil L. Williams and Mary Fish, *Convicts, Codes and Contraband: The Prison Life of Men and Women*, 1974.

ARIZONA CORRECTIONAL SYSTEM. The state system consists of four adult facilities, three institutions for juveniles, and six halfway houses. In June 1975, almost 2,300 adult inmates and slightly more than 400 juveniles were incarcerated in Arizona. By far the largest institution in the state is Arizona State Prison at Florence, a facility that was known as the Yuma Territorial Prison before Arizona became a state. It houses most of the adult inmates in the state (1,800 men and almost 100 women). Women inmates are housed in a separate ten-acre complex near the men's division of the prison.

Smaller institutions in the system are Fort Grant Training Center at

Wilcox, holding about 300 adult men, and Safford Conservation Center, housing 165 adult males. Adobe Mountain School, near Phoenix, is a coeducational facility holding more than 200 juveniles. The Alpine Conservation Center is home for about 100 boys, and Arizona Youth Center, near Tucson, holds 145 boys.

In the 1970s, the most pressing problem of the system was overcrowding. Both adult and juvenile institutions in the state have populations well above their rated capacity. Part of the reason why the inmate population is growing faster than new prison construction can provide new space is simply that Arizona is one of the fastest growing states in the nation. Another factor is that the Arizona courts are handing down longer sentences than they did in the past. In recent years, the legislature has established long mandatory minimum sentences for a number of crimes. Parole is granted cautiously. The minimum average length of sentences is 8.7 years and the maximum average is 11.5 years.

Administrative control of parole in the state is vested in the Arizona Department of Corrections under the deputy director for community services. Some forty-seven parole officers oversee about 2,500 adult and juvenile parolees with an average caseload of forty. Probation in the state, with 6,000 adult and 3,000 juvenile probationers, is administered by each of the fourteen counties in the state.

Arizona is one of only eight states in which the prison population declined in 1977. Between January 1, 1977, and January 1, 1978, the prison population declined 9 percent from 3,072 to 2,806. This decline provides the officials in the state with a welcome respite after annual increases in the prison population in most years of this decade; however, the recent decline is not sufficient to reduce worries about prison overcrowding.

REFERENCES: Edgar May, "Profile/Arizona," *Corrections Magazine,* 1975; Michael Serrill, "Prison Population Rises Again, But at a Slower Rate," *Corrections Magazine,* 1978.

ARKANSAS CORRECTIONAL SYSTEM. Institutions in Arkansas are administered by two separate agencies. Adult institutions are operated under the authority of the Department of Corrections, and juvenile institutions under the aegis of the Department of Social and Rehabilitation Service, Division of Rehabilitation.

The majority of adult males are confined in two prison farm complexes: Cummins Unit and Tucker Unit. Cummins Unit, located at Grady, is the largest and oldest facility in Arkansas. The original Cummins Unit was opened in 1842 and the new facility was completed in 1934. Cummins is designed for a normal capacity of 1,117 male felons, but has been overcrowded in recent years, with an average population of 1,450 in 1974. Tucker Unit at Tucker is a smaller complex used for males under twenty-one years of age. With a normal capacity of 325, it has also been overcrowded, with an average population of 448 in 1974. The Women's Unit, with room for 134 female felons, is located at Pine Bluff. Unlike the male institutions, it has been operating below capacity with an average population of eighty in 1974.

State Commissioner of Corrections Terrell Don Hutto opened five smaller community correctional centers in 1975. A work release center at Benton operates at full capacity with sixty male offenders; the pre-release center, also at Benton, operates at its full 100 capacity of adult males. Benton's complex includes an alcohol/narcotic center designed to serve forty males. The Blytheville work release center, also operating at full capacity, is located at Luxora. A small livestock production center serving ten males is located at Booneville.

Incarcerated juveniles are served by a reception and classification center at Benton where juveniles up to age eighteen are committed for evaluation before being placed in one of the state's three training schools. Youths placed in a training school are committed for an indefinite period of time, with the average length of stay being six months. Two juvenile male institutions, both bearing the name Arkansas Training School for Boys and both of the same size, are located at Pine Bluff and at Wrightsville. The Pine Bluff institution was opened in 1917, and the Wrightsville facility in 1928. The Arkansas Training School for Girls, opened in 1917, is located at Alexander and has been operating slightly below its 121 capacity.

The recent history of the Arkansas prison system is replete with difficulties that began to be widely publicized with a January 28, 1968, story in the *New York Times* while Tom Murton was superintendent of the state's prison system. Murton was appointed to his position by Governor Winthrop Rockefeller in February 1967 to carry out Rockefeller's prison reform campaign promises. Murton, acting on statements from long-time inmates in the system, created extensive national and international publicity when he publicly stated that a number of inmates had been shot or beaten to death in the past and were buried in unmarked graves on prison farm property. In the furor of media coverage that resulted when several bodies were indeed dug up at Cummins, many of the improper prison practices that Murton had been trying to end for several months were brought to the attention of the nation. Murton, on the basis of statements from inmates, believed that the bodies were those of inmates murdered over the years by the armed inmate guards who constituted the bulk of the staff in the system. State Police investigating the discovery of the bodies, however, concluded that Murton had discovered no more than a pauper's graveyard. Murton, charging that a coverup was being staged because of political pressures, was fired on March 7, 1968, and the investigation was dropped.

Despite the end of Murton's controversial tenure as a reform penologist, reforms are continuing in the Arkansas system. The state's correctional system was the object of one of the first of the sweeping court decisions in recent years when a federal court in *Holt* v. *Sarver* (1969), declared virtually all of the system to be unconstitutional because of overcrowding and primitive living conditions.

The Arkansas prison system experienced moderate population growth with a 1 percent increase from 2,445 to 2,466 inmates between January 1, 1977, and January 1, 1978.

REFERENCES: American Correctional Association, *Directory,* 1975–1976 edition; Thomas O. Murton and Joe Hyams, *Accomplices to the Crime; The Arkansas Prison Scandal,* 1969; Michael Serrill, "Prison Population Rises Again, But at a Slower Rate," *Corrections Magazine,* 1978.

ASKLEPIEION THERAPY. Martin Groder, a psychiatrist, developed this treatment approach while working at the federal penitentiary at Marion, Illinois, from 1968 to 1972. Asklepieion was selected as the name of the approach by inmates participating in the Marion program; the term, located by inmates in a medical textbook, comes from the name of a temple built to honor Asklepios, the Greek god of healing.

The technique, which has been categorized as a variety of behavior modification, is a self-help program that Groder developed by combining two approaches: transactional analysis (*q.v.*) techniques associated with the name of Eric Berne, and the group-living "attack therapy" developed in Synanon (*q.v.*), the California program for treatment of drug addicts.

Asklepieion therapy, as practiced at Marion, involves placing twenty-five to thirty-five men in a separate living unit where, without being cut off from the rest of the prison population, they can receive group exposure to the positive philosophy taught in transactional analysis under the leadership of a role-model. Groder initially served as the role-model for the group (the function is often performed by an experienced inmate in the treatment group). The program is normally run by inmates after its inception. The group-living arrangement allows program participants to practice the basics of transactional analysis on one another: the analysis of transactions or units of social exchange. It also facilitates the holding of nightly discussion groups wherein inmates' criticisms of one another can become heated and abrasive in the manner of Synanon groups.

Groder feels that many inmates and staff members dislike Asklepieon therapy because it challenges their usual patterns of behavior. Nonetheless, it is an effective technique; Groder points out that the first twenty-five men to be released from prison after spending two years in the program have not committed any new crimes. Stuart Saken, current director of the Asklepieion unit at Marion, reports that the recidivism (*q.v.*) rate is now about 10 percent of the 156 program participants released.

Some of the program participants have started Asklepieion groups in other prisons either before their release or after they were paroled. Ken Windes, for example, was transferred to the federal correctional institution at Terminal Island in Los Angeles where he started a program shortly before being offered parole. He delayed acceptance of parole for a year to stay on and act as a role-model for the new program. After his release on parole, he joined the Asklepieion Foundation, which Groder established in 1970 to provide a new mode of therapy, and he still works for the foundation, starting transactional analysis groups in other prisons. Groder has recommended paroled inmates as role-models to start Asklepieion programs in several state prisons. For discussion of the basic elements of the treatment techniques, see SYNANON and TRANSACTIONAL ANALYSIS THERAPY. For further information on Martin Groder's role in corrections, see FEDERAL CENTER FOR CORRECTIONAL RESEARCH.

REFERENCES: Steve Gettinger, "Dr. Martin Groder: An Angry Resignation," *Corrections Magazine*, 1975.

ATTICA CORRECTIONAL FACILITY. A maximum security institution for adult male offenders, Attica is part of the New York State correctional system (*q.v.*). It became one of the best known prisons in America in September 1971 when millions of Americans watched comprehensive television coverage of a bloody inmate uprising that lasted four days. When the prison was retaken from inmates with an assault by the state police, the result was ten hostages and twenty-nine inmates killed. The news media further stirred public alarm when it initially reported that inmates had carried out their threats to slaughter the hostages if attacked; within twenty-four hours, however, it became apparent that the hostages had been killed by gunfire from the assault force. In the months of followup investigation that ensued, Attica became a household word. To liberal-minded people, it symbolized government misuse of power and a highly visible token of a corrupt society that produced an inadequate correctional system; those at the opposite end of the ideological spectrum, noting the revolutionary rhetoric of the inmates and their attorneys, took it as a sign of the growing power of a Communist conspiracy.

Ironically, Attica prison was constructed to put an end to prison uprisings, following the nation's experience of a wave of such uprisings in the late 1920s. Both Clinton and Auburn prisons in New York State had serious riots in 1929. Attica, opened in 1931 following investigations of the 1929 prison riots, was acclaimed to be the ultimate in prison design. At a cost exceeding $9 million, it was clearly the most expensive prison ever built and it was thought to be the most secure prison in the world. The wall alone cost $1,275,000; it enclosed fifty-five acres, and was thirty feet high and extended twelve feet below ground level. The separated cellblocks had individual cells for 500 men in each of its four areas. Fourteen gun towers were constructed on top of the expensive, two-foot thick wall to provide perimeter security.

The institution has changed little over the years; currently, there are eighteen buildings inside the walls, five of which are cellblocks. The four main cellblocks form a square surrounding a huge open area that is divided into four exercise yards by narrow corridors called tunnels running from one cellblock directly across to the cellblock on the opposite side. The middle of the open space, where the four tunnels meet, is a security area known as "Times Square" and is designed to seal off the cellblocks from one another as part of the "divide and conquer" strategy of prison security. The cellblocks, still holding some 500 men each, are divided into twelve groups called "companies." A fifth cellblock, constructed in 1966, sits apart from the large cellblocks forming the square around the exercise yards. Service buildings are located outside of the square formed by the four cellblocks; a laundry building contains a bathhouse where inmates shower twice weekly. Other buildings house mess areas, disciplinary units, metal trades shops, the garage, the auditorium-chapel, the school, clothing issue shops, and the powerhouse.

The annual budget for Attica exceeds $8 million. Slightly more than 60 percent of that sum is used to pay the salaries of corrections officers; 25 percent is used for general administrative and maintenance costs; and less than 14 percent is spent for medical supplies, food, inmate clothing, and inmate wages. As in most maximum security prisons, the correctional staff (almost 400 people) is organized as a semimilitary force and is conceptually apart from the almost 150 employees making up the "civilian" staff. Civilians work in education, industry, medicine, religion, counseling, parole, plant operation, and clerical capacities; corrections officers are concerned mainly with the custody and security aspects of the prison.

Attica inmates characteristically spend fourteen or more hours per day in their cells. Those with assignments to attend school or work normally are out of their cells about five hours per day for that purpose. Recreation in an exercise yard is limited to sixty to ninety minutes on weekdays, but slightly more time is allowed on weekends. Each of three meals requires the inmate to be out of his cell for only twenty to forty minutes. Other special occasions for being out of cells are normally scheduled during the inmate's work or school day; these include visits to the commissary, bathhouse, sick call, or special appointments. For related subject matter, see ATTICA UPRISING and McKAY COMMISSION.

REFERENCES: New York State Special Commission on Attica, *Attica: The Official Report,* 1972.

ATTICA UPRISING. Between September 9 and 13, 1971, inmates of the Attica Correctional Facility in New York State carried out the largest scale prison riot in American history. The retaking of the prison and the freeing of the hostages on September 13, with forty-three people killed and hundreds wounded, constituted one of the bloodiest one-day encounters between Americans since the Civil War.

Important precedents in the management of prison disturbances were broken during the Attica riot. Some months before, on January 1, 1971, New York State correctional services were reorganized to merge the former Division of Parole and Department of Correction into the new Department of Correctional Services. Russell G. Oswald was selected as the new commissioner of correctional services, and he, in turn, selected Walter Dunbar as his executive deputy commissioner. In the months after Oswald took office, he became aware that trouble might break out in the system. The prisons were full of young, politically aware inmates who sent him a series of letters protesting prison conditions.

On July 2, 1971, Commissioner Oswald received a letter from five Attica inmates listing specific problems of the system that they perceived. The letter had documents written in inflammatory rhetoric calling prisons "the fascist concentration camps of modern America" and the prison system "the authoritative fangs of a coward in power." However, the actual demands of these five inmates, who called themselves the "Attica Liberation Faction," were fairly traditional prison reform items. They asked for legal representation when they appeared before the parole board, improved medical care, better visiting facilities, better food and sanitation in food preparation, better opportunity for good personal hygiene, improved clothing, improved recreational facilities, improved working conditions in the shops, a uniform set of rules in all prisons throughout the New York State prison system, adjustment of prices of items sold in the prison commissary, and an end to the practice of segregating prisoners from the main population because of their political beliefs. Oswald agreed with many of these grievances and planned a number of reforms.

During Oswald's first months in office, and before he could implement any reforms, a series of incidents at Attica indicated that the prison was a likely trouble spot. Attica inmates held a peaceful day of fasting and mourning on August 22, 1971, after receiving news that George Jackson had been killed at San Quentin. Then, on August 30, 1971, 300 inmates signed up for sick call to protest the low level of medical care at the institution. After these incidents, as well as other minor occurrences, Oswald sent a taped message to the Attica inmates urging patience while he worked on reforms.

An important sign of the imminence of violence came on September 8 when an inmate struck a lieutenant with his fist. It was the first time in the memory of either inmates or officers that an inmate had struck an officer. After evening lockup, officers moved the inmate to solitary confinement; other inmates, responding to rumors that the inmate had been severely beaten, created a disturbance by shouting and throwing items from their cells.

The tension in the prison culminated in a riot the following morning. The large acreage inside of Attica is divided into four exercise yards by covered tunnels which allow inmates passage across the area and serve as interior walls to divide the yards. Another lieutenant was walking through one of these tunnels where inmates were standing in formation when an inmate struck him on the head. Subsequently, inmates began beating the lieutenant and other correctional officers who were inside the tunnel, but these officers were able to escape from the group of inmates. Meanwhile, the rioting inmates had obtained keys that gave them access to Exercise Yard A and Cellblock A where they gathered baseball bats, rakes, wood from benches, and other items that could be used for weapons. The inmates again entered the tunnel with their weapons and moved to the area where the four tunnels come together (called Times Square). A mechanical defect in the prison construction was to play a major role in the incident as the inmates reached Times Square. The area has four heavy gates designed to allow any one cellblock to be sealed off to confine trouble to one area. Unexpectedly, the gate to A tunnel opened as inmates surged against it. A faulty weld in a rod, made decades ago, gave way to allow the inmates to break into Times Square, overpower the guards stationed there, and obtain keys that opened the other tunnel gates. The first hostages were taken by collecting five officers in the tunnels.

Within a short time, inmates controlled all five cellblocks and several other buildings within the walls. They assembled in D Exercise Yard after looting supplies from prison shops, the commissary, and the officers' mess. Subsequent investigation showed that 1,281 inmates assembled there with fifty hostages. Off-duty correctional officers and state police were assembling at Attica's administration building while inmates assembled in D Yard. Since most of the prison had been taken over by the inmates, it was obvious to officials that they would need to delay long enough to gather a large force to retake the prison. However, officers secured some parts of the prison that were abandoned by inmates moving to the D Yard assembly where inmate leaders were organizing the group and urging other inmates to compile a list of demands for prison reform. Inmate factions—Panthers, Young Lords, Five Percenters, and Muslims—formed an uneasy alliance that brought some order to the group. One outcome of the coalition was the forming of a security guard to act as an internal police force. This security guard kept inmates from leaving the yard; officials believe that many inmates simply milled around in the yard during the following days without taking an active part in the rebellion.

Commissioner Oswald came to the facility that afternoon to take command, but when he arrived, the state police still had not mustered enough manpower to attempt to retake the institution. It was during this delay that Oswald decided to break the established prison tradition of refusing to negotiate with inmates holding hostages. Oswald had two civilian volunteers willing to contact the inmates in D Yard. Faced with the prospect of further delay or the attempt to negotiate, Oswald allowed the volunteers to enter D Yard. They emerged with a list of demands, one of which was that Oswald personally negotiate with the inmates. Oswald did enter the yard for negotiations soon afterward and broke a second precedent by allowing members of the news media to accompany him on the visit. Little was accomplished except to receive a list of preconditions for further negotiations.

Negotiations with the inmates lasted through Sunday, September 12. Oswald agreed to many of the reforms demanded by inmates, but negotiations began to falter when the inmates demanded total criminal anmesty. Not only did they require amnesty for crimes committed but they also asked for transportation out of the country for a number of inmates. Oswald assured the inmate leaders that he would guarantee that there would be no administrative reprisals and that the department would not file any criminal charges for the property damage caused by the riot. These assurances did not go far enough to satisfy the inmates, and no official, including the governor, felt they had authority to grant criminal amnesty.

After negotiations broke down, the New York State police mounted an assault on September 13; corrections officers were excluded from the attack force because of their possible emotional involvement. At 9:46 A.M., a helicopter dropped CS gas on Times Square, and riflemen stationed on roofs began firing. Other troopers immediately moved out onto catwalks overlooking the yard, and they, too, started firing. Heavy firing continued for six minutes. When it stopped, ten hostages and twenty-nine inmates were dead of gunshot wounds inflicted by officials; eighty-five inmates and three hostages suffered gunshot wounds that were not fatal; and one State Police lieutenant was wounded by his own men. Although inmates had insisted that they would kill all of the hostages if force was used to enter the yard, later investigations showed that inmates did not kill any hostages. Two hostages who survived the assault did receive serious knife wounds from inmates, and two other hostages killed by the assault force had knife wounds. Nearly 10 percent of everyone in the yard when the assault started was struck by gunfire; thirteen of the thirty-eight hostages still being held were killed or wounded by gunfire. The death toll of thirty-nine during the assault, when added to the death of an officer from injuries received while hostages were being taken and the deaths of three prisoners at the hands of other inmates, made the total death count forty-three for the four-day period.

The daily operation of Attica is not greatly different today from what it was before the riot. Physical damage to the plant has been repaired; inmates are allowed slightly more recreation time in the yard each day; but most conditions are about the same as those included among the inmates' grievances during the disturbances.

For related topics, see ATTICA CORRECTIONAL FACILITY and McKAY COMMISSION.

REFERENCES: Herman Badillo and Milton Haynes, *A Bill of No Rights: Attica and the American Prison System,* 1972; William R. Coons, *Attica Diary,* 1972; John Irwin, "Replaying Attica," *Human*

Behavior, 1973; Samuel Melville, *Letters from Attica,* 1972; New York State Special Commission on Attica, *Attica: The Official Report,* 1972; Tom Wicker, *A Time to Die,* 1975.

AUBURN SILENT SYSTEM. New York State's disciplinary and administrative system of imprisonment, developed as a variation of the Pennsylvania System of Prison Discipline (*q.v.*), became the model for virtually all American prisons. The Pennsylvania system was characterized by solitary confinement of inmates chiefly to avoid the supposed evils of allowing criminals to associate with one another. Work was believed to be an indication that reformation was beginning, but the inmate was required to do the work in the isolation of his cell in order to avoid any interaction with his fellow inmates. Under the Pennsylvania plan, the handicraft work completed by inmates in their individual cells was a source of funds that contributed to the operation of the prison. The congregate work shops of the Auburn system proved to be much more productive and more capable of making a prison self-supporting. A scheme that provided economic self-sufficiency for prisons, thereby reducing the burden on taxpayers, was more attractive politically than the intangible benefits claimed for the Pennsylvania system, and so the Auburn system was widely copied in the United States.

The original prison built by New York State at Auburn had large rooms built to hold a relatively large number of inmates. By 1821, the increasing population in the state, and the attendant increases in the crime rate, combined with less frequent use of capital and corporal punishment to create a need for additional prison capacity at Auburn. Members of New York's legislative assembly, aware of events in Pennsylvania, were interested in adopting the cellular system employed there. A legislative committee drew up a plan for expanding Auburn Prison facilities incorporating the use of solitary cells as developed in Pennsylvania. Only the most hardened of criminals would be confined in solitary cells. Following the approval of the new plan in 1821, William Brittin, prison architect and governor of Auburn Prison, constructed a new cellblock at Auburn to implement the Pennsylvania system. Two rows of cells, built on five floors, were placed back to back, facing corridors lined with high windows providing indirect light. For the sake of economy, Brittin constructed the cells so that they were much smaller than those in Pennsylvania; each cell measured three and one-half feet wide, seven feet long, and seven feet high. The new cellblock was ready for occupancy on Christmas Day 1821, and eighty-three men were placed in the cells.

The experiment in solitary confinement at Auburn proved disastrous. The men in the solitary cells were assigned no work to relieve the relentless monotony, nor were they permitted to leave the cells for any purpose or to speak with anyone other than the prison chaplain. Within one year, the prison officials were convinced that the system of solitary confinement in tiny cells without work could not be continued. Five of the original eighty-three men placed in the cells had died, one had become insane, one had attempted to kill himself, and the remainder had become seriously demoralized.

William Brittin died in 1821 and was succeeded as governor of Auburn Prison by Captain Elam Lynds and his deputy, John D. Cray. Lynds and Cray are traditionally credited with establishing the Auburn Silent System, which was to become the world's second great system of prison discipline (the Pennsylvania system being the first). Lynds found an opportunity to introduce a new system when the governor of New York pardoned the remaining men in the solitary confinement cells in 1823 and 1824. Under Lynds' scheme, prisoners were taken out of cells to work in small, strictly supervised congregate shops during daylight hours, but were locked in the individual cells at night. In effecting this compromise with the previous system, Lynds enforced a rule of silence to overcome any tendencies the prisoners might have to corrupt one another. At dawn, prisoners were aroused from sleep to prepare for a new day; cell doors were opened fifteen minutes after reveille, and the men were made to march in lock-step with their eyes downcast. They emerged from their individual cells carrying their chamber pot, food bowl, and water jug. After emptying their chamber pots in a courtyard and washing their faces, they marched to the workshops for an hour of work before breakfast. For breakfast, and again at noon, the men were marched to the dining room where they were required to sit in silence at narrow tables all facing in the same direction. The convicts used hand signals to indicate the need for additional food. The work day ended a little before sunset. Inmates again were allowed to wash their faces and hands en route to their cells. They picked up their personal chamber pots, food bowls, and water jugs before passing through a narrow hallway adjacent to the kitchen where their food bowls were filled for a solitary meal in their cells. After the guards had ascertained that each man was properly locked in his cell, the inmates were still required to remain silent. They had no means of diversion in their cells other than a Bible.

All rules were strictly enforced by flogging. Prisoners were expected to obey orders instantly, to work quickly and efficiently without pause, to maintain silence and downcast eyes, and to avoid creating even the slightest distraction. There were few occasions for speaking. They were not allowed to speak to guards about matters that did not concern their most pressing personal needs or their work. Their daily routine never varied except on Sundays. In some ways, however, inmates found Sundays more trying, because of boredom, than other days. They were awakened at dawn to leave their cells for a time to wash and empty their chamber pots. Following this brief interlude, prisoners were locked in their cells to await issue of a clean shirt. In their clean shirts, they were marched to the dining hall for a brief breakfast and from there to the chapel to attend church services. After the services, their evening meal was dumped in their food bowl as they were marched back to their cells to be locked up until Monday morning. Sunday afternoon offered one of the few occasions for a prisoner to speak if he were among the few that the chaplain could visit.

The Auburn prison system became a model for other states largely through the efforts of Reverend Louis Dwight, the first American prison reformer to operate on a national scale. Dwight became an advocate for the Auburn style of prison operation and chose to oppose the Pennsylvania system. He organized the Boston Prison Discipline Society in 1825 and continued to function as its leader until his death in 1854. The Society's annual reports, which were issued for thirty years, until 1855, became penal textbooks for politicians and penologists throughout the nation. Through Dwight's vigorous efforts to promote the use of the Auburn system, together with its lower building costs and the greater economic efficiency of congregate shops, the system ultimately superseded the Pennsylvania system.

The Auburn style of prison discipline continues to be used in the twentieth century, though sometimes in radically changed form. Prisons still tend to employ cellular construction that allows inmates to be locked in cells at night, and congregate workshops where inmates work together in the day time are still in practice. John D. Cray's old practice of forming inmates into squadrons or batteries for purposes of marching them to and from the shops remains prevalent in American prisons, although use of the lock-step died out decades ago. Enforcing a rule of silence is no longer part of the Auburn style, but the practice of requiring inmates to be silent in the dining hall persisted for at least a hundred years (a diligent search might still discover an American prison using this rule). Corporal punishment, in the form of flogging for disobedience to rules, has disappeared from the Auburn style, but rule violations are still punished by loss of privileges and solitary confinement on reduced rations. In modern prisons, the cells tend to be somewhat larger and are designed to hold at least two inmates. In short, the emphasis on keeping inmates from conversing with one another is gone from the Auburn system, but many of the original vestiges remain. For related information see ARCHITECTURE and PENNSYLVANIA SYSTEM OF PRISON DISCIPLINE.

REFERENCES: Henry Burns, Jr., *Corrections: Organization and Administration,* 1975; Torsten Eriksson, *The Reformers: An Historical Survey of Pioneer Experiments in the Treatment of Criminals,* 1976; George G. Killinger and Paul F. Cromwell, Jr. (eds.), *Penology: The Evolution of Corrections in America,* 1973; Blake McKelvey, *American Prisons: A Study in American Social History Prior to 1915,* 1968.

C

CALIFORNIA CORRECTIONAL SYSTEM. This system is the largest of the state systems, with more prisons, jails, prisoners, and guards than any other state. As a progressive state, it has been willing to fund a great variety of treatment programs, with the result that it also has more psychologists, psychiatrists, counselors, and other professionals than any other state system.

The correctional bureaucracy is divided into two branches. The Department of Corrections operates the state's thirteen adult institutions, which house slightly more than 22,000 inmates (1974) and, in addition, oversees almost 19,000 parolees besides operating five halfway houses. Juveniles in the state are handled by the Department of the Youth Authority, which operates ten institutions housing some 4,500 youths between the ages of thirteen and twenty-five. The Youth Authority supervises another 9,500 parolees.

As overwhelming as these numbers are, they do not reflect the entire correctional operation in the state. Probation is administered by county government; collectively, the counties supervise some 185,000 adults and juveniles. County jails, correctional facilities, and juvenile detention centers incarcerate another 25,000 people. The large number of convicted persons handled by local government has a definite impact on the state's prison system in that it keeps the inmate population from being even larger and more unwieldy than it is now. The local handling of offenders is partly a result of California's probation subsidy plan begun in 1966. Probation subsidy is a scheme for transferring money from the state budget to county probation offices to enable the local governments to reduce the caseloads of its probation officers for more effective supervision of the clients. The impact of this program is illustrated by estimates that the scheme keeps an average of 5,000 offenders per year from being sent to state prisons.

Several of the institutions operated by the Department of Corrections are well known to the general public by virtue of having been in news stories regularly or depicted in movies, television productions, and popular books. Male prisons in this category include San Quentin, the state's oldest prison, with a capacity of 2,602; San

Quentin has been in continuous operation since 1852. Folsom prison has a normal capacity of 1,958 and has been in operation since 1880. Prisons opened in the 1940s include Chino and Soledad, both of which have frequently been in the public limelight. Chino has a capacity of 2,632, and Soledad 2,655.

In most states, few women serve prison sentences, and it is not economically feasible to establish a separate prison with good facilities and programs for a small number of women. In contrast, California has more than enough female inmates to justify separate prisons. The California Institution for Women at Frontera has a capacity for 913 women ages eighteen and above. Furthermore, the Youth Authority operates the Ventura School housing more than 300 females (1974) between the ages of eight and twenty-one years.

The less well-known adult prisons in the state include some rather large institutions: San Luis Obispo with a capacity of 2,694; Sierra with 1,564; Vacaville Medical Facility with 1,911; the Deuel Vocational Institution at Tracy with 1,369; and Tehachapi with 1,126. Some of the institutions operated by the Youth Authority are larger than might be expected: the Youth Training School at Ontario holds 1,200; the Preston School of Industry has a capacity of 750; and the Fred C. Nelles School for Boys can house 500.

In a large, well-funded correctional system such as California has, it is natural to find a variety of treatment programs and approaches. California's Department of Corrections has two institutions that serve only psychotic inmates and one facility devoted entirely to the treatment of drug addicts. It operates an extensive conjugal and family visiting program. The Youth Authority has institutions that specialize in a primary treatment strategy such as behavior modification or transactional analysis (*q.v.*). In various parts of the adult and youth systems, emphasis is given to psychiatric counseling, academic improvement, vocational training and drug treatment. There is disagreement on the results of these massive efforts, and there is no strong evidence that the treatment programs have lowered recidivism (*q.v.*) rates.

One of California's strategies that has produced mixed reactions in the field is the use of the indeterminate sentence (*q.v.*). In the pure theoretical form, an indeterminate sentence would mean that a judge sentences a person to prison without specifying any length of sentence. In accordance with the therapeutic ideology, the sentenced offender would be received by the correctional system, tested, evaluated, classified, and given academic/vocational skills, if needed, in addition to any psychological treatment to bring about attitude change. Once these tasks were accomplished, the offender would theoretically be ready to be returned to the community for successful reintegration into normal community life. The tasks might require a long time, or they might be accomplished within a few months. Regardless of the amount of time involved, the correctional staff members would make the determination because they are presumably in a better position to do so than the sentencing judge.

The indeterminate sentence used in California is a variant of the "pure" form. Legislation enabling the indeterminate sentence was passed in a 1944 reform movement. The law does not set up the pure form because the legislature preserves the right to specify maximum and minimum terms for different offenses and according to whether the offender has previous convictions. Over the years since 1944, the maximum and minimum terms have been changed—usually to exact longer minimum terms. For example, a third conviction for the sale of narcotics carries a mandatory sentence of fifteen years to life, with no possibility of parole until the minimum fifteen years has been served. Under the indeterminate sentence law, an inmate does not receive time off for good behavior.

California's indeterminate sentence law applies to all adult offenders other than those who have committed the few crimes carrying the death penalty or life without possibility of parole. Inmates and some prison reformers have complained that the indeterminate sentence has been misused in California and that it should be abolished because it results in prisoners serving longer sentences than they would in a state that uses less innovative sentencing procedures. Instead of serving the ends of rehabilitation, opponents charge, the indeterminate sentence gives the correctional system a tool that results in arbitrary punishment of inmates who hold the "wrong" political views. Statistics on the median time served do show that inmates in California are serving longer sentences. In 1960, the median sentence was twenty-four months, whereas by 1972, the median sentence was almost forty months. Correctional officials defend the use of the indeterminate sentence by pointing out that the probation subsidy program has been so successful in diverting people from prison that only the most dangerous people receive prison sentences.

California is one of only eight states that experienced a decline in prison population between January 1, 1977, and January 1, 1978. Its population declined 6 percent from 20,914 to 19,623.

REFERENCES: Michael S. Serrill, "California," *Corrections Magazine,* 1974; Michael Serrill, "Prison Population Rises Again, But at a Slower Rate," *Corrections Magazine,* 1978.

CARLSON, NORMAN A. (1933–   ). Norman Carlson was appointed the fourth director of the Federal Bureau of Prisons on March 25, 1970, succeeding retiring Director Myrl E. Alexander. He is president of the American Correctional Association, serving a two-year term that began in August 1978.

As top executive of the Federal Bureau of Prisons, a branch of the Justice Department, Carlson is in a position to play a key role in shaping the future direction of penal policy in the United States and, to a lesser extent, throughout the western world. Congress has always intended for the bureau to exert leadership in the field of penology and to provide a model for the state systems. Since the bureau was established in 1930, it has assumed that leadership role. The bureau has had excellent leadership in its nearly five decades, and its funding has been good during most of that time.

Carlson's impact on the philosophy of penology is gradually becoming clear as he adjusts Bureau of Prisons procedures to conform with his latest thinking on what prison authorities can hope to accomplish. Carlson differs from previous directors of the bureau in that he is much less confident that prisons can ever rehabilitate inmates. He denies that he has made any basic changes in the bureau's policies, but there are not-too-subtle differences between his philosophy in the mid-1970s and that of the first few years of his leadership. Carlson presented his philosophy in some detail in an article he wrote for *Federal Probation* for the forty-fifth anniversary of the bureau in 1975. He believes that Americans have been oversold on the potential of rehabilitation programs for changing offenders. He notes that following the prison riot at Attica in 1971 the public increasingly demanded prison reform with emphasis on rehabilitation. However, Carlson is critical of the medical model of corrections wherein penologists speak of diagnosis and treatment of offenders as if their criminality were a disease subject to systematic analysis and correction. He maintains that corrections personnel do not have the knowledge to rehabilitate offenders; rather, he believes that corrections is an art and cannot be a science, given the state of human knowledge. When too much emphasis is placed on rehabilitation, the other reasons for incarceration can be overlooked. A balanced mission for corrections, he proposes, requires recognition of the deterrence and retribution roles of incarceration as well as the rehabilitation role.

One result of Carlson's views within the bureaucracy was the abrupt resignation of Dr. Martin Groder on April 3, 1975. Groder, a young psychiatrist who was scheduled to become the warden at the Bureau of Prisons' new Federal Center for Correctional Research in

Butner, North Carolina, called a press conference to announce his resignation and attacked Carlson for abandoning rehabilitation as a goal of the prison system. Groder had spent a number of years establishing transactional analysis as the primary treatment technique at the United States Penitentiary at Marion, Illinois. While there is nothing necessarily coercive about transactional analysis, Groder was accused by inmates of coercive treatment in securing inmate participation in his transactional analysis program at Marion. Inmates with reputations as violent, disruptive prisoners were isolated from the rest of the inmate population until they volunteered for transactional analysis treatment.

One of Carlson's basic policy shifts is evident in the issue of using coercion to get inmates to participate in treatment programs such as the one Groder operated. In the early part of Carlson's career as director, the bureau took the position that disruptive inmates should be coerced into participation in rehabilitation efforts (for additional information, see RIGHT TO "NO TREATMENT" CONTROVERSY and TRANSACTIONAL ANALYSIS THERAPY). In 1975, Carlson clearly denounced this type of coercion. He now feels that rehabilitation is possible only when it occurs at the volition of the offender. Penologists can do no more than make educational, vocational, counseling, psychotherapy, medical, and community services programs available for those offenders who decide to change their lives and avail themselves of the opportunity provided by such programs.

REFERENCES: Norman A. Carlson, "The Federal Prison System: Forty-five Years of Change," *Federal Probation,* 1975; Steve Gettinger, "Dr. Martin Groder: An Angry Resignation," *Corrections Magazine,* 1975.

CHAPLAINCY SERVICES. Most prisons in the United States accept the principle that religion is a necessary part of a treatment program for inmates, a belief that dates back to the beginning of penology. Practices with regard to providing staff to administer to the spiritual needs of the inmates vary widely from one state prison system to another, with some prisons relying solely on volunteers from the surrounding community to provide chaplain services and other prisons formalizing the pastoral function by hiring their own chaplain and staff.

The appropriate qualifications for prison chaplains have been worked out by Correctional Chaplains Associations representing the predominant faiths of American inmates: The American Catholic Chaplains Correctional Association headquartered in the reformatory of Anamosa, Iowa; the American Jewish Correctional Chaplains Association at 10 East 73rd Street, New York; and the American Protestant Chaplains Correctional Association in the U.S. reformatory at El Reno, Oklahoma. These associations can furnish details on the role that their denomination plays in prison ministry.

Ideal standards in establishing a proper ratio of chaplains to serve an inmate population suggest that one full-time chaplain be assigned to each faith group represented by at least fifty inmates, with an additional full-time chaplain for each 300 inmates in the particular faith group. When the prison population includes faith groups with fewer than fifty persons, the services of part-time chaplains may be utilized. Ideally, at least one of the chaplains from each faith group should be clinically trained. In assigning chaplains to prison systems, the first priority should be assignment to reception centers in order to have chaplains available to see newly committed inmates.

The duties of prison chaplains include the administering of the holy rites, worship services, and special rites as deemed appropriate by the respective churches. Chaplains are also expected to develop and conduct a religious education program that will develop inmate character as well as inform inmates about the doctrines and rituals of their faith. Chaplains also have a major responsibility for interviewing and counseling individually with inmates. Pastoral visiting to all parts of the institution is conducted on a regular basis, with special attention to visits in the hospital, psychiatric unit, isolation units, and the cells for condemned prisoners. Chaplains often meet with members of the inmate's family during one of their visits to the prison, in recognition of the rehabilitation potential inherent in assisting inmates in maintaining social ties with persons outside the prison. Chaplains must act as spokesmen for the inmate populations with religious organizations in the surrounding communities to attempt to instill a sense of responsibility for offenders and their families. At least a small portion of the prison chaplain's time is spent in looking after the spiritual welfare of fellow workers on the prison staff who occasionally need counseling in a personal crisis.

The work of the prison chaplain requires the use of special facilities and equipment within the prison. The chaplain must assume administrative duties in order to provide and maintain the necessary facilities, supplies, and equipment; procure and distribute religious literature; determine the need for inmate assistance in running the program and provide supervision for these assistants; and maintain records. The diversity and magnitude of these activities are such that the chaplain's office will normally have a separate budget. Along with other administrative duties, the chaplain is expected to prepare the budget and to defend budget requests.

Major facilities and equipment for the religious program normally include a chapel and office space suitable for private counseling. Although the state or federal government will actually own the chapel, it is recommended that it not be utilized for nonreligious activities; rather, it should be kept open for meditation in privacy by inmates. Also, an appropriately diverse program of religious activities will assure that it is used almost daily.

REFERENCES: American Correctional Association, *Manual of Correctional Standards,* 1966; American Bar Association, Commission on Correctional Facilities and Services and Council of State Governments, *Compendium of Model Correctional Legislation and Standards,* 1975.

CLASSIFICATION. Current correctional ideology views the criminal offender as being "sick" in the sense that there is some fault in the offender's socialization or personality. Accordingly, it is thought that an offender's faults can be diagnosed and treated. Classification is an orderly procedure applied to inmates to facilitate diagnosis, treatment planning, and the process of treatment. It came into use in 1790 in the Walnut Street Jail in Philadelphia, through the efforts of Quakers, and is now used in all federal prisons.

The objective of classification is to develop and administer a treatment program for the individual inmate. In practice, however, inmates rarely receive highly individualized treatment programs. Rather, inmates with similar problems are grouped together and treated as a homogeneous group since an institution will normally have relatively few programs thought to be beneficial for rehabilitation purposes.

New inmates are usually segregated in a reception process before being assigned to the living quarters that they will occupy for the greater part of their period of incarceration. Classification procedures begin during this initial period of isolation. The diagnostic aspect of classification is conducted during the normal four- to eight-week interval required for medical quarantine, orientation, and testing. Staff members administer medical, psychiatric, and psychological examinations; compile social histories; test for academic and vocational achievement and aptitude; make religious and recreational studies; and observe the inmate's characteristics directly. The results of all these procedures are brought together to constitute the inmate's file. Conclusions drawn from the data in the file make up the diagnosis and provide the basis for a treatment plan.

A common name for the compiled results of the diagnostic studies is the admission summary. The admission summary is the first document in the inmate's case history. Elements of the admission summary are (1) a summary of the legal aspects of the case; (2) a summary of previous criminal history, if any; (3) a social history; (4) a statement of physical condition; (5) information about vocational interests and abilities; (6) educational attainments; (7) recreational interests; (8) religious information; (9) evaluations by psychiatrist and psychologist; (10) a statement of the reception center staff about the inmate's behavior while in the center; and (11) the inmate's initial reaction to counseling or group psychotherapy. The inmate's point of view on his case, as well as the evaluations of staff members, are obtained for the admission summary. The final page of the document is used to list recommendations concerning the treatment program to be administered to the inmate.

Information compiled about an individual is placed in a case folder and is normally kept in a central records office within an institution in an area providing staff members easy access to records. Inmates generally are denied access to this area. All papers pertaining to the individual inmate, from the time he enters the institution until he is released, are kept in this central file.

The institutional classification process is coordinated by a classification committee made up of staff representatives from the diagnostic, treatment, and security segments of the prison facility. Often, department heads from the various segments belong to the committee. The ex officio chairman of the committee is usually the chief executive of the institution. In larger prisons, it is customary to have two associate wardens serving directly under the warden, one of whom oversees treatment in the institution and the other who supervises security tasks. In these larger prisons, the associate warden for treatment typically chairs the classification committee. Other committee members might include (1) the supervisor of education programs; (2) the supervisor of vocational training programs; (3) the supervisor of the prison industries; (4) the chaplain; (5) the chief medical officer; (6) the psychiatrist; (7) the psychologist; and (8) a representative from the security force who often will be the correctional officer in charge of the admission unit.

When the classification process is conducted within the institution where the inmate is expected to serve his sentence, it is termed classification within the institution. Increasingly, however, the federal system and the larger state systems are making use of central classification, a process that is essentially the same as classification within the institution except that the inmate does not go directly to the institution where he will serve his sentence after being committed to the prison system. Instead, many of the larger correctional systems use one of the facilities in their system as a receiving institution for all newly committed inmates. The most common name for such facilities is the diagnostic and classification center. In systems using diagnostic and classification facilities, the classification committee decides on the appropriate institution within the system to which each new inmate will be assigned after the initial classification process is complete. Thus, the use of a diagnostic and classification center is "central classification" as opposed to "classification within an institution."

Central classification is feasible only if the correctional system has a number of institutions that vary in their custody grades and treatment programming. It has economic advantages in that it is economically feasible to have the wide variety of treatment staff available in a diagnostic and reception center needed for the classification process, whereas it may not be possible to have as large a staff in each institution within the system. In systems where central classification is used, it is customary to also use classification within the institution once the inmate is assigned to the facility where he will serve the bulk of his sentence. Thus, the classification process can be carried on at two different levels.

Decisions made by the classification committee, other than those decisions necessary to assign the inmate to an institution within the system, include recommendations concerning the degree of custody needed for the individual offender. Escape risks, inmates with unusually low intelligence, and overt homosexuals present management problems that must be considered in assigning living quarters to inmates. The inmate's work assignment is also a matter for consideration by the classification committee; past work experience, physical condition, and attitudes must be determined. Assignments to academic or vocational programs, if any, must be determined by the classification committee. It may also make recommendations for participation in recreational activites to fill leisure-time hours that might otherwise be spent in discussing criminal activity with other inmates.

The classification process does not end after initial recommendations are made about a new inmate. Continuous review and study of an inmate's progress or lack of progress are also a part of the classification committee's task. Program changes, called "reclassification," will be necessary from time to time while the inmate is incarcerated. The committee normally prepares a progress report on an individual inmate who is scheduled for an appearance before the parole authority. This report provides current information that will help the parole officials decide whether the inmate is ready for release from the institution.

In summary, classification is cumulative recording of all significant information about an individual offender from the time he is convicted until his release. A probation officer normally prepares a presentence investigation report for the sentencing judge. The presentence investigation report goes with the inmate who is committed to prison and forms the first in a series of papers that will be added to his folder during incarceration. In terms of the medical model of corrections (*q.v.*), classification serves as the diagnostic and coordinating procedure to initiate and oversee the treatment program for the individual offender. For a critique of this approach to corrections, see MEDICAL MODEL OF CORRECTIONS.

REFERENCES: American Bar Association, Commission on Correctional Facilities and Services and Council of State Governments, *Compendium of Model Correctional Legislation and Standards,* 1975; American Correctional Association, *Correctional Classification and Treatment,* 1975; American Correctional Association, *Manual of Correctional Standards,* 1966; Ernst A. Wenk, Thomas V. Halatyn, and Nora Harlow, *An Analysis of Classification Factors for Young Adult Offenders: Volume 1: Background of the Study and Statistical Description of the Total Study Population,* 1974.

COED CORRECTIONS. The present policy of making correctional institutions sexually integrated may be regarded either as an innovative intervention in corrections or as a reversion to an earlier time in history, when women were placed within men's institutions solely for reasons of limited numbers and economy of scale, depending upon one's perspective. Regardless, it is a phenomenon on the correctional horizon that has received support at both federal and state levels. The National Advisory Commission on Criminal Justice Standards and Goals has called for the abandonment of "the current system of separate institutions based upon sex" and development of "a fully integrated system based on all offenders' needs." The Federal Bureau of Prisons has been experimenting with coed institutions since 1971. In addition, over a dozen states have either opened a coed correctional institution or are at the operational planning stage of opening one.

The evolution of the sexually integrated prison has occurred against a background dominated by surging costs of institutionalization, legal decisions regarding equal opportunities as a result of the women's movement, shifts in crime patterns among women, and changes in correctional philosophy from restraint to rehabilitation and from rehabilitation to integration.

The principal purposes behind the development of coed prisons are to reduce the corrosive aspects of confinement; to reduce institutional control problems; to separate troublesome populations; to normalize the institutional environment; to reduce adjustment problems experienced by releasees; to realize the economies of scale (that is, to reduce the high per capita costs of single-sex institutions); to relieve anticipated overcrowding of single-sex institutions; to provide an inexpensive light to heavy work force (for example, transferring male prisoners to women's prisons and using them as maintenance workers); to expand treatment and program options not only through medical, religious, counseling, vocational, academic, recreational, and industrial programs, but also by providing the means for developing healthy relationships with the other sex; to comply with immediate and anticipated court decisions regarding rights of women to equal protection; and to provide an experimental or demonstration model.

Research on the effectiveness of coed corrections has been difficult for two reasons. First, isolating coed corrections and evaluating it apart from other factors such as unit management, the existence of a coed staff, institution size, inmate population characteristics, and engagement of the institution with the community is difficult. Furthermore, administrators modify what they perceive to be critical variables, such as sex proportion, age distribution, program content, physical contact restrictions, and security levels, within relatively short periods of time. Second, it is not clear what constitutes success in coed corrections, or cocorrections. Because cocorrections has been introduced for a wide range of reasons, the measurement of success is dependent on the clarification of the objectives and the specification of measures appropriate to those objectives. Multiple goals, such as normalization and integration, access to work and educational programs, inmate control and improvement of inmate morale, inmate attitude and behavioral changes, and space utilization, bring about a complicated network of internal and external measures. Related issues are the presence or absence of data to provide measurements, the degree to which comparative data may be obtained from other institutions, and the degree to which we can design experimental control groups to compare cocorrections with itself and with one-sex prisons.

Most of the available research on coed corrections has been sponsored by the Federal Bureau of Prisons. It points out that inmates prefer sexually integrated incarceration over one-sex incarceration. There are fewer problems associated with prison sex and violence in sexually integrated prisons, and as a result, there are fewer institution control problems. Viewing sexually integrated prisons at the level of constitutional rights, researchers have also argued that coed incarceration helps eliminate or reduce problems that have plagued the prison system for years. It can be argued that legitimate state interests are substantively furthered in coed prisons and that a coed prison system would undoubtedly withstand a challenge under the equal protection clause of the Fourteenth Amendment.

REFERENCES: Koba Associates, "Phase I: Evaluation of Coeducational Corrections," Washington, D.C.: National Institute on Law Enforcement and Criminal Justice, 1977; Barry Ruback, "The Sexually Integrated Prison: A Legal and Policy Evaluation," *American Journal of Criminal Law* 3 (1975): 301–330; John Ortiz Smykla, *Cocorrections: A Case Study of a Coed Federal Prison,* Washington, D.C.: University Press of America, 1978.

COLORADO CORRECTIONAL SYSTEM. Penal institutions in Colorado operate under the State Department of Institutions with four separate divisions. The divisions involved in caring for incarcerated offenders are the Division of Correctional Services, which operates the adult institutions and provides parole services for adults; and the Division of Youth Services, which operates the juvenile institutions of the state and provides aftercare services. The Division of Youth Services, which operates the juvenile institutions of the state and provides aftercare services. The other two divisions are the Division of Developmental Disabilities and the Division of Mental Health. Both adult and juvenile probation services are provided by the state under the jurisdiction of twenty-two separate judicial administrators. The State Board of Parole operates independently to grant parole to adult offenders.

The majority of Colorado's adult offenders are confined in a correctional complex located in Canon City. Under Colorado law, anyone adjudicated in adult court as a felon or as a misdemeanant is committed to an adult institution. The sentencing options include a fixed maximum sentence or a fixed minimum sentence. Sex offenders receive an indeterminate sentence (*q.v.*) of from one day to life. The maximum security unit at Canon City, the Colorado State Penitentiary, began operation in 1871. It has a normal capacity of 1,105 males but has been operating at about 50 percent capacity in recent years, due to increased use of probation and parole. The complex includes a medium security unit for males that was opened in 1962 with space for 600 males; recently, it has been operating at about 80 to 85 percent capacity. The Colorado Women's Correctional Institution, also located at Canon City, was opened in 1968 with space for ninety and has been operating at near capacity. The Colorado State Reformatory, a medium-size institution, is located at Buena Vista. It was opened in 1889 with a normal capacity of 500 and has been operating at near capacity in recent years. A few adult male offenders are assigned to two camps: the Delta Conservation Camp at Delta, with facilities for 125 inmates, and the Camp George West Conservation Camp at Golden, with housing for sixty offenders.

The Office of Community Services, a part of the Division of Correctional Services, has statewide jurisdiction for providing parole services to adult offenders. This office oversees the Bail Work Release Center in Denver; opened in 1968, it has space for forty-three males. It also operates the Grand Junction Work/Education Center at Grand Junction. This facility opened in 1974 with space for twenty males. The Office of Community Services is also establishing the Fort Logan Correctional Center in Denver.

The Division of Youth Services operates a variety of institutions and programs around the state without using a large facility. Five facilities serve to provide secure custody for juveniles being held pending disposition by the court or pending execution of court order for placement: (1) the Adams County Detention Center, opened in Brighton in 1969 with space for thirty youths; (2) the Arapahoe County Evaluation Center in Englewood, opened in 1968 with space for fifteen youths; (3) the Denver Juvenile Hall, opened in 1936 with room for 100 youths; (4) the Jefferson County Youth Center in Golden, opened in 1970 with space for twenty-six youths; and (5) the Zebulon Pike Detention Center in Colorado Springs, opened in 1962 with space for twenty-nine youths. Five institutions provide longer term care of juvenile delinquents and Children in Need of Supervision (CHINS): (1) the Golden Gate Youth Camp, opened in 1965 at Golden with space for forty-eight males; (2) the Lookout Mountain School for Boys, opened in 1881 at Golden with room for 138; (3) the Mount View Girl's School, opened in 1899 at Denver with room for ninety-six; (4) the Closed Adolescent Treatment Center, opened in 1972 at Denver with room for twenty-six youths; and (5) the Lathrop Park Youth Camp, opened in 1966 at Walsenburg with space for forty-eight boys.

Unlike many other states, Colorado has not been experiencing large increases in its institution population. During calendar year 1975, the state's prison population grew only 7 percent, to a total of 2,104. In 1977, it grew from 2,324 to 2,401 for only a 3 percent increase.

REFERENCES: American Correctional Association, *Directory, 1975–1976* edition; Steve Gettinger, "U.S. Prison Population Hits All-Time High," *Corrections Magazine,* 1976; Michael Serrill, "Prison Population Rises Again, But at a Slower Rate," *Corrections Magazine,* 1978.

COMMUNITY TREATMENT CENTERS. The U.S. Bureau of Prisons uses this term to designate its small residential centers that serve some twenty-five to seventy inmates each. The bureau prefers this terminology to the older phrase "halfway houses" (*q.v.*). A few halfway houses for offenders are known to have existed in Boston in the 1920s for a brief period of time. European countries had experimented with residential centers much earlier; the European efforts were made in the latter half of the nineteenth century and include Crofton's "Irish System" proposal.

In the United States, the movement to establish halfway houses for offenders did not gain much ground until after World War II when a few private organizations, state correctional systems, and federal correctional institutions began to experiment with pre-release programs. As early as 1946, the Children's Bureau was discussing the possibility of establishing residential centers for juvenile offenders to ease their transition from institutions to the community. However, it was 1961 before the U.S. Bureau of Prisons opened a few residential centers to determine the effectiveness of this type of facility for juvenile and youth offenders who were soon to be paroled. The facilities opened in 1961 were called pre-release guidance centers and operated in Chicago and Los Angeles.

One impetus for expanding the use of small, community-based corrections programs came from the recommendations of the Corrections Task Force of the President's Commission of Law Enforcement and Administration of Justice in 1967. Recommendations emphasized the need for corrections to assist the offender in building or rebuilding ties with the community, specifically, restoring family ties, and contact with employers, educational institutions, and, in general, with the noncriminal population. Assuming that an offender is motivated to give up his criminal career when he is ready for release from the institution, he needs assistance in avoiding the social role of "ex-con." In theoretical terms, such assistance must maintain his motivation to adopt a noncriminal career, provide opportunities for testing this new possibility, and reward experiences to reinforce his determination to sustain his new role.

In pragmatic terms, using a community treatment center to assist the offender is simply a means of gradually easing him into a community setting. Its proper place in corrections can best be assessed by considering the degrees of control exercised by the correctional system. An inmate serving time in a maximum security prison is subjected to complete control. All of his daily activities are highly regimented and are conducted in unison with blocks of inmates under rigorous surveillance by staff members who are concerned mainly with custody and security. Under these conditions, the inmate has few decisions to make. He experiences the daily tensions, gradually loses his ability to make decisions, and is oblivious to the changes taking place in the free world. Ideally, the inmate serving a long term in a maximum security prison will be transferred to a medium or minimum security prison during the last year of his sentence. In the new location, he will be subjected to a lesser degree of regimentation and surveillance. With less tension and slightly more personal autonomy, he begins exercising responsibility for his own actions and making simple decisions. Without the use of community treatment centers, the next relaxing of control over the inmate would be the partial control of parole. The parolee suddenly experiences a frightening surge of freedom. He is faced with almost complete responsibility for his own conduct as well as a bewildering array of personal decisions concerning employment, finding a place to live, how to clothe and feed himself, and so on. While the parole officer will provide some help in these matters, his role is limited as he is likely to have a caseload of 50 to 100 parolees to supervise. The community treatment center provides a useful bridge between prison and parole.

In 1965, the U.S. Bureau of Prisons began to expand the number and scope of its residential facilities. It opened additional units in metropolitan areas, established facilities to serve adult and youthful offenders, as well as facilities for female offenders, and experimented with serving offenders without reference to parole eligibility. In addition, the centers have experimented with direct commitments of selected short-sentence offenders, direct commitments of low-risk offenders sentenced to longer terms for observation before disposition, and the temporary housing of probationers and parolees who without the stabilizing influence of residential care might otherwise be subject to violation proceedings. Future plans of the bureau call for contracting with private agencies and state and local governments for operation of the centers.

In establishing centers, the bureau's experimental programs suggest some guidelines that may well determine future trends. The facilities should be accessible to public transportation and be located near centers of business and industry to cut down on commuting time. Managers of some pioneering facilities have sought out large old houses to provide a "family" type of setting. Current practice suggests that inmate needs are better served by using commercial hotels and YMCAs where food services and recreational facilities can be obtained as part of a package contract. Using such facilities frees staff time, enabling staff to spend more time working with the offenders. These facilities can operate with a fair degree of anonymity, which is an important advantage inasmuch as communities frequently oppose efforts to locate a group of offenders in their midst.

Typically, a Federal Community Treatment Center is staffed with a director who manages the entire program; one or two counselors who deal directly with the residents; either full-time or part-time clerical staff; students who work under supervision on a part-time basis to provide additional counseling and therapeutic services; a resource developer to provide employment placement; and various specialists such as psychologists and medical doctors who serve only as needed. The costs for staff, facilities, and other operating expenses are reduced by requiring the residents to pay for their room and food. Residents, whose length of stay in the facility ranges from thirty to ninety days, receive employment placement, residence placement, and counseling relating to their particular needs. There are about fifteen centers in existence today.

REFERENCES: Nora Klapmuts, "Community Alternatives to Prison," *Crime and Delinquency Literature,* 1973; National Council on Crime and Delinquency Research Center, *Residential Corrections: Alternatives to Incarceration,* 1973; U.S. Bureau of Prisons, *The Residential Center: Corrections in the Community* (no date); U.S. Law Enforcement Assistance Administration, *Guidelines and Standards for Halfway Houses and Community Treatment Centers,* 1973; U.S. National Advisory Commission on Criminal Justice Standards and Goals, *Corrections,* 1973.

CONJUGAL VISITATION. Whether conjugal visits are a viable part of prison programs in the United States depends upon how narrowly one defines the concept. A narrow definition of the term assumes that the inmate is confined in an institution, is allowed to receive a visitor of the opposite sex in a place provided by the institution, and engages in sexual intercourse. A broader definition of the term includes situations wherein the inmate receives a furlough (*q.v.*), leaves the institution temporarily, and is presumed to have sexual intercourse with a member of the opposite sex during the furlough interval at some location away from prison property. The stated purposes of a furlough may or may not give official recognition of conjugal visiting as an objective of the furlough, but prison officials are likely to view conjugal visiting as a desirable aspect of the furlough. For example, an inmate may be granted a three-day furlough for employment interviews if parole eligibility is near, but it is expected that he or she engages in social and sexual activities in addition to seeking employment.

Under the narrow definition of the term, prisons in the United States have few experiments in conjugal visiting as compared to prison systems in other countries. The California prison system has experimented with allowing a select few inmates spend up to three days per month with their families in apartments provided for that purpose by the prison system. The California program, started in 1968, was limited to male inmates from Soledad, San Quentin, and the Rehabilitation Center at Corona who had already earned parole consideration. According to many correctional officials in California, the rationale for the program was to reduce the incidence of homosexuality. However, Raymond K. Procunier, then California's director of corrections, said that the program's purpose was to help the inmate maintain family ties so that his prison term would not cost him his family in addition to his freedom.

The Mississippi State Penitentiary at Parchman is the only penal institution in the United States that permits conjugal visits for all married men throughout their prison sentences. The program is informal, unofficial, and has no legal status or control; it can only be described as a tradition at the institution. Prison records are not helpful in determining when the program started, but the Parchman facilities for conjugal visitation were constructed around 1940. Strangely enough, the program was originally available only to black males, in line with the prevalent notion of that time that blacks were more "promiscuous" than whites and had stronger sex drives. Penologists who have studied the development of conjugal visitation in Mississippi have identified several variables believed to be directly or indirectly related to the development of the practice: (1) the Mississippi penitentiary is primarily an agricultural plantation that is a self-contained, sociocultural system functioning much as a culture in and of itself; (2) emphasis is placed on the welfare of the plantation labor force for the sake of achieving economic efficiency; (3) the plantation prison is divided into a number of smaller camps where the guard force usually knows each inmate on a personal basis; and (4) family ties are stronger in rural societies. The lack of records at Parchman makes it impossible to determine if the program has been successful in reducing either the recidivism (*q.v.*) rate or the incidence of homosexuality.

A survey conducted in 1964 showed that fewer than 14 percent of all prison wardens in the United States favored conjugal visiting programs for their institutions; most wardens felt that such a program would heighten rather than relieve tensions in their prisons. Their opposition appears to reflect the chief objection to conjugal visitation in the United States: that is, that it would be incompatible with existing mores because of the apparent emphasis on the physical aspects of sex. The cultural values in the United States favor spontaneity in sexual relations and abhor the appearance of deliberate, preplanned sexual activity. Related objections are the fear of unfavorable public reaction, a loss of human dignity, and a perceived incompatibility of the legal system and conjugal visitation. Some wardens argue that a conjugal visiting program for married inmates would create a demand from single inmates for visits from their lovers, and, then, those inmates who had neither spouses nor lovers would demand the services of prostitutes at taxpayer expense. Such an argument is not necessarily logical, but it does illustrate the nature of the opposition to conjugal visiting programs.

The advantages of conjugal visiting programs are probably not to be found in the reduction of the incidence of homosexuality in prison populations. Virtually all serious studies of prison homosexuality conclude that those inmates who have homosexual relations while confined in institutions, but prefer heterosexual relations otherwise, engage in homosexual relations in an attempt to compensate for their social isolation rather than for any sexual gratification. It seems unlikely that occasional heterosexual relations would offset the cause of prison homosexuality as conceptualized by most sociologists. At any rate, studies do show that inmates make better adjustments to freedom when they are able to maintain contacts with persons outside the prison. The philosophy expressed by Procunier is perhaps the most logical rationale for conjugal visiting.

Considering the sparse number of conjugal visiting experiments in the history of American penology and the attitude of prison wardens, it does not seem likely that the use of conjugal visiting will increase under the narrow definition of the concept. Conversely, the use of furloughs for inmates is increasing, and the inclusion of a conjugal visit in a furlough setting does not seem to raise as many objections as conjugal visiting conducted on prison property. For related topics, see FURLOUGHS; HOMOSEXUALITY IN FEMALE PRISONS; and HOMOSEXUALITY IN MALE PRISONS.

REFERENCES: Michael Braswell and Paul DeFrancis, "Conjugal Visitation; A Feasibility Study," *Georgia Journal of Corrections,* 1972; Jules Quentin Burstein, *Conjugal Visits in Prison: Psychological and Social Consequences,* 1977; Columbus B. Hopper, *Sex in Prisons: The Mississippi Experiment with Conjugal Visiting,* 1969.

CONNECTICUT CORRECTIONAL SYSTEM. Adult institutions in Connecticut are operated by the Department of Correction, which is further divided into the Division of Parole, Community Service Centers, and the Division of Community Release. The department was established in 1968 in a move to centralize corrections as recommended in several studies over a period of years. Before the establishment of the department, the existing prisons operated autonomously. The 1968 reform move also placed all county jails under the jurisdiction of the Department of Correction. The state's six county jails were redesignated community corrections centers, but continue to be used primarily for misdemeanants serving sentences and for detainees awaiting trial. In 1974, officials decided to upgrade these centers in accordance with the United Nations minimum standards of imprisonment. Construction programs are gradually replacing the nineteenth-century buildings that were used as county jails and as community corrections centers after the state took over their operation.

Connecticut's maximum security prison, located at Somers, was opened in 1963 to replace the original Wethersfield institution established in 1827. Somers Correctional Institution has a normal capacity of 994 male offenders aged sixteen and above. The population at the beginning of 1978 was 1,021. The Connecticut Correctional Institution at Cheshire was opened in 1913 with a normal capacity of 450 males aged sixteen to twenty-one. The Connecticut Correctional Institution at Enfield, Hazardville Station, was opened as a prison farm in 1930 but was replaced by Osborn Division in 1960; it has a normal capacity of 400 male offenders. Female offenders, aged sixteen and up, are incarcerated in the Connecticut Correctional Institution at Niantic which opened as a farm in 1917 and as a prison in 1930; it has space for 184.

The community corrections centers, which were county jails prior to 1968, include (1) a facility in Bridgeport, opened in 1974 with a normal capacity of 480 males; (2) a unit in Brooklyn, opened in 1842 housing eighty-six males; (3) a facility at Hartford, opened in 1873 with a normal capacity of 530 male offenders; (4) a unit at Litchfield, opened in 1812 with room for sixty-six male offenders; (5) a center at New Haven, opened in 1857 with space for 325 males; and (6) a facility at Montville, Uncasville, opened in 1957 with a normal capacity of 100 males.

Connecticut has committed itself rather heavily to the use of community-based corrections programs. The Division of Community Release, a part of the Department of Correction, receives adult offenders who are within one year of their earliest possible release date. The division operates a total of twenty-seven work release (*q.v.*) and education release programs. These programs allow inmates to work at outside jobs, attend classes in local schools and universities, and go home on furloughs (*q.v.*).

Juvenile institutions are operated under the aegis of the Department of Children and Youth Services which has jurisdiction over youths up to the age of sixteen. All children judged delinquent by the juvenile court are committed to the department for two years, but the commissioner of corrections may discharge a youth at any time during this period. The department operates two institutions, the Long Lane School at Middletown and the Community Service Unit at Hartford, which together incarcerate about 170 children in a co-educational setting. The Long Lane School was previously used only to house female offenders; in 1975, the Connecticut School for Boys at Meriden was abandoned. Now, boys and girls share classrooms and other programs at Long Lane School; the institution has seven cottages with living space for twenty-five boys or girls. Children aged sixteen and above who are considered dangerous and/or unmanageable are sent to the adult prison for young offenders at Cheshire.

Connecticut corrections is well known for its progress in improving the training of its corrections officers and upgrading salaries to attract and maintain better officers. Starting salaries range from $10,000 to $12,000, depending on the qualifications of the applicant. Since the state has a thirty-five hour work week, the pay is the highest in the country on an hourly basis, with the possible exception of Alaska. Innovative training for correctional officers is conducted at the Connecticut Justice Academy at Haddam. The mandatory four weeks of training includes a period of incarceration in the old Haddam jail constructed in 1786; the incarceration period is designed to give the officers a feel for the plight of inmates. Beyond this period of basic training, the state subsidizes the college-level correctional training of thirty-five officers each semester. The participating officers attend one full day of college classes in correctional subjects each week.

During the early part of the 1970s, the prison population in Connecticut's penal institutions declined as a result of the state's growing emphasis on the use of community-based corrections programs. This trend was halted in 1976 when the prison population increased 9 percent over the January 1975 figure, to a total of 3,060 inmates. However, the trend toward declining prison population resumed in 1977 with a 7 percent decline from 1,923 to 1,781 between January 1, 1977, and January 1, 1978.

REFERENCES: American Correctional Association, *Directory,* 1975–1976 edition; Roan Conrad, "Profile/Connecticut," *Corrections Magazine,* 1975; Steve Gettinger, "U.S. Prison Population Hits All-Time High," *Corrections Magazine,* 1976; Michael Serrill, "Prison Population Rises Again, But at a Slower Rate," *Corrections Magazine,* 1978.

COUNT. Since inmates perform most of the ordinary housekeeping and the industrial labor of institutions, they have considerable mobility within the prison. In addition, a fair number of inmates have permission to seek medical attention, use the commissary facilities, attend vocational or academic education classes, participate in therapy programs, or attend religious services. This movement of inmates within the prison confines makes the daily task of obtaining an exact head count extremely difficult. Some of the larger prisons, with several thousand inmates, issue what amount to estimates of their population.

The frequency of the counting procedure gives it a social aspect. The count continues day and night every day of the year. This unceasing regularity gives it the appearance of a ritual, although it has the serious purpose of detecting escapees. As an ever-present ritual, it contributes to the rhythm of the daily prison routine.

Any prison should have at least four official counts for each twenty-four hour period; many prisons have an official count every sixty minutes. In institutions that have only four counts per day, two of these should be made near the time for shift changes of officers so that a relatively large number of officers will be available if inmates are found to be missing.

Prison officers are taught several basic techniques for making a count of inmates under their supervision. They concentrate on the count by avoiding conversation with an inmate or with another staff member during the counting. A temporary count sheet is utilized to record the number of inmates counted when one segment of a building is completed. By using the temporary count sheet when changing from one part of a building to another, the officer is better able to give complete concentration to the task. Officers are taught to avoid being deceived by the skillful substitution of a dummy in a cell. Before counting an inmate present in his cell, the officer should hear sound from the inmate and see movement or flesh. The skillful inmate can condition the officer to accept certain practices over a period of weeks. For example, prison rules may require an inmate to stand by his cell door for the count. If the guard does not insist on strict observance of such a rule, the inmate may gradually condition the officer to expect to find him away from the door and eventually to see him in bed with a blanket over him. At that point, it is easier for the inmate to deceive the officer with a dummy. Counting inmates in a dormitory requires two officers—one officer to do the actual counting and the second to watch, keeping inmates from moving from one side of the room to the other.

REFERENCES: American Bar Association, Commission on Correctional Facilities and Services and Council of State Governments, *Compendium of Model Correctional Legislation and Standards,* 1975; American Correctional Association, *Manual of Correctional Standards,* 1966.

D

DEINSTITUTIONALIZATION. Deinstitutionalization is the process of closing down large traditional institutions in correctional systems by shifting inmates to small community residential treatment programs or simply relying on probation and parole supervision to keep offenders in the community. It is a form of decentralization.

Much of the national impetus toward deinstitutionalization is a result of interest and controversy surrounding the 1972 closing of all training schools for juveniles in Massachusetts by Jerome Miller, commissioner of the Massachusetts Department of Youth Services from October 1969 to January 1973. *Corrections Magazine* has designated the closing of the Massachusetts juvenile institutions, which was the first instance of deinstitutionalization, as "one of the most revolutionary changes in the history of American corrections." Miller, who may be classified ideologically as an abolitionist (*q.v.*), believes that institutions are unnecessary, harmful to the incarcerated, and excessively expensive. In lieu of its training schools, the Massachusetts Department of Youth Services now places youths in some 200 different programs, with about fifty of the programs absorbing 75 percent of the youths. Out of some 2,000 juveniles for whom the agency is responsible, about seventy-five are in facilities designated as "secure," some 300 are in group care facilities, and the remainder are in nonresidential programs such as foster care homes or on parole.

Deinstitutionalization does not mean that all inmates are shifted to locations and programs where they have a significant degree of personal freedom and autonomy. Some offenders are still confined because they are thought to be dangerous. However, it does involve a different conceptualization of the potential danger of offenders; fewer offenders are labeled dangerous. The closing of the larger training schools in Massachusetts shifted some youths to smaller facilities that resemble jails in their custody aspects. Massachusetts officials say that such facilities differ from the traditional training school in that they are better staffed and smaller, and provide more intensive programming.

Deinstitutionalization does not necessarily mean that all traditional institutions in a system are closed. Philosophically, it is a commitment to less reliance on traditional institutions. Dozens of states have altered their pattern of institutionalizing offenders during a period of increasing convictions or commitments to corrections systems without the national publicity received by Massachusetts. Illinois, for example, has closed nine of its seventeen juvenile institutions to achieve deinstitutionalization on a scale almost as great as that in Massachusetts. Michigan has reduced the number of juveniles institutionalized by one half during the last few years. California uses a probation subsidy plan to keep large numbers of adult offenders in the community rather than having them committed to its prisons. Vermont has closed its only maximum security prison for adult male offenders and has shifted the inmates to smaller community treatment centers (*q.v.*).

Deinstitutionalization has become a national trend, even though it is not readily apparent to a casual observer because more and more offenders are being convicted and committed to correctional systems. The nation's prison population reached a record number in the decade of the 1970s, but the proportion of offenders being assigned probation and parole increased faster than the proportion being held in institutions. Furthermore, correctional systems are establishing community-based residential treatment programs at an ever-increasing rate. For discussions of related matters, see ABOLITIONISTS and MORATORIUM ON PRISON CONSTRUCTION.

REFERENCES: Benedict Alper, *Prison Inside-Out*, 1974; Yitzhak Bakal, *Closing Correctional Institutions: New Strategies for Youth Services*, 1973; Calvert R. Dodge (ed.), *A Nation Without Prisons: Alternatives to Incarceration*, 1975: Gordon Hawkins, *The Prison; Policy and Practice*, 1976; Norval Morris, *The Future of Imprisonment*, 1974; Andrew T. Scull, *Decarceration: Community Treatment and the Deviant—A Radical View*, 1977; Michael S. Serrill, "Juvenile Corrections in Massachusetts," *Corrections Magazine*, 1975; Robert Sommer, *The End of Imprisonment*, 1976.

DELAWARE CORRECTIONAL SYSTEM. Delaware's Bureau of Adult Correction is a part of its Department of Correction. The bureau, under the leadership of Chief Paul W. Keve, operates two facilities for adult male offenders and one for adult females. The Delaware Correctional Center, located at Smyrna, was opened in 1971 to serve a normal capacity of 441 males aged eighteen and above. Both felons and misdemeanants may be sentenced to Delaware's institutions. The Sussex Correctional Institution at Georgetown was opened in 1932 with a normal capacity of 228 adult male offenders. The Correctional Institution for Women is located at Wilmington; it was opened in 1929 with a normal capacity of sixty-five.

The Bureau of Juvenile Correction is under the same department and operates a slightly more diversified group of institutions that hold children whose ages range from eight to eighteen. The Ferris School for Boys in Wilmington opened in 1885 to serve a normal capacity of 100. The Woods Haven-Kruse School for girls in Claymont was opened in 1893 with a normal capacity of seventy-five. Bridge House, a detention home for both male and female juveniles, opened in 1958 in Wilmington. Stevenson House in Milford was opened in 1970 with a normal capacity of twenty boys and girls held for disposition by the court. The Delaware Youth Center was opened in Dover in 1970 with a normal capacity of thirty-two male juvenile delinquents.

Delaware has been experiencing an increase in its prison population in recent years, as a result of which several of the facilities have become overcrowded. The institution population increased from 555 at the beginning of 1975 to 701 early in 1976, or by 27 percent. In 1977, the prison population continued to grow from 858 to 918 for a 7 percent increase in twelve months.

REFERENCES: American Correctional Association, *Directory*, 1975–1976 edition; Steve Gettinger, "U.S. Prison Population Hits All-Time High," *Corrections Magazine,* 1976; Michael Serrill, "Prison Population Rises Again, But at a Slower Rate," *Corrections Magazine,* 1978.

DISPARITY OF SENTENCES. A major source of inmate complaint is the wide disparity of sentences given different inmates convicted of like crimes committed under similar circumstances. The inmate who learns from another prisoner that he has received a much harsher sentence than another inmate with a similar background and a legally identical crime naturally experiences a profound sense of injustice and frustration.

It is a basic principle in American jurisprudence that the law be so constructed that every citizen know his obligations and the legal consequences of misconduct. Our laws are generally specific enough to fulfill this principle. The consequences of misconduct, however, are not as clear-cut. They involve an extremely wide range of permissible punishments as a result of the amount of discretion given to sentencing judges. An example from the federal criminal code illustrates the problem. Rape is punishable by death, or imprisonment for any term of years or for life, under Title 18, section 2031, of the U.S. Code. In many of the codes, the range of permissible punishment is specified with the phrase "not more than." Driving a stolen car across state lines calls for a term of not more than five years; robbery of a federally insured bank calls for a term of not more than twenty-five years. The sentencing judge can decide to grant probation and not incarcerate the offender at all, or he can sentence the felon to serve any term of years up to the maximum specified by the offense.

Federal Judge Marvin E. Frankel is a prominent critic of how judicial discretion is exercised. His highly acclaimed book, *Criminal Sentences* (1973), gives numerous examples of sentencing practices that are stupid at best and vicious at worst. Judges have no clear rationale for the purposes of sentencing, nor do federal or state laws provide adequate guidelines. The legal profession even neglects to provide criteria, training, or traditions to guide judges in the exercise of what Frankel calls "excessive judicial power."

The large amount of discretion allowed sentencing judges stems from the philosophy of corrections which states that the treatment of offenders should be individualized. For at least a century, Western civilization has avoided the use of criminal codes that rigidly assign a punishment to the crime to be applied evenly to all violators. Rather, the punishment should fit the individual criminal instead of the particular crime. Thus, criminal statutes are written to give judges a broad range of sentencing alternatives, in order to give them the flexibility to tailor the punishment to the offender's characteristics. Those characteristics are identified after conviction by a presentence investigation conducted by probation officers. The presentence investigation report is basically a social and legal history which guides the sentencing judge in imposing the sentence.

While the philosophy of individualized sentencing has its positive side, Frankel believes that it has not proven to be a viable policy since judges are not uniformly humane and sensitive. Their training as lawyers gives them little knowledge of criminal law and none of the problems of sentencing. During their twenty or thirty years of law practice after completing law school and before becoming judges, relatively few of these future judges gain experience in defending criminals and almost none experiences the socioeconomic conditions under which offenders live. In short, nothing in the judges' training or experience prepares them for understanding criminals. It is not surprising that they devote little time to the sentencing decision, nor is it surprising that they do not rank it as a meaningful aspect of their work. They must make a given number of decisions in the course of a work day, and they consider it more important that the decisions be made than that they be right.

As a result of the judges' lack of preparation for sentencing offenders, the amount of punishment meted out for the same crime often varies widely. Two men who collaborate in the same armed robbery may find that, upon conviction, one receives probation while the second is sentenced to five years in the state penitentiary. Upon arrival in the prison, the robber who is serving a five-year sentence may find that his cellmate has received a one-year sentence for a similar crime. Some criminologists believe that under such circumstances offenders become career criminals. After brooding over his harsh sentence for years inside the prison walls, the offender decides to "get even with society" when released by committing a series of crimes. For further information, see INDETERMINATE SENTENCES.

REFERENCES: Alan M. Dershowitz, "Criminal Sentencing in the United States: An Historical and Conceptual Overview," *Annals of the American Academy of Political and Social Science,* 1976; Marvin E. Frankel, *Criminal Sentences: Law Without Order,* 1973; John Hogarth, *Sentencing As a Human Process,* 1971; Pierce O'Donnell, Michael J. Churgin, and Dennis E. Curtis, *Toward a Just and Effective Sentencing System: Agenda for Legislative Reform,* 1977; Leo H. Whinery and others, *Predictive Sentencing: An Empirical Evaluation,* 1976.

DISTRICT OF COLUMBIA CORRECTIONAL SYSTEM. With a total population of only 760,000, Washington, D.C., had more than 2,500 adults and juveniles incarcerated in its correctional facilities as of 1975. (These facilities are the equivalent of state correctional systems elsewhere.) An additional 1,200 adults and juveniles are held in detention facilities (jails). This prison population, extremely large for a city the size of the District, is attributed to the number of violent crimes in Washington rather than to harsh sentences. Several state correctional systems serving vastly larger populations—for example, Arkansas, Colorado, or Massachusetts—have smaller inmate populations. Like other jurisdictions, the District sentences the less dangerous offenders to probation and paroles inmates who have made satisfactory adjustments to prison life. In 1975, the District had almost 5,000 adult and youthful probationers and nearly 3,000 adult and youthful parolees in addition to its incarcerated adults and juveniles.

Washington's largest complex of correctional institutions is located in Fairfax County, Virginia. The D.C. Department of Corrections, which administers parole, detention, and correctional institutions for adults, operates three of the five institutions located in the correctional complex known widely as Lorton Reformatory. These three separate institutions for adult males are set up by the three security grades minimum security, medium security, and maximum security. The other two prisons in the correctional complex serve youthful offenders sentenced under the Youth Corrections Act of 1950. This act specifies that sentenced persons must be between the ages of sixteen and twenty-two years and that they be entitled to be held apart from adult offenders. Youths are required to serve indeterminate sentences and, under the act, must be given treatment programs.

Female offenders are sent to the U.S. Bureau of Prisons' Federal Reformatory for Women in Alderson, West Virginia. Even though the U.S. Bureau of Prisons does house the female offenders from Washington and some male prisoners, the bureau is entirely separate from the D.C. system. The bureau receives persons from all parts of the country who are sentenced for violation of federal laws, while the D.C. system receives persons convicted of offenses that would ordinarily be crimes under state laws.

Another complex of correctional facilities is located near Laurel, Maryland. Three separate institutions for juveniles ranging in age from eight to eighteen are located here and are administered by the Bureau of Youth Services, a part of the D.C. Department of Human Resources: Oak Hill School, a maximum security facility; Cedar Knoll School, with a lower custody grade (inmates are not as likely to escape); and Maple Glen School, which is for Persons in Need of Supervision (PINS), that is, children who have been neglected or abused by their parents and who have committed delinquent acts. The Bureau of Youth Services also administers aftercare (parole) for juveniles and operates nine group homes.

While the District of Columbia correctional system is by no means free of disturbances and escape attempts, the administrators of the system believe that they have managed to eliminate one source of friction that plagues most systems: racial conflict. In many state systems, the proportion of black inmates is rather high compared to the total black population in the state. Most penologists agree that this disproportionately large black inmate population, rather than indicating a racial propensity for crime, suggests a bias in the criminal justice system that causes poor people to be arrested, convicted, and imprisoned more frequently than the rich or middle class. Racial conflict often arises in U.S. prisons when the prison staff is dominated by whites. In such prisons, black inmates can easily see themselves as victims of a racist white society. The District of Columbia is unique in that it does not have this problem. The top layer of executives in the system consists of black administrators who point out that their rapport with the inmates (about 95 percent black) is possible because they themselves are black and also because many of them have a ghetto background.

The District of Columbia prison population continues to grow with a 5 percent increase from 2,342 to 2,464 between January 1, 1977, and January 1, 1978.

REFERENCES: Michael S. Serrill, "Profile/District of Columbia," *Corrections Magazine,* 1975; Michael Serrill, "Prison Population Rises Again, But at a Slower Rate," *Corrections Magazine,* 1978.

E

EASTERN PENITENTIARY. For 141 years this penitentiary in Phildelphia was one of the most famous prisons in the world. The cornerstone for construction of the massive structure bounded by Fairmount Avenue, 21st and 22nd streets, was laid on May 23, 1823. It was abandoned as a state prison in 1970 because of its age, and the last of its inmates were transferred on April 13. But it was soon pressed into service again by the city government as a detention center. About 75,000 men and several hundred women served prison sentences at Eastern since Charles Williams, a black man from Delaware County, became its first prisoner on October 25, 1829.

Eastern Penitentiary, known simply as Cherry Hill because of a cherry orchard on the construction site, is renowned both for its architecture (q.v.) and for representing the epitome of the unique penal philosophy known as the Pennsylvania System of Prison Discipline (q.v.). John Haviland, the architect of the institution, gave it the beauty and durability of the castles of the Middle Ages; architects and artists have hailed it as a work of art. Even the wall surrounding the ten-acre site draws admiration from architects; built of Falls of Schuylkill stone, it is twelve feet thick at the base, thirty feet high, and almost three feet thick at the top.

In the nineteenth century, many well-known visitors came to see the architectural features of Cherry Hill and to study the correctional philosophy practiced there. In 1831, France sent two officials to study the prison—Gustave de Beaumont and Alexis de Tocqueville—both of whom talked to Charles Williams before he finished his two-year sentence. Fredrika Bremer, a Swedish novelist, and Harriett Martineau, the British author, also visited Cherry Hill and wrote about their favorable impressions. Dickens became the most famous critic of the prison after a visit on March 8, 1842. One of the Cherry Hill prisoners interviewed by Dickens is believed to be the "Dutchman" in Dickens' works. Louis Dwight, founder of the Boston Prison Discipline Society, was also a vocal critic of Cherry Hill and of its approach to corrections. In contrast, Dorothea Lynde Dix praised Eastern as a model prison. All of these writers contributed to the fame of the prison. Alexis de Tocqueville was especially influential in promoting the style of prison it represented, and as a result it has been widely copied in Europe. For a discussion of the philosophy of corrections practiced at Cherry Hill, see PENNSYLVANIA SYSTEM OF PRISON DISCIPLINE.

REFERENCES: Harry Elmer Barnes, *The Evolution of Penology in Pennsylvania: A Study in American Social History,* 1968 (1927); Norman Johnston, *The Human Cage: A Brief History of Prison Architecture,* 1973; Negley K. Teeters, "The Passing of Cherry Hill: Most Famous Prison in the World," *Prison Journal,* 1970.

F

FEDERAL CENTER FOR CORRECTIONAL RESEARCH. The center, located in Butner, North Carolina, and one of the U.S. Bureau of Prisons' newest facilities, began receiving inmates in the early part of 1976. The institution has two sections: (1) a mental health section for mentally disturbed prisoners consisting of a thirty-eight bed facility for young male offenders, a sixty-four bed facility for adult male offenders, and a thirty-eight bed facility for female offenders; and (2) a research section that will house 200 inmates in four sections containing fifty beds each. The 340 inmates will be watched over by slightly more than 200 staff members. The two sections of the institution share a chapel, gymnasium, commissary, infirmary, and other necessary support buildings.

Designated as a medium security facility, the institution utilizes heavy-duty plastic windows with wiring instead of traditional iron bars over the windows. An underground electrical sensing field around the double fences serves as perimeter security instead of the usual guard towers. Inmates live in single rooms that are air conditioned. The site was selected for its proximity to university research facilities at Chapel Hill, Durham, and Raleigh.

The new facility was in the planning and construction phases for more than fifteen years. In 1961, the Bureau of Prisons first received appropriations from Congress for a planned 750-bed mental hospital for inmates that was to be named the Eastern Psychiatric Institute. Construction was postponed during the 1960s as bids were consistently too high, and plans were laid aside altogether during the latter part of the 1960s. The bureau finally revived the project in 1971 when it proposed that the smaller institution be used for correctional research as well as for conventional treatment of mentally disturbed prisoners. Construction of the $14 million facility was started in 1972, but difficulties with the contractor postponed its completion from 1974 to the early months of 1976.

The institution became controversial long before the actual construction was completed. In 1972, as construction began, Martin Groder was named warden of Butner Center; at age thirty-five, he would be the youngest warden in the federal system and the only warden with psychiatric training. Groder became a widely known figure in the field ·of corrections in the years prior to 1972, when he pioneered the treatment program in the new federal penitentiary at Marion, Illinois. The Marion institution, a maximum security facility replacing Alcatraz (*q.v.*), established a therapeutic milieu in the new facility in hopes of avoiding the oppressive atmosphere long associated with Alcatraz. Groder pioneered a treatment program at Marion that initially was heavily oriented toward the use of transactional analysis therapy (*q.v.*) that he had learned while working with Eric Berne. Groder developed his own eclectic mode of therapy during his 1968 to 1972 tour of duty at Marion by combining transactional analysis techniques with the attack therapy and group-living approaches associated with the California drug treatment program at Synanon. Groder's hybrid treatment mode has become known as Asklepieion therapy (*q.v.*). His use of Asklepieion techniques brought Groder a large measure of praise and national recognition. The praise was not universal, however. Aware that as warden Groder would use his Asklepieion therapy at the Butner institution, his critics attempted to discredit Groder. Inevitably, the controversy surrounding Groder became attached to the Federal Center for Correctional Research. Alvin J. Bronstein, executive director of the National Prison Project of the American Civil Liberties Union (ACLU) and a leading critic of Groder's techniques, maintained that techniques altering personality and behavior could not be used in prison settings without violating the prisoners' civil rights. Peter Breggin, executive director of the Center for the Study of Psychiatry, also opposed Groder's techniques. Breggin is a member of the United Church of Christ's Commission for Racial Justice, a group that investigated Groder's program. Breggin's group expressed fear that Groder would use drug therapy, hypnotic therapy, electroshock treatment, and aversion therapy at Butner Center—techniques that they considered equivalent to torture. Groder answered these charges by explaining that his program had a number of built-in safeguards. He stated that inmates in the program had to be volunteers, they were free to withdraw whenever they wished, and the parole board would not be given reports on their progress in the program.

On April 3, 1975, Groder added to the controversy by calling a press conference and reading his letter of resignation from the Bureau of Prisons. In the letter, he accused Director Norman A. Carlson (*q.v.*) of abandoning the treatment ideology in the federal system, discarding the bureau's plans to conduct research at Butner Center, and secretly making plans to convert the new facility into a conventional prison or mental hospital for inmates. Carlson replied that while he was reevaluating some of the planned programs at Butner, he had not changed the basic purpose of the new facility.

Following Groder's abrupt resignation, Carlson appointed Donald A. Deppe warden of the new center. Deppe plans a variety of educational, vocational training, and treatment programs for the facility, but he does not intend to use Groder's Asklepieion techniques. To dispel rumors about the use of the institution, Deppe announced that only conventional treatment modes would be used. Hence, the program would not employ aversive conditioning, drugs in therapy, or other controversial techniques. Groder, now in private practice, continues as an influence in the field of corrections by working with Asklepieion programs in various prisons around the country. For treatment of related ideas, see ASKLEPIEION THERAPY, PRAGMATISTS, AND RIGHT TO "NO TREATMENT" CONTROVERSY.

REFERENCES: "Follow-Up," *Corrections Magazine,* 1975; Steve Gettinger, "Dr. Martin Groder: An Angry Resignation," *Corrections Magazine,* 1975; Constance Holden, "Butner: Experimental U.S. Prison Holds Promise, Stirs Trepidation," *Science,* 1974.

FEDERAL CORRECTIONAL SYSTEM. The U.S. Bureau of Prisons, a part of the U.S. Department of Justice, was established on May 14, 1930, by an act of Congress to provide care for persons convicted of crimes against the United States. Currently, the bureau operates forty-seven facilities administered by directors in five regions.

In 1930, when President Herbert Hoover signed the act creating the U.S. Bureau of Prisons, a detention facility, an institution for delinquents, a prison for women, and three penitentiaries for adult males were operating autonomously. The 12,300 population in the six facilities was well above their rated capacity of 7,400. Services for these inmates were limited to some academic training at the elementary school level, religious services provided by prison chaplains, and farm or maintenance work designed to occupy the time of inmates and keep the costs of operating the institution within reason. When the bureau was created, management of the federal prisons was centralized under the bureau director, and centralization has brought about many changes in the system.

The bureau has had four directors: Sanford Bates (1930–1937); James V. Bennett (1937–1964); Myrl E. Alexander (1964–1970); and Norman A. Carlson (*q.v.*) (1970 to the present).

Over the years the number of federal prisoners has grown steadily with the increase in crime and the addition of new criminal laws to federal statutes. In adding new institutions to accommodate an increasing number of prisoners, the bureau, over a period of twenty years, has developed a graded system of institutions to care for offenders who have different needs and who constitute varying degrees of security risk.

Offenders who are serving sentences longer than five years are housed in maximum security prisons if they are deemed to be security risks. The bureau has six such institutions, all of which are designated U.S. penitentiaries; hence, they can be distinguished only in terms of their location: (1) the penitentiary at Atlanta, Georgia, opened in 1902 with a normal capacity of 1,900 adults; (2) the penitentiary at Terre Haute, Indiana, opened in 1940 with a rated capacity of 1,075; (3) the system's newest and smallest penitentiary, that at Marion, Illinois, opened in 1963 with a capacity of 620; (4) the penitentiary at Leavenworth, Kansas, opened in 1895 with a normal capacity of 1,900; (5) the facility at Lewisburg, Pennsylvania, opened in 1932 with a normal capacity of 1,150; and (6) the oldest penitentiary still in use, that on McNeil Island, Steilacoom, Washington, opened in 1889 with a current rated capacity of 1,000. All six penitentiaries are used for adult male felons only.

The bureau's medium security prisons are known as correctional institutions, and all are officially called federal correctional institutions. The bureau has twelve such facilities. These prisons normally house offenders serving sentences of two to five years; on the whole, they tend to be much smaller than the penitentiaries and may house both male and female prisoners. The locations of the twelve prisons, with their opening dates and rated capacities are as follows: Danbury, Connecticut, 1940, 600 males; Lompoc, California, 1959, 1,350 males; Terminal Island, Los Angeles, California, 1955, 600 males and 160 females; Tallahassee, Florida, 1938, 480 males; Lexington, Kentucky, 1974, 500 males and 100 females; Milan, Michigan, 1933, 535 males; Sandstone, Minnesota, 1959, 450 males; Fort Worth, Texas, 1971, 400 males and 100 females; La Tuna, Texas, 1932, 550 males; Seagoville, Texas (once used to house female prisoners), 1940, 400 males; Texarkana, Texas, 1940, 475 males; and Oxford, Wisconsin, 1973, 250 males.

In 1975, the U.S. Bureau of Prisons opened three medium security facilities designated as metropolitan correctional centers. Each facility holds both adult males and females serving sentences of two to five years. These centers are located in Chicago, New York City, and San Diego.

Two federal detention centers, used to hold suspects awaiting trial, are also classified as medium security facilities: the center in Florence, Arizona, opened in 1963 with a normal capacity of 130; and the center in El Paso, Texas, opened in 1974 with a normal capacity of 155.

The Medical Center for Federal Prisoners opened in 1933 at Springfield, Missouri, with a rated capacity of 1,003 males; it is designated a medium security prison.

In addition, the U.S. Bureau of Prisons operates three medium security prisons known as reformatories: El Reno, Oklahoma, 1933, 900 males; Petersburg, Virginia, 1930, 500 males; and Alderson, West Virginia, 1927, 475 females. These facilities were opened during a period of penal history (1927–1933) when the name reformatory indicated institutions that provided rehabilitation programs in addition to the traditional custody. The name does not necessarily indicate any difference in treatment programming in the contemporary systems; even the maximum security penitentiaries now provide a substantial range of treatment programs.

The bureau's federal youth centers are minimum security facilities for persons serving sentences of less than two years. Four facilities of this type hold juvenile and youth offenders: Pleasanton, California, 1974, 190 males and 60 females eighteen to twenty-five years of age; Englewood, Colorado, 1940, 325 males fifteen to nineteen years of age; Ashland, Kentucky, 1940, 425 males eighteen to twenty-three years of age; and the Robert F. Kennedy Youth Center at Morgantown, West Virginia, 1968, 310 males. The Morgantown facility replaced the old Boy's School in the District of Columbia; female offenders were also held there for several years, but it became an all-male facility in 1975.

Other minimum security facilities hold adult offenders who are serving short sentences. Four federal prison camps serve this purpose: Maxwell Air Force Base, Montgomery, Alabama, 1930, 250 males; Safford, Arizona, 1958, 250 males; Eglin Air Force Base, Florida, 1962, 450 males; and Allenwood at Montgomery, Pennsylvania, 1952, 410 males.

The thirty-five institutions listed above are traditional prisons in the sense that most are immediately recognizable as prisons by any casual passerby. The bureau has been operating a newer type of residential facility in recent years that is not characterized by the usual architectual prison features. Called community treatment centers (*q.v.*), these facilities provide living quarters for twenty to eighty offenders who pursue a vocation in the surrounding community. These centers do not necessarily operate out of government buildings. Their program can be operated out of hotels, YMCAs, and other privately owned accommodations where living space can be leased. All of the twelve centers operated by the bureau are in large cities: Phoenix, Arizona; Los Angeles, California; Long Beach, California; Oakland, California; Miami, Florida; Atlanta, Georgia; Chicago, Illinois; Detroit, Michigan; Kansas City, Missouri; New York City; Houston, Texas; and Dallas, Texas.

The Federal Correctional Institution (FCI) is the latest name for the newest addition to the federal prison system. Despite its newness, the institution has a long history because it has been in the planning stages since the latter part of the 1950s. The official name of the facility changed several times before it ever opened and, for the sake of simplicity, it is simply called "Butner" on an informal basis for its location at Butner, North Carolina. Originally, it was intended to be an institution for emotionally disturbed offenders, and the location was picked due to its proximity to local universities with psychiatric and psychological training programs. However, funds were not available for the project until the 1970s, when the project was revived. By the time the institution was actually built and ready to receive inmates in March 1976, its missions were to develop and evaluate a number of treatment modalities and to house federal prisoners who were acutely suicidal or severely psychotic.

The inmate population in federal prisons is growing as it is in state prison systems. The number of federal prisoners increased 6 percent from 27,665 to 29,457 between January 1, 1977, and January 1, 1978.

For additional information on the uses of residential centers, see COMMUNITY TREATMENT CENTERS. For a discussion of the controversy surrounding FCI, see FEDERAL CENTER FOR CORRECTIONAL RESEARCH.

REFERENCES: American Correctional Association, *Directory,* 1975–1976 edition; Norman A. Carlson, "The Federal Prison System: Forty-five Years of Change," *Federal Probation,* 1975; William G. Nagel, *An American Archipelago: The Federal Bureau of Prisons,* 1974; Michael Serrill, "Prison Population Rises Again, But at a Slower Rate," *Corrections Magazine,* 1978.

FEDERAL PRISON INDUSTRIES, INC. This government-owned corporation, established in 1934, operates as a part of the U.S. Bureau of Prisons, and is run by a board of directors appointed by the president of the United States. The current board members are James L.

Palmer, representing retailers and consumers; John Marshall Briley, representing the secretary of defense; George Meany, labor; Berry N. Beaman, industry; William E. Morgan, agriculture; and Peter B. Bensinger, the U.S. attorney general.

Federal Prison Industries provides full-time employment for about one-fourth of all inmates in the federal prison system; the services and products produced throughout the system are sold only to other federal agencies. Inmate employees of the system earn modest wages, usually less than a dollar per hour, and receive training in work skills that often give them employment opportunities after their release. The corporation studies the array of activities performed from time to time and phases out those operations that have minimal work training value in favor of activities that provide marketable skills for the inmates involved.

Money earned from the sale of goods and services produced by the corporation is used to finance the U.S. Bureau of Prisons' vocational training program. Profits also finance the work of employment placement officers located in metropolitan areas; these officers assist probationers and releasees in finding employment. Remaining profits are paid to the U.S. Treasury as dividends.

In 1975, sales from goods and services produced by some 13,300 inmates employed by the corporation totaled $68.8 million. Profits of $8.9 million financed the bureau's vocational training program for 12,000 federal prisoners. Part of the profits were used to give special monetary awards to about 26,000 inmates, and the remainder increased the net worth of the corporation by $2.8 million.

During 1975, the corporation operated factories located at twenty-three federal institutions; 580 civilian employees trained the inmate workers and supervised their work; and more than forty different types of goods and services were produced for sale to other federal agencies. The seven major groups of products and services were automated data processing; electronics; graphics; metals; shoe and brush; textiles; and wood and plastics.

The automated data processing division provides computer programming and data encoding services such as keypunch, key-to-disk, and key-to-tape. Four plants are involved in this division: Alderson, West Virginia; Fort Worth, Texas; Leavenworth, Kansas; and Terminal Island, California. The main federal customers for this division are the Department of Agriculture, the Department of Defense, and the Department of Commerce.

The electronics division produces all types of wiring devices, electrical cable assemblies, electronic wiring harnesses, printed circuits, electronic systems, and support systems. Five plants are involved in the production of this division: Danbury, Connecticut; Lompoc, California; McNeil Island, Washington; Oxford, Wisconsin; and Petersburg, Virginia. The Department of Defense is the major customer of this division.

The graphics division does general and special custom printing, produces wood and metal signs and decals, and provides drafting services. Five plants are involved in the division: Atlanta, Georgia; Lompoc, California; Marion, Illinois; Oxford, Wisconsin; and Sandstone, Minnesota. Customers of the division include the Department of Defense.

The metals division produces metal office furniture, steel shelving, aluminum lockers, military beds, casters, bore brushes, tools, and dies. The division also supervises the production of several nonmetal items including brooms, dairy products, automotive repair, and tire rebuilding. Nine plants participate in these operations: Ashland, Kentucky; El Reno, Oklahoma; La Tuna, Texas; Lewisburg, Pennsylvania; Marion, Illinois; Milan, Michigan; Petersburg, Virginia; Tallahassee, Florida; and Terminal Island, California.

The shoe and brush division produces military dress shoes, safety shoes, orthopedic and custom shoes, institutional shoes, several varieties of paint, varnish, and maintenance brushes. The three plants involved in the operations of this division are at La Tuna, Texas; Leavenworth, Kansas; and Springfield, Missouri. Primary federal customers are the Department of Defense, the General Services Administration, and the Department of Justice.

In terms of total sales, the textile division is the largest division in the corporation with sales in excess of $25 million out of the corporation's total sales of almost $69 million. This division produces cotton and wool textiles, canvas, canvas goods, synthetic textile products, mattresses, gloves, clothing, and weather parachutes. The seven plants for these products are at Alderson, West Virginia; Atlanta, Georgia; Danbury, Connecticut; Lewisburg, Pennsylvania; Safford, Arizona; Sandstone, Minnesota; and Terre Haute, Indiana. Major customers of the division include the U.S. Postal Service, the Department of Defense, the General Services Administration, and the Veterans Administration.

The wood and plastics division produces Allenwood walnut furniture, solid wood furniture, molded fiberglass with chrome trim furniture, plastic laminated particle-board furniture, lifeboat repair, fiberglass molding, and furniture refinishing. Eleven plants participate in this production: Allenwood, Pennsylvania; La Tuna, Texas; Leavenworth, Kansas; Lompoc, California; McNeil Island, Washington; Oxford, Wisconsin; Seagoville, Texas; Tallahassee, Florida; Terminal Island, California; Terre Haute, Indiana; and Texarkana, Texas. Primary customers include the Department of Defense, the General Services Administration, the Department of Justice, and the Veterans Administration.

REFERENCES: Federal Prison Industries, Inc., *1975 Annual Report,* printed at the printing plant in the U.S. Penitentiary at Marion, Illinois, 1976; Georgetown University Law Center, Institute of Criminal Procedure, *The Role of Prison Industries Now and in the Future,* 1974.

FEMALE OFFENDERS. Information on the characteristics of incarcerated females was sparse prior to the 1970s. By 1972, however, many researchers had become sensitive to the neglect of this area of study, and as a result there is a rapidly growing body of literature on the characteristics and problems of the female offender. The reported results of surveys and research projects reveal the following profile of women in prison: (1) they come from poor families; (2) they have been neglected by their parents; (3) they have a rather poor self-image; (4) about 67 percent are mothers; (5) about 50 percent are under thirty years of age; (6) almost half have less than a tenth grade education; and (7) they have held low-paying, low-status jobs.

Their offenses are predominantly prostitution, shoplifting, forgery, larceny, and burglary. One of the few encouraging crime statistics available is the 4.5 percent decrease in homicides by women in the United States during the 1964–1970 period. On the other hand, wardens of federal women's prisons believe that female commitments for bank robbery are rising, but statistics are not available to confirm their impressions. The question of whether women are committing more bank robberies is part of a broader question being raised by some writers: are women committing different types of crime because of the impact of the women's rights movement? Some writers speculate that the movement may have made American women less passive and more assertive. If so, they state, it is not unreasonable to look for evidence of an increased number of violent crimes committed by women. However, there is no convincing evidence that the patterns of criminal behavior are changing in this respect. The impact of the women's rights movement probably has not touched the lives of the lower class females who make up the bulk of the population of women's prisons, and no one can be sure that they would tend to commit more violent crimes if the impact did reach them. In 1972, Walter Miller, in a longitudinal study of a girls' gang made over thirty months, noted that the females involved in the study had the same opportunities to commit street crimes as did males, but their most frequent offense was truancy.

Incarceration statistics show that more women were being sent to prison in the 1970s than in previous decades. In 1974, for instance, 3 percent of the prison population was female, compared to 2.5 percent in 1964. Current research efforts are exploring a number of promising leads in an attempt to account for these increased commitments. The obvious avenue of inquiry is the attempt to discover whether women really are committing more crimes than ever before, but such studies, thus far, do not support that hypothesis. An increased commitment rate for women could be the result of a shift in the types of crimes committed from less to more serious crimes, but as yet no evidence supporting the possibility that they are indeed committing more serious crimes has emerged.

No one really knows why more women are being committed to prison. Perhaps the research that is being conducted on shifts in society's reaction to offenses committed by women may finally provide the answer. A growing population in women's prisons could be the result of subtle changes in the way women are processed through the criminal justice system. In the past, the predominantly male personnel in the criminal justice system may have been exhibiting a patronizing attitude toward women offenders that resulted in less severe punishment for women than for men found guilty of the same type of crime. While it is highly doubtful that the women's rights movement has had an impact on the socioeconomic strata from which U.S. female convicts are drawn, it is possible that it may have influenced the more highly educated male prosecutors and judges to begin meting out sentences for women that are as harsh as those given to male offenders. Based on our historical experience with the impact of discrimination on the criminal trial process, there is a certain logic to exploring this possibility. When members of minority groups were allowed to take their places on juries and on the judges' bench, their lack of patronization toward other minority group members resulted in harsher treatment. Likewise, when enlisted men took their places on military court martial boards beside officers, their higher expectations of standards of conduct appropriate for enlisted men resulted in harsher treatment for offenders. It appears that achievement of equality is hard on criminals.

REFERENCES: Freda Adler, *Sisters in Crime: The Rise of the New Female Criminal,* 1975; American Bar Association, Female Offender Resource Center, *Female Offenders: Problems and Programs,* 1976; Phyllis Jo Baunach and Thomas O. Murton, "Women in Prison: An Awakening Minority," *Crime and Delinquency,* 1973; Annette M. Brodsky (ed.), *The Female Offender,* 1975; Edna Walker Chandler, *Women in Prison,* 1973; Laura Crites (ed.), *The Female Offender,* 1976; Richard Deming, *Women: The New Criminals,* 1977; Joy S. Eyman, *Prisons for Women: A Practical Guide to Administration Problems,* 1971; Rose Giallombardo, *The Social World of Imprisoned Girls: A Comparative Study of Institutions for Juvenile Delinquents,* 1974; Rose Giallombardo, *Society of Women: A Study of a Women's Prison,* 1966; Esther Heffernan, *Making It in Prison: The Square, the Cool, and the Life,* 1972; Walter B. Miller, "The Molls," *Society,* 1973; Rita Simon, "American Women and Crime," *Annals of the American Academy of Political and Social Science,* 1976; Carol Smart, *Women, Crime and Criminology: A Feminist Critique,* 1977; Elizabeth M. Suval and Robert C. Brisson, "Neither Beauty Nor Beast: Female Criminal Homicide Offenders," *International Journal of Criminology and Penology,* 1974; Clyde B. Vedder and Dora B. Somerville, *The Delinquent Girl,* 1975; Margery L. Velimesis, "The Female Offender," *Crime and Delinquency Literature,* 1975; David A. Ward and Gene G. Kassebaum, *Women's Prison: Sex and Social Structure,* 1965.

FLORIDA CORRECTIONAL SYSTEM. Florida's adult prison system has been crowded in recent years and appears to be getting increasingly more so. In 1974, the adult system in Florida had 10,400 inmates at a time when the total state population was 7.5 million. In the same year, the state of Illinois, with a total population of 13 million, had 6,000 adults in its prisons. Since 1974, the situation has worsened. The prison population of the Florida correctional system increased from 11,420 on January 1, 1975, to 15,709 on January 1, 1976, an increase of 38 percent in one year. The nationwide increase for this period was 11 percent.

One reason for the high proportion of inmates to total population in Florida is that parole is not as easily obtainable there as in most other states; about 40 percent of all adult inmates complete their sentences without receiving parole. For their part, correctional officials in Florida attribute it to the rapid growth of the state's total population and to a substantial increase in the use of drugs. The typical inmate in the Florida adult system is a young black male. Some 70 percent of all inmates are less than twenty-six years of age, and 57 percent of all inmates are black. (The statewide black population is 16 percent.)

Two prisons for adult males are located in a north-central Florida complex collectively called Raiford: the Union Correctional Institution (UCI) at Raiford and the Florida State Prison at Starke. The state prison at Starke was opened in 1961 with a normal capacity of 1,255 males aged fourteen and above; UCI was opened in 1914 with a normal capacity of 1,050 and serves the same kind of population as the Starke facility. The Starke facility was officially a part of the Raiford complex until 1972 when it was renamed the Florida State Prison and given a separate administration, but among Floridians it is still widely known simply as Raiford. The Starke prison was designated a maximum security prison when it was split off from the Raiford complex in 1972; UCI has housed inmates of all security classifications since the 1972 split. UCI is one of the most overcrowded facilities in the Florida system; most of its inmates are housed in one building built in 1927 with cells intended to house four men each. The UCI building, known to inmates as "The Rock," has had seven men in each four-man cell in recent years. UCI is also home of a forty-three cell punishment unit in a separate low concrete structure known to inmates as "The Flat Top." James Blake, a successful inmate author, publicized these two structures in his book *The Joint* (1971).

The adult prison system is administered under the aegis of the Department of Offender Rehabilitation headed by Secretary Louie L. Wainwright. As a past president of the American Correctional Association (*q.v.*), Wainwright has gained a national reputation in the field of corrections. Some of his critics contend that he is too conservative to manage the changes needed in Florida's rapidly growing system, but John Dussich, a staff member in the statewide criminal justice planning agency, is among those who point out that Florida is more progressive than other southern states in its approach to corrections. One recent change is the attempt to create nearly forty small facilities in urban areas to house groups of inmates engaged in work release (*q.v.*) or study release programs. The division planned to have all of these facilities in operation by the end of 1974, but their efforts were slowed by opposition launched by citizens in many communities who did not want one of the units located in their neighborhood. Another notable change is the reduction in the number of old-style road prisons from thirty-six to ten. The road prisons were established in 1917, and new road prisons were built until 1950. Now, there are only ten road prisons and three vocational centers, holding some 900 adult males, scattered throughout the state.

The Reception and Medical Center opened at Lake Butler in 1967 with a normal capacity of 600. Other adult prisons in the state, aside from those discussed above, are known as correctional institutions. The names of these institutions, together with their opening dates and normal capacities are as follows: Apalachee at Sneads, 1949, 565 males in its Youth Unit and 140 males in its Farm Unit; Avon Park at Avon Park, 1973, 300 males; Desoto at Arcadia, 1969, 510 males; Florida at Lowell—the Female Unit, 1956, 326, and the Male Unit, 1960, 195; Glades at Belle Glade, 1932, but replaced in 1951 with a facility housing 525 males; Lake at Clermont, 1973, 225 males; Lantana at Lantana, 1975, 150 males; River Junction at Chattahoochee, 1974, 350 males; and Sumter at Bushnell, 1965, 576 males.

Juvenile institutions in the state are administered by the Division of Youth Services, which is part of the Department of Health and Rehabilitative Services. The Division of Youth Services is further divided into the Bureau of Training Schools, the Bureau of Community Services, and the Bureau of Field Services. The division works with about 1,700 youths on a full-time basis; some 1,000 of these are in the state's four training schools: the Arthur G. Dozier School for Boys at Marianna, opened in 1900, with capacity for 450; the Florida School for Boys at Okeechobee, opened in 1959 with room for 500; the Lancaster Youth Development Center at Trenton, opened in 1971 with a rated capacity of 150; and the state's training school for girls, the Alyce C. McPherson School for Girls at Ocala, opened in 1914 with a rated capacity of 300.

Joseph R. Rowan has been director of the Division of Youth Services since 1973 when he replaced Oliver J. Keller, who was promoted to a cabinet-level job at that time. Both men have brought major changes to the system. Rowan is planning further modifications by reducing the population of the juvenile institutions from 1,000 to 400 by 1978 and eventually closing three of the four existing training schools. Under Rowan's plan, youths would be placed in a large network of foster group homes providing care for 1,000 young offenders.

The greatest credit for transforming Florida's juvenile correctional system belongs to State Senator Louis de la Parte, sponsor of the bill creating the Division of Youth Services. It was he who hired Oliver Keller to head the division in 1967. Keller, co-author of *Halfway Houses: Community-Centered Correction and Treatment* (1970), abandoned the traditional caseworker treatment approach to juvenile corrections and established Guided Group Interaction (GGI) (*q.v.*) as the primary mode of treatment for juveniles in the state.

In addition to its four training schools, the state's youth system includes nine halfway houses; three small halfway houses that have their own schools (designated START centers); five Group Treatment Homes, each consisting of a seven-bed facility administered by a husband and wife team caring for younger emotionally disturbed children; and seven nonresidential centers for youths who live at home and come to the center after school for GGI sessions on a regular basis.

Florida has involved private groups and nonprofessionals in juvenile corrections. About 800 volunteers work in youth corrections in the state, some 550 of whom spend twenty hours a month working with young probationers and parolees on a one-to-one basis. The Eckerd Foundation, a privately endowed organization, operates two camps for boys twelve years of age and younger; the boys learn wilderness lore while attending classes in the camps. The Associated Marine Institutes, another private group, has four centers serving a total of 130 young probationers who learn oceanography.

The prison population in Florida has increased steadily in recent years from 11,420 on January 1, 1975, to 18,602 on January 1, 1977, to 19,643 on January 1, 1978.

REFERENCES: American Correctional Association, *Directory,* 1975–1976 edition; Ronald H. Bailey, "Profile/Florida," *Corrections Magazine,* 1974; James Blake, *The Joint,* 1971; Michael Serrill, "Prison Population Rises Again, But at a Slower Rate," *Corrections Magazine,* 1978.

FOGEL, DAVID (1925–   ). While holding his current post as Executive Director of the Illinois Law Enforcement Commission, a position he has held since 1973, David Fogel published a controversial new book ". . . *We Are the Living Proof . . .": The Justice Model for Corrections* (1975). The book presents a plan for reshaping the rationale of corrections. Fogel began developing this plan while he was serving as commissioner of the Minnesota Department of Corrections from 1971 to 1973. His book argues convincingly that criminals cannot be rehabilitated while they are inmates of correctional institutions. In Fogel's plan, society should make massive efforts to rehabilitate its convicted criminals through probation, halfway houses, and similar community corrections techniques that would divert them from prison. He feels, along with many other experienced penologists, that the vast majority of inmates in prisons in the United States do not pose such a threat to the safety of the public that they need to be kept in prison. Thus, Fogel argues, our prisons should hold only a fraction of their present population, and those who are sent to prison should serve relatively short, "flat" sentences of specified length with no hope of parole.

Fogel's plan is the result of his belief that our efforts to conduct rehabilitation programs in our nation's prisons have not had any significant results. In the past four or five decades penologists have added and refined prison programs meant to change incarcerated criminals into productive citizens. They have promoted therapeutic psychological techniques such as transactional analysis, academic educational programs providing a range of courses from basic literacy to a college degree, vocational-training programs meant to prepare the inmate for productive work after release, and various recreational and religious activities. The framework for these rehabilitation efforts is the indeterminate sentence and parole. Penologists who do believe in the possibility of rehabilitation within the confines of the prison feel they need to have control over the length of an individual inmate's prison sentence. When treatment is successful, the inmate can be released from prison early, by means of the indeterminate sentence, under the partial supervision of parole.

With the publication of his 1975 book, Fogel became the leading spokesman for an increasing group of penologists who had lost faith in the standard prescriptions for penal rehabilitation. In their considerable experience, they found no convincing evidence that rehabilitation in prisons was possible. The early promise of indeterminate sentences and parole had faded in their opinion. Inmates who had roughly the same background and had committed similar crimes under similar circumstances served sentences of vastly different lengths without any apparent therapeutic justification. Inmates came to feel that the prison system was both irrational and unjust, and penologists like Fogel listened to their complaints, studied their records, and eventually came to agree with them. It is significant that Fogel served as chief executive of the Minnesota prison system, for Minnesota has an excellent reputation for supporting a progressive and humane prison system. Over the years, its penologists have exerted leadership by being among the first to install ever more progressive treatment modalities in their state penal system. Some states have not given progressive penal approaches a serious trial, but that can hardly be said of Minnesota. If rehabilitation is not working in that system, there is cause for concern.

Fogel's arguments are well reasoned. He urges us to rethink what we can hope to accomplish with prisons. He is humane because he advocates the use of shorter sentences and takes into consideration the typical inmate's distaste for the uncertainty of the indeterminate sentence. Under the flat sentences he proposes, inmates would know precisely when they would be released and would have some sense of the fairness of the system. The best we can hope for from prisons, Fogel believes, is that they will help to deter some crimes and not that they will rehabilitate.

Fogel's plan is unpopular with traditional penologists who are trained in the usual medical model of corrections wherein the offender is sick and must be treated in the prison. Some of these penologists refuse to even read his book and wrongfully classify him among reactionary primitives who want to lock offenders up for life whatever their crime. Others, dedicated enough to the profession to give Fogel's plan the careful reading it deserves, disagree with him on more rational grounds. Fogel's opponents feel that if states enacted flat sentence statutes and abolished indeterminate sentences and parole, his plan would work initially, but, legislators would react to rising crime rates by periodically increasing the length of the flat sentences until the prisons would become overflowing with inmates with no hope and little to lose.

Fogel's importance to contemporary penology lies in his ability to stir controversy in the profession, for that controversy makes its members reexamine their premises while gathering ammunition to defend what they are doing. Not only does he criticize the system in a perceptive manner, he also offers a humane and logical alternative to the status quo. His book presents the case for determinate sentences in such an eloquent way that he has become the leading spokesman for this important school of thought.

REFERENCES: David Fogel, ". . . *We Are the Living Proof . . .": The Justice Model for Corrections,* 1975; David Fogel, "For 'Flat Time,' " *Christian Science Monitor,* 1976; David Fogel, "The Case for Determinacy in Sentencing and the Justice Model in Correction," *American Journal of Correction,* 1976.

FORTUNE SOCIETY. This private, nonprofit organization located in New York City seeks to provide services and counseling for ex-inmates. With a full-time staff of fifteen and the assistance of nonpaid volunteers, the organization helps between 4,000 and 5,000 ex-inmates each year to reintegrate themselves into the mainstream of society. Five of the staff members devote full time to counseling, while three work exclusively on locating jobs for ex-inmates. Other staff members fill speaking engagements in the area, produce the organization's newspaper, *Fortune News,* or do clerical work.

With the exception of Executive Director David Rothenberg, virtually all of the staff and 38,000 members are ex-offenders, thereby making Fortune Society the largest organized group of ex-offenders. Its 20,000 financial contributors and fund-raising activities generate annual revenues in excess of $300,000. In evaluating the services they have received from the group, ex-inmates agree that its most valuable contribution is in helping ex-offenders overcome the debilitating effects of institutionalization immediately after their release.

David Rothenberg founded the group in March 1968, following the run of a play he had produced in a Greenwich Village theater. The play, "Fortune and Men's Eyes," written by John Herbert, an ex-convict from Canada, examines some of Herbert's prison experiences. As a result of the audience's lively discussion of the play, Rothenberg became interested in prison reform, and by 1970, he was devoting full time to the work. (The name of his organization was taken from the title of the play.)

Under the leadership of Jeanette Spencer, president of the organization, Fortune Society continues to expand the scope of its activities. Plans for the future include implementing programs that will provide contact with inmates before they leave the institution.

The basic philosophy of the society is that the prison system is counterproductive and harmful to society inasmuch as prisons contribute to the increase in crime. The idea that prisons are a cause of crime is based on statistics showing that the majority of crimes are committed by offenders who have been previously convicted. For discussion of related material, see ABOLITIONISTS.

REFERENCES: Michael S. Serrill, "The Fortune Society: Championing the Ex-Offender," *Corrections Magazine,* 1975.

FUNCTIONAL UNITS. This term describes an organizational arrangement for therapy programs developed by the U.S. Bureau of Prisons in the early 1970s and used in twenty-three federal prisons. Rather than build expensive, new, but more suitable, institutions for intensive therapy with groups of 50 to 100 offenders, the Bureau of

Prisons decided to operate self-contained institutions, of relatively small size, within the confines of the less suitable existing prisons. Offenders are assigned common living quarters, or units, in which they are housed together for twelve to eighteen months. This spatial arrangement allows the unit to be staffed with sufficient personnel to conduct an intensive treatment program. It also allows other arrangements conducive to rehabilitation, such as inmate government in matters of day-to-day life within the unit. Offenders can be assigned to different units on the basis of their need for a particular type of treatment program.

In reorganizing the prison population to form functional units, the prison becomes decentralized in terms of its organizational structure. The traditional hierarchic arrangements are so modified that a relatively large number of unit managers report to one executive. This change shortens the chain of command and broadens the span of control of correctional executives. From the standpoint of organization theory, the change makes it more difficult for superiors to supervise the activities of staff members. Ease and efficiency in supervision are sacrificed to attain the benefits of functional units.

The primary benefit associated with the innovation is improvement in delivery of services to the inmate. Psychologists, social workers, and members of the treatment staff are in daily contact with a fairly small group of inmates. Prisons operating with the traditional hierarchic form of organization often group such personnel together in a complex of offices where inmates have little access to their skills. The use of functional units constitutes decentralization in that it disperses treatment personnel among the inmate population being served rather than grouping them together in remote offices. The staffing pattern of a functional unit might consist of a unit manager, two correctional counselors, one social worker, and one educational specialist. In contrast, centralized hierarchic systems are prone to group all social workers together in one part of an administration building and all educational personnel together in a school facility.

One disadvantage of the functional unit is that it destroys unity of command, that is, the principle that each employee be reponsible to only one supervisor. For example, a social worker assigned to a functional unit is responsible to the unit supervisor in day-to-day operation of the unit. However, the same social worker is normally also responsible to a second supervisor who exercises control over all social workers employed by the institution for the purpose of overseeing matters of professional demeanor. Through this arrangement, the employee could conceivably receive conflicting orders from the two supervisors involved—a situation that violates a sound principle of management. On the other hand, the shorter chain of command associated with the use of functional units gives staff members who are in daily contact with inmates more access to executives at the policy-making level.

Flexibility is another advantage of functional units. Individual units can be altered, new units added, or old units disbanded without much difficulty or expense. Inmates get more individual attention since programs can be designed for their unique needs. The administrative ability to offer the inmate greater options in treatment approaches and an improved staff/inmate ratio helps achieve decentralized case management. Staff members forming the treatment team for a unit have a continuing program responsibility. The result is often better interpersonal relations between staff members and inmates, which tends to improve the inmate's chances of early, successful parole.

Functional units also promote greater efficiency in the use of economic resources by providing a mechanism for implementing treatment approaches thought to be desirable without the expense of constructing new buildings. In recent years, many penologists have come to feel that large maximum security prisons hamper contemporary treatment goals in that they have a dehumanizing impact on the inmate by making him a faceless number in a crowd. Modern treatment ideology advocates smaller institutions that are less imposing in terms of architectural features designed to make prisons escape-proof. Such Bastille-like facilities constitute a barrier to achieving the degree of permissiveness believed necessary for successful rehabilitation programs. An optimum solution, from the standpoint of treatment ideology alone, is to build small prisons that have fewer bars and locks. However, since the American prison system has so many large maximum security facilities, it is not economically feasible to replace them with a large number of small institutions. Functional units provide a means for grouping inmates into relatively small groups within the confines of large prisons. The technique is helpful in reducing the anonymity of the inmate but does nothing to change the intimidating architecture (*q.v.*).

REFERENCES: Douglas Lansing, Joseph B. Bogan, and Loren Karacki, "Unit Management: Implementing a Different Correctional Approach," *Federal Probation,* 1977; Robert B. Levinson and Roy E. Gerard, "Functional Units: A Different Correctional Approach," *Federal Probation,* 1973; Vergil Williams and Mary Fish, "Optimum Prison Size: Cost Behavior vs. Rehabilitation Goals," *American Journal of Correction,* 1972.

FURLOUGHS. Furloughs are variously known as temporary leaves, home visits, or temporary community release. For decades, prisons have occasionally granted short furloughs to inmates who were suddenly faced with a severe family crisis such as a death or grave illness in the immediate family. Furloughs of that type are treated as special circumstances, and often the inmate must be accompanied by an officer as part of the terms of the temporary release.

In contemporary usage, the term *furlough* is most often applied to formalized programs operated by prisons as part of their treatment programs. Inmates are given temporary releases to visit their homes and are allowed to travel alone. Treatment objectives include the provision of a mechanism whereby the inmate can maintain contacts with family and other persons outside the prison; have an opportunity to engage in heterosexual activity and feel less pressure to join in prison homosexual relations; and exercise responsibility and personal decision-making. The common practice is to grant the inmate leave for a forty-eight to seventy-two hour period during a weekend. Furlough statistics do not include inmates who leave the institution and return daily for work release (*q.v.*) or school release programs.

In 1975, *Corrections Magazine* completed a national survey of prison furlough programs; the findings relate to the number of furloughs granted by a jurisdiction in fiscal 1974. Since some inmates receive a number of furloughs during the course of a year, the information does not reflect the number of individuals involved. (Agencies contacted could not supply that information with the records they had available.) The survey results show that the District of Columbia, the federal prison system, and all state systems except Hawaii, Montana, Oklahoma, Texas, West Virginia, Wisconsin, and Wyoming have furlough programs for their adult inmates. With regard to furlough programs for incarcerated juveniles, the states of Missouri, South Carolina, West Virginia, and Wyoming do not have such programs. (The federal prison system does not have juvenile institutions, nor does Massachusetts.)

Before 1969, relatively few states had furlough programs. The current popularity of the furlough concept is reflected in the fact that Nevada, New Hampshire, Ohio, and Rhode Island had just approved their furlough programs shortly before the survey.

A comparison of the *Corrections Magazine* survey with an earlier survey completed in 1971 by Carson W. Markley is helpful in understanding the recent growth of furlough programs in American prisons. The Markley survey revealed that Mississippi had the only furlough program in the United States from its inception in 1918 until Arkansas started a similar program in 1923. It was 1964 before Louisiana started the third such program in the United States. In 1965, the growth of these programs began to accelerate with the District of Columbia, the U.S. Bureau of Prisons, North Carolina, and Utah adding programs. Oregon, South Carolina, and Vermont started programs in 1967. Two years later, furlough operations began in California, Connecticut, Delaware, Illinois, Iowa, Maine, and Maryland. In 1970, programs were initiated in Alaska, Arizona, and North Dakota. In 1971, the last year covered in the Markley survey, Florida, Idaho, Kansas, Michigan, Minnesota, Nebraska, New Jersey, New Mexico, Pennsylvania, and Washington were added to the roster of states allowing furloughs. The Markley survey polled all fifty state departments of corrections, plus the District of Columbia and the U.S. Bureau of Prisons. Twenty-two departments of corrections reported that they did not have a program in 1971, but sixteen of the twenty-two indicated plans to implement one.

The *Corrections Magazine* survey shows that by 1975 sixteen states had been added to the list of those offering furloughs: Alabama, Colorado, Georgia, Indiana, Kentucky, Massachusetts, Missouri, Nevada, New Hampshire, New Mexico, New York, Ohio, Rhode Island, South Dakota, Tennessee, and Virginia. At the time of the Markley survey, Kentucky, Nevada, New Mexico, and South Dakota did not indicate any future plans for implementation of furlough programs, but they have since established the programs. Hawaii, Montana, and Oklahoma expressed interest in 1971 but later established such programs only for their juvenile institutions.

Both Markley and *Corrections Magazine* list some important influences affecting the growth of furlough programs. Both point out that penologists have been disillusioned with institution treatment programs and are now basing their hopes for future success in rehabilitation efforts on community-based programs. *Corrections Magazine* further notes that their successes in operating work release programs have given prison administrators confidence in the viability of furlough programs. Their rationale is that inmates who can be trusted to return to prison after working in the community can be trusted to visit their homes.

REFERENCES: Carson W. Markley, "Furlough Programs and Conjugal Visiting in Adult Correctional Institutions," *Federal Probation,* 1973; Michael S. Serrill, "Prison Furloughs in America," *Corrections Magazine,* 1975; Robert T. Sigler, *Furlough Programs for Inmates: Final Report,* 1976.

G

GEORGIA CORRECTIONAL SYSTEM. The State Board of Corrections under the Department of Offender Rehabilitation is responsible for the 9,738 adult males and 373 adult females incarcerated in Georgia's institutions. Large prisons in the state include Georgia State Prison at Reidsville with a normal capacity of 2,100 males twenty-one years of age and older; Georgia Industrial Institute with a normal capacity of 1,000 males sixteen years of age and up; and Georgia Diagnostic and Classification Center at Jackson with a normal capacity of 820 male felons aged sixteen and up. Adult women are housed at the Georgia Rehabilitation Center for Women at Hardwick; this institution has a normal capacity of 320 for females seventeen years of age and older. The State Board of Corrections also oversees the operation of thirteen smaller prisons for adult males: Atlanta Advancement Center; Chatham Correctional Institution in Savannah; Colony Farms at Hardwick for males fifty years old and over; Decatur Correctional Institution at Bainbridge; Georgia Training and Development Center at Buford; Lee Correctional Institution at Leesburg; Lowndes Correctional Institution at Valdosta; Montgomery Correctional Institution at Mt. Vernon; Putnam Correctional Institution at Eatonton; Stone Mountain Correctional Institution at Stone Mountain; Walker Correctional Institution at Lafayette; Ware Correctional Institution at Waycross; and Wayne Correctional Institution at Jesup.

Overcrowding and idleness are important problems in the adult institutions. The 10,111 adult inmates are housed in institutions that have a normal capacity of only half that size. Georgia has more prisoners on a per capita basis than any other state, and these prisoners serve sentences that average five years or double the national average. At least 40 percent of the inmates in the system are idle on any given day.

The Division for Children and Youth under the Department of Family and Children Services administers ten institutions for juveniles below the age of seventeen. Most of these institutions are known as Youth Development Centers. The center at Milledgeville is the largest with a normal capacity of 420 males. Augusta has a facility with a normal capacity of 372, while the Macon Center houses 140.

An Atlanta center for females has a normal capacity of 100. The remaining six centers have normal capacities of thirty each.

Throughout most of the state's history, Georgia's correctional practices have been the subject of widespread criticism. The state played a leading role in the development of the chain gang, inevitably gaining notoriety with the use of penal slavery. The Georgia legislature established a lease system in 1867 whereby railroads paid $25.00 per year for the labor of each inmate leased. Thus, the chain gang originated. This type of lease system continued only until 1898, but the use of the chain gang continued long after the lease labor system ended. Inmates were committed to county work camps where their labor was utilized for maintenance of county roads. They were made to wear striped suits for easy identification and chains for prevention of escape. From the turn of the century to the 1950s, these road camps served as housing for Georgia inmates.

Georgia began a prison construction program to replace these road camps in the 1950s after several decades of periodic scandals surfaced over conditions in the camps. Some of these institutions, like the Rock Quarry Prison built in 1951, achieved their own measure of notoriety. The state's correctional system continued to be one of the nation's most primitive until Jimmy Carter was elected governor in 1970 on a platform that included prison reform. Under Carter's administration, the Department of Offender Rehabilitation was created to oversee adult probation, parole, and institutions, while jurisdiction over juvenile corrections was assigned to the newly created Department of Human Resources.

Governor Carter hired Ellis MacDougall as his commissioner of corrections to help carry out his campaign promises to improve the prison system. MacDougall had already achieved a reputation as an active, capable prison reformer as head of the South Carolina system from 1962 to 1968 and head of the Connecticut system from 1968 to 1971. MacDougall resigned in 1973, but his successor, Dr. Allen Ault, is continuing the reforms. Programs started since 1970 include academic and vocational education and counseling reaching 2,000 inmates and a work release (*q.v.*) arrangement serving 500 inmates. Some twenty-five of the state's seventy work camps have been closed since 1970. Other recent improvements include the establishment of a legal services program for inmates and the opening of four restitution centers for probationers and parolees who will work in the community while using part of their salaries to pay back their victims.

An ironic, but important, indicator of Georgia's commitment to penal reform in the 1970s is the site of the old Rock Quarry Prison at Buford. Once one of the cruelest of the old-style punative prisons, it was reopened in 1964 as the Georgia Training and Development Center and designated for use as a facility for youths between the ages of seventeen and twenty-four after the legislature passed its Youthful Offender Act of 1972. The 200 inmates at Buford are guaranteed treatment, and all participate in group therapy, as well as either academic or vocational training. The old rock quarry, where fifty-two inmates protested conditions in 1956 by purposely smashing the bones in their legs with twenty-pound sledgehammers, has been covered over to make a baseball field.

The prison inmate population in Georgia grew rapidly in 1975 and 1976 from 9,772 on January 1, 1975, to 11,956 on January 1, 1977. In the twelve months following January 1, 1977, the state's prison system experienced only a modest 1 percent growth to 12,135.

REFERENCES: Lewis E. Powell and Michael S. Serrill, "Profile/Georgia," *Corrections Magazine,* 1974; Michael Serrill, "Prison Population Rises Again, But at a Slower Rate," *Corrections Magazine,* 1978.

GOOD TIME. Good time, an idea proposed by reformer Jeremy Bentham around 1776, refers to the practice of reducing an inmate's sentence in a correctional institution for good behavior. Most American correctional systems use good time, but states vary considerably in the amount of good time they allow and in the manner of awarding the allowance. In a fairly typical system, an inmate's sentence is reduced by one day per month if the inmate has not been the subject of disciplinary action; thus, it is said that the inmate can earn one day of good time per month. The objective is to give the inmate an incentive for good behavior in the institution. Normally, good time is established by legislative fiat rather than by administrative discretion.

National surveys in recent years show that all state correctional systems in the United States have good time laws with the exceptions of California, Hawaii, Pennsylvania, and Utah. The authors of these surveys feel that some of the positive benefits of good time practices have been lost because many systems have incorporated the forfeiture of good time accumulated into the range of punishments provided for misbehavior. For example, a prison policy might require the forfeiture of five days of accumulated good time if their disciplinary committee finds that the inmate has been guilty of fighting.

REFERENCES: Robert R. Smith, "A Survey of Good-Time Policies and Practices in American Correctional Agencies," *Journal of Criminal Justice,* 1975; Texas Corrections Department, Research and Development Division, *A National Survey of Good Time Laws and Administrative Procedures*, 1973.

GRADUATED RELEASE. All prisons exercise substantial control over the daily activities of inmates. Maximum security prisons are designed to control inmates who are either violence prone or escape risks, or both. In exercising such control, staff members maintain constant surveillance, observing the inmates directly and indirectly by means of closed circuit television cameras. Inmates are highly regimented in their daily round of activities, for the staff enforces rigid schedules for rising in the morning, attending meals, performing work, and any other daily activity. Surveillance, regimentation, and the danger of attack from other violence-prone inmates create an atmosphere of extreme tension in such prisons. After a lengthy period of confinement under such conditions, many inmates are no longer able even to make simple decisions about diet or wearing apparel because all such decisions are made for them by the rules and routines of the prison. In recognition of these undesirable social consequences of prison life, many prison administrators gradually shift the inmate from highly regimented to somewhat less regimented situations to provide an adjustment period before complete freedom is granted. Graduated release is assumed to give the inmate a better chance of avoiding recidivism (*q.v.*).

Pre-release programs are one means of providing graduated release. Some four to six weeks before scheduled release from the institution, the inmate is transferred to a living area where regulations are more relaxed, and he is expected to take greater responsibility for his own conduct. Counselors prepare the inmate for release by focusing upon possible solutions to problems that will confront him immediately after release. Representatives from surrounding communities may be called in to inform the inmate about the job market, modes of dress, parole requirements, and similar matters of concern to a person who has been incarcerated. Staff members in the pre-release program usually give classes in techniques of job applications, personal budgeting, motor vehicle operation, family responsibilities, and other matters thought to be helpful for the particular locality and prison population.

Work release (*q.v.*) is a plan for accomplishing graduated release. An inmate assigned to a work release program is allowed to leave the institution during normal business hours to obtain employment. Having obtained employment, he is allowed to leave the prison each work day to fulfill the conditions of employment, but he is required to return to the institution and its routine when not working. Most work release programs place a number of restrictions upon the use of the money earned. Typically, the inmate is required to pay the institution a portion of his wages for room and board. If he has a family, he may be required to contribute to their support. Any remaining funds, other than small sums used for lunches and transportation, must be saved for use after release.

School release is a variation of work release. It is relatively new in the practice of penology and is not widely used. The few inmates involved in such programs are unique among the inmate population in that they have the academic background and the potential for college training. A school release program permits the inmate to leave the institution to attend classes in a nearby college or university. The inmate returns to the institution each night.

Halfway houses (*q.v.*) also constitute a form of graduated release. They serve as a temporary residence for offenders immediately after their release from prison. These facilities are located in population centers for easy access to employment possibilities and public transportation. They may provide living space for as few as fifteen offenders but seldom more than fifty. Offenders living in these transitional institutions ordinarily locate employment and attempt to become settled into a stable routine of work before their parole or release from institutional supervision.

REFERENCES: Daniel Glaser, *Handbook of Criminology,* 1974; Nora Klapmuts, "Community Alternatives to Prison," *Crime and Delinquency Literature,* 1973; National Council on Crime and Delinquency Research Center, *Residential Corrections: Alternatives to Incarceration,* 1973; U.S. Law Enforcement Assistance Administration, *Guidelines and Standards for Halfway Houses and Community Treatment Centers,* 1973; U.S. National Advisory Commission on Criminal Justice Standards and Goals, *Corrections,* 1973; U.S. Public Health Service, *Graduated Release,* 1971.

GRIEVANCE PROCEDURES FOR INMATES. As defined by Linda R. Singer, director of the Center for Correctional Justice, grievance procedures are "distinct, formal methods for responding to written complaints from inmates." The Center for Correctional Justice identifies two basic types of grievance mechanisms: (1) investigatory, a procedure in which an official investigates a complaint and writes a reply that may be appealed to an official higher in the administrative structure; and (2) participatory, a scheme wherein inmates and staff members cooperate to develop suitable grievance procedures and attempt to settle grievances by negotiation, with opportunity for appeal to higher authority. Typical grievance mechanisms include ombudsmen (*q.v.*) systems, inmate representative councils, and legal services programs.

The number of correctional institutions with formal grievance procedures has been increasing during the past decade largely because of pressure from the courts. Prior to 1961, in following a policy that has been termed the "hands-off" doctrine, the court system was extremely reluctant to intervene in the internal administration of prisons. Since 1961, however, a number of important court decisions have whittled away at the "hands-off" doctrine; judicial scrutiny of the internal policies and procedures of prisons has become more common. Inmates, recognizing the fundamental change in attitude of the court system, drastically increased the number of court petitions filed. Only about 2,000 petitions per year were being received by federal courts in 1961, whereas some 17,000 were being received annually in 1975. The willingness of judges to consider inmate complaints has greatly increased the workload in the court system to the point where judges have called upon prison administrators to establish grievance procedures. As early as 1972, Chief Justice Warren E. Burger urged correctional executives to establish formal complaint procedures that would remedy valid grievances as well as expose those that are spurious.

Prison administrators are heeding the jurists' calls for action on this front partly because many are convinced that a viable grievance mechanism will relieve tension in their institutions and present the type of uprising experienced at Attica. Perhaps more significantly, administrators are more willing to evaluate their rules, policies, and procedures and to grant inmate requests for change if the security of the institution is not threatened. This new openness of attitude stems from a fear that inmate petitions to the court could win judicial intervention in the operation of the prison and thus limit the administrator's discretion much more than would be the case if the administrator made concessions to avoid litigation.

The judicial call for viable inmate grievance procedures has been supplemented by that of other groups. The National Council on Crime and Delinquency (*q.v.*) published a Model Act for the Protection of Rights of Prisoners in 1972. The model law includes a provision for establishing grievance mechanisms with review by a disinterested third party. President Nixon's 1973 National Advisory Commission on Criminal Justice Standards and Goals urges all correctional institutions to adopt similar grievance procedures and to protect complaining inmates from reprisals. The Center for Correctional Justice, a nonprofit organization under the leadership of Linda R. Singer, was established in 1971 to assist administrators in exploring ways to deal with inmate problems without the need for court petitions. This organization conducted a national survey in May 1973 in an attempt to learn how many institutions utilized grievance mechanisms. The survey produced 209 replies indicating that 166 institutions had formal grievance mechanisms; half of these were established since March 1972. In interpreting the survey results, the center concluded that many of the newer grievance procedures were simply informal mechanisms hastily elevated to official status to appear to be in vogue with the times.

An important legal controversy has developed around a 1973 court ruling in Maryland specifying that inmates' petitions shall not be considered by the court until the inmate has exhausted all administrative grievance procedures provided by the state. The exhaustion requirement is not accepted by many attorneys who represent inmates. They argue that rulings by the U.S. Supreme Court give the inmate the right to sue in federal court without exhausting state remedies if his civil rights have been denied. Supporters of Maryland's position concede that the ruling may delay inmate access to courts but that it does not deny access to federal court hearings. For discussion of the grievance procedure used by federal prisons, see ADMINISTRATIVE REMEDY PROCEDURE. For a unique approach to processing grievances, see OMBUDSMEN IN PRISON.

REFERENCES: R. V. Denenberg and Tia Denenberg, "Prison Grievance Procedures: A National Survey of Programs Underway," *Corrections Magazine,* 1975; J. Michael Keating, Jr., and others, *Grievance Mechanisms in Correctional Institutions,* 1975; Virginia McArthur, "Inmate Grievance Mechanisms: A Survey of 209 American Prisons," *Federal Probation,* 1974; Linda R. Singer and J. Michael Keating, *Grievance Mechanisms in American Corrections: The State of the Art,* 1975.

GUIDED GROUP INTERACTION. Guided group interaction (GGI) is a treatment method used in correctional institutions in a number of locations throughout the United States. At least two states (Florida and Georgia) have adopted it as their primary approach to the rehabilitation of juvenile offenders, and other state correctional systems make extensive use of the technique.

The ultimate goal of GGI is to keep the juvenile from committing additional offenses. GGI is thought to accomplish this goal by modifying the juvenile's self-concept. The assumption underlying this rationale is that the behavioral problems of the delinquent stem from his self-concept as inadequate, hostile, and aggressive. Modification of this self-image is thought to reduce the nonconforming behavior of the youth.

GGI utilizes the setting of the small group for treatment. Several juveniles of similar age and background are brought together for discussion and problem-solving at regular intervals under the supervision of a therapist. Some forms of group therapy may be classified as "group psychotherapy" in that the therapist is giving individual therapy in a group setting. GGI, however, is one form of group treatment wherein the group itself is an important treatment agent. GGI group participants have similar problems and are encouraged to express themselves freely by revealing their intimate experiences, fears, and anxieties to other group members. Behavior is assumed to be social in nature, so that deviant behavior can only be changed within the context of group association. The GGI participant has new learning experiences in the group context that may modify his socially unacceptable qualities.

In GGI groups, the delinquent who is participating should be made to feel that he can work up to acceptable behavior gradually rather than have to adopt new standards of behavior immediately. The therapist attempts to develop situations that give an individual participant the opportunity to choose from several alternative courses of action and to discuss the choice he makes. This type of group learning experience helps the participant because he obviously must choose between alternative courses of action when he is returned to the community. The group is important in this process because the offender can receive both criticism and approval from his peers instead of from an authority figure.

GGI participants are usually allowed to work out their own rules and regulations for group sessions, thereby creating an atmosphere that is supportive but not so inflexible that it inhibits individual development. The appropriate atmosphere encourages the participant to discuss his problems and eventually to realize that the problems result from his own attitudes, values, and motives rather than from the environment. Hopefully, the juvenile will gain insight into his problems and stop projecting blame onto others. Through GGI, he has an opportunity to learn new methods of social interaction; if these new methods are satisfactory to him, he may change the patterns of behavior that caused him trouble.

GGI aids the juvenile in facing the reality of his life instead of rationalizing his problems away with weak justifications of his deviant behavior. His interaction with his peers in the group setting helps him to understand the source of his problems. Such insight into one's problems, along with the opportunity to ventilate feelings of frustration, is the heart of the process of reformation. No less important is the fact that the experience the participant gains in conforming to the rules and regulations established by his peer group helps him to conform to the rules of the world outside of the prison. In effect, the juvenile learns to act as a law-abiding person through his attempts to help other participants to reform. His identification with reformation and his anticriminal stance during the group process give him experience that may carry over into his future life.

Individual group members are generally defensive about their criminal behavior. Such an attitude constitutes a barrier to the learning and accepting of new modes of socially acceptable behavior and must be undermined in the course of group therapy. One way of eliminating this defensive stance is to break down the participant's identification with criminal groups and criminal value systems. Participation in a group where criminal behavior is deprecated subjects the juvenile participant to social pressure from peers and causes him anxiety about his past deviant behavior. He may switch his allegiance from a delinquent group to a conforming group. Accomplishing this switch involves overcoming the participant's outlook on criminal behavior. Delinquent subcultures nearly always socialize their members to disparage conventional values and behavior as being "square." The GGI participant must learn that conventional behavior can be rewarding and satisfying.

The Minnesota State Training School at Red Wing is thought to be the first juvenile institution to adopt GGI as the preferred mode of treatment for its clientele.

REFERENCES: National Council on Crime and Delinquency Training Center, *Guided Group Interaction,* 1972; Richard M. Stephenson and Frank R. Scarpitti, *Group Interaction as Therapy: The Use of the Small Group in Corrections,* 1974.

H

HALFWAY HOUSES. Halfway houses for ex-inmates have been called "decompression chambers" because they provide an intermediate step between the highly regimented atmosphere of the traditional prison and the freedom of parole. The inmate's transition from prison to a free community is eased by living in a residential center of this type, for staff members exercise some control over the residents while they are readjusting to the necessity of making their own decisions. Many halfway houses provide treatment in the form of counseling or psychological therapy; others merely offer meals, a place to sleep, and help in obtaining employment and in finding a permanent residence. Halfway houses of this type are halfway "out" of prison, but halfway houses may also be halfway "in" if they are used to house offenders who are deemed to need more supervision than probation would provide, but less regimentation than prison.

The first halfway house for convicts is believed to have been operated by St. Leonard in a monastery in France during the first century. The Reverend James G. Jones, Jr. carried on St. Leonard's tradition when he founded the first halfway house in the United States in Chicago in 1954; he named it after St. Leonard. Soon afterward, the Reverend Charles Dismas Clark founded St. Dismas, a halfway house in St. Louis (St. Dismas was the penitent thief of the first Good Friday).

Ten years after the founding of the first halfway house in the United States, the movement had gained sufficient momentum for organization of the International Halfway House Association representing some fifty such facilities in Canada and the United States.

While religious organizations have been instrumental in establishing halfway houses, prison systems have also been an important influence in the movement. In the 1850's, Sir Walter Crofton's "Irish Ticket of Leave" system employed halfway houses in establishing the practice of parole in Ireland. In the early 1960s, Attorney General Robert F. Kennedy promoted the halfway house idea in the United States. He helped to establish three such facilities called pre-release guidance centers in 1961 to house young men from federal youth institutions.

The U.S. Department of Defense uses a similar arrangement for military prisoners by assigning them to a retraining center after they have served prison sentences but before they are returned to regular duty.

The halfway house is used for several types of offenders: (1) probationers who may benefit from a "halfway-in" type of facility; (2) inmates on gradual release programs in order to get the decompression effect; (3) parolees as a means of helping them establish themselves in the community; and (4) persons who are released because they have served their entire sentences. The last-named probably needs the service more than any other group because they do not have the supportive services offered by correctional personnel unless they can be assigned to a halfway house.

Since halfway houses are intended to help offenders overcome institutionalized dependency (or avoid developing it), residents do not usually spend much time in the facilities. Hostels are a type of very short-term halfway houses for ex-inmates; they offer dormitory living, meals, and perhaps employment counseling for a term that usually does not exceed six weeks. Most halfway houses, however, are in the medium-term range as to length of stay; the resident is expected to stay a minimum of six weeks and may stay as long as three or four months. Halfway houses designed for long-term care of offenders have been called "three-quartering houses." These serve elderly inmates and others who have little likelihood of becoming completely independent and may provide "boarding house" living facilities for residents over a period of years. For additional information, see COMMUNITY TREATMENT CENTERS and GRADUATED RELEASE.

REFERENCES: Reverend J. T. L. James, "The Halfway House Movement," in Gary R. Perlstein and Thomas R. Phelps (eds.), *Alternatives to Prison: Community-Based Corrections,* 1975; Nora Klapmuts, "Community Alternatives to Prison," *Crime and Delinquency Literature,* 1973; National Council on Crime and Delinquency Research Center, *Residential Corrections: Alternative to Incarceration,* 1973; Andrew T. Scull, *Decarceration: Community Treatment and the Deviant—A Radical View,* 1977; Robert Sommer, *The End of Imprisonment,* 1976; U.S. Law Enforcement Assistance Administration, *Guidelines and Standards for Halfway Houses and Community Treatment Centers,* 1973.

HAWAII CORRECTIONAL SYSTEM. Prisons in Hawaii are administered under the Corrections Division of its Department of Social Services and Housing. Persons over the age of eighteen who are convicted of a felony or a misdemeanor are committed to the director of Social Services preliminary to placement in one of the state's correctional facilities.

Most of Hawaii's adult institutions are smaller than those of other states. Hawaii State Prison, the largest facility, opened in 1918 and currently has a normal capacity of 250; it is located in Honolulu. The Halawa Correctional Facility in Oahu, formally known as Honolulu Jail, was opened in 1962. It holds both male and female offenders who may be felons or misdemeanants or persons awaiting trial. The prison has a rated capacity of 224. The Kulani Honor Camp in Hilo was opened in 1946 with a normal capacity of 120 males. The Maui Community Correctional Center at Wailuku, Maui, opened in 1973 with a normal capacity of twenty-five. The state's newest adult facility is the Hawaii Community Correctional Facility opened in Hilo in 1975 with a normal capacity of twenty-five. Two small conditional release centers, each with a normal capacity of fifteen, are located in Honolulu: the Laumaka Conditional Release Center opened in 1968 and Kamehameha Conditional Release Center opened in 1971.

The state juvenile facility, the Hawaii Youth Correctional Facility, was opened in 1950 and receives both male and female offenders aged twelve to eighteen. The Honolulu facility has space for 200 but has held less than half that number in recent years. The Program Committee of this facility establishes the parole date for incarcerated juveniles, but the parole services are administered under the separate Division of Vocational Rehabilitation.

The prison population in Hawaii is growing as it is in most other states. The prison population increased 18 percent from January 1, 1975, to January 1, 1976; however, the total numbers are small. In absolute terms, the increase was from 310 to 366. The system experienced a 19 percent increase from 413 to 491 between January 1, 1977, and January 1, 1978.

REFERENCES: American Correctional Association, *Directory,* 1975–1976 edition; Steve Gettinger, "U.S. Prison Population Hits All-Time High," *Corrections Magazine,* 1976; Michael Serrill, "Prison Population Rises Again, But at a Slower Rate," *Corrections Magazine,* 1978.

HOMOSEXUALITY IN FEMALE PRISONS. The pattern of homosexuality in women's institutions is substantially different from that in male prisons. Most investigators of the social structure of female prisons report that the dyad, or homosexual marriage alliance, forms the most basic social unit of the female inmate subculture (*q.v.*). This unit is expanded with imaginary kinship ties. Researchers believe that the rather extensive involvement of female inmates in homosexual relations reflects their orientation toward social structures and constitutes a mode of adjustment to prison life. That is, women are most familiar with the family as a unit of social organization and logically tend to organize their lives in prison around the family unit.

Rose Giallombardo, a prominent investigator of the female inmate subculture, believes that extensive kinship ties are developed by dyads with other inmates with whom it is necessary to have considerable interaction. The kinship ties decrease jealousy, suspicion, and misunderstanding by defining the type of interaction between them. For example, a married couple who plays cards frequently with another married couple might agree to pretend that the two wives were sisters. By this means, the dyad is expanded to sisters and brothers-in-law. These imaginary kinship relations can be extensive with the adoption of sons, daughters, fathers, mothers, grandfathers, grandmothers, and even cousins. Having formed such kinship bonds, an inmate can maintain close friendly relations with many inmates without triggering a jealous reaction from her mate.

There are no reliable statistics on the extent of homosexuality in female prisons. One problem of determining the number of inmates involved is a definitional one; there is considerable variation among prison staff members as to what constitutes homosexual conduct. Examples of homosexual actions cited in disciplinary reports include two women showering in the same stall, two women walking with arms around the partner's waist, and two women kissing while lying on a bed together. David Ward and Gene Kassebaum, authorities on the social structure of women's prisons, have stated that defining homosexual behavior in prison is difficult for both staff and inmates because behavior that is permissible outside the prison becomes problematic in prison.

Another problem in gathering reliable statistics on the extent of homosexuality in prisons obviously stems from the fact that it is forbidden behavior. Like other forbidden activity, inmates attempt to hide homosexual activities from the staff, and it is reasonable to assume that they are successful in many cases. Ward and Kassebaum, after careful research at the California Institution for Women at Frontera, one of the larger women's prisons, have reported that about 50 percent of the inmates were involved in homosexual activity at some time during their confinement. Other research on the topic indicates that the Ward and Kassebaum estimate may be typical, or even conservative, for female correctional institutions. Whatever the exact extent of involvement in homosexuality, it clearly is high enough so that all female inmates live in an atmosphere dominated by homosexual behavior. Even if they do not become involved directly, they must at least consider homosexuality as a mode of adapting to prison life at some point in their period of confinenent.

Most of the researchers into the inmate subculture (*q.v.*) have been sociologists who have developed typologies of inmates. In labeling the typologies, they generally use the argot (*q.v.*) terms invented by inmates instead of applying new, more neutral terms. In women's prisons, many of these typologies, or social roles, refer to homosexual activity. The "penitentiary turnout," a social role identified by Giallombardo, is a term reflecting the inmate's concern with differentiating between those women they consider to be "true" homosexuals (lesbians) and those who participate in homosexual activity in prison but return to heterosexual activity after release. The penitentiary turnout, in the view of inmates, uses homosexual relations as a mode of adjustment to prison life but has no real preference for homosexuality as does the lesbian. The penitentiary turnout usually plays the role of "femme" or "mommy" in the homosexual dyad. The femme acts out the stereotyped, traditional role of the wife in outside society. The "stud broad" or "daddy" is the complementary role to the femme. The stud broad must provide the prison with a male image and, in attempting to do so, adopts male mannerisms and appearance to the extent possible. A stud and femme who have established a marriage alliance are said to be "making it" or to be "tight." The stud has prestige in the inmate subculture (*q.v.*) because it is considered difficult for a woman to play the male role over a long period of time. Occasionally, a stud will become enamored with another stud to the point of switching to a femme role. Inmates call this role switch "dropping the belt." An inmate who drops the belt generally loses some prestige in the inmate population and causes some adverse comment because the femmes outnumber the studs. To decrease the stud population by dropping the belt is disturbing to inmates because it reduces the predictability in their environment.

The social roles centering on homosexuality include argot labels that define exploitative elements in homosexual alliances. An expressed ideal in the inmate subculture is to form a sincere relationship based on romantic love. A "trick" is a woman who allows herself to be exploited instead of forming the more prestigious "sincere" relationship. "Commissary hustlers" are studs who exploit several tricks for economic purposes. The hustler forms homosexual alliances with several femmes in living quarters scattered around the prison;

the economic exploitation is carried out by the hustler demanding that each of the tricks buy her cigarettes and other items at the prison commissary. However, the commissary hustler does maintain a "sincere" relationship with one of the women involved and thus avoids the label of "chippie." A chippie participates in homosexual activity with a number of women without forming a sincere relationship with any one woman. Inmates consider the chippie to be promiscuous.

The above description of homosexual roles in female prisons is not a comprehensive listing, nor does it attempt to delineate social roles that are nonsexual. However, a careful consideration of the homosexual roles does verify the overall impressions of systematic observers of women's prisons, that the prevalence of homosexual dyads reflects women's general orientation to social organization in terms of the family unit. It is obvious that far more than sexual gratification is involved for the participants: the family units provide a unified front against prison officials and serve as vehicles for economic and moral support for women who would otherwise have to face the harsh realities of prison alone. For related topics, see HOMOSEXUALITY IN MALE PRISONS and INMATE SUBCULTURE.

REFERENCES: Edna Chandler, *Women in Prison,* 1973; Thomas W. Foster, "Make-Believe Families: A Response of Women and Girls to the Deprivations of Imprisonment," *International Journal of Criminology and Penology,* 1975; Rose Giallombardo, *The Social World of Imprisoned Girls: A Comparative Study of Institutions for Juvenile Delinquents,* 1974; Rose Giallombardo, *Society of Women: A Study of a Women's Prison,* 1966; Esther Heffernan, *Making It in Prison: The Square, the Cool, and the Life,* 1972; Margery L. Velimesis, "The Female Offender," *Crime and Delinquency Literature,* 1975; David A. Ward and Gene G. Kassebaum, *Women's Prison: Sex and Social Structure,* 1965; Vergil L. Williams and Mary Fish, *Convicts, Codes and Contraband: The Prison Life of Men and Women,* 1974.

HOMOSEXUALITY IN MALE PRISONS. Estimates of the incidence of homosexuality in prisons vary widely for a number of reasons. It is difficult to obtain estimates from inmates because homosexual acts in prison are punished by denial of parole or removal to a segregation unit. As for ex-inmates, they tend to keep their prison experiences secret. Prison staff members also are prone to suppress information they may have concerning homosexual behavior among inmates. When prison staff members do discuss homosexuality in their institutions, it becomes apparent that different officers have different definitions of what constitutes a homosexual act. One officer may report a homosexual occurrence after observing two inmates holding hands, while another officer may ignore the incident.

Nonetheless, there is a range of agreement among a number of researchers as to estimates of the incidence of homosexuality in men's prisons. These estimates cluster in the range of 30 to 45 percent and refer to the male penal population having homosexual relations at some time during their incarceration. To obtain a better perspective on the significance of this amount of homosexuality, other researchers have attempted to determine the proportion of these inmates having preinstitutional homosexual experience. According to these studies, 5 to 10 percent of male inmates have no homosexual experience before coming to prison, about the same number have extensive homosexual commitment prior to incarceration, and 25 to 30 percent have intermittent homosexual experience before imprisonment.

Statistics on the incidence of prison homosexuality, even if accurate, do not reveal anything about the frequency of sexual contacts. An inmate is counted in the statistics if only one sexual contact occurred during a five-year sentence. Available data indicate that the frequency of homosexual contacts is normally very low except for a few inmates who had vigorous homosexual commitments prior to their incarceration.

Most researchers believe that inmates do not experience much sexual desire during incarceration. Reasons given for low sex drive in prison include the lack of social cues associated with stimuli; there are no opportunities to visit cocktail lounges, attend dances, or engage in other activities that arouse sexual responses. Furthermore, studies show that lower class males, who make up the overwhelming percentage of the prison population, do not employ sexual fantasies as do middle-class males. Since sexual fantasies are at least as important as social cues in stimulating sexual desire, the sterile environment of the prison offers few occasions for appropriate stimuli for male inmates whose past sexual experiences have been of a concrete nature.

Lower class males also have a taboo against masturbation; it is helpful to remember that taboo when evaluating the sexual behavior of men in prison. By understanding that masturbation is taboo in the value system of male prisoners and that their preinstitutional sexual experiences have been concrete experiences with little fantasy, it is easier to comprehend the involved sexual roles. Penologists believe that prison homosexuality is much more complex than the simple desire for relief of sexual tension.

Three basic role configurations occur in male prison populations; distinguishing among the three roles is vital to understanding the inmates' social setting and sexual behavior. Inmates place great emphasis on defining the roles in terms of active or passive behaviors. The "wolf" or "jocker" has an active (inserter) role. The inmates do not consider the jocker to be engaging in a homosexual act if he avoids a passive (insertee) sexual contact. Thus, an inmate may be defined as a nonhomosexual by other inmates either because he has no sexual contacts or because his sexual contacts are all of the active type. The "punk" has a passive (insertee) role that is forced on him. Inmates accord low status to the punk because they feel he lacks the strength of character to avoid the dilemma he is in. He is defined as a reluctant homosexual. The "fag" is one who assumes a passive role because of personal preference; he has an even lower status role than the punk does.

While the motives of the inmates involved in passive roles are relatively clear, those of the jockers are more complex. Jockers have pre-institutional experiences that give them a set of attitudes towards heterosexual relationships. In the prison setting where there are no females, the jockers manifest these attitudes towards punks and fags. For jockers, aggressive sex defines maleness and must be validated periodically; sexual conquest and the dominance that it symbolizes are also necessary for conversation purposes. Maleness is validated by aggressive sexual conquest, but these conquests must be discussed to obtain the desired approval from peers.

Homosexual behavior in male prisons is thought to be a problem largely because it generates an atmosphere where there is a constant awareness of homosexual behavior and because it threatens the inmate's self-esteem. Daily conversations are full of jokes, verbal games, and rumors that impute homosexuality to others. Most inmates appear to believe in a "contagious theory" of homosexuality; that is, they fear that imprisonment will change a heterosexual man into a homosexual. Such omnipresent fears make prison sentences even harsher than they are intended.

REFERENCES: Peter C. Buffum, *Homosexuality in Prisons,* 1972; Leo Carroll, *Hacks, Blacks and Cons: Race Relations in a Maximum Security Prison,* 1974; Azmy Ishak Ibrahim, "Deviant Sexual Behavior in Men's Prisons," *Crime and Delinquency,* 1974; Paul M. Keve, *Prison Life and Human Worth,* 1974; Eve Pell (ed.), *Maximum Security: Letters from Prison,* 1972; Karel Weiss (ed.), *The Prison Experience: An Anthology,* 1976.

I

IDAHO CORRECTIONAL SYSTEM. Idaho's Department of Correction is responsible for operation of adult probation and parole services as well as adult prisons. The adult institutions receive convicted offenders over the age of eighteen on an indeterminate sentence (*q.v.*) that has no minimum number of years specified.

The adult institutions are the Idaho Correctional Institution at Boise originally opened in 1870 (a new facility was opened in 1973 with a normal capacity of 516); and the North Idaho Correctional Institution at Cottonwood, opened in 1974 with a normal capacity of 150.

The Department of Health and Welfare receives juveniles from the District Court; the court cannot commit a juvenile directly to an institution but may recommend placement. Juveniles are not subject to any minimum sentence; the department's jurisdiction over a juvenile committed prior to age eighteen may continue until the youth is twenty-one years old. Idaho law makes no distinction between status offenders (*q.v.*) (children who are truants, runaways, or who have committed some other act that would not be a crime if they were adults) and those children who have committed crimes. Idaho's juvenile facility is the Youth Services Center at St. Anthony, opened in 1904 with a rated capacity of 150 males and females aged ten to eighteen.

Idaho, like most other states, experienced an increase in its prison population between January 1, 1977, and January 1, 1978, with an 11 percent growth from 725 to 805.

REFERENCES: American Correctional Association, *Directory, 1975–1976* edition; Michael Serrill, "Prison Population Rises Again, But at a Slower Rate," *Corrections Magazine,* 1978.

ILLINOIS CORRECTIONAL SYSTEM. Penal institutions in Illinois, other than those in Chicago, are operated under the jurisdiction of the Department of Corrections located in Springfield. Cook County (Chicago) has a separate Department of Corrections.

The Cook County Department of Corrections operates three facilities in Chicago. Division No. 1, as it is now known, was formerly the
Cook County Jail; it was opened in 1929 with a rated capacity of
2,009 felons and misdemeanants seventeen years of age and above.
Division No. 2, once known as the House of Correction, was opened
in 1871 with a normal capacity of 1,438 adult felons and misdemeanants. Division No. 3, formerly known as the Women's Division, was opened in 1973 with a normal capacity of 256 female felons and misdemeanants; it also holds federal women prisoners.

The Department of Corrections at Springfield operates the Adult
Institution Services Division which receives both male and female
felons over the age of seventeen. The division also receives some offenders who are serving a sentence of at least sixty days for a misdemeanor. Misdemeanants are housed in the Dwight and Vandalia facilities along with felons who are serving time at those locations.
Adult facilities for felons are as follows: Dwight Correctional Center
at Dwight, opened in 1930 with space for about 130 inmates (it became coeducational in 1974); Joliet Correctional Center at Joliet,
opened in 1860 for about 730 males; Menard Correctional Center, located on the bank of the Mississippi River on the outskirts of
Chester, opened in 1878 and holding about 1,400 males; Menard Psychiatric Center, located on a bluff overlooking Menard Correctional
Center, opened in 1934 to serve as the state's facility for the criminally insane and holding some 230 males; Sheridan Correctional Center at Sheridan, opened in 1973 as an adult male facility holding about
210 offenders (from 1950 to 1973, it served as the Illinois Industrial
School for Boys); Stateville Correctional Center at Joliet, opened in
1919 and housing nearly 2,000 males; Vandalia Correctional Center at
Vandalia, opened in 1921 with a capacity of about 630 males; and Vienna Correctional Center at Vienna with 425 felons, opened in 1965
as the state's first major experiment in minimum security prisons (it
became coeducational in 1975).

The Division of Juvenile Institutions and Field Services, a part of
the Department of Corrections at Springfield, receives both males
and females under the age of twenty-one (juveniles who have reached
the age of seventeen in Illinois can be transferred to an adult institution). Both felons and misdemeanants are received by the division.
The Illinois Youth Center—Channahon at Morris was opened in
1958; it holds about twenty-five males thirteen to fifteen years of age.
The Illinois Youth Center—Dixon Springs at Brownfield opened in
1970; it holds some thirty-five males ages sixteen to nineteen. Illinois
Youth Center—DuPage at Naperville opened in 1964; in 1974, it

moved to a new facility built by Standard Oil Company of Indiana in exchange for the site of the old facility. It houses about fifty males thirteen to seventeen years of age. The Illinois Youth Center—Geneva at Geneva opened in 1895 and became coeducational in 1971. It holds about 100 youths thirteen to eighteen years of age. The Illinois Youth Center—Hanna City at Hanna City opened in 1968 and holds some sixty males ages thirteen to seventeen. The Illinois Youth Center—Joliet at Joliet opened in 1974 with a capacity of seventy males fourteen to twenty-one years of age. Illinois Youth Center—Kankakee at Manteno opened in 1960 and holds some forty males ages fifteen to eighteen. The Illinois Youth Center—St. Charles at St. Charles opened in 1901; it houses some 250 males ages thirteen to seventeen and also serves as the state's Reception and Diagnostic Center for boys. The Illinois Youth Center—Valley View at St. Charles opened in 1967 and holds some 135 males ages fourteen to eighteen.

Illinois prison officials like to point out that relatively few juveniles are incarcerated considering the large total population of the state. Illinois has been able to carry out deinstitutionalization of its juvenile facilities on a large scale in recent years without incurring the publicity generated by similar efforts in other states. (For additional information, see DEINSTITUTIONALIZATION.)

The institution populations cited above (based on average populations for calendar year 1974) underestimate the number of incarcerated persons because there is a lag in the reporting of statistics to the American Correctional Association (*q.v.*). It is known, however, that in Illinois, as in many other states, the inmate population has grown rapidly in recent years. Its prison population increased 22 percent from January 1, 1975, to January 1, 1976. The total prison population at the beginning of 1975 was 6,672 and increased to 8,110 a year later. Between January 1, 1977, and January 1, 1978, it grew 6 percent from 10,002 to 10,608.

REFERENCES: American Correctional Association, *Directory,* 1975–1976 edition; Steve Gettinger, "U.S. Prison Population Hits All-Time High," *Corrections Magazine,* 1976; Michael Serrill, "Prison Population Rises Again, But at a Slower Rate," *Corrections Magazine,* 1978.

INDETERMINATE SENTENCES. Any prison sentence for which the exact term of confinement is not known at the time of sentencing is known as an indeterminate sentence. The decision as to when the offender will be released is made at a later date by a parole board or an agency with paroling authority. Theoretically, the indeterminate sentence could commit the convicted felon to an institution for an indefinite period of time. In practice, however, there are various degrees of indeterminacy in our federal and state criminal laws. In the federal criminal codes, the indeterminacy of sentences stems largely from the discretion granted to the Board of Parole to order the release of the offender at any point after completion of from one-third to two-thirds of the sentence imposed by the court. The Adult Authority in California sets a maximum term for the offender after sentencing that may range from one year to life.

The rationale of the indeterminate sentence, which is closely linked to the ideology of offender rehabilitation, is to provide flexibility to individualize the treatment of the offender. It sets up a mechanism whereby correctional personnel can follow the progress of the individual offender and be allowed to determine the proper time for release from the highly regimented supervision of the prison to the less restrictive supervision of parole. Given that viewpoint, the sentencing judge cannot be expected to foresee how long it will take correctional institutions to effect a cure for his criminality.

The use of indeterminate sentencing is part of the medical model of corrections (*q.v.*) in that its advocates believe in the feasibility of treating crime as a form of illness. A diagnosis of the offender's defects can be made, a treatment plan devised, and a treatment program provided for the incarcerated offender. Periodic reviews of progress are made to determine whether or not program adjustments would be appropriate. The parole board reviews the individual's activities within the institution to fix the release date. Indeterminate sentencing is a logical vehicle for carrying out the mandates of the rehabilitative ideal, but is criticized by many scholars for the underlying premise that criminals are "sick," that their illness can be adequately "diagnosed" and "treated." Critics of the rehabilitative ideal contend that criminals who appear to have made rational economic decisions to defraud, evade taxes, counterfeit money, or engage in other acquisitive crime are not emotionally disturbed or sick in any meaningful sense of the word. Lacking a defendable rationale, critics maintain, advocates of the rehabilitative ideal can only use the indeterminate sentence to set whimsical release dates.

Since the use of indeterminate sentences has become more widespread in the past decade, inmates have become increasingly vocal in their opposition to it. From the inmate's perspective, the uncertainty of not knowing how long he may be confined is cause for complaint rather than celebration. Jack Griswold and his fellow inmate co-authors devote an entire chapter of their book, *An Eye for an Eye,* to criticism of the indeterminate sentence as used in the Indiana prison system. They charge that its use resulted in Indiana prisoners serving longer sentences than inmates convicted of identical crimes in states not claiming allegiance to the rehabilitative ideal. More recently, prisoners' unions (*q.v.*) have called for the abolition of the indeterminate sentence in California, citing the abuses in its administration. Some inmates feel strongly that prison administrators use the indeterminate sentence as a tool for increasing the length of time served by inmates who are vocal in expressing radical political ideologies.

Judge Marvin Frankel seriously questions the usefulness of indeterminate sentencing procedures that are based on the assumptions that rehabilitation is possible for all offenders and that indeterminate sentences are always desirable. He would prefer the use of the definite sentence in most cases and would restrict use of indeterminate sentences to cases where definite needs could be established for the offender and appropriate resources for effective rehabilitation could be located. Offenders who might benefit from this approach include drug users, some sex offenders, and many young offenders. Use of indeterminate sentencing for dangerous offenders is reasonable because of the potential benefit to society that would come from keeping the offender locked up until cured. However, there exist formidable obstacles to identifying which offenders are dangerous and especially to determining when they can safely be released. For additional information, see DISPARITIES OF SENTENCES.

REFERENCES: Alan Dershowitz, "Let the Punishment Fit the Crime," *New York Times Magazine,* 1975; Alan Dershowitz, "Criminal Sentencing in the United States: An Historical and Conceptual Overview," *Annals of the American Academy of Political and Social Science,* 1976; Marvin E. Frankel, *Criminal Sentences: Law Without Order,* 1973; H. Jack Griswold and others, *An Eye for an Eye,* 1971; Gordon Hawkins, *The Prison: Policy and Practice,* 1976; Jessica Mitford, *Kind and Unusual Punishment: The Prison Business,* 1973; Pierce O'Donnell, Michael J. Churgin, and Dennis E. Curtis, *Toward a Just and Effective Sentencing System: Agenda for Legislative Reform,* 1977; Lawrence W. Pierce, "Rehabilitation in Corrections: A

Reassessment,'' *Federal Probation,* 1974; Michael S. Serrill, "Profile/California," *Corrections Magazine,* 1974; Leo H. Whinery and others, *Predictive Sentencing: An Empirical Evaluation,* 1976; Marvin Zalman, *Indeterminate Sentence Laws: Present, Past and Future,* 1976.

INDIANA CORRECTIONAL SYSTEM. The correctional system in Indiana consists of a Department of Correction with two major divisions: the Indiana Adult Authority and the Indiana Youth Authority. In 1974, the Department of Correction opened a Correctional Training Institute in Plainfield to provide training for correctional personnel in the state.

The largest adult institution in the state is the Indiana State Prison at Michigan City; it was opened in 1859 with a normal capacity of 1,800 males age thirty and above. All who receive life commitments and the death penalty are sent to this institution regardless of age. Younger adult offenders, ages fifteen to thirty, are sent to the Indiana State Reformatory at Pendleton. The Pendleton facility was opened in 1923 with a normal capacity of 1,200 within the confines of the main prison; an additional 200 inmates can be housed in dormitory accommodations outside the main Pendleton prison. The Indiana State Farm was opened in 1914 at Greencastle with space for 1,000 male inmates. Indianapolis is the site of the Indiana Women's Prison; it was opened in 1873 with a rated capacity of 160. Other adult facilities are the Reception and Diagnostic Center at Plainfield, opened in 1971 with a normal capacity of 200 males; the Indianapolis Urban Center, opened in 1969 with a normal capacity of 100; and the South Bend Urban Center, opened in 1975 with a normal capacity of twenty.

The Indiana Youth Authority operates institutions, camps, and centers of incarceration for juvenile offenders. These facilities, together with their opening dates and normal capacities, are as follows: the Indiana Boys' School in Plainfield, 1867, 400 juvenile delinquents ages twelve to twenty-one; the Indiana Girls' School in Indianapolis, 1907, 175 juveniles ages twelve to twenty; the Rockville Training Center at Rockville, 1954, about 115 males ages twelve and up; the Indiana Youth Center at Plainfield, 1965, 400 male felons ages fifteen and over who are first offenders; the Chain O'Lakes Youth Camp at Albion, 1964, fifty felons ages sixteen to twenty-five; the Clark County Youth Camp at Henryville, 1961, sixty juvenile delinquents ages fifteen to eighteen; and the Jasper-Pulanski Youth Camp at Medaryville, 1964, sixty male felons ages sixteen to twenty-five.

The prison population in Indiana is relatively stable: it increased by only 1 percent in 1975, when the average increase for all prison systems in the nation was 11 percent. The total prison population in the state increased from 4,360 to 4,392 between January 1975 and January 1976, and it increased 5 percent from 4,430 to 4,648 between January 1977 and January 1978.

REFERENCES: American Correctional Association, *Directory, 1975–1976* edition; Steve Gettinger, "U.S. Prison Population Hits All-Time High," *Corrections Magazine,* 1976; Michael Serrill, "Prison Population Rises Again, But at a Slower Rate," *Corrections Magazine,* 1978.

INMATE SUBCULTURE. In general, the term *subculture* refers to a subgroup within a culture displaying some deviance from the generally accepted pattern of the culture. Specifically, the term *inmate subculture* refers to the habits, customs, mores, values, beliefs, or superstitions of the body of inmates incarcerated in correctional institutions.

Prison subcultures have been a distinct topic of study in the United States at least since the 1930s when Donald Clemmer did research in a maximum security state prison. His research culminated in the publication of the first edition of his classic work *The Prison Community* (1940). Clemmer analyzed the population of the male prison in terms of social stratification and informal organization theories. His work introduced his colleagues to the existence of the inmate subculture and to the possibilities of using this captive group as a human laboratory for further research. Clemmer set the tone for future inmate subculture studies by concentrating largely on prison argot (*q.v.*) to determine how inmates use language to classify their experiences in the prison world and their interaction with other inmates. He used quotations from inmates to illustrate theoretical points. Researchers who followed Clemmer used the same approach and have produced a colorful and fascinating body of literature.

Gresham M. Sykes, another pioneer in inmate subculture studies, produced a book as widely distributed as Clemmer's classic—*The Society of Captives* (1971). Sykes' research was done in the New Jersey State Maximum Security Prison at Trenton, a prison for adult male felons. Part of Sykes' analysis focuses on the sociological relationships between guards and inmates to clarify how guards make use of the principle of reciprocity in their efforts to control inmates. That is, since it is not feasible for guards to use force to control inmates, they maintain control by overlooking minor rule violations in return for the inmates' general compliance with requirements.

Sykes develops an intriguing set of inmate typologies in terms of argot roles. The roles are prescriptions for behavior that inmates use to classify one another according to preconceived characteristics. For example, the "rat" is the prisoner who violates the inmate code of behavior by allowing information to flow across forbidden communication barriers by their giving information to guards. The "real man" lives up to all the requirements of the inmate value system; he minds his own business, can take punishment without excessive complaint, does not exploit other inmates, and never gives information or prestige to a guard. The "gorilla" takes cigarettes and other goods from his fellow inmates by force. The "merchant" is not respected by other inmates because he attempts to profit from other inmates rather than freely sharing scarce goods such as cigarettes and candy.

From the small sample of argot roles listed above, it can be seen that the terms are descriptive of behavior considered to be deviations from the norm. The inmate subculture is a value system that unifies inmates in their opposition to prison staff attempts to control them and modify their attitudes. Prison subculture researchers have come to view the tenets of the inmate subculture as imposing an important obstacle to achieving the custody and rehabilitation goals of the prison. The Clemmer and Sykes studies of male prisons found strong inmate subcultures in operation and considerable evidence that inmates were able to thwart the goals of the institutions to some extent. Later studies, such as one by Bernard B. Berk in 1966, demonstrated that inmate subcultures were likely to be strong in the atmosphere of the maximum security prison but a rather insignificant barrier to rehabilitation in the more relaxed atmosphere of medium or minimum security prisons in which rehabilitation received more emphasis than custody. It has also been found that a strong inmate subculture can be managed by a knowledgeable prison staff. John C. Watkins, warden of Draper Correctional Center in Alabama during the 1960's, made use of the body of literature on the inmate subculture to devise a strategy that weakened the influence of the subculture on Draper and enhanced his rehabilitation efforts during his tenure at the institution.

Watkin's technique involved surveillance of the inmate population to identify clique leaders. Once these leaders were identified, he worked with them one at a time to try to convert them to prosocial types who would be more likely to stay out of prison once their sentence was completed. Watkins believed that, if he was successful in converting the inmate, the inmate's leadership ability would result in the conversion of his entire clique.

Another major issue addressed in the inmate subculture literature is the question of whether it is unique to prison populations. Clarence Schrag has identified various preinstitutional factors that influence the inmates' adaptation to prison life and make some inmates prone to adopt particular roles in prison. The "real man" ("right guy" in Schrag's terminology) is the staid upholder of the inmate subculture values. He typically has had a career of many arrests starting when he was a juvenile and gradually advancing from petty thefts in his youth to a pattern of unsophisticated crimes like robbery and burglary as an adult. He is often from urban slum areas and may have earned his living by performing minor duties for organized crime. Rebellion against the generally accepted norms of society was a pattern of his life before entering prison, and the pattern continues while he is incarcerated.

With the growth in interest in the male inmate subculture, investigators have become curious as to whether women's prisons have a similar subculture. David A. Ward and Gene G. Kassebaum have conducted such research in California's Institution for Women at Frontera, and Rose Giallombardo has investigated the social structure of the Federal Reformatory for Women at Alderson, West Virginia. These researchers have found that the inmate subculture in women's prisons differs from that in male prisons in important ways: (1) the social roles in women's prisons emphasize homosexual relations to a larger extent as a mode of adaptation to prison life and (2) the mode of adaptation selected by a female inmate is best assessed by studying the preinstitutional experiences of the inmate.

While the initial excitement of discovery has worn off, the body of literature on inmate subcultures continues to grow as investigators occasionally add new contributions to the field. Leo Carroll and R. Theodore Davidson, in separate studies, have analyzed the factor of ethnic backgrounds in inmate subcultures, and Vergil L. Williams and Mary Fish have studied the economic system in the inmate subculture. For related materials, see ARGOT, HOMOSEXUALITY IN FEMALE PRISONS, HOMOSEXUALITY IN MALE PRISONS, and IRWIN, JOHN.

REFERENCES: Bernard B. Berk, "Organizational Goals and Inmate Organization," *Americal Journal of Sociology,* 1966; Seth Allan Bloomberg, "Participatory Management: Toward a Science of Correctional Management," *Criminology,* 1977; Leo Carroll, *Hacks, Blacks and Cons: Race Relations in a Maximum Security Prison,* 1974; Donald Clemmer, *The Prison Community* 2d ed. rev., 1958; Richard A. Cloward and others, *Theoretical Studies in Social Organization of the Prison,* 1960; R. Theodore Davidson, *Chicano Pris-*

oners: The Key to San Quentin, 1974; Thomas W. Foster, "Make-Believe Families: A Response of Women and Girls to the Deprivations of Imprisonment,"*_International Journal of Criminology and Penology,* 1975; John H. Gagon and William Simon, "The Social Meaning of Prison Homosexuality," *Federal Probation,* 1968; Rose Giallombardo, *The Social World of Imprisoned Girls: A Comparative Study of Institutions for Juvenile Delinquents,* 1974; Rose Giallombardo, *Society of Women: A Study of a Women's Prison,* 1966; Seymour L. Halleck and Marvin Hersko, "Homosexual Behavior in a Correctional Institution for Adolescent Girls," *American Journal of Orthopsychiatry,* 1962; F. E. Haynes, "The Sociological Study of the Prison Community," *Journal of Criminal Law and Criminology,* 1948; Esther Heffernan, *Making It in Prison: The Square, the Cool, and the Life,* 1972; John Irwin, *The Felon,* 1970; Elmer H. Johnson, "Sociology of Confinement; Assimilation and the Prison 'Rat'," *Journal of Criminal Law, Criminology and Police Science,* 1961; Sidney Kosofsky and Albert Ellis, "Illegal Communication Among Institutionalized Female Delinquents," *Journal of Social Psychology,* 1958; Gresham M. Sykes, *The Society of Captives,* 1971; A. J. W. Taylor, "The Significance of 'Darls' or 'Special Relationships' for Borstal Girls," *British Journal of Criminology,* 1965; Charles W. Thomas and David M. Peterson, *Prison Organization and Inmate Subcultures,* 1977; Charles R. Tittle, "Inmate Organization: Sex Differentiation and the Influence of Criminal Subcultures," *American Sociological Review,* 1969; Charles R. Tittle and Drollene P. Tittle, "Social Organization of Prisoners: An Empirical Test," *Social Forces,* 1964; Margery L. Velimesis, "The Female Offender," *Crime and Delinquency Literature,* 1975; David A. Ward and Gene S. Kassebaum, *Women's Prison: Sex and Social Structure,* 1965; Stanton Wheeler, "Socialization in Correctional Communities," *American Sociological Review,* 1961; Vergil L. Williams and Mary Fish, *Convicts, Codes and Contraband: The Prison Life of Men and Women,* 1974.

IOWA CORRECTIONAL SYSTEM. The correctional system in Iowa consists of the Department of Social Services with its five divisions: (1) the Division of Correctional Institutions for adult inmates; (2) the Division of Community Services which is divided into (3) the Bureau of Community Correctional Services for adult probation and parole services; (4) the Bureau of Youth Services for juvenile institutions and services; and (5) the Adult Parole Board.

Iowa's adult facilities, with opening dates and normal capacities, are the State Penitentiary at Fort Madison, 1839, 1,096 males; the Men's Reformatory at Anamosa, 1872, 700 males; the Women's Reformatory at Rockwell City, 1915, seventy-eight; and the Iowa Security Medical Facility at Oakdale, 1968, 100 dangerous patients from the state's mental health institutions and mentally ill offenders. In addition, the Bureau of Community Correctional Services operates the Riverview Release Center at Newton. The Center, serving adult offenders, was opened in 1965 with a rated capacity of 126 males.

The Bureau of Youth Services operates two institutions for juvenile offenders, but under Iowa law, a child in need of assistance, as opposed to a child who has committed a crime, cannot be incarcerated in either facility. The Iowa Training School for Boys at Eldora opened in 1868 with a capacity of 235 boys twelve to eighteen years of age. The Iowa Training School for Girls at Mitchellville opened in 1880 with a rated capacity of sixty girls ages twelve to seventeen.

Iowa experienced a very large increase (22 percent) in its institutional population during calendar year 1975. The number of prisoners on January 1, 1975, was 1,520, with an increase to 1,857 a year later, and the population increased 9 percent from 1,956 to 2,125 between January 1, 1977, and January 1, 1978.

REFERENCES: American Correctional Association, *Directory, 1975–1976* edition; Steve Gettinger, "U.S. Prison Population Hits All-Time High," *Corrections Magazine,* 1976; Michael Serrill, "Prison Population Rises Again, But at a Slower Rate," *Corrections Magazine,* 1978.

IRWIN, JOHN KEITH (1929–   ). John Irwin, an associate professor in San Francisco State University's Department of Sociology, has been a leader in the field of corrections through his research, writing, teaching, leadership in professional organizations, and active role in prison reform. Irwin brings a balanced perspective to his work; he has the scientific rigor of the Ph.D. sociologist and at the same time manages to maintain a consumer's perspective of penology.

Irwin's interest in education began in the 1950s while he was serving a sentence in San Quentin for a felony offense. He continued his studies after serving his sentence and earned a B.A, in sociology from the University of California at Los Angeles in 1962. He received his Ph.D. in sociology in 1968 from the University of California at Berkeley. As a graduate student, Irwin held several fellowships: the Woodrow Wilson Graduate Fellowship (1963); a National Institute of Mental Health Predoctoral Fellowship (1964 and 1965); and the Woodrow Wilson Dissertation Fellowship (1966).

Irwin entered his university teaching career in 1967. During his years of teaching, Irwin has exercised leadership in a number of prison-related projects designed for research and/or evaluation of corrections programs. In 1972, he was project director of an Office of Economic Opportunity grant to evaluate NewGate (*q.v.*) and other prison education programs. In 1973, he served as project director of a National Institute of Mental Health study of the social careers of heroin addicts. He was project director on a Law Enforcement Assistance Administration (*q.v.*) grant-funded evaluation study of the Eagle River, Alaska, prison program from 1975 to 1977.

Irwin's involvement in prison reform has been evident in direct action programs as well as in research and evaluation efforts. He has served as a member of the Board of Directors of the Prisoners' Union since 1969, and in that key position, he constitutes a power in the National Prison union movement. He sponsors "Rebound," a project to assist ex-offenders attending San Francisco State University. Between 1969 and 1973, he was a member of the San Francisco Prison Committee of the American Friends Service Committee. In 1970–1971, he served as a member of the American Friends Service Committee Working Party on Criminal Justice; he is one of the co-authors of the resulting book, *Struggle for Justice* (1971).

Irwin's most widely distributed publications focus on the sociology of prison subcultures. Indeed, Irwin is one of the leading authors in the body of literature on the prison subculture. His first publication, "Thieves, Convicts and the Inmate Culture," co-authored with Donald R. Cressey and appearing in *Social Problems* in the fall of 1962, has become a classic familiar to hundreds of corrections students. It has been reprinted in Howard S. Becker's *The Other Side* (1964); William Rushing's *Deviant Behavior and Social Process* (1969); and David O. Arnold's *The Sociology of Subcultures* (1970). Arnold's book contains an original contribution by Irwin: "Deviant Behavior as Subculture Phenomenon." Irwin's first book, *The Felon* (1970), has also received widespread attention in the field. Prison subculture typologies developed in *The Felon* are often noted, discussed, and critiqued in other publications on prisons. A portion of the work is excerpted as "The Prison Experience, The Convict World" in *Correctional Institutions* (1972), a popular book of readings edited by Robert Carter, Daniel Glaser, and Leslie Wilkins. Excerpts also appear in Earl Rubington and Martin Weinberg's *Deviance: Interactionist Perspective* (1973). Continuing interest in *The Felon* is evidenced by the most recent reprinting of excerpts from it in George F. Cole's *Criminal Justice: Law and Politics* (2d edition, 1976). Irwin has a contribution, "Adaptation to Being Corrected," in Daniel Glaser's monumental *Handbook of Criminology* (1974).

Irwin is editor of *Urban Life* and an associate editor of *Contemporary Sociology*. He is working on a new book on prisons that will incorporate some of the newer studies on prison subcultures into the framework of his analysis. For related information, see PRISONERS' UNIONS.

REFERENCES: American Friends Service Committee, *Struggle for Justice*, 1971; David O. Arnold (ed.), *The Sociology of Subcultures*, 1970; Howard S. Becker (ed.), *The Other Side*, 1964; Robert Carter, Daniel Glaser, and Leslie Wilkins (eds.), *Correctional Institutions*, 1972; George F. Cole (ed.), *Criminal Justice: Law and Politics*, 2d ed., 1976; John Irwin, *The Felon*, 1970; Earl Rubington and Martin Weinberg (eds.), *Deviance: Interactionist Perspective*, 2d ed., 1973; William Rushing (ed.), *Deviant Behavior and Social Process,* 1969.

J

JACKSON PRISON. The State Prison of Southern Michigan at Jackson, with a normal capacity of 4,899, is the largest prison in the United States. Even when operating below its maximum capacity (4,450 inmates in 1975), it ordinarily holds a larger average inmate population than any other prison in the country. The outer walls of Jackson enclose fifty-seven acres. An additional 4,000 acres beyond the walls belong to the Trusty Division of the prison operation.

The size of Jackson Prison is an important point of discussion in the field of penology. This prison, and other prisons of large size, achieve economies of scale of operation that result in a relatively low average daily cost per inmate. For example, the 750-inmate prison at Marquette, Michigan, spends almost twice as much per inmate because of its smaller size. The potential for cost savings is a powerful inducement for units of government at all levels to build large prisons or jails. Jackson Prison was opened in 1929 when such cost advantages seemed especially important. However, the staff members at Jackson, along with most penologists, recognize that large prisons present a significant disadvantage in attempts to provide rehabilitation for inmates. The individual inmate becomes an anonymous number in the masses, with little chance of establishing a relationship with a staff member that will be conducive to diverting him from a criminal career. Penologists, in general, so strongly agree on the therapeutic value of smaller prisons that in recent years they have been able to block the building of new prisons as large as Jackson.

The Michigan Department of Corrections has long-range plans to replace the Jackson institution with smaller prisons holding from 600 to 1,000 men each. Some of the smaller prisons are now being built, but completion of the whole project will require twenty years. Meanwhile, the department is coping with the huge inmate population at Jackson by offering a number of treatment programs and by maintaining reasonable regulations that allow inmates to have wide choice of clothing, to grow mustaches, to wear their hair fairly long, and to own an array of personal property items including television sets, radios, tape players, typewriters, wall decorations, and musical instruments. Academic and vocational education involves more than 1,500 of the Jackson inmates in a rehabilitation effort. Thirty-four full-time teachers offer the inmates 125 sections of vocational education courses, remedial education, and high school courses. Inmates can take college-level courses through the offerings of Jackson Community College. The college has 500 inmates taking courses and is believed to be operating the largest prison program of any college in the United States. In 1974, Detroit's Wayne State University began offering junior and senior level courses in the prison.

Jackson's prison industries employ more than 600 inmates in the production of textiles, clothing, printing, shoes, and metal goods. These products are used by the prison or are sold to other government agencies.

Jackson's rehabilitation programs and custody procedures work well in keeping down disturbances. Any large prison is potentially a powder keg that can explode into a violent riot, but at the time of this writing, Jackson had not had a major disturbance since 1952.

REFERENCE: Jerry Ziegler, "America's Largest Prison," *Corrections Magazine,* 1975.

JOHNSON, ELMER HUBERT (1917–   ). Perhaps Johnson's most outstanding contribution to penology was his early recognition that a partnership between higher education and penology was possible. He began to study the problems of the prison system long before it became a popular pursuit for academics in the United States. From the first, Johnson viewed penological problems from the perspective of those who make the system work. Unlike most academics, Johnson has never criticized and blamed penology practitioners for the failures of the prison system; rather, he regards them as individuals who have attempted to deal with unmanageable problems that have largely been created by conditions outside their control.

Remarkably, through the abstract theories of sociology Johnson has been able to shed light on practical problems encountered in the daily operation of prison systems. His keen insights, awesome productivity, and lucid discussion of issues in the field have made him a substantial force in corrections. He is one of the most widely published and most frequently quoted academic penologists. Thousands of practitioners and preservice students have learned the basics of corrections from Johnson's texts and scholarly articles. One rarely encounters a scholarly treatise on corrections that does not quote from one of Johnson's works. A new generation of academics who studied under Johnson is writing materials that reflect his philosophy and approach to corrections.

Johnson developed his interest in corrections in 1949 while he was an assistant professor in the Department of Sociology and Anthropology at North Carolina State University at Raleigh. His identification with penology was firmly established when he took a two-year academic leave (1958–1960) from his university to serve as assistant director of the North Carolina Prison Department, at a time when the state system had 140 units and 12,000 inmates.

Johnson's expertise in deviance and criminology was well developed when he left North Carolina in 1966 to accept a professorship at the Center for the Study of Crime, Delinquency and Corrections, College of Human Resources, Southern Illinois University at Carbondale. He is continuing his career as professor of sociology and criminal justice at Southern Illinois University; his most recent interests include gerontology, as well as criminal justice administration and corrections.

Johnson's contributions to the corrections literature date back to a 1957 article on capital punishment in *Social Forces*. The 1960s found him publishing articles that almost exclusively pertained to the administration of criminal justice and corrections. Articles appeared regularly in periodicals such as *Journal of Criminal Law, Criminology and Police Science, Social Forces, Crime and Delinquency, Prison Journal, Criminologica, Journal of Correctional Education, Police, Canadian Journal of Corrections, Federal Probation, American Journal of Correction,* and *The Correctional Trainer.* The quality of these articles is reflected in the demand for them by editors of anthologies; Johnson's articles have been reprinted in more than a dozen professional books currently in print.

Johnson's most obvious impact on the field has been through the widespread use of his college text *Crime, Correction, and Society,* published by Dorsey Press in three editions (1964, 1968, and 1974). The large text (671 pages) surveys a massive amount of currently accepted literature in the field and in addition is replete with his own contributions to the field. He views crime from the perspective of society's reaction to it and scrupulously avoids making correctional practitioners the scapegoats. Johnson's broad perspective of the social scene is demonstrated in his second text *Social Problems of Urban Man* (1974).

Johnson's insights into corrections derive both from his original research and from his interludes as a practitioner. He has completed several research projects for the National Institute of Mental Health:

a study of felon self-mutilations, the status of social work in prisons, and a pilot study on age, race, and recidivism (*q.v.*). He completed a research project for the Vocational Rehabilitation Administration on work release (*q.v.*) programs in North Carolina. In recent years, his interest in prison systems has extended to the international scene; he has examined systems in Japan, Taiwan, and Hong Kong (1970); eight countries in Western Europe (1972), and Australia (1974).

REFERENCES: Elmer H. Johnson, letter to author dated October 25, 1976; Elmer H. Johnson, *Crime, Correction, and Society,* 3d ed., 1974; Elmer H. Johnson, *Social Problems of Urban Man,* 1974.

JUST COMMUNITY. The Connecticut Department of Correction is experimenting with a unique treatment program, called the Just Community, based on Lawrence Kohlberg's moral development theory (*q.v.*). The program was initiated in a cottage of the state's prison for adult females, the Connecticut Correctional Institution at Niantic, in 1971. Since then, more than 120 women who have participated in the program have been released, only 15 percent of whom later returned to custody—a figure that is only half the usual recidivism (*q.v.*) rate for female offenders. These results, even though measured without the use of an experiment control group, have led corrections Commissioner John R. Manson to expand the program to a group of young male offenders transferred to one of the cottages in the Niantic complex. Although Manson does not necessarily consider the group interaction technique to be a panacea, he does believe that it provides staff members with a viable set of guidelines for administering a therapeutic setting for offenders. Manson feels that, at the very least, the use of moral development theory helps staff members do a better job and that their competence must inevitably improve the inmate's prospects. As support for his belief in the value of the technique, he observes that the women graduates of the Just Community program who are transferred to the halfway house (*q.v.*) in New Haven before their ultimate release from custody cause fewer problems than the graduates of conventional social work counseling who are transferred to a halfway house in Hartford.

Inmates who participate in the Just Community program receive the same kind of correctional services as those provided to other inmates: academic and vocational training, along with the usual institution work assignments. In addition, they join in the group processes of moral development theory which allows individuals to learn the impact of their decisions about their personal life on other people with whom they associate daily. The result is more mature decisions after a few months of practice. Inmates learn to see moral dilemmas from the viewpoint of other people involved as well as from their own perspective. For an additional explanation, see MORAL DEVELOPMENT THEORY.

REFERENCES: William E. Cockerham, "Connecticut's 'Just Community,' " *Corrections Magazine,* 1975; Lawrence Kohlberg, "The Cognitive-Developmental Approach to Moral Education," *Readings in Human Development: Annual Editions: 1976–1977,* 1976.

JUSTICE MODEL OF CORRECTIONS. The justice model of corrections is essentially a proposal for a shift in the goals of the correctional system in the United States. While a number of prominent authorities in the field have been discussing similar proposals since about 1970, the best known spokesman for the justice model is David Fogel (*q.v.*), executive director of the Illinois Law Enforcement Commission. In 1975, Fogel revealed an elaborate plan that, if adopted, would redefine the goals of the Illinois correctional system. His justice model has attracted national attention and has stimulated a great deal of debate among penologists. His book ". . . *We Are the Living Proof . . .": The Justice Model for Corrections* elucidated his plan to the general public and to penologists nationwide.

Fogel's plan is based on the use of flat sentencing to switch the emphasis of corrections from rehabilitation to "fairness." This shift is accomplished by abolishing the use of the indeterminate sentence (*q.v.*) and greatly limiting the discretion of sentencing judges to make sentences uniform for categories of crimes specified in the plan. Fogel views his scheme as a rehabilitation plan for the prison system rather than for inmates. Underlying the concepts of the justice model is a pessimistic conclusion that offenders cannot be rehabilitated in prisons and that penologists must stop trying to convince themselves and the public that prisons can be turned into therapeutic settings. The justice model openly recognizes that prisons serve only to punish offenders; no claim is made for the therapeutic value of incarceration. The justice model proposal has aroused great interest among penologists because inmates participating in major prison riots during the past decade have so consistently complained about the injustice of sentencing disparities.

Both the indeterminate sentence and parole are tools of the medical model of corrections (*q.v.*)—the model that views the offender as being emotionally ill, with the logical conclusion that the illness can be diagnosed, treated, and cured. In abandoning lip service to diagnosis and treatment, Fogel's plan would abolish parole as well as replace indeterminate sentences with determinate sentences. He does not, however, propose that more offenders be incarcerated; he carefully emphasizes his identification with groups seeking the abolition of the traditional, fortress-type prison. Fogel believes that his plan would greatly reduce the number of offenders being incarcerated by forcing trial courts to rely more on diversion to community corrections programs such as probation or halfway houses (*q.v.*). His plan has attracted critics from the ranks of other abolitionist groups, such as the John Howard Association and the National Council on Crime and Delinquency (*q.v.*). These groups fear that the adoption of Fogel's plan by state legislators would ultimately result in even more people being sent to prison because the state legislatures would tend to modify the plan over the years to achieve even harsher determinate sentences.

As support for the use of flat sentences, Fogel cites the findings of judicial authorities showing that offenders given the supposedly humane indeterminate sentence often serve longer terms than those given definite sentences. Fogel also views the decision-making of parole boards as similar to the discretion exercised by sentencing judges, but amenable to more "whim, caprice, and arbitrariness." Flat sentences, along with the abolition of parole, would make "fairness" the basic mission of the prison. Fogel argues that offenders are "volitional," by which he means that they must exercise complete freedom of choice as to whether they will participate in any treatment programs within the institution. Fogel's concept of volition is the key to the humanitarian dimensions of his plan. He does not propose to be humanitarian by reforming the inmates but rather by treating them with dignity and fairness. Inmates could choose to participate in self-improvement programs while incarcerated, but programs not in demand would be phased out.

Fogel's flat sentencing plan would severely narrow the discretion of judges by providing a schedule of sentences constructed by grouping felonies into five categories. Discretion would be exercised by judges in that they could choose from a range of alternatives to incarceration once an offender was convicted. If, however, the court found incarceration to be appropriate for the convicted felon, the judge would be required to use the schedule to select a sentence within a narrow range of possible terms. When the offender left the courtroom after sentencing, he would know the exact number of years he would be required to serve less the amount of good time (*q.v.*) he could earn ("good time" being a specified number of days per month subtracted from a sentence as a reward for cooperation from the inmate).

In the categories proposed by Fogel (patterned after the classification of felonies currently in use by Illinois), murder is a separate category calling for a fixed sentence ranging from twenty-five years to life (or death, if permissible). The other four classifications group felonies as Class 1 to Class 4, with Class 1 felonies being the more serious offenses. Class 4 felonies would receive a flat time sentence of two years, Class 3 three years, Class 2 five years, and Class 1 eight years. Fogel refers to the sentencing schedule as the "2,3,5,8" scheme. He also provides a second schedule of "enhanced" sentences that would be used to provide extended terms of incarceration for repeat offenders or those considered to be especially dangerous; the enhanced schedule is a "5,6,9,15" scheme. For discussions of related material, see ABOLITIONISTS, DISPARITY OF SENTENCES, FOGEL, DAVID, INDETERMINATE SENTENCES, MAINE CORRECTIONAL SYSTEM, MEDICAL MODEL OF CORRECTIONS, and PRAGMATISTS.

REFERENCES: Alan M. Dershowitz, "Criminal Sentencing in the United States: An Historical and Conceptual Overview," *Annals of the American Academy of Political and Social Sciences,* 1976; David Fogel, *". . . We are the Living Proof . . .": The Justice Model for Corrections,* 1975; Gordon Hawkins, *The Prison: Policy and Practice,* 1976; Pierce O'Donnell, Michael J. Churgin, and Dennis E. Curtis, *Toward a Just and Effective Sentencing System: Agenda for Legislative Reform,* 1977; Lawrence W. Pierce, "Rehabilitation in Corrections: A Reassessment," *Federal Probation,* 1974; Michael S. Serrill, "Critics of Corrections Speak Out," *Corrections Magazine,* 1976; Twentieth Century Fund, Task Force on Criminal Sentencing, *Fair and Certain Punishment,* 1976.

K

KANSAS CORRECTIONAL SYSTEM. Adult institutions, adult parole, and adult probation services in Kansas are all administered under the Department of Corrections. Juvenile correctional services are administered under the Department of Social and Rehabilitation Services, which is divided into the Division of Mental Health and Retardation Services and the Division of Children and Youth.

The Department of Corrections receives all convicted male felons eighteen years of age or above; in some cases, males as young as sixteen are received if the Juvenile Court certifies them as not being amenable to juvenile offender treatment programs. Female offenders convicted of a misdemeanor cannot serve more than thirty days in a county jail; if their misdemeanor sentences are longer than thirty days, they are held in the Kansas Correctional Institution for Women, even though they are not actually committed to the Department of Corrections. Thus, the Kansas Correctional Institution for Women, opened in 1918 at Lansing, holds both felons and misdemeanants; it has a normal capacity of eighty-two.

Adult facilities include the Kansas State Industrial Reformatory at Hutchinson, opened in 1895 with a normal capacity of 692 male felons; the Kansas State Penitentiary at Lansing, opened in 1864 with a rated capacity of 738 males; and the Kansas State Reception and Diagnostic Center at Topeka, opened in 1974 with a rated capacity of 180. The Department of Corrections also operates two honor camps for male felons: Tuttle Creek Reservoir Honor Camp at Randolph, opened in 1962 with a normal capacity of twenty-eight, and Toronto Reservoir Honor Camp at Toronto, opened in 1963 with a normal capacity of ninety-six.

The Division of Mental Health and Retardation Services operates the juvenile institutions in the state; youths between the ages of thirteen and eighteen are committed by the Juvenile Court. All commitments are to age twenty-one, but the superintendent of an institution may release a youth at any time. The institutions are as follows: the Youth Center at Beloit, opened in 1888 with a normal capacity of ninety-seven females; the Youth Center at Topeka, opened in 1881 with a rated capacity of 198 males ages fourteen to eighteen; the Youth Center at Atchison, opened as an orphanage in 1885 (in 1972, a section was added for sixty-two delinquent boys ages thirteen to fifteen); the Larned Youth Rehabilitation Center at Larned, opened in 1914 as a hospital (in 1972, a unit for thirty male delinquents was added to the hospital); and the Osawatomie Youth Rehabilitation Center, a unit for sixty male juveniles that was added to the Osawatomie State Hospital in 1972.

The state has recently experienced a significant increase in the size of its prison population—a 19 percent increase between January 1, 1975, and January 1, 1976, with a rise in population from 1,421 to 1,696. The prison population continued to grow with a 9 percent increase from 2,126 to 2,249 between January 1977 and January 1978.

REFERENCES: American Correctional Association, *Directory, 1975–1976 edition*; Steve Gettinger, "U.S. Prison Population Hits All-Time High," *Corrections Magazine*, 1976; Michael Serrill, "Prison Population Rises Again, But at a Slower Rate," *Corrections Magazine*, 1978.

KENTUCKY CORRECTIONAL SYSTEM. The Kentucky Department of Corrections, responsible for the state's adult offenders, operates seven prisons holding more than 3,000 inmates. Two of the prisons are relatively large: Kentucky State Reformatory at LaGrange with a normal capacity of 1,750 and Kentucky State Penitentiary at Eddyville with a normal capacity of 1,150. Adult females are incarcerated in the Kentucky Correctional Institution for Women located at Pewee Valley. The women's facility has a normal capacity of eighty but has been slightly overcrowded in recent years.

The department is beginning to renovate its physical facilities, with an emphasis on smaller prisons that can be more treatment oriented. The Kentucky legislature has approved the construction of a small $15 million maximum security prison.

In addition to the two large facilities for males and the women's prison, the department operates four small units for males: Bell County Forestry Camp at Chenoa; Blackburn Correctional Complex at Lexington; Frenchburg Correctional Facility at Frenchburg; and Harlan County Forestry Camp at Harlan. The Frenchburg Correctional Facility was opened in 1969 as the state's first effort to provide a special institution for a particular kind of offender: first offenders sixteen years of age and over. In establishing the new facility, the department adopted the policy of accepting its inmates directly from the state's reception center at LaGrange so that the inmate population would consist of persons who had never lived in a large prison. By accepting first offenders inexperienced in the destructive subculture values learned in large prisons, the Frenchburg penologists hope to be more successful in their rehabilitation efforts. Inmate subculture (*q.v.*), which is so prevalent in large, traditional prisons, hampers rehabilitation efforts because its values prohibit inmate cooperation with prison staff members. Young inmates often are especially eager to win the social acceptance of other inmates who are upholding the anti-institution norms of the prison subculture. Officials believe that the atmosphere at the small Frenchburg prison (112 normal capacity) helps to reduce the recidivism (*q.v.*) rate. The apparent success at Frenchburg encouraged the department to open Blackburn Correctional Complex at Lexington in 1972. With a normal capacity of 180, the facility offers differential treatment for inmates (assignment to different types of activities based upon needs determined in the classification [*q.v.*] process). Since the opening of the Blackburn facility, two small forestry camps were opened in 1973: Bell County at Chenoa and Harlan County at Harlan.

The Division of Community Services, a branch of the Department of Corrections, administers adult probation and parole in the state. Like most other states, Kentucky has been making more use of probation and parole in recent years as part of the general trend in the United States towards greater reliance on community-based corrections to deal with offenders and less on institutionalization. For example, between 1970 and 1975, the number of probationers doubled in the state and the number of parolees increased by 50 percent. To some extent, such figures reflect an increasing number of convictions. However, the most accurate interpretation of the statistics is simply that fewer convicted felons are being sent to prison in the first place, and those who are incarcerated are being released on parole earlier if the parole board believes they can adjust to freedom successfully.

Under enabling legislation passed in 1972, probation and parole officials operate two programs not commonly used in other states. One unusual program is "shock probation," which allows a sentencing judge to send an offender to prison for sixty days before he is released on probation. If the judge has some doubts about whether the convicted felon is a good risk for probation, the procedure is used to give the offender a taste of prison life. The second program provides for the supervision of prisoners released after serving their full sentence. In most states, inmates who serve the full term of their sentence because the parole board does not deem it advisable to release them early are simply released without supervision at the end of their term. The Kentucky program, known as conditional release, allows the probation and parole officers to supervise such offenders for a time after their release from prison. This type of supervision is designed to help the offender readjust to life in the community.

Juvenile offenders in Kentucky must be over eleven years of age and younger than sixteen in order for the Juvenile Court to commit them to an institution. Once committed to a juvenile facility, a youth may stay until age twenty-one. All juvenile sentences are indeterminate. The Bureau of Social Services, a part of the Department for Human Resources, receives commitments from juvenile judges and decides whether to place the youth in an institution. Kentucky has a residential treatment policy for juveniles that stresses alternatives to incarceration for youngsters. If the youths are incarcerated, they must be grouped according to their treatment needs, with no more than fifty in any one facility. Some 700 per year, out of 35,000 appearing before the courts, are placed in residential programs.

As a result of the state's juvenile policies, Kentucky's largest institution for children, Kentucky Village, was closed in 1971, and six other institutions have been closed or converted to day treatment since 1972. The Bureau of Social Services now operates five special institutions, along with three camps, two group homes, and five day-treatment programs. The five special institutions for youthful public offenders are the Central Kentucky Treatment Center at Lynden, opened in 1956 with a normal capacity of forty boys; the Frenchburg Boys' Center, opened in 1969 with a normal capacity of fifty culturally deprived boys; the Morehead Treatment Center, opened in 1971 with a normal capacity of forty-eight boys and girls; and two facilities for status offenders: the Kentucky Children's Home Resource Home in Lynden with room for forty females and the Lynwood Treatment Center in Anchorage with space for fifty juveniles. The three camps are Green River Boys' Camp at Cromwell, opened in 1972 with a normal capacity of fifty male public offenders; Lake Cumberland Boys' Camp at Monticello, opened in 1965 with space for forty public offenders; and Woodsbend Boys' Camp at West Liberty, opened in 1964 with a normal capacity of fifty public offenders. The five day-treatment programs include the Christian County Day Treatment Program at Hopkinsville; the Daniel Boone Treatment Center at Burlington; the Hardin County Day Treatment at Elizabethtown; the Jewel Manor Treatment Center at Louisville, and the Kentucky Children's Home-Day Treatment at Lynden. Reception for juvenile offenders is provided at two locations: Northern Kentucky Reception

Center at Crittenden and the Diagnostic Detention Center at Louisville.

The state's prison population grew from 2,958 in January 1975 to 3,659 in January 1977, but growth leveled off so that the January 1978 population was 3,661.

REFERENCES: American Correctional Association, *Directory,* 1975–1976 edition; Lauren Katzowitz, "Profile/Kentucky," *Corrections Magazine,* 1975; Michael Serrill, "Prison Population Rises Again, But at a Slower Rate," *Corrections Magazine,* 1978.

L

LAW ENFORCEMENT ASSISTANCE ADMINISTRATION (LEAA).
The Omnibus Crime Control and Safe Streets Act of 1968 created
LEAA as part of the U.S. Department of Justice. While the general
public has generally thought of LEAA as an agency designed to provide financial assistance to law enforcement agencies, it has pumped
about $1.5 billion of its $5 billion expenditures into some 30,000 corrections projects since its inception in October 1968. This sum is
thought to be about 5 to 10 percent of the amount spent on corrections by state and local governments during the 1968–1976 period.
The impact of LEAA funds on corrections is much greater, however,
than the percentage of total expenditures on corrections would indicate because so much of the LEAA funds have been spent on innovative and experimental programs.

LEAA distributes money to various components of the criminal
justice system through a system of grants of federal tax revenues. In
1976, total LEAA expenditures were $810.7 million. One obvious im-
pact of LEAA funding has been the establishment of state planning
agencies throughout the country. The Safe Streets Act encouraged responsibility and planning for criminal justice needs by specifying that
the bulk of LEAA funds be awarded in block grants to states based
on state populations. Part B of the Safe Streets Act enables LEAA to
finance the preparation of state plans by awarding annual planning
grants of at least $200,000 to state planning agencies. These grants as-
sist them in the preparation of comprehensive plans analyzing all of
the state's problems in criminal justice and establishing goals, priorities, and standards before federal grant money will be made available
for use in the field. State planning agencies are normally made up of
members of criminal justice agencies in the state and local governments involved. State planning agencies have supervisory boards
whose members are appointed by governors and chief executives of
local government jurisdictions.

Planning grants from LEAA to state planning agencies usually have
matching requirements and pass-through provisions. The matching requirement requires the state receiving the planning grant to appropri-

ate 10 percent of the total amount to be spent so that the federal grant is paying $90 out of every $100 being spent in the planning process. The pass-through provision requires each state to make a minimum of 40 percent of its planning grant available to local government units. When a state submits its annual comprehensive plan to LEAA, it must be approved or disapproved by the federal agency within ninety days.

When a state's comprehensive plan is approved, the state is eligible to receive block action grants from LEAA to implement the provisions of the plan. Parts C and E of the Safe Streets Act authorize LEAA to award block grants to fifty-five eligible jurisdictions: all fifty states, Puerto Rico, the District of Columbia, American Samoa, Guam, and the Virgin Islands. The state planning agencies in these fifty-five jurisdictions then subgrant the money for use by agencies, groups, and organizations throughout the jurisdiction. Part E funds are important for penology in that they must be used solely for corrections (institutions and community corrections). These funds supplement, but do not supplant, funds due to state planning agencies under the block action and discretionary grant programs. Part E grant money can be used to acquire, construct, or renovate prisons, as well as to improve correctional programs. State planning agencies must subgrant to local governments the proportion of block action grants received that local governments normally spend on criminal justice as compared to the state government. Thus, if local governments usually provide 70 percent of all nonfederal funds spent on criminal justice in a state, then local governments must receive 70 percent of the state's block action grants. Block grants require a 10 percent nonfederal match, with the state providing at least half of that match for local projects. If Part C block funds are spent on construction projects, the nonfederal match must be 50 percent. Correctional facilities built with Part E funds require only a 10 percent nonfederal match. In cases where a state's plan is not approved, LEAA will reallocate that state's block action grants to its discretionary grants program. Block action funds not exhausted by a state in a given year may be reallocated to other states.

The LEAA discretionary grant program provides action grant money for LEAA to award funds directly to states, cities, counties, and nonprofit organizations for innovative and experimental projects that address priorities established by LEAA. Amounts allocated to the discretionary grant program total some 15 percent of the Part C block action grant budget and 50 percent of the Part E corrections budget.

LEAA operates with a total of about 850 employees, 250 of whom work out of the agency's ten regional offices established in 1970 to ease the difficulties of operating the program from the Washington office. Regional offices audit the expenditures of the state planning agencies, review and approve the comprehensive annual plans submitted by the states, process applications for discretionary grants, and provide technical assistance.

Part E of the Safe Streets Act is of special significance to penologists. Part E is legislation added to the 1968 Safe Streets Act in 1970 as a result of lobbying by corrections officials who felt that law enforcement and courts were getting a disproportionate share of LEAA funds. Part E simply earmarks a portion of the LEAA budget for the exclusive use of corrections. LEAA, with authority to determine the method of distributing Part E funds, has chosen to distribute half of the earmarked funds to states via the block grant program and to distribute half through its discretionary grant program. Under present policies, corrections programs can receive LEAA funds in four different ways: (1) through Part E block grants; (2) through regular block grants which are allocated among law enforcement, courts, and corrections programs at the discretion of state planning agencies; (3) through Part E discretionary grants; and (4) through Part C discretionary grants. The Part E legislation has apparently been a factor in increasing the amount of LEAA funds being channeled into corrections. The proportion of LEAA funds being spent on corrections rose from 22 percent in 1970 to 37 percent in 1971. Some $450 million in Part E funds was spent on corrections programs between 1971 and 1975. More than 30 percent of the total LEAA budget was spent on corrections in 1976 as compared to 8 percent in 1969.

LEAA efforts to make an impact on crime have been hampered by a constant shifting of priorities resulting largely from staff turnover in LEAA and in the state planning agencies. In one two-year interval, from 1974 to 1976, twenty-seven of the fifty-five directors of state planning agencies were replaced. Since LEAA began, five different LEAA administrators (Patrick Murphy, 1968–1969; Charles H. Rogovin, 1969–1970; Jerris Leonard, 1971–1973; Donald Santarelli, 1973–1974; and Richard Velde, 1974–present) have headed LEAA under the supervision of seven different attorneys general.

One indirect impact of LEAA funding on American penology has been through the largest single program funded by LEAA: the Law Enforcement Education Program (LEEP). Based on the rationale that the criminal justice system needs well-educated personnel, LEEP has provided funds to assist some 290,000 criminal justice personnel to attend colleges and universities at a total cost of $234.7 million between 1969 and 1976. Some 40,000 of the personnel assisted by the LEEP program are prison guards and probation and parole personnel.

LEEP grants are awarded annually to colleges and universities participating in the program. The schools then distribute the money to personnel from local criminal justice agencies who enroll in academic programs. LEEP funds cannot be used to pay teaching salaries or to provide the school with facilities or equipment. Criminal justice personnel participating in the LEEP program can receive grants to cover the cost of tuition, fees, and books up to $250 per academic quarter, or $400 per semester. The grant recipient is not required to repay the grant if he continues as a full-time employee in a criminal justice agency for two years following completion of a course financed by LEEP funds. LEEP also makes loans to a limited number of preservice students who plan careers in criminal justice and to in-service students. Loans pay for direct education costs up to $2,200 per academic year. Recipients of these loans receive a 25 percent cancellation of LEEP indebtedness for each year of full-time employment in a criminal justice agency after they complete their full-time study. For discussion of two other LEAA programs, see NATIONAL CLEARINGHOUSE FOR CRIMINAL JUSTICE PLANNING AND ARCHITECTURE and NATIONAL INSTITUTE OF LAW ENFORCEMENT AND CRIMINAL JUSTICE.

REFERENCES: Charles Rogovin, "The Genesis of the Law Enforcement Assistance Administration: A Personal Account," *Columbus Human Rights Law Review,* 1973; Michael S. Serrill, "LEAA," *Corrections Magazine,* 1976; U.S. Department of Justice, *The Law Enforcement Assistance Administration: A Partnership for Crime Control,* 1976.

LEENHOUTS, KEITH J. (1925–   ). Judge Keith J. Leenhouts, director of the VIP (Volunteers in Prevention, Prosecution, Probation, Prison, Parole) of the National Council on Crime and Delinquency (*q.v.*) has devoted his life to the development of volunteerism in criminal justice. In 1959, as a young judge of the Royal Oak Municipal Court in Michigan, he developed a compassionate concern for the plight of misdemeanant offenders appearing before the bench. With little information about the offender, only the briefest time available to consider the sparse information, and only the limited options to fine, imprison, or release the offender, he was helpless to assist the offenders and felt he was punishing them for the symptoms of their problems. As a result, Leenhouts began to use citizen volunteers as a means of overcoming some of the deficiencies he saw in the role of judge. His early experiences with volunteers convinced him that using volunteers was an effective way to convert criminal offenders into productive, law-abiding citizens. Within a few years of starting a volunteer program in his court, 500 citizens devoting 50,000 hours were involved in the probation program of the court. By utilizing volunteers, he found that the court could spend some twelve hours per month on each offender instead of the usual three minutes. Many offenders had never had someone who took a personal interest in their problems and who was willing to provide highly individualized services as well as to serve as a "significant other" or "inspirational personality."

Leenhouts estimates that at least 500,000 hours were devoted to refining the concept of volunteers in criminal justice programs from 1959 to 1969. During those ten years, he subjected his program to close scrutiny by calling in independent professional evaluators of the National Institute of Mental Health. The evaluators found a misdemeanant recidivism (*q.v.*) rate of only 7 percent in the Royal Oak Court compared to the national average of 37 percent in misdemeanant courts.

Leenhouts began to encourage other criminal justice agencies to develop volunteer programs. In the early years of his efforts to promote the program, Leenhouts helped others on his own time and at his own expense. In 1965, he received a small grant from the Methodist church which helped cover some of his expenses and enabled him to make the concept more widespread. In 1969, a wealthy industrialist heard of his work and agreed to fund Project Misdemeanant if Leenhouts would step down from the bench to devote full time to promoting volunteerism in criminal justice. When Leenhouts resigned from the bench in 1969 to run Project Misdemeanant, some 100 courts, jails, prisons, juvenile institutions, and diversion programs were using volunteers. Project Misdemeanant ultimately became VIP, a division of the NCCD.

The goals of VIP are to help new programs begin utilizing volunteers in criminal justice and to assist existing programs to expand and improve their services. The National Association of Volunteers in Criminal Justice was formed as a forum for annual meetings to unite criminal justice volunteers and to allow them to share their experiences. In addition, VIP assists states in the development of organizations to foster volunteerism. Through these activities and countless consultations around the United States, the number of involved citizen volunteers grew by 1978 to approximately 750,000 citizen volunteers active in over 3,000 volunteer programs in criminal justice.

Leenhouts' work in the court-corrections volunteer movement received further major impetus in 1977 when VIP-NCCD, the University of Alabama, and the W. K. Kellogg Foundation planned and established the National Education—Training Program (NETP) with offices at Royal Oak, Michigan, and in the Criminal Justice Program at the University of Alabama. For additional information, see NATIONAL EDUCATION—TRAINING PROGRAM FOR COLLEGES-PROFESSIONALS-CITIZENS.

Leenhouts' work has been described in two articles by Joe Alex Morris which appeared in the October 1965 and April 1968 issues of *Reader's Digest.* Morris published a book, *First Offender,* about Leenhouts' work in 1970. Leenhouts published his own book about his work, *A Father . . . a Son . . . and a Three Mile Run,* in 1975. He has published articles for *Crime and Delinquency, Federal Probation, American Judicature Society,* and various other professional journals, magazines, and newspapers. He is the publisher of *V.I.P. Examiner,* a quarterly newspaper with a circulation of 45,000.

REFERENCES: Keith J. Leenhouts, *A Father . . . a Son . . . and a Three Mile Run,* 1975; Joe Alex Morris, *First Offender,* 1970.

LOCKDOWN. During a lockdown, all inmates are kept in their cells twenty-four hours a day. The term is best known from events and procedures established in 1973 in the California prison system. Raymond K. Procunier, then California's director of corrections, ordered Folsom, San Quentin, Soledad, and Tracy prisons to be ''locked down.'' His order meant that inmate work assignments, recreation, and participation in rehabilitation programs would cease immediately for the some 9,000 inmates in the four prisons. As a result of the order, inmates were locked in their cells almost twenty-four hours a day for weeks; they left their cells only for meals and then only in small groups. The lockdown of the four institutions came in late November 1973. A few days later, in early December, a lockdown was also ordered for the Vacaville Medical Facility.

Events that led to Procunier's lockdown order reached back over a three-year period of increasing violence in the prisons at Folsom, San Quentin, Soledad, and Tracy; almost 500 men had been stabbed. Of the ninety-three who died of stab wounds, eleven were staff members. In the weeks just prior to the order, the violence had intensified. On August 30, 1973, Lynwood Bell, an inmate in San Quentin, was stabbed to death in the exercise yard by two other inmates in full view of a guard on the gunwalk. After firing warning shots, the guard had to wound one of the attackers to break up the fight. During the next ninety days in the four prisons, a dozen more men were stabbed, several of them fatally. Four men were stabbed in a single day in San Quentin. On November 27, 1973, Jerry V. Sanders, a correctional officer at Tracy, was found stabbed to death in the corridor of a cell-block. Following this incident, Procunier met for two days with his wardens and staff members and then ordered the lockdown. Vacaville was added to the list of facilities to be locked down when Juan Corona, a convicted mass murderer, received thirty-two stab wounds on December 2, 1973.

Vacaville soon returned to its normal mode of operation, but the other four prisons were reorganized to achieve greater safety for the inmates and guards. Inmate freedom of movement was reduced drastically in the four prisons by cutting down on the number of inmates allowed to work in prison industries and maintenance shops where weapons could be manufactured, and by rigorous screening of inmates allowed to participate in rehabilitation programs. Dining arrangements were changed so that inmates in work areas could eat their meals on the work site instead of being marched to the dining room. In some instances, classrooms and shops were moved closer to the cellblocks. Metal detectors, similar to those used in airports, were installed in corridors where inmates were marched to and from school or work assignments. Inmates were required to remove their clothes before passing through the metal detector and to put on a new set of clothing after passing through. Additional space was converted into areas where inmates could be held in protective custody if they had reputations as informers or if some rival gang had threatened their lives. A new type of security arrangement known as a "control unit" was established. The 1,000 or so men placed in these units did not experience the maximum security precautions that they would have in segregation, but they were more highly regimented than the inmates in the general population.

California officials attribute most of the prison violence leading to the lockdown to various prison gangs who war with one another and employ "hit men" in putting out contracts on individuals. Two Chicano gangs appear to have caused about 50 to 75 percent of the stabbings. The two gangs, warring with one another, are the Mexican Mafia, whose members come from east Los Angeles, and the Nuestra Familia (Our Family) consisting of rural Chicanos. Some stabbings are also attributed to the Aryan Brotherhood, a white group that is successor to the old Nazi party in the prison system. The Brotherhood is believed to consist of former members of motorcycle gangs and long-term offenders willing to hire out as hit men for the Chicano gangs. The death of the Tracy corrections officer is blamed on the Black Guerrilla Family.

These measures continue and to a degree have helped contain the violence. Although stabbings still occur, the bulk of them have been confined to the control unit sections of San Quentin and Tracy.

REFERENCES: "Procunier: A Candid Conversation," *Corrections Magazine*, 1975; Michael S. Serrill, "Profile/California," *Corrections Magazine*, 1974.

LOUISIANA CORRECTIONAL SYSTEM. The majority of the state's adult inmates serve their time in Louisiana State Penitentiary at Angola which, in recent years, has had an average population exceeding its normal capacity of 3,478 male felons seventeen years old and up. Angola, originally a cotton plantation, extends over 18,000 acres of bottomland surrounded on three sides by the Mississippi River. The Angola complex contains eight different living areas: the "New Prison" which houses more than 2,300; the five outcamps, about 1,000; the Reception Center, 450; and the hospital, some 100.

Louisiana, like several other Southern states, once used a convict lease system under which private entrepreneurs leased inmates from the state for their labor. Major Samuel L. James obtained the lease in 1869 and transferred the state's inmates from the Baton Rouge prison to his Angola plantation. This form of penal slavery lasted until 1901 when the state took control of the inmates.

Other than penal slavery, Angola had another long tradition: beginning in 1917, the prison used armed inmate guards in order to cut expenses. This practice continued until 1972 when Elayn Hunt became director of corrections and stopped the practice.

In June 1975, a federal court order was issued requiring Angola to hire additional staff and to improve its food, security, and medical services. Decentralization of the state system was also ordered so that some of the Angola inmates would be moved out of the crowded complex to other parts of the state.

Other institutions which receive adult offenders are (1) the Louisiana Correctional Institute for Women at St. Gabriel with a capacity of 150; (2) the Louisiana Correctional and Industrial School at DeQuincy with a normal capacity of 500; and (3) work release centers at four locations.

The receiving center for juveniles committed to the system is the Juvenile Reception and Diagnostic Center at Baton Rouge. Under state law, children up to seventeen years of age are sent to one of the state's juvenile institutions: the largest Baton Rouge Training Institute, which houses both male and female juveniles and has a normal capacity of 557; Monroe Training Institute, which takes care of some 250 male juveniles; Pineville Training Institute, with a normal capacity of 115 juvenile girls; and Bridge City Training Institute, with a normal capacity of 150.

Orleans Parish Prison has presented many problems for the state, primarily because of its overcrowding. ("Parish" is Louisiana's equivalent of "county" and, technically, the Orleans Parish Prison is a county jail.) On June 30, 1975, it held 261 sentenced males, 627 pretrial detainees, and thirty-five on appeal. In addition, the women's wing held fifty pretrial and sentenced offenders. Thus, the more than 900 inmates were being housed in a facility considered to be large enough for a maximum of only 450 when it was built in 1929.

The overcrowding at the prison will be alleviated somewhat by the 1977 opening of a new parish prison containing 448 beds, but the size of the jail population requires that the old jail continue to be used. Conditions in the Orleans Parish Prison have improved under the guidance of Criminal Sheriff Charles C. Foti, Jr., and his administrative assistant, Terry Alarcon. Upon taking office on April 1, 1974, Foti intensified efforts to reduce violence and drug use in the jail, to reduce the number of escapes, to complete remodeling of cells, to hire additional staff, to improve staff training, and to implement treatment programs for the inmates. New treatment programs include a work release (*q.v.*) program, a restitution center, a group therapy effort, an academic education program, and a counseling program.

Between January 1, 1977, and January 1, 1978, there was a 6 percent increase in the Louisiana prison population from 4,695 to 6,032.

REFERENCES: Anthony Astrachan, "Louisiana's Orleans Parish Prison," *Corrections Magazine,* 1975; Anthony Astrachan, "Profile/ Louisiana," *Corrections Magazine,* 1975; Michael Serrill, "Prison Population Rises Again, But at a Slower Rate," *Corrections Magazine,* 1978.

M

MCKAY COMMISSION. The McKay Commission is a shorthand reference to the New York State Special Commission on Attica, a citizens' committee appointed in October 1971 to investigate the September 8–13, 1971, riot at Attica Correctional Facility (*q.v.*). Chief Judge Stanley H. Fuld and the four presiding justices of New York State's Court of Appeals selected the nine members of the committee: (1) Robert B. McKay, dean of the New York University School of Law, chairman; (2) Edwin B. Broderick, Roman Catholic bishop of the Albany diocese; (3) Robert L. Carter, a member of a New York City law firm; (4) Amalia R. Guerrero, president and founder of the Society of Friends of Puerto Rico; (5) Amos Henix, an ex-inmate who directs a Manhattan drug rehabilitation program; (6) Burke Marshall, deputy dean of the Yale University Law School; (7) Walter Rothschild, chairman of the Board of the New York Urban Coalition; (8) Dorothy Wadsworth, director of development at the Rochester Institute of Technology; and (9) William Wilbanks, a doctoral candidate for a degree in criminal justice at Albany's State University of New York.

The commission formally received its powers in an executive order signed by Governor Nelson Rockefeller on November 15, 1971, mandating it to make a full investigation of and report on the events and circumstances surrounding the Attica riot. The commission investigation was independent of the investigation of criminal acts being conducted by Deputy Attorney General Robert E. Fischer for purposes of prosecution. The commission was given the power to subpoena witnesses, to examine witnesses under oath, and to require the production of any books or papers thought to be helpful. There were no restrictions on the commission's geographical limitations or right to hold public hearings. State agencies were ordered to cooperate fully.

By February 1972, the commission's investigation was at its peak. It had hired a permanent staff consisting of thirty-six persons, and additional assistance was provided by more than sixty persons who were either volunteers or were paid on a per diem basis as consultants. The commission established offices inside the prison walls, in New York City, Rochester, and Batavia. At the outset of the investigation, the McKay Commission announced its intentions to interview some 3,000 persons thought to have personal knowledge of the events at Attica. Inmates constituted by far the largest group of interviewees, since Attica held 2,243 inmates when the riot started. Most of the inmates cooperated with the commission in the lengthy individual interviews that ensued. About eighty inmates who were suspected by prison officials of being leaders in the riot refused to cooperate with the commission for fear that criminal charges would be brought against them.

The commission also interviewed 400 of the 450 correctional officers who comprised the custodial staff at the time of the uprising; an additional fifty civilian employees of Attica; 300 of the 550 state police officers present at Attica who were known to have some direct knowledge of events inside the facility; more than 100 sheriffs, undersheriffs, and deputies from five counties; and about 200 National Guardsmen who were identified as having personal knowledge of the events.

The commission secured the services of its own pathologist, Alan Moritz, to review the work done by other pathologists in autopsies of the inmates and hostages who died at Attica. Other medical doctors worked for the commission as psychiatric consultants and also reviewed the health care facilities at the prison. H. P. White Laboratories of Bel Air, Maryland, assisted in the analysis of ballistics information and the testing of weapons used by the state police in the assault on Attica. Additional research was conducted on all aspects of daily life at the Attica facility.

The public hearings were held in public television studios. The commission decided to provide the raw evidence to the public in order to enable any interested parties to independently evaluate the commission's ultimate conclusions and to lessen the expense for public television coverage. The hearings were televised live each afternoon during April 17–28, 1972.

The basic questions surrounding the uprising at the Attica prison were (1) why did the uprising happen?; (2) how was the prison taken over by the inmates?; (3) why was not a peaceful solution achieved?; and (4) why did forty-three persons die and hundreds others suffer injuries during the riot? These basic questions are given comprehensive treatment in the official report of the commission and are widely available to the public. One of the most important conclusions of the study was that the riot was not the result of an inmate conspiracy, as charged by Russell G. Oswald who was commissioner of New York's Department of Correctional Services at the time and in command of the Attica facility during most of the uprising. For related information, see ATTICA CORRECTIONAL FACILITY and ATTICA UPRISING.

REFERENCES: New York State Special Commission on Attica, *Attica: The Official Report,* 1972; Russell G. Oswald, *Attica: My Story,* 1972.

MAINE CORRECTIONAL SYSTEM. Three adult institutions hold the 545 male and seventeen female inmates (as of March 1, 1975) of the Maine correctional system. Maine State Prison at Thomaston is the largest, with 340 inmates within the institution proper and seventy-five more prisoners at two minimum security locations. The Men's Correctional Center is located at South Windham and houses 130 male offenders between the ages of sixteen and thirty-six. The female inmates are confined in the Women's Correctional Center at Hallowell. Steven's School, Maine's institution for juvenile girls, shares the Hallowell facilities with the Women's Correctional Center. Twenty-four girls eleven to seventeen years of age are confined in Steven's School. The state's institution for young males, Boys' Training Center, is located at South Portland and houses 160 males between the ages of eleven and seventeen.

Both the adult and the juvenile facilities are administered by the Maine Bureau of Corrections. Ward Murphy, director of the Bureau of Corrections, assumed her present position in 1970 and became the nation's first woman to head a state correctional system.

On June 18, 1975, Governor James B. Longley signed into law a new criminal code that makes significant changes in the operation of the state's correctional system by abolishing both the indeterminate sentence (*q.v.*) and parole. These innovations also constitute firsts for the state in penological experimentation. Inmates are sentenced to flat terms under the new codes. Judges must set a prison term according to the number of years specified in the code for the particular category of offense. The inmate cannot be released early on parole, but the Bureau of Corrections does have the discretion to assign inmates to a work release (*q.v.*) or education release program in their home communities. For any sentence over six months, the inmate can earn good time (*q.v.*) (time subtracted from the sentence) at the rate of ten to twelve days per month. These changes reflect Maine's belief that indeterminate sentences and parole have not produced the benefits originally intended. Prison reform groups oppose the new code on the basis that the maximum sentences are too long rather than on the basis that the indeterminate sentence and parole practices should be retained.

The recent history of the state's juvenile institutions indicates that Maine has been experimenting in this area of corrections as well. The population of the state's two juvenile prisons declined substantially in 1973 and 1974 after the legislature eliminated the practice of incarcerating status offenders (*q.v.*), that is, children who have committed an act such as running away from home, that would not be a crime if they were adults.

The Maine prison system held 678 inmates on January 1, 1978, a 9 percent increase over the 622 inmates imprisoned there on January 1, 1977.

REFERENCES: Steve Gettinger, "Profile/Maine," *Corrections Magazine,* 1975; Michael Serrill, "Prison Population Rises Again, But at a Slower Rate," *Corrections Magazine,* 1978.

MARTINSON, ROBERT M. (1927–   ). Martinson, a sociologist and a vocal critic of corrections in recent years, has conducted extensive research into the effectiveness of rehabilitation programs and has recommended some unusual alternatives to traditional correctional programs.

Martinson became a prominent name in corrections in 1975, when he and his co-authors, Douglas Lipton and Judith Wilks, published *The Effectiveness of Correctional Treatment: A Survey of Treatment Evaluation Studies. Criminal Justice Newsletter* described the book as a landmark study. The *Effectiveness of Correctional Treatment* surveys 231 research studies conducted during 1945–1967 for the purpose of evaluating the treatment of criminal juvenile offenders. Based on these data covering virtually every research study on the topic printed in the English language during this time period, Martinson concludes that, except in isolated instances, rehabilitation efforts have had almost no effect on recidivism (*q.v.*). He posits that treatment programs founded on the premise that criminality is similar to illness, and subject to the same kind of diagnosis and treatment strategy, are useless.

In defense of the treatment ideology, the adherents of the medical model of corrections (*q.v.*) have presented numerous written critiques of Martinson's research findings. Ted Palmer, a corrections official who does research for the California Youth Authority, is among those who have attempted to rebut Martinson's conclusions. Using Martinson's data, Palmer argues that Martinson's own findings demonstrate positive, or at least partly positive, results in almost one-half of the programs studied. Palmer further contends that Martinson's methodology is inappropriate in that he is seeking to find one treatment strategy that benefits all types of offenders; Palmer feels that some treatment programs do benefit some offenders. Another critic, Milton Luger, former chairman of the Division for Youth in New York State, notes that a reduction in the recidivism rate is only one criteria for judging the value of a correctional program. Offenders may be returned to prison for a less serious crime or for a technical parole violation. This type of unfortunate occurrence, he states, officially swells the recidivism rate, but it does not mean that the offender has failed to make progress. Likewise, the offender who normally is convicted of a new crime within six months of release from prison may not be convicted of a new crime for twelve months if treatment is partially successful.

Martinson counterargues that Palmer's positive findings of a 48 percent success rate in the data are amiss because the individual research findings vary widely in reliability and cannot simply be tabulated. Martinson, deeply concerned for the plight of victims of crimes, believes that today the public is more interested in reducing the crime rate than in programs that promise small improvements in the recidivism rate. He offers the provocative counterproposition that, because of the neglect of the study of deterrence, a reported drop in recidivism in a particular corrections program may not stem from the positive features of the program, but rather from the offender's determination to avoid repeating the ordeal of being rehabilitated again.

Martinson does not view the use of prisons as a viable means of reducing the crime rate. While incarcerating more offenders would provide some protection of the public, this expedient would be far too costly to achieve the desired results. The alternative he proposes is to revise the functions of probation and parole in the direction of making more extensive use of them. In Martinson's view, parole boards could be abolished because the offender should be given a fixed sentence, part of which would be served in a prison and the other part under field supervision. Offenders serving sentences under field supervision would in effect be assigned their own personal police officer who would maintain close surveillance over their activities. Rather than attempting to provide rehabilitation for a large number of offenders, the role of the officer involved would be similar to that of a police officer. One "community restraint" officer could be hired for each six offenders to be supervised. Martinson argues that this arrangement is economically feasible because it would release 90 percent of all inmates now in prison, thereby creating a vast savings in the operation of prisons. He maintains that only 10 percent of those incarcerated need the degree of restraint provided by prisons. To further ease the potentially high cost of providing one agent for a small group of offenders, 10 percent of the personnel in police departments could be diverted into the proposed role of community restraint officer.

Community restraint officers would closely supervise the activities of those persons whom the courts determined could not be deterred from committing additional crimes. Rather than send this type of offender to prison, the court would make him a *restrainee* and the subject of much surveillance by a community restraint officer. A person who would receive probation under our present system would be a *suspendee* under Martinson's proposal, that is, one thought to be easily deterred from committing more crimes. The suspendee would not be assigned an agent for surveillance, but rather would be sent home to live—under the threat of being sent to prison to serve twice the amount of the full sentence assigned his crime if he committed a new crime during his term as suspendee.

Martinson is advocating a new emphasis on deterrence to replace our present reliance on rehabilitation. However, unlike other critics of corrections who advocate an emphasis on deterrence, he does not believe it can be achieved by incarcerating even more offenders while abolishing treatment programs. He has, at the very least, spurred a great deal of introspective debate on the proper role of corrections. For a related discussion, see ABOLITIONISTS.

REFERENCES: "Critique of Martinson by Ted Palmer Says Abandonment of 'Treatment' not Justified," *Criminal Justice Newsletter,* 1976; Douglas Lipton, Robert Martinson, and Judith Wilks, *The Effectiveness of Correctional Treatment: A Survey of Treatment Evaluation Studies,* 1975; Milton Luger, "Reaction to Robert Martinson," *American Journal of Correction,* 1975; Robert Martinson, "Restraint in the Community: A Modest Proposal, " *Criminal Justice Newsletter,* 1975; Judith Wilks and Robert Martinson, "Is the Treatment of Criminal Offenders Really Necessary?" *Federal Probation,* 1976.

MARYLAND CORRECTIONAL SYSTEM. Maryland's adult correctional services are administered under the aegis of the Department of Public Safety and Correctional Services, which is divided into the Division of Correction, the Division of Parole and Probation, and the Board of Parole. The secretary of the Department of Public Safety and Correctional Services, who acts as the department's chief executive, is appointed by the governor of the state. The secretary appoints a deputy secretary for correctional services, who is responsible for overseeing all adult corrections in the state. Persons reporting to the deputy secretary include the commissioner of the Division of Correction, the director of the Division of Parole and Probation, the chairman of the Board of Parole, the director of the Inmate Grievance Commission, and the director of Patuxent Institution.

The Patuxent Institution at Jessup opened in 1955 with a normal capacity of 640. It is operated within the state's administrative structure for adult corrections, but it is an autonomous institution designed as a psychiatric correctional facility for defective delinquents. Patuxent has its own paroling authority.

More than 1,000 male inmates are housed in a group of camps administered by the Maryland Correctional Camp Center at Jessup. These camps include (1) the Central Laundry and Correctional Camp at Sykesville; (2) the Community Vocational Rehabilitation and Release Center at Baltimore; (3) the Eastern Correctional Camp at Church Hill; (4) the Poplar Hill Correctional Camp at Quantico; and (5) the Southern Maryland Correctional Camp at Hughesville.

Other adult facilities are the Maryland Correctional Institution at Hagerstown, opened as a penal farm in 1931 but converted to a reformatory in 1945, with a normal capacity of 598 males; the Maryland Correctional Institution for Women at Jessup, opened in 1940 with room for 184; (in 1967, a small reception center large enough for fifteen women was added to the facility); the Maryland House of Correction at Jessup, opened in 1879 with a rated capacity of 912 males; the Maryland Penitentiary at Baltimore, opened in 1811 with space for 743 males; and the Reception Center in Baltimore opened in 1967 with a normal capacity of 266.

The Community Correction Task Force in Baltimore oversees the operation of five centers with a combined capacity of 188: (1) Dismas House, Inc., a privately owned center operating under contract with the state, located in Baltimore; (2) the Montgomery County Pre-Release Center at Kensington; (3) the O'Brien House in Baltimore; (4) the St. Ambrose Community Corrections Center for Women in Baltimore; and (5) the Women's Detention Center, leased from the Baltimore City Jail.

The Department of Health and Mental Hygiene's Juvenile Services Administration operates the juvenile institutions in the state and receives all juveniles under eighteen committed to institutions for indeterminate sentences (*q.v.*). The Boys' Forestry Camps Headquarters at Cumberland opened in 1955. It has a normal capacity of 140 juvenile delinquent boys placed in the following facilities: (1) Boys' Forestry Camp No. 1 at Flintstone; (2) Boys' Forestry Camp No. 2 at Lonaconing; (3) Boys' Forestry Camp No. 4 at Swanton; and, (4) Boys' Forestry Camp No. 5 at Flintstone. The Boys' Village of Maryland at Cheltenham opened in 1870 with a normal capacity of 275. In 1975, it was converted to a multiservice center with a fifty-six bed detention program (coed) and a twenty-four bed developmental disabilities program (male). Maryland Children's Center in Baltimore opened in 1959 with a normal capacity of 112; it houses both males and females and provides living facilities for delinquents and children in need of supervision (CHINS). The Maryland Training School for Boys in Baltimore opened in 1910 with a rated capacity of 301 juvenile delinquents between the ages of sixteen and eighteen. The Montrose School in Reisterstown opened in 1922 with a normal capacity of 250; it houses both male and female juvenile delinquents. The Thomas J. S. Waxter Children's Center in Laurel opened in 1963 with a normal capacity of forty; it also houses both male and female juvenile delinquents.

The prison population in Maryland is growing at a somewhat slower rate than that in other states. Maryland's prison population grew from 6,128 on January 1, 1975, to 6,606 on January 1, 1976, for an 8 percent increase. The total prison population was 7,211 on January 1, 1978. This figure represents a 2 percent increase over the previous twelve months.

REFERENCES: American Correctional Association, *Directory,* 1975–1976 editon; Michael Serrill, "Prison Population Rises Again, But at a Slower Rate," *Corrections Magazine,* 1978.

MASSACHUSETTS CORRECTIONAL SYSTEM. Massachusetts' Department of Correction receives convicted felons and misdemeanants over the age of seventeen. Adults committed to state prisons must serve a minimum of thirty months, but persons committed to reformatories receive indefinite terms without a minimum term being imposed.

Massachusetts has attempted large-scale prison reform in recent years. A package of prison reform legislation, the Correctional Reform Act of 1972, called for the establishment of comprehensive community-based corrections programs, including furlough (*q.v.*) programs, pre-release centers, halfway houses (*q.v.*), and work release (*q.v.*) programs, in order to get more inmates out of traditional prisons and into the community. John O. Boone, an experienced prison administrator, was hired in 1972 to implement the planned reforms. Boone served as commissioner of corrections until June 1973, when Governor Francis Sargent fired him because of controversy (see NATIONAL PRISONERS REFORM ASSOCIATION for a description of the controversy). Boone began implementing the planned reforms by establishing community corrections programs, and he also attempted reform in the five main adult prisons in the system.

The five main adult prisons are each designated a Massachusetts Correctional Institution (MCI). (1) The MCI located at Bridgewater opened in 1855 and currently has a capacity of 1,257. Bridgewater is actually composed of several institutions; it receives inmates from other institutions who are in need of protective custody, aged and infirm inmates, inmates who are criminally insane, alcoholics and drug addicts (including voluntary commitments), and residents of a treatment center for about 100 men thought to be sexually dangerous.

(2) The MCI located at Norfolk opened in 1931 with a normal capacity of 630 males. It is a medium security facility housing many inmates who are serving long sentences. (3) The MCI at South Walpole, which is often simply called Walpole Prison, is the state prison (the only maximum security facility in the state). It opened in 1956 with a normal capacity of 607. (4) The MCI at West Concord, opened in 1878 with a rated capacity of 375 males, is used to hold younger inmates between the ages of eighteen and twenty-four. These youths serve indeterminate sentences (*q.v.*) under the youthful offenders' law which makes them eligible for parole at any time during their incarceration. (5) The smallest of the MCIs is located at Framingham; it opened in 1877 with a normal capacity of 175 and receives all of the female prisoners in the state. In 1973, Commissioner Boone made the institution coeducational; in the latter part of 1975, it housed 100 women and forty-five men.

In addition to the MCIs, the Department of Correction operates the Reception Diagnostic Center at Norfolk, which was opened in 1974 with a normal capacity of sixty males; and three forestry camps: (1) the facility at Plymouth, opened in 1952 with space for fifty-four males; (2) the Monroe Bridge facility (receiving mail through the Readsboro, Vermont, post office), opened in 1955 with room for fifty males; and (3) the Warwick facility, opened in 1964 with a normal capacity of fifty males.

Frank Hall, who replaced Boone as commissioner of correction in 1973, is continuing to expand the community corrections programs mandated in the 1972 legislation. One-third of the state's inmates are now paroled from community programs, and Hall eventually plans to shift almost 90 percent of the system's inmates to community programs before they are eligible for parole. These community treatment centers include (1) the Boston State Pre-Release Center at Dorchester, opened in 1972 with space for fifty inmates (both male and female); (2) Brooke House in Boston, opened in 1973 with a normal capacity of thirty-five males; (3) Charlotte House at Dorchester, opened in 1973 with a rated capacity of twelve females; (4) Coolidge House in Boston, opened in 1973 with space for thirty; (5) Norfolk Pre-Release Center in South Walpole, opened in 1975 with a normal capacity of twenty-six; (6) Project 699 in Boston, opened in 1975 with a normal capacity of fifteen; (7) the Roxbury Community Rehabilitation Center in Dorchester, opened in 1973 with room for twenty-five; and (8) the Shirely Pre-Release center in Shirley, opened in 1972 with a rated capacity of seventy-five males.

Juvenile corrections in Massachusetts received extensive national publicity during October 1969–January 1973 when all of the state's traditional juvenile institutions were closed under the leadership of Jerome Miller, the commissioner of the Department of Youth Services. All of the state's juvenile offenders are now placed in community programs. However, the Department of Youth Services does operate three "secure" facilities for juveniles that are similar to jails, except that they are better staffed than most jails: (1) the Intensive Care Division in Boston which can place eighty-nine juveniles in secure settings in three different locations; (2) the Westfield Intensive Treatment Center at Westfield which has a normal capacity of twenty-five juveniles (both male and female); and (3) the Worcester Intensive Treatment Center at Worcester which has a normal capacity of twenty-five juveniles (both male and female). For additional information on the closing of juvenile institutions in Massachusetts, see DEINSTITUTIONALIZATION.

Massachusetts, like other states, has experienced some growth in its prison population in recent years. However, the prison population was 2,047 in January 1975 and only 2,820 in January 1978.

REFERENCES: American Correctional Association, *Directory,* 1975–1976 edition; Michael S. Serrill, "Massachusetts Adult Corrections System," *Corrections Magazine,* 1975; Michael Serrill, "Prison Population Rises Again, But at a Slower Rate," *Corrections Magazine,* 1978.

MEDIA IN PRISONS. The news media operated within prisons consist of inmate-published newspapers, inmate-operated radio stations, and one television station.

The prison media are believed to have started in New York Prison with the weekly newspaper, *The Forlorn Hope,* published by William Keteltas in 1800. By 1967, when the most recent survey of prison newspapers was conducted, some 222 prison newspapers reached more than 200,000 readers. Russell Baird, author of *The Penal Press,* conducted the 1967 survey and notes that the number of prison newspapers increased during the 1960s. According to his estimates, however, the number of publications is no greater today than it was in 1967.

Cost factors and the availability of facilities within an institution are more likely to determine the quality and frequency of publication than the availability of editorial talent. Some prison publications are no more than simple newsletters produced on mimeograph machines. Others are sophisticated newspapers printed in shops with elaborate equipment provided for vocational training programs. Some of the most widely known prison newspapers are (1) *The Menard Time* published in the Menard Correctional Center in Illinois; (2) the *San Quentin News* published in California; (3) the *Jefftown Journal* published in the Missouri State Penitentiary; (4) the *Spectator* published in the State Prison of Southern Michigan (Jackson); and (5) *The Echo* published in the Texas prison system.

The main purpose of prison newspapers is to keep inmate audiences entertained and informed. Typical coverage includes sports events and other recreational activity; the reprinting of statements from the warden to distribute institutional policies; editorials and investigative reports in prisons where censorship does not interfere with this type of reporting; creative writing pages; cartoons; statistics on releases, new admissions and total population; interviews with inmates and staff members; and legal articles that provide commentary on recent court decisions.

Much of what is known about the overall quality of prison newspapers comes from the annual American Penal Press Contest sponsored by the School of Journalism of Southern Illinois University in Carbondale. David Saunders is a judge for the contest and a staff member in the School of Journalism. (He built *The Menard Time* into a well-known newspaper while serving as inmate editor from 1952 to 1961.)

Radio broadcasts in prisons developed during the past twenty years when many prisons had to install equipment to rebroadcast signals from commercial radio stations because the prison construction and rural locations of prisons severely interfered with reception. Once the rebroadcast equipment was available, the practice of producing programs by inmates naturally developed. The prison radio station normally rebroadcasts programs from local radio stations during most of its hours of operation; the broadcasts of commercial stations are periodically interrupted to program inmate-produced news coverage of events within the institution.

Arizona State Prison's rural location accounts for the operation of ASP-TV—the sole television station in any American prison. Early in the 1970s inmate funds purchased equipment to install antennas and cables necessary to receive broadcasts from distant commercial television stations. After the receiving equipment was installed, the inmates decided to use two blank channels to rebroadcast network programs broadcast at hours inconvenient for the institution audience. Actual inmate programming was initiated with the help of a federal grant that provided funds necessary to equip a television broadcast studio. Programs produced by inmates include entertainment events filmed by inmate crews, documentaries on prison life, and a weekly news show on Fridays.

REFERENCE: Steve Gettinger, "Prison Media: Getting the News Inside," *Corrections Magazine,* 1976.

MEDICAL MODEL OF CORRECTIONS. Many penal institutions in America view their function as that of providing both custody and treatment for convicted felons. The custody function is straightforward, involving keeping inmates confined to a designated geographical area and protecting them from one another. The treatment function, however, is based on a complex set of ideas that constitute the medical model of corrections. Terminology is borrowed from the medical profession to describe the administrative processing of offenders. Within this framework of thought, offenders are considered to be "sick" in the sense that some defect in their personality structure or socialization has caused them to commit crimes. Prison procedures include admission processes known as diagnosis and classification (*q.v.*). In making diagnoses, it is assumed that crime is a symptom of a personal maladjustment or defect, and if the defect can be identified, the offender can be classified. Classification is a relatively comprehensive plan detailing how the inmate will spend his time in the institution with respect to living quarters, work assignments, requirements for academic or vocational training, and participation in psychological treatment modes. It is assumed that the inmate's involvement in the planned activities will cure the defect that caused him to commit crimes.

Paul E. Lehman, chief of the National Institute of Mental Health Clinical Research Center, advises caution in making the medical model of corrections the standard treatment model in corrections. He believes that it has a place in a spectrum of treatment rationales and that its primary value has been to make corrections more humane. Lehman maintains that the medical model has been widely accepted as the standard for correctional treatment largely for historical reasons rather than for any proven value of the approach. In the early twentieth century, professionals in the mental health field came to believe that determination had replaced individual free will—a concept that supports the idea that crime is a symptom of disease. This change in ideology is reflected in the 1917 *Proceedings of the National Conference of Social Work* in a report by E. E. Southard entitled "The Desirability of Medical Wardens for Prisons." Thomas Mott Osborne, warden of Sing Sing in 1916, became an early critic of the ideology when he observed that the disease theory relieved the offender of the responsibility for his acts. Osborne preferred to give inmates educational experiences that would improve their outlook on life and increase their sense of responsibility.

Lehman feels that the medical model of corrections has been widely adopted in part because of the prestige of the medical profession. Professionals in the correctional field have closely followed developments in the field of mental health. A significant problem, however, in attempting to apply the talk therapy of the mental health field to the clients in corrections is the use of the one-to-one social casework relationship. Not only must the therapists applying the techniques be highly trained to be effective, but also it is nearly impossible to find the funds necessary to attract enough therapists to the field of corrections to handle the 250,000 people in prisons, plus the countless hundreds of thousands on probation or parole, with a one-to-one casework relationship. Those medical model techniques that lend themselves to small-group therapy are most generally applied in prison settings.

Susan Rose, from the University of Oregon, is more critical of the medical model of corrections than Lehman. She believes that medical science was an especially poor choice of models to follow in establishing a rationale for corrections. Medical doctors, she states, have a relatively complete store of knowledge about the human body. Conversely, social scientists have a most imperfect set of theories about human behavior, and many of those theories conflict with one another. The basic problem of the medical model, according to Rose, is that, not knowing the cause of crime, we do not know what it is that we are trying to cure with our diverse treatment approaches. The treatment plan may be bizarre and even harmful to the client.

Given the pervasiveness of the medical model of corrections, there are literally hundreds of prominent professionals in corrections who defend it. Even many of its defenders, however, are troubled by the problem of obtaining enough therapists to make an impact on the large number of offenders incarcerated.

REFERENCES: Paul E. Lehman, "The Medical Model of Treatment: Historical Development of an Archaic Standard," and Susan Rose, "The Fallacy of the Medical Model as Applied to Corrections," in Edward E. Peoples (ed.), *Readings in Correctional Casework and Counseling,* 1975.

MICHIGAN CORRECTIONAL SYSTEM. The Department of Corrections has jurisdiction over adult prisons and the adult Parole Board in Michigan. The Department of Social Services controls juvenile institutions and the Youth Parole and Review Board.

Adult institutions receive offenders at least eighteen years of age who have been convicted of a felony and sentenced to serve at least one year. However, the courts may waive juvenile status for persons under eighteen, usually in cases of homicide, and adult prisons may hold inmates as young as seventeen. The state's adult prison system has a severe overcrowding problem. On January 1, 1975, the system was comfortably below its rated capacity with a total of 8,702, but some 150 additional inmates have been coming into the system each month. As of June 17, 1976, there were 11,840 inmates in prisons designed to hold 10,800. In January 1977 there were 12,462 inmates in the state's prison system, and by January 1978 that figure had increased 12 percent to 13,901.

Michigan has a large building program underway to accommodate the increases in the size of the prison population. One of the building projects involves remodeling the State Prison of Southern Michigan at Jackson (*q.v.*). The huge Jackson facility was originally opened in 1839 but was rebuilt in 1929 with a capacity of 4,899 male felons twenty-three years of age and above. Remodeling plans involve sealing off two cellblocks on the north side of the prison and combining them with three new buildings to establish a 1,100-bed medium security prison within the confines of the Jackson Prison property.

Other building programs involve a new women's facility at Ypsilanti which opened in 1977 with space for 270. A new men's prison is also being built on the Ypsilanti site. At Ionia, a former state mental hospital is being remodeled to house older male inmates and inmates in need of psychiatric care. Two 600-bed male prisons and a 100-bed facility are being planned for construction near Detroit. New dormitories will be built at three camps in the system, and a new hospital will be built at Jackson Prison. The prison construction projects completed or planned for the decade of the 1970s cost the state $100 million.

Almost half of the adult inmates in the state are housed in the huge State Prison of Southern Michigan at Jackson. The remainder of the adult inmates are located in seven adult institutions, eleven conservation camps, and fourteen community corrections centers. The Cassidy Lake Technical School at Chelsea was opened in 1944 with a normal capacity of 259 males; it is a minimum security facility utilizing cottages for living quarters. The Corrections-Conservation Camps are supervised by a superintendent located at Grass Lake; the camps have a total capacity of 1,225 males.

The Michigan Intensive Program Center (MIPC) is a relatively new facility (opened in 1973) located adjacent to the very old (opened in 1889) State House of Corrections and Branch Prison at Marquette. The ninety-eight cell MIPC is a maximum security prison used to house the most assaultive and disruptive male inmates in the Michigan prison system. Staff members of MIPC operate a behavior modification program designed to reinforce positive behavior through the use of a "token economy" and a "step program." The token economy allows the staff to provide immediate rewards for desired behavior by giving tokens to an inmate for activities ranging from cleaning up his cell to academic achievement in the school program. The tokens can be used to purchase canteen items or privileges such as watching television. The step program involves allowing inmates to progress from one wing of the institution to another in which more privileges are available. As inmates become more tractable, they are allowed to progress from Orange wing to Blue wing and eventually to Yellow wing, with increasing access to privileges at each stage of advancement. A fourth wing, Green wing, is used as a punishment area for inmates who violate regulations and as a holding area for inmates who refuse to participate in the program.

The Michigan Reformatory at Ionia was opened in 1877 with a rated capacity of 1,144 males. It is used to house the youthful offenders in the state; the ages of the inmates in the Ionia facility range from seventeen to twenty-five. The average age of the reformatory inmates is nineteen, and they are serving an average sentence of two years. Other young offenders are housed in the Michigan Training Unit at Ionia; it was opened in 1958 with a normal capacity of 724 males ages seventeen to twenty-one. The Muskegon Correctional Facility at Muskegon was opened in 1974 with space for almost 600 males between the ages of twenty and twenty-six; this modern prison provides individual rooms that inmates can lock with their own keys and utilizes male and female correctional officers. The State House of Correction and Branch Prison at Marquette was opened in 1889 with a rated capacity of 877 males. All adult males sentenced to prison in Michigan are processed through the Reception and Guidance Center in Jackson; it was opened in 1956 with a normal capacity of 477.

While the new women's prison at Ypsilanti was under construction, female offenders were housed in the Women's Division of the Detroit House of Corrections (DeHoCo) under contract with the city. In 1976, some 360 women were confined in the facility. Female and male offenders are housed in the sixteen community corrections centers operated by the Department of Corrections in Detroit and other large cities. The centers are temporary living quarters for offenders who are nearing their parole dates, and they are rented from Young Men's Christian Associations and other organizations as needed. Each center is staffed with case workers.

Juvenile institutions in Michigan are the responsibility of the Institutional Services Division within the Department of Social Services. The division receives juvenile delinquents between the ages of twelve and seventeen years on indeterminate sentences (*q.v.*). The jurisdiction of the department continues until the juvenile reaches the age of nineteen. The W. J. Maxey Campus at Whitmore Lake consists of five separate facilities for boys: (1) the Reception/Diagnostic Center, opened in 1962 with space for forty-five; (2) the Campus Center A, opened in 1964 with room for eighty; (3) the Campus Center B, opened in 1965 with room for 100; (4) the Campus Center C, opened in 1967 with space for eighty; and (5) the Green Oak Center, opened in 1960 with space for ninety. Two Youth Rehabilitation Camps provide space for males: Camp Nokomis, opened in 1964 at Prudenville with space for fifty, and Camp Shawono, opened in 1963 at Grayling with space for fifty. Two of Michigan's juvenile facilities are coeducational: Adrian Training School, opened at Adrian in 1881 with a capacity of 140, and the Arbor Heights Center, opened at Ann Arbor in 1935 with a capacity of twenty-eight. For additional information on Michigan's correctional system, see JACKSON PRISON.

REFERENCES: American Correctional Association, *Directory,* 1975–1976 edition; William Hart, "Profile/Michigan," *Corrections Magazine,* 1976; Michael Serrill, "Prison Population Rises Again, But at a Slower Rate," *Corrections Magazine,* 1978.

MINNESOTA CORRECTIONAL SYSTEM. The Department of Corrections oversees both adult and juvenile institutions in Minnesota.

The Minnesota Corrections Authority handles the parole of adult felons.

Minnesota correctional officials profess to have been influenced by the philosophy of David Fogel (*q.v.*), who was the state's commissioner of corrections from 1971 to 1973 before becoming director of the Illinois Law Enforcement Commission. Specifically, they have accepted Fogel's justice model of corrections (*q.v.*) which proposes that rehabilitation not be the main objective of the prison. The rationale is that it is probably not possible to conduct effective rehabilitation programs in prisons because of the basic nature of confinement and the limited knowledge of correctional personnel as to what constitutes rehabilitation. Minnesota may be the first state to abandon rehabilitation as the primary goal of its prison system. The justice model that Minnesota correctional officials are attempting to implement under the leadership of Commissioner Kenneth F. Schoen focuses on fairness and justice for offenders. A basic element of the model is that no one should be locked up if his freedom is not a threat to other people.

Given this approach to corrections, Minnesota is attempting to develop community alternatives to incarceration to handle all but the most dangerous offenders. Minnesota is a pioneer in the development of community corrections, but despite its efforts to create community corrections programs and despite its ratio of inmates in state prisons compared to those in alternative programs (one of the lowest in the United States), the prison population in Minnesota is rising dramatically. Following a brief interval of decrease in 1976, the prison population rose from 1,684 in January 1977 to 1,755 in January 1978.

All adult male felons committed to prison are sent to the Minnesota State Prison at Stillwater; it was opened in 1913 with a normal capacity of 1,000. Youthful offenders between the ages of eighteen and twenty-four are sent to the State Reformatory for Men at St. Cloud, a facility that opened in 1889 with a normal capacity of 700. Women are committed to the Minnesota Correctional Institution for Women at Shakopee, opened in 1920 with space for sixty women ages eighteen and above. Adult male prisoners at the Stillwater and St. Cloud facilities are eligible for transfer to Willow River Camp at Willow River, a forestry camp and vocational center opened in 1951 with a normal capacity of fifty.

The Minnesota Metropolitan Training Center at Circle Pines was opened in 1963 with a normal capacity of 192; it houses juvenile delinquents and felons and has living facilities for adult and juvenile males and females.

Minnesota operates three juvenile institutions. One is the State Training School at Red Wing which opened in 1889 with a normal capacity of 162; this facility was the first training school to adopt guided group interaction (*q.v.*) as the mode of treatment for juvenile delinquents. The other two juvenile institutions are the Minnesota Home School at Sauk Centre, opened in 1912 with a normal capacity of 125, and the Thistledew Forestry Camp, opened in 1960 with a normal capacity of fifty. All three institutions are coeducational.

REFERENCES: American Correctional Association, *Directory,* 1975–1976 edition; Steve Gettinger, "U.S. Prison Population Hits All-Time High," *Corrections Magazine,* 1976; Michael S. Serrill, "Profile/Minnesota," *Corrections Magazine,* 1975; Michael Serrill, "Prison Population Rises Again, But at a Slower Rate," *Corrections Magazine,* 1978.

MISSISSIPPI CORRECTIONAL SYSTEM. Adult felons in Mississippi are sentenced to the State Penitentiary at Parchman, the only adult institution in the state. It is a plantation-type of prison with relatively small housing facilities scattered over a large amount of acreage. It was opened in 1900 with a rated capacity of 1,900, but it has been overcrowded in recent years with 2,429 inmates assigned to the institution on the first day of 1976. Female offenders assigned to the prison normally constitute only about 5 percent of the population.

The Mississippi Department of Youth Services operates two training schools and one camp for juvenile delinquents. The Columbia Training School was opened in 1917 at Columbia with a normal capacity of 270; it is a coeducational facility with its population divided about evenly between males and females. The ages of the males range from ten to twenty. The Oakley Training School was opened in 1943 at Raymond with a normal capacity of 300 males age fifteen to twenty. The Willie Simmons Forestry Camp is located at Columbia.

The prison system experienced a 12 percent increase in population between January 1, 1977, and January 1, 1978, and had 2,526 inmates on the latter date.

REFERENCES: American Correctional Association, *Directory,* 1975–1976 edition; Michael Serrill, "Prison Population Rises Again, But at a Slower Rate," *Corrections Magazine,* 1978.

MISSOURI CORRECTIONAL SYSTEM. Missouri's Department of Social Services oversees both the adult and juvenile corrections in the state.

George M. Camp, deputy director of the department, is responsible for many of the changes that the Missouri correctional system is currently undergoing. Camp is unusual as a prison administrator in that he is younger than most top correctional executives (he assumed his present post at the age of thirty-four in 1974) and is one of the few top prison administrators with a Ph.D. Earlier in his career as associate warden at the U.S. Penitentiary at Marion, Illinois, Camp met Martin Groder, the psychiatrist, running a treatment program at the facility. Groder's work (see ASKLEPIEION THERAPY) influenced Camp's philosophy of corrections.

The changes that Camp has brought to the Missouri system include an "open door" policy that has welcomed the news media and citizens' groups into the prisons to study the problems of the system. As a result of his policy, large numbers of Missouri citizens who might otherwise have ignored the correctional system have developed a keen interest in the state's corrections problems. Camp, in carrying out prison reforms planned by Governor Christopher Bond, finally managed to rid the prison system of racial segregation. He has also introduced change into the administration of corrections by implementing a management by objectives (MBO) system. MBO is currently a popular approach to management that involves defining and working toward the attainment of specific objectives.

Most of the adult inmates in Missouri's prison system are housed in seven institutions. (1) Missouri State Penitentiary for Men was opened in 1835 with a normal capacity of 1,500 but held 2,000 early in 1976; it is the largest prison in the state. (2) The Missouri Training Center for Men, a medium security prison, opened at Moberly in 1963 with a normal capacity of 800. (3) The Missouri Intermediate Reformatory opened in 1932 at Algoa with a normal capacity of 500 males and holds younger offenders seventeen to twenty-five years of age. (4) The State Correctional Center for Women was rebuilt in 1960; it is located in Tipton and has a rated capacity of eighty. (5) The Fordland Honor Camp at Fordland opened in 1961 with space for 175 males. Adult males are also housed in two minimum security farms: (6) the Church Farm Facility at Jefferson City, opened in 1938 with a rated capacity of 300, and (7) Renz Farm, opened at Cedar City in 1961 with space for 175.

Community Service Centers (halfway houses [*q.v.*]) are located in Cape Girardeau, Columbia, Kansas City, Saint Louis (two facilities), and Springfield.

Juvenile institutions are administered by the Division of Youth Services within the Department of Social Services. The division receives youths between the ages of twelve and sixteen from the Juvenile Division of the Circuit Court for an indeterminate sentence (*q.v.*). Unlike the population of the adult system, that of the juvenile system is not growing; the number of juveniles in the division's jurisdiction has been fairly stable at about 1,300 youths. Some 600 of the 1,300 are in institutions, while the remainder are on parole. The state had only two juvenile facilities—the Training School for Boys, opened at Boonville in 1889 with a normal capacity of 150, and the Training School for Girls, opened at Chillicothe in 1889 with a normal capacity of 120—before 1970 when the Youth Center opened at Poplar Bluff with a normal capacity of seventy-five. Since 1970, the division has opened a series of group homes, each of which holds eight to twelve children. Kansas City has three group homes for boys and one for girls; St. Louis, three for boys; Cape Girardeau, two for boys; Booneville, one for boys; St. Joseph, one for boys; Joplin, one for girls; and Sikeston, one for girls. More group homes are scheduled to open in the near future.

The principal treatment approach in Missouri juvenile correctional systems is positive peer culture (PPC), a treatment approach based on the premise that juveniles get into trouble because of peer pressure. Juveniles are assigned to small groups to operationalize the therapy. Group members live together, analyze one another's problems, and vote on whether an individual has progressed sufficiently to be paroled—all based on the idea that peer pressure can get the youths out of trouble as well as into it. PPC was developed by Harry Vorrath and associates as an outgrowth of guided group interaction (see GUIDED GROUP INTERACTION for details of the method), and has also been implemented in state juvenile institutions in West Virginia and Michigan.

Missouri experienced a 6 percent increase in its prison population from 4,748 on January 1, 1977, to 5,040 on January 1, 1978.

REFERENCES: American Correctional Association, *Directory,* 1975–1976 edition; Anthony Astrachan, "Close Up/George Camp of Missouri," *Corrections Magazine,* 1975; Clemens Bartollas and Stuart J. Miller, *The Juvenile Offender: Control, Correction, and Treatment,* 1978; Edgar May, "Profile/Missouri," *Corrections Magazine,* 1976; Michael Serrill, "Prison Population Rises Again, But at a Slower Rate," *Corrections Magazine,* 1978.

MONTANA CORRECTIONAL SYSTEM. In 1975, a reorganization of state agencies in Montana created the Division of Corrections within the Department of Institutions to provide services for adult and juvenile offenders. The division oversees one adult institution and three facilities for juveniles. Other correctional services are provided through the department's Adult Probation and Parole Field Services Bureau, the Juvenile Aftercare Bureau, and the office of Correctional Information Systems.

Persons convicted of a felony are committed to the Department of Institutions to be placed in the Montana State Prison if they are adults or the Swan River Forest Camp for juveniles. The Montana State Prison at Deer Lodge, the state's only adult facility, opened in 1869 and currently has a normal capacity of 420 inmates sixteen years of age or older; the institution holds both male and female felons. The three juvenile facilities are the Swan River Youth Forest Camp at Swan Lake, opened in 1968 with a normal capacity of fifty males between the ages of sixteen and eighteen; the Pine Hills School at Miles City, opened in 1894 with a normal capacity of 150 males ages ten to eighteen; and the Mountain View School at Helena, opened in 1921 with a normal capacity of seventy-five girls ages ten to eighteen.

Although Montana has a relatively small prison system, its prison population has been growing rapidly in recent years. Its inmate population was 344 in January 1975. By January 1977, it was 500, and the next twelve months brought a 10 percent increase to 550.

REFERENCES: American Correctional Association, *Directory*, 1975–1976 edition; Steve Gettinger, "U.S. Prison Population Hits All-Time High," *Corrections Magazine*, 1976; Michael Serrill, "Prison Population Rises Again, But at a Slower Rate," *Corrections Magazine*, 1978.

MORAL DEVELOPMENT THEORY. Lawrence Kohlberg, a psychologist employed by Harvard's Graduate School of Education, has spent more than twenty years developing his theory of moral development. He posits that moral development occurs universally in six stages. He divides moral development into three distinct levels with two stages in each level. At the lowest level is the criminal who can view moral dilemmas solely in terms of his own interests; in the middle stage is the person who can view a moral dilemma both in terms of his self-interest and of the perspective of other people involved; and at the highest stage of moral development is the person who can look at a moral dilemma from a universal perspective.

Kohlberg believes that criminals, in operating at the first level of moral development, tend to think they should do anything they can get away with and allow others the same privilege. The result in an institution is a code of morality that allows the inmate to steal or commit acts of violence against others, but prohibits informing on another inmate for committing such acts.

Joseph Hickey, one of Kohlberg's students and now with the Connecticut Department of Corrections, convinced Corrections Commissioner John R. Manson of the value of experimenting with moral development theory in the setting of the correctional institution. In 1971, a Just Community (*q.v.*) was established in one of the cottages that make up the living facilities of the Connecticut Correctional Institution at Niantic, the state's prison for adult female offenders. In a program that can accommodate as many as twenty participants, the women in the cottage receive moral development instruction in addition to their normal academic education, vocational training, or work assignments.

William Jennings acts as training supervisor and oversees the moral development training in the experimental program. The group of cottage residents and staff members attempt to maintain a relaxed atmosphere in which equality prevails to the extent possible. Rules for the governance of the cottage are made and enforced by the group members, with each inmate and staff member having one vote. Two discussion groups operate to give the women a forum for discussing personal problems and attempting to resolve the day-to-day issues that arise. Staff members or inmates can call meetings of either of these discussion groups at any time. Both groups meet together on a regular weekly basis to resolve issues that prove too difficult for resolution in the smaller groups. The treatment objective of the program is to teach the women to think about the ways in which their decisions about their personal lives affect other people. The group may vote to let one of the group members transfer to a halfway house (*q.v.*) program in New Haven. Those with a minimum of three months' participation in the Just Community and the ability to make mature decisions become eligible for transfer. In terms of moral development theory, Kohlberg believes that at least a portion of the women in the program move up from the first stage of moral development to the middle stage. For related information, see JUST COMMUNITY.

REFERENCES: William E. Cockerham, "Connecticut's 'Just Community,' " *Corrections Magazine,* 1975; Lawrence Kohlberg, "The Cognitive-Developmental Approach to Moral Education," *Readings in Human Development: Annual Editions, 1976–1977,* 1976.

MORATORIUM ON PRISON CONSTRUCTION. The moratorium on prison construction is more of a philosophical position than a reality.

In part, the call for a halt to the building of major institutions is a reflection of economic difficulties in financing the extensive construction at today's prices. Estimates of building costs are ranging from $30,000 to $50,000 per bed for initial building costs, with a similar sum added to the construction costs to cover debt service and the obtaining of equipment. The costs are rather prohibitive. Florida is spending $38 million for 2,280 beds in five new institutions; Michigan has committed $30 million for five new facilities; North Carolina is projecting a need for 11,000 new beds by 1980; and the Ohio legislature is considering an appropriations bill seeking $250 million for new prison construction.

A complicating factor in the high cost of prison construction is the trend toward the building of smaller institutions that are considered to be more conducive to the establishment of a therapeutic milieu. Penologists have long maintained that large prisons (3,000 to 5,000 beds) are cheaper to operate on a per inmate, per day basis because capital costs are amortized over the larger number of inmates, resulting in economies of scale. A 1972 study by Williams and Fish cast some doubt on the economy of scale hypothesis by noting that economies of scale, if any, seem to be associated with the central administration of prison operations rather than with the physical plant. Savings could be achieved by centralizing management and clerical functions while placing inmates in small regional centers.

Sociologists have been critical of the use of large prisons because the large size is believed to result in anonymity and anomie for the inmate in the general prison population. Prison administrators, while favoring smaller institutions (200 to 800 beds), are still groping for a compromise between what they feel would be a cost savings in the operation of larger institutions and the therapeutic advantages thought to be associated with smaller prisons. The Ohio Department of Corrections feels that the proper compromise is the intermediate institution that houses from 1,500 to 2,000 inmates. California corrections officials believe that the small prisons cost 50 percent more to build and 35 percent more to operate as compared with large prisons. A 2,400-bed replacement for the aging San Quentin prison would cost California $86 million.

Even if public financing can be obtained for new prison construction, it is time consuming, expensive, and difficult to find a suitable location for a new prison. Penologists have been criticized for locating prisons in remote areas where it is difficult for families to visit inmates and where the social services of settled areas are not readily available. But when prison officials attempt to locate new facilities in the outskirts of cities, they normally encounter substantial opposition from adjoining communities whose residents fear the inmates and believe that property values will decline as a result of the construction. Tennessee corrections officials had already constructed three buildings on a site for a new prison when dynamiting and shooting incidents forced them to abandon the location and turn the buildings over to a community college.

The issue is not simply a matter of economics. Many are opposed to building new prisons on the ground that they do more harm than good. Prisons are durable by virtue of the concrete and steel construction thought necessary to prevent escapes. Once constructed, these structures last for a century or more. Opponents of prison construction maintain that the building of these long-lasting facilities necessarily locks corrections into a commitment to an obsolete strategy for dealing with offenders. William Nagel, director of the American Foundation's Institute of Corrections, is a prominent critic of new construction. The National Moratorium on Prison Construction, sponsored by the National Council on Crime and Delinquency (*q.v.*), is a lobbying group that has compiled records of prison construction plans around the nation. They note that some 522 new prisons are in the planning stages; estimated building costs for 274 of them total $1.85 billion. Brian Willson, coordinator of the moratorium, considers it as both an economic and philosophical issue: we cannot afford such construction programs, he says, and most of the offenders do not need to be in prison. With growing inmate populations, new prisons intended to replace older institutions that are unfit for human habitation may simply supplement the old prisons as more people are sentenced.

Many penologists are caught in the middle of the controversy. Those whose existing facilities are outdated and overcrowded may not necessarily believe that prisons are the best means of dealing with offenders, but they see new and larger facilities as a means of alleviating the suffering of inmates now incarcerated. For discussion of related material, see ABOLITIONISTS.

REFERENCES: Steve Gettinger, "U.S. Prison Population Hits All-Time High," *Corrections Magazine,* 1976; William G. Nagel, "On Behalf of a Moratorium on Prison Construction," *Crime and Delinquency,* 1977; William G. Nagel, *The New Red Barn: A Critical Look at the Modern American Prison,* 1973; Milton G. Rector, "The Extravagance of Imprisonment," *Crime and Delinquency,* 1975; Vergil L. Williams and Mary Fish, "Optimum Prison Size: Cost Behavior vs. Rehabilitation Goals," *American Journal of Correction,* 1972.

MUTUAL AGREEMENT PROGRAM. In 1964, the U.S. Department of Labor began to fund training programs in prisons with the objective of improving inmate work skills to assure them decent jobs after release. The Department of Labor involvement in prison rehabilitation efforts, under the authority of the Manpower Development and Training Act of 1962, produced evaluation reports indicating a problem area. The problem appeared to be a paucity of coordination and communication between institutional staff and parole authorities that resulted in poor utilization of the federally financed training. Parole boards were not consulted about the training, nor did they consider it in making parole decisions in individual cases. Compounding the problem was the fact that inmate training cycles were not coordinated with release dates. In order to make the inmate training economically justifiable, it was obviously necessary to allow an inmate to be released as soon as the job training was completed so that he could be placed in an occupation related to the training.

The lack of coordination and cooperation was found to be related to the administrative structure of corrections. Many states administer their parole systems and their institutions under different departments to give parole boards complete independence in deciding to grant or revoke paroles. Given that administrative structure, it is possible, even likely, that parole and institution managers will blame one another for parole failures. Parole boards do not inform institutions about the release criteria they expect, nor do prison wardens necessarily inform parole agencies as to what programs are available to inmates.

The American Correctional Association (ACA) (*q.v.*) attempted to deal with the problem through a parole-corrections project funded by the Labor Department. The concept of Mutual Agreement Programming (MAP) was the solution developed by ACA. In developing a change model, ACA has instituted a system of cooperation in which a legally binding contract is negotiated between a parole board and an institution with the knowledge and full participation of the inmate concerned. The contract delineates the goals to be accomplished by the inmate, the program services that the institution will provide for him, and the specific release date to be approved by the parole board if and when the inmate satisfactorily completes the training. If successful completion is delayed or is not possible, the system provides for renegotiation of the contract among everyone concerned.

In 1967, the ACA began to implement the scheme by holding workshops for corrections and parole administrators, compiling information from questionnaires, and holding additional workshops in which the administrators could discuss the MAP concept. These efforts represented an attempt to work out a consensus among parole administrators, who were somewhat reluctant to give up any of the traditional parole board discretion in determining a parole date, and institution staff members, who feared change. In the initial phase, the MAP project staff had the objective of selecting several states suitable for implementation of the system. A significant opposition to MAP's idea of a definite parole date to be set by the parole board at the beginning of the contract period developed. While parole administrators already had some experience in giving "favorable consideration" to inmates who completed an agreed-upon program, the notion of establishing a definite release date several months in advance was entirely new to them. In negotiating to overcome such resistance, the project staff visited Wisconsin, Alabama, California, Arizona, and Idaho in roughly that order. Then came additional visits to Wisconsin and Alabama, with first visits to Kansas, New Jersey, Massachusetts, New York, the District of Columbia, and the Federal Parole Board. These visits to "sell" the MAP concept were made between March 1972 and March 1973. From the jurisdictions visited, the project staff selected three states for implementation of the model: Wisconsin, Arizona, and California.

The states selected for participation in the MAP project established procedures for achieving the necessary communication and cooperation between agencies and among inmates who would participate. Inmates began signing contracts in the latter part of 1973. At first, inmates displayed suspicion, fear, and distrust of the program, but they soon gained confidence when they discovered that the states would actually honor a contract for a release. Such confidence improved inmate participation in treatment programming. Both institution staff and parole board personnel found the program to be viable and, in general, expressed their willingness to continue the program.

The Mutual Agreement Program, as established by the ACA, has only temporary federal funding. Federal funding of this type of project normally ends after three years, when the state or local government is expected to assume the costs. The three states selected expressed willingness to continue the techniques beyond the life of the federal funding. For the future, Arizona, California, and Wisconsin may utilize the scheme more fully by allowing significant numbers of inmates to contract a release date contingent upon fulfilling a specified program.

The basic technique of MAP, or some variation of it, may become popular with other state correctional systems where it will be adopted and funded with state revenues. On the other hand, the MAP concept may gradually wither away, as have many other penological innovations. Ultimately, the real test of the value of these innovations is whether they achieve the rehabilitation goal of corrections to the point of lowering the recidivism (*q.v.*) rate. A basic, and debatable, assumption underlying the MAP concept is that vocational training can reduce commitment to criminality. The focus of the program is on the economic disadvantages experienced by many offenders in our system. Whether treatment via the teacher-pupil model to provide marketable skills will divert a person from a criminal career is yet unknown. For related discussions, see PAROLE CONTRACTS.

REFERENCES: American Correctional Association, *An Evaluative Summary of Research: MAP Program Outcomes in the Initial Demonstration States,* 1975; American Correctional Association, *The Mutual Agreement Program,* 1973; Ellen R. Dunbar, *Organizational Change and the Politics of Bureaucracy: Illustrations from the Initiation of Mutual Agreement Programming in Three State Correctional Agencies,* 1976; Robin Eptein and others, *The Legal Aspects of Contract Parole,* 1976; Leon Leiberg and William Parker, "Mutual Agreement Programs with Vouchers: An Alternative for Institutionalized Female Offenders," *American Journal of Correction,* 1975.

N

NATIONAL CLEARINGHOUSE FOR CRIMINAL JUSTICE PLAN-NING AND ARCHITECTURE. The clearinghouse was created in 1971 on the campus of the University of Illinois at Champaign/Urbana, with the help of a federal grant from the Law Enforcement Assistance Administration (LEAA) (*q.v.*). The need for the clearinghouse arose when the Crime Control and Safe Streets Act of 1968 was amended in 1970 to provide federal grant money to be used exclusively by corrections agencies. This amendment, officially known as Part E, established a vehicle for awarding grant money that could be used for prison construction as well as for correctional programs.

In order to establish appropriate guidelines for awarding Part E funds that would be used for the construction of institutions, LEAA sponsored competition among universities. The University of Illinois won the contest by putting together the best set of construction guidelines. Subsequently, the clearinghouse was set up at Champaign/Urbana to review grant applications asking for Part E construction funds. Since 1970, however, the scope of the work undertaken by the clearinghouse has expanded to include providing technical assistance to corrections agencies throughout the country. In 1974, the clearinghouse made its services available to courts and law enforcement agencies, but it continues to do most of its work for correctional agencies.

The clearinghouse provides analysis of problems, planning, and recommendations as part of its short-term services; it does not design or build any institutions. Its recommendations nearly always encourage total systems planning that encourages the use of small, community-based corrections facilities and discourages the building of large, fortress-type maximum security prisons. Officials from state and local governments get free technical advice from the clearinghouse. This advice can be ignored by state and local governments determined to build the traditional large prisons or jails, but federal funding for such projects cannot be obtained without plans that meet the approval of clearinghouse staff. Clearinghouse Director Frederick Moyer has a staff consisting of eight persons: architects, data analysts, planners, and a cross-section of other specialists from several fields. All staff members are employees of the University of Illinois, but LEAA provided $5.6 million to fund the clearinghouse from 1971 to 1976.

Despite its emphasis on total planning to increase the use of community corrections programming such as probation and parole, a considerable number of prison facilities have been built by units of government after seeking technical assistance from the clearinghouse. Estimates covering the period 1971–1975 show that some 17,000 new beds were constructed at a cost of roughly $366 million. William Nagel, head of the Institute of Corrections of the American Foundation and formerly a member of the Clearinghouse Advisory Board, resigned from the board in 1975 after charging that the clearinghouse was not making sufficient efforts to resist pressures from state and local government officials who sought money to build large maximum security prisons. Nagel was especially critical of clearinghouse assistance to the state of Nevada in planning a new prison. To refute such criticism, Director Moyer points out that prisons of this type would be built in any case since the clearinghouse cannot enforce its recommendations unless federal money is used in the construction. Moyer believes that the analysis and planning services provided by the clearinghouse encourage many state and local government officials to use more community corrections programs and to build smaller institutions. Some grant seekers completely ignore advice from the clearinghouse and build traditional institutions with local tax revenue, but many others make significant changes in their construction plans after receiving advice from clearinghouse personnel.

A representative project undertaken by the clearinghouse is illustrated by assistance given to the state correctional system in Alabama. Alabama prison officials, under a federal court order of 1975 mandating the improvement of living conditions in the state prisons, contracted with the University of Alabama to complete a study of the cost of redesigning the state's correctional system to meet the requirements of constitutionality. The University of Alabama, in turn, sought assistance from the clearinghouse in completing its study. Director Moyer spent several days studying the Alabama prison system in March 1976. A short-term assistance project of this kind normally requires clearinghouse staff to spend a week studying a system and an additional week compiling recommendations.

While the example refers to assistance of a state system, about 50 percent of the clearinghouse projects involve city and county governments. The example illustrates another dimension of service provided by the clearinghouse in that the call for assistance came as the result of a crisis. New York City officials sought clearinghouse help under similar circumstances in 1974 after a federal judge ordered the Tombs detention center closed; clearinghouse officials recommended design changes and computed the cost of reopening the facility. In another crisis situation, Oklahoma officials called for clearinghouse help in redesigning their penitentiary at McAlester after it was destroyed in an eleven-day riot in 1973. For a discussion of the relationship between correctional architecture and correctional philosophy, see ARCHITECTURE.

REFERENCES: Norman Johnston, *The Human Cage: A Brief History of Prison Architecture,* 1973; Thomas O. Murton, *The Dilemma of Prison Reform,* 1976; Charles Rogovin, "The Genesis of the Law Enforcement Assistance Administration: A Personal Account," *Columbia Human Rights Law Review,* 1973; Michael S. Serrill, "LEAA's National Clearinghouse for Criminal Justice Planning and Architecture," *Corrections Magazine,* 1976; U.S. National Advisory Commission on Criminal Justice Standards and Goals, *Corrections,* 1973.

NATIONAL COUNCIL ON CRIME AND DELINQUENCY (NCCD). The NCCD is a nonprofit citizen organization with an active membership of about 60,000 professionals or lay persons. It was originally established in 1907 and was incorporated as a national service agency in 1921. The NCCD considers itself to be the largest citizens' action program in the United States in the area of criminal justice. Its interests encompass the entire spectrum of activities in criminal justice: law enforcement, juvenile and criminal courts, and correctional institutions and programs. It is supported by contributions from community chests, foundations, business corporations, and individuals. Membership is open to any interested person for $15 per calendar year and may be obtained by writing to:

National Council on Crime and Delinquency
Continental Plaza
411 Hackensack Avenue
Hackensack, New Jersey 07601

Membership includes a subscription to the quarterly journal *Crime and Delinquency.*

One function of NCCD is the drafting of model legislation that can be used by legislators, criminal justice agencies, and citizen groups interested in reform. Examples of model legislation currently available include (1) Model Act for the Protection of Rights of Prisoners; (2) Model Sentencing Act, 2d edition; (3) Standard Family Court Act; (4) Standard Juvenile Court Act, 6th edition; and (5) Standard Probation and Parole Act, 2d edition.

Specialized staff members of the NCCD study criminal justice agencies and provide guides to action. Examples of printed guidelines available for general distribution include (1) Guides for Juvenile Court Judges; (2) Guides for Juvenile Court Judges on News Media Relations; (3) Guides for Sentencing, 2d edition; (4) Guides to the Judge in Medical Orders Affecting Children; (5) Guides to the Judge in Sentencing in Racketeering Cases; and (6) Guides to Sentencing the Dangerous Offender.

Volunteers in Probation (VIP), a division of NCCD, operates nationwide out of a central office in Royal Oak, Michigan, to develop programs involving citizens as volunteers in court and corrections rehabilitative programs. VIP has offices in twenty states and in the District of Columbia.

NCCD serves as a clearinghouse for information about crime and maintains an extensive library at its Information Center. The center publishes *Crime and Delinquency Literature*. This quarterly, available for $40 per year, contains in-depth abstracts of books and journal articles published about criminal justice. Each issue also has at least one comprehensive bibliographic essay that synthesizes and summarizes the knowledge on or developments in a certain subject of interest to the profession.

The NCCD also conducts an annual conference and organizes training institutes. Its Research Center carries out major projects in criminal justice research. Its other periodic publications are *Criminal Justice Newsletter,* a biweekly publication available for $55 per year, and *Journal of Research in Crime and Delinquency,* a semiannual publication available for $10 per year.

From time to time, the NCCD Board of Directors publishes policy statements. In recent years, a number of these statements have stirred controversy in the field. For controversial positions of the NCCD discussed in other entries, see ABOLITIONISTS, MORATORIUM ON PRISON CONSTRUCTION, and STATUS OFFENDERS.

REFERENCES: National Council on Crime and Delinquency, *Crime and Delinquency,* 1976; Kathleen Yaskiw Perl, "Policy Statements and Model Acts," *Crime and Delinquency Literature,* 1976.

NATIONAL EDUCATION—TRAINING PROGRAM FOR COLLEGES–PROFESSIONALS–CITIZENS (NETP). NETP is a program for promoting the use of citizen volunteers in corrections. It was established in 1977 through the efforts of Judge Keith J. Leenhouts (*q.v.*), director of the VIP Division of the National Council on Crime and Delinquency (*q.v.*); Dr. Robert T. Sigler and Mr. Philip Grote, staff members of the University of Alabama; and Dr. Peter Ellis of the W. K. Kellogg Foundation. Funding for the program is provided by the W. K. Kellogg Foundation, one of the five largest philanthropic organizations in the United States, and the University of Alabama.

NETP has offices at Royal Oak, Michigan, and at the University of Alabama. The University NETP effort is part of the Criminal Justice Program and is formally known as the National Criminal Justice Volunteer Resource Service (NCJVRS). NCJVRS assists colleges and universities throughout the nation in establishing college-level courses in criminal justice volunteerism, organizes conferences on criminal justice volunteerism, oversees the establishment of regional resource centers, develops programs for volunteer coordinators, develops models for evaluation of volunteer programs in the field, and operates a rental library of videotapes that can be used for training volunteers.

By establishing college-level courses on criminal justice volunteerism, NCJVRS insures the future of the volunteer court-corrections movement by informing thousands of students about the possibilities of citizens working in corrections settings to achieve rehabilitation of offenders. Some of the students in the courses plan to become professionals in criminal justice. They are learning to recruit, train, and coordinate the work of citizen volunteers who spend a few hours each month working for one of the 2,500 courts, jails, prisons, and juvenile institutions utilizing the services of volunteers. Many students in the volunteerism classes go into other careers, but maintain a personal commitment to the court-corrections movement and frequently volunteer their services in their spare time.

One of the services offered by NCJVRS is its library of high-quality audiovisual TV color cassettes covering all phases of volunteerism in criminal justice. The cassettes, made by outstanding leaders of the volunteer court-corrections movement, are used in college classes and by criminal justice agencies training volunteers to work with offenders. The cassettes are in forty-five segments and provide a total of thirty-four hours of instruction. Persons wishing to utilize the cassettes and other resources offered by NCJVRS can obtain a free manual describing each cassette, suggesting training and educational curriculum, and providing instructions for obtaining materials by writing to either of two addresses:

VIP-NCCD
200 Washington Square Plaza
Royal Oak, Michigan 48067
(313) 398–8550

NCJVRS
The University of Alabama
P.O. Box 6365
University, Alabama 35486
(205) 348-6738

For additional information on the volunteer court-corrections movement, see LEENHOUTS, KEITH J.

NATIONAL INSTITUTE OF LAW ENFORCEMENT AND CRIMINAL JUSTICE. This institute, the research arm of the Law Enforcement Assistance Administration (LEAA) (*q.v.*), has been funded by Congress since 1969, with $185.6 million allocated to its operations between 1969 and 1976. Under the direction of its former director, Martin Danziger, and its present director, Gerald Caplan, the institute awards grants to study issues important to corrections, in addition to those issues important to law enforcement and courts. In 1976, the institute had thirty-seven corrections research projects funded and underway, including a large grant to Robert Martinson (*q.v.*) to update his studies published between 1967 and 1975. (For additional information, see MARTINSON, ROBERT.)

Although LEAA has never felt that the mission of the institute should be the monitoring and evaluation of LEAA's block and discretionary grants to state and local criminal justice agencies, the Congress has insisted on such activities, with the result that the institute launched a phased evaluation program in 1974 to study clusters of different programs. Between 1974 and 1976, the institute conducted Phase I of its evaluation program by spending $6.4 million on "state-of-the-art" studies of several hundred programs. Phase II of the program during 1977 and 1978 involved more intensive study of the impact of the best programs identified in Phase I; some $3.5 million was allocated for the effort in 1978.

There have been problems both in getting research done and in determining what use should be made of the research findings. According to George Bohlinger, who supervised research efforts for the institute for several years, the problem with getting research done involves finding persons capable of doing high-quality research as well as getting them to meet deadlines. Bohlinger feels there are very few persons in the United States whom he would trust to do high-quality research in corrections. He also complains that researchers do not complete their final reports until they are long overdue. There is disagreement over the proper use of research findings that are timely and of good quality. Some critics of the institute believe that it should use research findings to make recommendations for correctional policy. Gerald Caplan's answer to such criticisms is that research findings are seldom conclusive enough for such direct action. Research findings, he believes, are more useful for discovering those procedures that do not work well than for determining which procedures should be used. As an example, Caplan cites research on deterring habitual criminals from committing additional crimes by increasing the probability of punishment. Research findings that would support the hypothesis of deterrence would not necessarily mean that the United States should imprison more offenders. The financial and social costs involved in adopting a harsh deterrence policy would also have to be considered.

One way in which the Institute has attempted to influence correctional policy as a result of its research findings is by identifying correctional programs on a state or local level that seem to be working well and encouraging replication of these efforts. The institute has been identifying and designating outstanding programs as "exemplary" since 1973. It prints brochures on exemplary programs and, in some cases, handbooks on program replication. The brochures and/or handbooks are widely distributed to criminal justice personnel; eight of the seventeen exemplary programs are in the area of corrections. As an example of how the exemplary program technique works, the institute designated the Des Moines Community Based Corrections Program in Iowa as an exemplary program and distributed brochures on the program. It has also provided funds for design and evaluation for six other jurisdictions interested in implementing the program.

REFERENCES: Charles Rogovin, "The Genesis of the Law Enforcement Assistance Administration: A Personal Account," *Columbia Human Rights Law Review,* 1973; Michael S. Serrill, "LEAA," *Corrections Magazine,* 1976; U.S. Department of Justice, *The Law Enforcement Assistance Administration: A Partnership for Crime Control,* 1976.

NATIONAL PRISONERS REFORM ASSOCIATION (NPRA). The NPRA is the only inmate union in the history of United States prisons that ever obtained official sanction. It was established in 1972 in the Massachusetts Correctional Institution at South Walpole and lasted until 1975.

In 1972, John O. Boone became commissioner of correction in Massachusetts with a mandate from the governor to revamp the rehabilitation programs at Walpole. Boone reports that he encouraged the inmates to organize themselves so that they could take more responsibility for their own lives and help plan their own rehabilitation programs. Boone's primary objective for the inmates was to alleviate the restrictive control that the guards exercised over them.

The experiment in inmate self-government was a disaster. The guards lost control of the institution in 1972 and did not completely regain it during the three-year period that the NPRA was powerful. During this interval, fifteen inmates were killed by other inmates by stabbings, beatings, burning of cells, or by being thrown off tiers. Hundreds of acts of violence occurred, with serious injuries inflicted on both guards and inmates. Authorities charge that much of the violence was committed by inmates under the influence of drugs. Drugs became plentiful in the prison after the NPRA negotiated more liberal visiting rules that made it easier to smuggle drugs into the facility. One of the casualties during this period of violence was Albert DeSalvo, who claimed to be the Boston Strangler; DeSalvo was found dead in his cell with nine stab wounds in his chest. In attempting to control the violent episodes, officials triggered several major disturbances and a number of less serious incidents in which inmates broke fixtures, burned cells, and hurled debris, feces, and urine at guards. In May 1973, guards staged a walkout that lasted fourteen days.

Governor Francis Sargent fired Boone in June 1973. Boone, whom a number of people blamed for the chaotic conditions in Walpole, contends that the guard force sabotaged his reform efforts to lessen their control over the inmates by not carrying out their duties properly. The guards concede that they did not cooperate with Boone, but as justification for their lack of cooperation they state that they feared for their safety. A state police colonel and two acting wardens attempted to halt the violence and restore order to Walpole for more than a year after Boone's dismissal.

Frank Gunter was appointed warden at Walpole on December 31, 1974. His plan for restoring order to the institution involved dividing the prison into two sections, with the A section of the institution operating as a normal medium security prison, while the B section inmates spent most of their time locked in their cells. Implementing the plan to transfer inmates to different parts of the facility led to a riot that Gunter hopes was the last episode associated with the reign of the NPRA. (The NPRA is no longer recognized as the official bargaining agent for the inmates.) Guards began moving inmates on January 20, 1975. Five days later, the transfer of more than 200 inmates was complete, but inmates in the maximum security B section staged a controlled riot for two weeks afterward by wrecking their cells, breaking fixtures, throwing their garbage on the floor after eating, and throwing human wastes at guards.

Prison guards and a number of inmates feel that the NPRA was controlled by a band of ruthless men who terrorized the inmate population during their reign. Penologists and other inmates disagree. Nevertheless, as a result of the long period of turmoil associated with the NPRA, the Walpole institution began to emphasize security and custody over treatment programming—an emphasis that may last for decades. For a related discussion, see PRISONERS' UNIONS.

REFERENCES: J. E. Baker, *The Right to Participate: Inmate Involvement in Prison Administration,* 1974; C. Ronald Huff, "Unionization Behind the Walls," *Criminology,* 1974; Michael S. Serrill, "Walpole Prison: After the Storm," *Corrections Magazine,* 1975; Linda R. Singer and J. Michael Keating, *Grievance Mechanisms in American Corrections: The State of the Art,* 1975; U.S. National Advisory Commission on Criminal Justice Standards and Goals, *Corrections,* 1973.

NEBRASKA CORRECTIONAL SYSTEM. Nebraska's Department of Correctional Services is responsible for both adult and juvenile correctional institutions. Any person convicted of a felony is committed to the department. Although no minimum age is specified, state statutes require that persons below the age of sixteen be segregated from the adult prison population.

The Youth Development Center at Geneva was opened in 1892 with a normal capacity of 100 special supervision cases and juvenile delinquents up to age nineteen. The Youth Development Center at Kearney was opened in 1881 with a normal capacity of 150 special supervision cases and juvenile delinquents up to age nineteen. The Nebraska Center for Women at York was opened in 1920 with a normal capacity of sixty women fifteen years of age and above. The Nebraska Penal and Correctional Complex at Lincoln was originally opened as a penitentiary in 1869. A reformatory unit was added in 1921, and it became a correctional complex in 1963. It has a normal capacity of 1,168 felons. The Diagnostic and Evaluation Center at Lincoln was completed in 1976 with a normal capacity of 180 male felons and evaluatees.

Nebraska is one of the few states that experienced a decrease in prison population in 1977. (Others were Arizona, California, Connecticut, Montana, Ohio, Utah, West Virginia, and Wisconsin.) The population decreased 7 percent from 1,339 on January 1, 1977, to 1,241 on January 1, 1978.

REFERENCES: American Correctional Association, *Directory,* 1975–1976 edition; Michael Serrill, "Prison Population Rises Again, But at a Slower Rate," *Corrections Magazine,* 1978.

NEVADA CORRECTIONAL SYSTEM. The state's three adult institutions are operated by Nevada State Prisons. The state's maximum security prison, Nevada State Prisons at Carson City, was opened in 1861 with a normal capacity of 454 male felons. The Northern Nevada Correctional Center at Stewart was opened in 1964 with a normal capacity of 432 male felons. Nevada Women's Correctional Center at Carson City was opened in 1964 with a normal capacity of thirty-three.

The Youth Services Agency, which is part of the Department of Human Resources, oversees the two juvenile institutions in the state. District Courts commit felons and misdemeanants between the ages of eight and eighteen to one of these facilities to serve an indeterminate sentence (*q.v.*). The Nevada Girls Training Center at Caliente opened in 1962 with a normal capacity of 100 girls. The Nevada Youth Training Center at Elko was originally established in 1865; it was rebuilt in 1913 and new buildings were added in 1962 and in 1964. It has a normal capacity of 160 boys.

Nevada is experiencing relatively large increases in its prison population. In January 1975, the population was 854. In January 1977, it had grown to 953. By January 1978, there had been a 19 percent increase over the previous twelve months to 1,137.

REFERENCES: American Correctional Association, *Directory,* 1975–1976 edition; Michael Serrill, "Prison Population Rises Again, But at a Slower Rate," *Corrections Magazine,* 1978.

NEWGATE PROGRAM. The NewGate program offers post-secondary education to inmates. The first NewGate programs, established in the 1960s, were funded by the federal government's Office of Economic Opportunity. Following the NewGate experiments in the 1960s, a number of state correctional systems have made college courses available to inmates, but NewGate is the only national post-secondary education program for inmates. Many state and federal prisons incorporated post-secondary education into their rehabilitation efforts as the 1970s got underway. Such programs resemble the NewGate effort in many respects, but they are most often extension programs of colleges in the vicinity of the prison being served. Unlike these extension course operations, NewGate programs employ a full-time staff and operate as residence programs within an institution.

A brief survey of the history of education in prisons is helpful in understanding the NewGate operations. The first prison school was probably established in 1798 at the Walnut Street Jail in Philadelphia. Its purpose was to teach inmates a few basic subjects at the elementary school level during their leisure time. Relatively few prisons felt the need to establish similar programs in the following century. In 1870, the American Prison Association endorsed academic learning as a contributing factor in the reform of inmates, but despite this endorsement, education programs in prisons did not begin to expand rapidly until the 1930s. Elementary and secondary education, along with vocational training and business courses, soon became common in institutions. Offerings of high school education flourished throughout the 1940s and 1950s, but prior to the 1960s college courses were available only by correspondence.

College courses were offered in a number of prisons as pilot programs between 1962 and 1967. One pilot program, the Upward Bound Oregon Prison Project, combined the features of several of the better programs; this project offered post-secondary education in a maximum security prison for the first time. The Oregon education program was evaluated and eventually funded by the Office of Economic Opportunity and became the prototype Project NewGate. By 1971, the federal agency had funded additional NewGate programs in Colorado, Kentucky, Minnesota, New Mexico, and Pennsylvania.

NewGate programs are designed primarily for inmates who are capable of doing university study. Inmates with deficiencies in their previous educational backgrounds are given college preparatory courses to enable them to become eligible for college classes. The NewGate staff members provide inmates with individual or group counseling in addition to education, inasmuch as the program is based on the notion that the inmate should be helped with his personal adjustment as well as with his academic attainments. These efforts to provide the NewGate participant with psychological counseling extend to the post-release phase. NewGate staff members feel that the educational process itself has therapeutic value. They reason that inmates with low self-esteem who experience success in the classroom may develop better self-concepts.

The structure of NewGate programs is geared to reintegrating the offender into the community. College courses offered at the freshman or sophomore level can readily be transferred to college programs which the inmates will enter after their release from prison. Participating inmates are required to keep up a grade point average that is acceptable to sponsoring colleges; tutors are available for those who fall behind in their studies. Some NewGate programs operate residential facilities outside of the prison for inmates who are assigned to a study release operation. These facilities are usually available to those offenders who are nearing the end of their sentences. They have taken college courses in the NewGate program inside of the prison and become eligible for some type of pre-release program as they near the time when they will be eligible for parole. A study release program with housing away from the prison creates an ideal pre-release setting. Inmates assigned to such facilities attend regular college classes away from the institution but return to the residential facility at night. The arrangement allows the inmate to make a gradual transition from the restrictive atmosphere of the prison to the freer setting of the residential center before being released.

NewGate staff members help newly released or paroled inmates to locate housing, and to select educational programs. They also provide instruction in applying for financial aid from colleges. As a means of facilitating the releasee's personal adjustment to freedon, NewGate programs continue to make their counselors available to participants.

The early efforts of the NewGate programs have been deemed a success. Recidivism (*q.v.*) rates for program participants are estimated to be in the range of 15 to 20 percent as compared with estimated rates of 60 to 70 percent for the total nationwide inmate population. NewGate participants are also believed to have lower dropout rates from academic programs than college students who are not offenders. More than 50 percent of offenders who earn B.A. degrees enter graduate school.

Current information about the status of NewGate programs and information on funding sources for institutions interested in starting such projects can be obtained from the NewGate Resource Center, a clearinghouse operation established in 1971 by the National Council on Crime and Delinquency in Paramus, New Jersey (see Appendix A for address).

REFERENCES: Stuart Adams and John J. Connolly, "Role of Junior Colleges in the Prison Community," *Junior College Journal,* 1971; Alfred Blumstein and Jacqueline Cohen, *An Evaluation of a College-*

Level Program in a Maximum Security Prison, 1974; Rex Herron, *Project NewGate—Past, Present and Future: Issues of the Change Agent Role in the Replication of a Demonstration Program,* 1973; M. Joselson, "Prison Education: A Major Reason for Its Impotence," *Corrective Psychiatry and Journal of Social Therapy,* 1971; John J. Marsh, "Higher Education in American Prisons," *Crime and Delinquency Literature,* 1973; National Council on Crime and Delinquency, "NewGate: New Hope Through Education," in Gary R. Perlstein and Thomas R. Phelps (eds.), *Alternatives to Prison: Community-Based Corrections,* 1975.

NEW HAMPSHIRE CORRECTIONAL SYSTEM. New Hampshire has the smallest state prison system population (240 in 1978). Its one adult prison, New Hampshire State Prison, was opened in 1880. It is located at Concord and has a normal population of 314 adult males ages eighteen and above. The prison warden is responsible to a Board of Trustees. Any adult females sentenced to prison in New Hampshire are boarded outside of the state with another state prison system or the federal system.

Staff members at the Youth Development Center at Manchester are responsible for overseeing all detention, aftercare, and residential services for juveniles. The New Hampshire Youth Development Center was opened in 1858 with a normal capacity of 187. It houses both male and female juvenile offenders ages eleven to eighteen. Friendship House in Manchester was opened in 1975 with a normal capacity of twenty juvenile males ages eleven to eighteen years.

The prison population in New Hampshire is running counter to the national trend by showing a 20 percent decrease in 1977 as compared to an average 5 percent increase for all prison systems in the country.

REFERENCES: American Correctional Association, *Directory,* 1975–1976 edition; Michael Serrill, "Prison Population Rises Again, But at a Slower Rate," *Corrections Magazine,* 1978.

NEW JERSEY CORRECTIONAL SYSTEM. The state of New Jersey operates a graded system of institutions under the guidance of the Division of Correction and Parole within the Department of Institutions and Agencies. The system is divided into training schools, youth correctional institutions, prisons, residential group centers, community treatment centers, community service centers, and a parole resource and orientation facility to provide crisis service to parolees.

The training school category includes a facility for juvenile boys at Skillman, which houses boys from eight to thirteen years of age, and a facility at Jamesburg which is for boys thirteen to fifteen years of age. A training school for juvenile girls at Trenton provides services for girls in the eight to seventeen year age bracket. A correctional institution for women ages sixteen and above located at Clinton is also classified as a training school.

A youth reception and correction center at Yardville provides reception for all youth correctional institution commitments for the Youth Correctional Institution Complex. The ages of the male offenders received at Yardville range from fifteen to thirty years. With subsidiaries at West Trenton and Wharton Forest, the 1972 average population at the Yardville Youth Reception and Correction Center was 800. Both Annandale and Bordentown have youth correction institutions, each of which holds around 700 inmates received from the Yardville reception unit. The Annandale institution has subsidiaries at High Point and Stokes Forest, while the Bordentown institution has subsidiaries at the Neuro-Psychiatric Institute and at New Lisbon.

The New Jersey Prison Complex includes the historic New Jersey State Prison at Trenton. It was first opened in 1798 and was replaced with the present facilities in 1836. It houses some 1,400 to 1,500 males ages sixteen and up. Subsidiaries include the Prison Unit at West Trenton and the Trenton Prison Readjustment Unit of the Trenton Psychiatric Hospital. Two other large prisons in the complex receive transfers from Trenton: the New Jersey State Prison at Rahway, with its subsidiary at Marlboro, and the New Jersey State Prison at Leesburg.

Four short-term residential group centers, each with a capacity of twenty, provide treatment for adolescents as a condition of their probation: Highfields Residential Group Center at Hopewell, Turrell Residential Group Center for females at Allaire, Warren Residential Group Center at Oxford, and Ocean Residential Group Center at Forked River.

Camden, Paterson, and Plainfield are sites for three community treatment centers that receive male delinquents fourteen to sixteen years of age for short-term remedial treatment upon recommendation of the juvenile court.

Three community service centers capable of housing fifty inmates each attempt to ease the problems of adult male offenders ready for release. Such pre-release centers provide housing for four months while the residents are working or attending vocational education classes. These centers are located in Newark, Hudson County, and Trenton.

As of August 1, 1974, there were 3,517 state prison inmates above the age of fifteen (3,323 males and 194 females); 2,140 Youth Correctional Institution inmates, fifteen to thirty years of age; and 324 male and 49 female juvenile inmates ranging in age from eight to eighteen. In addition, the correctional system is responsible for 9,261 parolees and almost 45,000 probationers.

The rapid increase in the state's population and a corresponding increase in crime have created serious problems for the state's correctional officials. The population of the state has doubled within the last thirty years, so that New Jersey, with 953 people per square mile, is now the most densely populated state in the union. From 1962 to 1972, the state's correctional institutions experienced a 100 percent increase in average daily population.

The historic Trenton State Prison once represented the most progressive thinking in corrections. The original prison, constructed in 1798, is now used as a home for the superintendent. The building bears a plaque proclaiming the ideology of the times: "Labor, Silence, Penitence." With the massive ideological changes that have taken place in penology over the years, modern penologists have come to regard the institution as the antithesis of what an institution should be. The ancient prison has eighty-eight cells which were built in 1836 for occupancy by one man. The cells have solid steel doors instead of bars. Each of these small, dark cells now holds three or four men. Most of the inmates are housed in cells that are stacked four tiers high, with three inmates or less in each cell. Living conditions are so primitive that inmates who fail to adjust to other prisons in the system are transferred to Trenton as punishment. Ann Klein, commissioner of the Department of Institutions and Agencies, has vowed to close down the facility as soon as room can be found for its population.

The New Jersey prison population increased slightly from 6,187 on January 1, 1977, to 6,282 on January 1, 1978.

REFERENCES: American Correctional Association, *Directory,* 1975–1976 edition; Michael S. Serrill, "Profile/New Jersey," *Corrections Magazine,* 1974; Michael Serrill, "Prison Population Rises Again, But at a Slower Rate," *Corrections Magazine,* 1978.

NEW MEXICO CORRECTIONAL SYSTEM. All of New Mexico's adult felons (at least eighteen years of age, except those who commit certain violent crimes) must be committed to the Department of Corrections upon conviction to serve a minimum six-month sentence in an institution. The department oversees the operation of five adult and juvenile institutions under the Division of Adult Institutions and the Division of Juvenile Institutions; it is also responsible for adult probation and parole services and juvenile parole services.

Adult offenders, both male and female, are initially sent to the Penitentiary of New Mexico at Cerrillos, which is located a few miles south of Santa Fe. This institution was constructed in 1956 to replace the original penitentiary opened in 1884. It is a medium security prison built in the classic telephone-pole style of prison architecture: wings branching off a long, central corridor. The institution has a normal capacity of 1,000 but has been overcrowded in recent years. Inmates who are nearing the end of their sentences may be transferred to the Los Lunas Correctional Center, a minimum security facility near Albuquerque; it was opened in 1940 and now serves as a pre-release center. Women offenders are housed in the Women's Division, a subsidiary of the Penitentiary of New Mexico, which consists of a concrete building on the grounds of the main institution. The Women's Division holds fewer than twenty women.

The Division of Juvenile Institutions operates one facility for males and one for females, and uses two camps as subsidiaries. These detention homes normally house children below the age of eighteen (the dividing line between adults and juveniles in New Mexico), but the secretary of corrections has discretion to order persons up to age twenty-one to be confined in a juvenile facility. The New Mexico Boys' School has a normal capacity of 262, counting the space in its subsidiary camps at Eagle Nest and Camp Sierra Blanca at Fort Stanton. It originally opened in 1910 and was replaced by a new institution in 1956. The institution, holding about 200 boys, operates a step program in which a boy progresses through four steps in the institution with the fifth step being parole. Privileges are severely restricted in step one, which every boy enters when arriving at the facility. Good behavior earns the boy progression through the steps, with enjoyment of additional privileges at each step; the minimum amount of time required to pass through the step program is four months. The New Mexico Girls' School at Albuquerque opened in 1919 with a normal capacity of fifty-two.

The Penitentiary of New Mexico at Santa Fe, the state's main prison, operates a Psychological Services Unit that makes evaluations of all incoming inmates, inmates being considered for parole or the furlough (*q.v.*) program, and those individuals requiring pretrial sanity hearings. The unit involves some 130 inmates in either individual or group therapy. A limited number of inmates participate in two education programs operated in the main prison: the Adult Basic Education program, with an enrollment of slightly more than 100 enrollees, and a Project Newgate program wherein Eastern New Mexico University and the College of Santa Fe offer precollege and college courses leading to an associate of arts or bachelor of arts degree in a limited number of fields. The college section of the educational program has a little more than 100 enrollees.

The usual vocational training and prison industry programs are offered in the state's main prison. Vocational training consists of auto repair, cabinetmaking, carpentry, electronics, and welding. The prison industries, which generate about $250,000 annually, employ some seventy inmates in a furniture repair shop, a highway sign shop, and a license plate plant. Inmates are chosen for the program on the basis of their academic achievements and the length of their sentences. Inmates can earn up to twenty-five cents an hour in prison industry or other jobs around the institution.

New Mexico's prison system is one of the few in the United States which have overcome the substantial barriers to hiring ex-inmates as system employees. Lloyd McClendon, the administrative assistant to the top official in the state's correctional system, Secretary of Corrections Mike Hanrahan, served a total of seventeen years in prisons for a number of convictions. He was given the death sentence for murder in 1964; this sentence was later overturned, but he did serve ten years in the New Mexico State Penitentiary after another appeal during which he was again convicted for the crime. Many officials in the state point to him as a product of the system's rehabilitation programs, but McClendon himself steadfastly maintains that he was able to rebuild his life in spite of the system, and not because of it. He does not, however, deny the value of the educational program, for it was through this program that he earned a four-year degree in business. He hopes to use his experience and perspective to reshape rehabilitation programming in the system. He believes strongly that rehabilitation programs are useless unless the inmate's participation is completely voluntary. He states that an inmate should be left alone to serve his time if that is what he wants. McClendon also advocates that prison officials should hear out those who criticize the operation of prisons.

Prison population has been increasing rapidly in recent years from 979 in January 1975 to 1,359 in January 1977 to 1,622 in January 1978.

REFERENCES: American Correctional Association, *Directory,* 1975–1976 edition; William Hart, "Profile/New Mexico," *Corrections Magazine,* 1976; Michael Serrill, "Prison Population Rises Again, But at a Slower Rate," *Corrections Magazine,* 1978.

NEW YORK CITY CORRECTIONAL SYSTEM. On an average day, the New York City system holds 7,500 inmates. Some 55,000 inmates are processed through the city system every year, thereby making it larger than the prison systems of forty states. The penal facility at Riker's Island has almost 8,000 beds and is the largest complex of penal institutions in the United States. As an aid in comprehending the magnitude of the operation, Benjamin Malcolm, New York City commissioner of corrections, points out that the U.S. Bureau of Prisons handles only 30,000 inmates each year.

Since the system is a jail rather than a prison operation, the magnitude of the operation is even more awesome. Jails hold sentenced prisoners and persons charged with crimes who are awaiting trail (detainees). The presence of detainees makes the administration of a penal facility more difficult because detainees have more visitors than prisoners and must be transported to and from court for hearings and trials. The New York City system has 250 buses and vans to transport a total of 500,000 inmates per year from institutions to courts or hospitals and from one institution to another.

The large complex on Riker's Island has seven separate institutions on a 400-acre landfill about seven miles from Manhattan in the East River. The largest facility in the complex is the Manhattan House of Detention for Men with a total capacity of 1,879. The second largest facility is the Correctional Institution for Men with a capacity of 1,872. The Adolescent Reception and Detention Center (ARDC), slightly smaller with a total capacity of 1,080, houses sixteen to twenty-one-year-old males awaiting trial. The newest facility is designed to hold 1,016 inmates; it is known as Project C-95. The Mental Health Unit has a total capacity of 992 but was closed in 1975 to save money during the height of the city's budget crisis. Prior to its closing, it was known as the Adolescent Remand Shelter. In 1976, one wing of the facility was reopened to hold about 150 inmates believed to be potential suicides. The New York City Correctional Institution for Women has a capacity of 680, but two wings were closed in 1976 because it normally held only 350 inmates including adults and adolescents, sentenced and detainees. The Infirmary has room for 279 inmates with medical problems that do not require hospitalization.

The system has several facilities other than those operating on Riker's Island. The Bronx, Brooklyn, and Queens each have a jail. The Bronx House of Detention for Men holds 465 adult males; the Brooklyn House of Detention for Men, 840 inmates; and the Queens House of Detention for Men, 520. Manhattan's jail, the Tombs, was closed in 1974 after U.S. District Court Judge Morris Lasker, in a 1972 opinion, declared conditions there to be unconstitutional; city officials eventually decided to close the facility rather than improve it. Three city hospitals have prison wards: the Bellevue Hospital Prison Ward with a normal capacity of eighty-four, the Elmhurst Hospital Prison Ward with a normal capacity of thirty, and the Kings County Hospital Prison Ward with a normal capacity of 105.

Since the closing of the Tombs, facilities for adult males have been crowded. To alleviate the problem, some 500 men are normally housed in a state prison, with New York City paying for their care. The Ossining Correctional Facility (commonly known by its older name, Sing Sing) is used for this purpose; Ossining is reached via a thirty-mile train ride.

While the system's facilities for adult males are presently overcrowded, the system as a whole was less crowded in 1977 than in 1970 when the city had 14,000 prisoners in cells intended to hold fewer than 8,000. Much of the overcrowding has been alleviated by effective bail reform. The Vera Institute of Justice, founded by Louis Schweitzer in 1961, is responsible for successful experiments in bail reform; "release on recognizance" (ROR) began to be used widely by New York City courts following a trial period conducted by Vera Institute's Manhattan Bail Project. Release on one's own recognizance is based on the idea that a person who has strong roots in the community will appear for trial without being required to put up a cash bond. Since so many of the city's detainees are too poor to post bond, or even to pay the fee for a professional bondsman, ROR greatly reduces the number of persons being held in jail pending trial. At present, employees of the Pretrial Services Agency interview persons booked in jail to determine if they do qualify for ROR.

A number of diversion programs for drug addicts, established in recent years, are keeping hundreds of people out of the jails. There are several public and private drug addiction programs in New York City, and judges now routinely refer drug offenders to these programs rather than sending them to jail.

REFERENCE: Steve Gettinger, "Profile/New York City's Adult Corrections System," *Corrections Magazine*, 1976.

NEW YORK STATE CORRECTIONAL SYSTEM. Adult institutions and adult parole services in New York State are administered by the Department of Correctional Services. The Executive Department has two governmental units for juvenile correctional services: the Division of Youth, which administers juvenile institutions, and the Bureau of Placement and Counseling, which administers juvenile parole services.

The New York State prison system has a variety of institutions. Attica Correctional Facility (*q.v.*) at Attica was opened in 1931 with a normal capacity of 2,370 male felons. The facility suffered major damage in the 1971 riot and has been operating below maximum capacity in recent years while repairs are being made. Attica receives male offenders age twenty-one or above from judicial districts five through eight and male offenders at least sixteen years of age as transfers from other institutions.

Auburn Correctional Facility at Auburn was opened in 1817 and has a normal capacity of 1,700 male felons ages sixteen and above. The Bedford Hills Correctional Facility at Bedford Hills was opened in 1933 with a normal capacity of 360 felons and misdemeanants; the facility receives female offenders from judicial districts one, two, three, nine, ten, and eleven, and females from all judicial districts if they are committed under an indeterminate sentence (*q.v.*) with a minimum of five years. The Clinton Correctional Facility at Dannemora was opened in 1845 with a normal capacity of 2,200 male felons and misdemeanants ages sixteen and above. Clinton receives offenders at least twenty-one years of age from judicial districts three and four, and receives offenders who are at least sixteen years by transfer from other institutions.

Coxsackie Correctional Facility at West Coxsackie opened in 1935 with a normal capacity of 750 male felons and misdemeanants sixteen to nineteen years of age. The facility receives these youngsters by transfer from other institutions; the institution stresses vocational training and intense academic work. The Eastern New York Correctional Facility at Napanoch was opened in 1900 with a normal capacity of 1,250 male felons and misdemeanants between the ages of sixteen and thirty. The Elmira Reception Center was opened in 1945 with a normal capacity of 400 male felons and misdemeanants aged sixteen to twenty-one; the center receives all young males sentenced to institutions except those who are insane or mentally retarded. The Great Meadow Correctional Facility at Comstock opened in 1911 with a normal capacity of 1,525 male felons and misdemeanants ages sixteen to thirty. Great Meadow receives young males as transfers from other prisons in the system; in most instances, the transferee has personality problems and is serving a rather long minimum sentence. The population of the Great Meadow facility includes Narcotic Control Commission inmates who are housed under contract. The Green Haven Correctional Facility at Stormville was opened in 1949 with a normal capacity of 2,300 male felons and misdemeanants ages sixteen and above. Inmates at Green Haven are received by transfer from other institutions in the system; the population includes 325 Narcotic

Addiction Control Commission inmates housed under contract. The Ossining Correctional Facility (formerly known as Sing Sing) at Ossining was opened in 1825 with a normal capacity of 1,600 male felons and misdemeanants aged sixteen and above. The facility receives male offenders twenty-one years of age or older from judicial districts one, two, nine, ten, and eleven, and receives younger males by transfer from other institutions. The Wallkill Correctional Facility at Wallkill opened in 1932 with a normal capacity of 504 male felons sixteen years of age and above. The facility has an open environment and a strong emphasis on rehabilitation. It receives inmates by transfer from other institutions in an attempt to select inmates who are able to profit from the atmosphere.

The Division of Correctional Camps, part of the Department of Correctional Services, operates five camps for offenders: Camp Adirondack at Dannemora, opened in 1972 with a normal capacity of 100 male felons and misdemeanants at least twenty-one years of age; Camp Georgetown at Georgetown, opened in 1961 with a normal capacity of 100 male offenders aged sixteen to twenty-five; Camp Monterey at Beaver Dams, opened in 1958 with a normal capacity of eighty male offenders sixteen to twenty-five years of age; Camp Pharsalia at South Plymouth, opened in 1956 with a normal capacity of eighty male offenders sixteen to twenty-five years of age; and Camp Summit at Summit, opened in 1961 with a normal capacity of 100 males between the ages of sixteen and twenty-five.

The Executive Department's Division for Youth receives three different categories of juveniles: (1) Persons in Need of Supervision (PINS)—those children between the ages of seven and sixteen who are deemed to be incorrigible or habitually truant; (2) children between the ages of seven and sixteen who are juvenile delinquents by virtue of having committed an act that would be a criminal offense if they were adults; and (3) youthful offenders ages sixteen to nineteen who are committed as a condition of their probation or who volunteer for commitment.

New York State's juvenile institutions, together with opening dates and normal capacities, are as follows: Brookwood Center at Claverack, 1965, sixty female PINS ages seven to sixteen; the Goshen Center for Boys, 1947, 100 delinquent boys ages seven to thirteen; Overbrook Center at Red Hook, 1966, twenty-five boys ages seven to thirteen (it houses juvenile delinquents and PINS); South Kortright Center at South Kortright, 1963, fifty boys ages fifteen to sixteen (it holds juvenile delinquents and PINS); the South Lansing Center at South Lansing, 1969, fifty-five girls ages thirteen to seventeen (it holds juvenile delinquents and PINS); Highland School at Highland, 1957, 120 juvenile boys and girls ages seven to sixteen (all the juveniles are PINS); Hudson School at Hudson, 1904, 100 female PINS ages thirteen to sixteen; the Industry School at Industry, 1849, 200 male delinquents ages thirteen to sixteen; Tryon School at Johnstown, 1966, 120 male PINS ages thirteen to sixteen; and the Warwick School at Warwick, 1933, 160 male delinquents ages thirteen to sixteen.

The population of New York State prisons was 14,387 on January 1, 1975, and increased 12 percent to 16,056 by January 1, 1976. The population increased 11 percent in 1977 from 17,791 on January 1, 1977, to 19,754 on January 1, 1978.

REFERENCES: American Correctional Association, *Directory,* 1975–1976 edition; Steve Gettinger, "U.S. Prison Population Hits All-Time High," *Corrections Magazine,* 1976; Michael Serrill, "Prison Population Rises, But at a Slower Rate," *Corrections Magazine,* 1978.

NORTH CAROLINA CORRECTIONAL SYSTEM. North Carolina has a sprawling array of prisons holding a relatively large number of inmates considering the size of the state. There are seventy-seven adult prison facilities in the state, sixty-six of which are administered by six geographical area offices: The Eastern, Western, North Central, South Central, North Piedmont, and South Piedmont area offices.

On January 1, 1976, the prison population of the state was 12,486. One reason for the large prison population is that any adult male felon or misdemeanant who receives a minimum sentence of thirty days is committed to the Department of Corrections. Thus, misdemeanants who would serve their sentences in county jails in other states are counted as part of the prison population in North Carolina. Adult women committed to the Department of Corrections must be at least sixteen years of age and have a minimum sentence of six months to serve. Persons who are awaiting trial or appellate review of their cases may also be committed to the Department of Correction.

The Division of Prisons, which belongs to the Department of Correction, operates all adult institutions and facilities used to house juveniles who are tried as adults and assigned to the division's Youth Services Complex. Most of the adult prisons are administered under the six area offices, but the central office in Raleigh oversees six adult institutions and five facilities in the Youth Services Complex. Adult institutions administered by the central office of the Division of Prisons include Central Prison at Raleigh, opened in 1871 with a normal capacity of 1,000 male felons age twenty-one and above. Central Prison is a maximum security prison serving as a reception center for male felons with sentences longer than five years. The Correctional Center for Women at Raleigh was opened in 1934 with a normal capacity of 500 female felons and misdemeanants; it serves as a holding facility for all women committed to prison in the state. The Caledonia and Odom Complex consists of two male prisons under the supervision of one director: (1) the Caledonia unit at Tillery, opened in 1900 with a normal capacity of 480 male felons in a medium security setting; and (2) the Odom unit at Jackson, opened in 1960 with a normal capacity of 300 male felons in a close security setting. Blanch Prison at Blanch opened in 1956 with a normal capacity of 126 males in a close security setting. The Halifax facility at Halifax is a minimum security facility.

All male offenders below the age of twenty-one are segregated from older offenders by being placed in the Youth Services Complex. Within the complex, the young offenders are further segregated by age by separating those under age eighteen from those who are eighteen to twenty-one. The five youth facilities are as follows: the Western Correctional Center at Morgantown, a reception/evaluation center and holding facility for males under eighteen; the Sandhills Youth Center at McCain housing youths under eighteen who have attained minimum custody status; Burke Youth Center at Morgantown holding felon and misdemeanant youths under age eighteen in a minimum custody status; Harnett Youth Center at Lillington, a reception/evaluation center and holding facility for felons ages eighteen to twenty-one from the southern half of the state (it is a medium security prison); and the Polk Youth Center at Raleigh, a reception/evaluation center and holding facility for felons ages eighteen to twenty-one from the northern half of the state (it is a medium security prison).

In addition to the sixty-six facilities administered by the six geographic area commands, there are seven additional youthful offender units in these area commands which segregate offenders eighteen to twenty-one years of age from older offenders. All adult male offenders sentenced to five-year terms or less are received in these seven area commands at a facility designated as a reception/diagnostic center. After evaluation, the offender is assigned to one of the prisons in the area command.

The central office of the Eastern Area is located at Greenville and oversees nine facilities: Carteret, a minimum security facility at Newport; Corrituck, a medium and minimum security facility at Maple; Duplin, a minimum security unit at Kenansville used as a youthful offender facility; Gates, a facility for adult misdemeanants located at Gatesville; Goldsboro Youth Center, a minimum security facility at Goldsboro used as a youthful offender unit; Greene, a minimum security prison located at Maury and serving as the reception center for Eastern Area; Martin, a minimum security facility at Williamston; Pender, a minimum security unit at Burgaw; and Washington, a medium security prison located at Creswell.

The offices for the Western Area are located at North Wilkesboro. Eleven prison units are under the jurisdiction of its area administrator: Alexander, a minimum security unit at Taylorsville; Avery, a medium security facility at Newland; Caldwell, a minimum security unit at Hudson; Craggy, a medium and minimum security facility at Ashville; Haywood Subsidiary, a minimum security unit at Hazelwood; Henderson, a minimum security unit at Hendersonville; McDowell, a minimum security unit at Marion; Rutherford, a minimum security unit at Forest City; Watauga, a minimum security facility at Boone serving as reception center for Western Area; Wilkes, a minimum security facility at Wilkesboro; and Yancey, a medium security prison at Burnsville.

Offices for the North Central Area are located in Raleigh. The area administrator oversees thirteen facilities: Durham, a minimum security unit at Durham; Franklin, a minimum security unit at Bunn serving as the reception center for North Central Area; Granville, a minimum security unit at Oxford; Johnston Youth Center at Smithfield, a youthful offender unit; Nash Advancement Center, a pre-release facility at Nashville; Orange, a medium security unit at Hillsborough; Person, a minimum security unit at Roxboro; Sanford Advancement Center, a pre-release center at Sanford; Triangle Correctional Center, a minimum security prison in Raleigh; Umstead Youth Center, a minimum security youthful offender prison at Butner; Vance, a minimum security unit at Henderson; Wake Advancement Center, a pre-release facility in Raleigh; and Warren, a medium security facility at Warrenton, which used to hold escapees and detainees in the North Central Area.

Offices for the South Central Area are located at Fayettesville. Its area administrator oversees eleven prisons: Anson, a minimum security unit at Wadesboro; Bladen, a minimum security unit at Elizabethtown; Columbus, a medium security unit at Brunswick; McCain Correctional Center at McCain, serving as reception center for the South Central Area and as a prison hospital for tubercular and other patients; Montgomery, a youthful offender unit located at Troy; Moore, a medium security facility located at Carthage; New Hanover, a minimum security unit at Wilmington; Richmond Advancement Center, a pre-release facility located at Rockingham; Robeson, a medium and minimum security facility at Luberton; Sampson, a medium security facility at Clinton; and Scotland at Wagram, a holding facility for escapees and detainees from the South Central and North Piedmont areas.

Offices for the North Piedmont Area are located in Greensboro. The area administrator oversees eleven prisons: Alamance, a minimum security prison located at Graham; Caswell, a medium security facility at Yanceyville; Davidson, a minimum security facility at Lexington; Davie, a minimum security facility at Mocksville; Forsyth, a minimum security unit at Winston-Salem, serving as a pre-release center; Guilford I at High Point, another pre-release center; Guilford II at McLeansville, the reception center for the North Piedmont Area; Randolph, a medium security unit at Asheboro; Rockingham, a medium security prison at Reidsville; Stokes, a minimum security unit at Walnut Cove; and Yadkin, a medium security unit at Yadkinville.

Offices for the institutions in the South Piedmont Area are located at Huntersville. The eleven institutions are as follows: Cabarrus, a minimum security unit located at Mt. Pleasant; Catawba, a minimum security prison at Newton; Cleveland, a medium security prison at Shelby; Gaston at Dallas, serving as a youthful offender unit; Iredell, a medium security facility at Statesville; Lincoln, a medium security prison at Lincolnton; Mecklenburg I, Advancement Center, a minimum security facility at Charlotte; Mecklenburg II at Huntersville, a minimum security unit serving as the reception center for the South Piedmont Area; Rowan, a minimum security facility at Salisbury; Stanly, a medium security unit at Albermarle; and Union at Monroe, a medium and minimum security unit.

Offenders under the age of eighteen who are adjudicated delinquent by the court are committed to the Department of Human Resources' Division of Youth Services. The Division of Youth Services oversees the operation of seven co-educational institutions: the Richard T. Fountain Reception and Diagnostic Center at Rocky Mount, opened in 1926 with a normal capacity of 125 and serving as reception center for juvenile delinquents; the C. A. Dillon School at Butner, 1968, 110; Dobbs School at Kinston, 1944, 150 (it houses younger children up to age fourteen); the Juvenile Evaluation Center at Swannanoa, 1961, 270; the Cameron Morrison School at Hoffman, 1925, 290;

Samarkand Manor at Eagle Springs, 1918, 240; and the Stonewall Jackson School at Concord, 1909, 240.

The North Carolina correctional system held 13,261 inmates on January 1,1977. By January 1, 1978, the system had experienced a 7 percent increase in population to 14,189.

REFERENCES: American Correctional Association, *Directory*, 1975–1976 edition; Michael Serrill, "Prison Population Rises Again, But at a Slower Rate," *Corrections Magazine*, 1978.

NORTH DAKOTA CORRECTIONAL SYSTEM. North Dakota experienced a 19 percent increase (from 173 to 205) in its prison population during calendar year 1975. Even so, its institutions are not overcrowded. The director of institutions operates the state's one juvenile institution and two adult facilities: the North Dakota Industrial School at Mandan, opened in 1903 with a normal capacity of 160 male and female juvenile delinquents ages twelve to twenty-one; the North Dakota Penitentiary at Bismarck, opened in 1885 with a normal capacity of 360 felons (it holds mostly male offenders, but has a wing for females); and the North Dakota State Farm, opened in 1943 with space for forty felons and first offenders either male or female.

Only New Hampshire has fewer inmates in its system, but the prison population in North Dakota is growing. It reached 273 on January 1, 1978.

REFERENCES: American Correctional Association, *Directory*, 1975–1976 edition; Steve Gettinger, "U.S. Prison Population Hits All-Time High," *Corrections Magazine*, 1976; Michael Serrill, "Prison Population Rises Again, But at a Slower Rate," *Corrections Magazine*, 1978.

O

OFFENDER AID AND RESTORATION (OAR). OAR is a nonprofit organization formed in Virginia during the early part of the 1970s to recruit, train, and supervise the activities of volunteers who work with young adult offenders sixteen to twenty-one years of age. The group has chapters in various Virginia communities working with youth in county jails, but its major impact appears to have resulted from the efforts of its New York City chapter where 450 volunteers are working with inmates under the supervision of sixteen full-time staff members. The New York City chapter was formed by Kenneth Jackson, founder of the Fortune Society, a New York City-based prison reform group, and put its first group of volunteers to work in 1974. The volunteers undergo a six-week training period and agree to spend at least one evening per week with the one prisoner they are assigned to work with. Each volunteer is initially assigned to a young prisoner who is in jail awaiting trial. The volunteer works with the assigned offender for a full year whether the offender remains in jail, is released, or is sent to a state prison. The ultimate objective of the volunteers is to get youths out of jail and to keep them out.

Volunteers make weekly visits to jails, spending two hours with their client. Some young offenders simply need a friend to talk with for this period of time, but many ask, and receive, assistance in processing their cases. Volunteers contact the offender's lawyer, help to locate witnesses, or aid in investigating the offender's case. In some instances, the volunteers are able to get bail amounts reduced to an amount that OAR staff members can raise (about $250). The volunteers appear at court hearings and make it known to the judge that they are working with the prisoner. If the youth is released from jail, the volunteer provides assistance by helping him to find a job, get into school, or enter some type of community treatment program. In cases where the offender is sent to prison, the volunteer is expected to correspond regularly with the youth and to visit if possible.

OAR staff members report that only three youths out of 600 are known to have returned to jail after receiving the service of a volunteer. This success is attributed to the volunteer training program and efforts to recruit minority group members who have backgrounds similar to those of the offenders.

REFERENCE: Steve Gettinger, "Close-up/OAR," *Corrections Magazine,* 1976.

OHIO CORRECTIONAL SYSTEM. The Department of Rehabilitation and Correction operates the eight adult institutions and their subsidiaries in Ohio and is also responsible for adult parole services. The Ohio Youth Commission oversees juvenile institutions and parole services.

The Ohio State Reformatory at Mansfield was opened in 1896 with a normal capacity of 1,800 male felons who are first offenders. Under Ohio law, male felons between the ages of eighteen and twenty-one years must be sentenced to a reformatory (rather than a penitentiary) if they are first offenders. First offenders between the ages of twenty-one and thirty years may be sentenced to a reformatory. Felons of any age are sentenced to a penitentiary if they are convicted of first or second degree murder. The State Reformatory population is normally somewhat above the rated capacity of the institution because the population count includes several hundred inmates in its subsidiaries: (1) the Osborn Honor Farm; (2) the Grafton State Farm; and (3) the Mt. Vernon Honor Camp.

The Lebanon Correctional Institution at Lebanon was opened in 1959 with a normal capacity of 1,400 male felons who are transfers from the Reformatory. The Marion Correctional Institution at Marion was opened in 1955 with a normal capacity of 1,400 male felons twenty-one years of age and above. The London Correctional Institution at London was opened in 1925 with a rated capacity of 1,800 male felons twenty-one years of age and over. All women sentenced to serve sentences for felony convictions are sent to the Ohio Reformatory for Women at Marysville; the Marysville facility was opened in 1916 with a normal capacity of 2,500 felons. The Chillicothe Correctional Institute at Chillicothe opened in 1966 with a normal capacity of 1,200 male felons; the institution was formerly a U.S. reformatory. It has a subsidiary, the Hocking Honor Camp at Logan. The Southern Ohio Correctional Facility at Lucasville was opened in 1972 with a normal capacity of 1,600 male felons.

Two institutions operated by the Division of Forensic Psychiatry, Department of Mental Health and Mental Retardation, house offenders over eighteen years of age who are found incompetent to stand trial, "not guilty" by reason of insanity, or mentally ill or mentally retarded prior to sentencing. They are the Lima State Hospital at Lima, opened in 1915 with a normal capacity of 500 (both male and female); and the Junction City Treatment Center at Junction City, opened in 1968 with a normal capacity of ninety.

The Ohio Youth Commission receives youths between the ages of twelve and seventeen who have been adjudicated delinquent by county juvenile courts. The commission operates eleven facilities for these juveniles: (1) the Buckeye Youth Center, at Columbus, a co-educational facility which opened in 1914 as a diagnostic center and became a treatment center in 1973 with a normal capacity of 200 youths ages fifteen to seventeen; (2) the Child Study Center in Columbus, which opened in 1914 as part of the Buckeye Youth Center and became a diagnostic center in 1974 with a normal capacity of 100 juveniles ages ten to seventeen (males) and twelve to seventeen (females); (3) the Cuyahoga Hills Boys School at Warrensville, opened in 1969 with a normal capacity of 200 boys ages fourteen to sixteen; (4) the Fairfield School for Boys at Lancaster (formerly known as the Boys' Industrial School), opened in 1858 with a normal capacity of 650 boys ages fifteen to seventeen; (5) the Indian River School at Massilcon, opened in 1973 with a normal capacity of 184 male delinquents ages sixteen to seventeen; (6) the Maumee Youth Camp at Liberty Center, opened in 1966 with a normal capacity of 120 males ages twelve to fourteen; (7) the Mohican Youth Camp at Loudonville, opened in 1959 with a normal capacity of 120 boys ages fourteen to sixteen; (8) the Riverview School for Girls at Powell, opened in 1968 with a normal capacity of 152 delinquent girls ages fifteen to seventeen; (9) Scioto Village (formerly known as the Girls' Industrial School), opened in 1869 with a normal capacity of 200 girls ages twelve to seventeen; (10) the Training Center for Youth at Columbus, opened in 1963 with a normal capacity of 113 males ages twelve to seventeen; and (11) the Training Institute in Columbus, opened in 1961 with a normal capacity of 192 males ages sixteen to seventeen.

Ohio experienced significant increases in the size of its prison population in the mid-1970s. Its prison population grew from 9,326 on January 1, 1975, to 11,451 on January 1, 1976—a 23 percent increase in a state with a relatively large prison system and facilities operating near normal capacity before the increase. Subsequent increases have been on a smaller scale with a modest 2 percent increase between January 1, 1977, and January 1, 1978, from 12, 626 to 12,846.

REFERENCES: American Correctional Association, *Directory,* 1975–1976 edition; Steve Gettinger, "U.S. Prison Population Hits

All-Time High," *Corrections Magazine,* 1976; Michael Serrill, "Prison Population Rises Again, But at a Slower Rate," *Corrections Magazine,* 1978.

OKLAHOMA CORRECTIONAL SYSTEM. Adult offenders in Oklahoma are the responsibility of the Department of Corrections, which is divided into the Division of Institutions and the Division of Community Services. The Division of Institutions' Social and Rehabilitative Services receives juvenile offenders.

Oklahoma's adult prison system experienced a riot in 1973 that resulted in major damage to its main prison; the state's correctional system will be recovering from the event for many years. On July 27, 1973, the inmates of the Oklahoma State Penitentiary at McAlester staged a riot that lasted for eleven days and virtually destroyed the institution erected in 1908. While the riot in Attica Correctional Facility (*q.v.*) in 1971 was the bloodiest prison uprising in American history, the 1973 riot at McAlester is thought to be America's most expensive prison riot to date. David Hall, governor of Oklahoma at the time of the riot, requested $30 million in federal aid to rebuild the prison, and the request was referred to the National Clearinghouse for Criminal Justice Planning and Architecture (*q.v.*). Clearinghouse Director Frederick Moyer would not approve federal funding for restoration of the prison to its original fortress-style condition. Moyer, viewing the disaster as an opportunity for Oklahoma to restructure its entire correctional system, insisted that any federal funding be given only in conjunction with a comprehensive master plan to reform all of the state's correctional system. Oklahoma officials initially rejected Moyer's advice and spent several million dollars of the state government's funds to rebuild parts of the McAlester institution.

The clearinghouse staff nevertheless continued to work with Oklahoma officials, and, in 1975, a master plan for reform of the state system evolved. The clearinghouse approved a $600,000 grant to help rebuild the McAlester facility as part of the master plan. The master plan incorporates the clearinghouse philosophy of utilizing smaller institutions in conjunction with expanded use of probation and parole and the establishment of community treatment centers (*q.v.*). Thus, the 1973 McAlester riot has resulted in a prison reform movement in Oklahoma that will be implemented with the help of more than $5 million in federal funds. The renovation of the McAlester prison as part of the master plan has reduced its normal capacity of 2,000 to 516 male felons. McAlester's Trusty Installation, opened in 1974, has space for 300 males, and its Women's Ward, opened in 1971, has a normal capacity of fifty female felons.

Other penal institutions, with their opening dates and normal capacities, are as follows: the Oklahoma State Reformatory at Granite, 1909, 500 male felons; the Women's Treatment Facility in Oklahoma City, 1973, seventy; the Vocational Training School at Stringtown, 1955, 400 male felons; the Lexington Regional Treatment Center at Lexington, 1971, 400 male felons; the McLeod Honor Farm at Farris, 1961, 400 male felons; and the Ouachita Vocational Training Center at Hodgens, 1970, 100 male felons.

The Division of Community Services, under the Department of Corrections, provides probation and parole services for adult offenders in the state and oversees the operation of five community-based treatment centers: the Enid Community Treatment Center, opened in 1974 with a normal capacity of thirty-five male felons; the Lawton Community Treatment Center, opened in 1973 with a normal capacity of forty-three male felons; the Muskogee Community Treatment Center, opened in 1974 with a normal capacity of thirty-five male felons; the Oklahoma City Community Treatment Center, opened in 1970 with a normal capacity of 100 male felons; and the Tulsa Community Treatment Center, opened in 1973 with a normal capacity of fifty male felons.

On January 1, 1975, the total prison population in Oklahoma stood at 2,867. One year later, it had increased to 3,435, or by 20 percent. This increase in prison population continued throughout 1976, so the population was 4,106 on January 1, 1977. However, it decreased slightly in 1977 to 4,006 on January 1, 1978. Oklahoma is one of relatively few states to experience a decrease in prison population in 1977. (Others were Arizona, California, Connecticut, Nebraska, New Hampshire, Utah, West Virginia, and Wisconsin.)

REFERENCES: American Correctional Association, *Directory,* 1975–1976 edition; Steve Gettinger, "U.S. Prison Population Hits All-Time High," *Corrections Magazine,* 1976; Michael S. Serrill, "LEAA's National Clearinghouse for Criminal Justice Planning and Architecture," *Corrections Magazine,* 1976; Michael Serrill, "Prison Population Rises Again, But at a Slower Rate," *Corrections Magazine,* 1978.

OMBUDSMEN IN PRISON. The office of ombudsman, which originated in Sweden more than 167 years ago and soon spread to other parts of the world, is responsible for seeing that government authority is not abused. This task is accomplished by giving the ombudsman independent powers of investigation and censure.

Prison ombudsmen, sometimes known as "conflict mediators," are recent arrivals on the American corrections scene. In 1971, David Fogel (*q.v.*), then corrections commissioner for Minnesota, suggested a prison ombudsman for the state corrections system. As a result of his suggestion, the first such office was established in the United States by an executive order of Governor Wendell Anderson in February 1972. Theartrice Williams was recruited to fill the post and, for a time, became the nation's senior prison ombudsman.

Early experiences with prison ombudsmen efforts indicate that success requires that the persons filling the role win the confidence of both prison staff and inmates. Inmate confidence is extremely difficult to gain if the ombudsman is employed by the correctional system itself. On the other hand, if the conflict mediator is an outsider, then staff confidence becomes elusive. Overall, the early ombudsmen programs confirm the view of experts who believe that ombudsmen must be independent of the bureaucracy that they oversee. Most of the first fourteen states which established ombudsmen programs in the early 1970s failed to establish the degree of ombudsmen independence that authorities thought necessary. Notable exceptions were Minnesota and Connecticut where the ombudsmen were independent of the corrections commissioner from the beginning of the programs. In Minnesota, the office is independent of supervision by the corrections commissioner, but it is a state office responsible to the governor. In Connecticut, the ombudsman works under the aegis of a private agency, the Hartford Institute of Criminal Justice. Michigan and Kansas followed the same pattern. States that located their prison ombudsmen within their own correctional system, and thus reduced their independence, included New Jersey, South Carolina, Kentucky, Ohio, and New York's Division for Youth. Some states follow the European practice of using ombudsmen to deal with all government functions. In these states, which include Hawaii, North Carolina, Iowa, Nebraska, and Oregon, prison complaints are only one facet of the ombudsman's responsibilities.

Use of the correctional ombudsmen approach to deal with inmate complaints has received impetus from several sources. Without an effective grievance mechanism, the inmate often takes his complaint directly to the courts. Judges who become overburdened with such cases may urge other solutions, including the use of ombudsmen, to the problems. Correctional administrators find that appearing before the courts to answer inmate charges is time consuming; furthermore, administrators fear that they will lose some of their administrative discretion if the Court defines acceptable prison practices or if prisoners' unions (*q.v.*) become powerful enough to dictate operating policies.

The practice of making ombudsmen independent of the correctional bureaucracy gives the office credibility with inmates, as has been demonstrated in Connecticut and Minnesota. The ombudsman's more difficult task—achieving credibility with correctional workers—can be effected by building a reputation for fairness and impartiality. For related information, see GRIEVANCE PROCEDURES FOR INMATES.

REFERENCES: J. E. Baker, *The Right to Participate: Inmate Involvement in Prison Administration*, 1974; Timothy L. Fitzharris, *The Desirability of a Correctional Ombudsman*, 1973; Edgar May, "Prison Ombudsmen in America," *Corrections Magazine*, 1975; Linda R. Singer and J. Michael Keating, *Grievance Mechanisms in American Corrections: The State of the Art*, 1975; U.S. National Advisory Commission on Criminal Justice Standards and Goals, *Corrections*, 1973.

OREGON CORRECTIONAL SYSTEM. Oregon's Corrections Division, under the Department of Human Resources, oversees adult prisons and work release (*q.v.*)/education release centers, and provides probation and parole services for adult offenders. Juvenile institutions are the responsibility of the department's Children's Services Bureau.

Persons eighteen years of age or older who are convicted of a felony, and juveniles sixteen to seventeen years of age who are remanded to juvenile courts, become the responsibility of the Corrections Division. Offenders committed to the division serve an indeterminate sentence (*q.v.*) and are eligible for parole or participation in a work release program at any time after being committed, regardless of the nature of their offense.

Oregon's main prison is Oregon State Penitentiary which was originally opened in Portland in 1853 but was transferred to Salem in 1866. It has a normal capacity of 1,254; additional space is provided in an annex holding 200 and in a forest camp holding sixty-five. The facility holds males sixteen years of age and above. Other adult institutions are the Oregon State Correctional Institution at Salem, which opened in 1959 with a normal capacity of 476 male felons who are first offenders, and the Oregon Women's Correctional Center at Salem, which opened in 1965 as part of the Oregon State Penitentiary but became a separate facility in 1971 with a normal capacity of seventy-six female felons sixteen years of age and over.

Community corrections efforts in Oregon are manifested in the operation of a series of work release/education release centers at various locations around the state: (1) Milwaukie Work Release Center; (2) Portland Women's Community Treatment Center; (3) Portland Men's Center; (4) the Albany-Corvallis Center at Corvallis; (5) Eleventh Avenue Center at Eugene; (6) Lincoln Street Center at Eugene; (7) Alder Street Center at Eugene; and (8) Bay Area Community Center at North Bend.

Juveniles between the ages of twelve and eighteen are committed to the Children's Services Bureau for an indeterminate period of time; jurisdiction may continue to age twenty-one. The juvenile facilities are MacLaren School, opened at Woodburn in 1891 with a normal capacity of 365 youths ages twelve to eighteen; and Hillcrest School of Oregon at Salem, opened in 1913 with a normal capacity of 150 youths ages twelve to eighteen. The Children's Services Bureau also operates two camps, each of which holds twenty-five male releasees from MacLaren and Hillcrest: Florence Work Study Camp and Tillamook.

Oregon experienced a 22 percent increase in its total prison population between January 1, 1975, and January 1, 1976, the figures increasing from 2,001 to 2,442. Later increases have been more moderate with a mere 3 percent increase between January 1, 1977, and January 1, 1978, from 2,848 to 2,924.

REFERENCES: American Correctional Association, *Directory, 1975–1976* edition; Steve Gettinger, "U.S. Prison Population Hits All-Time High," *Corrections Magazine,* 1976; Michael Serrill, "Prison Population Rises Again, But at a Slower Rate," *Corrections Magazine,* 1978.

P

PAROLE CONTRACTS. Parole contracts are written, legally enforceable contracts involving inmates, prisons, and parole authorities. If the inmate fulfills the conditions of the contract, the paroling authority grants parole on the date specified in the contract. Provisions of the contract ordinarily establish goals for the inmate in measurable terms. Typically the goals are defined in terms of desired accomplishments in the areas of academic education, vocational training, participation in therapy programs such as Alcoholics Anonymous, and standards of institutional behavior. The inmate's institution is a party to the contract in that it agrees to make services available in order for the inmate to be able to complete the requirements on schedule. The parole authority agrees to grant parole, without additional evaluation of the inmate's suitability for release, if and when the inmate fulfills the conditions of the contract.

Much of the credit for the concept of parole contracts belongs to Leon Leiberg, a former probation officer skilled in developing alternatives to incarceration. The concept has been promoted through the efforts of the Parole-Corrections Project of the American Correctional Association under the acronym of MAP (Mutual Agreement Programming). Florida, Georgia, Maine, Maryland, Massachusetts, Michigan, Minnesota, North Carolina, Wisconsin, and the District of Columbia presently use parole contracts; Delaware, New Jersey, and South Carolina plan to start similar programs. For additional information, see MUTUAL AGREEMENT PROGRAM.

REFERENCES: American Correctional Association, *An Evaluative Summary of Research: MAP Program Outcomes in the Initial Demonstration States,* 1975; Robin Eptein and others, *The Legal Aspects of Contract Parole,* 1976; Steve Gettinger, "Parole Contracts: A New Way Out," *Corrections Magazine,* 1975.

PENNSYLVANIA CORRECTIONAL SYSTEM. Adult corrections in Pennsylvania are administered under the state's Department of Justice. The commissioner of the state's Bureau of Correction oversees the operation of adult institutions and reports to the attorney general, as does the chairman of the Board of Probation and Parole. Juvenile institutions are operated under the aegis of the Department of Public Welfare's Office of Children and Youth.

The Bureau of Correction cares for some 7,000 offenders, 95 percent of whom are incarcerated in seven state prisons and one regional facility. The state's prison system is of great historical interest to penologists. In 1829, Pennsylvania built the first fortress-style prison in the United States, in Philadelphia, at the urging of the Philadelphia Society for Alleviating the Miseries of Public Prisons (the name of this organization was changed to the Pennsylvania Prison Society in 1887) to establish the Pennsylvania Solitary System of imprisonment. This orginal prison, Eastern Penitentiary (*q.v.*), continued as a prison until 1970 and was used by the city as a jail for another year after it was abandoned as a state prison. Western State Penitentiary at Pittsburgh was the state's second penitentiary. The site of the original Western Penitentiary is now the State Correctional Institution and Correctional Diagnostic and Classification Center. The original buildings at Western Penitentiary (1826) are no longer standing, but some buildings in the complex date back to 1876. This facility has a normal capacity of 1,048 male felons.

The State Correctional Institution and Correctional Diagnostic and Classification Center at Graterford (near Philadelphia) is the state's largest prison with a normal capacity of 2,067 male felons. It was opened in 1928 as a branch of Eastern Penitentiary and in 1954 in its present capacity. The State Correctional Institution at Camp Hill was opened in 1941 with a rated capacity of 1,325. The Camp Hill facility, unlike other prisons administered by the Bureau of Correction, holds juveniles as well as adult offenders. Under Pennsylvania law, offenders under eighteen years of age can be tried in adult courts if their offense is serious. Whether an offender is committed to the adult system or the juvenile system depends not on age but on the court where the offender is tried. Thus, boys as young as fifteen are committed to Camp Hill, while older boys who commit less serious crimes are sent to juvenile institutions by the juvenile court. The Camp Hill inmate population is in the age range of fifteen to twenty-one.

The state's female offenders are sent to the State Correctional Institution at Muncy, which opened in 1920 with a normal capacity of 360 and holds females ages sixteen and above. The State Correctional Institution and Correctional Diagnostic and Classification Center at Dallas opened in 1960 with a normal capacity of 952 male felons. The State Correctional Institution and Correctional Diagnostic and

Classification Center at Huntingdon, with space for 1,094 male felons, is an old facility that has been used for several purposes over the years. It opened in 1889 as an industrial school, was converted to an institution for defective delinquents in 1945, and began serving in its present capacity in 1960. The State Correctional Institution and Correctional Diagnostic and Classification Center at Rockview, with a normal capacity of 988 male felons, opened in 1912 as a branch of Western Penitentiary and was converted to its present use in 1954. The Regional Correctional Facility at Greensburg opened as a county prison in 1966 but was converted to its present use in 1969; it has a normal capacity of 126 male felons.

In 1975, Pennsylvania's Governor Shapp appointed Jerome Miller commissioner of the Department of Public Welfare's Office of Children and Youth. Miller's move to Pennsylvania from the Illinois correctional system is generally interpreted by penologists to mean that Pennsylvania is considering deinstitutionalization (*q.v.*) of its juvenile system. Penologists have followed Miller's career with interest since he closed down all of the juvenile institutions in Massachusetts in the early 1970s. Miller has indeed expressed a desire to shut down a number of Pennsylvania's juvenile prisons, but the task will require a great deal of planning since the state has more than 2,000 juvenile inmates in nine institutions owned by the state and in eight privately owned facilities operated with public funding.

Pennsylvania's juvenile facilities include the Youth Development Center at Cornwells Heights, opened in 1968 with a normal capacity of 136 delinquent males ages twelve to eighteen; the Youth Development Center at Loysville, opened in 1963 with a normal capacity of 130 delinquent males ages twelve to eighteen; the Youth Development Center at New Castle, opened in 1968 with a normal capacity of 250 delinquent males ages fifteen to eighteen; the Youth Development Center Complex in Philadelphia, opened in 1965 for sixteen to nineteen year olds, with space for 100 in its residential program and for an additional 200 in a day treatment program; the Youth Development Center at Warrendale, opened in 1962 with a normal capacity of 130 male delinquents ages twelve to fifteen; and the Youth Development Center at Waynesburg, opened in 1960 and replaced in 1969 with a facility having a normal capacity of 144 female delinquents ages twelve to eighteen.

The Bureau of Youth Services also operates three forestry camps for male delinquents ages fifteen through eighteen: Youth Forestry Camp No. 1 at Hookstown, Youth Forestry Camp No. 2 at White Haven, and Youth Forestry Camp No. 3 at James Creek. The capacity of each of the three camps is fifty-two.

The city government's prison system is larger than that of many states. The Philadelphia superintendent of prisons works for the Philadelphia Department of Public Welfare and oversees the operation of three prisons: the House of Correction, opened in 1874 but rebuilt in 1928, holding both males and females in facilities with a normal capacity of 710; the Holmesburg Prison, opened in 1896 with a rated capacity of 720 males; and the Detention Center, opened as Moyamensing Prison in 1835 but replaced in 1963, with a normal capacity of 792 males being held for trial.

The prison population in Pennsylvania is fairly stable with 7,584 inmates on January 1, 1977, and 7,600 on January 1, 1978.

For related material, see EASTERN PENITENTIARY and PENNSYLVANIA SYSTEM OF PRISON DISCIPLINE.

REFERENCES: American Correctional Association, *Directory, 1975–1976 edition;* Anthony Astrachan, "Profile/Pennsylvania," *Corrections Magazine,* 1975; Michael Serrill, "Prison Population Rises Again, But at a Slower Rate," *Corrections Magazine,* 1978.

PENNSYLVANIA SYSTEM OF PRISON DISCIPLINE. Penal reform was mandated by Pennsylvania's original state constitution adopted in 1776. The constitution clearly states that offenders should serve sentences in houses provided for that purpose and that their punishment should include hard labor designed to benefit the general public or for reparation of injuries done to a private citizen. This philosophy does not seem remarkable to contemporary Americans, but when considered in light of the history of punishment prior to 1776, one realizes that Pennsylvania was officially committing itself to a radical departure from the standard methods of handling offenders.

The experiments that ultimately resulted in the official adoption of the philosophy expressed in the state constitution was begun many years before 1776 by William Penn. In founding Philadelphia, Penn had greatly reduced the number of offenses for which persons could be given the death penalty; he also reduced the number of occasions for administering corporal punishment. These experiments were unique because capital and corporal punishments were standard in England and in the American colonies. In essence, Penn's experiments were designed to substitute incarceration for capital or corporal punishment. Jails had traditionally been used to hold prisoners only until they went to trial and until the sentences of convicted prisoners could be executed. The development of long-term incarceration as punishment was interrupted by Penn's death, whereupon control of the Pennsylvania colony reverted to England and traditional punishments were restored for a time. By 1776, however, the time was ripe for further experimentation with Penn's ideas.

It was 1786 before the Pennsylvania legislature passed a law implementing the correctional ideology incorporated into the state constitution. At that time, a statute was adopted authorizing imprisonment at hard labor for a number of offenses previously punishable by death or corporal punishment. Following passage of the 1786 statute, gangs of fettered prisoners from the Walnut Street Jail could be seen cleaning the streets in Philadelphia. Public indignation, aroused both by the sight of fettered prisoners in the streets and by the disturbances they caused, resulted in the formation of one of the nation's earliest prison reform groups—the Philadelphia Society for Alleviating the Miseries of Public Prisons—in May 1787. Benjamin Franklin and Benjamin Rush were among the more prominent members of the society.

In 1788, the society urged the Pennsylvania legislature to abolish public labor by prisoners and to substitute more solitary or private labor. Benjamin Franklin signed the 1788 message advocating convict labor reforms. Franklin agreed that convict labor could benefit the state, but believed that its potential for transforming the prisoner required that the labor be carried out in a setting of solitude. The legislature responded in 1790 by creating a statute authorizing an additional cell house to be built on the Walnut Street Jail property. The new cell house would provide individual cells for hardened criminals who were serving a term of years for their crimes. A 1789 statute had already abolished public labor and had authorized all Pennsylvania counties to send their long-term prisoners to the Walnut Street Jail if they so desired.

The "penitentiary house" authorized in the 1790 statute was completed in 1791. It contained sixteen individual cells with each cell eight feet long, six feet wide, and eight feet high. An additional six cells, probably built at the same time, were located on the ground floor of one of the workshops occupying the jail yard. Although information on this period of penal history is sparse, it does not appear that the penitentiary house at the Walnut Street Jail was used for any extensive experimentation with the new concept of long-term incarceration since the number of cells available was limited and a relatively large number of prisoners were known to be confined there (45 to 145 per year during the period 1791–1799). The 1789 statute had established a vehicle for centralizing imprisonment by authorizing county jails to send their prisoners to the Walnut Street Jail, but it appears that county judges used this privilege rather infrequently. It is logical to assume that for many years after its construction the cells in the penitentiary house were used mostly for short-term disciplinary purposes.

The experimentation with long-term incarceration as punishment did not get a real trial until Pennsylvania opened Eastern Penitentiary (*q.v.*) in 1829. The Philadelphia Society for Alleviating the Miseries of Public Prisons (which became the Pennsylvania Prison Society in 1887) eventually claimed credit for originating the system of prison discipline used in Eastern Penitentiary during its early history. The Pennsylvania system of prison discipline is based on the idea that convicts should be separated from one another by confining only one inmate in a cell. The inmate living in total isolation from other inmates as well as from society was expected to do productive work in his cell. Aside from his work, the only pastimes available to the convict were an hour or so in an enclosed exercise yard and the reading of his Bible. "Separation," "long-term confinement," and "cellular labor" were the key elements in the Pennsylvania system of prison discipline. The convict was to be reformed by virtue of spending much time alone with nothing to do but work, read his Bible, meditate on his sins, and do penance.

Despite the society's claims that it originated this approach to penology, there is evidence that the innovation was actually a British import. John Howard, a British prison reformer, made reform recommendations in 1777 which resulted in Parliament's passage of a bill urging the erection of at least one national penitentiary. The bill became law in 1779. No national penitentiaries were built for many years, but Howard's later writings (1789) describe his visit to the Reading county bridewell where he observed convicts being placed in solitary confinement much as Eastern Penitentiary's inmates were following its opening in 1829.

The Philadelphia society nevertheless achieved reforms in Pennsylvania that ultimately resulted in the construction of Eastern Penitentiary and a large-scale venture into testing the reformation ideology of the society. Europeans visited and studied Eastern Penitentiary, and its architecture and approach to reformation of convicts were widely copied by European countries. New York State initially attempted to copy the Pennsylvania Separate System but soon developed its own competing system at its Auburn prison. The Pennsylvania Separate System and the Auburn Silent System became competing approaches to penology in the United States, and their relative merits were debated for decades in the United States. Most states finally chose to copy the Auburn system, while the Pennsylvania system attracted far more adherents in Europe than in America.

The Pennsylvania system of prison discipline is important to modern penologists only because it established long-term incarceration as the standard punishment for serious crime. A summary of its basic elements illustrates the quaintness of its approach today: (1) imprisonment should be unpleasant enough to convince the convict that the way of the transgressor is hard; (2) the convict should be separated from other convicts to keep him from being further corrupted by his confinement; (3) seclusion, combined with religious instruction, is conducive to reformation in that the sinner will come to see the error of his ways; (4) separate confinement provides a means for varying the intensity of punishment and discipline in that the punishment can be intensified by withholding the opportunity to work or read; and (5) the system should be economical because the ability to vary the intensity of punishment will bring about reformation without holding the convict for as many years as would be necessary in a more relaxed prison. For related topics, see AUBURN SILENT SYSTEM and EASTERN PENITENTIARY.

REFERENCES: Harry Elmer Barnes, *The Evolution of Penology in Pennsylvania: A Study in American Social History,* 1968 (1927); Torsten Eriksson, *The Reformers: An Historical Survey of Pioneer Experiments in the Treatment of Criminals,* 1976; Norman Johnston, *The Human Cage: A Brief History of Prison Architecture,* 1973; Andrew T. Scull, *Decarceration: Community Treatment and the Deviant —A Radical View,* 1977; Thorsten Sellin, "The Origin of the 'Pennsylvania System of Prison Discipline,' " *Prison Journal,* 1970.

PLASTIC SURGERY. Only a limited amount of research has been done on the potential for rehabilitating offenders by surgical correction of disfigurements. One three-year long study found that inmates whose disfigurements were corrected had significantly lower recidivism (*q.v.*) rates than disfigured inmates who did not receive the surgery. This study, and the earlier studies that it confirmed, indicate that the technique is especially useful if the disfigurements are on the face.

Cosmetic disfigurements may impair the offender's social or vocational adjustment, even though they do not impair his physical ability. Common cosmetic disfigurements among inmates include needle marks on former narcotics addicts, some types of tattoos, scars, and protruding ears. Some tattoos and scars reduce vocational adjustment prospects because employers associate them with a criminal life. Plastic surgeons also correct functional deformities that impair use of the limbs.

Successful use of plastic surgery for purposes of rehabilitation requires careful planning and cooperation on the part of surgeons and correctional personnel from the behavioral sciences. Some offenders are screened out of such treatment programs on the basis of severe psychosis, the potential for severe psychological disruptiveness during hospitalization, or pathological overemphasis of the potential of the defect to create a handicap. An additional aspect of screening is the obvious decision as to whether the offender's disfigurement can be repaired.

The number of disfigured offenders is fairly large. One study of 450 consecutive commitments to a reception center showed that, excluding those offenders with needle marks from heroin addiction, 47 percent of the inmates had at least one disfigurement. Out of this relatively large number of persons with multiple handicaps, a few will be likely to benefit from surgical repair of one kind of handicap. An offender who is ashamed to go to job interviews because of a scarred face can benefit from plastic surgery, but it is only one part of a rehabilitation program: the offender's academic and vocational skills may also need attention for any significant change in his life-style to occur.

REFERENCE: Richard Kurtzberg and others, "Plastic Surgery in Corrections," *Federal Probation,* 1969.

PLEASANTON YOUTH CENTER. The Federal Youth Center at Pleasanton, California, illustrates the relationship between architecture (*q.v.*) and treatment ideology as elucidated in contemporary correctional thought. As the U.S. Bureau of Prisons expresses it in a descriptive brochure, "This correctional facility [Pleasanton] represents a clear architectural response to the human needs of its inmate population. . . ."

The architectural features of Pleasanton are thought to complement the correctional programming philosophy of the institution. Pleasanton resembles a small, modern college campus (such facilities are often described as open campuses). Open space and freedom of movement are stressed by the architecture, while security and custody are deemphasized. The security measures that do exist, such as motorized patrol around the perimeter of the property, tend to be unobtrusive. Escapes, usually called "walk aways," are easy, but most inmates are deterred from escape by the knowledge that they will likely be captured and placed in a more traditional prison.

Four buildings, each with living space for sixty persons, are arranged around a central core that provides space for recreation, education, and offices. The housing units offer single rooms for inmate privacy and personal space. There are no bars, walls, or fences. The design incorporates an attempt to avoid all appearances of the traditional prison. The pleasing architecture, freedom of movement, and use of color schemes are all intended to influence attitudes and behavior to set the tone for the correctional programming. Both the programming and the architecture attempt to stimulate motivation, learning, and personal responsibility among the residents.

Correctional programming includes academic education through the post-secondary level, vocational training, work release (*q.v.*), social awareness programs, and individual and group therapy.

The Pleasanton facility, which has a normal capacity of 190 male and 60 female felons and misdemeanants, is classified as one of the bureau's four institutions for juvenile and youth offenders. (The others are located at Englewood, Colorado; Ashland, Kentucky; and Morgantown, West Virginia.) These institutions provide minimum security conditions for young people serving short sentences. The age range of inmates eligible for assignment to Pleasanton is eighteen to twenty-five years.

As demonstrated by the Pleasanton facility, the current trend in the Bureau of Prisons' correctional rehabilitation thought is to focus its resources on building better facilities to house young offenders. The best correctional programming and the most architecturally pleasing institutions are given over to the young, first offenders on the assumption that the young are more pliable and are therefore better candidates for rehabilitation. This priority is logical in that young offenders who are not rehabilitated during their incarceration will live longer to commit more offenses as compared with adult offenders. The economic payoff would be greater in terms of cost-benefit analysis if young offenders could be reformed. However, there is little hard evidence to support the assumption that young offenders are more likely to be rehabilitated than older offenders by virtue of being more vulnerable to treatment methodologies. One of the most recent and most comprehensive studies of the effectiveness of correctional treatment programs for young offenders offers virtually no support for the assumption (see MARTINSON, ROBERT M.). It could as easily be argued that the best efforts at rehabilitation should be focused on offenders above the age of forty because they have matured enough to be vulnerable to extant treatment methodologies. Instead, older recidivist offenders are defined as hardened and hopeless, and they are generally denied the benefits of whatever innovations in institutional architecture and correctional programming are available.

Pleasanton's coeducational status illustrates another contemporary trend in correctional ideology. The facility has a normal capacity of 190 males and sixty females. The one-sex society created by imprisonment throughout much of the United States' history of corrections has long been debated as a problem resulting in aggression and homosexuality (*q.v.*) among inmates. Prior to the development of classification (*q.v.*) procedures, men, women, and children were all placed in the same detention areas to mix freely together. Segregation by sex and age was considered an advance in penology that could be attributed to classification and the medical model of corrections (*q.v.*). However, segregation by sex resulted in complete separation and isolation of the sexes. This trend is currently being reversed by institutions like Pleasanton, which provide not only privacy for the sexes but also the opportunity for them to mingle. Corrections officials sometimes object to coeducational prisons on the basis that male and female inmates will find ways to get together for heterosexual activity, but it is not clear why they view this possibility as a threat.

REFERENCE: U.S. Bureau of Prisons, *Breaking with the Past: The Changing View of Correctional Facilities* (no date).

POLITICAL PRISONERS. This term does not have the same meaning in U.S. prisons that it might have in European prisons. European jurisprudence specifies the nature of a political offense and prescribes the method of dealing with the political prisoner (generally less harshly than with ordinary criminals). In countries that do recognize political crimes, a category excluded in the United States, the political offender is a participant in a political uprising in a struggle for political power. The offense that comes closest to this concept in the United States would be the act of treason, which is treated as a crime more reprehensible than murder in American legal philosophy. Otherwise, our legal framework has no mechanism for recognizing political motivations.

The inmates in American prisons who view themselves as political prisoners are serving time for ordinary offenses such as armed robbery, forcible rape, murder, auto theft, burglary, and selling heroin. In describing themselves as political prisoners, they have expanded the meaning of the term to include those persons who are victims of social ills in a society. They believe that they are the products of the slum environment and, as such, are not responsible for their actions. In their view, society has failed to provide them with adequate educational opportunities, decent housing, entry into the job market, and, in general, the ability to compete favorably in the American way of life. They feel that society is in need of rehabilitation, but that they are normal and have no need to be changed.

A more extreme view of the American meaning of political prisoner has been expressed by Howard Moore, the defense attorney for Angela Davis. He defines the concept in racial terms, stating that *all* blacks are political prisoners as a result of the economic and social impact of racial discrimination.

The self-concepts of inmates have undergone change in the past two or three decades. Most treatment approaches now used in American prisons view the offender as a "sick" person in the sense that there is something wrong with either his personality or his socialization that requires him to be cured. Perhaps understandably, inmates reject this view. In the 1950s, inmates adopted a "bad" role as being more acceptable to their self-image than the "sick" role that correctional workers were trying to impose on them. As a part of the criminal subculture in the "bad" role, inmates could gain status in their peer groups and easily rationalize away any guilt feelings. An additional advantage of the "bad" role is that criminals have often been depicted as glamorous people in movies and television productions.

The majority of inmates in the 1970s continue to reject the "sick" role, but a significant number of them have now adopted the "political prisoner" role. It is more acceptable to them than the customary inmate "bad" role or the "sick" role that treatment staff attempt to impose on them. The "political prisoner" role has enormous potential for rationalization. The inmate can easily avoid guilt feelings by blaming social conditions for his own plight, and he can conceive of himself as a victim. Support for this rationalization is readily available from within the prison population and from significant segments of the world outside as well. In the 1960s, outside support was available from the Berkeley free speech movement, the black power movement, the antiwar movement, campus dissidents, and all those who accepted violence as a legitimate form of protest.

Black Muslim inmates first expressed the political prisoner ideology sometime around 1964–1965, and it soon spread to include all races and ethnic groups. White inmates began to identify with ethnic minorities or simply to use a rich versus poor dichotomy in order to think of themselves as a minority group.

The political prisoner role gravely lessens the potential of rehabilitation programs in prisons, for it is almost impossible to change the attitudes of inmates who believe they are victims of a corrupt society. Authorities in the field have not offered many possible solutions to the problem, and it is by no means certain that the few solutions offered will have any impact. One fairly obvious answer is to recruit and train more minority group members for prison staffs. With the large number of minority group representatives in the prison population, it is possible that inmates might consequently identify more with staff values. Such minority staff recruiting is, of course, only a short-run solution. It is easy for inmates to think of themselves as political prisoners because there are indeed inequities in the American social system. A long-term solution requires ending the social problems that provide the basis of the political prisoner rationale.

REFERENCES: Burton M. Atkins and Henry R. Glick, *Prisons, Protest and Politics*, 1972; Stuart A. Brody, "The Political Prisoner Syndrome: Latest Problem of the American Penal System," *Crime and Delinquency*, 1974; James W. L. Park, "What Is a Political Prisoner? The Politics of Predators," *American Journal of Correction*, 1972; Charles E. Reasons, "The Politicizing of Crime, the Criminal and the Criminologist," *Journal of Criminal Law and Criminology*, 1973; Stephen Schafer, *The Political Prisoner: The Problem of Morality and Crime*, 1974; U.S. House of Representatives, Internal Security Committee, *Revolutionary Target: The American Penal System*, 1973.

PRAGMATISTS. Persons or groups interested in prison reform who are working on what they feel to be short-term, practical measures that will make prisons more humane and effective are referred to as pragmatists among penologists. Some pragmatists, like the abolitionists (*q.v.*), favor a large reduction in the size of the prison population. They differ from the abolitionists by concentrating on changes in the correctional system itself rather than changing all of society along with the correctional system. A basic premise of the pragmatists is that prisons are inevitable and that their failure has been the result of a misguided emphasis on attempting to reform inmates. They believe that the attempt to rehabilitate inmates has been a failure and that prisons should be used only to punish persons who commit serious crimes. Justice, they maintain, is to be achieved by assigning roughly the same punishment for anyone convicted of the same crime. They point out that the reform ideology has resulted in the use of parole and the indeterminate sentence (*q.v.*) as abortive attempts to release inmates when rehabilitation has been achieved. The use of parole and indeterminate sentences merely results in inmates convicted of the same crime serving sentences of different lengths and feeling unjustly treated. The solution to this dilemma, many pragmatists believe, is to abolish parole and indeterminate sentences and to use flat sentencing in order to treat everyone uniformly and justly.

Norval Morris in *The Future of Imprisonment* (1974) describes a potential use of prisons which places him in the pragmatist category. Both Tom Wicker, author of *A Time to Die* (1975), and Norman Carlson (*q.v.*), director of the U.S. Bureau of Prisons, share Morris's approach to prison reform. Morris suggests that uniformity of punishment is a desirable goal of corrections and can be achieved by making the seriousness of the crime, rather than the relative danger to society posed by the offender, the key variable in deciding whether to incarcerate a person. He believes that corrections officials are not equipped to make an accurate determination of the offender's propensity for violence. Morris differs from other pragmatists in that he does not propose complete abolition of indeterminate sentences and parole. However, he does recommend setting limits on the discretion of sentencing judges and parole boards to eliminate much of the uncertainty of the length of sentence.

David Fogel (*q.v.*) is one of the most widely known pragmatists. In 1975, Fogel, as executive director of the Illinois Law Enforcement Commission, proposed a scheme that he calls the justice model of corrections (*q.v.*). Flat sentencing is a key element of his proposal. He groups crimes in five categories with a fixed term of years associated with each category. The judge's discretion is limited under the plan, with a provision that judges raise or lower the fixed term by no more than 20 percent because of individual circumstances in a case. According to Fogel, implementation of his plan will not cause an increase in the Illinois prison population because offenders who do not constitute a clear and present danger to the community will be diverted to community-based corrections programs. For a conflicting ideology, see ABOLITIONISTS.

REFERENCES: David Fogel, ". . . *We Are the Living Proof* . . .," *The Justice Model for Corrections,* 1975; Gordon Hawkins, *The Prison: Policy and Practice,* 1976; Norval Morris, *The Future of Imprisonment,* 1974; Thomas O. Murton, *The Dilemma of Prison Reform,* 1976; Michael S. Serrill, "Critics of Corrections Speak Out," *Corrections Magazine,* 1976; Tom Wicker, *A Time to Die,* 1975.

PRINCIPLE OF LESS ELIGIBILITY. This doctrine, formulated by the Utilitarians in the eighteenth century, has been, and remains, thoroughly entrenched in the deliberations of government officials who are responsible for funding prison operations. Even though most contemporary penologists disclaim any belief in its validity, it is not uncommon to hear correctional officers, or even prison wardens, express the sentiments of the doctrine. Like many other laws and doctrines of English origin, it has become part of the American heritage in penology.

Jeremy Bentham, the Utilitarian philosopher, defined the principle in 1791. As a leader in the humanitarian reform movement in England, Bentham was interested in establishing deterrence as the proper basis of the criminal law. Punishment, in his view, was not justified in a civilized society if that punishment was administered in the spirit of retaliation as it had been in countless centuries past. According to the English Utilitarian philosophy, punishment was justified only to the extent that it would deter people from committing crimes, either by impressing upon offenders that the pain associated with punishment offset the utility of the criminal act or, in the case of potential offenders, by serving as an example to offset the temptation to commit a crime. It was in the course of his attempt to give precision to deterrence that Bentham introduced the principle of less eligibility into penology. He promoted the idea that a convict's life should be severe and that the convict's standard of living should be slightly lower than that enjoyed by the poorest citizens who were not in prison. If living standards inside the prisons were not sufficiently harsh, the threat of a prison sentence might not deter the poor (from whom Bentham correctly assumed the bulk of the prison population would be drawn) from committing crimes.

Hermann Mannheim, a British criminologist, made use of Bentham's concept in his in-depth study of English penal reforms in 1938. He coined the phrase "principle of non-superiority" and used it to discuss the social and economic implications of its application to penology. Mannheim believed that the doctrine became thoroughly rooted in public opinion when deterrence as the goal of punishment came to be supplemented by a reformation ideology that provided a rationale for having constructive activities for convicts. In Mannheim's view, public opinion could tolerate providing reformation services for the offender only if it was assured that the offender's condition would not be improved too much in relation to that of the nonoffender. As a contemporary illustration of such logic, many working-class citizens often express resentment of the free college education some inmates receive, and they need to be reassured that inmates are not living in luxury at the expense of taxpayers.

The principle of less eligibility in modern penology has indirect economic consequences for the individual inmate. The typical prison diet provides an excellent example. The poor quality of food served to prisoners is high on nearly every list of inmate grievances leading to the not infrequent prison strikes and disturbances. Yet, most state prison systems till thousands of acres of state-owned farmland where, in addition to cash crops, tons of fresh vegetables, meat, and dairy products are harvested regularly for consumption by the prison community. Given the availability of good food in most prison systems, it is difficult to explain the inferior meals served to inmates without reference to the principle of less eligibility—especially when excellent meals are often provided in separate dining halls for staff members, while inmates are eating meatless meals on the "main line" and buying their sweets at the prison commissary.

Judges can sentence offenders to do hard labor; farms provide such hard labor and have the additional advantage of making the prison economically self-sufficient, thereby relieving the tax burden that would otherwise arise. In practice, however, prison labor both satisfies and disturbs that segment of public opinion that yearns for inmate toil. The working class objects to the use of cheap inmate labor to create goods to compete in the free market on the basis that it would take jobs from "decent" men. This objection is actualized via the collective power yielded by labor unions. Business interests, fearful that competitors can utilize cheap inmate labor to produce a low-cost product that would undercut their price, are quick to side with labor on this issue. The combined forces of labor unions and business interests easily persuade legislators to pass laws preventing prison-made products from competing with the free market goods. Inmates must labor, but the products of their labor can be used only to reduce taxes by making the prison self-supporting or by providing products for other government agencies in a state-use system.

The principle has further economic implications. Prison industry, existing primarily for creating economic self-sufficiency, becomes loosely linked to reformation ideology. Prison administrators, perceiving that progressive prisons should provide vocational training for inmates, begin to regard inmate labor in their automobile license plate plants, broom factories, and textile mills as "training" that prepares inmates for their return to society. Almost invariably, however, the job skills learned in prison industry are obsolete for outside industry.

Yet another consequence of applying the principle of less eligibility arises in the stigma that society attaches to ex-inmates. Stigma creates both economic and social handicaps. Parolees have difficulty finding employers who will hire them to do anything other than the most menial of tasks; more lucrative occupations often require licensing or certification that specifically and systematically excludes ex-offenders. In addition, the ex-convict predictably has difficulty finding a desirable place to live since landlords may require references. Social, church, and civic organizations may all reject ex-inmates, and acquaintances may fear them because of their ex-convict labels. The stigma makes any prison term a life sentence in a practical sense in that ex-inmates remain "less eligible" and "inferior beings" for as long as they live.

The principle of less eligibility has been a force in penology ever since the idea of long-term incarceration as punishment was introduced, and there is no indication that it will ever disappear from our social thought. It is largely an emotional response rather than a logical construction.

REFERENCES: Fry Consulting Group, *Employment Problems of Ex-Offenders,* 1973; Hermann Mannheim, *The Dilemma of Penal Reform,* 1939; J. P. Martin and D. Webster, *The Social Consequences of Conviction,* 1971.

PRISONERS' UNIONS. In 1970, California's Folsom Prison became the site of the first prisoners' union in the United States. Following a series of disturbances and a prisoners' strike that lasted nineteen days, Folsom inmates presented the prison administration with a list of twenty-nine demands. One of the demands specified the right to form a labor union. Ex-inmates and other interested observers outside of the prison supported the move to win collective bargaining and organizing rights for prisoners. The strike resulted in the forming of a California prisoners' union, with locals in fourteen of the state's institutions. As set up in the original constitution, the union organization was to be controlled by members who were not incarcerated, that is, ex-inmates and other interested persons who were not in prison. Inmates participating in forming the union felt that negotiations with prison officials would be virtually impossible if the union officers were under the control of correctional personnel. Incarcerated union members could engage in work stoppages in prison industry to support a strike but could not negotiate with prison staff.

The California prisoners' union was adequately staffed by personnel who were not serving sentences. Part of the plan to assist inmates included the launching of a nationwide prisoners' union movement. California apparently provided leadership for prisoners seeking unions in other states. In 1972, a union was established in New York's Greenhaven Prison; Massachusetts inmates formed the National Prisoners Reform Association (NPRA) (*q.v.*) at Walpole

Prison; and NPRA locals were formed at Framingham, Norfolk, and Concord. In 1973, the North Carolina prisoners' union listed more than 2,000 members in the state's institutions; Michigan inmates claimed union membership in excess of 2,000 in the Jackson and Marquette institutions; and on May 15 of that year, the New England Prison Coalition was formed to consolidate prisoners' union efforts in Vermont, Maine, Rhode Island, Massachusetts, and New Hampshire, a region where prisons are separated by long distances. By 1973, inmate interest in establishing labor unions was evident in some federal prisons as well (e.g., in Leavenworth in Kansas and in the facility in Atlanta, Georgia).

C. Ronald Huff has studied the development of the prisoners' union movement in Ohio. Huff believes that contemporary inmates are more sophisticated politically and are more inclined toward formal organization than earlier when inmate collective behavior was usually expressed in mass escape attempts. He also points out that modern inmates are more prone to consider themselves victims of our social system or "political prisoners" (*q.v.*)—a view that is supported by other scholars in the field. Inmates with this viewpoint emphasize that the prison population consists of disproportionately large numbers of persons from minority groups and the lower socioeconomic class. They believe that they are incarcerated primarily because of their status rather than because of their behavior. Huff believes that the rise of such inmate ideology plays a key role in the movement to form prisoners' unions. Outsiders provide financial and other types of support, but the pressure to organize comes from the inmates.

The goals of prisoners' unions are similar to those of labor unions in that both focus on economic conditions. For example, a typical salary goal of inmates working in prison industry is to receive at least the minimum wage (a goal that has also been suggested in a policy statement of the National Council on Crime and Delinquency [*q.v.*]). Other typical union goals are to correct dangerous working conditions, develop apprenticeship programs, affiliate with outside labor unions, and have access to Workmen's Compensation insurance.

Some correctional administrators have resisted the inmates' efforts to form unions. A standard technique for dealing with inmate leaders who create problems for the prison staff is to transfer them to another institution in the system and perhaps place them in a security unit at the new location. In California and in Ohio, prison administrators have employed this tactic to slow the development of the unions, but it has only limited utility for the administrators. The California prisoners' union, in offering advice to inmates in other states, suggests that such "union busting" strategy can be averted by training a succession of leaders. The reasons for administration opposition vary. In Ohio, a policy memorandum suggests that official recognition of prisoners' unions might cause adverse public opinion that would set off a backlash against other prison programs. More commonly, prison officials oppose unions because of their possible threat to the security and orderly operation of the prison.

Huff, and other writers, note that inmates have always negotiated with penologists on an informal basis. Inmates do have considerable power to disrupt the routine of an institution if they so desire; conversely, they can keep a prison running smoothly. The real issue may be whether bargaining will continue to be informal or whether it will become overt and collective. For a brief account of the rise and fall of one prisoners' union, see NATIONAL PRISONERS REFORM ASSOCIATION.

REFERENCES: J. E. Baker, *The Right to Participate: Inmate Involvement in Prison Administration,* 1974; "Bargaining in Correctional Institutions: Restructuring the Relation Between the Inmate and the Prison Authority," *Yale Law Journal,* 1972; C. Ronald Huff, "Unionization Behind the Walls," *Criminology,* 1974; U.S. National Advisory Commission on Criminal Justice Standards and Goals, *Corrections,* 1973.

PROGRAM FOR THE INVESTIGATION OF CRIMINAL BEHAVIOR. A pioneering study in criminology has been in process since 1961 at St. Elizabeth's Hospital in Washington, D.C., under the auspices of the National Institute of Mental Health. The late Samuel Yochelson, M.D., was director of the massive research effort for more than fifteen years. In 1970, Stanton E. Samenow, a young Ph.D. in psychology, joined Yochelson as clinical research psychologist for the project. Yochelson and Samenow have studied 255 persons charged with every conceivable crime. Samenow estimates that a total of 150,000 to 200,000 hours have been spent in intensive examination of the 255 criminals studied, with as much as 8,000 hours devoted to an individual criminal. During the first few years of the project, the study was limited to patients of St. Elizabeth's Hospital, but it was later expanded to include persons on probation and parole, and even criminals who, although they confessed their crimes to these psychiatric workers, had never been arrested.

Their research began to attract widespread attention in the field in 1976 when they published findings that challenged the traditional concepts of criminal responsibility. The first volume of the findings, *The Criminal Personality: A Profile for Change,* explains the methodology and nature of the project. The first volume identifies fifty-three thinking and action patterns, all of which were present in every one of the 255 criminals studied. Yochelson, a practicing Freudian psychoanalyst before taking the post as director of the program, did not begin to attempt to identify the "thinking and action patterns" of criminals until the fifth year of the project, when his approach to the problem of criminality changed radically. At this time, he decided it would be necessary to abandon the traditional Freudian focus on unconscious forces to explain why criminals turn to crime. Despite his training and preconceptions, Yochelson ultimately rejected the usual deterministic view of man that explains criminality mostly in terms of environmental influences. The abrupt change in methodology came with the realization that the criminals under study were willing to say whatever the researchers believed they wanted to hear to receive sympathy. Both Yochelson and Samenow gradually rejected the Freudian view of impulsive and compulsive behavior and replaced it with the view that criminals are in control of their behavior and commit crimes as a matter of preference and deliberate, knowing choice.

The first volume of the findings of the program has stirred controversy for placing blame squarely on the criminal himself instead of on unconscious drives or environmental conditions. Yochelson began to reassess his work in the program when the criminals he was studying continued to commit serious crimes while being treated and were able to discuss them because of his guarantee of privileged communication. The later focus on the distinctive thinking and behavior patterns of criminals convinced Yochelson and Samenow that the conventional methods of therapy and rehabilitation are ineffective because the popular premise that criminals think and reason as noncriminals do is simply erroneous. Since the thinking patterns of criminals are different, they do not respond to reasoning and to love as noncriminals do. The work has profound implications for American jurisprudence, which holds that a person is not criminally responsible if the conduct is caused by mental disease or defect. Yochelson and Samenow have put aside mental illness as a cause of crime.

Samenow is carrying on the research Yochelson started and is completing the final volume of the findings. Three volumes are planned. The second volume, *The Criminal Personality: The Change Process,* published in May 1977, consists of a detailed presentation of the techniques the researchers developed in order to completely restructure the thinking patterns of criminals and thereby make them into productive noncriminals. The approach used is a phenomenological process in which the criminal participating in therapy reports all of his thinking over the previous twenty-four hour period. The phenomenological reporting becomes raw material for the therapist to use in discovering "errors" in thinking patterns and developing "correctives" that are taught to the criminal. The change agent (the person working with the criminal) remains cold and detached enough to place any blame for failure on the criminal and to make the criminal realize that he must change into a responsible person, or face prison or suicide. The change agent enhances the criminal's guilt feelings instead of relieving them as a traditional therapist might.

The third volume will present new concepts with respect to the drug-using criminal.

REFERENCES: Joseph Borkin, Review of *The Criminal Personality: Volume I* in *Federal Bar Journal,* 1976; Judy Sedgeman, Review of *The Criminal Personality: Volume II* in *Psychotherapy and Social Science Review,* 1977; Samuel Yochelson and Stanton E. Samenow, *The Criminal Personality: Volume I: A Profile for Change,* 1976; Samuel Yochelson and Stanton E. Samenow, *The Criminal Personality: Volume II: The Change Process,* 1977.

PROPERTY OFFENDERS PROGRAM (POP). The Property Offenders Program (POP) is an experimental program of some twenty women property offenders in the Minnesota Corrections Institution for Women at Shakopee. It was started in 1974 in order to make a restitution center available for female offenders.

The state opened the Minnesota Restitution Center for male inmates in 1972 (see RESTITUTION CENTER). It was a pioneering corrections project designed to experiment with the concept of allowing nonviolent property offenders to hold ordinary jobs in the community while living in an institutional setting with minimal custody emphasis. These offenders use part of their earnings to repay the victim a sum of money that they took illegally. When the victim is repaid, the offender is granted parole with its greater degree of personal freedom. Possible advantages of the restitution center concept include a therapeutic effect on the offender due to his awareness of the victim's plight; less resentment on the part of the victim due to the possibility of recovering financial losses; smoother reintegration of the offender into the community because of the minimum security living arrangements and the normal employment; and less hardship for financially dependent members of the offender's family, who can receive a part of the offender's wages.

In order to facilitate the beginnings of a restitution center program for women, staff members of the Minnesota Correctional Institution for Women designated one of their cottages as a special cottage to provide living quarters for the twenty women in the program. It is preferable to have separate living quarters for inmates in such programs because they are subjected to considerable pressure to bring forbidden items such as alcohol into the prison if they live with inmates who cannot leave the institution.

Initial evaluations deem the POP a success. Such programs have not been in operation long enough to determine whether the restitution concept really does have a significant impact on the attitudes of the offender and the victim. It is clear, however, that the minimum security living arrangements and contact with the community make reintegration of the offender into society easier. Also, the cost to taxpayers of keeping an inmate in a restitution center are about $14.50 per day compared to the $16.00 to $25.00 per day cost of keeping an offender in a traditional prison.

REFERENCE: Michael S. Serrill, "The Minnesota Restitution Center," *Corrections Magazine*, 1975.

R

RECIDIVISM. Recidivism refers to the failure of a criminal offender to avoid further problems with the law after having served a prison sentence. Much of the literature on corrections discusses recidivism as the failure of prisons and community-based corrections programs to rehabilitate the offender during the first period of incarceration, as evidenced by subsequent rearrest and conviction for another crime or revocation of parole.

It is difficult to determine exactly how many offenders are reimprisoned after serving a sentence. In the first place, it is costly to trace the people released from prison for a period of years. A second complication is the possibility that excessive checking on their whereabouts may violate the civil rights of offenders released from prison. Even when studies can be conducted with adequate funding and civil rights violations can be avoided, however, researchers disagree as to what to measure. For example, if an ex-inmate is rearrested and returned to prison for a lesser offense, should that failure be counted the same as a return to prison for the same type of offense that originally got the offender convicted? Or should the researcher count the return to prison of a parolee who has his parole revoked for technical volations such as disobeying parole rules (drinking in public or going out of state without permission, for example)? And how long must the ex-inmate remain free of rearrest before the rehabilitation can be considered a success?

The difficulties inherent in studying recidivism rates result in some inaccurate reporting. Daniel Glaser, a professor widely known for his studies of recidivism, observes that journalists have promoted a myth that two-thirds of the people in prison will become recidivists. This overly high projection stems from the practice of examining the files of people in a particular prison to determine how many have a record of prior imprisonment. The technique yields a false impression because people who have served prior sentences tend to receive longer sentences for a second or third offense, and they therefore form an inordinately high proportion of the institution population at any given time. The researcher choosing to predict future failures on the basis of past performance can obtain more accurate projections by examining the files of people being received or released from a prison for a given period. Even this technique, however, will be inaccurate because past performance is not necessarily an indication of future problems. Glaser's research, completed in the 1950s, revealed that a one-third recidivism rate is closer to reality than the two-thirds rate of popular myth.

A number of more recent studies on recidivism provide further insights into recidivism. In 1974, Irvin Waller published a large study on recidivism research conducted in Canada. He used a representative sample of 423 ex-inmates released from federal penitentiaries in Ontario during 1968. Of these, 213 men were released without supervision at the end of their sentence and 210 received early release on parole. Of the group released without supervision, one-third were rearrested and subsequently convicted of another offense within six months of release; two-thirds of them were rearrested and convicted two years after release. In the two-year period, slightly less than one-half of the men on parole were rearrested and convicted. Length of sentence served did not influence the probability of reconviction following release for either group. Waller's study seems to suggest that parole may delay rearrest.

In 1974, the U.S. Bureau of Prisons released a report on the results of a recidivism study of 1,800 inmates released from federal prisons in 1970. The bureau found that 67 percent were not recidivists during the two-year period following release. (The bureau defined recidivism as either parole revocation or any new sentence of at least sixty days resulting from an arrest reported to the FBI.) This two-thirds success rate is similar to the success rate discovered in Glaser's study of federal prisoners in 1956. In comparing the success rates on the basis of age and race, minority group members were found to have a lower success rate than older inmates. Female offenders had a higher success rate than males.

The Bureau of Prisons compared its study with the earlier study of federal prisoners done by Glaser. They concluded that the composition of the prison population had changed between 1956 and 1970, so that the 1970 population constituted a higher risk group more likely to fail. The percentage of bank robbers, for example, increased from 6 to 20 percent. In addition, there was a 10 percent increase in the proportion of violent offenders. Despite the factors creating a higher risk group in 1970 compared with 1956, the 1970 recidivism rate was no worse. The reason for this improvement is not apparent.

Available studies on recidivism do not permit the projection of a "typical" recidivism rate. However, careful studies generally show that the recidivism rate is lower than the 60 to 70 percent figure frequently publicized.

REFERENCES: Daniel Glaser, *The Effectiveness of a Prison Parole System,* 1969; U.S. Bureau of Prisons, *Success and Failure of Federal Offenders Released in 1970,* 1974; Irvin Waller, *Men Released from Prison,* 1974.

RECTOR, MILTON G. (1919–   ). Rector, the president and chief executive officer of the National Council on Crime and Delinquency (NCCD) since 1972, has profoundly influenced the field of corrections during his distinguished career. The NCCD is one of the largest private organizations dealing with crime (see NATIONAL COUNCIL ON CRIME AND DELINQUENCY). As its chief executive, Rector has worked with the heads of major organizations in labor, business, government, and industry to help them understand crime and what they can do about it.

Almost every one of the NCCD position statements and policies was first conceived by Rector, then debated by the NCCD staff and ultimately adopted by the Board of Directors of NCCD. These policies and position papers have often been controversial when practitioners in the field first received them. The policies have been so well conceived and forward looking, however, that ultimately the controversy dies away and the policies become guidelines for action. In conceiving these policies, Rector has been a leading spokesman for (1) abolishment of capital punishment; (2) compensation of inmate labor at a rate no lower than the minimum wage; (3) removal from the criminal codes of laws making acts with no victim other than the offender illegal; (4) elimination of statutes making drug possession a crime so that the medical profession can be induced to deal systematically with the problem of drug addiction; (5) establishment of a moratorium on the construction of new prisons until alternatives to incarceration have been fully explored; (6) eliminating the use of preventive detention; (7) limiting imprisonment of nondangerous offenders; (8) making comprehensive criminal justice planning a permanent part of state government; (9) guidelines to assure that privacy is protected when electronic eavesdropping is used as a tool of law enforcement; and (10) removal of all restrictions to equal employment of women in criminal justice.

These ten policy positions do not provide a comprehensive listing of the issues currently receiving Rector's attention, but they do provide an idea of the scope and significance of his work. In advocating these NCCD positions, Rector travels extensively across the United States to fill speaking engagements before all types of groups and publishes articles regularly. He authors a weekly nationally syndicated newspaper column "Of Crime and Punishment." On sixteen different occasions between 1961 and 1978, he appeared before various subcommittees of the U.S. Congress to present statements of policy on criminal justice problems.

Rector's influence on policy in the field has extended to the international sphere through his service as Delegate to the United Nations' World Congresses on Prevention of Crime and Treatment of Offenders. He was appointed delegate by Presidents Kennedy, Johnson, and Nixon. He attended Congress Sessions in London (1960), Stockholm (1965), and Kyoto, Japan (1970).

Milton Rector is still active in formulating and promoting rational, human policies for dealing with offenders. His influence in the field will be felt for many decades.

For additional information on some of his policies, see ABOLITIONISTS; MORATORIUM ON PRISON CONSTRUCTION; NATIONAL COUNCIL ON CRIME AND DELINQUENCY (NCCD); and STATUS OFFENDERS.

REEDUCATION OF ATTITUDES AND REPRESSED EMOTIONS (ROARE). This treatment program for sex offenders has been conducted at the Rahway Treatment Unit (RTU) of the New Jersey State Prison for adult males at Rahway since 1969. It was developed for New Jersey by William Prendergast, a clinical psychologist who directs the program.

The purpose of the program is to uncover traumas that sex offenders have experienced in the belief that they are the source of sex crimes. Past sex traumas and other psychological difficulties are dredged from the repressed memories of rapists and child molesters, most of whom were sexually abused when they were children. Prendergast believes that the techniques of the ROARE program constitute a major breakthrough in psychotherapy.

A basic assumption of the treatment mode is the idea of compulsion in the commission of sex crimes. Prendergast's experience in working with sex offenders has suggested that almost none of the offenders know why they have committed their crime. Thus, a logical step in therapy is to find the source of their unconscious urges. A single incident, or sometimes a single series of incidents, in early childhood is thought to be the source of deviant behavior resulting in abnormal sex drives.

ROARE differs from traditional psychotherapy by deliberately attempting to force the sex offender to remember the sex traumas of his past and to relive them as well. This regression process is so vivid that the inmate experiences the unpleasant events all over again. While regression is a standard tool of psychiatry, Prendergast believes that his program approach is unique in inducing such regression without resort to the use of drugs or hypnotism. The technique is a variant of the primal therapy approach of Arthur Janoff, wherein the recall of repressed memories is the heart of the treatment process. To be effective, clients must internalize what they are able to learn about themselves, and Prendergast contends that his techniques better enable clients to do that.

Inmates run the ROARE group therapy sessions in a special room in which all the participants forego the use of any furniture and sit on the carpet. Therapists do not enter the room; instead, they watch the progress of the group on a videotape monitor in another room. The treatment session focuses on a single inmate in an atmosphere of trust and security. The inmate who is the object of the session assumes responsibility for his own treatment by selecting group members he trusts to assist him and by deciding on the frequency of the sessions. He may ask other group members to hasten his regression by badgering him, or he may request that they simply listen as he talks. In this situation which Prendergast calls "comfortably naked," the offender who is the object of the session tells the group more details of his private life than he would ordinarily be able to reveal to a therapist. The environment encourages the discarding of inhibitions to facilitate the regression process.

The inmate who does regress to relive a trauma during a session will usually forget the experience again. The videotape of the session is then shown to him as many times as he feels is necessary until he can remember. Prendergast believes that remembering the repressed traumas is a necessary and vital part of the treatment process. Ralph Brancale, formerly Prendergast's superior, recognizes the value of Prendergast's contribution to the treatment of sex offenders, but cautions that his apparent success does not necessarily indicate that a cure for sex offenses has been discovered. The regression and the ultimate ability to remember repressed traumas provide insight for the patient—which is not per se a cure for sexual deviance. To be fully recovered, a patient must reintegrate himself successfully toward reality at the conscious level. There is always a danger that the client will revert to previous behavior patterns, given certain kinds of situations.

New Jersey, along with Massachusetts, Washington, and Wisconsin, is among the few states that offer special treatment programs for sex offenders. All men convicted of a sex crime in New Jersey, under the provisions of a 1947 Sex Offender Act, must submit to psychiatric examination before sentencing. They are sentenced to an indeterminate period of confinement not to exceed the maximum sentence for their crime if they are found to be "compulsive, repetitive" sex offenders. They are treated as mental patients. Almost 200 inmates have participated in ROARE since its inception in 1969; sixty of these have been paroled, only three of whom have committed new crimes and have been returned to prison.

REFERENCE: Michael S. Serrill, "Treating Sex Offenders in New Jersey," *Corrections Magazine,* 1974.

RESTITUTION CENTER. Restitution centers are small residential facilities which house convicted felons who work at jobs in the outside community and return to the center after working hours. Their earnings are budgeted to allow them to pay for their room and board, to pay their incidental expenses associated with their jobs, to contribute toward support of their dependents, and to repay their victims. This last-named use distinguishes restitution centers from similar facilities known as work release (*q.v.*) centers. The center residents, almost always property offenders who have no record of violent crimes, sign contracts agreeing to repay their victims a specified amount of money from their own earnings. In return for fulfilling their part of the contract, inmates are allowed to live in the less restrictive setting of the restitution center rather than a traditional prison. More significantly, the state contracts with the inmate to release him or her when the victim has been repaid.

Restitution programs claim several advantages over traditional incarceration. The offender gets the therapeutic value available from working at a job in the community as well as on-the-job association with persons who are not criminals. Community friendships and contacts are maintained in the work setting. The offender's ability to support himself and his dependents and to pay taxes results in an improved self-image that may have long-term psychological benefits. The programs express concern for the plight of the victim; victims, often in dire financial need themselves, take a more positive outlook toward the criminal justice system and towards the offenders. An additional advantage is highly theoretical at this point but may prove to be a valuable contribution to corrections: criminologists and penologists alike have long expressed the belief that restitution has an educational and therapeutic impact on the offender by making him vividly aware of the damage done by his crime. Restitution allows the offender to redress his crime. The more complete the restitution, the more complete the offender's sense of responsibility and accomplishment. Social reformers, penologists, and criminologists have discussed the possiblity of incorporating restitution into the correctional process for decades, but only very recently has a viable mechanism for using restitution been discovered.

The pioneering effort in establishing restitution centers was made in Minnesota in 1972 in Hennepin County (Minneapolis). The federal Law Enforcement Assistance Administration (LEAA) (*q.v.*), which provided most of the funding for the innovative project, was so impressed with the results that it has provided federal funding to open four restitution centers in Georgia (in Albany, Atlanta, Macon, and Rome) and one in Des Moines, Iowa. The concept is rapidly gaining in popularity. Other centers will be funded by LEAA in a number of states.

The concept of restitution centers was developed in 1972 by Joe Hudson and Burt Galaway, both of whom were sociologists at the University of Minnesota when they learned about the use of restitution in their studies of punishments in ancient feudal and tribal societies. The two sociologists presented a paper on restitution in 1971 before the Minnesota Penal Coalition. David Fogel (*q.v.*), commissioner of corrections in Minnesota between 1971 and 1973, was in attendance and asked Hudson and Galaway to assist the Minnesota Department of Corrections in developing a program incorporating their ideas. A proposal for funding was approved by the Minnesota Crime Commission to initiate the center on August 1, 1972. Hudson and Galaway became the first and second directors of the center, respectively.

Some ideological differences arose in the early phases of the center's operation. Fogel, an advocate of the justice model of corrections (*q.v.*), did not think it would be necessary to operate treatment programs in the center; he felt justice would be served if offenders repaid the victim. As the center developed, however, Alcoholics Anonymous and drug counseling programs were made available for center residents. A multistep behavior modification procedure was installed, and individual counseling was provided by staff members trained in transactional analysis (*q.v.*). The present director, Robert Mowatt, defends the need for these programs by pointing out that offenders entering the program have personal problems that must be addressed if they are to fulfill their restitution contracts.

During the Minnesota Restitution Center's first three years of operation, its residents repaid $16,000 to their victims. Some 100 offenders participated in repaying money to 300 victims.

The center is a relatively small operation with space for twenty-two offenders at one time. Those who will be paroled to the center are strictly screened, with those who have committed violent crimes being screened out, and as a result the program has operated below capacity much of the time. See also PROPERTY OFFENDERS PROGRAM (POP).

REFERENCES: Burt Galaway and Joe Hudson, "Restitution and Rehabilitation: Some Central Issues," *Crime and Delinquency,* 1972; Stephen Schafer, *The Victim and His Criminal,* 1968; Michael S. Serrill, "The Minnesota Restitution Center," *Corrections Magazine,* 1975; Vergil L. Williams and Mary Fish, "A Proposed Model for Individualized Offender Restitution Through Victim Compensation," in Israel Drapkin and Emilio Viano (eds.), *Victimology: A New Focus: Volume II: Society's Reaction to Victimization,* 1974.

RHODE ISLAND CORRECTIONAL SYSTEM. Rhode Island's Department of Corrections operates the state's adult and juvenile institutions and is responsible for all probation and parole services. The state has seven distinct facilities for handling adult offenders eighteen years of age and above. All adult (and juvenile) facilities are located in a complex at Cranston. The Awaiting Trial Facility was opened as the Providence County Jail in 1878 and was converted to its present use in 1956 with space for ninety-nine offenders. The Admission and Orientation Unit is located in the same facility and has a normal capacity of thirty-three. The Maximum Security Facility, called the Rhode Island State Prison when it opened in 1878, was converted to its present use in 1956 with a normal capacity of 346. The Medium Security Facility opened in 1932 as the Reformatory for Men and was converted to its present use in 1956 with space for 260. The Minimum Security Facility opened in 1973 with a normal capacity of twenty-five; it once served as the Training School for Girls. The Adult Correctional Institution—Women's Division was opened in 1972 with a normal capacity of twenty-five. The Work Release Unit was opened in 1966 with a normal capacity of forty-five.

Four facilities serve juvenile delinquents and wayward juveniles up to age eighteen: the Rhode Island Training School for Boys, opened in 1850 and converted to its current use in 1965 with space for 120; the Rhode Island Training School for Girls, opened in 1882, with a new school constructed in 1965 for twenty-five; the Youth Correctional Center with a normal capacity of twenty; and the Juvenile Diagnostic Center, opened in 1971 with a normal capacity of twenty-two.

Rhode Island's total prison population stood at 594 on January 1, 1976, an increase of 8 percent over the 550 population a year earlier. By January 1978, the prison population had decreased to 523.

REFERENCES: American Correctional Association, *Directory,* 1975–1976 edition; Steve Gettinger, "U.S. Prison Population Hits All-Time High," *Corrections Magazine,* 1976; Michael Serrill, "Prison Population Rises Again, But at a Slower Rate," *Corrections Magazine,* 1978.

RIGHT TO "NO TREATMENT" CONTROVERSY. In July 1972, a group of inmates in the segregation unit of the federal penitentiary at Marion, Illinois, prepared a report which was addressed to the United Nations Economic and Social Council. The inmates, calling their group the Federal Prisoners' Coalition, claimed they had been placed in the segregation unit for refusing to take part in the behavioral research programs of the institution. The cause of the complaint was the therapeutic milieu established in the Marion facility by Martin Groder, the prison psychologist, who used transactional analysis (*q.v.*) as the main vehicle of treatment.

The issue raised by the Federal Prisoners' Coalition report was whether convicted felons have a right to resist rehabilitation techniques designed to change their attitudes, values, or personalities. Complicating the basic issue was the question of whether prison treatment personnel could use coercive means to secure inmate cooperation in the therapeutic programs designed by the staff. The Marion inmates viewed the program as "brainwashing" and accused Groder of forcing inmates to participate in the transactional analysis program by having them transferred to a prison where their families could not visit them, then further isolating them by placing them in segregation, depriving them of mail and other privileges. The report indicated that inmates who gave in to such pressures were moved to living quarters where they were surrounded by a "prison thought-control team" (inmates who had received training in transactional analysis). There they were subjected to intense group pressure which would ultimately heighten their suggestibility and weaken their character structure to the point where their thoughts and emotional responses could be brought under the control of the staff and inmates assisting the staff. The process was considered "psychogenocide" by the Federal Prisoners' Coalition.

Eventually, the coalition brought these charges before a federal court. The issue considered by the court was the extent to which prison staff could use coercion to get inmates to participate in programs designed to alter their attitudes. The controversy does not often arise because many penologists are convinced that such treatment programs will fail unless the inmate's participation is completely voluntary. Thus, treatment programs are made available to inmates, but no pressure is applied to secure their participation. In the case of the Marion institution and the Federal Prisoners' Coalition, however, the Bureau of Prisons was experimenting with a nontraditional approach to treatment programming wherein inmates thought to be troublemakers on account of their assaultive behavior or general lack of cooperation were pressured to cooperate in treatment programs. The position of the inmates was that they had a right to be left alone to serve their sentences without being subjected to efforts to change their attitudes. Prison officials, on the other hand, maintained that no one had the right to continue in such antisocial attitudes. Ultimately, the National Prison Project of the American Civil Liberties Union won a court order in December 1975 on behalf of the Federal Prisoners' Coalition ending some coercive aspects of the Marion program. The court did not uphold the right of inmates to avoid rehabilitation efforts, but it did set limits on the use of coercive measures that officials could use in an attempt to secure cooperation from inmates.

Inmates at Marion were not the only prisoners to protest programs designed by behavioral scientists. In 1973, eight inmates incarcerated in the Springfield, Missouri, federal facility filed suit against prison officials charging them with "human destructiveness" for forcing them into a new U.S. Bureau of Prisons rehabilitation program called START (Special Treatment and Rehabilitative Training). The START project was a "levels" type of program wherein an inmate could advance through three levels of privileges, providing his behavior was deemed appropriate. In 1974, court-appointed investigators filed unfavorable reports and the START program was dropped.

Inmate complaints have originated in state correctional systems as well. In 1973, the Eighth Circuit Court of Appeals ruled that Iowa's use of apomorphine, a vomit-inducing drug, was unconstitutional unless the inmate gave knowing, written permission, which he was free to revoke at any time. In that same year, a Michigan court blocked a scheduled brain operation on a violent, criminally insane inmate. The inmate had volunteered for surgery, but the court ruled that the coercive atmosphere of incarceration made informed consent impossible.

Inmates and libertarian lawyers have singled out a number of experimental techniques in prison rehabilitation programs for special criticism: sensory deprivation, stress assessment, chemotherapy, aversion therapy, and neurosurgery. Sensory deprivation can be accomplished by lengthy confinement in an adjustment center. Stress assessment is carried out by placing the inmate in an open dormitory (for irritation due to lack of privacy), assigning him menial chores, and subjecting him to intense pressure in group therapy sessions to determine how much stress he can stand without losing his temper. Chemotherapy is the use of drugs, often tranquilizers, as behavior modifiers. Aversion therapy utilizes drugs, electrical shock, or other procedures designed to cause the inmate to associate unpleasant consequences with the behavior the therapist wants to eliminate. Finally, neurosurgery is surgical removal of a portion of the brain to make the patient passive.

Inmate resistance to experimental rehabilitation programs has helped shape correctional policy. Early in 1974, Donald E. Santarelli, then administrator of the Law Enforcement Assistance Administration (LEAA) (*q.v.*), banned the use of LEAA funds for programs utilizing "psychosurgery, medical research, behavior modification, chemotherapy, and physical therapy of mental disorders." Santarelli based his decision on the findings of an LEAA study he had requested in November 1973. The report indicated that LEAA did not have the technical skill needed to screen, evaluate, or monitor such federally funded projects; and that a decision on federal funding for these projects could be made only by agencies such as the Department of Health, Education and Welfare to which Congress has given oversight responsibility for medical research projects. For related topics, see ASKLEPIEION THERAPY, FEDERAL CENTER FOR CORRECTIONAL RESEARCH, and TRANSACTIONAL ANALYSIS.

REFERENCES: "Behavior Mod Behind the Walls," *Time*, 1974; Lynn Bergman Kassirer, "The Right to Treatment and the Right to Refuse Treatment—Recent Case Law," *Journal of Psychiatry and Law*, 1974; Jill K. McNulty, "The Right to Be Left Alone," *American Criminal Law Review*, 1972; Jessica Mitford, *Kind and Usual Punishment*, 1973; "Santarelli Bans Funding for Modifying Behavior," *LEAA Newsletter*, 1974.

S

SERRILL, MICHAEL S. (1947–   ). Although Serrill is neither a practitioner nor an academician in the field of corrections, he has become an important influence in penology.

In May 1974, Serrill became executive editor of *Corrections Magazine,* a magazine produced by journalists to provide timely coverage of issues affecting the U.S. prison system. As executive editor, Serrill has been responsible for editorial decisions, as well as the magazine's design, circulation, and production. He has personally researched and written dozens of the magazine's articles since the first issue appeared in September 1974 and has edited most of the articles written by other staff members and outside contributors. As a result of these efforts, Serrill is likely writing and disseminating more information about American prisons, and has a better grasp of the current state of the art of penology, than any other individual in the United States. No one else has visited as many U.S. correctional systems to make first-hand observations of a variety of problems and to report the findings to the public. A number of journals serve the field, but most tend to be refereed journals publishing articles by contributors who provide in-depth analysis of narrow issues. While such periodicals provide a much needed service, they do not present current information inasmuch as the lead time for article publication may be as much as three to five years. By contrast, *Corrections Magazine* can report on developments in the field within weeks.

Serrill's work may ultimately be viewed in the same light as the writings of England's John Howard who became sheriff of Bedford in 1773. Howard, although not a philosopher or scholar, became an important influence on penology through his tireless travels to personally inspect and analyze prison conditions throughout England, Europe, and the Middle East. After four years of such travel, Howard published his findings in the classic volume *The State of the Prisons in England and Wales, with Preliminary Observations, and an Account of Some Foreign Prisons.* Howard's original volume, published in 1777, was followed by an *Appendix* in 1780 after additional travels. Further travels and observations were reported in books he published in 1784 and 1789. By gathering, analyzing, and making available a vast amount of information to other reformers, Howard made lasting contributions to penology. He created awareness of undesirable conditions and promoted the use of desirable techniques that he found during the 42,000 miles he covered on horseback and in horsedrawn carriages. Serrill's contemporary work has some of the same elements as Howard's work: wide travel for direct observation of contemporary prison conditions, and the publication of voluminous information on the positive and negative aspects of penology.

Serrill was introduced to penology in 1971 in his capacity as an investigative reporter for *The News Tribune* in Woodbridge, New Jersey, while covering a riot in Rahway State Prison and examining the New Jersey prison system as a followup. His coverage of the Rahway riot won him a prize for interpretative reporting.

In April 1973, Serrill became a project specialist for Ford Foundation, serving as assistant director in the development of the Correctional Information Service. The project laid the groundwork for the new publication, *Corrections Magazine,* which was first published in 1974. In the course of the project, Serrill made a detailed examination of a dozen state correctional systems. In May 1974, he became vice-president and secretary of the Correctional Information Service and the executive editor of *Corrections Magazine.*

Serrill's considerable exposure to the contemporary scene in American penology has gradually modified the views he adopted when he first came into contact with penology in New Jersey. He initially accepted the conventional wisdom of the rehabilitative model of corrections. He believed that there was a direct relationship between the commission of crime and the social and economic deprivation so apparent in the background of most inmates. He felt that academic/vocational training would indeed provide a cure for these offenders by overcoming their deprivations. As for other offenders, those who committed violent crimes without clear economic justification, he believed that they were simply mentally ill and could surely benefit from the services of psychiatrists and psychologists. Thus, having accepted the standard tools of institutional rehabilitation (academic/vocational training and therapy), Serrill also accepted the indeterminate sentence (*q.v.*) and parole as valuable tools for implementing the rehabilitative model.

Today Serrill is convinced that prison rehabilitation programs are sadly lacking in quality as well as in quantity. He cannot foresee a time when it will be possible for such programs to be funded at the levels recommended by traditional reformers. He is no longer certain that social and economic deprivations constitute a cause of crime. He sees a void in the state of knowledge about the origin of the criminal impulse and has grown wary of therapists who would provide "treatment"—sometimes at the expense of civil liberties. He has come to believe that while treatment programs should be available to inmates, society should not make the inmate's release date contingent on participation in prison programs. Prison administrators or parole authorities, he asserts, do not have the ability to judge whether an inmate has been rehabilitated.

Nor does Serrill any longer believe in the usefulness of the indeterminate sentence; he now supports the trend in California of returning to determinate sentences. This is not to say that Serrill advocates sending more offenders to prison. He sees a potential for abuse in fixed sentencing schemes in that legislators might set unnecessarily long sentences as a response to public concern about crime, or might provide mandatory prison sentences for offenders who could actually be managed without incarceration. Offsetting the risk of those abuses is the huge expense of building additional prison cells. Serrill believes that fixed sentences will result in just treatment for inmates and will eliminate some of the faults of the criminal justice system.

REFERENCE: Michael S. Serrill, letter to the author dated October 1, 1976.

SOUTH CAROLINA CORRECTIONAL SYSTEM. The Department of Corrections receives all convicted persons in South Carolina who are seventeen years of age or older if they are sentenced to a term greater than three months. Thus, the South Carolina prison system holds persons who would be held in county jails in other states. The state has a youthful offender act that allows persons between the ages of seventeen and twenty-one to be sentenced to serve an indeterminate term of one to six years. Incarcerated offenders below the age of seventeen are the responsibility of the Department of Youth Services.

The adult prison system has two groups of prisons (the Appalachian Correctional Region and the Upper Savannah Correctional Region) administered under the supervision of regional directors. In addition, there are nineteen institutions and centers that are not under regional directors; these are administered by Commissioner of Corrections William D. Leeke's office in Columbia.

Ten adult facilities are administered under the aegis of the Appalachian Correctional Region with a central office in Spartanburg. The names of these centers, together with their opening dates and rated capacities, are the Intake Service Center in Greenville, 1974, forty-two males; the Givens Youth Correction Center at Simpsonville, 1969, seventy-six males; the Cherokee Correctional Center at Gaffney, 1974, fifty-six males; the Duncan Correctional Center at Duncan, 1973, forty males; the Hillcrest Correctional Center at Greenville, 1974, sixty males; the Northside Correctional Center at Spartanburg, 1974, thirty males; the Oaklawn Correctional Center at Pelzer, 1974, sixty males; the Travelers Rest Correctional Center at Travelers Rest, 1974, fifty males; the Blue Ridge Community Pre-Release Center at Greenville, 1972, 115 males; and the Piedmont Community Pre-Release Center at Spartanburg, 1970, ninety males.

The Upper Savannah Correctional Region oversees the operation of two small prisons from its central office at Greenwood: the Greenwood Correctional Center, which opened in 1974 with a normal capacity of forty-eight males, and the Laurens Correctional Center at Laurens, which opened in 1974 with room for forty males.

The nineteen facilities that are not administered by regional directors, together with their opening dates and normal capacities, are as follows: the Reception and Evaluation Center at Columbia, 1967, 180 males; the Maximum Detention Retraining Center at Columbia, 1968, eighty males; the Kirkland Correctional Institution at Columbia, 1975, 448 males (because of overcrowding, it has been used to hold the overflow from the Reception and Evaluation Center in recent years); Lexington Correctional Center at Lexington, 1974, forty, and the Sumter Correctional Center at Sumter, 1975, fifty, both of which also hold part of the overflow from the Reception and Evaluation Center; the Central Correctional Institution at Columbia, the oldest and largest prison facility in the state, 1868, 1,100 males; the Goodman Correctional Institution at Columbia, 1970, eighty-four males; the Manning Correctional Institution at Columbia, 1963, 300 males; the Walden Correctional Institution at Columbia, 1951, ninety-eight males; the Wateree River Correctional Institution at Rembert, 1892, 240 males; the Women's Correctional Center at Columbia, 1973, ninety-six; the MacDougall Youth Correction Center at Ridgeville, 1966, 240 youthful offenders ages seventeen to twenty-five; and the Thomas P. Stoney Psychiatric Center in Columbia, 1970, forty-eight males.

The Columbia office of the Department of Corrections also oversees the operation of six pre-release facilities among the non-regionalized institutions: the Campbell Pre-Release Center at Columbia, opened in 1975 to replace the Mid-State Community Pre-Release Center and with a normal capacity of 100; the Catawba Community Pre-Release Center at Rock Hill, opened in 1971 with a normal capacity of fifty males; the Coastal Community Pre-Release Center at Charleston, opened in 1970 with space for sixty-two males; the Palmer Pre-Release Center at Florence, opened in 1975 with a normal capacity of sixty males; the Savannah River Community Pre-Release Center at Aiken, opened in 1974 with room for fifty males; and the Watkins Pre-Release Center at Columbia, opened in 1964 with space for 129 males.

The Division of Institutional Services, which is part of the Department of Youth Services, supervises the operation of five facilities for juveniles from its Columbia office. It receives children between the ages of ten and seventeen years who are adjudicated delinquent or declared to be status offenders (*q.v.*) by a family court judge. They must serve a minimum sentence of six months. The five youth facilities are as follows: the William J. Goldsmith Reception and Evaluation Center at Columbia which receives all children committed to the system for assignment to a facility or other disposition; the John G. Richards School for Boys at Columbia, established in 1900 with room for 120 boys fifteen and sixteen years old when committed; the South Carolina School for Boys, founded in 1908 for younger boys; the Willow Lane School at Columbia, a coeducational facility for 120, most of whom are females; and the Intensive Care Unit at Columbia, started in 1970 for children who had trouble adjusting to the open campus programs of the Willow Lane and John G. Richards facilities.

South Carolina has been experiencing severe overcrowding in its prison system in recent years, and the problem seems to be growing worse, despite efforts to build new prisons in the state. In calendar year 1975, the state's 38 percent increase in prison population was one of the highest in the nation. During the twelve-month period, the total grew from 4,422 to 6,100. In 1977, the prison population grew from 6,985 to 7,322.

REFERENCES: American Correctional Association, *Directory,* 1975–1976 edition; Steve Gettinger, "U.S. Prison Population Hits All-Time High," *Corrections Magazine,* 1976; Michael Serrill, "Prison Population Rises Again, But at a Slower Rate," *Corrections Magazine,* 1978.

SOUTH DAKOTA CORRECTIONAL SYSTEM. Adult and juvenile institutions in South Dakota are supervised by the State Board of Charities and Corrections. This five-member board also oversees three state hospitals.

Adult offenders, male and female, are committed to the South Dakota Penitentiary which opened in 1882 at Sioux Falls with a normal capacity of 500. Juvenile offenders, up to age seventeen, are committed to the South Dakota Training School at Plankinton; it was opened in 1887 with a normal capacity of 150 and holds both male and female offenders. The Youth Forestry Camp at Custer is the state's only other correctional facility. It was opened in 1967 with a normal capacity of fifty selected youthful offenders ages fifteen to twenty-one.

In recent years, these three penal institutions have been operating at about half their normal capacity. However, the prison population in South Dakota is growing faster than it is in some other states; it grew from 277 on January 1, 1975, to 372 on January 1, 1976, or 34 percent during the twelve-month period. Growth continued and reached 555 on January 1, 1978.

REFERENCES: American Correctional Association, *Directory, 1975–1976* edition; Steve Gettinger, "U.S. Prison Population Hits All-Time High," *Corrections Magazine,* 1976; Michael Serrill, "Prison Population Rises Again, But at a Slower Rate," *Corrections Magazine,* 1978.

STATUS OFFENDERS. Status offenders are children who have committed acts that would not be considered crimes if committed by adults, but subject children to the jurisdiction of the juvenile courts. Typical status offenses include truancy from school, running away from home, consensual sexual behavior, smoking, drinking, curfew violations, chronic disobedience of parents or other authority figures, ungovernability, and waywardness.

For purposes of court jurisdiction, distinguishing children from adults is a matter of definition in the statutes of the various states, and the definitions are necessarily somewhat arbitrary. Many states use the ages of sixteen or seventeen as the dividing line to distinguish children from adults; thus, a particular state may have a statute that designates sixteen as the age at which a person becomes an adult and is subject to the jurisdiction of the adult court. Children below the age of sixteen, in a state using that age as the dividing line, may come under the jurisdiction of the juvenile court because they commit an act that would be a crime if they were adults or because they commit a status offense.

Each year, some 600,000 children are confined in jails temporarily while awaiting a court hearing; about 200,000 of these are status offenders. Approximately 85,000 children each year are committed to juvenile institutions after hearings in juvenile courts. Of these 85,000, about 23 percent of the boys and 70 percent of the girls are committed as status offenders.

In 1975, the Board of Directors of the National Council on Crime and Delinquency (NCCD) (*q.v.*) released a policy statement which urged that juvenile courts no longer have jurisdiction over status offenses. The NCCD policy statement recognizes that the philosophy of juvenile courts is to provide rehabilitative service to children rather than punishment. However, the NCCD argues that the imprisonment of status offenders constitutes punishment, regardless of the rationale used by the court, and that imprisonment can serve no rehabilitative purpose. The NCCD considers the imprisonment of status offenders unjust because it is an unduly harsh societal response to the acts committed by the status offenders. Among the NCCD's criticisms is the tendency of juvenile institutions to incarcerate status offenders for as long as or longer than juvenile offenders who have committed felonies such as rape or aggravated assault. Because juvenile courts tend to commit status offenders to an institution until they reach their majority, the younger the status offender at the time of commitment, the longer the period of incarceration. The NCCD further notes that children who serve the longest sentences in institutions have the highest rate of parole revocation.

The purpose of incarcerating status offenders is to help them become law-abiding, productive adults, but the NCCD points out that there is a dismal lack of evidence that promiscuous girls who have been imprisoned have fewer illegitimate children than those who have not been imprisoned, or that disobedient boys who have been imprisoned end up in adult prisons less frequently than those who have not been incarcerated as juveniles. The NCCD's 1975 policy statement makes it clear that it does not believe that juvenile courts can deliver rehabilitative services. The organization feels that juvenile courts do have coercive powers that can be used effectively on children who commit crimes that threaten the safety of the community, but that the juvenile courts' commitment to salvaging the lives of status offenders is merely rhetoric.

Juvenile court personnel have developed special terminology for status offenders in an attempt to differentiate them from those children who have committed adult crimes. The latter are often called juvenile delinquents, while status offenders are designated as Persons in Need of Supervision (PINS) or Children in Need of Supervision (CHINS). Nonetheless, the NCCD argues that any action on the part of a juvenile court results in stigma for the child subjected to the juvenile court process.

The essence of the NCCD policy statement is that jurisdiction over the noncriminal behavior of children be removed from juvenile courts and that they become the agency of last resort for children involved in criminal conduct.

Opponents of the NCCD position on jurisdiction over status offenders point out that children are rarely incarcerated solely because of status offenses. Such children, they argue, usually commit crimes in addition to their status offenses, and these crimes are "plea bargained" down to lessen the stigma of the youth being imprisoned. Furthermore, the critics of the NCCD argue, commitments to juvenile institutions are rarely made because of a single status offense. More often, the child in question has established a pattern of repeatedly running away from home or being truant from school, and this pattern of behavior is symptomatic of more serious problems that need attention. Not infrequently, parents have exhausted all noncoercive means of control over their children before petitioning the juvenile court for help. There is some reason to believe that status offenders are incarcerated longer than juvenile delinquents because status offenders are more troubled and more difficult to manage. An adult who serves a term of incarceration can be expected to be able to care for himself after release, but a troubled child cannot be released unless there is a capable family ready to care for him. The critics of the NCCD policy statement agree that more community resources should be available to serve status offenders, but maintain that these services should be available to the juvenile court to serve either status offenders or juvenile delinquents.

It is difficult to assess the relative merits of the two sides in the debate. The more important issue may ultimately be the availability of a social institution that is ready to serve status offenders. At present, status offenders seem to have fallen into the jurisdiction of juvenile courts largely by default. Apparently, no other social institution is equipped to deal with them.

REFERENCES: Lawrence H. Martin and Phyllis R. Snyder, "Jurisdiction over Status Offenses Should *Not* Be Removed from the Juvenile Court," *Crime and Delinquency,* 1976; National Council on Crime and Delinquency, Board of Directors, "Jurisdiction over Status Offenses Should Be Removed from the Juvenile Court: A Policy Statement," *Crime and Delinquency,* 1975.

SYNANON. Synanon, a privately owned and operated organization, was formed in the late 1950s in Santa Monica, California. It is not a correctional institution, but rather a residential program for drug addicts. Its importance for American penology is not the facility itself, but the treatment techniques developed there. The literature on correctional counseling and treatment programs in prisons frequently refers to the "Snyanon-type" aspects of such programs. Synanon symbolizes a type of group therapy approach to the treatment of offenders. It also symbolizes "success" in treatment because addicts living in the Synanon facility have demonstrated ability to stay free from drug use for long periods of time.

As an approach to group therapy, Don C. Gibbons has characterized Synanon as representative of "milieu management." It involves a group of clients pursuing the same goals as group therapy, but it is a somewhat more ambitious undertaking than the usual group therapy program. The Synanon group member's entire life is an experiment in social adjustment to the institution, and such an experiment will eventually enhance adjustment to life in the outside community. The advantage of the therapeutic community created in this social experiment is that it does not have antitreatment influences such as custody-oriented guards who may be critical of treatment staff, or antisocial inmate subcultures which create barriers to constructive change.

At the time new addicts are received into the facility, the Synanon program immediately begins to instill self-discipline in the new resident. Withdrawal from the drug habit is accomplished "cold turkey" (without the support of any drugs or chemicals). Although this type of withdrawal is uncomfortable for the addict, it is not the extremely painful process popularly depicted in movies and television dramatizations. Following physical withdrawal from the drug habit, the new resident receives a series of indoctrinations. The addict is told that he has the opportunity to work for the Synanon Foundation and that in return for working will receive room and board, cigarettes, and therapy sessions three times a week. The addict is also informed that he must meet the high standards of conduct required of residents and will not be allowed to use any drugs; when he gets rid of his drug habit, he will become part of the Foundation staff. Indoctrinations are designed to emphasize to the addict that he is an emotionally immature failure and to get the addict to accept himself as he really is. The harshness of the indoctrination is part of the "attack therapy" (see below) that is characteristic of Synanon. It is based on the proposition that a person must be stripped of his defenses before he can begin to be cured.

The group psychotherapy sessions conducted three times a week are called synanons. Each synanon session includes ten to fifteen residents, and enough sessions are held each week to allow each resident to participate in three. The ten to fifteen persons taking part in an individual synanon settle in a circle facing one another. The ensuing discussion is an intensive emotional discussion of group and personal problems, with emphasis on uncompromising candor about one another. Verbal attacks are launched repeatedly on various group members' delusions, distorted self-images, and inappropriate behaviors. This attack therapy is believed to "toughen up" a person so that he will see himself as others see him, get information about himself, and gain insight into his problems. Any defenses that remain after an individual has been subjected to relentless verbal attacks in a synanon are said to be "valid" defenses. The synanons also help socialize the group member into the norms of the Synanon society.

Groups are formed by Synanon members who have been in the program for a long time. They are designated "Synamasters" and make up the group lists from a list containing the names of everyone living in the facility at the time. The groups are balanced in terms of male/female ratios, age, and length of time in the program. A senior Synanist, or resident, is included in each group to provide leadership. The composition of the groups shifts from one session to the next, so it is unlikely that the same collection of individuals will gather in a synanon more than once.

The use of senior Synanists as role-models is one example of how synanons differ from professional group therapy sessions. The senior Synanist, unlike the professional therapist, uses self-revelation in therapy sessions. He can point out to the newcomer that he has experienced the same difficulties but is now performing at a more acceptable level. The role-model gives the newcomer a chance to identify with a person who has been a total failure, but who has now greatly improved his life. He also can give the newcomer some idea of the problems he will face in achieving the improvement.

One of the most controversial aspects of the Synanon program is its commitment to the idea that people can help themselves without professional therapists. Many professionals resent the claim that patients can become therapists. Other professionals, however, have offered their help and support. The definition of mental health at Synanon is largely rational behavior. A resident who stays free from the use of alcohol and drugs and shows a high degree of predictable and consistent behavior is apt to be considered healthy, regardless of some quirks in his behavior. Some professional therapists refuse to consider such residents "cured" and argue that their progress at Synanon simply prepares them for professional therapy.

References in the literature to "Synanon-type" treatment programs are partly to the self-help dimension of group therapy programs, but more commonly they attempt to invoke an image of the "attack therapy" aspect of synanons. Attack therapy, a unique and unorthodox approach, is associated with the treatment strategy used at Synanon. Attack therapy occurs in the course of a synanon when the entire group places one group member on the "hot seat" by vicious cross-examination of his behavior. The comments from various group members exaggerate, caricature, and ridicule the behavior problems of the person being subjected to the process. The recipient of the group attack is forced to face the truth and examine it, and ultimately to put aside the delusions about himself that previously led him to use drugs. Given this outcome to attack therapy, Synanists see the attacks as expressions of love and sympathy.

Lewis Yablonsky, a prominent sociologist who has studied and written about Synanon, believes that the Synanon movement and its founder, Charles E. Dederich, represent a new treatment methodology administered by a new breed of professional people. In Yablonsky's view, it is a unique approach to treating social deviance and a point of reference in other programs that use elements of the methodology.

Success, and the attendant publicity, have brought a number of changes to the Synanon operation, as illustrated by a 1976 report on the operation by *People* magazine. Since its modest beginning as a storefront operation in 1958, Charles Dederich has expanded the non-profit corporation to provide living facilities in Tomales and Badger as well as in Santa Monica. The Synanon Foundation has assets valued at $22 million, including 300 land vehicles, ten airplanes, and a small airport to serve the 1,300 residents. The foundation solicits substantial amounts of clothing, foodstuff, and building materials from business corporations each year and has become the nation's second largest supplier of promotional specialties, such as ballpoint pens, T-shirts, and other advertising gimmicks. More than 15,000 people have been Synanon residents since 1958.

One new dimension of the Synanon program is the presence of residents who do not need treatment. More than 30 percent of the current residents simply enjoy Synanon's highly structured, communal way of life. These residents, called "squares" or "life-stylers," pay fees for the privilege of living in the Synanon community. Fees for life-stylers are $450 a month for a single person, $750 a month for a couple, and an additional $400 per month for each child.

REFERENCES: Don C. Gibbons, *Changing the Lawbreaker: The Treatment of Delinquents and Criminals,* 1965; Barbara Wilkins, "Bio," *People,* 1976; Lewis Yablonsky, *Synanon: The Tunnel Back,* 1965.

T

TENNESSEE CORRECTIONAL SYSTEM. Tennessee's Department of Correction is divided into Adult Services and Juvenile Services. Adult Services oversees the operation of the adult prisons, and its Division of Probation and Paroles provides probation and parole services for adult offenders.

All persons committed to an adult institution serve a minimum of one year. In most cases, persons committed to adult prisons are at least eighteen years old, but fifteen-year-old juveniles who commit capital offenses, as well as sixteen year olds who are declared incorrigible and sentenced as adults, may be placed in an adult prison.

The Tennessee State Penitentiary at Nashville was opened in 1898 with a normal capacity of 1,600 male felons. The overcrowding of the state's prison system in recent years is illustrated by the average population figures for 1974–1975 of 2,550. The Tennessee Prison for Women at Nashville was opened in 1898, and the facility in use now was opened in 1966 with a normal capacity of 100. It is unusual for a women's prison to be overcrowded, but the average population of the women's prison for 1974–1975 was 160. The Fort Pillow State Farm at Fort Pillow was opened in 1938 with room for 600 male felons. The Turney Center at Memphis has a normal capacity of 562 and has been somewhat overcrowded in recent years. Adult Services hoped to alleviate some of its overcrowding problems by opening two new prisons before 1980: the Bushy Mountain Prison at Petros and the Shelby County Regional Correctional Center at Memphis.

Tennessee's metropolitan areas have work release (*q.v.*) centers that add to the capacity of the state prisons. The Chattanooga Community Release Center has space for seventy-five; the Memphis Community Release Center, for 100; the Nashville Community Release Center, for 175; and the Knoxville Community Release Center, for 110.

The Division of Juvenile Services receives juveniles between the ages of twelve and eighteen who are given an indefinite sentence regardless of the nature of the offense committed. The juvenile centers, together with their opening dates and normal capacities, are as follows: the Tennessee Reception and Guidance Center at Nashville, 1920, 150 youths ages twelve to fifteen; the Spencer Youth Center at Nashville, 1912, 350 youths ages twelve to fifteen; the Taft Youth Center at Pikeville, 1920, 375 youths ages sixteen to eighteen; the Tennessee Youth Center at Joelton, 1962, 125 males ages fifteen to eighteen; the Wilder Youth Development Center at Somerville, 1971, 192 males and females, ages twelve to fourteen and twelve to thirteen, respectively; and the Highland Rim School for Girls at Tullahoma, 1917, 208.

Tennessee has experienced substantial increases in prison population in recent years. For example, its inmate population increased 14 percent from 5,350 on January 1, 1977, to 6,085 on January 1, 1978.

REFERENCES: American Correctional Association, *Directory, 1975–1976 edition;* Michael Serrill, "Prison Population Rises Again, But at a Slower Rate," *Corrections Magazine,* 1978.

TEXAS CORRECTIONAL SYSTEM. The Department of Corrections is responsible for operation of the adult prisons in the state, while the Texas Youth Council oversees the operation of the juvenile institutions. Adult offenders are those persons seventeen years of age or older; if convicted of a felony, they are committed to the Department of Corrections. The department also receives some juvenile offenders between the ages of fifteen and seventeen if the courts have certified them for trial as adults.

The adult facilities, together with their opening dates and normal capacities, are: the Huntsville Unit at Huntsville, 1849, 2,000 adult males, used mainly to house older first offenders (its "Treatment Center" houses offenders deemed to be mentally irresponsible and mentally deficient); the Diagnostic Unit at Huntsville, 1964, 790 male felons; Central Unit at Sugar Land, 1902, 720 male felons, used mainly for first offenders; Clemens Unit at Brazoria, also used for first offenders, 1902, 1,050 male felons; Coffield Unit at Tennessee Colony, 1973, 2,000 male felons (a minimum security unit for inmates who have been convicted of nonviolent crimes); the Darrington Unit at Rosharon, 1919, 785 male felons, used to house recidivists under twenty-five years of age; the Eastham Unit at Weldon, 1917, 2,224 (a number of handicapped recidivists are sent to this facility for male felons); the Ellis Unit at Huntsville, a maximum security prison, 1963, 1,722 male felons; the Ferguson Unit at Midway, 1917, 1,525 male felons who are first offenders and in the age range of seventeen to twenty-one; the Goree Unit at Huntsville, 1901, 600 female felons; the Jester Unit at Richmond, 1885, 925 male felons, used as a pre-release center; the Mountain View Unit at Gatesville, 1975, 250 female felons; Ramsey Unit at Rosharon, 1908, 1,880 male felons, used mainly for recidivists above age twenty-five; Retrieve Unit at Angleton, 1919, 700 male felons, also used for recidivists above age twenty-five; and the Wynne Unit at Huntsville, 1899, 1,878 male felons, used as a maximum security unit for physically handicapped offenders.

The Texas Youth Council operates five facilities for delinquent juveniles and four facilities for dependent and neglected children. Those persons between the ages of ten and seventeen who have committed a felony offense, or an offense that would be punishable by jail confinement for an adult, are considered juvenile delinquents in Texas. The sentences for delinquents are indeterminate, and the Texas Youth Council can retain custody until the youth reaches age eighteen.

The facilities for delinquent juveniles follow: (1) Gatesville State Schools for Boys is composed of a number of facilities in Gatesville housing delinquent boys ten to seventeen years of age. Two of the smaller facilities house 160 boys each, four of the facilities 240 boys each, and the two larger facilities 320 and 480 boys, respectively. The largest facility, Mountain View School for Boys, is a prison for chronic, serious juvenile offenders. (2) The Giddings State Home and School at Giddings was opened in 1972 with a normal capacity of 480; it is a coeducational facility. (3) The Statewide Reception Center at Brownwood was opened in 1970 with room for 100; it serves as a receiving facility for all juvenile delinquents. (4) The Brownwood State Home and School at Brownwood was opened in 1970 with a normal capacity of 240; it is a coeducational facility. (5) Gainesville State School at Gainesville was opened in 1915 with space for 390; it is a co-educational facility.

The four facilities for dependent and neglected children are the Corsicana State Home, with space for about 160 children ages three to twelve; the Crockett State Home at Crockett, with room for about twenty children ages three to eighteen; the Waco State Home at Waco, housing about twenty children ages three to eighteen; and the West Texas Children's Home at Monahans, with capacity for about 180 children ages three to eighteen.

The Texas prison population increased 12 percent between January 1, 1975, when the population was 16,833, and January 1, 1976, when it was 18,934. In January 1978, the prison population reached 22,439 to make Texas the state with the largest prison population. By contrast, California had 19,623 inmates, New York 19,754, and Florida 19,643.

REFERENCES: American Correctional Association, *Directory, 1975–1976* edition; Steve Gettinger, "U.S. Prison Population Hits All-Time High," *Corrections Magazine,* 1976; Michael Serrill, "Prison Population Rises Again, But at a Slower Rate," *Corrections Magazine,* 1978.

TRANSACTIONAL ANALYSIS THERAPY. This treatment methodology, developed by psychiatrist Eric Berne in the 1950s, has played an important role in prison treatment programs following Martin Groder's introduction of the approach into the federal penitentiary at Marion, Illinois, in 1968.

Berne developed his own unique approach to psychotherapy based on his observation that all men share three ego states which he designated as the Parent, Adult, and Child. These three ego states are all operational in any one individual, and shifts from one ego state to another occur many times in the course of a normal day in response to different types of stimuli. Such shifts are evidenced by changes in voice intonations, facial expressions, vocabulary used, and gestures. The three ego states stem from the way in which the human brain functions in what Berne called "memory tapes." Different stimuli trigger memories that replay past events and emotions in a person's life.

According to Berne, the Parent ego state represents memories that are formed before a person reaches five years of age. Such memories are provided primarily by parents who alternatively make the child feel good or bad as they admonish or praise. Without much objectivity, the Parent tapes of an individual give one the sense of an act, event, or situation being "right" or "wrong" depending upon the relationship between the parent and child.

The Child ego state involves memories formulated before a person reaches adolescence. Since the child does not have the experience to evaluate and understand the events around him, memories from this period of life are mainly in terms of feelings and emotions. Many of the memories arouse anxiety or "not okay" feelings in Berne's terminology. The Adult ego state is likened to a computer in that it has the capacity to process data on an objective basis. It considers data on a what, where, when, and why basis, without the commands and exhortations of the Parent ego state or the anxiety of the child. The Adult ego state is free to decide that parachuting is not dangerous as mother said it was and to put aside the childish fear of falling. The ability to make this type of analysis is the basis of Berne's therapy.

The Adult ego state should be in control of the personality in a healthy person—able to accept or reject the memory messages being received from the Parent or Child tapes.

Clients in transactional analysis therapy often receive classroom instruction in the principles of the technique. It therefore differs from conventional psychoanalysis wherein the client is not expected to learn to be a psychoanalyst. Once the client in transactional analysis therapy has mastered the concepts discussed above, he is taught to analyze transactions. A transaction is a unit of social intercourse. Two people who come into contact with one another will eventually react to one another's presence by some form of verbal or nonverbal behavior. This acknowledgment by one of the parties is called a transactional stimulus. The second party's reaction to the transactional stimulus is called a transactional response. Analysis, usually done with diagrams, is designed to determine whether the stimulus originates from the Parent, Adult, or Child ego state and to make a similar determination for the response. If both the stimulus and response make parallel lines between the two diagrams, the transaction is complementary and the exchange can go on indefinitely. Conversely, if the stimulus and response make crossed lines between the two diagrams, communication stops. When advocates of the technique say that communication stops as a result of one person communicating from, say, the Adult ego state while the second person communicates from the Parent or Child ego state to make crossed lines on the diagrams, they do not mean that the conversation literally ends. Rather, the conversation takes a predictable turn and ends up in what Berne calls a game. Games, a subject to which Berne devoted an entire book, are "crooked," i.e., they have ulterior motives. Clients learning the techniques of transactional analysis are able to determine which ego state their stimulus or response comes from in a particular situation and to make a similar determination for the other party in a conversation. This ability enables the client to communicate in an open, honest manner with the rational adult in full control of his personality. The client knows that the Parent ego state and the Child ego state are useful, but that they should be released only on appropriate occasions. (An appropriate occasion for release of the Child ego state is for relaxation and play, while the Parent ego state might be released to discuss the "good old days.") In short, the client strives to place his Adult ego state in charge of his personality and to avoid the destructive playing of games.

Some games occur with such regularity that they become "life scripts." One such possibility illustrates Berne's unique view of the nature of criminality. Prison inmates are "compulsive losers" who play the game of "cops and robbers." They commit crimes because they are playing a game, the object of which is to prove that they are "not okay." They may make it difficult for the police to catch them for a time, but they intend to be caught. In considering this aspect of Berne's theories, the penologist is reminded of the many inmates who tattoo themselves with the phrase Born to Lose. The other category of criminal, Berne maintains, is the "compulsive winner"—the professional criminal who is rarely convicted of a crime.

Transactional analysis lends itself to use in correctional institutions because it is best practiced in a group setting. Advocates note that patients can conduct analysis of transactions and certain other less complicated aspects of the therapy without much training. Analysis of games and scripts is more difficult and requires the services of a highly trained therapist. For related topics, see ASKLEPIEION THERAPY and FEDERAL CENTER FOR CORRECTIONAL RESEARCH.

REFERENCES: Eric Berne, *Games People Play,* 1964; Eric Berne, *Principles of Group Treatment,* 1966; Eric Berne, *Transactional Analysis in Psychotherapy,* 1961; Thomas A. Harris, *I'm OK—You're OK,* 1969; Richardson C. Nicholson, "Transactional Analysis: A New Method for Helping Offenders," *Federal Probation,* 1970.

U

UTAH CORRECTIONAL SYSTEM. The Division of Corrections, which is part of the Department of Social Services, operates Utah's one prison and oversees adult probation and parole services. The Utah State Prison at Draper was opened in 1868, but a facility on a new site was opened in 1951. It has a normal capacity of 876 and houses male and female felons eighteen years of age or older. The Department of Social Services' Division of Family Services is responsible for operation of the Utah State Industrial School at Ogden, opened in 1888 as a territorial reformatory. The Ogden facility became the State Industrial School in 1896 with a normal capacity of 210; it houses male and female juvenile delinquents ages eight to nineteen.

The Utah prison population decreased 3 percent from 827 on January 1, 1977, to 800 on January 1, 1978, after several years of growth.

REFERENCES: American Correctional Association, *Directory,* 1975–1976 edition; Michael Serrill, "Prison Population Rises Again, But at a Slower Rate," *Corrections Magazine,* 1978.

V

VERMONT CORRECTIONAL SYSTEM. Under the leadership of Commissioner R. Kent Stoneman and Deputy Commissioner Cornelius D. Hogan, Vermont's correctional system has embarked on an unusual course of action in operating a prison system without a maximum security institution. Alaska is the only other state that lacks a maximum security prison. The State Correctional Facility at Windsor was closed in August 1975 because the institution, built in 1809, had become too dilapidated and too expensive to run. Inmates who need to be in a maximum security prison are now placed in a federal penitentiary under a lease agreement costing Vermont between $7,000 and $9,000 per year for each inmate housed in federal facilities. This per inmate cost is only half of what it cost to house the inmates in the Windsor institution, and no more than forty inmates out of the 300 that Windsor is capable of holding were deemed to be in need of maximum security supervision. Inmates not transferred to federal facilities were placed in the state's community correctional centers.

Adult community correctional centers include the Chittenden Community Correctional Center at South Burlington, which opened, after being relocated, in 1975 and houses eighty male and female prisoners. The Corrections Diagnostic/Treatment Center at St. Albans was opened in 1969 with room for eight male offenders. The Rutland Community Correctional Center at Rutland was also opened in 1969; it has a normal capacity of thirty-five male offenders. The St. Johnsburg Community Correctional Center at St. Johnsburg is designed to hold thirty-five males and has been in operation since 1969. The Woodstock Community Correctional Center at Woodstock was opened in 1969 to house a total of sixty male and female offenders. The Residential Treatment Facility at Windsor was opened in 1973 to house forty-five males. The Weeks School at Vergennes is the state's only institution for juveniles; it is designed to accommodate 180 boys and girls ages twelve to eighteen and has been in operation since 1865.

Since the Vermont Department of Corrections operates all the correctional facilities in the state, the population of the institutions includes misdemeanants who would be housed in county jails in other states. The state established its correctional centers beginning in 1969 as it moved to close its fourteen existing county jails. The correctional code was rewritten in 1972 to authorize the transfer of felons from the Windsor maximum security prison to the community correctional centers. This development paved the way for the subsequent closing of Windsor in 1975. Vermont's commitment to the large-scale use of community-based corrections is illustrated not only in the relatively recent move to establish community correctional centers to replace the Windsor prison and county jails, but also in probation and parole statistics: the number of persons on probation and parole increased from 1,500 in 1969 to 3,200 in 1975, while the total population in institutions remained near 350 during the six-year period.

The Vermont Division of Probation and Parole is part of the Department of Corrections; its officers supervise almost 3,000 adult probationers and more than 300 adult parolees.

The Vermont prison population grew 14 percent in 1977 from 244 on January 1, 1977, to 279 on January 1, 1978.

A historical footnote to Vermont's commitment to the use of community-based correction is that it is believed to be the first state to operate work release programs (see WORK RELEASE).

REFERENCES: American Correctional Association, *Directory,* 1975–1976 edition; Michael Kiernan, "Profile/Vermont," *Corrections Magazine,* 1975; Michael Serrill, "Prison Population Rises Again, But at a Slower Rate," *Corrections Magazine,* 1978.

VIRGINIA CORRECTIONAL SYSTEM. Adult institutions in Virginia are operated under the supervision of the Division of Adult Services, and juvenile institutions are the responsibility of the Division of Youth Services. Both divisions operate under the aegis of the State Department of Corrections.

The Division of Adult Services receives persons over the age of eighteen who have been convicted of a misdemeanor that requires them to serve at least six months. On occasion, the court may certify an offender below the age of eighteen for confinement in an adult prison. The adult institutions, with opening dates and normal capacities, include the Bland Correctional Center at Bland, 1946, 487 males; the Bureau of Correctional Units at Richmond, 1906, 2,153 males (the capacity of field units operated as pre-release centers is included in the 2,153 figure); the James River Correctional Center, 300 males, and the Powhatan Correctional Center, 711 males (these became separate institutions in 1974 after operating as the State Farm since 1895); the St. Brides Correctional Center at Chesapeake, 1973, 210 males; the Southampton Correctional Center at Capron, 1937, 534 youthful first offenders; the Virginia Correctional Center for Women at Goochland, 1932, 300; the Virginia State Penitentiary at Richmond, 1800, 840 males; and the Pre-Release Activities Center at Chesterfield, 1971, 112 males.

The Division of Youth Services operates eight institutions that are listed as holding "juvenile delinquents" without reference to gender. The institutions group children by age. (1) The Reception and Diagnostic Center for Children at Bon Air, opened in 1969 with a rated capacity of 200 children ages eight to eighteen; (2) the Barrett Learning Center at Hanover, opened in 1915 with a normal capacity of 100 children ages ten to fifteen; (3) the Beaumont Learning Center at Beaumont, opened in 1898 with room for 300, ages fifteen to twenty-one; (4) the Bon Air Learning Center at Bon Air, opened in 1919 with a normal capacity of 160, ages fifteen to twenty-one; (5) the Hanover Learning Center at Hanover, opened in 1898 with space for 225 children ages ten to fifteen; (6) the Natural Bridge Learning Center at Natural Bridge Station, opened in 1964 housing ninety, ages sixteen to twenty-one; (7) the Pinecrest Learning Center at Richmond, opened in 1969 with space for forty children ages eight to twelve; and (8) the Appalachian Learning Center at Honaker, opened in 1967 with a normal capacity of fifty, ages sixteen to twenty-one.

Compared to most other states, the prison population in Virginia has not been growing rapidly. It increased 8 percent between January 1, 1975, and January 1, 1976, rising from 5,635 to 6,092. The period from January 1, 1977, to January 1, 1978, saw a 2 percent increase in the prison population from 8,376 to 8,550.

REFERENCES: American Correctional Association, *Directory,* 1975–1976 edition; Steve Gettinger, "U.S. Prison Population Hits All-Time High," *Corrections Magazine,* 1976; Michael Serrill, "Prison Population Rises Again, But at a Slower Rate," *Corrections Magazine,* 1978.

W

WARD GRIEVANCE PROCEDURE OF THE CALIFORNIA YOUTH AUTHORITY.

The Ward Grievance Procedure (WGP) is one of seventeen programs designated as exemplary programs by the National Institute of Law Enforcement and Criminal Justice (*q.v.*) to encourage replication by other agencies. The exemplary projects include law enforcement, courts, and corrections; only eight of the seventeen exemplary projects are in the area of corrections.

The goal of WGP is to reduce conflict between inmates who have grievances and prison administrators, without violence or costly and time-consuming litigation. The techniques used are basically negotiation and mediation. As a grievance mechanism, it is an alternative to the use of ombudsman programs or inmate councils elected by inmates to represent them before the administration. The unique features claimed for WGP are problem-solving by line staff and inmates, who exercise equal decision-making authority in the context of an open hearing, and inmate opportunity to appeal a decision to outside arbitration.

The principles established for the WGP operations are that (1) inmates must help to resolve grievances as well as to file them; (2) workable solutions to grievances can only be obtained by the mutual efforts of inmates and line staff members who are in daily contact with inmates; and (3) both inmates and staff need recourse to a third party for an unbiased point of view. Inmates in a particular living unit elect one of their members to serve as a grievance clerk for the group. A grievant is allowed to have an inmate representative at a hearing; the elected grievance clerk often serves in this advocate role. A feature of WGP is that decisions are put in writing at each stage of the hearing and review process. The elected grievance clerk provides a form to an inmate who wants to file a grievance. The clerk sees that the grievant reduces the description of the complaint to ten typewritten lines on the form provided and that the grievance committee gets the form. The committee must consider the grievance and rule on it within five days after it has been reduced to writing on the form provided.

The grievance committee is composed of two inmates and two line staff members, all four of whom have voting privileges. A fifth member of the grievance committee is a middle management staff member who chairs the committee but who does not have a voting privilege. The grievance clerk attends the committee meetings to observe the proceedings. The grievant can elect to represent himself at the committee meeting or to be represented by the grievance clerk or by an inmate or staff member of his choice. The committee hears grievances and makes decisions by majority vote. The grievance can be resolved by the vote of the committee if it involves only the policy of the grievant's living unit. If the grievance involves institution-wide or state-wide policy, the committee can do no more than suggest a remedy to the administrator at the proper level. The grievance committee's handling of the complaint is a formal recourse for the inmate that may not be necessary. Once the grievance is turned over to the grievance clerk, it may be settled informally by staff members without the need for a formal hearing.

A grievant who is not satisfied with the decision of the grievance committee has the right to appeal the decision to the superintendent of the institution or the director of the California Youth Authority (depending on which level of authority has power to deal with the policy in question). This right to appeal the decision for administrative review puts pressure on the grievance committee to work hard to achieve fair solutions to grievances. It also gives correctional management a role in the WGP and helps to break up inmate stereotyping of staff members as the "enemy" in cases where grievants are appealing a decision of their peers to management officials.

If the appeal on the grievance goes against the inmate, he can carry the procedure one step further to an arbitration board. One of twelve professional arbitrators, recruited by the American Arbitration Association as volunteers, chairs a three-member review panel consisting of the arbitrator, a member selected by the grievant, and a member selected by the California Youth Authority. The review board conducts a hearing on the appeal and issues an advisory opinion that is not binding on the administration. If the inmate loses the appeal, he still has recourse to court action.

The types of grievances processed by WGP involve situations that would be considered minor if the grievant were not an inmate. Inmates, however, are continuously aware of their powerlessness, and minor complaints can become the source of serious tensions in a prison if the complaints are ignored. A sample of 1,496 grievances processed through WGP in seven California institutions over a nineteen-month period reveals that approximately 40 percent of the grievances involved individual problems relating to how rules were applied to individual inmates; about 33 percent dealt with policy issues in the sense that the grievance questioned the need for the rule itself; 17 percent called attention to some seemingly arbitrary act by a staff member; and 10 percent involved complaints about inadequate equipment and facilities or other miscellaneous matters. Disciplinary matters are exluded from the grievance mechanism, both because the California Youth Authority has a disciplinary procedure that incorporates its own due process standards and because penologists feel that complaints about discipline cannot effectively be resolved by consensus decision-making techniques.

The WGP appears to be working well from the perspective of both the inmates and the staff. Institution tensions have been relieved, and the amount of litigation reduced, by the ability to settle grievances internally. Only 2 percent of the grievances need outside arbitration to produce a settlement. From the inmate perspective, inmates find that they can bring constructive change to their environment through the WGP. About 51 percent of the grievance dispositions favor the grievants, and an additional 20 percent partially favor the grievants through some sort of compromise. For related materials, see ADMINISTRATIVE REMEDY PROCEDURE, GRIEVANCE PROCEDURES FOR INMATES, NATIONAL INSTITUTE OF LAW ENFORCEMENT AND CRIMINAL JUSTICE, and OMBUDSMEN IN PRISON.

REFERENCES: R. V. Denenberg and Tia Denenberg, "Prison Grievance Procedures: A National Survey of Programs Underway," *Corrections Magazine*, 1975; National Institute of Law Enforcement and Criminal Justice, *Controlled Confrontation: The Ward Grievance Procedure of the California Youth Authority: An Exemplary Project*, 1976.

WASHINGTON STATE CORRECTIONAL SYSTEM. The Adult Corrections Division, part of the Department of Social and Health Services, operates one female prison, three large male prisons, and two honor camps for male offenders in Washington State. Each of these facilities has a specialized function in the system.

Washington Corrections Center at Shelton was opened in 1964 with a normal capacity of 720 male felons; it serves as a diagnostic reception center for all male offenders who come into the prison system, and it is also a training center for relatively young, first offenders.

The Shelton facility uses its architectural features and treatment programs to create a therapeutic setting for first offenders. Inmates live in modern dormitory units with concrete latticework substituting for traditional iron bars over the windows. The local school district operates a high school that normally serves about 250 of the inmate population at any one time. Many of the inmates who are not in the high school take vocational training from a variety of courses offered. By using the facility to house only first offenders, officials are attempting to prevent the development of a prison subculture.

Washington's other modern prison is the Purdy Treatment Center for Women opened in 1970 with space for 170 women. Women at Purdy are housed in small units that provide single bedrooms and a lounge. The treatment program provides high school education and some vocational training, but emphasis is on work release (*q.v.*) and school release. Some thirty-five to forty of the Purdy inmates make a daily twenty-minute bus trip to Tacoma to participate in these programs. The philosophy and architecture (*q.v.*) of the Purdy institution have drawn praise from William G. Nagel, author of *The New Red Barn,* and the National Commission on Criminal Justice Standards and Goals.

Washington State Penitentiary at Walla Walla opened in 1887 as the state's first prison; it has a normal capacity of 1,420 male felons. The penitentiary is the only prison in the state that is not near Puget Sound where most of the state's population is clustered. It has the traditional fortress-style appearance from the outside, but the interior has been modified by a policy which allows inmates to express their individuality and to form self-help groups. Prison uniforms and personal appearance regulations were abolished years ago; inmates wear their own clothes, grow beards, and wear their hair long if they choose to do so. Cell doors are left open much of the day and are decorated according to the occupants' individual tastes. The inmates have organized a variety of different self-help groups based on age, length of sentence, ethnic background, and other factors on which group distinctions can be made. Some of the groups are the Black People's Forum Unlimited, a Lifers' Club, a Senior Citizens' Club, and the Confederated Indian Tribes. Activities of the self-help groups vary according to the needs and preferences of the members, but each group is allocated space for its activities. The Black People's Forum Unlimited conducts Swahili language courses and other cultural self-awareness activities. The Lifers' Club repairs appliances for needy persons in the outside community, tape records books for the blind, and holds handicraft classes for Head Start children. The Confederated Indian Tribes operates a furniture refinishing shop to help make up for the lack of meaningful jobs in prison. Although the penitentiary has severely limited opportunities for productive work, it does offer a strong education program that includes the opportunity to earn college degrees through courses offered in the institution by faculty members of Walla Walla Community College and Washington State University at Pullman.

The Washington State Reformatory at Monroe opened in 1908 with a normal capacity of 700 male felons; it is said to be modeled after the reformatory at Elmira, New York. Tensions ran high among the inmates during the early part of the 1970s, partially because of extensive drug use in the facility. These tensions were eased in 1973 when a new superintendent was appointed who changed some of the regulations and allowed inmates a greater voice in decision-making.

In addition to these four prisons for adult offenders, the Adult Corrections Division operates two small camps: the Larch Mountain Honor Camp at Yacolt, which opened in 1956 with a normal capacity of 100 males, and the Indian Ridge Treatment Center at Arlington, which opened in 1969 with space for sixty males.

The Bureau of Juvenile Rehabilitation receives juveniles eight to eighteen years of age for incarceration in one of its thirteen facilities. These facilities, together with their opening dates and normal capacities, are the Cascadia Juvenile Reception-Diagnostic Center in Tacoma, 1963, 136 male and female juvenile delinquents; the Echo Glen Children's Center at Snoqualmie, 1968, 160 male and female juvenile delinquents eight to fourteen years of age; Green Hill School at Chehalis, 1891, 112 males ages fourteen to eighteen; Maple Lane School at Centralia, 1914, 139 female juvenile delinquents ages fourteen to eighteen; Canyon View Group Home at East Wenatchee, 1969, fourteen children ages fifteen to eighteen; Oakridge Group Home at Tacoma, 1969, fourteen children ages fifteen to eighteen; Pioneer Group Home in Tacoma, 1962, fourteen males ages sixteen to eighteen; Sunrise Group Home in Ephrata, 1967, sixteen boys ages eight to fourteen; Twin Rivers Group Home at Richland, 1975, fourteen boys ages fourteen to sixteen; Woodinville Group Home, 1965, sixteen females ages fifteen to eighteen; Cedar Creek Youth Camp at Littlerock, 1952 and rebuilt in 1959, ninety males ages fifteen to eighteen; Mission Creek Youth Forest Camp at Belfair, 1961, sixty males ages fifteen to eighteen; and Naselle Youth Forest Camp at Naselle, 1966, 114 males ages fourteen to eighteen.

The total prison population in Washington State is showing significant increases. On January 1, 1975, the population was 2,698;

one year later, it stood at 3,063—a 14 percent increase. By January 1, 1978, the prison population stood at 4,099.

REFERENCES: American Correctional Association, *Directory,* 1975–1976 edition; R. V. Denenberg, "Profile/Washington State," *Corrections Magazine,* 1974; Steve Gettinger, "U.S. Prison Population Hits All-Time High," *Corrections Magazine,* 1976; Michael Serrill, "Prison Population Rises Again, But at a Slower Rate," *Corrections Magazine,* 1978.

WEST VIRGINIA CORRECTIONAL SYSTEM. The Division of Correction, under the Department of Public Institutions, oversees the operation of adult and juvenile correctional facilities in West Virginia.

The adult facilities, together with opening dates and normal capacities, are the West Virginia Penitentiary at Moundsville, 1866, 600 male felons ages sixteen and above; the West Virginia Medium Security Prison at Huttonsville, 1939, 600 male felons ages sixteen and above; and the West Virginia State Prison for Women at Pence Springs, 1948, sixty female felons ages sixteen and above.

The juvenile facilities are the Anthony Correctional Center at Neola, 1970, 168 delinquents ages sixteen to twenty-one; the West Virginia Industrial School for Boys at Grafton, 1891, 180 delinquents ages ten to eighteen; the West Virginia Industrial Home for Girls at Salem, 1899, 100 delinquents ages ten to eighteen; the West Virginia Forestry Camp for Boys at Davis, 1956, eighty boys ages sixteen to twenty-one; and the West Virginia Forestry Camp for Boys at Leckie, 1970, eighty boys ages sixteen to twenty-one.

The state also operates three work/study release centers for adult male felons: the Beckley Work/Study Release Center at Beckley, opened in 1974 with a normal capacity of twenty-five; the Charleston Work/Study Release Center at Charleston, opened in 1972 with space for twenty-five; and the Grafton Work/Study Release Center at Grafton, opened in 1975 with a normal capacity of twenty-five.

West Virginia experienced a large growth in its prison population between January 1, 1975, and January 1, 1976, with a 29 percent increase from 940 to 1,213. However, the prison population decreased by 1 percent in 1977 to 1,206 in January 1978.

REFERENCES: American Correctional Association, *Directory,* 1975–1976 edition; Michael Serrill, "Prison Population Rises Again, But at a Slower Rate," *Corrections Magazine,* 1978.

WISCONSIN CORRECTIONAL SYSTEM. Within Wisconsin's Division of Corrections, which is under the Department of Health and

Social Services, is the Bureau of Institutions, responsible for the operation of prisons.

Adult offenders in Wisconsin are defined as persons eighteen years old or above, but persons between the ages of sixteen and eighteen may be sent to adult prisons if the court so directs.

The state has five adult prisons: the Wisconsin State Prison at Waupun, opened in 1851 with a normal capacity of 876 male felons; the Wisconsin State Reformatory at Green Bay, opened in 1898 with space for 623 male felons (it is used as a reception center for adult males and houses mostly first offenders between the ages of sixteen and thirty); the Wisconsin Correctional Institution at Fox Lake, opened in 1962 with a normal capacity of 576 male felons (it holds transfers from Wisconsin State Prison and Wisconsin State Reformatory); the Wisconsin Home for Women at Taycheedah, opened in 1921 with room for 161 female felons (it serves as the receiving center for female offenders); and the Kettle Moraine Correctional Institution at Plymouth, opened in 1962 with a normal capacity of 260 (it receives adult male transfers from Wisconsin State Prison and Wisconsin State Reformatory).

Juvenile offenders are imprisoned in three institutions (which are coeducational despite their names) and a series of camps for boys. The Wisconsin School for Boys at Wales was opened in 1959 with a normal capacity of 344 youths ages twelve to eighteen. The Wisconsin School for Girls at Oregon was opened in 1941 with room for 331 youths ages twelve to eighteen. The Lincoln Boys School at Irma was opened in 1970 with space for 287 youths ages twelve to eighteen. The Wisconsin Correctional Camp System, with a central office at Oregon, was opened in 1962 with a total capacity of 418 males ages twelve to eighteen housed in the following units: (1) McNaughton Forestry Camp at Lake Tomahawk; (2) Gordon Forestry Camp at Gordon; (3) Oregon Farm at Oregon; (4) Thompson Farm at Cambridge; (5) Union Grove Farm at Union Grove; (6) Winnebago Farm at Winnebago; (7) Black River Camp at Black River Falls; (8) Community Corrections Center at Milwaukee; and (9) Flambeau Forestry Camp at Hawkins.

The prison population in Wisconsin increased from 2,591 on January 1, 1976, to 3,055 one year later for a growth rate of 18 percent. By January 1, 1978, the prison population was 3,249.

REFERENCES: American Correctional Association, *Directory,* 1975–1976 edition; Steve Gettinger, "U.S. Prison Population Hits All-Time High," *Corrections Magazine,* 1976; Michael Serrill, "Prison Population Rises Again, But at a Slower Rate," *Corrections Magazine,* 1978.

WORK RELEASE. Work release programs allow selected incarcerated individuals to leave their place of custody so that they can fulfill the requirements of their employment in the free community. An inmate participating in a work release program typically leaves his place of confinement in the morning, travels to the place of his employment, works an eight-hour day at an ordinary job among other employees who are not inmates, and returns to his place of confinement immediately after the workday ends. The participating inmate is supervised much as any other inmate would be during the hours spent at the place of incarceration, but he is not supervised by correctional personnel during his working hours. The work release inmate is free for a part of each day, but only for purposes of holding a job in the community. The place of confinement can be a traditional prison or jail, or it may be a minimum security, community-based facility housing only inmates participating in the work release program.

Programs of this type are operated by correctional facilities at all levels of government from city jails to the U.S. Bureau of Prisons and are used by all fifty-one state systems. The earnings of work release inmates go for incidental expenses associated with their employment, the welfare of their dependents, room and board (paid to the place of incarceration), and savings to be used by the inmate at the time he is released from custody.

Work release is essentially a twentieth-century phenomenon in the United States. Vermont is believed to have operated the first work release program in the United States. The state passed a law in 1906 authorizing sheriffs to allow extramural civilian employment for prisoners. Sheriff Frank H. Tracy of Montpelier, Vermont, operated a program that had all of the basic elements of modern work release. In 1913, Wisconsin's Senator Henry A. Huber sponsored legislation that established a work release procedure for county jail inmates; references to the Huber Law often appear in discussions of work release operations. Massachusetts is thought to be the first state (in 1918) to allow female inmates to participate in work release; the state had enabling legislation as a result of an ancient indenture law that had rarely been used. A flu epidemic created an emergency that prompted the superintendent of the women's institution to allow female prisoners to be employed by a hospital. North Carolina has been a pioneer in work release, for it used work release several years before other states. In 1957, the state enacted legislation allowing work release for offenders in state institutions, but only for certain misdemeanor offenders who were recommended by the sentencing judge. In 1959, North Carolina changed its law to extend work release eligibility to some felons. The first work release program operated entirely away from prison grounds is thought to be that of the San Diego County Department of Camps and Honor Farms; it was operated from Crofton House, a residence in the urban area.

The Prisoner Rehabilitation Act of 1965 authorizes the U.S. Bureau of Prisons to use work release. In that same year, the growing popularity of work release programs was recognized when the American Correctional Association (*q.v.*) scheduled a special section on work release at its annual conference.

As work release programs have evolved over the years, a number of significant trends have emerged: (1) work release programs are more likely to be located in community correctional centers than in traditional prisons; (2) selection of inmates for participation is more likely to be made by administrators than by judges; (3) inmates have more responsibility in handling their earnings; (4) a specialized staff is used in work release programming; (5) there is less emphasis on applying inmate earnings to recovery of program costs; and (6) more reliance is placed on existing community programs for inmate self-improvement activities as opposed to staging the activities in the work release center.

Benefits claimed for work release programs include the rehabilitative potential inherent in keeping the offender on his job in the community to care for his family. The offender's personal dignity and work skills are therefore preserved. In cases where the offender's family does not use up all of his earnings, the work release inmate is able to accumulate savings. The offender is able to pay part of the costs of his rehabilitation program by paying taxes as well as room and board while in the program. In some cases, the inmate pays restitution to the victim.

Work release can be employed at different points in the criminal justice process. It can be used as an alternative to release on bond after the offender has been arrested, but before sentencing. Wisconsin has used this procedure, but it is rarely used elsewhere. Work release can also be used as part of the sentence for a crime. In this case, the court may authorize work release to begin immediately after the sentence is imposed, or it may simply be an option exercised by correctional officials in programming activities for the convicted offender. Work release may also be used as a pre-release program to ease the transition of offenders back into the community after they have been incarcerated for a substantial part of their sentence. The practice followed depends upon the provisions of the enabling legislation in the jurisdiction involved.

REFERENCES: Richard K. Brautigam, "Work Release: A Case Study and Comment," *Prison Journal,* 1973; Barry S. Brown and John D. Spevacek, "Work Release in Community and Institutional Settings," *Corrective Psychiatry and Journal of Social Therapy,* 1971; Walter H. Busher, *Ordering Time to Serve Prisoners: A Manual for the Planning and Administering of Work Release,* 1973; Elmer H. Johnson, *Work Release: Factors in Selection and Results,* 1969; Lawrence S. Root, "Work Release Legislation," *Federal Probation,* 1972.

WYOMING CORRECTIONAL SYSTEM. Operation of the one adult and two juvenile institutions in the state is the responsibility of the State Board of Charities and Reform. The board is made up of five state-elected officials, the governor, the secretary of state, the state auditor, the treasurer, and the state superintendent of public instruction.

The juvenile institutions are the Wyoming Girls School at Sheridan, opened in 1925 with a normal capacity of ninety girls ages eight to twenty; and the Wyoming Industrial Institute at Worland, opened in 1915 with space for 110 males whose ages range up to twenty-one. The adult institution, the Wyoming State Penitentiary at Rawlins, was opened in 1892 with a normal capacity of 325 adult male felons, including the space available at its subsidiary, the Wyoming State Penitentiary Farm at Riverton. The state has less than a dozen adult female felons; they are housed under contract in the Nebraska Reformatory for Women.

Between January 1, 1975, and January 1, 1976, the prison population of the state increased from 222 to 384, or by 73 percent. Such an increase would be extremely alarming if the prison population were not a moderate size compared with the normal capacity available. By January 1, 1978, the state's prison population stood at 436.

REFERENCES: American Correctional Association, *Directory,* 1975–1976 edition; Steve Gettinger, "U.S. Prison Population Hits All-Time High," *Corrections Magazine,* 1976; Michael Serrill, "Prison Population Rises Again, But at a Slower Rate," *Corrections Magazine,* 1978.

PRISON REFORM ORGANIZATIONS

The following listing of prison reform groups in the United States constitutes a small sample of the 490 active groups that have been identified by Urban Information Interpreters, Inc. This listing attempts to provide the name and location of at least one such group in each state for readers who may desire to participate in prison reform efforts, seek assistance from such groups, or obtain information on local prison conditions.

Alabama

Joint Committee of Lawyers and Interested Citizens to Study Alabama's Correctional Institutions and Procedures: P.O. Box 4483, Mobile, Alabama 36604, phone (205) 269–1515. Research on the prison system and public awareness campaign.

Link Society, Inc.: 48 North Kraft Highway, Prichard, Alabama 36610, phone (205) 452–0568. Social services to inmates and ex-inmates.

Alaska

Alaska Legal Services Corporation: 524 West Sixth Avenue, Suite 204, Anchorage, Alaska 99501, phone (907) 272–9431. Specialists in prison reform activity, including class action suits.

Arizona

Arizona Citizens Committee on Corrections: 715 North Park Avenue, Tucson, Arizona 85719, phone (602) 623–7575. Advocates of reform through education of the public.

SOURCE: Mary Lee Bundy and Kenneth R. Harmon (eds.), *The National Prison Directory*, 1975.

California

All for One Community Counseling Center: 44 East San Fernando, San Jose, California 95113, phone (213) 998–9307. Social services to offenders, ex-offenders, and potential offenders.

Black Panther Party: 8501 East 14th Street, Oakland, California 94621, phone (415) 638–0195. Social services and legal assistance to inmates.

Coordinating Council of Prisoner Organizations: Austin MacCormick Center, 1251 Second Avenue, San Francisco, California 94122, phone (415) 681–6750. Coordination of prisoner support groups.

Prison Information Center: Box 6751, Stanford, California 94305, phone (415) 497–2677. Lobbying for prison reform and social services to inmates.

Prisoner's Union: 1315 18th Street, San Francisco, California 94107, phone (415) 648–2880. Law union for inmates (national scope).

Colorado

Colorado Correctional Association: 3656 West Princeton Circle, Denver, Colorado 80236, phone (303) 761–1969. Resources for public education on prison reform.

Indian Corrections Project: 1506 Broadway, Boulder, Colorado 80302, phone (303) 447–8760. Class-action litigation to assure rehabilitation for Indian inmates and clearinghouse for information on Indian prisoners (national scope).

Connecticut

Connecticut Prison Association: 340 Capitol Avenue, Hartford, Connecticut 06115, phone (203) 566–2030. Social services to inmates.

Poor People Federation, Inc.: 1491 Main Street, Hartford, Connecticut 06120, phone (203) 278–7570. Social services and legal assistance to inmates.

Delaware

Delaware Council on Crime and Justice, Inc.: 701 Shipley Street, Wilmington, Delaware 19801, phone (302) 658–7174. Consultation, public education, and community organization for reform.

Florida

American Friends Service Committee: 3005 Bird Avenue, Cocoanut Grove, Miami, Florida 33133, phone (305) 443–9836. Resources on prison reform and limited amount of social services to inmates.

Georgia

Clearinghouse on Georgia Prisons and Jails: 88 Walton Street, N.W., Atlanta, Georgia 30303, phone (404) 525–0848. Coordination of a coalition of organizations interested in prison reform.

Hawaii

John Howard Association of Hawaii: 200 North Vineyard Boulevard, Room 102, Honolulu, Hawaii 96817, phone (808) 537–2917. Lobbying for reform and public education.

Idaho

Idaho Correctional Association: Box 375, Lewiston, Idaho 83501, phone (208) 746–2625. Seminars on prison problems.

Illinois

American Penal Press Contest: School of Journalism, Southern Illinois University, Carbondale, Illinois 62901, phone (618) 536–3361. Improvement of prison publications and encouragement of inmate authors (national scope).

Chicago Connections: P.O. Box 469, Chicago, Illinois 60601, phone (312) 939–4227. Social services to inmates.

John Howard Association: 67 East Madison, Room 1216, Chicago, Illinois 60603, phone (312) 263–1901. Public education, consultation, and technical assistance (national scope).

Safer Foundation: 343 South Dearborn, Room 400, Chicago, Illinois 60604, phone (312) 922–5301. Employment services for ex-offenders.

World Correctional Service Center: 2849 West 71st Street, Chicago, Illinois 60629, phone (312) 925–6591. Information on corrections (national scope).

Indiana

Coalition on Justice and Correctional Reform: 1100 West 42nd Street, Indianapolis, Indiana 46208, phone (317) 923–3674. Reform legislative program and liaison with other groups working for prison reform.

National Association of Training Schools and Juvenile Agencies: 5256 North Central Avenue, Indianapolis, Indiana 46220, phone (317) 257–3955. Research and legislation for improvement of juvenile institutions (national scope).

PACT (Prisoner and Community Together): Pact Community Resource Center, 431 Willard Avenue, P.O. Box 177, Michigan City, Indiana 46360. Social services to ex-inmates.

Iowa

Iowa Council of Churches: 317 East 5th Street, Des Moines, Iowa 50309, phone (515) 244–2253. Reform of penal codes.

Prison Reform Committee: Box 578, Newton, Iowa 50208. Vocational training in prisons and employment for ex-inmates.

Kansas

Seventh Step Foundation of Topeka, Inc.: P.O. Box 635, 935 Kansas Avenue, Topeka, Kansas 66601, phone (913) 232–8203. Social services to ex-inmates.

Kentucky

NAACP Project Rebound, Inc.: 1224 South 28th Street, Louisville, Kentucky 40211, phone (502) 774–2336. Social services to ex-inmates.

Prisons and Jails Subcommittee, Kentucky Civil Liberties Union: 630 Maxwelton Court, Lexington, Kentucky 40508. Litigation on behalf of inmates.

Louisiana

Community Service Center: 4000 Magazine Street, New Orleans, Louisiana 70115, phone (504) 897–6277. Social services to ex-inmates and public education.

Maine

SCAR: 374 Fore Street, Portland, Maine 04111, phone (207) 772–2303. Social services to inmates and public education.

Maryland

American Correctional Association: 4321 Hartwick Road, Suite L 208, College Park, Maryland 20740, phone (301) 854–1070. Education of the general public on prison issues and education for correctional professional (national scope).

Clearinghouse to End Medical Experimentation on Prisoners: P.O. Box AH, College Park, Maryland 20740, phone (301) 864–7628. Information on medical experimentation in prisons (national scope).

Prisoner Assistance Project: Baltimore Legal Aid Bureau, Inc., 341 North Calvert Street, Baltimore, Maryland 21202, phone (301) 539–5340. Legal services to inmates.

Massachusetts

Prison Information Center: Correctional Change Group, Inc., 48 Queen Street, Worchester, Massachusetts 01610, phone (617) 753–7167. Social services to inmates and public education.

Prisons Committee: Phillips Brooks House, Harvard College, Cambridge, Massachusetts 02138, phone (617) 495–5526. Lobbying and political action for prison reforms.

Self Development Group, Inc.: Three Joy Street, Boston, Massachusetts 02108, phone (617) 523-7965. Social services to inmates and ex-inmates.

Michigan

The Committee for the Rehabilitation and Reinvolvement of Ex-Offenders: Church of Scientology, 19 Clifford, Detroit, Michigan 48226, phone (313) 963–0886. Investigation of prison conditions and political action for reform.

Community Corrections Resource Programs, Inc.: P.O. Box 327, Ann Arbor, Michigan 48104, phone (313) 763–4276. Research and resource material for correctional programming.

Volunteers in Probation Division: National Council on Crime and Delinquency, 200 Washington Square Plaza, Royal Oak, Michigan 48067, phone (313) 398–8550. Promotion of use of volunteers in courts and corrections throughout the United States and in Canada.

Minnesota

F.O.C.U.S., Inc. (Former Offenders Creating Understanding in Society): 1212 Yale Place, Minneapolis, Minnesota 55403, phone (612) 336–4061. Social services to offenders and public education.

H.I.R.E. (Helping Industry Recruit Ex-Offenders): 1009 Nicollet Mall, Minneapolis, Minnesota 55403, phone (612) 348–8560. Employment assistance to ex-inmates and public education.

Minnesota Prisoners Union: 1427 Washington Avenue, South, Minneapolis, Minnesota 55404, phone (612) 339–8511. Labor union for inmates.

The Murton Foundation for Criminal Justice, Inc.: 810 Thorton Street, S.E. #403, Minneapolis, Minnesota 55415, phone (612) 338–3285. Research and publications on prison conditions (national scope).

Mississippi

Mississippi Prisoners' Defense Committee: Lawyers' Committee for Civil Rights Under Law, 233 North Farish Street, Jackson, Mississippi 39201, phone (601) 948–5400. Litigation on behalf of inmates and public education.

Missouri

Citizens Lobby for Penal Reform: 6429 Main Street, Kansas City, Missouri 64113, phone (816) 333–9636. Grassroots lobbying for prison reform.

Corrections Task Force: Missouri Association for Social Welfare, 411 Madison Street, Jefferson City, Missouri 65101, phone (314) 634–2901. A prison ombudsman program and other social services for offenders.

Montana

Correctional Facilities and Services Committee: Montana Bar Association, 501 Western Bank Building, Missoula, Montana 59801, phone (406) 543–3005. Drafting of legislation to remove work restrictions for ex-inmates.

Nebraska

7th Step Foundation of Nebraska, Inc.: 3212 Dodge Street, Omaha, Nebraska 68131, phone (402) 422–1477. Social and rehabilitation services to ex-inmates.

New Hampshire

New England Prisoners Association: Franconia, New Hampshire 03580, phone (603) 823–8501. Coalition of prison reform groups in the New England states.

New Jersey

Coalition for Penal Reform: New Jersey Council of Churches, 116 North Oraton Parkway, East Orange, New Jersey 07017, phone (201) 675–8600. Coalition of groups offering about seventy different programs to effect change in the correctional system.

Forum Project: 6 West Hanover Street, Trenton, New Jersey 08608, phone (609) 393–3544. Social services to inmates.

National Council on Crime and Delinquency: Continental Plaza, 411 Hackensack Avenue, Hackensack, New Jersey 07106, phone (201) 488–0400. Research, collection of information, and publications to promote prison reform (national scope).

New Mexico

Women's Prison Project, Inc.: P.O. Box 1911, Santa Fe, New Mexico 87501. Social services to women inmates.

New York

Bridge Volunteers/Associates Inc.: 1766 Main Street, Buffalo, New York 14208, phone (716) 885–0660. Social services to inmates and training of volunteers to work with inmates.

Citizens' Inquiry on Parole and Criminal Justice, Inc.: 84 Fifth Avenue, Room 307, New York, New York 10011, phone (212) 929–2955. Public education through research, distribution of publications, and maintaining a speakers' bureau.

Fight Ex-Offender Employment Program: Fight, Inc., 14 Lamberton Park, Rochester, New York 14611, phone (716) 328–9770. Social services to ex-inmates and visitation to prisons.

Fortune Society, Inc.: 29 East 22nd Street, New York, New York 10010, phone (212) 677–4600. Social services to ex-inmates and to families of inmates (national scope).

Midnight Special: National Lawyers Guild, 23 Cornelia Street, New York, New York 10014, phone (212) 989–3222. Publication of inmates' writings on prison reform issues (national scope).

New York Thresholds: Correctional Solutions, Inc., 593 Park Avenue, New York, New York 10021, phone (212) 838–0808. Teaching of decision-making skills to inmates and training of volunteers to work in prisons.

Offender Aid and Restoration of New York City: 473 Hudson Street, New York, New York 10014, phone (212) 255–6463. Training of volunteers to work with inmates and social services to inmates.

Salvation Army: 120 West 14th Street, New York, New York 10011, phone (212) 243–8700. Social services to inmates and ex-inmates.

Think Tank Concept: Green Haven Correctional Facility, Drawer B, Stormville, New York 12582, phone (212) 628–7400. Research and political action for prison reform.

North Carolina

Prisoners' Rights Project: North Carolina Civil Liberties Union Legal Foundation, Inc., 858 Southeastern Building, P.O. Box 3094, Greensboro, North Carolina 27402, phone (919) 273–1641. Assistance to inmates with grievances.

North Dakota

National Association for Justice, Inc., North Dakota Chapter: P.O. Box 1985, Minot, North Dakota 58701, phone (701) 839–5211. Legislative action for prison reform.

Ohio

Central Ohio Seventh Step, Inc.: 145 North High Street, Columbus, Ohio 43215, phone (614) 224–5783. Pre-release instruction for inmates.

Ex-Cons for a Better Society, Inc.: 2426 Salem Avenue, Dayton, Ohio 45406, phone (513) 223–9374. Social services to inmates and ex-inmates.

Prisoner Helper, Inc.: Box 424 (Midcity Station), Dayton, Ohio 45401, phone (513) 866–3398. Social services to inmates.

Oklahoma

H.O.P.E., Inc.: 431 Southwest 11th, P.O. Box 24031, Oklahoma City, Oklahoma 73103, phone (405) 272–0271. Social services to inmates.

Volunteers in Corrections: 55 North Western, Suite 104, Oklahoma City, Oklahoma 73118, phone (405) 848–4832. Recruiting and training of volunteers to work with offenders.

Oregon

Prisoner Assistance Project: 732 Southwest Third Avenue, Room 603, Portland, Oregon 97204, phone (503) 223–3490. Legal assistance to inmates.

Pennsylvania

Black Economic Development Conference, Inc.: 1007 West Somerset Street, Philadelphia, Pennsylvania 19133, phone (215) 221–5150. Social services to inmates.

Correctional Service Federation—U.S.A., International Prisoners Aid Association: 311 South Juniper Street, Room 300, Philadelphia, Pennsylvania 19107, phone (215) 732–5990. Clearinghouse for public information about volunteer correctional service agencies and development of agencies in areas where none exist (national scope).

Medical Committee for Human Rights, National Office: P.O. Box 7155, Oakland Station, Pittsburgh, Pennsylvania 15213, phone (412) 682–1200. Establishment of improved health care for inmates (national scope).

Pennsylvania Program for Women and Girl Offenders: 1530 Chestnut Street, Philadelphia, Pennsylvania 19102, phone (215) 563–9386. Social services to female inmates and ex-inmates.

Rhode Island

National Prisoners' Reform Association: 384 Elmwood Avenue, Providence,

Rhode Island 02907, phone (401) 461–2285. Social services to inmates and public education on prison reform (national scope).

South Carolina

Corrections Clinic: University of South Carolina Law School, Columbia, South Carolina 29208, phone (803) 777–8194. Legal advice to inmates.

South Carolina Association for Improved Justice: Columbia Building, Suite 200, Columbia, South Carolina 29203, phone (803) 253–8325. Social services to inmates.

South Dakota

Jail Reform Committee: Mueller and Bennett, c/o Dan Hanson, 618 State Street, Belle Fourche, South Dakota 57717, phone (605) 892–2641. Jail visitations and publicity designed to create public awareness of jail conditions.

Tennessee

Operation Reachback: 4010 Izlar Lane, Route 3, Ooltewah, Tennessee 37363. Social services to inmates.

Southern Coalition on Jails and Prisons: P.O. Box 12044, Nashville, Tennessee 37312, phone (615) 255–2959. Public education on prison conditions and coordination of six-state coalition.

Southern Prison Ministry: P.O. Box 12044, Nashville, Tennessee 37212, phone (615) 255–2959. Promotion of prison reform in the South.

Texas

Christian Reorientation and Prisoners Aid Center: 1207 21st Street, Huntsville, Texas 77340, phone (713) 295–7843. Social services to inmates and ex-inmates.

Community Prison Coalition: 1713 East 6th Street, Austin, Texas 78702, phone (512) 476–6321. Social services to inmates and political action for prison reform.

Vermont

Prisoner Community Center, Inc.: 87 Main Street, Windsor, Vermont 05089, phone (802) 674–2708. Social services to inmates and advocacy for prison reform.

Virginia

Tysk Magazine: P.O. Box 27264, Richmond, Virginia 23261, phone (804) 770–2101. Creation of greater public awareness of prison problems.

Incarcerated Veterans Assistance Organization: Box 25, Lorton Reformatory, Lorton, Virginia 22079. Social services to veterans who are in prison.

Lorton Voices: Box 25, Lorton, Virginia 22079, or 2242 Ontario Road, N.W., Washington, D.C. 20009, phone (202) 234–4114. A group that gives dramatic performances on prison conditions that need attention.

Offender Aid and Restoration of the U.S., Inc.: 414 4th Street, N.E., Charlottesville, Virginia 22901, phone (804) 295–0089. Training of volunteers to work with offenders (national scope).

Post-Conviction Assistance Project: Marshall-Wythe School of Law, College of William and Mary, Williamsburg, Virginia 23185, phone (804) 229–3000, extension 582. Legal assistance to inmates.

Washington

Prison Legal Services Project: Seattle-King County Legal Services Center, 618 Second Avenue, Seattle, Washington 98104, phone (206) 464–5911. Legal services to inmates.

Prisons Component: Operational Emergency Center, 2214 South Jackson, Seattle, Washington 98144, phone (206) 329–5881. Social services to inmates.

West Virginia

West Virginia Citizens and Offenders Resources, Inc.: Box 5032, Charleston, West Virginia 25311, phone (304) 346–9366. Public education, political action, and social services to inmates.

West Virginia Civil Liberties Union: American Civil Liberties Union, 1332 Washington Boulevard, Huntington, West Virginia 25701, phone (304) 525–3951. Litigation for prison reform.

Wisconsin

Commando Project I: 522 West North Avenue, Milwaukee, Wisconsin 53212, phone (414) 372–6260. Social services to inmates and ex-inmates.

Coordinated Volunteer Services: American Friends Service Committee, 2006 Monroe Street, Madison, Wisconsin 53711, phone (608) 233–0185. Social services to inmates.

Corrections Legal Services Program: Wisconsin Correctional Service, 436

West Wisconsin Avenue, Milwaukee, Wisconsin 53203, phone (414) 224-9074. Legal services to inmates.

Jewish Vocational Service of Milwaukee: 1339 North Milwaukee Street, Milwaukee, Wisconsin 53202, phone (414) 275-1344. Social services to ex-inmates.

Offender Reintegration Project: Center for Public Representation, 520 University Avenue, Madison, Wisconsin 53703, phone (608) 251-4008. Working for removal of civil disabilities.

Project Phoenix, Inc.: 1410 North 27th Street, Milwaukee, Wisconsin 53208, phone (414) 933-7100. Social services to native American offenders.

Self Help Coalition, Inc.: 2510 West Capitol Drive, Suite 207, Milwaukee, Wisconsin 53206, phone (414) 444-0753. Education and employment services for inmates.

Wisconsin Program for Women and Girl Offenders: 1015 North Ninth Street, Milwaukee, Wisconsin 53233, phone (414) 765-9344. Political action, public education, and monitoring of criminal justice activities having an impact on women offenders.

District of Columbia

Americans for Democratic Action: 1424 16th Street N.W., #704, Washington, D.C. 20036, phone (202) 265-5771. Lobbying for prison reform (national scope).

Capitol Hill Citizens for Better Education, Inc.: 603 A Street, S.E., Washington, D.C. 20009, phone (202) 543-4680. Efforts to secure education programs for area prisons.

Center for Correctional Justice: 1616 H Street, N.W. #505, Washington, D.C. 20006, phone (202) 628-6094. Analysis and development of grievance procedures in prisons (national scope).

Commission on Correctional Facilities and Services: American Bar Association, 1705 DeSales Street, N.W., Washington, D.C. 20036, phone (202) 223-1528. Eleven different programs for improvement of prisons, including the publication of *Corrections Magazine* (national scope).

Correctional Economics Center: American Bar Association, 1705 DeSales Street, N.W., Suite 501, Washington, D.C. 20036, phone (202) 223-8547, extension 48. Technical assistance to penologists on financial and economic matters (national scope).

National Association for Justice, Inc.: 1100 17th Street, N.W., Washington, D.C. 20036, phone (202) 833-9530. Research, analysis, and advocacy for prison reform (national scope).

National Prison Project of the American Civil Liberties Union Foundation: 1346 Connecticut Avenue, N.W., #1031, Washington, D.C. 20036, phone (202) 331–0500. Public education and class action suits on behalf of inmates (national scope).

National Moratorium on Prison Construction: National Council on Crime and Delinquency and the Unitarian Universalist Service Committee, 2215 M Street, N.W., Washington, D.C. 20037, phone (202) 296–8290. Clearinghouse on prison construction plans (national scope).

One America Rehabilitation Division: One America, Inc., 1330 Massachusetts Avenue, N.W., Suite 205, Washington, D.C. 20005, phone (202) 628–2216. Training of volunteers to work with offenders and design of rehabilitation programs.

ADDRESSES OF STATE PLANNING AGENCIES

State planning agencies prepare and revise comprehensive annual plans for the purposes of reducing crime, improving criminal justice, and preventing juvenile delinquency. The state planning agencies are funded by planning grants from the Law Enforcement Assistance Administration and must submit their plans to LEAA in order to be eligible for LEAA funds awarded in their block grant program. The state planning agencies can supply application forms for state or local agencies or for nonprofit organizations seeking subgrants for criminal justice activities.

Alabama

Alabama Law Enforcement Planning Agency
2863 Fairlane Drive, Suite 49
Executive Park
Montgomery, Alabama 36111   205/277–5440

Alaska

Alaska Criminal Justice Planning Agency
Pouch AJ
Juneau, Alaska 99801   907/465–3530

American Samoa

Territorial Criminal Justice Planning Agency
Office of the Attorney General
Box 7
Pago Pago, American Samoa 96920   33431

SOURCE: U.S. Department of Justice, *The Law Enforcement Assistance Administration: A Partnership for Crime Control,* 1976.

Arizona

Arizona State Justice Planning Agency
Continental Plaza Building, Suite M
5119 North 19th Avenue
Phoenix, Arizona 85015   602/271–5466

Arkansas

Commission on Crime and Law Enforcement
1000 University Tower Building
12th at University
Little Rock, Arkansas 72204   501/371–1305

California

Office of Criminal Justice Programs
California Council on Criminal Justice
7171 Bowling Drive
Sacramento, California 95823   916/445–9156

Colorado

Division of Criminal Justice
Department of Local Affairs
328 State Service Building
1526 Sherman Street
Denver, Colorado 80203   303/892–3331

Connecticut

Governor's Planning Committee on Criminal Administration
75 Elm Street
Hartford, Connecticut 06115   203/566–3020

Delaware

Delaware Agency to Reduce Crime
Room 405—Central YMCA
11th and Washington Streets
Wilmington, Delaware 19801   302/571–3431

District of Columbia

Office of Criminal Justice Plans and Analysis
Munsey Building, Room 200
1329 E Street, N.W.
Washington, D.C. 20004   202/629–5063

Florida

Bureau of Criminal Justice Planning and Assistance
620 South Meridian
Tallahassee, Florida 32304   904/438–6001

Georgia

Office of the State Crime Commission
Suite 306
1430 West Peachtree Street, N.W.
Atlanta, Georgia 30309   404/656–3825

Guam

Comprehensive Territorial Crime Commission
Office of the Governor
Soledad Drive
Amistad Building, Room 4, 2d Floor
Agana, Guam 96910   772–8781

Hawaii

State Law Enforcement and Juvenile Delinquency Planning Agency
1010 Richard Street
Kamamalu Building, Room 412
Honolulu, Hawaii 96800   808/548–3800

Idaho

Law Enforcement Planning Commission
State House, Capitol Annex No. 3
Boise, Idaho 83707   208/384–2364

Illinois

Illinois Law Enforcement Commission
120 South Riverside Plaza, 10th Floor
Chicago, Illinois 60606   312/454–1560

Indiana

Indiana Criminal Justice Planning Agency
215 North Senate
Indianapolis, Indiana 46202   317/633–4773

Iowa

Iowa Crime Commission
3125 Douglas Avenue
Des Moines, Iowa 50210   515/281-3241

Kansas

Governor's Committee on Criminal Administration
535 Kansas Avenue, 10th Floor
Topeka, Kansas 66612   913/296-3066

Kentucky

Executive Office of Staff Services
Kentucky Department of Justice
209 St. Clair Street, 5th Floor
Frankfort, Kentucky 40601   502/564-6710

Louisiana

Louisiana Commission on Law Enforcement and Administration of Criminal
   Justice
1885 Wooddale Boulevard, Room 615
Baton Rouge, Louisiana 70806   504/389-7515

Maine

Maine Law Enforcement Planning and Assistance Agency
295 Water Street
Augusta, Maine 04330   207/289-3361

Maryland

Governor's Commission on Law Enforcement and Administration of Justice
Executive Plaza One, Suite 302
Cockeysville, Maryland 21030   301/666-9610

Massachusetts

Massachusetts Committee on Criminal Justice
80 Boylston Street, Suite 740
Boston, Massachusetts 02116   617/727-5497

Michigan

Office of Criminal Justice Programs
Lewis Cass Building, 2d Floor
Lansing, Michigan 48913   517/373-3992

Minnesota

Governor's Commission on Crime Prevention and Control
444 Lafayette Road, 6th Floor
St. Paul, Minnesota 55101   612/296-3052

Mississippi

Mississippi Criminal Justice Planning Division
Suite 200, Watkins Building
510 George Street
Jackson, Mississippi 39201   601/354-6591

Missouri

Missouri Council on Criminal Justice
P.O. Box 1041
Jefferson City, Missouri 65101   314/751-3432

Montana

Board of Crime Control
1336 Helena Avenue
Helena, Montana 59601   406/499-3604

Nebraska

Nebraska Commission on Law Enforcement and Criminal Justice
State Capitol Building
Lincoln, Nebraska 68509   402/471-2194

Nevada

Commission on Crime, Delinquency and Corrections
430 Jeanell Street
Carson City, Nevada 89701   702/885-4404

New Hampshire

Governor's Commission on Crime and Delinquency
169 Manchester Street
Concord, New Hampshire 03301   603/271-3601

New Jersey

State Law Enforcement Planning Agency
3535 Quaker Bridge Road
Trenton, New Jersey 08625   609/292-3741

New Mexico

Governor's Council on Criminal Justice Planning
P.O. Box 1770
Santa Fe, New Mexico 87501   505/827-5222

New York

State of New York, Division of Criminal Justice Services, Office of Planning
    and Program Assistance
270 Broadway, 10th Floor
New York, New York 10007   212/488-3891

North Carolina

Division of Law and Order
North Carolina Department of Natural and Economic Resources
P.O. Box 27867
Raleigh, North Carolina 27611   919/829-7974

North Dakota

North Dakota Combined Law Enforcement Council
Box B
Bismarck, North Dakota 58501   701/224-2594

Ohio

Ohio Department of Economic and Community Development
Administration of Justice Division
30 East Broad Street, 26th Floor
Columbus, Ohio 43215   614/466-7610

Oklahoma

Oklahoma Crime Commission
3033 North Walnut Street
Oklahoma City, Oklahoma 73105   405/521–2821

Oregon

Executive Department, Law Enforcement Council
2001 Front Street, N.E.
Salem, Oregon 97310   503/378–4347

Pennsylvania

Governor's Justice Commission
Department of Justice
P.O. Box 1167
Federal Square Station
Harrisburg, Pennsylvania 17108   717/787–2042

Puerto Rico

Puerto Rico Crime Commission
G.P.O. Box 1256
Hato Rey, Puerto Rico 00936   809/783–0398

Rhode Island

Governor's Committee on Delinquency and Criminal Administration
265 Melrose Street
Providence, Rhode Island 02907   401/277–2620

South Carolina

Office of Criminal Justice Programs
Edgar A. Brown State Office Building
1205 Pendleton Street
Columbia, South Carolina 29201   803/758–3573

South Dakota

Division of Law Enforcement Assistance
118 West Capitol
Pierre, South Dakota 57501   605/224–3665

Tennessee

Tennessee Law Enforcement Planning Agency
Suite 205, Capitol Hill Building
301—7th Avenue, North
Nashville, Tennessee 37219   615/741–3521

Texas

Criminal Justice Division
Office of the Governor
P.O. Box 1828
Austin, Texas 78767   512/475–9239

Utah

Utah Council on Criminal Justice Administration
Room 304—State Office Building
Salt Lake City, Utah 84114   801/533–5731

Vermont

Governor's Commission on the Administration of Justice
149 State Street
Montpelier, Vermont 05602   802/828–2351

Virginia

Division of Justice and Crime Prevention
8501 Mayland Drive
Richmond, Virginia 23229   804/786–7421

Virgin Islands

Virgin Islands Law Enforcement Commission
Box 280—Charlotte Amalie
St. Thomas, Virgin Islands 00801   809/774–6400

Washington

Law and Justice Planning Office
Planning and Community Affairs Agency
Insurance Building, Room 107
Olympia, Washington 98504   206/753–2235

West Virginia

Governor's Committee on Crime, Delinquency and Corrections
Morris Square, Suite 321
1212 Lewis Street
Charleston, West Virginia 25301   304/348–8814

Wisconsin

Wisconsin Council on Criminal Justice
122 West Washington
Madison, Wisconsin 53702   608/266–3323

Wyoming

Governor's Planning Committee on Criminal Administration
State Office Building East
Cheyenne, Wyoming 82002   307/777–7716

Appendix C

PRISON SYSTEM ADDRESSES

Alabama

Alabama State Board of Corrections
101 S. Union Street
Montgomery, Alabama 36130   205/832–6800

Alaska

Alaska Department of Health and Social Services
Division of Corrections
Pouch H 03, Health and Social Services Building
Juneau, Alaska 99811   907/465–3376/77

Arizona

Arizona Department of Corrections
1601 West Jefferson
Phoenix, Arizona 85007   602/271–5536

Arkansas

Arkansas Department of Correction
Post Office Box 8707
Pine Bluff, Arkansas 71601   501/535–7231

California

California Department of Corrections
714 P Street
State Office Building No. 8
Sacramento, California 95814   916/445–7688

Colorado

Colorado State Department of Institutions
4150 South Lowell Boulevard
Denver, Colorado 80236   303/761–0220

Connecticut

Connecticut Department of Correction
340 Capitol Avenue
Hartford, Connecticut 06115   203/566–4457

Delaware

Delaware Department of Correction
Box 343
Smyrna, Delaware 19977   203/653–7545

District of Columbia

Department of Corrections, D.C.
614 H Street, N.W.
Washington, D.C. 20001   202/629–3532

Florida

Florida Department of Offender Rehabilitation
1311 Winewood Boulevard
Tallahassee, Florida 32301   904/488–5021

Georgia

Department of Corrections/Offender Rehabilitation
Georgia State Board of Corrections
800 Peachtree Street, N.E.
Atlanta, Georgia 30308   404/894–5548

Hawaii

Hawaii Department of Social Services and Housing
Corrections Division
P.O. Box 339
Honolulu, Hawaii 96809   808/548–6441

Idaho

Idaho Department of Correction
Box 7309
Boise, Idaho 83707   208/342–7442

Illinois

Illinois Department of Corrections
201 Armory Building
Springfield, Illinois 62706   217/782–4777

Indiana

Indiana Department of Correction
804 State Office Building
Indianapolis, Indiana 46204   317/633–4697

Iowa

Iowa Department of Social Services
Division of Correctional Institutions
Robert Lucas Building
Des Moines, Iowa 50319   515/281–5459

Kansas

Kansas Department of Corrections
KPL Tower Building, Suite 500
818 Kansas Avenue
Topeka, Kansas 66612   913/296–3317

Kentucky

Kentucky Bureau of Corrections
State Office Building
Frankfort, Kentucky 40601   502/564–4726

Louisiana

Louisiana Department of Corrections
P.O. Box 44304
State Capitol Station
Baton Rouge, Louisiana 70804   504/389–5641

Maine

Maine Department of Mental Health and Corrections
411 State Office Building
Augusta, Maine 04333   207/289–3161

Maryland

Maryland Department of Public Safety and Correctional Services
Executive Plaza One, Suite 500
Hunt Valley, Maryland 21031   301/667–1100

Massachusetts

Massachusetts Department of Correction
Saltonstall Office Building
Government Center
100 Cambridge Street
Boston, Massachusetts 02202   617/727–3312

Michigan

Michigan Department of Corrections
Stevens T. Mason Building
Lansing, Michigan 48913   517/373–0720

Minnesota

Minnesota Department of Corrections
430 Metro Square Building
Seventh and Robert Streets
St. Paul, Minnesota 55101   612/296–6133

Mississippi

Mississippi State Penitentiary
Parchman, Mississippi 38738   601/745–6611

Missouri

Missouri Department of Social Services
Broadway Building
Jefferson City, Missouri 65101   314/751–4815

Montana

Montana Department of Institutions
1539 11th Avenue
Helena, Montana 59601   406/449–3930

Nebraska

Nebraska Department of Correctional Services
P.O. Box 94661
Lincoln, Nebraska 68509   402/471–2654

Nevada

Nevada State Prisons
P.O. Box 607
Carson City, Nevada 89710   702/885–5069

New Hampshire

New Hampshire State Prison
Box 14
Concord, New Hampshire 03301   603/224–6554

New Jersey

New Jersey Department of Institutions and Agencies
Division of Correction and Parole
135 West Hanover Street
Trenton, New Jersey 08625   609/292–4223

New Mexico

New Mexico Department of Corrections
P.O. Box 2325
Santa Fe, New Mexico 87501   505/827–2348

New York City

New York City Department of Corrections
100 Centre Street
New York, New York 10013   212/374–4414

New York State

New York Department of Correctional Services
State Office Building Campus
Albany, New York 12226   518/457–8134

North Carolina

North Carolina Department of Correction
840 West Morgan Street
Raleigh, North Carolina 27603   919/829–4926

North Dakota

North Dakota Director of Institutions
State Capitol
Bismarck, North Dakota 58505   701/224–2474

Ohio

Ohio Department of Rehabilitation and Correction
1050 Freeway Drive North
Columbus, Ohio 43229   614/466–6190

Oklahoma

Oklahoma Department of Corrections
3400 N. Eastern
Oklahoma City, Oklahoma 73111   405/521–2371

Oregon

Oregon Department of Human Resources
Corrections Division
2575 Center Street, N.E.
Salem, Oregon 97310   503/378–2467

Pennsylvania

Pennsylvania Department of Justice
Bureau of Correction
Box 598
Camp Hill, Pennsylvania 17011   717/787–7482

Rhode Island

Rhode Island Department of Corrections
75 Howard Avenue
Cranston, Rhode Island 02920   401/464–2611

South Carolina

South Carolina Department of Corrections
4444 Broad River Road
P.O. Box 766
Columbia, South Carolina 29202   803/758–6444

South Dakota

South Dakota State Board of Charities and Corrections
Department of Social Services
Division of Corrections
402 West Sioux
Pierre, South Dakota 57501   605/224–3398

Tennessee

Tennessee Department of Correction
11th Floor, 1st American Center
Nashville, Tennessee 37238   615/741–2071

Texas

Texas Department of Corrections
Box 99
Huntsville, Texas 77340   713/295–6371

Utah

Utah Department of Social Services
Division of Corrections
2525 South Main Street
Suite #15
Salt Lake City, Utah 84115   801/533–6541

Vermont

Vermont Agency of Human Services
Department of Corrections
79 River Street
Montpelier, Vermont 05602   802/828–2452

Virginia

Virginia State Department of Corrections
22 East Cary Street
Richmond, Virginia 23219   804/779–8575

Washington

Washington Department of Social and Health Services
Adult Corrections Division
P.O. Box 1788
Olympia, Washington 98504   206/753–2500

West Virginia

West Virginia Department of Public Institutions
Division of Correction
State Capitol Building
Charleston, West Virginia 25305   304/348–2091

Wisconsin

Wisconsin Department of Health and Social Services
Division of Corrections
P.O. Box 669
Madison, Wisconsin 53701   608/266–2471

Wyoming

Wyoming State Board of Charities and Reform
Capitol Building
Cheyenne, Wyoming 82002   307/777–7405

United States

United States Department of Justice
Bureau of Prisons
320 First Street, N.W.
Washington, D.C. 20534   202/739–2226

American Samoa

Government of American Samoa
Department of Public Safety
Pago Pago, American Samoa 96799   33431

Guam

Guam Department of Corrections
P.O. Box 3236
Agana, Guam 96910   734–2458/59

Commonwealth of Puerto Rico

Puerto Rico Administration of Corrections
Box 71308
San Juan, Puerto Rico 00936   763/1558

Virgin Islands

Virgin Islands Department of Public Safety
P.O. Box 668
St. Thomas, Virgin Islands 00801   809/774–1330

Appendix D

UNITED STATES GOVERNMENT STATISTICS PERTAINING TO CORRECTIONAL ACTIVITIES

SOURCE: U.S. Department of Justice, Law Enforcement Assistance Administration, National Criminal Justice Information and Statistics Service, *Sourcebook of Criminal Justice Statistics—1977*. Albany, New York: Criminal Justice Research Center, February 1978.

Table 1 Direct current expenditure for State correctional activities, by type of activity and State, fiscal year 1975

[Dollar amounts in thousands. — represents zero or rounds to zero.]

State [a]	Total direct current expenditure	Institutions Total	For men	For women	For juveniles	Other and combined	Corrections administration	Probation, parole, and pardon	Miscellaneous
Total	$2,015,826	$1,550,973	$989,979	$44,270	$419,306	$97,418	$155,747	$271,824	$37,282
Alabama	17,538	14,255	10,644	644	2,967	—	157	2,706	420
Alaska	12,323	9,945	3,125	—	3,527	3,293	397	1,649	332
Arizona	18,117	14,271	2,991	—	3,627	7,653	1,519	2,216	111
Arkansas	9,644	8,845	5,711	124	3,010	—	83	521	195
California	266,447	192,953	135,657	5,677	51,619	—	25,836	34,707	12,951
Colorado	30,144	21,939	15,140	—	6,799	—	1,215	6,931	59
Connecticut	40,036	27,599	19,716	2,061	3,952	1,870	4,849	6,584	1,004
Delaware	10,634	9,002	4,832	226	3,211	733	880	695	57
Florida	119,073	78,395	51,432	204	23,187	3,572	5,790	34,888	—
Georgia	49,061	33,104	21,663	973	10,468	—	5,560	9,815	582
Hawaii	6,800	5,303	—	—	1,427	3,876	270	1,123	104
Idaho	6,428	5,373	3,804	95	1,474	—	—	1,055	—
Illinois	82,578	60,192	37,190	1,752	21,250	—	12,150	10,236	—
Indiana	30,943	25,402	19,486	888	5,028	—	1,431	1,825	2,285
Iowa	20,564	17,943	12,168	608	5,167	—	660	1,250	711
Kansas	27,587	26,608	13,558	732	4,257	8,061	309	670	—
Kentucky	19,903	15,114	10,379	521	4,003	211	898	3,177	714
Louisiana	26,743	18,806	11,212	726	6,868	—	1,632	3,559	2,746
Maine	8,154	6,840	3,918	25	2,897	—	195	814	305
Maryland	79,705	58,357	35,392	1,620	17,028	4,317	5,661	15,443	244
Massachusetts	60,012	49,086	32,023	2,148	14,915	—	5,593	5,315	18
Michigan	61,322	53,548	40,750	—	12,798	—	2,894	4,880	—
Minnesota	26,465	20,799	13,324	637	6,838	—	4,702	253	711
Mississippi	11,227	9,435	—	—	1,936	7,499	135	1,657	—
Missouri	31,388	21,951	16,034	474	5,443	—	4,842	4,366	229

290

Montana	6,948	5,421	3,285	20	2,116	—	425	1,102	—
Nebraska	11,584	9,098	6,460	439	2,199	—	426	2,060	—
Nevada	9,402	7,626	4,826	—	2,724	76	—	1,776	—
New Hampshire	5,232	4,110	2,091	—	2,019	—	—	1,098	24
New Jersey	59,201	51,641	25,635	3,335	11,931	10,740	1,726	5,193	641
New Mexico	8,235	6,113	3,598	53	2,462	—	190	1,932	—
New York	213,630	177,516	123,769	4,036	22,564	27,147	11,546	21,708	2,860
North Carolina	71,297	53,521	39,228	1,841	11,554	898	4,196	10,703	2,877
North Dakota	3,461	3,167	1,533	62	1,572	—	—	294	—
Ohio	110,416	81,661	44,415	2,594	26,513	8,139	22,241	5,958	556
Oklahoma	19,427	14,113	10,308	464	3,341	—	3,567	1,747	—
Oregon	25,814	19,239	11,267	414	7,558	—	837	5,738	—
Pennsylvania	88,631	74,065	41,840	2,618	29,607	—	2,693	10,786	1,087
Rhode Island	11,192	8,655	6,784	—	1,871	—	889	1,648	—
South Carolina	31,097	21,937	15,578	524	5,835	—	2,955	2,458	3,747
South Dakota	4,247	3,741	—	—	1,238	2,503	8	333	165
Tennessee	29,043	24,264	15,128	869	8,267	—	933	3,846	—
Texas	53,683	46,088	32,466	1,459	12,163	—	3,207	4,388	—
Utah	9,572	6,259	—	133	2,103	4,023	138	3,129	46
Vermont	6,474	4,866	2,473	—	2,093	300	333	875	400
Virginia	62,809	45,346	34,939	1,685	8,722	—	7,994	8,416	1,053
Washington	43,963	35,368	20,513	2,129	12,726	—	348	8,247	—
West Virginia	9,472	8,240	5,463	219	2,558	—	—	1,184	48
Wisconsin	44,577	30,635	16,722	1,197	10,209	2,507	3,342	10,600	—
Wyoming	3,583	3,218	1,509	44	1,665	—	95	270	—

[a] Data are based on a field compilation from records of each State government; see Source for data limitations.

Source: U.S. Department of Justice, Law Enforcement Assistance Administration and U.S. Bureau of the Census, *Expenditure and Employment Data for the Criminal Justice System 1975* (Washington, D.C.: U.S. Government Printing Office, 1977), p. 276.

Table 2 Employment and payroll for correctional activities, by State and level of government, October 1971– October 1975

[Dollar amounts in thousands. — represents zero or rounds to zero.]

State and level of government	October 1971 Full-time equivalent employment	October 1971 October payroll	October 1972 Full-time equivalent employment	October 1972 October payroll	October 1973 Full-time equivalent employment	October 1973 October payroll	October 1974 Full-time equivalent employment	October 1974 October payroll	October 1975 Full-time equivalent employment	October 1975 October payroll
States–local, total	172,821	$129,119	177,864	$142,905	187,298	$159,518	203,230	$185,577	213,813	$208,942
States	106,045	78,648	107,785	86,710	112,176	95,565	121,160	110,710	126,933	123,252
Local, total	66,776	50,470	70,079	56,193	75,122	63,953	82,070	74,867	86,880	85,690
Counties	49,261	36,028	53,014	40,958	56,905	46,742	62,482	55,027	67,942	64,478
Municipalities	17,515	14,442	17,065	15,235	18,217	17,211	19,588	19,840	18,938	21,213
Alabama	1,425	730	1,590	892	1,763	1,103	2,036	1,393	2,171	1,676
State	939	486	1,003	563	1,066	695	1,243	850	1,281	1,042
Local, total	486	244	587	330	697	409	793	544	890	634
Counties	333	163	414	234	536	319	620	411	736	508
Municipalities	153	81	173	95	161	90	173	132	154	125
Alaska	380	401	442	559	385	403	445	571	455	701
State	335	364	370	476	341	360	412	534	424	667
Local, total	45	37	72	83	44	43	33	37	31	33
Boroughs	—	—	—	—	—	—	—	—	—	—
Municipalities	45	37	72	83	44	43	33	37	31	33
Arizona	1,374	881	1,450	1,020	1,845	1,403	2,099	1,811	2,237	2,110
State	745	512	744	539	950	761	1,070	943	1,103	1,075
Local, total	629	369	706	481	895	642	1,029	868	1,134	1,035
Counties	576	334	649	437	847	601	1,013	856	1,115	1,018
Municipalities	53	35	57	44	48	41	16	13	19	17
Arkansas	665	313	761	405	821	479	892	561	1,148	766
State	452	215	543	306	560	348	643	420	792	560
Local, total	213	98	218	99	261	132	249	141	356	206
Counties	157	65	165	67	176	80	197	107	283	157
Municipalities	56	33	53	32	85	51	52	34	73	49

California	26,754	25,266	29,039	28,329	29,589	31,039	31,996	35,768	32,572	39,914
State	10,159	9,925	11,891	11,687	11,714	12,691	12,807	14,913	12,704	16,017
Local, total	16,595	15,342	17,148	16,643	17,875	18,348	19,189	20,855	19,868	23,896
Counties	15,802	14,543	16,310	15,806	17,094	17,528	18,321	19,963	19,014	22,938
Municipalities	793	799	838	836	781	820	868	892	854	959
Colorado	1,710	1,265	1,778	1,360	1,910	1,601	2,053	1,884	2,331	2,453
State	1,327	1,012	1,399	1,101	1,470	1,268	1,535	1,443	1,702	1,896
Local, total	383	253	379	259	440	333	518	441	629	556
Counties	148	76	161	87	217	131	280	184	353	264
Municipalities	235	177	218	172	223	202	238	258	276	292
Connecticut	2,058	1,660	2,087	1,806	2,312	1,907	2,703	2,542	2,593	2,446
State	2,048	1,654	2,087	1,806	2,312	1,907	2,701	2,539	2,593	2,446
Local, total	10	6	—	—	—	—	2	3	—	—
Counties	10	6	—	—	—	—	2	3	—	—
Municipalities	—	—	—	—	—	—	—	—	—	—
Delaware	583	493	690	565	654	522	683	637	791	760
State	583	493	690	565	654	522	683	637	791	760
Local, total	—	—	—	—	—	—	—	—	—	—
Counties	—	—	—	—	—	—	—	—	—	—
Municipalities	—	—	—	—	—	—	—	—	—	—
District of Columbia:										
Local, total	2,625	2,390	2,850	2,917	2,922	2,883	3,333	3,486	2,741	3,766
Florida	7,367	4,572	8,472	5,674	9,827	7,116	10,816	9,058	11,861	9,362
State	4,698	3,019	5,831	4,037	7,065	5,157	8,274	7,035	9,022	6,985
Local, total	2,669	1,553	2,641	1,637	2,762	1,959	2,542	2,024	2,839	2,377
Counties	2,037	1,188	2,031	1,256	2,219	1,603	1,999	1,615	2,268	1,937
Municipalities	632	365	610	381	543	357	543	409	571	440
Georgia	3,896	2,164	4,050	2,561	4,970	3,291	5,315	3,867	5,695	4,158
State	2,503	1,412	2,593	1,736	3,183	2,170	3,427	2,566	3,637	2,713
Local, total	1,393	752	1,457	824	1,787	1,124	1,888	1,301	2,058	1,445
Counties	1,214	649	1,269	717	1,548	978	1,662	1,151	1,753	1,222
Municipalities	179	103	188	108	239	145	226	150	305	223
Hawaii	434	400	432	384	444	450	453	494	380	454
State	358	337	351	320	360	371	372	412	371	446
Local, total	76	62	81	64	84	79	81	82	9	8
Counties	17	13	17	11	20	18	17	12	9	8
Municipalities	59	49	64	53	64	61	64	69	—	—
Idaho	425	253	458	293	542	346	469	337	531	420
State	360	223	369	245	441	292	364	276	394	334
Local, total	65	30	89	48	101	54	105	61	137	86
Counties	63	29	85	46	97	52	102	59	135	85
Municipalities	2	1	4	2	4	2	3	2	2	1

See footnote at end of table.

293

Table 2 (continued)

[Dollar amounts in thousands. — represents zero or rounds to zero.]

State and level of government	Employment and payroll [a]									
	October 1971		October 1972		October 1973		October 1974		October 1975	
	Full-time equivalent employment	October payroll	Full-time equivalent employment	October payroll	Full-time equivalent employment	October payroll	Full-time equivalent employment	October payroll	Full-time equivalent employment	October payroll
Illinois	7,161	5,213	7,391	5,865	6,877	6,340	7,437	6,855	7,914	7,624
State	4,959	3,634	4,910	4,031	4,502	4,380	4,767	4,668	4,981	5,102
Local, total	2,202	1,579	2,481	1,834	2,375	1,960	2,670	2,186	2,933	2,522
Counties	2,165	1,549	2,459	1,815	2,337	1,931	2,654	2,175	2,923	2,516
Municipalities	37	29	22	20	38	29	16	12	10	6
Indiana	3,042	1,812	2,828	1,818	3,024	2,085	3,284	2,461	3,480	2,827
State	1,999	1,234	1,856	1,257	1,869	1,397	1,969	1,598	2,072	1,847
Local, total	1,043	578	972	560	1,155	688	1,315	863	1,408	980
Counties	542	271	644	356	836	485	880	566	977	661
Municipalities	501	307	328	204	319	202	435	298	431	319
Iowa	1,563	979	1,508	1,059	1,549	1,209	1,806	1,417	2,005	1,814
State	1,134	752	1,115	843	1,131	964	1,271	1,061	1,377	1,307
Local, total	429	227	393	216	418	245	535	356	628	507
Counties	424	223	389	211	412	240	527	349	617	499
Municipalities	5	4	4	4	6	5	8	7	11	8
Kansas	2,379	1,445	2,208	1,326	2,300	1,445	2,570	1,694	2,713	2,011
State	2,045	1,280	1,911	1,171	1,945	1,241	2,114	1,422	2,194	1,682
Local, total	334	165	297	155	355	204	456	272	519	328
Counties	297	143	252	127	290	159	400	233	484	302
Municipalities	37	23	45	28	65	45	56	39	35	26
Kentucky	1,710	903	1,763	1,048	1,971	1,358	2,032	1,389	2,286	1,754
State	1,487	784	1,332	819	1,458	1,040	1,448	1,011	1,525	1,224
Local, total	223	120	431	229	513	318	584	377	761	530
Counties	201	106	403	210	462	279	517	332	620	427
Municipalities	22	14	28	19	51	39	67	45	141	103

Louisiana	2,395	1,292	2,556	1,499	3,043	1,838	3,146	2,155	3,639	2,823
State	1,582	867	1,742	1,070	2,095	1,289	2,139	1,486	2,466	1,959
Local, total	813	425	814	429	948	549	1,007	669	1,173	864
Parishes	308	159	417	214	422	248	490	303	578	386
Municipalities	505	266	397	215	526	301	517	366	595	478
Maine	737	439	751	529	785	583	806	631	780	621
State	629	388	641	474	672	519	668	548	639	529
Local, total	108	51	110	55	113	64	138	83	141	92
Counties	108	51	106	53	109	61	138	83	141	92
Municipalities	—	—	4	2	4	2	—	—	—	—
Maryland	5,095	3,896	5,323	4,902	5,356	5,041	5,522	5,559	5,800	6,113
State	4,336	3,385	4,508	4,136	4,652	4,454	4,683	4,773	4,822	5,176
Local, total	759	512	815	767	704	586	839	786	978	937
Counties	320	236	406	333	333	284	400	367	485	487
Municipalities	439	276	409	433	371	303	439	419	493	450
Massachusetts	4,670	3,772	4,709	3,883	4,966	4,312	5,273	4,937	5,381	5,278
State	3,016	2,587	2,895	2,315	3,100	2,578	3,187	2,885	3,085	2,950
Local, total	1,654	1,185	1,814	1,568	1,866	1,734	2,086	2,052	2,296	2,327
Counties	1,235	825	1,363	1,166	1,441	1,301	1,640	1,583	1,760	1,765
Municipalities	419	360	451	402	425	433	446	469	536	562
Michigan	5,575	4,924	5,782	5,228	5,903	5,850	6,613	6,754	7,420	8,063
State	3,178	2,963	3,132	3,013	3,143	3,310	3,312	3,538	3,659	4,146
Local, total	2,397	1,961	2,650	2,215	2,760	2,540	3,301	3,217	3,761	3,917
Counties	2,063	1,675	2,354	1,945	2,464	2,229	2,970	2,853	3,361	3,458
Municipalities	334	287	296	270	296	311	331	363	400	459
Minnesota	2,670	2,084	2,671	2,283	2,544	2,314	2,635	2,500	2,848	2,779
State	1,534	1,132	1,811	1,536	1,494	1,361	1,442	1,329	1,524	1,387
Local, total	1,136	952	860	747	1,050	953	1,193	1,171	1,324	1,393
Counties	944	776	779	671	975	877	1,118	1,089	1,249	1,313
Municipalities	192	176	81	75	75	76	75	82	75	80
Mississippi	595	297	760	397	927	558	1,122	688	1,213	836
State	485	242	578	311	754	473	924	581	933	669
Local, total	110	55	182	86	173	84	198	107	280	167
Counties	72	34	102	45	123	57	142	74	232	136
Municipalities	38	21	80	40	50	27	56	33	48	32
Missouri	2,833	1,650	3,229	1,896	3,467	2,237	3,669	2,572	4,030	2,974
State	1,630	916	1,744	946	1,847	1,115	1,972	1,312	2,217	1,631
Local, total	1,203	735	1,485	950	1,620	1,122	1,697	1,259	1,813	1,343
Counties	742	424	768	448	848	536	944	645	1,059	733
Municipalities	461	311	717	502	772	586	753	615	754	609

See footnote at end of table.

Table 2 (continued)

[Dollar amounts in thousands. — represents zero or rounds to zero.]

Employment and payroll [a]

State and level of government	October 1971		October 1972		October 1973		October 1974		October 1975	
	Full-time equivalent employment	October payroll	Full-time equivalent employment	October payroll	Full-time equivalent employment	October payroll	Full-time equivalent employment	October payroll	Full-time equivalent employment	October payroll
Montana	538	329	556	349	587	408	609	463	665	615
State	437	279	455	294	485	344	490	382	507	500
Local, total	101	50	101	54	102	65	119	81	158	115
Counties	95	46	93	49	94	59	115	77	143	105
Municipalities	6	4	8	5	8	6	4	4	15	10
Nebraska	823	483	870	533	909	639	1,022	773	1,210	964
State	689	416	707	427	669	465	780	590	859	684
Local, total	134	67	163	106	240	174	242	182	351	280
Counties	117	55	146	91	203	143	216	160	307	238
Municipalities	17	13	17	15	37	31	26	23	44	42
Nevada	767	607	842	721	876	776	958	963	1,110	1,217
State	398	325	418	367	445	389	477	475	572	637
Local, total	369	282	424	354	431	388	481	488	538	580
Counties	323	244	361	294	397	355	440	446	493	530
Municipalities	46	38	63	60	34	33	41	42	45	50
New Hampshire	367	226	454	283	425	296	457	363	561	447
State	256	158	277	189	274	206	311	271	374	321
Local, total	111	68	177	94	151	91	146	93	187	126
Counties	100	60	158	81	130	73	126	79	167	109
Municipalities	11	8	19	13	21	18	20	13	20	17
New Jersey	6,383	5,025	6,573	5,406	7,119	5,962	7,700	7,078	7,995	7,640
State	3,243	2,660	3,082	2,553	3,252	2,863	3,398	3,340	3,362	3,274
Local, total	3,140	2,364	3,491	2,853	3,867	3,099	4,302	3,737	4,633	4,366
Counties	3,133	2,360	3,485	2,849	3,863	3,096	4,287	3,731	4,605	4,347
Municipalities	7	4	6	4	4	3	15	7	28	19

	1	2	3	4	5	6	7	8	9	10
New Mexico	780	404	802	469	823	534	835	593	860	647
State	624	317	633	382	590	388	617	445	658	511
Local, total	156	86	169	87	233	146	218	147	202	136
Counties	102	45	108	46	104	53	97	56	66	33
Municipalities	54	41	61	41	129	93	121	92	136	103
New York	25,797	21,874	20,512	20,214	21,733	22,336	23,550	26,026	23,284	27,348
State	15,124	13,181	10,632	11,490	10,999	11,799	11,959	13,664	12,299	14,468
Local, total	10,673	8,693	9,880	8,724	10,734	10,537	11,591	12,363	10,985	12,880
Counties	4,367	3,053	4,559	3,501	4,830	3,927	5,213	4,627	5,471	5,287
Municipalities	6,306	5,640	5,321	5,223	5,904	6,610	6,378	7,735	5,514	7,593
North Carolina	4,989	3,005	5,332	3,491	5,300	3,682	5,905	4,620	6,563	5,187
State	4,377	2,722	4,744	3,197	4,682	3,341	5,196	4,180	5,722	4,644
Local, total	612	283	588	294	618	341	709	440	841	543
Counties	612	283	583	291	612	337	702	436	836	540
Municipalities	—	—	5	3	6	3	7	4	5	3
North Dakota	267	174	233	151	259	156	296	208	336	258
State	215	152	192	129	205	125	247	178	274	215
Local, total	52	23	41	22	54	31	49	30	62	43
Counties	49	20	38	19	51	28	46	27	59	40
Municipalities	3	2	3	3	3	3	3	3	3	3
Ohio	7,563	5,163	8,881	6,839	9,155	7,562	9,447	8,319	9,903	9,695
State	5,220	3,656	6,246	5,064	6,427	5,526	6,389	5,952	6,476	6,790
Local, total	2,343	1,507	2,635	1,775	2,728	2,035	3,058	2,368	3,427	2,905
Counties	1,766	1,108	2,120	1,346	2,126	1,500	2,476	1,816	2,820	2,267
Municipalities	577	399	515	429	602	536	582	552	607	638
Oklahoma	1,465	726	1,759	846	1,927	1,004	2,004	1,212	2,533	1,809
State	1,081	523	1,435	666	1,526	753	1,603	942	2,108	1,511
Local, total	384	203	324	180	401	250	401	271	425	297
Counties	301	148	222	115	311	183	298	186	346	232
Municipalities	83	55	102	65	90	68	103	84	79	66
Oregon	1,990	1,507	2,094	1,702	2,060	1,780	2,248	2,036	2,472	2,500
State	1,262	981	1,394	1,172	1,236	1,090	1,427	1,283	1,631	1,633
Local, total	728	526	700	530	824	690	821	752	841	867
Counties	643	451	643	478	802	678	812	745	832	857
Municipalities	85	75	57	52	22	13	9	7	9	10
Pennsylvania	6,592	4,809	7,855	6,198	8,139	6,996	8,739	7,980	9,299	8,892
State	3,269	2,354	3,946	3,199	3,944	3,717	4,008	4,143	4,054	4,342
Local, total	3,323	2,456	3,909	2,999	4,195	3,279	4,731	3,838	5,245	4,550
Counties	1,998	1,126	2,318	1,414	2,543	1,628	2,797	1,980	3,211	2,446
Municipalities	1,325	1,329	1,591	1,585	1,652	1,651	1,934	1,858	2,034	2,104

See footnote at end of table.

Table 2 (Continued)

State and level of government	Employment and payroll [a]									
	October 1971		October 1972		October 1973		October 1974		October 1975	
	Full-time equivalent employment	October payroll	Full-time equivalent employment	October payroll	Full-time equivalent employment	October payroll	Full-time equivalent employment	October payroll	Full-time equivalent employment	October payroll
Rhode Island	440	390	519	458	563	565	739	790	694	787
State	440	390	519	458	563	565	739	790	694	787
Local, total	—	—	—	—	—	—	—	—	—	—
Municipalities	—	—	—	—	—	—	—	—	—	—
South Carolina	2,024	1,077	2,267	1,310	2,345	1,491	2,616	1,784	3,144	2,363
State	1,354	772	1,576	965	1,715	1,150	2,048	1,445	2,514	1,987
Local, total	670	306	691	345	630	340	568	338	630	376
Counties	640	290	660	330	597	320	531	314	567	332
Municipalities	30	16	31	16	33	21	37	24	63	45
South Dakota	341	188	329	198	332	222	312	229	331	258
State	265	154	242	157	224	160	214	170	266	219
Local, total	76	35	87	41	108	61	98	59	65	39
Counties	72	33	84	40	104	59	96	58	64	38
Municipalities	4	2	3	2	4	2	2	1	1	1
Tennessee	2,665	1,422	2,844	1,608	3,278	2,035	3,570	2,366	3,754	2,804
State	1,966	1,019	2,015	1,137	2,247	1,388	2,379	1,562	2,464	1,872
Local, total	699	403	829	471	1,031	647	1,191	803	1,290	932
Counties	556	317	673	381	684	408	823	536	913	637
Municipalities	143	86	156	90	347	240	368	267	377	295
Texas	6,565	3,601	6,451	3,921	7,181	4,696	7,460	5,230	7,927	6,458
State	3,898	2,094	3,679	2,285	4,080	2,721	4,124	2,890	4,203	3,604
Local, total	2,667	1,507	2,772	1,636	3,101	1,975	3,336	2,340	3,724	2,854
Counties	2,300	1,304	2,432	1,435	2,777	1,741	3,019	2,090	3,288	2,442
Municipalities	567	204	340	202	324	233	317	250	436	412

Utah	612	397	683	457	767	544	701	901	904	820
State	499	341	552	386	587	441	549	653	699	661
Local, total	113	56	131	71	180	103	152	248	205	159
Counties	113	—	131	71	179	102	151	246	201	157
Municipalities	—	—	—	—	1	(b)	1	2	4	2
Vermont	439	333	438	418	437	352	350	420	422	349
State	435	330	438	418	435	351	349	418	418	347
Local, total	4	2	—	(b)	2	1	1	2	4	2
Counties	1	—	—	(b)	2	1	1	2	3	1
Municipalities	3	2	—	—	—	—	—	—	1	1
Virginia	3,320	1,981	3,732	2,431	4,092	2,976	3,862	5,430	5,735	4,818
State	2,535	1,548	2,722	1,830	2,958	2,218	2,932	4,159	4,229	3,688
Local, total	785	434	1,010	601	1,134	758	930	1,271	1,506	1,131
Counties	317	178	375	231	399	299	374	488	611	451
Municipalities	468	256	635	371	735	459	557	783	895	680
Washington	3,510	2,686	3,718	2,773	3,697	2,928	3,288	3,851	3,955	3,859
State	2,597	2,031	2,427	1,875	2,369	1,932	2,112	2,408	2,457	2,487
Local, total	913	655	1,291	898	1,328	996	1,176	1,443	1,498	1,372
Counties	775	540	1,159	785	1,193	866	1,095	1,362	1,445	1,303
Municipalities	138	115	132	113	135	130	81	81	53	69
West Virginia	983	443	867	454	949	519	617	1,040	1,004	631
State	736	343	628	335	676	379	459	744	759	486
Local, total	247	100	239	119	273	140	158	296	245	145
Counties	245	99	237	118	271	139	157	295	244	144
Municipalities	2	1	2	1	2	1	1	1	1	1
Wisconsin	3,188	2,625	3,362	3,009	3,340	3,169	3,486	3,571	3,787	3,809
State	2,365	1,968	2,526	2,292	2,550	2,436	2,640	2,657	2,740	2,812
Local, total	823	657	836	717	790	732	847	914	1,047	998
Counties	823	657	836	717	790	732	847	914	1,047	998
Municipalities	—	—	—	—	—	—	—	—	—	—
Wyoming	292	148	313	167	309	176	219	342	350	264
State	239	120	254	140	260	150	187	288	286	221
Local, total	53	28	59	30	49	27	32	54	64	44
Counties	45	23	50	24	37	19	29	50	51	31
Municipalities	8	5	9	6	12	7	4	4	13	12

a Data for municipalities, and the local governments totals which include municipal data, are estimates subject to sampling variation; data for counties (boroughs, parishes) are based on a canvass of all county governments and therefore are not subject to sampling variation; see Source for data limitations.
b Less than half the unit of measurement shown.

Source: U.S. Department of Justice, Law Enforcement Assistance Administration and U.S. Bureau of the Census, *Trends in Expenditure and Employment Data for the Criminal Justice System 1971–1975* (Washington, D.C.: U.S. Government Printing Office, 1977), pp. 94–101.

Table 3 Employment and payroll for State correctional activities, by type of activity and State, October 1975

[Dollar amounts in thousands. — represents zero or rounds to zero.]

State [a]	Total corrections activities				Institutions							
	Number of employees			October payroll [b]	Total				For men			
	Total	Full-time only	Full-time equiva-lent [b]		Number of employees			October payroll	Number of employees			October payroll
					Total	Full-time only	Full-time equivalent		Total	Full-time only	Full-time equivalent	
Total	128,523	126,196	126,933	$123,252	98,983	97,285	97,824	$94,322	60,638	60,071	60,259	$59,656
Alabama	1,302	1,268	1,281	1,042	980	961	969	758	609	607	608	473
Alaska	432	412	424	667	333	320	329	517	122	119	122	192
Arizona	1,103	1,103	1,103	1,075	931	931	931	878	170	170	170	162
Arkansas	792	792	792	560	682	682	682	487	363	363	363	256
California	13,237	12,455	12,704	16,017	10,124	9,515	9,698	11,865	6,648	6,403	6,486	8,034
Colorado	1,734	1,690	1,702	1,896	1,104	1,088	1,091	1,281	677	663	666	830
Connecticut	2,624	2,582	2,593	2,446	1,891	1,866	1,872	1,744	1,311	1,298	1,301	1,260
Delaware	810	789	791	760	673	652	654	640	324	323	323	349
Florida	9,147	8,954	9,022	6,985	6,154	6,001	6,057	4,579	3,742	3,674	3,698	2,915
Georgia	3,637	3,637	3,637	2,713	2,491	2,491	2,491	1,787	1,572	1,572	1,572	1,198
Hawaii	371	371	371	446	276	276	276	357	NA	NA	NA	NA
Idaho	401	392	394	334	306	298	299	246	186	180	181	150
Illinois	4,981	4,981	4,981	5,102	3,970	3,970	3,970	3,954	2,543	2,543	2,543	2,468
Indiana	2,081	2,064	2,072	1,847	1,889	1,872	1,880	1,648	1,404	1,399	1,403	1,227
Iowa	1,389	1,370	1,377	1,307	1,201	1,183	1,190	1,143	773	768	770	780
Kansas	2,194	2,194	2,194	1,682	2,091	2,091	2,091	1,591	873	873	873	723
Kentucky	1,525	1,525	1,525	1,224	1,176	1,176	1,176	931	772	772	772	660
Louisiana	2,466	2,466	2,466	1,959	1,629	1,629	1,629	1,275	903	903	903	750
Maine	654	634	639	529	568	560	563	461	283	283	283	231
Maryland	4,826	4,820	4,822	5,176	3,329	3,326	3,327	3,616	2,093	2,093	2,093	2,353

State												
Massachusetts	3,085	3,085	3,085	2,950	2,454	2,454	2,454	2,304	1,920	1,920	1,920	1,894
Michigan	3,714	3,651	3,659	4,146	3,221	3,158	3,166	3,533	2,487	2,444	2,450	2,725
Minnesota	1,568	1,485	1,524	1,387	1,226	1,161	1,193	1,216	733	705	719	848
Mississippi	990	914	933	669	808	732	751	542	—	—	—	—
Missouri	2,339	2,194	2,217	1,631	1,427	1,399	1,405	1,009	1,005	982	987	695
Montana	526	496	507	500	420	392	402	396	214	202	207	218
Nebraska	886	843	859	684	694	668	675	538	459	449	452	369
Nevada	578	568	572	637	456	451	453	501	306	302	303	335
New Hampshire	377	373	374	321	291	289	290	244	142	142	142	124
New Jersey	3,384	3,327	3,362	3,274	2,926	2,875	2,908	2,835	1,264	1,251	1,261	1,226
New Mexico	658	658	658	511	426	426	426	328	225	225	225	172
New York	12,392	12,269	12,299	14,468	10,349	10,226	10,257	11,926	7,049	7,049	7,049	8,268
North Carolina	5,722	5,722	5,722	4,644	4,362	4,362	4,362	3,430	3,302	3,302	3,302	2,616
North Dakota	278	268	274	215	247	239	244	188	110	103	107	85
Ohio	6,528	6,462	6,476	6,790	5,496	5,430	5,444	5,703	2,782	2,782	2,782	2,935
Oklahoma	2,108	2,108	2,108	1,511	1,287	1,287	1,287	883	908	908	908	645
Oregon	1,639	1,624	1,631	1,633	1,192	1,181	1,187	1,183	745	745	745	760
Pennsylvania	4,054	4,054	4,054	4,342	3,314	3,314	3,314	3,505	1,891	1,891	1,891	2,055
Rhode Island	694	694	694	787	496	496	496	581	370	370	370	455
South Carolina	2,528	2,510	2,514	1,987	1,710	1,692	1,696	1,252	1,066	1,066	1,066	775
South Dakota	283	254	266	219	238	223	229	188	—	—	—	1,001
Tennessee	2,464	2,461	2,464	1,872	2,036	2,033	2,036	1,542	1,214	1,214	1,214	2,147
Texas	4,278	4,165	4,203	3,604	3,623	3,544	3,568	3,016	2,493	2,457	2,465	—
Utah	735	678	699	661	458	433	445	416	106	98	100	85
Vermont	433	413	418	347	319	300	304	247	—	—	—	—
Virginia	4,239	4,224	4,229	3,688	2,857	2,842	2,847	2,487	1,997	1,995	1,995	1,797
Washington	2,493	2,437	2,457	2,487	1,956	1,917	1,931	1,942	1,065	1,061	1,063	1,083
West Virginia	762	759	759	486	644	641	641	395	413	410	410	260
Wisconsin	2,790	2,718	2,740	2,812	1,999	1,984	1,987	2,045	905	897	899	994
Wyoming	292	283	286	221	253	248	251	189	99	95	97	78

See footnotes at end of table.

Table 3 (continued)

[Dollar amounts in thousands. — represents zero or rounds to zero.]

State [a]	For women — Number of employees				Institutions — For juveniles — Number of employees				Institutions — Other and combined — Number of employees			
	Total	Full-time only	Full-time equivalent [b]	October payroll [b]	Total	Full-time only	Full-time equivalent	October payroll	Total	Full-time only	Full-time equivalent	October payroll
Total	3,007	2,975	2,988	$2,793	28,760	27,762	28,082	$25,266	6,578	6,477	6,508	$6,607
Alabama	42	42	42	33	329	312	319	252	—	—	—	—
Alaska	—	—	—	—	107	97	104	151	104	104	104	174
Arizona	—	—	—	—	248	248	248	237	513	513	513	479
Arkansas	10	10	10	7	309	309	309	224	—	—	—	—
California	295	289	291	354	3,181	2,823	2,921	3,477	—	—	—	—
Colorado	NA	NA	NA	NA	427	425	426	451	—	—	—	—
Connecticut	139	135	136	122	300	292	294	245	141	141	141	117
Delaware	16	16	16	17	266	246	248	210	67	67	67	64
Florida	24	24	24	17	2,112	2,032	2,063	1,423	276	271	273	224
Georgia	75	75	75	51	844	844	844	538	—	—	—	—
Hawaii	—	—	—	—	107	107	107	107	169	169	169	250
Idaho	—	—	—	—	120	118	118	96	—	—	—	—
Illinois	129	129	129	125	1,298	1,298	1,298	1,361	—	—	—	—
Indiana	80	78	79	67	405	395	397	354	—	—	—	—
Iowa	43	42	42	36	385	373	378	327	—	—	—	—
Kansas	63	63	63	47	345	345	345	252	810	810	810	569
Kentucky	46	46	46	34	350	350	350	229	8	8	8	8
Louisiana	56	56	56	42	670	670	670	483	—	—	—	—
Maine	—	—	—	—	285	277	279	230	—	—	—	—
Maryland	99	99	99	112	839	836	837	829	298	298	298	322

State												
Massachusetts	133	133	133	119	401	401	401	291	—	—	—	—
Michigan	44	36	39	—	734	714	717	808	—	—	—	—
Minnesota	—	—	—	—	449	420	438	326	—	—	—	—
Mississippi	—	—	—	—	237	232	234	140	571	500	515	402
Missouri	47	45	46	32	375	372	373	282	—	—	—	—
Montana	X	X	X	—	206	190	196	178	—	—	—	—
Nebraska	43	41	42	32	192	178	182	137	—	—	—	—
Nevada	—	—	—	—	140	140	140	157	10	9	9	9
New Hampshire	—	—	—	—	149	147	148	120	—	—	—	—
New Jersey	278	275	277	248	720	696	708	702	664	653	662	659
New Mexico	12	12	12	9	189	189	189	147	1,575	1,575	1,575	1,976
New York	198	198	198	208	1,527	1,404	1,439	1,474	—	—	—	—
North Carolina	133	133	133	104	831	831	831	636	96	96	96	74
North Dakota	—	—	—	—	137	136	137	103	—	—	—	—
Ohio	186	186	186	202	1,923	1,857	1,871	1,930	605	605	605	636
Oklahoma	54	54	54	40	325	325	325	198	—	—	—	—
Oregon	28	26	27	29	419	410	415	394	—	—	—	—
Pennsylvania	139	139	139	147	1,284	1,284	1,284	1,303	—	—	—	—
Rhode Island	NA	NA	NA	NA	126	126	126	126	—	—	—	—
South Carolina	51	51	51	38	593	575	579	439	—	—	—	—
South Dakota	—	—	—	—	117	107	111	82	121	116	118	106
Tennessee	71	71	71	50	751	748	751	491	—	—	—	—
Texas	110	110	110	96	1,020	977	994	773	303	295	298	291
Utah	14	12	12	12	141	126	136	113	21	21	21	17
Vermont	—	—	—	—	192	181	184	145	—	—	—	—
Virginia	118	118	118	100	742	729	734	590	—	—	—	—
Washington	110	110	110	111	781	746	758	748	—	—	—	—
West Virginia	18	18	18	10	213	213	213	125	226	298	226	291
Wisconsin	103	103	103	100	765	758	760	721	226	226	226	230
Wyoming	—	—	—	—	154	153	153	111	—	—	—	—

See footnotes at end of table.

Table 3 (continued)

[Dollar amounts in thousands. — represents zero or rounds to zero.]

State [a]	Corrections administration				Probation, parole, and pardon				Miscellaneous			
	Number of employees			October payroll [b]	Number of employees			October payroll	Number of employees			October payroll
	Total	Full-time only	Full-time equivalent [b]		Total	Full-time only	Full-time equivalent		Total	Full-time only	Full-time equivalent	
Total	8,264	8,116	8,161	$8,283	19,731	19,295	19,429	$19,112	1,545	1,500	1,515	$1,530
Alabama	73	68	69	68	249	239	242	216	—	—	—	—
Alaska	18	18	18	30	81	74	77	120	—	—	—	—
Arizona	91	91	91	103	75	75	75	87	6	6	6	7
Arkansas	60	60	60	36	50	50	50	37	—	—	—	—
California	924	888	900	1,140	1,595	1,497	1,536	2,305	594	555	569	707
Colorado	68	52	56	68	550	538	542	537	12	12	12	10
Connecticut	273	263	266	243	445	438	440	446	15	15	15	13
Delaware	66	66	66	60	63	63	63	55	8	8	8	5
Florida	338	319	324	306	2,655	2,634	2,641	2,100	—	—	—	—
Georgia	237	237	237	224	854	854	854	653	55	55	55	49
Hawaii	12	12	12	8	68	68	68	68	15	15	15	13
Idaho	NA	NA	NA	NA	95	94	94	88	—	—	—	—
Illinois	368	368	368	447	643	643	643	701	—	—	—	—
Indiana	48	48	48	53	140	140	140	143	4	4	4	3
Iowa	42	42	42	48	98	97	98	77	48	48	48	39
Kansas	25	25	25	26	78	78	78	65	—	—	—	—
Kentucky	30	30	30	31	297	297	297	241	22	22	22	21
Louisiana	368	368	368	258	234	234	224	209	235	235	235	217
Maine	9	8	8	6	77	66	68	62	16	16	16	15
Maryland	222	222	222	258	1,259	1,256	1,257	1,287	—	—	—	—
Massachusetts	314	314	314	313	317	317	317	333	—	—	—	—
Michigan	110	110	110	137	383	383	383	476	—	—	—	—
Minnesota	331	313	318	160	11	11	11	11	—	—	—	—
Mississippi	10	10	10	10	172	172	172	117	—	—	—	—
Missouri	412	396	401	300	500	399	411	322	—	—	—	—

State												
Montana	30	30	30	36	76	74	75	68	—	—	—	—
Nebraska	21	20	20	23	171	155	164	123	—	—	—	—
Nevada	NA	NA	NA	NA	122	117	119	136	—	—	—	—
New Hampshire	NA	NA	NA	NA	86	84	85	77	—	—	—	—
• New Jersey	84	84	84	95	366	360	362	337	8	8	8	7
New Mexico	9	9	9	10	223	223	223	173	—	—	—	—
New York	667	667	667	926	1,338	1,338	1,338	1,572	38	38	38	44
North Carolina	270	270	270	273	909	909	909	804	181	181	181	137
North Dakota	NA	NA	NA	NA	31	29	30	27	—	—	—	—
Ohio	568	568	568	610	464	464	464	476	—	—	—	—
Oklahoma	418	418	418	304	403	403	403	324	—	—	—	—
Oregon	188	187	187	165	259	256	257	285	—	—	—	—
Pennsylvania	102	102	102	138	638	638	638	699	—	—	—	—
Rhode Island	51	51	51	58	147	147	147	148	—	—	—	—
South Carolina	258	258	258	274	298	298	298	237	262	262	262	224
South Dakota	—	—	—	—	32	23	29	22	13	8	8	9
Tennessee	62	62	62	55	366	366	366	275	—	—	—	—
Texas	270	265	268	262	385	356	366	326	—	2	2	2
Utah	12	10	11	13	263	233	241	230	11	10	10	8
Vermont	18	18	18	20	85	85	85	72	2	10	10	8
Virginia	550	550	550	440	832	832	832	761	—	—	—	—
Washington	NA	NA	NA	NA	537	520	526	545	—	—	—	—
West Virginia	NA	NA	NA	NA	118	118	118	91	—	—	—	—
Wisconsin	227	209	215	241	564	525	538	526	—	—	—	—
Wyoming	10	10	10	10	29	25	25	22	—	—	—	—

[a] Data are based on a field compilation from records of each State government; see Source for data limitations.
[b] Because of rounding, the detail figures may not add precisely to the totals shown.

Source: U.S. Department of Justice, Law Enforcement Assistance Administration and U.S. Bureau of the Census, *Expenditure and Employment Data for the Criminal Justice System 1975* (Washington, D.C.: U.S. Government Printing Office, 1977), pp. 299–301.

Table 4 Public juvenile detention and correctional facilities, by level of government, region, and State, June 30, 1973 and June 30, 1974

NOTE: Data in this report are from the 1971, 1972-73, and 1974 censuses of State and local juvenile facilities. These censuses covered residential facilities operated by State and local governments for delinquent juveniles. The 1974 census also included private residential facilities. Excluded from the censuses were juvenile detention centers operated as part of a jail and without a separate staff or budget, nonresidential facilities, facilities for drug abusers or for dependent and neglected children, foster homes, and Federal juvenile correctional facilities.

[— represents zero]

Region and State	State facilities			Local facilities		
	1973	1974	Percent change	1973	1974	Percent change
United States, total	367	396	7.9	427	433	1.4
Region 1	18	19	5.6	1	—	-100.0
Connecticut	5	5	—	—	—	—
Maine	2	2	—	—	—	—
Massachusetts	6	7	16.7	—	—	—
New Hampshire	1	1	—	1	—	-100.0
Rhode Island	3	3	—	—	—	—
Vermont	1	1	—	—	—	—
Region 2	60	60	—	23	26	13.0
New Jersey a	10	11	10.0	15	17	13.3
New York	50	49	-2.0	8	9	12.5
Region 3	47	46	-2.1	46	56	21.7
Delaware	6	6	—	10	11	10.0
District of Columbia	X	X	X	—	—	—
Maryland	14	13	-7.1	—	—	—
Pennsylvania	9	9	—	22	20	-9.1
Virginia	13	14	7.7	10	20	100.0
West Virginia	5	4	-20.0	4	5	25.0
Region 4	73	95	30.1	59	42	-28.8
Alabama	3	3	—	3	8	166.7
Florida	22	44	100.0	22	5	-77.3
Georgia	15	18	20.0	7	4	-42.9
Kentucky	10	9	-10.0	7	7	—
Mississippi	3	3	—	6	5	-16.7
North Carolina	9	7	-22.2	8	7	-12.5
South Carolina	5	5	—	1	1	—
Tennessee	6	6	—	5	5	—

Region 5	57	57	—	87	91	4.6
Illinois	15	14	-6.7	13	11	-15.4
Indiana	3	3	—	10	10	—
Michigan	18	19	5.6	27	29	7.4
Minnesota	6	5	-16.7	5	7	40.0
Ohio	10	11	10.0	26	28	7.7
Wisconsin	5	5	—	6	6	—
Region 6	20	19	-5.0	38	40	5.3
Arkansas	4	4	—	5	5	—
Louisiana	5	5	—	9	9	—
New Mexico [b]	2	2	—	2	2	—
Oklahoma	3	3	—	5	7	40.0
Texas	6	5	-16.7	17	17	—
Region 7	25	30	20.0	38	38	—
Iowa	5	6	20.0	6	4	-33.3
Kansas	6	7	16.7	5	8	60.0
Missouri	12	15	25.0	25	24	-4.0
Nebraska	2	2	—	2	2	—
Region 8	21	24	14.3	14	12	-14.3
Colorado	9	10	11.1	1	1	—
Montana	3	3	—	1	—	-100.0
North Dakota [c]	1	3	200.0	4	3	-25.0
South Dakota	2	2	—	1	1	—
Utah	4	4	—	7	7	—
Wyoming	2	2	—	—	—	—
Region 9	27	27	—	101	108	6.9
Arizona	7	7	—	8	8	—
California	15	15	—	89	96	7.9
Hawaii	3	3	—	4	4	—
Nevada	2	2	—	—	—	—
Region 10	19	19	—	20	20	—
Alaska	2	2	—	—	—	—
Idaho	1	1	—	1	—	-100.0
Oregon	4	4	—	6	6	—
Washington	12	12	—	13	14	7.7

[a] In New Jersey, two annex training schools were reported combined with the parent State training school as one facility for both 1971 and 1973. These training schools were out of the census scope in 1974.

[b] In New Mexico, two State camps were reported combined with a State training school as one facility in 1971, 1973, and 1974.

[c] In North Dakota, three State group homes were reported combined with a State training school as one facility in 1973 and 1974. In 1971, two of these group homes were nonexistent, and data for the remaining facilities were reported separately.

Source: U.S. Department of Justice, Law Enforcement Assistance Administration, *Children in Custody: Advance Report on the Juvenile Detention and Correctional Facility Census of 1974* (Washington, D.C.: U.S. Government Printing Office, 1977), pp. 18, 19.

Table 5 Public juvenile detention and correctional facilities, by type of facility, level of government, region, and State, June 30, 1974

[— represents zero]

Region and State	Total facilities			Short-term facilities					
				Detention centers			Shelters		
	Total	State	Local	Total	State	Local	Total	State	Local
United States, total	829	396	433	331	50	281	21	—	21
Region 1	19	19	—	8	8	—	—	—	—
Connecticut	5	5	—	4	4	—	—	—	—
Maine	2	2	—	4	4	—	—	—	—
Massachusetts	7	7	—	—	—	—	—	—	—
New Hampshire	1	1	—	—	—	—	—	—	—
Rhode Island	3	3	—	—	—	—	—	—	—
Vermont	1	1	—	—	—	—	—	—	—
Region 2	86	60	26	23	—	23	2	—	2
New Jersey	28	11	17	16	—	16	1	—	1
New York	58	49	9	7	—	7	1	—	1
Region 3	102	46	56	39	4	35	8	—	8
Delaware	6	6	—	2	2	—	—	—	—
District of Columbia	11	X	11	1	X	1	6	X	6
Maryland	13	13	—	1	1	—	—	—	—
Pennsylvania	29	9	20	19	—	19	—	—	—
Virginia	34	14	20	14	1	13	—	—	—
West Virginia	9	4	5	2	—	2	2	—	2
Region 4	137	95	42	62	30	32	—	—	—
Alabama	11	3	8	7	—	7	—	—	—
Florida	49	44	5	21	21	—	—	—	—
Georgia	22	18	4	13	9	4	—	—	—
Kentucky	16	9	7	5	—	5	—	—	—
Mississippi	8	3	5	4	—	4	—	—	—
North Carolina	14	7	7	7	—	7	—	—	—
South Carolina	6	5	1	1	—	1	—	—	—
Tennessee	11	6	5	4	—	4	—	—	—

Region 5	148	57	91	61	—	61	5	—	5
Illinois	25	14	11	10	—	10	—	—	—
Indiana	13	3	10	8	—	8	4	—	4
Michigan	48	19	29	17	—	17	—	—	—
Minnesota	12	5	7	3	—	3	—	—	—
Ohio	39	11	28	19	—	19	1	—	1
Wisconsin	11	5	6	4	—	4	—	—	—
Region 6	59	19	40	26	—	26	6	—	6
Arkansas	9	4	5	2	—	2	2	—	2
Louisiana	14	5	9	7	—	7	—	—	—
New Mexico [a]	4	2	2	2	—	2	—	—	—
Oklahoma	10	3	7	2	—	2	4	—	4
Texas	22	5	17	13	—	13	—	—	—
Region 7	68	30	38	21	—	21	—	—	—
Iowa	10	6	4	3	—	3	—	—	—
Kansas	15	7	8	7	—	7	—	—	—
Missouri	39	15	24	9	—	9	—	—	—
Nebraska	4	2	2	2	—	2	—	—	—
Region 8	36	24	12	14	5	14	—	—	—
Colorado	11	10	1	5	5	5	—	—	—
Montana	3	3	—	—	—	—	—	—	—
North Dakota [b]	6	3	3	1	—	1	—	—	—
South Dakota	3	2	1	1	—	1	—	—	—
Utah	11	4	7	7	—	7	—	—	—
Wyoming	2	2	—	—	—	—	—	—	—
Region 9	135	27	108	57	2	57	—	—	—
Arizona	15	7	8	8	—	8	—	—	—
California	111	15	96	44	—	44	—	—	—
Hawaii	3	3	—	2	2	2	—	—	—
Nevada	6	2	4	3	—	3	—	—	—
Region 10	39	19	20	20	1	20	—	—	—
Alaska	2	2	—	1	1	1	—	—	—
Idaho	1	1	—	—	—	—	—	—	—
Oregon	10	4	6	5	—	5	—	—	—
Washington	26	12	14	14	—	14	—	—	—

[a] In New Mexico, two State camps were reported combined with a State training school as one facility in 1971, 1973 and 1974. In 1971, two of these group homes were nonexistent, and data for the remaining facilities were reported separately.
[b] In North Dakota, three State group homes were reported combined with a State training school as one facility in 1973 and 1974.

Table 5 (continued)

Region and state	Short-term facilities			Long-term facilities					
	Reception or diagnostic centers			Training schools			Ranches, forestry camps, and farms		
	Total	State	Local	Total	State	Local	Total	State	Local
United States, total	19	17	2	185	151	34	107	61	46
Region 1	1	1	—	7	7	—	1	1	1
Connecticut	—	—	—	1	1	—	—	—	—
Maine	—	—	—	2	2	—	—	—	—
Massachusetts	—	—	—	—	—	—	1	1	—
New Hampshire	—	—	—	1	1	—	—	—	—
Rhode Island	1	1	—	2	2	—	—	—	—
Vermont	—	—	—	1	1	—	—	—	—
Region 2	—	—	—	13	13	—	7	7	—
New Jersey	—	—	—	3	3	—	2	2	—
New York	—	—	—	10	10	—	5	5	—
Region 3	2	2	—	24	19	5	11	11	—
Delaware	—	—	—	3	3	—	—	—	—
District of Columbia	X	X	—	3	X	3	—	X	—
Maryland	1	1	—	3	3	—	4	4	—
Pennsylvania	—	—	—	7	6	1	3	3	—
Virginia	1	1	—	5	5	—	2	2	—
West Virginia	—	—	—	3	2	1	2	2	—
Region 4	5	5	—	30	27	3	11	10	1
Alabama	—	—	—	3	3	—	—	—	—
Florida	—	—	—	6	4	2	4	3	1
Georgia	—	—	—	5	5	—	—	—	—
Kentucky	2	2	—	1	—	1	6	6	—
Mississippi	—	—	—	2	2	—	—	—	—
North Carolina	1	1	—	6	6	—	—	—	—
South Carolina	1	1	—	3	3	—	—	—	—
Tennessee	1	1	—	4	4	—	1	1	—

310

Region 5	2	2	—	—	36	26	10	15	14	1
Illinois	—	—	—	—	8	7	1	6	6	—
Indiana	1	1	—	—	3	2	1	1	1	—
Michigan	—	1	—	—	5	3	2	3	2	1
Minnesota	1	—	—	—	5	3	2	1	1	—
Ohio	—	—	—	—	12	8	4	2	2	—
Wisconsin	—	—	—	—	3	3	—	2	2	—
Region 6	2	2	—	—	21	17	4	7	3	4
Arkansas	1	1	—	—	3	3	—	1	1	—
Louisiana	1	1	—	—	5	4	1	—	—	—
New Mexico [a]	—	—	—	—	2	2	—	2	2	—
Oklahoma	—	—	—	—	4	3	1	—	—	—
Texas	—	—	—	—	7	5	2	4	—	4
Region 7	1	—	1	—	15	13	2	7	3	4
Iowa	—	—	—	—	2	2	—	1	1	—
Kansas	1	—	1	—	6	6	—	—	—	—
Missouri	—	—	—	—	5	3	2	6	2	4
Nebraska	—	—	—	—	2	2	—	—	—	—
Region 8	1	1	—	—	10	10	—	4	4	—
Colorado	—	—	—	—	3	3	—	2	2	—
Montana	—	—	—	—	2	2	—	1	1	—
North Dakota [b]	1	1	—	—	1	1	—	—	—	—
South Dakota	—	—	—	—	1	1	—	1	1	—
Utah	—	—	—	—	1	1	—	—	—	—
Wyoming	—	—	—	—	2	2	—	—	—	—
Region 9	4	3	1	—	22	12	10	45	6	39
Arizona	—	—	—	—	2	2	—	1	1	—
California	4	3	1	—	17	7	10	43	5	38
Hawaii	—	—	—	—	1	1	—	—	—	—
Nevada	—	—	—	—	2	2	—	1	—	1
Region 10	1	1	—	—	7	7	—	6	5	1
Alaska	—	—	—	—	1	1	—	—	—	—
Idaho	—	—	—	—	1	1	—	—	—	—
Oregon	—	—	—	—	2	2	—	3	2	—
Washington	1	—	—	—	3	3	—	3	3	1

Source: U.S. Department of Justice, Law Enforcement Assistance Administration, *Children in Custody: Advance Report on the Juvenile Detention and Correctional Facility Census of 1974* (Washington, D.C.: U.S. Government Printing Office, 1977), pp. 22, 23.

Table 5 (continued)

Region and State	Long-term facilities		
	Halfway houses and group homes		
	Total	State	Local
United States, total	166	117	49
Region 1	2	2	—
Connecticut	—	—	—
Maine	—	—	—
Massachusetts	2	2	—
New Hampshire	—	—	—
Rhode Island	—	—	—
Vermont	—	—	—
Region 2	41	40	1
New Jersey	6	6	—
New York	35	34	1
Region 3	18	10	8
Delaware	1	1	—
District of Columbia	1	X	1
Maryland	4	4	—
Pennsylvania	—	—	—
Virginia	12	5	7
West Virginia	—	—	—
Region 4	29	23	6
Alabama	1	—	1
Florida	18	16	2
Georgia	4	4	—
Kentucky	2	1	1
Mississippi	2	1	1
North Carolina	1	1	—
South Carolina	1	1	—
Tennessee	1	—	1

Region 5	29	15	14
Illinois	1	1	—
Indiana	1	—	1
Michigan	18	13	5
Minnesota	3	1	2
Ohio	5	—	5
Wisconsin	1	—	1
Region 6	4	—	4
Arkansas	1	—	1
Louisiana	1	—	1
New Mexico [a]	—	—	—
Oklahoma	—	—	—
Texas	2	—	2
Region 7	24	14	10
Iowa	4	3	1
Kansas	1	1	—
Missouri	19	10	9
Nebraska	—	—	—
Region 8	7	4	3
Colorado	1	—	1
Montana	—	—	—
North Dakota [b]	3	1	2
South Dakota	—	—	—
Utah	3	3	—
Wyoming	—	—	—
Region 9	7	4	3
Arizona	4	4	—
California	3	—	3
Hawaii	—	—	—
Nevada	—	—	—
Region 10	5	5	—
Alaska	—	—	—
Idaho	—	—	—
Oregon	—	—	—
Washington	5	5	—

Table 6 Selected characteristics of private juvenile detention and correctional facilities, by type of facility, United States, June 30, 1974

[— represents zero]

Characteristic	Total facilities	Short-term facilities				Long-term facilities			
		Total	Detention centers	Shelters	Reception or diagnostic centers	Total	Training schools	Ranches, forestry camps, and farms	Halfway houses and group homes
Number of facilities, June 30, 1974	1,337	76	4	67	5	1,261	61	395	805
Number of facilities by sources of juveniles:									
Police	179	40	[a]	37	[a]	139	4	42	93
Parents of juveniles in custody	664	43	[a]	40	[a]	621	26	243	352
Juvenile court	1,207	74	4	65	5	1,133	58	358	717
State correctional authority	463	26	[a]	21	[a]	437	19	129	289
Welfare department	1,099	61	3	54	4	1,038	51	334	653
Other sources	522	33	[a]	29	[a]	489	20	185	284
Number of facilities by sources of financial support:									
Public agencies and courts	1,224	64	3	56	5	1,160	60	358	742
Private agencies	120	7	—	[a]	[a]	113	5	60	48
Parents	487	21	[a]	[a]	—	466	20	190	256
Federal grants:									
Law Enforcement Assistance Administration	231	26	[a]	[a]	—	205	8	41	156
Department of Health, Education, and Welfare	112	9	—	[a]	[a]	103	5	31	67
Other	64	3	—	[a]	[a]	61	5	24	32
United Fund	273	11	—	11	—	262	21	91	150
Fund-raising drives of facilities	523	24	[a]	[a]	[a]	499	25	164	310
Bequests and other individual contributions	643	39	[a]	36	[a]	604	24	219	361
Endowments or investments	292	9	[a]	[a]	—	283	16	116	151
Sponsoring denominational body	268	14	—	[a]	—	254	11	80	163
Other sources	159	11	—	11	—	148	7	45	96

[a] Data withheld to avoid disclosure and maintain confidentiality guarantees.

Source: U.S. Department of Justice, Law Enforcement Assistance Administration, *Children in Custody: Advance Report on the Juvenile Detention and Correctional Facility Census of 1974* (Washington, D.C.: U.S. Government Printing Office, 1977), pp. 62, 63.

Table 7 Type of expenditure, average population, and per capita operating expenditures of public juvenile detention and correctional facilities, by region and State, fiscal years 1973-74

"Operating expenditures" includes salaries, wages, and other operating expenditures such as the purchase of food, supplies, and contractual services. "Capital expenditures" includes expenditures for new buildings, major repairs or improvements, and new equipment.

[Dollar amounts in thousands]

Region and State	Total expenditures			Capital expenditures		
	1973	1974	Percent change	1973	1974	Percent change
United States, total	483,941	507,903	+5.0	30,127	24,536	−18.6
Region 1	14,963	15,309	2.3	781	319	−59.1
Connecticut	3,776	3,391	−10.2	38	23	−39.5
Maine	3,297	3,712	12.6	311	186	−40.3
Massachusetts	2,597	2,743	5.7	13	18	35.5
New Hampshire	1,771	1,888	6.6	127	—	−100.0
Rhode Island	2,086	2,048	−1.8	238	10	−95.7
Vermont	1,436	1,527	6.4	53	83	54.3
Region 2	54,696	45,579	−16.7	6,145	831	−86.5
New Jersey [a]	17,707	15,175	−14.3	2,324	465	−80.0
New York	36,988	30,404	−17.8	3,821	366	−90.4
Region 3	53,493	61,502	15.0	3,321	7,083	113.3
Delaware	3,370	2,375	−29.5	1,352	285	−79.0
District of Columbia	6,770	7,468	10.3	184	28	−84.7
Maryland	12,061	11,121	−7.8	364	633	73.8
Pennsylvania	19,526	26,478	35.6	133	5,184	3,804.0
Virginia	8,850	11,513	30.1	393	853	117.3
West Virginia	2,916	2,547	−12.7	895	101	−88.7
Region 4	61,360	66,073	7.7	5,528	4,439	−19.7
Alabama	2,590	4,118	59.0	124	227	83.5
Florida	19,204	19,859	3.4	1,424	445	−68.7
Georgia	12,224	11,668	−4.6	2,534	552	−78.2
Kentucky	4,080	4,218	3.4	78	47	−39.2
Mississippi	2,537	2,333	−8.0	189	223	17.7
North Carolina	9,970	10,229	2.6	560	2,121	278.5
South Carolina	3,666	4,271	16.5	511	254	−50.3
Tennessee	7,090	9,377	32.3	107	569	431.8
Region 5	101,405	101,711	0.3	3,181	2,753	−13.5
Illinois	27,229	23,382	−14.1	196	762	287.7
Indiana	6,507	6,691	2.8	1,511	785	−48.1
Michigan	17,912	21,283	18.8	103	528	413.7
Minnesota	10,835	10,204	−5.8	718	256	−64.3
Ohio	27,539	29,908	8.6	566	206	−63.6
Wisconsin	11,383	10,244	−10.0	87	216	147.5
Region 6	30,552	33,702	10.3	1,309	2,602	98.7
Arkansas	2,172	3,635	67.4	154	1,020	561.2
Louisiana	6,727	7,927	17.8	154	250	63.0
New Mexico	2,807	2,813	0.2	126	98	−22.6
Oklahoma	3,948	3,857	−2.3	633	852	34.5
Texas	14,898	15,471	3.8	242	382	57.8
Region 7	20,741	23,656	14.1	2,245	2,619	16.6
Iowa	4,934	5,474	11.0	113	245	115.9
Kansas	4,500	6,749	50.0	468	1,619	245.8
Missouri [b]	9,356	9,252	−1.1	1,648	725	−56.0
Nebraska	1,951	2,180	11.7	16	31	98.1

See footnotes at end of table.

Because of rounding, detail may not add to total. For definitions of terms, see Appendix 4.

Operating expenditures			Average populations			Per capita operating expenditures (whole dollars)		
1973	1974	Percent change	1973	1974	Percent change	1973	1974	Percent change
453,814	483,368	6.5	47,363	46,753	−1.3	9,582	10,339	7.9
14,182	14,990	5.7	1,095	970	−11.4	12,951	15,453	19.3
3,738	3,368	−9.9	193	145	−24.9	19,368	23,224	19.9
2,986	3,527	18.1	219	220	0.5	13,634	16,030	17.6
2,584	2,726	5.5	208	179	−13.9	12,420	15,226	22.6
1,644	1,888	14.9	205	206	0.5	8,018	9,164	14.3
1,848	2,038	10.3	142	131	−7.7	13,015	15,555	19.5
1,382	1,444	4.5	128	89	−30.5	10,797	16,227	50.3
48,551	44,478	−8.4	3,494	2,824	−19.2	13,895	15,750	13.4
15,384	14,710	−4.4	1,589	972	−38.8	9,681	15,133	56.3
33,168	30,038	−9.4	1,905	1,852	−2.8	17,410	16,219	−6.8
50,172	54,419	8.5	5,140	5,001	−2.7	9,761	10,881	11.5
2,017	2,090	3.6	232	230	−0.9	8,694	9,088	4.5
6,586	7,439	13.0	549	536	−2.4	11,995	13,879	15.7
11,697	10,488	−10.3	1,436	1,182	−17.7	8,145	8,873	8.9
19,393	21,294	9.8	1,274	1,300	2.0	15,222	16,380	7.6
8,458	10,660	26.0	1,309	1,350	3.1	6,461	7,896	22.2
2,021	2,446	21.0	340	403	18.5	5,945	6,069	2.1
55,832	61,634	10.4	8,220	8,153	−0.8	6,792	7,559	11.3
2,466	3,891	57.8	473	548	15.9	5,213	7,100	36.2
17,781	19,414	9.2	2,184	2,150	−1.6	8,141	9,029	10.9
9,690	11,116	14.7	1,391	1,446	4.0	6,965	7,687	10.4
4,002	4,171	4.2	456	483	5.9	8,776	8,635	−1.6
2,347	2,110	−10.1	618	589	−4.7	3,798	3,582	−5.7
9,409	8,108	−13.8	1,266	1,072	−15.3	7,432	7,563	1.8
3,154	4,017	27.3	582	618	6.2	5,420	6,499	19.9
6,983	8,808	26.1	1,250	1,247	−0.2	5,586	7,063	26.4
98,223	98,958	0.7	8,418	8,471	0.6	11,668	11,682	0.1
27,033	22,620	−16.3	1,751	1,353	−22.7	15,438	16,718	8.3
4,996	5,906	18.2	826	918	11.1	6,048	6,433	6.4
17,809	20,755	16.5	1,541	1,610	4.5	11,556	12,891	11.6
10,117	9,948	−1.7	710	730	2.8	14,249	13,626	−4.4
26,973	29,702	10.1	2,813	3,014	7.1	9,588	9,854	2.8
11,295	10,028	−11.2	777	846	8.9	14,537	11,853	−18.5
29,242	31,100	6.4	4,734	3,899	−17.6	6,177	7,976	29.1
2,017	2,615	29.6	492	455	−7.5	4,100	5,747	40.2
6,573	7,676	16.8	1,199	1,193	−0.5	5,482	6,434	17.4
2,681	2,715	1.3	307	329	7.2	8,734	8,252	−5.5
3,314	3,004	−9.4	412	460	11.7	8,044	6,531	−18.8
14,656	15,089	3.0	2,324	1,462	−37.1	6,306	10,321	63.7
18,495	21,037	13.7	2,049	2,167	5.8	9,026	9,707	7.5
4,821	5,230	8.5	405	395	−2.5	11,903	13,239	11.2
4,032	5,131	27.3	394	490	24.4	10,232	10,470	2.3
7,707	8,528	10.6	1,033	1,088	5.3	7,461	7,837	5.0
1,935	2,149	11.0	217	194	−10.6	8,919	11,077	24.2

Table 7 (continued)

Region and State	Total expenditures			Capital expenditures		
	1973	1974	Percent change	1973	1974	Percent change
Region 8	13,431	8,650	−35.6	337	330	−2.1
Colorado [c]	5,669	446	−92.1	54	15	−72.1
Montana	2,026	2,197	8.5	44	53	22.5
North Dakota	878	1,157	31.8	64	29	−54.4
South Dakota	998	921	−7.7	71	52	−26.6
Utah	2,679	2,728	1.8	91	51	−43.4
Wyoming	1,182	1,200	1.6	14	129	829.6
Region 9	107,594	125,703	16.8	5,181	3,193	−38.4
Arizona	6,929	5,613	−19.0	1,850	1,252	−32.3
California [a,d]	95,881	115,025	20.0	3,292	1,696	−48.5
Hawaii	1,190	1,355	13.9	5	1	−76.3
Nevada	3,594	3,710	3.2	34	243	609.9
Region 10	25,708	26,019	1.2	2,099	368	−82.5
Alaska	3,479	1,951	−43.9	1,800	18	−99.0
Idaho	1,283	1,504	17.2	69	64	−6.9
Oregon	6,154	7,057	14.7	128	236	84.5
Washington	14,791	15,506	4.8	102	49	−51.9

[a]These State facilities held an unspecified number of adults or youthful offenders included in the calculations for the average populations: One New Jersey facility, 1973; and 15 California facilities, 1973 and 1974. Per capita operating expenditures were affected.

[b]For 1973, "other operating expenditures" (exclusive of salaries and wages) and capital expenditures of six Missouri facilities were not available. Therefore, all Missouri expenditure data for 1973 are understated.

[c]For 1974, expenditure data for nine Colorado facilities were unavailable.

[d]For 1973, total and capital expenditures are understated because capital expenditures reported for 15 State facilities included outlays for equipment only.

Source: U.S. Department of Justice, Law Enforcement Assistance Administration, Children in Custody: Advance Report on the Juvenile Detention and Correctional Facility Census of 1974 (Washington, D.C.: U.S. Government Printing Office, 1977), pp. 56-59.

Operating expenditures			Average populations			Per capita operating expenditures (whole dollars)		
1973	1974	Percent change	1973	1974	Percent change	1973	1974	Percent change
13,094	8,320	−36.5	1,206	1,380	14.4	10,858	6,028	−44.5
5,615	431	−92.3	425	492	15.8	13,211	875	−93.4
1,982	2,144	8.2	218	242	11.0	9,093	8,860	−2.6
814	1,128	38.6	91	119	30.8	8,945	9,478	6.0
927	869	−6.2	102	108	5.9	9,083	8,046	−11.4
2,589	2,677	3.4	254	301	18.5	10,192	8,892	−12.8
1,168	1,072	−8.2	116	118	1.7	10,067	9,080	−9.8
102,413	122,510	19.6	11,138	12,013	7.9	9,195	10,198	10.9
5,080	4,360	−14.2	708	499	−29.5	7,174	8,737	21.8
92,589	113,329	22.4	10,004	11,074	10.7	9,255	10,233	10.6
1,185	1,354	14.3	116	112	−3.4	10,214	12,091	18.4
3,560	3,467	−2.6	310	328	5.8	11,483	10,568	−8.0
23,609	25,651	8.6	1,869	1,875	0.3	12,631	13,680	8.3
1,679	1,933	15.1	84	92	9.5	19,992	21,006	5.1
1,215	1,440	18.6	111	135	21.6	10,941	10,667	−2.5
6,026	6,821	13.2	527	504	−4.4	11,435	13,534	18.4
14,689	15,457	5.2	1,147	1,144	−0.3	12,806	13,511	5.5

Table 8 Type of expenditure, average population, and per capita operating expenditures of private juvenile detention and correctional facilities, by region and State, fiscal year 1974

[Dollar amounts in thousands; — represents zero]

Region and State	Total expenditures	Capital expenditures	Operating expenditures	Average population	Per capita operating expenditures (whole dollars)
United States, total	$294,036	$25,905	$268,131	31,384	$ 8,543
Region 1	23,791	1,799	21,992	2,316	9,495
Connecticut	5,570	483	5,087	519	9,801
Maine	2,215	393	1,822	314	5,803
Massachusetts	11,959	668	11,291	1,043	10,825
New Hampshire	2,054	136	1,918	273	7,024
Rhode Island	1,777	(ª)	1,664	120	13,866
Vermont	217	(ª)	210	47	4,476
Region 2	60,882	3,507	57,375	4,131	13,888
New Jersey	1,955	206	1,750	182	9,613
New York	58,927	3,301	55,626	3,949	14,086
Region 3	27,419	2,425	24,994	2,873	8,699
Delaware	60	—	(ª)	18	3,350
District of Columbia	5,677	—	(ª)	651	8,079
Maryland	18,639	1,286	17,353	1,816	9,555
Pennsylvania	2,704	575	2,129	335	6,354
Virginia	340	(ª)	193	53	3,632
West Virginia					
Region 4	16,766	1,820	14,946	2,488	6,007
Alabama	259	33	226	76	2,971
Florida	6,301	780	5,521	871	6,338
Georgia	3,906	516	3,390	572	5,926
Kentucky	1,106	34	1,072	256	4,186
Mississippi	1,336	175	1,160	183	6,340
North Carolina	1,403	13	1,390	224	6,203
South Carolina	854	107	746	74	10,086
Tennessee	1,601	160	1,441	232	6,211

Region 5	56,176	6,094	50,082	5,464	9,165
Illinois	9,141	912	8,230	1,006	8,180
Indiana	6,748	1,108	5,641	932	6,052
Michigan	17,078	1,659	15,420	1,360	11,338
Minnesota	7,687	1,670	6,018	741	8,120
Ohio	6,860	396	6,464	801	8,069
Wisconsin	8,661	350	8,310	624	13,317
Region 6	18,329	3,087	15,242	3,410	4,469
Arkansas	1,682	(a)	(a)	370	3,642
Louisiana	2,272	503	1,769	448	3,948
New Mexico	909	(a)	(a)	192	4,388
Oklahoma	3,073	434	2,639	631	4,182
Texas	10,393	1,750	8,643	1,769	4,886
Region 7	14,167	799	13,368	2,024	6,604
Iowa	2,420	224	2,196	268	8,193
Kansas	2,405	153	2,252	346	6,508
Missouri	5,827	251	5,576	764	7,298
Nebraska	3,515	171	3,344	646	5,176
Region 8	9,340	1,030	8,311	1,337	6,215
Colorado	3,844	163	3,682	620	5,938
Montana	(a)	(a)	(a)	(a)	(a)
North Dakota	1,147	(a)	(a)	119	8,909
South Dakota	1,247	91	1,156	232	4,983
Utah	1,866	239	1,627	215	7,566
Wyoming	(a)	(a)	(a)	(a)	(a)
Region 9	51,348	3,680	47,668	5,556	8,579
Arizona	5,515	529	4,986	813	6,133
California	44,709	3,073	41,635	4,584	9,082
Hawaii	877	(a)	818	50	16,367
Nevada	246	18	228	109	2,091
Region 10	15,817	1,665	14,153	1,785	7,928
Alaska	905	(a)	(a)	109	8,200
Idaho	1,262	(a)	(a)	107	11,134
Oregon	6,314	919	5,395	551	9,791
Washington	7,337	664	6,673	1,018	6,554

[a] Data withheld to avoid disclosure and maintain confidentiality guarantees.

Source: U.S. Department of Justice, Law Enforcement Assistance Administration, *Children in Custody: Advance Report on the Juvenile Detention and Correctional Facility Census of 1974* (Washington, D.C.: U.S. Government Printing Office, 1977), pp. 60, 61.

Table 9 Staff of public and private juvenile detention and correctional facilities, by employment status, region, and State, June 30, 1974

Nonpayroll staff included those personnel of a parent agency or other public agency (including school systems) who were assigned for some or all of their working time to a facility. Community volunteers, college interns, and persons paid under contractual agreements or Federal grants were also included.

[— represents zero]

Region and State	Public facilities				Private facilities			
	Payroll staff		Nonpayroll staff		Payroll staff		Nonpayroll staff	
	Full-time	Part-time	Full-time	Part-time	Full-time	Part-time	Full-time	Part-time
United States, total	37,842	3,708	1,549	3,177	19,694	4,520	906	3,492
Region 1	1,203	133	26	113	1,521	356	43	307
Connecticut	275	74	—	19	320	62	(a)	49
Maine	282	17	—	17	137	12	(a)	(a)
Massachusetts	230	14	20	—	777	217	34	219
New Hampshire	153	12	—	14	141	29	4	15
Rhode Island	161	8	6	6	116	31	—	(a)
Vermont	102	8	—	57	30	5	—	(a)
Region 2	3,252	534	69	182	3,754	905	181	528
New Jersey	1,203	176	42	134	150	16	(a)	9
New York	2,049	358	27	48	3,604	889	(a)	519
Region 3	4,231	290	211	502	1,909	547	32	183
Delaware	252	3	—	—	8	—	—	—
District of Columbia	482	4	2	—	—	(a)	—	(a)
Maryland	850	5	16	38	369	126	(a)	41
Pennsylvania	1,289	125	147	398	1,328	399	21	124
Virginia	1,100	118	44	64	185	(a)	—	(a)
West Virginia	258	35	2	2	19	(a)	(a)	10
Region 4	6,063	224	188	221	1,259	192	69	242
Alabama	496	32	22	42	32	14	(a)	10
Florida	1,830	45	22	73	472	38	18	25
Georgia	1,056	33	40	25	255	46	11	56
Kentucky	441	22	75	6	104	30	(a)	40
Mississippi	280	16	5	20	92	(a)	9	(a)
North Carolina	727	29	15	32	108	20	(a)	(a)
South Carolina	386	24	1	—	48	(a)	(a)	(a)
Tennessee	847	23	8	23	148	14	11	49

Region 5	7,354	704	268	540	3,741	791	121	631
Illinois	1,609	96	40	37	611	122	(a)	96
Indiana	626	45	46	23	508	70	6	66
Michigan	1,379	226	38	61	1,055	206	(a)	95
Minnesota	651	38	30	107	450	145	45	102
Ohio	2,369	240	100	267	532	116	13	240
Wisconsin	720	59	14	45	585	132	(a)	32
Region 6	3,331	175	71	261	1,346	216	132	489
Arkansas	297	7	12	3	165	28	(a)	17
Louisiana	840	69	6	122	132	65	14	86
New Mexico	246	5	—	7	88	8	(a)	14
Oklahoma	422	20	2	93	259	38	62	189
Texas	1,526	74	51	36	702	77	(a)	183
Region 7	2,069	220	84	150	1,064	280	27	243
Iowa	465	31	4	18	172	48	3	15
Kansas	527	43	50	26	181	87	—	35
Missouri	872	117	30	102	449	99	(a)	131
Nebraska	205	29	—	4	262	46	(a)	62
Region 8	981	138	13	90	644	162	16	116
Colorado	325	17	4	2	323	85	4	68
Montana	176	25	4	1	(a)	(a)	—	(a)
North Dakota	95	6	1	8	59	14	—	(a)
South Dakota	69	9	1	21	96	17	(a)	(a)
Utah	221	71	3	58	96	26	(a)	20
Wyoming	95	10	—	—	(a)	(a)	(a)	7
Region 9	7,533	1,068	526	832	3,339	775	187	486
Arizona	409	26	—	6	482	76	8	(a)
California [b]	6,767	1,027	492	823	2,779	686	157	410
Hawaii	104	6	13	—	(a)	5	—	(a)
Nevada	253	9	21	3	(a)	8	22	—
Region 10	1,825	222	93	286	1,117	296	98	267
Alaska	111	—	21	12	81	13	—	(a)
Idaho	109	1	—	—	62	26	7	(a)
Oregon	490	75	16	21	437	121	33	72
Washington	1,115	146	56	253	537	136	58	171

[a] Data withheld to avoid disclosure and maintain confidentiality guarantees.
[b] Although some California public facilities held youthful offenders in addition to juveniles, all their staff were included.

Source: U.S. Department of Justice, Law Enforcement Assistance Administration, *Children in Custody: Advance Report on the Juvenile Detention and Correctional Facility Census of 1974* (Washington, D.C.: U.S. Government Printing Office, 1977), pp. 54, 55.

Table 10 Number of State correctional institutions and number of inmates, by type of institution and State, 1974

NOTE: The Census of State Correctional Facilities was conducted in January 1974, to obtain basic administrative, environmental, and program characteristics for all of the adult or youthful offender correctional facilities operated or funded by State governments. To have been considered for inclusion in the census, a facility must have been (1) operational on Jan. 31, 1974; (2) administratively capable of providing a unique inmate count, staffing pattern, payroll figure, and budgetary information; and (3) defined as a State correctional facility for adults or youthful offenders, or a non-State-operated facility where the clear majority of residents were State inmates. Federal, military, county, local, and municipal correctional institutions, except as noted above, were not included in the census. However, certain of the surveyed facilities housed some non-State inmates, such as Federal prisoners or presentenced offenders, but these inmates comprised only a small percentage of the total inmate population.

Following these criteria, State representatives initially submitted 700 institutions for inclusion in the census. Of this total, 608 eligible facilities remained after it was determined that some functionally distinct units were not able to separate themselves administratively from parent institutions.

Data were obtained through a mail canvass in which the warden or designated representative was requested to complete a questionnaire. Telephone calls were made to obtain missing data items or to clarify inconsistent entries. Responses were received from all facilities except for two in Georgia and a majority of institutions in Massachusetts. The two Georgia facilities were small, and the missing data could not have materially altered State totals for Georgia. Because more than half of Massachusetts' institutions failed to respond, it was decided not to publish any data for that State, as the incomplete information could be misleading.

State	All institutions		Reception, classification, diagnostic centers		Community centers	
	Institutions	Inmates	Institutions	Inmates	Institutions	Inmates
Total	592	187,982	33	9,766	158	8,975
Alabama	20	3,995	1	503	2	64
Alaska	8	466	0	0	1	16
Arizona	6	1,756	0	0	4	208
Arkansas	3	1,755	0	0	0	0
California	35	22,923	2	604	4	160
Colorado	7	2,070	0	0	3	83
Connecticut	12	2,731	0	0	1	20
Delaware	4	683	0	0	1	26
District of Columbia	(a)	(a)	(a)	(a)	(a)	(a)
Florida	46	10,334	1	1,025	19	895
Georgia [b]	30	7,593	2	1,027	3	137
Hawaii	5	303	0	0	3	46
Idaho	1	489	0	0	0	0
Illinois	15	5,843	2	470	6	133
Indiana	10	4,071	1	133	2	78
Iowa	9	1,462	1	93	4	140
Kansas	7	1,446	1	114	0	0
Kentucky	8	2,886	0	0	0	0
Louisiana	7	4,063	0	0	3	299
Maine	6	465	0	0	3	97

State					
Maryland	12	6,489	1	462	4	749
Massachusetts	(c)	(c)	(c)	(c)	(c)	(c)
Michigan	21	8,104	1	987	3	314
Minnesota	6	1,401	0	0	1	14
Mississippi	1	1,736	0	0	0	0
Missouri	9	3,449	1	174	1	32
Montana	1	336	0	0	0	0
Nebraska	4	1,010	0	0	1	34
Nevada	1	790	0	0	0	0
New Hampshire	2	279	0	0	1	8
New Jersey	13	5,655	0	0	2	74
New Mexico	2	775	0	0	0	0
New York	23	14,311	4	1,595	1	32
North Carolina	76	11,809	5	1,041	29	2,986
North Dakota	2	176	0	0	0	0
Ohio	11	7,873	2	201	0	0
Oklahoma	11	3,175	0	0	4	191
Oregon	12	1,686	0	0	7	139
Pennsylvania	22	6,065	1	122	13	434
Rhode Island	1	569	0	0	0	0
South Carolina	17	3,615	2	237	6	411
South Dakota	1	233	0	0	0	0
Tennessee	10	3,504	1	202	4	354
Texas	14	17,136	1	493	0	0
Utah	3	599	0	0	2	40
Vermont	7	368	1	43	5	240
Virginia	38	5,394	1	48	3	234
Washington	14	2,592	1	192	8	182
West Virginia	4	1,051	0	0	1	17
Wisconsin	12	2,183	0	0	2	73
Wyoming	3	281	0	0	1	15

[a] District of Columbia correctional facilities are considered to be local institutions.
[b] Excludes the Andromeda Work Release and Drug Treatment Center.
[c] No data are given for Massachusetts because of a lack of response from certain institutions.

Table 10 (continued)

| State | Prisons | | | | | | | |
| | All prisons | | Farms | | Road camps | | Forest camps | |
	Institutions	Inmates	Institutions	Inmates	Institutions	Inmates	Institutions	Inmates
Total	401	169,241	41	25,402	80	6,369	41	2,483
Alabama	17	3,428	3	1,187	10	469	0	0
Alaska	7	450	0	0	0	0	0	0
Arizona	2	1,548	0	0	0	0	0	0
Arkansas	3	1,755	1	1,287	0	0	0	0
California	29	22,163	0	0	1	67	15	933
Colorado	4	1,987	0	0	0	0	1	89
Connecticut	11	2,711	0	0	0	0	0	0
Delaware	[a]	657	0	0	[a]	[a]	[a]	[a]
District of Columbia	26	8,414	[a]	[a]	13	812	0	0
Florida	25	6,429	0	0	13	957	0	0
Georgia [b]								
Hawaii	2	257	0	0	0	0	0	0
Idaho	1	489	0	0	0	0	2	58
Illinois	7	5,240	0	0	0	0	0	0
Indiana	7	3,860	1	628	0	0	1	26
Iowa	4	1,229	0	0	0	0	0	0
Kansas	6	1,332	1	82	0	0	2	66
Kentucky	8	2,886	0	0	0	0	1	19
Louisiana	4	3,764	1	3,138	0	0	0	0
Maine	3	368	0	0	0	0	0	0

Maryland	7	5,278	0	0	1	135	0	0
Massachusetts	(c)	(c)	(c)	(c)	(c)	(c)	(c)	(c)
Michigan	17	6,803	0	0	0	0	10	756
Minnesota	5	1,387	1	63	0	0	0	0
Mississippi	1	1,736	1	1,736	0	0	0	0
Missouri	7	3,243	2	322	0	0	0	0
Montana	1	336	0	0	0	0	0	0
Nebraska	3	976	0	0	0	0	0	0
Nevada	1	790	0	0	0	0	0	0
New Hampshire	1	271	0	0	0	0	0	0
New Jersey	11	5,581	0	0	0	0	2	91
New Mexico	2	775	1	72	0	0	0	0
New York	18	12,684	0	0	0	0	3	260
North Carolina	42	7,782	3	855	15	1,939	0	0
North Dakota	2	176	1	22	0	0	0	0
Ohio	9	7,672	1	257	0	0	0	0
Oklahoma	7	2,984	1	234	0	0	1	33
Oregon	5	1,547	1	71	0	0	0	0
Pennsylvania	8	5,509	0	0	0	0	0	0
Rhode Island	1	569	0	0	0	0	0	0
South Carolina	9	2,967	1	68	0	0	0	0
South Dakota	1	233	0	0	0	0	0	0
Tennessee	5	2,948	2	666	0	0	0	0
Texas	13	16,643	10	13,187	0	0	0	0
Utah	1	559	0	0	0	0	0	0
Vermont	1	85	0	0	0	0	0	0
Virginia	34	5,112	3	965	27	1,990	1	80
Washington	5	2,218	0	0	0	0	0	0
West Virginia	3	1,034	1	388	0	0	0	0
Wisconsin	10	2,110	4	163	0	0	2	72
Wyoming	2	266	1	11	0	0	0	0

Source: U.S. Department of Justice, Law Enforcement Assistance Administration, *Census of State Correctional Facilities 1974—Advance Report*, National Prisoner Statistics Special Report No. SD-NPS-SR-1 (Washington, D.C.; U.S. Government Printing Office, 1975), pp. 18, 19.

Table 10 (continued)

State	Prisons			
	Closed prisons		Other prisons	
	Institutions	Inmates	Institutions	Inmates
Total	172	118,708	67	16,279
Alabama	3	1,670	1	102
Alaska	1	56	6	394
Arizona	1	1,417	1	131
Arkansas	2	468	0	0
California	11	19,224	2	1,939
Colorado	2	1,852	1	46
Connecticut	4	1,674	7	1,037
Delaware	3	657	0	0
District of Columbia	(a)	(a)	(a)	(a)
Florida	8	6,466	5	1,136
Georgia [b]	8	3,950	4	1,522
Hawaii	1	200	1	57
Idaho	1	489	0	0
Illinois	7	5,240	0	0
Indiana	4	3,174	0	0
Iowa	3	1,203	0	0
Kansas	3	1,251	3	81
Kentucky	4	2,626	1	112
Louisiana	2	607	0	0
Maine	3	368	0	0

State				
Maryland	4	3,879	2	1,264
Massachusetts	(c)	(c)	(c)	(c)
Michigan	6	5,861	1	186
Minnesota	3	1,288	1	36
Mississippi	0	0	0	0
Missouri	2	1,579	3	1,342
Montana	1	336	0	0
Nebraska	1	647	2	329
Nevada	1	790	0	0
New Hampshire	1	271	0	0
New Jersey	4	3,587	5	1,903
New Mexico	1	703	0	0
New York	10	11,259	5	1,165
North Carolina	20	4,646	4	342
North Dakota	1	154	0	0
Ohio	6	7,237	2	178
Oklahoma	3	1,893	3	857
Oregon	3	1,443	0	0
Pennsylvania	7	4,845	1	664
Rhode Island	1	569	0	0
South Carolina	4	2,412	4	487
South Dakota	1	233	0	0
Tennessee	3	2,282	0	0
Texas	2	2,611	1	845
Utah	1	559	0	0
Vermont	1	85	0	0
Virginia	3	2,033	1	124
Washington	4	2,138	0	0
West Virginia	2	646	0	0
Wisconsin	4	1,875	0	0
Wyoming	1	255	0	0

Table 11 Number of State correctional institutions and number of inmates, by type of institution and security confinement classification, United States, 1974

Type of institution	All types		Type of security confinement					
			Minimum		Medium		Maximum	
	Institu-tions[a]	Inmates	Institu-tions[a]	Inmates	Institu-tions[a]	Inmates	Institu-tions[a]	Inmates
Total -------	592	187,982	509	49,983	246	63,786	187	74,213
Reception, classification, diagnostic centers -------	33	9,766	11	1,015	14	3,286	23	5,465
Community centers -------	158	8,975	157	8,791	6	159	4	25
Prisons -------	401	169,241	341	40,177	226	60,341	160	68,723
Farms -------	41	25,402	35	5,436	13	6,039	18	13,927
Road camps -------	80	6,369	68	3,157	67	2,937	10	275
Forest camps -------	41	2,483	41	2,483	0	0	0	0
Closed prisons -------	172	118,708	138	21,210	116	44,683	111	52,815
Other prisons -------	67	16,279	59	7,891	30	6,682	21	1,706

[a] The number of institutions with inmates in specific types of security classifications exceeds the total number of institutions because an institution may have inmates in more than one type of security classification.

Source: U.S. Department of Justice, Law Enforcement Assistance Administration, *Census of State Correctional Facilities 1974—Advance Reports*, National Prisoner Statistics Special Report No. SD–NPS–SR–1 (Washington, D.C.: U.S. Government Printing Office, 1975), p. 20.

Table 12 State correctional institutions, by type of institution and size of inmate cells, United States, 1974

Type of institution	One-inmate cells	Two-inmate cells	Three- or four-inmate cells	Other quarters [a]
All institutions_____	100,563	15,245	900	2,055
Classification or medical centers_____	5,943	671	44	84
Community centers_____	24	104	3	296
All prisons_____	94,596	14,470	853	1,675
Prison farms_____	3,451	3,936	134	264
Road camps_____	12	0	5	163
Forest camps_____	0	0	0	82
Closed prisons_____	82,870	10,419	650	882
Other prisons_____	8,263	115	64	284

[a] Includes dormitories and cells for five or more inmates.

Source: U.S. Department of Justice, Law Enforcement Assistance Administration, *Census of State Correctional Facilities 1974—Advance Report*, National Prisoner Statistics Special Report No. SD–NPS–SR–1 (Washington, D.C.: U.S. Government Printing Office, 1975), p. 25.

Table 13 State correctional institutions, by size of inmate cells and type of amenity, United States, 1974

Type of amenity	Size class of cell							
	One-inmate cell		Two-inmate cell		Three- or four-inmate cell		Other quarters [b]	
	Number [a]	Percent	Number [a]	Percent	Number [a]	Percent	Number [a]	Percent
Total institutions	205	100.0	58	100.0	28	100.0	503	100.0
Flush toilet	176	85.9	53	91.4	25	89.3	456	90.7
Drinking fountain	77	37.6	21	36.2	14	50.0	362	72.0
Sink	171	83.4	50	86.2	25	89.3	446	88.7
Desk and chair	105	51.2	14	24.1	9	32.1	264	52.5
Reading lamp	84	41.0	20	34.5	5	17.9	226	44.9
Seating space (except beds)	106	51.7	18	31.0	13	46.4	369	73.4
Window	103	50.2	26	44.8	14	50.0	446	88.7
Fan	41	20.0	17	29.3	12	42.9	259	51.5
Ventilation other than window or fan	110	53.7	30	51.7	11	39.3	193	38.4

[a] The number of institutions with specific amenities in cells may exceed the total number of institutions with cells because an institution may have more than one type of amenity.
[b] Includes cells for five or more inmates and dormitories.

Source: U.S. Department of Justice, Law Enforcement Assistance Administration, *Census of State Correctional Facilities 1974—Advance Report*, National Prisoner Statistics Special Report No. SD-NPS-SR-1 (Washington, D.C.: U.S. Government Printing Office, 1975), p. 27.

Table 14 State correctional institutions, by type of institution and medical facilities, United States, 1974

Type of medical facility	All institutions		Reception, classification, diagnostic centers		Community centers		Prisons														
							All prisons		Farms		Road camps		Forest camps		Closed prisons		Other prisons				
	Num-ber[a]	Per-cent	Num-ber[a]	Per-cent	Num-ber[a]	Per-cent	Num-ber[a]	Per-cent	Num-ber[a]	Per-cent	Num-ber[a]	Per-cent	Num-ber[a]	Per-cent	Num-ber[a]	Per-cent	Num-ber[a]	Per-cent			
Total institutions	592	100.0	33	100.0	158	100.0	401	100.0	41	100.0	80	100.0	41	100.0	172	100.0	67	100.0			
With dispensary	489	82.6	30	90.9	87	55.1	372	92.8	36	87.8	68	85.0	34	82.9	171	99.4	63	94.0			
With sick bay	358	60.5	25	75.8	48	30.4	285	71.1	25	61.0	49	61.3	9	22.0	159	92.4	43	64.2			

[a] The number of institutions with specific types of medical facilities may exceed the total number of institutions because an institution may have more than one type of medical facility.

Source: U.S. Department of Justice, Law Enforcement Assistance Administration, *Census of State Correctional Facilities 1974—Advance Report*, National Prisoner Statistics Special Report No. SD-NPS-SR-1 (Washington, D.C.: U.S. Government Printing Office, 1975), p. 28.

Table 15 State correctional institutions, by type of institution and rehabilitative program, United States, 1974

Type of program	All institutions		Reception, classification, diagnostic centers		Community centers		Prisons												
							All prisons		Farms		Road camps		Forest camps		Closed prisons		Other prisons	
	Num-ber[a]	Per-cent	Num-ber[a]	Per-cent	Num-ber[a]	Per-cent	Num-ber[a]	Per-cent	Num-ber[a]	Per-cent	Num-ber[a]	Per-cent	Num-ber[a]	Per-cent	Num-ber[a]	Per-cent	Num-ber[a]	Per-cent
Total	592	100.0	33	100.0	158	100.0	401	100.0	41	100.0	80	100.0	41	100.0	172	100.0	67	100.0
Group counseling	487	82.3	23	69.7	136	86.1	328	81.8	30	73.2	50	62.5	37	90.2	153	89.0	58	86.6
Individual counseling	540	91.2	31	93.9	148	93.7	361	90.0	36	87.8	61	76.3	34	82.9	167	97.1	63	94.0
Remedial education	526	88.9	21	63.6	135	85.4	370	92.3	38	92.7	63	78.8	36	87.8	170	98.8	63	94.0
College degree	384	64.9	17	51.5	121	76.6	246	61.3	26	63.4	29	36.3	11	26.8	132	76.7	48	71.6
Assessment of vocational potential	471	79.6	30	90.9	133	84.2	308	76.8	30	73.2	39	48.8	26	63.4	155	90.1	58	86.6
Vocational training	477	80.6	17	51.5	134	84.8	326	81.3	35	85.4	47	58.8	30	73.2	163	94.8	51	76.1
Pre-vocational training	436	73.6	24	72.7	128	81.0	284	70.8	28	68.3	45	56.3	28	68.3	128	74.4	55	82.1
Job placement	496	83.8	21	63.6	157	99.4	318	80.3	34	82.9	52	65.0	25	70.7	146	84.9	61	91.0
Alcoholic treatment	489	82.6	22	66.7	143	90.5	324	80.8	33	80.5	46	57.5	33	80.5	152	88.4	60	89.6
Drug treatment	436	73.6	20	60.6	126	79.7	294	73.3	29	70.7	36	45.0	31	75.6	145	84.3	53	79.1
Religious services	571	96.5	32	97.0	145	91.8	394	98.3	40	97.6	75	93.8	41	100.0	171	99.4	67	100.0

[a] The number of institutions offering specific programs exceeds the total number of institutions because an institution may offer more than one type of program.

Source: U. S. Department of Justice, Law Enforcement Assistance Administration, *Census of State Correctional Facilities 1974—Advance Report, National Prisoner Statistics Special Report No. SD-NPS-SR-1* (Washington, D.C.: U.S. Government Printing Office, 1975), p. 30.

Table 16 Number of State correctional institutions and number of custodial personnel, by type of institution, United States, 1974

Type of institution	Number of institutions	Number of custodial personnel	Average number of custodial personnel per institution
All institutions_____	592	37,929	64
Classification or medical centers_____	33	2,253	68
Community centers_____	158	1,131	7
All prisons_____	401	34,545	86
Prison farms_____	41	3,247	79
Road camps_____	80	1,277	16
Forest camps_____	41	329	8
Closed prisons_____	172	26,357	153
Other prisons_____	67	3,335	50

Source: U.S. Department of Justice, Law Enforcement Assistance Administration, *Census of State Correctional Facilities 1974—Advance Report*, National Prisoner Statistics Special Report No. SD–NPS–SR–1 (Washington, D.C.: U.S. Government Printing Office, 1975), p. 6, Table C.

Table 17 Movement of persons under supervision of the Federal Probation System, by circuit and district, fiscal year 1976

"Special parole" refers to a specified period of parole attached to a term of imprisonment at sentencing. This provision is applicable to violations of certain drug laws (see Drug Abuse Prevention and Control Act of 1970, Public Law 91-513, Oct. 27, 1970, 84 Stat. 1260). Excludes Canal Zone, Guam, and the Virgin Islands.

Circuit and district	Persons under supervision July 1, 1975	Total received	Received for supervision							
			Total less transfers	Court probation	Deferred prosecution	U.S. magistrate probation	Parole	Mandatory release	Military parole	Special parole
Total all districts	64,261	44,620	35,102	18,375	1,711	5,358	6,286	1,935	232	1,205
District of Columbia	2,285	1,197	1,043	430	0	215	328	54	2	14
First Circuit	1,584	1,148	932	576	33	101	121	46	8	47
Maine	116	74	50	32	0	3	10	5	0	0
Massachusetts	963	716	611	388	24	58	71	29	4	37
New Hampshire	106	72	44	34	0	3	7	0	0	0
Rhode Island	140	100	78	46	0	14	15	3	0	0
Puerto Rico	259	186	149	76	9	23	18	9	4	10
Second Circuit	5,410	3,432	2,720	1,704	195	36	442	162	20	161
Connecticut	533	343	267	177	16	1	48	18	0	7
New York:										
Northern	263	160	123	60	19	9	21	6	3	5
Eastern	2,089	1,169	865	534	28	3	196	49	11	44
Southern	2,014	1,459	1,219	758	131	0	155	75	5	95
Western	364	221	187	127	1	23	14	14	1	7
Vermont	147	80	59	48	0	0	8	0	0	3
Third Circuit	4,751	3,425	2,983	1,477	124	838	346	111	8	79
Delaware	231	145	127	69	3	36	17	1	0	1
New Jersey	1,529	1,221	1,005	469	8	346	111	46	3	22
Pennsylvania:										
Eastern	1,850	1,411	1,279	582	62	417	133	37	3	45
Middle	289	192	156	102	15	19	12	5	1	2
Western	852	456	416	255	36	20	73	22	1	9
Fourth Circuit	6,475	4,312	3,622	1,800	157	859	647	107	25	27

Maryland	1,442	1,242	1,116	356	21	553	149	28	4	5
North Carolina:										
Eastern	592	411	322	178	7	67	55	12	3	0
Middle	816	326	254	155	20	5	56	16	0	2
Western	700	402	345	173	0	100	57	12	0	3
South Carolina	953	616	510	313	53	42	84	9	5	4
Virginia:										
Eastern	1,022	765	627	334	33	61	163	20	8	8
Western	565	285	239	165	22	18	30	3	0	1
West Virginia:										
Northern	117	67	48	32	0	0	13	1	1	1
Southern	268	198	161	94	1	13	40	6	4	3
Fifth Circuit	13,220	10,473	7,783	3,637	313	1,484	1,531	477	67	274
Alabama:										
Northern	930	662	570	397	31	13	92	31	5	1
Middle	402	230	190	113	6	16	43	10	2	0
Southern	277	162	130	93	0	4	25	6	0	2
Florida:										
Northern	312	171	115	42	1	8	44	9	3	8
Middle	1,283	907	643	348	14	30	180	38	7	26
Southern	1,245	839	608	330	0	48	116	35	8	71
Georgia:										
Northern	1,141	858	715	248	36	187	170	46	2	26
Middle	398	307	242	171	23	8	32	6	1	1
Southern	641	443	394	87	6	268	23	9	1	0
Louisiana:										
Eastern	671	611	523	284	55	25	102	43	0	14
Middle	133	114	74	41	2	5	21	5	0	0
Western	462	384	263	121	62	30	32	10	4	4
Mississippi:										
Northern	236	121	87	60	0	7	18	2	0	0
Southern	356	184	130	70	0	25	22	9	3	1
Texas:										
Northern	1,354	987	642	302	23	23	183	79	12	20
Eastern	322	280	157	93	3	13	29	11	4	4
Southern	1,665	2,177	1,568	627	22	593	192	56	9	69
Western	1,392	1,036	732	210	29	181	207	72	6	27

Table 17 (continued)

Circuit and district	Received by transfer	Total removed	Total less transfers	Removed from supervision						
				Court probation	Deferred prosecution	U.S. magistrate probation	Parole	Mandatory release	Military parole	Special parole
Total all districts	9,518	44,635	35,086	19,373	1,205	4,701	6,775	2,349	200	483
District of Columbia	154	1,442	1,343	795	1	254	246	41	1	5
First Circuit	216	1,060	906	521	14	131	163	62	3	12
Maine	24	76	63	41	1	4	12	5	0	0
Massachusetts	105	630	551	307	4	82	106	40	1	11
New Hampshire	28	86	66	44	0	12	9	1	0	0
Rhode Island	22	114	94	52	0	20	19	3	0	0
Puerto Rico	37	154	132	77	9	13	17	13	2	1
Second Circuit	712	3,307	2,531	1,648	155	38	421	192	20	57
Connecticut	76	301	245	181	2	3	42	16	0	1
New York:										
Northern	37	184	169	125	13	8	14	7	0	2
Eastern	304	1,110	886	603	14	1	173	64	13	18
Southern	240	1,406	997	579	120	6	159	95	5	33
Western	34	240	200	137	6	20	23	10	2	2
Vermont	21	66	34	23	0	0	10	0	0	1
Third Circuit	442	3,121	2,632	1,318	87	757	303	128	13	26
Delaware	18	166	131	63	10	35	22	1	0	0
New Jersey	216	1,157	965	476	6	303	115	55	2	8
Pennsylvania:										
Eastern	132	1,220	1,067	482	42	387	87	46	6	17
Middle	36	178	135	84	17	15	15	2	1	1
Western	40	400	334	213	12	17	64	24	4	0
Fourth Circuit	690	4,236	3,400	1,761	122	731	643	119	12	12

338

Division									
Maryland	3	0	34	170	331	12	320	870	1,110	126
North Carolina:										
Eastern	0	2	12	51	51	4	119	239	326	89
Middle	0	1	14	63	13	12	215	318	369	72
Western	2	0	16	55	184	10	152	419	503	57
South Carolina	5	3	13	76	55	27	294	473	553	106
Virginia:										
Eastern	2	3	19	155	61	38	303	581	779	138
Western	0	0	4	31	21	15	223	294	345	46
West Virginia:										
Northern	0	1	1	13	2	3	38	58	70	19
Southern	0	2	6	29	13	1	97	148	181	37
Fifth Circuit	106	56	551	1,567	1,059	251	3,828	7,418	10,289	2,690
Alabama:										
Northern	1	4	39	105	24	37	335	545	646	92
Middle	1	3	10	34	9	13	141	211	263	40
Southern	0	2	7	29	3	0	67	108	146	32
Florida:										
Northern	1	2	9	55	10	3	75	155	207	56
Middle	11	4	39	154	46	8	399	661	904	264
Southern	35	8	51	112	40	7	387	640	869	231
Georgia:										
Northern	9	2	66	142	199	15	303	736	861	143
Middle	4	2	12	25	26	13	97	179	221	65
Southern	0	0	12	33	169	2	214	430	565	49
Louisiana:										
Eastern	1	3	35	110	25	30	234	438	536	88
Middle	0	0	7	14	2	4	47	74	106	40
Western	1	6	13	35	21	22	144	242	356	121
Mississippi:										
Northern	0	0	2	16	0	0	86	104	138	34
Southern	0	2	11	19	15	2	123	172	216	54
Texas:										
Northern	12	6	83	231	59	17	285	693	933	345
Eastern	2	2	10	35	13	15	89	166	259	123
Southern	22	7	69	214	275	24	494	1,105	1,987	609
Western	6	3	76	204	123	39	308	759	1,076	304

339

Table 17 (continued)

Circuit and district	Removed by transfer	Persons under supervision June 30, 1976
Total all districts	9,549	64,246
District of Columbia	99	2,040
First Circuit	154	1,672
Maine	13	114
Massachusetts	79	1,049
New Hampshire	20	92
Rhode Island	20	126
Puerto Rico	22	291
Second Circuit	776	5,535
Connecticut	56	575
New York:		
Northern	15	239
Eastern	224	2,148
Southern	409	2,067
Western	40	345
Vermont	32	161
Third Circuit	489	5,055
Delaware	35	210
New Jersey	192	1,593
Pennsylvania:		
Eastern	153	2,041
Middle	43	303
Western	66	908
Fourth Circuit	836	6,551

Maryland	240	1,574
North Carolina:		
Eastern	87	677
Middle	51	773
Western	84	599
South Carolina	80	1,016
Virginia:		
Eastern	198	1,008
Western	51	505
West Virginia:		
Northern	12	114
Southern	33	285
Fifth Circuit	2,871	13,404
Alabama:		
Northern	101	946
Middle	52	369
Southern	38	293
Florida:		
Northern	52	276
Middle	243	1,286
Southern	229	1,215
Georgia:		
Northern	125	1,138
Middle	42	484
Southern	135	519
Louisiana:		
Eastern	98	746
Middle	32	141
Western	114	490
Mississippi:		
Northern	34	219
Southern	44	324
Texas:		
Northern	240	1,408
Eastern	93	343
Southern	882	1,855
Western	317	1,352

Table 18 Movement of persons under supervision of the Federal Probation System, by circuit and district, fiscal year 1976

Circuit and district	Persons under supervision July 1, 1975	Total received	Total less transfers	Received for supervision						
				Court probation	Deferred prosecution	U.S. magistrate probation	Parole	Mandatory release	Military parole	Special parole
Sixth Circuit	6,931	4,440	3,728	1,993	178	405	803	225	26	98
Kentucky:										
Eastern	496	285	214	124	3	7	60	19	0	1
Western	554	485	417	187	105	32	59	28	2	4
Michigan:										
Eastern	2,111	1,248	1,115	558	42	153	239	74	6	43
Western	413	277	217	129	16	38	27	3	2	2
Ohio:										
Northern	1,267	815	703	489	11	31	114	30	8	20
Southern	688	443	339	185	0	23	95	26	3	7
Tennessee:										
Eastern	523	333	252	115	0	37	85	12	1	2
Middle	392	313	272	104	1	83	52	21	1	10
Western	487	241	199	102	0	1	72	12	3	9
Seventh Circuit	4,636	2,730	2,160	1,170	214	51	467	164	14	80
Illinois:										
Northern	2,430	1,195	983	485	159	10	203	79	6	41
Eastern	346	242	175	103	8	3	40	13	1	7
Southern	330	188	132	89	2	0	31	9	1	0
Indiana:										
Northern	538	396	318	188	10	2	79	23	0	16
Southern	661	448	356	192	7	30	89	28	3	7
Wisconsin:										
Eastern	241	196	158	90	25	4	17	10	3	9
Western	90	65	38	23	3	2	8	2	0	0
Eighth Circuit	3,552	2,527	2,062	1,204	150	120	375	146	13	54
Arkansas:										
Eastern	349	260	207	137	1	9	38	12	0	10
Western	154	113	73	53	1	1	7	8	2	1

Iowa:										
Northern	125	103	82	65	2	0	10	4	0	1
Southern	204	154	117	72	0	3	29	6	1	6
Minnesota	569	369	307	158	14	25	53	29	4	24
Missouri:										
Eastern	832	457	393	179	47	7	125	28	1	6
Western	737	495	399	165	51	72	71	33	2	5
Nebraska	221	188	154	101	13	2	26	9	2	1
North Dakota	109	127	92	72	0	0	12	7	1	0
South Dakota	252	261	238	202	21	1	4	10	0	0
Ninth Circuit	12,400	8,611	6,418	3,600	300	943	906	313	34	322
Alaska	184	154	108	87	3	4	9	2	1	2
Arizona	1,153	982	809	434	12	69	137	52	2	103
California:										
Northern	1,864	1,253	914	339	35	348	128	37	1	26
Eastern	1,054	718	487	339	13	31	68	21	5	10
Central	4,453	2,515	1,839	1,027	99	212	276	129	10	86
Southern	1,064	1,232	1,023	701	1	187	69	16	2	47
Hawaii	282	140	105	76	0	4	15	7	0	3
Idaho	159	158	101	71	8	0	12	9	0	1
Montana	277	170	140	101	12	3	14	5	5	0
Nevada	287	202	117	81	3	3	18	6	0	6
Oregon	552	350	222	82	62	18	41	9	4	6
Washington:										
Eastern	230	176	125	84	9	7	12	4	2	7
Western	841	561	428	178	43	57	107	16	2	25
Tenth Circuit	3,017	2,325	1,651	784	47	306	320	130	15	49
Colorado	751	511	343	185	2	12	78	37	1	28
Kansas	591	485	387	165	37	50	86	33	11	5
New Mexico	478	351	235	103	2	46	47	27	1	9
Oklahoma:										
Northern	234	185	131	98	1	3	20	6	0	3
Eastern	144	102	53	38	0	0	12	1	1	1
Western	464	429	323	57	0	193	55	14	1	3
Utah	230	154	101	77	0	0	17	7	0	0
Wyoming	125	108	78	61	5	2	5	5	0	0

Source: Administrative Office of the United States Courts, 1976 Annual Report of the Director (Washington, D.C.: Administrative Office of the United States Courts, 1976), pp. I–46—I–49. (Preliminary Report)

Table 18 (continued)

Circuit and district	Received by transfer	Total removed	Total less transfers	Removed from supervision						
				Court probation	Deferred prosecution	U.S. magistrate probation	Parole	Mandatory release	Military parole	Special parole
Sixth Circuit	712	4,630	3,899	2,139	129	349	972	270	18	22
Kentucky:										
Eastern	71	339	262	128	16	6	81	27	1	3
Western	68	450	362	165	58	33	76	26	4	0
Michigan:										
Eastern	133	1,296	1,166	654	8	136	280	76	4	8
Western	60	258	214	145	10	22	30	5	1	1
Ohio:										
Northern	112	845	732	463	12	37	161	53	2	4
Southern	104	456	364	157	0	26	143	31	2	5
Tennessee:										
Eastern	81	383	323	175	19	22	89	16	2	0
Middle	41	305	235	108	6	63	40	17	1	0
Western	42	298	241	144	0	4	72	19	1	1
Seventh Circuit	570	2,919	2,453	1,402	153	65	574	215	15	29
Illinois:										
Northern	212	1,309	1,166	632	109	17	269	118	6	15
Eastern	67	240	187	97	9	9	53	16	2	1
Southern	56	203	145	90	7	1	35	9	3	0
Indiana:										
Northern	78	357	287	170	9	8	63	31	0	6
Southern	92	520	433	245	4	25	118	31	4	6
Wisconsin:										
Eastern	38	211	174	122	14	1	27	9	0	1
Western	27	79	61	46	1	4	9	1	0	0
Eighth Circuit	465	2,615	2,136	1,173	87	170	493	182	12	19
Arkansas:										
Eastern	53	214	163	103	10	2	32	13	1	2
Western	40	111	82	45	5	2	17	12	0	1

Iowa:

Northern	21	87	65	40	0	3	19	2	1	0
Southern	37	160	130	85	3	4	29	6	0	3
Minnesota	62	449	411	208	2	45	104	40	2	10
Missouri:										
Eastern	64	474	379	143	39	6	145	44	2	0
Western	96	605	494	232	16	103	97	40	4	2
Nebraska	34	195	161	117	3	3	28	9	0	1
North Dakota	35	118	90	75	1	0	8	5	1	0
South Dakota	23	202	161	125	8	2	14	11	1	0
Ninth Circuit	2,193	8,727	6,639	3,901	171	852	1,054	455	34	172
Alaska	46	152	116	80	1	14	13	3	1	4
Arizona	173	912	713	373	15	65	128	61	1	70
California:										
Northern	339	1,259	1,046	568	26	251	124	57	5	15
Eastern	231	796	595	420	2	61	68	31	7	6
Central	676	2,669	2,168	1,250	62	246	361	196	8	45
Southern	209	1,163	659	422	1	122	76	19	0	19
Hawaii	35	168	132	93	1	7	26	5	0	0
Idaho	57	128	102	72	1	6	12	10	1	0
Montana	30	170	135	89	19	0	22	5	0	0
Nevada	85	223	134	85	2	4	24	15	0	4
Oregon	128	361	274	156	29	16	47	19	5	2
Washington:										
Eastern	51	178	125	75	5	13	26	4	2	0
Western	133	548	440	218	7	47	127	30	4	7
Tenth Circuit	674	2,289	1,729	887	35	295	339	134	16	23
Colorado	168	497	372	233	6	21	70	34	2	6
Kansas	98	472	383	191	20	41	94	28	6	3
New Mexico	116	365	270	139	1	32	61	26	1	10
Oklahoma:										
Northern	54	150	98	63	2	2	16	12	3	0
Eastern	49	113	70	44	0	4	19	1	1	1
Western	106	461	364	95	1	189	52	23	2	2
Utah	53	130	99	69	0	2	22	6	0	0
Wyoming	30	101	73	53	5	4	5	4	1	1

Table 18 (continued)

Circuit and district	Removed by transfer	Persons under supervision June 30, 1976
Sixth Circuit	731	6,741
Kentucky:		
Eastern	77	442
Western	88	589
Michigan:		
Eastern	130	2,063
Western	44	432
Ohio:		
Northern	113	1,237
Southern	92	675
Tennessee:		
Eastern	60	473
Middle	70	400
Western	57	430
Seventh Circuit	466	4,447
Illinois:		
Northern	143	2,316
Eastern	53	348
Southern	58	315
Indiana:		
Northern	70	577
Southern	87	589
Wisconsin:		
Eastern	37	226
Western	18	76
Eighth Circuit	479	3,464
Arkansas:		
Eastern	51	395
Western	29	156

Iowa:		
Northern	22	141
Southern	30	198
Minnesota	38	489
Missouri:		
Eastern	95	815
Western	111	627
Nebraska	34	214
North Dakota	28	118
South Dakota	41	311
Ninth Circuit	2,088	12,284
Alaska	36	186
Arizona	199	1,223
California:		
Northern	213	1,858
Eastern	201	976
Central	501	4,299
Southern	504	1,133
Hawaii	36	254
Idaho	26	189
Montana	35	277
Nevada	89	266
Oregon	87	541
Washington:		
Eastern	53	228
Western	108	854
Tenth Circuit	560	3,053
Colorado	125	765
Kansas	89	604
New Mexico	95	464
Oklahoma:		
Northern	52	269
Eastern	43	133
Western	97	432
Utah	31	254
Wyoming	28	132

Table 19 Persons received for supervision by the Federal Probation System, by type of supervision, fiscal years 1974–76

These data represent persons who began supervision during the respective fiscal year.

[Excludes Canal Zone, Guam and the Virgin Islands]

Type of supervision	1974 Total	1974 Percent of total	1975 Total	1975 Percent of total	1976 Total	1976 Percent of total	Percent change 1976 over 1975
All cases	32,660	100.0	36,061	100.0	35,102	100.0	−2.7
Probation (court)	19,452	59.6	18,665	51.8	18,375	52.3	−1.6
Probation (U.S. magistrate)	3,351	10.2	4,884	13.5	5,358	15.3	9.7
Deferred prosecution	977	3.0	1,143	3.2	1,711	4.9	49.7
Parole	6,299	19.3	7,888	21.9	6,286	17.9	−20.3
Mandatory release	2,398	7.3	2,408	6.7	6,286	17.9	−19.6
Military parole	183	0.6	200	0.6	232	0.7	16.0
Special parole	—	—	873	2.4	1,205	3.4	38.0

Source: Administrative Office of the United States Courts, *Annual Report of the Director*, 1975, p. x–8; 1976, p. 17, Table 10 (Washington, D.C.: Administrative Office of the United States Courts). Table adapted by SOURCEBOOK staff.

Table 20 Persons under supervision of the Federal Probation System, by type of supervision, circuit, and district, on June 30, 1976

These data represent persons under supervision on one day, June 30.

Circuit and district	Total	Court probation	Parole	Mandatory release	Military parole	Deferred prosecution	U.S. magistrate probation	Special parole
Total all districts	64,246	39,234	14,090	1,352	339	1,763	6,038	1,430
District of Columbia	2,040	961	680	79	3	2	302	13
90 Districts	62,206	38,273	13,410	1,273	336	1,761	5,736	1,417
First Circuit	1,672	1,073	348	24	14	40	112	61
Maine	114	84	24	2	1	1	1	1
Massachusetts	1,049	654	233	16	6	28	73	39
New Hampshire	92	72	15	0	0	1	3	1
Rhode Island	126	93	24	1	0	0	8	0
Puerto Rico	291	170	52	5	7	10	27	20
Second Circuit	5,535	3,536	1,288	184	27	183	119	198
Connecticut	575	392	139	14	2	15	3	10
New York								
Northern	239	173	44	0	4	10	6	2
Eastern	2,148	1,449	554	46	13	30	2	54
Southern	2,067	1,143	474	114	7	126	90	113
Western	345	245	57	9	1	2	18	13
Vermont	161	134	20	1	0	0	0	6
Third Circuit	5,055	3,143	797	56	13	127	836	83
Delaware	210	132	41	1	0	3	31	2
New Jersey	1,593	901	253	27	4	11	376	21
Pennsylvania								
Eastern	2,041	1,260	293	11	5	54	374	44
Middle	303	218	42	3	2	16	18	4
Western	908	632	168	14	2	43	37	12

Fourth Circuit	6,551	4,131	1,262	60	34	171	842	51
Maryland	1,574	757	298	16	4	16	467	16
North Carolina								
Eastern	677	455	117	9	4	9	81	2
Middle	773	619	107	7	1	26	10	3
Western	599	396	81	4	1	4	108	5
South Carolina	1,016	658	194	11	6	54	85	8
Virginia								
Eastern	1,008	585	297	7	13	32	67	7
Western	505	379	70	2	1	29	19	5
West Virginia								
Northern	114	86	24	2	0	0	1	1
Southern	285	196	74	2	4	1	4	4

Table 20 (continued)

Circuit and district	Total	Type of supervision						
		Court probation	Parole	Mandatory release	Military parole	Deferred prosecution	U.S. magistrate probation	Special parole
Ninth Circuit	12,284	7,473	2,655	240	49	289	1,262	316
Alaska	186	135	31	5	1	3	11	0
Arizona	1,223	733	310	27	6	14	74	59
California								
Northern	1,858	954	391	34	3	41	410	25
Eastern	976	702	162	18	6	16	62	10
Central	4,299	2,678	960	85	13	79	384	100
Southern	1,133	712	170	8	4	4	192	43
Hawaii	254	188	38	14	0	2	5	7
Idaho	189	124	39	4	0	9	10	3
Montana	277	186	68	3	4	11	5	0
Nevada	266	191	47	1	1	4	8	14
Oregon	541	317	124	12	4	54	17	13
Washington								
Eastern	228	158	40	2	2	6	11	9
Western	854	395	275	27	5	46	73	33
Tenth Circuit	3,053	1,799	672	85	17	61	353	66
Colorado	765	458	185	21	1	7	57	36
Kansas	604	315	145	21	12	37	65	9
New Mexico	464	240	113	18	1	2	83	7
Oklahoma								
Northern	269	176	59	8	0	4	16	6
Eastern	133	107	18	1	1	0	2	4
Western	432	194	102	7	1	0	125	3
Utah	254	208	37	5	0	1	3	0
Wyoming	132	101	13	4	1	10	2	1

Source: Administrative Office of the United States Courts, 1976 Annual Report of the Director (Washington, D.C.: Administrative Office of the United States Courts, 1976), pp. 1–50, 1–51. (Preliminary Report)

Table 21 Persons in private juvenile detention and correctional facilities, by detention status, sex, region, and State, June 30, 1974

"The data indicate that juveniles were adjudicated delinquent for status offenses (i.e., those that would not be a crime if committed by adults), even in States with special statutes for such offenders, if the juveniles had previously committed a number of offenses. Furthermore, offenses of persons declared in need of supervision are not strictly limited to status offenses. At the discretion of the judge, a juvenile can be declared in need of supervision for an offense such as a felony or misdemeanor, especially if it is the first offense" (Source, p. 4). These data exclude juveniles (1) held pending disposition, (2) awaiting transfer to another jurisdiction, (3) held as voluntary commitments, (4) held as dependent and neglected juveniles, and (5) held for miscellaneous reasons.

[— represents zero. Juveniles who committed status offenses are found among the adjudicated delinquents and the juveniles declared in need of supervision.]

Region and State	Adjudicated delinquent			Declared in need of supervision (PINS)		
	Total	Male	Female	Total	Male	Female
United States, total	9,874	7,448	2,426	4,969	3,031	1,938
Region 1	723	585	138	129	75	54
Connecticut	218	182	36	—	—	—
Maine	[a]	[a]	[a]	—	—	—
Massachusetts	327	251	76	83	47	36
New Hampshire	86	70	16	—	—	—
Rhode Island	[a]	[a]	[a]	22	[a]	[a]
Vermont	[a]	[a]	[a]	24	[a]	[a]
Region 2	441	400	41	1,267	740	527
New Jersey	30	30	—	46	[a]	[a]
New York	411	370	41	1,221	[a]	[a]
Region 3	1,493	1,165	328	291	165	126
Delaware	[a]	[a]	[a]	—	—	—
District of Columbia	[a]	[a]	[a]	6	3	3
Maryland	[a]	[a]	299	285	162	123
Pennsylvania	1,283	984	[a]	—	—	—
Virginia	126	[a]	[a]	—	—	—
West Virginia	[a]	[a]	[a]	—	—	—
Region 4	753	532	221	234	[a]	[a]
Alabama	27	13	14	—	—	—
Florida	281	223	58	84	72	12
Georgia	120	83	37	63	[a]	[a]
Kentucky	36	[a]	[a]	48	10	38
Mississippi	99	64	35	[a]	[a]	[a]
North Carolina	44	[a]	[a]	[a]	[a]	[a]
South Carolina	31	[a]	[a]	—	—	—
Tennessee	115	72	43	[a]	[a]	[a]

354

Region 5	2,144	1,553	591	461	260	201
Illinois	247	185	62	165	76	89
Indiana	407	303	104	—	—	—
Michigan	651	477	174	—	—	—
Minnesota	393	253	140	—	—	—
Ohio	296	236	60	203	123	80
Wisconsin	150	99	51	93	61	32
Region 6	789	570	219	516	325	191
Arkansas	140	79	61	—	—	—
Louisiana	([a])	73	([a])	—	—	—
New Mexico	([a])	27	([a])	43	([a])	([a])
Oklahoma	136	131	5	180	([a])	([a])
Texas	349	260	89	293	172	121
Region 7	536	411	125	148	93	55
Iowa	78	44	34	—	—	—
Kansas	([a])	([a])	([a])	74	39	35
Missouri	337	258	79	—	—	—
Nebraska	([a])	([a])	([a])	74	54	20
Region 8	407	345	62	302	158	144
Colorado	145	121	24	162	73	89
Montana	32	([a])	([a])	([a])	—	([a])
North Dakota	([a])	([a])	([a])	66	([a])	([a])
South Dakota	89	71	18	57	39	18
Utah	95	([a])	([a])	—	—	—
Wyoming	([a])	([a])	([a])	([a])	([a])	([a])
Region 9	1,792	1,382	410	1,278	846	432
Arizona	410	([a])	([a])	149	117	32
California	1,299	1,052	247	1,090	720	370
Hawaii	([a])	([a])	([a])	([a])	([a])	([a])
Nevada	([a])	([a])	([a])	([a])	([a])	([a])
Region 10	796	505	291	343	218	125
Alaska	28	([a])	([a])	64	37	27
Idaho	54	([a])	([a])	—	—	—
Oregon	449	242	207	—	—	—
Washington	265	198	67	279	181	98

[a] Data withheld to avoid disclosure and maintain confidentiality guarantees.

Source: U.S. Department of Justice, Law Enforcement Assistance Administration, ***Children in Custody: Advance Report on the Juvenile Detention and Correctional Facility Census of 1974*** **(Washington, D.C.: U.S. Government Printing Office, 1977), pp. 46, 47.**

Table 22 Persons in private juvenile detention and correctional facilities, by type of facility, detention status, and sex, United States, on June 30, 1974

[— represents zero]

Detention status and sex	Total facilities	Short-term facilities				Long-term facilities			
		Total	Detention centers	Shelters	Reception or diagnostic centers	Total	Training schools	Ranches, forestry camps, and farms	Halfway houses and group homes
Total:									
Male	22,104	402	(a)	332	(a)	21,702	2,847	12,397	6,458
Female	9,645	395	(a)	302	(a)	9,250	1,231	4,558	3,461
Adjudicated delinquents:									
Male	7,448	53	(a)	43	(a)	7,395	1,640	3,239	2,516
Female	2,426	67	—	(a)	(a)	2,359	418	1,104	837
Declared in need of supervision (PINS):									
Male	3,031	56	(a)	33	(a)	2,975	413	1,710	852
Female	1,938	47	—	(a)	(a)	1,891	395	845	651
Held pending disposition by court:									
Male	330	127	(a)	(a)	—	203	29	98	76
Female	151	75	(a)	(a)	—	76	(a)	48	(a)
Awaiting transfer to another jurisdiction:									
Male	37	8	—	8	—	29	(a)	23	(a)
Female	26	8	—	8	—	18	5	—	13
Voluntary commitments:									
Male	5,272	94	—	(a)	(a)	5,178	279	3,879	1,020
Female	2,363	126	(a)	103	(a)	2,237	197	1,222	818
Dependent and neglected:									
Male	4,767	60	(a)	(a)	—	4,707	330	2,543	1,834
Female	2,337	70	—	(a)	(a)	2,267	140	1,117	1,010
Other population: b									
Male	1,219	4	—	4	—	1,215	155	905	155
Female	404	(a)	—	(a)	—	402	74	222	106

a Data withheld to avoid disclosure and maintain confidentiality guarantees.
b Examples are the emotionally disturbed and the mentally retarded.

Source: U.S. Department of Justice, Law Enforcement Assistance Administration, *Children in Custody: Advance Report on the Juvenile Detention and Correctional Facility Census of 1974* (Washington, D.C.: U.S. Government Printing Office, 1977), p. 63.

Table 23 Persons in public juvenile detention and correctional facilities, by sex, region, and State, on June 30, 1971, 1973, and 1974

[— represents zero]

Region and State	Number						Percent change					
	Male			Female			Male			Female		
	1971	1973	1974	1971	1973	1974	1971 to 1973	1973 to 1974	1971 to 1974	1971 to 1973	1973 to 1974	1971 to 1974
United States, total	41,781	35,057	34,783	12,948	10,637	10,139	−16.1	−0.8	−16.7	−17.8	−4.7	−21.7
Region 1	1,242	699	681	444	300	246	−43.7	−2.6	−45.2	−32.4	−18.0	−44.6
Connecticut	156	136	90	73	53	50	−12.8	−33.8	−42.3	−27.4	−5.7	−31.5
Maine	179	143	154	72	29	33	−20.1	7.7	−14.0	−59.7	13.8	−54.2
Massachusetts	577	156	116	147	61	45	−73.0	−25.6	−79.9	−58.5	−26.2	−69.4
New Hampshire	139	143	154	71	54	58	2.9	7.7	10.8	−23.9	7.4	−18.3
Rhode Island	135	77	110	39	53	17	−43.0	42.9	−18.5	35.9	−67.9	−56.4
Vermont	56	44	57	42	50	43	−21.4	29.5	1.8	19.0	−14.0	2.4
Region 2	3,357	2,443	2,218	857	679	668	−27.2	−9.2	−33.9	−20.8	−1.6	−22.1
New Jersey [a]	1,287	963	737	245	237	199	−25.2	−23.5	−42.7	−3.3	−16.0	−18.8
New York	2,070	1,480	1,481	612	442	469	−28.5	0.1	−28.5	−27.8	6.1	−23.4
Region 3	5,158	4,103	4,063	1,334	1,263	983	−20.5	−1.0	−21.2	−5.3	−22.2	−26.3
Delaware	255	155	144	135	79	60	−39.2	−7.1	−43.5	−41.5	−24.1	−55.6
District of Columbia	618	469	545	123	77	92	−24.1	16.2	−11.8	−37.4	19.5	−25.2
Maryland	1,096	1,131	1,005	301	341	143	3.2	−11.1	−8.3	13.3	−58.1	−52.5
Pennsylvania [a]	1,769	1,071	1,065	275	272	225	−39.5	−0.6	−39.8	−1.1	−17.3	−18.2
Virginia	1,109	990	995	382	416	374	−10.7	0.5	−10.3	8.9	−10.1	−2.1
West Virginia	311	287	309	118	78	89	−7.7	7.7	−0.6	−33.9	14.1	−24.6
Region 4	6,956	6,338	6,200	2,615	1,990	2,010	−8.9	−2.2	−10.9	−23.9	1.0	−23.1
Alabama	407	299	358	157	114	149	−26.5	19.7	−12.0	−27.4	30.7	−5.1
Florida	1,827	1,678	1,582	670	448	493	−8.2	−5.7	−13.4	−33.1	10.0	−26.4
Georgia	1,090	1,148	1,167	365	334	255	5.3	1.7	7.1	−8.5	−23.7	−30.1
Kentucky	445	387	359	208	107	112	−13.0	−7.2	−19.3	−48.6	4.7	−46.2
Mississippi	397	494	471	124	130	130	24.4	−4.7	18.6	4.8	—	4.8
North Carolina	1,258	887	719	554	447	370	−29.5	−18.9	−42.8	−19.3	−17.2	−33.2
South Carolina	609	385	549	184	145	240	−36.8	42.6	−9.9	−21.2	65.5	30.4
Tennessee	923	1,060	995	353	265	261	14.8	−6.1	7.8	−24.9	−1.5	−26.1

358

Region 5	8,555	6,539	6,703	2,704	2,013	1,992	-23.6	2.5	-21.6	-25.6	-1.0	-26.3
Illinois	2,156	1,452	1,207	461	259	203	-32.7	-16.9	-44.0	-43.8	-21.6	-56.0
Indiana	732	649	691	337	239	237	-11.3	6.5	-5.6	-29.1	-0.8	-29.7
Michigan	1,449	1,124	1,246	555	479	465	-22.4	10.9	-14.0	-13.7	-2.9	-16.2
Minnesota	654	545	543	175	156	178	-16.7	-0.4	-17.0	-10.9	14.1	1.7
Ohio	2,679	2,140	2,418	923	728	750	-20.1	13.0	-9.7	-21.1	3.0	-18.7
Wisconsin	885	629	598	253	152	159	-28.9	-4.9	-32.4	-39.9	4.6	-37.2
Region 6	4,319	3,761	3,020	1,242	874	704	-12.9	-19.7	-30.1	-29.6	-19.5	-43.3
Arkansas	375	360	334	131	137	126	-4.0	-7.2	-10.9	4.6	-8.0	-3.8
Louisiana	1,213	1,052	974	260	205	196	-13.3	-7.4	-19.7	-21.2	-4.4	-24.6
New Mexico	286	282	287	89	58	64	-1.4	1.8	0.3	-34.8	10.3	-28.1
Oklahoma	222	298	271	134	145	140	34.2	-9.1	22.1	8.2	-3.4	4.5
Texas	2,223	1,769	1,154	628	329	178	-20.4	-34.8	-48.1	-47.6	-45.9	-71.7
Region 7	1,608	1,468	1,614	616	524	551	-8.7	9.9	0.4	-14.9	5.2	-10.6
Iowa	341	225	269	151	119	102	-34.0	19.6	-21.1	-21.2	-14.3	-32.5
Kansas	298	285	387	119	107	137	-4.4	35.8	29.9	-10.1	28.0	15.1
Missouri	800	811	836	265	209	247	1.4	3.1	4.5	-21.1	18.2	-6.8
Nebraska	169	147	122	81	89	65	-13.0	-17.0	-27.8	9.9	-27.0	-19.8
Region 8	1,028	847	995	385	361	401	-17.6	17.5	-3.2	-6.2	11.1	4.2
Colorado	340	320	372	103	107	140	-5.9	16.3	9.4	3.9	30.8	35.9
Montana	138	141	171	68	69	60	2.2	21.3	23.9	1.5	-13.0	-11.8
North Dakota	95	58	66	31	28	46	-38.9	13.8	-30.5	-9.7	64.3	48.4
South Dakota	140	93	84	44	22	14	-33.6	-9.7	-40.0	-50.0	-36.4	-68.2
Utah	218	165	216	91	78	95	-24.3	30.9	-0.9	-14.3	21.8	4.4
Wyoming	97	70	86	48	57	46	-27.8	22.9	-11.3	18.8	-19.3	-4.2
Region 9	8,095	7,500	7,936	2,100	2,049	2,019	-7.4	5.8	-2.0	-2.4	-1.5	-3.9
Arizona	612	532	424	60	146	120	-13.1	-20.3	-30.7	143.3	-17.8	100.0
California [a]	7,007	6,678	7,173	1,911	1,767	1,762	-4.7	7.4	2.4	-7.5	-0.3	-7.8
Hawaii	87	79	81	18	29	32	-9.2	2.5	-6.9	61.1	10.3	77.8
Nevada	389	211	258	111	107	105	-45.8	22.3	-33.7	-3.6	-1.9	-5.4
Region 10	1,463	1,359	1,353	651	584	565	-7.1	-0.4	-7.5	-10.3	-3.3	-13.2
Alaska	112	49	74	32	32	33	-56.3	51.0	-33.9	—	3.1	3.1
Idaho	93	118	105	59	33	30	26.9	-11.0	12.9	-44.1	-9.1	-49.2
Oregon	346	411	342	174	143	106	18.8	-16.8	-1.2	-17.8	-25.9	-39.1
Washington	912	781	832	386	376	396	-14.4	6.5	-8.8	-2.6	5.3	2.6

[a] Excluded were the adults and youthful offenders held in addition to juveniles in some facilities.

Source: U.S. Department of Justice, Law Enforcement Assistance Administration, *Children in Custody: Advance Report on the Juvenile Detention and Correctional Facility Census of 1974* (Washington, D.C.: U.S. Government Printing Office, 1977), pp. 24, 25.

Table 24 Persons in public juvenile detention and correctional facilities, by detention status, sex, region, and State, on June 30, 1974

[— represents zero]

| Region and State | Total | | | Detention status | | | | | |
| | Total | Male | Female | Adjudicated delinquent[a] | | | In need of supervision (PINS)[a] | | |
				Total	Male	Female	Total	Male	Female
United States, total	44,922	34,783	10,139	31,270	25,575	5,695	4,644	2,701	1,943
Region 1	927	681	246	552	419	133	83	47	36
Connecticut	140	90	50	116	75	41	—	—	—
Maine	187	154	33	161	135	26	10	4	6
Massachusetts	161	116	45	37	24	13	—	—	—
New Hampshire	212	154	58	152	112	40	23	15	8
Rhode Island	127	110	17	55	55	—	50	28	22
Vermont	100	57	43	31	18	13	—	—	—
Region 2	2,886	2,218	668	1,085	981	104	1,058	725	333
New Jersey	936	737	199	550	471	79	78	36	42
New York	1,950	1,481	469	535	510	25	980	689	291
Region 3	5,046	4,063	983	3,684	3,035	649	193	118	75
Delaware	204	144	60	166	118	48	—	—	—
District of Columbia	637	545	92	306	295	11	94	48	46
Maryland	1,148	1,005	143	699	639	60	99	70	29
Pennsylvania	1,290	1,065	225	962	833	129	—	—	—
Virginia	1,369	995	374	1,198	865	333	—	—	—
West Virginia	398	309	89	353	285	68	—	—	—
Region 4	8,210	6,200	2,010	6,512	5,104	1,408	651	376	275
Alabama	507	358	149	435	315	120	180	63	117
Florida	2,075	1,582	493	1,330	1,137	193	85	50	35
Georgia	1,422	1,167	255	1,158	973	185	110	37	73
Kentucky	471	359	112	290	275	15	11	9	2
Mississippi	601	471	130	560	441	119	—	—	—
North Carolina	1,089	719	370	1,052	701	351	265	217	48
South Carolina	789	549	240	778	543	235	—	—	—
Tennessee	1,256	995	261	909	719	190	—	—	—

360

Region 5	8,695	6,703	1,992	6,640	5,350	1,290	156	81	75
Illinois	1,410	1,207	203	985	904	81	71	44	27
Indiana	928	691	237	666	510	156	—	—	—
Michigan	1,711	1,246	465	1,151	890	261	—	—	—
Minnesota	721	543	178	604	472	132	—	—	—
Ohio	3,168	2,418	750	2,638	2,075	563	64	29	35
Wisconsin	757	598	159	596	499	97	21	8	13
Region 6	3,724	3,020	704	2,832	2,377	455	398	240	158
Arkansas	460	334	126	444	321	123	—	—	—
Louisiana	1,170	974	196	1,026	854	172	—	—	—
New Mexico	351	287	64	197	163	34	63	43	20
Oklahoma	411	271	140	206	172	34	164	74	90
Texas	1,332	1,154	178	959	867	92	171	123	48
Region 7	2,165	1,614	551	1,635	1,288	347	147	55	92
Iowa	371	269	102	286	222	64	—	—	—
Kansas	524	387	137	319	274	45	93	40	53
Missouri	1,083	836	247	915	697	218	—	—	—
Nebraska	187	122	65	115	95	20	54	15	39
Region 8	1,396	995	401	999	787	212	231	105	126
Colorado	512	372	140	285	268	17	197	84	113
Montana	231	171	60	221	165	56	8	—	—
North Dakota	112	66	46	77	53	24	6	5	8
South Dakota	98	84	14	86	75	11	—	—	1
Utah	311	216	95	220	158	62	—	—	—
Wyoming	132	86	46	110	68	42	20	16	4
Region 9	9,955	7,936	2,019	5,922	5,120	802	1,511	886	625
Arizona	544	424	120	272	241	31	178	101	77
California [b]	8,935	7,173	1,762	5,249	4,588	661	1,309	769	540
Hawaii	113	81	32	84	64	20	11	6	5
Nevada	363	258	105	317	227	90	13	10	3
Region 10	1,918	1,353	565	1,409	1,114	295	216	68	148
Alaska	107	74	33	68	46	22	6	3	3
Idaho	135	105	30	135	105	30	—	—	—
Oregon	448	342	106	360	293	67	—	—	—
Washington	1,228	832	396	846	670	176	210	65	145

[a] Juveniles adjudicated for status offenses are found among the adjudicated delinquents and the juveniles declared in need of supervision.
[b] Excluded were the 2,346 youthful offenders—2,251 males and 95 females—held in addition to juveniles in some California facilities.

Source: U.S. Department of Justice, Law Enforcement Assistance Administration, Children in Custody: Advance Report on the Juvenile Detention and Correctional Facility Census of 1974 (Washington, D.C.: U.S. Government Printing Office, 1977), pp. 42–45.

Table 24 (continued)

Region and State	Detention status					
	Held pending disposition by court			Awaiting transfer to another jurisdiction		
	Total	Male	Female	Total	Male	Female
United States, total	7,373	5,462	1,911	458	326	132
Region 1	238	169	69	18	17	1
Connecticut	20	12	8	2	1	1
Maine	26	19	7	—	—	—
Massachusetts	80	61	19	—	—	—
New Hampshire	60	42	18	15	15	—
Rhode Island	34	25	9	1	1	—
Vermont	18	10	8	—	—	—
Region 2	423	288	135	27	19	8
New Jersey	209	162	47	2	—	2
New York	214	126	88	25	19	6
Region 3	1,087	857	230	62	46	16
Delaware	38	26	12	3	—	3
District of Columbia	234	202	32	—	—	—
Maryland	350	296	54	—	—	—
Pennsylvania	277	199	78	41	29	12
Virginia	143	110	33	18	17	1
West Virginia	45	24	21	—	—	—
Region 4	946	653	293	50	35	15
Alabama	51	30	21	2	1	1
Florida	532	358	174	22	15	7
Georgia	172	137	35	7	7	—
Kentucky	68	45	23	2	2	—
Mississippi	36	27	9	3	1	2
North Carolina	26	9	17	—	—	—
South Carolina	4	4	—	—	—	—
Tennessee	57	43	14	14	9	5

Region 5	1,393	966	427	85	56	29
Illinois	125	97	28	2	1	1
Indiana	252	176	76	19	15	4
Michigan	433	299	134	9	7	2
Minnesota	102	63	39	—	—	—
Ohio	409	281	128	54	32	22
Wisconsin	72	50	22	1	1	—
Region 6	360	304	56	49	30	19
Arkansas	6	4	2	1	—	1
Louisiana	92	73	19	9	6	3
New Mexico	86	79	7	5	2	3
Oklahoma	25	22	3	2	—	2
Texas	151	126	25	32	22	10
Region 7	276	215	61	16	12	4
Iowa	34	26	8	1	1	—
Kansas	75	48	27	6	4	2
Missouri	150	129	21	8	7	1
Nebraska	17	12	5	1	—	1
Region 8	121	75	46	17	13	4
Colorado	22	14	8	5	4	1
Montana	10	6	4	—	—	—
North Dakota	16	8	8	—	—	—
South Dakota	5	3	2	1	1	—
Utah	67	43	24	11	8	3
Wyoming	1	1	—	—	—	—
Region 9	2,270	1,785	485	120	89	31
Arizona	65	58	7	24	21	3
California b	2,166	1,704	462	86	60	26
Hawaii	18	11	7	—	—	—
Nevada	21	12	9	10	8	2
Region 10	259	150	109	14	9	5
Alaska	28	22	6	5	3	2
Idaho	—	—	—	—	—	—
Oregon	80	45	35	—	—	—
Washington	151	83	68	9	6	3

Table 24 (continued)

Region and State	Detention status					
	Voluntary commitments			Dependent and neglected		
	Total	Male	Female	Total	Male	Female
United States, total	679	472	207	498	247	251
Region 1	34	27	7	2	2	—
Connecticut	—	—	—	2	2	—
Maine	—	—	—	—	—	—
Massachusetts	34	27	7	—	—	—
New Hampshire	—	—	—	—	—	—
Rhode Island	—	—	—	—	—	—
Vermont	—	—	—	—	—	—
Region 2	278	196	82	15	9	6
New Jersey	82	59	23	15	9	6
New York	196	137	59	—	—	—
Region 3	9	4	5	11	3	8
Delaware	—	—	—	—	—	—
District of Columbia	—	—	—	—	—	—
Maryland	—	—	—	—	—	—
Pennsylvania	2	1	1	8	3	5
Virginia	7	3	4	3	—	3
West Virginia	—	—	—	—	—	—
Region 4	12	3	9	39	29	10
Alabama	—	—	—	19	12	7
Florida	2	1	1	9	8	1
Georgia	—	—	—	—	—	—
Kentucky	—	—	—	1	1	—
Mississippi	1	1	—	1	—	1
North Carolina	—	—	—	—	—	—
South Carolina	5	—	5	2	2	—
Tennessee	4	1	3	7	6	1

Region 5	240	164	76	181	86	95
Illinois	225	160	65	2	1	1
Indiana	7	3	—	10	5	5
Michigan	5	—	4	101	39	62
Minnesota	—	—	5	1	1	—
Ohio	—	1	—	3	1	2
Wisconsin	3	1	2	64	39	25
Region 6	54	44	10	31	25	6
Arkansas	—	—	—	9	9	—
Louisiana	27	27	—	16	14	2
New Mexico	—	—	—	—	—	—
Oklahoma	11	3	8	3	—	3
Texas	16	14	2	3	2	1
Region 7	31	21	10	60	23	37
Iowa	2	1	1	48	19	29
Kansas	28	20	8	3	1	2
Missouri	1	—	1	9	3	6
Nebraska	—	—	—	—	—	—
Region 8	13	8	5	15	7	8
Colorado	3	2	1	—	—	—
Montana	—	—	—	—	—	—
North Dakota	9	5	4	2	—	2
South Dakota	—	—	—	13	7	6
Utah	—	—	—	—	—	—
Wyoming	1	1	—	—	—	—
Region 9	4	2	2	128	54	74
Arizona	—	—	—	5	3	2
California [b]	4	2	2	121	50	71
Hawaii	—	—	—	—	—	—
Nevada	—	—	—	2	1	1
Region 10	4	3	1	16	9	7
Alaska	—	—	—	—	—	—
Idaho	—	—	—	—	—	—
Oregon	—	—	—	8	4	4
Washington	4	3	1	8	5	3

Table 25 Persons in public juvenile detention and correctional facilities, by type of facility, region, and State, on June 30, 1971, 1973, and 1974

[— represents zero]

Region and State	Detention centers			Short-term facilities					
				Shelters			Reception or diagnostic centers		
	1971	1973	1974	1971	1973	1974	1971	1973	1974
United States, total	11,767	10,782	11,010	360	190	180	2,153	1,734	1,376
Region 1	238	166	128	—	—	—	—	11	23
Connecticut	35	31	39	—	—	—	—	—	—
Maine	—	—	—	—	—	—	—	—	—
Massachusetts	203	135	89	—	—	—	—	—	—
New Hampshire	—	—	—	—	—	—	—	—	—
Rhode Island	—	—	—	—	—	—	—	11	23
Vermont	—	—	—	—	—	—	—	—	—
Region 2	909	765	727	15	—	38	—	—	—
New Jersey a	467	475	362	15	—	11	—	—	—
New York	442	290	365	—	—	27	—	—	—
Region 3	908	776	884	59	74	81	279	292	236
Delaware	44	26	38	—	—	—	—	—	—
District of Columbia	78	16	26	49	58	66	—	—	—
Maryland	66	34	45	—	—	—	103	111	111
Pennsylvania a	474	403	424	8	—	—	—	—	—
Virginia a	210	278	297	—	—	—	176	181	125
West Virginia	36	19	54	2	16	15	—	—	—
Region 4	1,699	1,249	1,360	36	24	—	211	355	323
Alabama	130	57	129	—	—	—	—	—	—
Florida	753	484	560	36	12	—	—	—	—
Georgia	484	414	405	—	—	—	—	—	—
Kentucky	79	58	78	—	12	—	56	70	60
Mississippi	30	48	37	—	—	—	—	—	37
North Carolina	78	63	40	—	—	—	—	—	—
South Carolina	11	7	17	—	—	—	155	160	136
Tennessee	134	118	94	—	—	—	—	125	90

Region 5	2,496	2,192	2,121	75	58	36	947	589	172
Illinois	585	392	343	—	—	—	274	164	—
Indiana	233	256	269	—	—	—	27	—	—
Michigan	925	809	819	22	30	25	185	50	45
Minnesota	60	96	90	—	—	—	—	—	—
Ohio	601	524	492	46	17	—	461	375	127
Wisconsin	92	115	108	7	11	11	—	—	—
Region 6	519	540	506	—	34	25	135	101	87
Arkansas	15	16	5	—	15	2	18	18	35
Louisiana	146	137	132	—	—	—	117	83	52
New Mexico b	51	54	70	—	—	—	—	—	—
Oklahoma	16	28	38	—	19	23	—	—	—
Texas	291	305	261	—	—	—	—	—	—
Region 7	384	396	438	110	—	—	—	—	11
Iowa	32	35	40	110	—	—	—	—	—
Kansas	126	128	162	—	—	—	—	—	11
Missouri	206	187	211	—	—	—	—	—	—
Nebraska	20	46	25	—	—	—	—	—	—
Region 8	231	216	286	—	—	—	—	—	25
Colorado	148	138	171	—	—	—	—	—	—
Montana	1	2	—	—	—	—	—	—	25
North Dakota c	—	—	—	—	—	—	—	—	—
South Dakota	17	14	6	—	—	—	—	—	—
Utah	64	62	109	—	—	—	—	—	—
Wyoming	—	—	—	—	—	—	—	—	—
Region 9	3,994	4,016	4,167	—	—	—	432	236	329
Arizona	140	146	165	—	—	—	116	—	—
California a	3,761	3,782	3,896	—	—	—	316	236	329
Hawaii	20	27	41	—	—	—	—	—	—
Nevada	73	61	65	—	—	—	—	—	—
Region 10	389	466	393	65	—	—	149	150	170
Alaska	7	5	6	—	—	—	—	—	—
Idaho	—	17	—	18	—	—	—	—	—
Oregon	160	162	93	—	—	—	—	—	—
Washington	222	282	294	47	—	—	149	150	170

a Excluded were the adults and youthful offenders held in addition to juveniles in some facilities. On June 30, 1971, the nonjuveniles were found in some California reception or diagnostic centers; some New Jersey, Pennsylvania, and California training schools; and some California ranches, forestry camps, and farms. On June 30, 1973, the nonjuveniles were found in the same facilities as in 1971, except for the Pennsylvania facility, which was no longer within the scope of the census. On June 30, 1974, the nonjuveniles found in the same California facilities as in previous years, and the New Jersey facility was no longer within the scope of the census.
b In New Mexico, two State camps were reported combined with a State training school as one facility in 1971, 1973, and 1974.

Table 25 (continued)

Region and State	Long-term facilities					
	Training schools			Ranches, forestry camps, and farms		
	1971	1973	1974	1971	1973	1974
United States, total	34,005	26,427	25,397	5,471	4,959	5,232
Region 1	1,423	735	704	25	26	31
Connecticut	194	158	101	—	—	—
Maine	251	172	187	25	26	31
Massachusetts	496	—	—	—	—	—
New Hampshire	210	192	212	—	—	—
Rhode Island	174	119	104	—	—	—
Vermont	98	94	100	—	—	—
Region 2	2,654	1,671	1,306	290	282	350
New Jersey [a]	987	625	387	—	—	70
New York	1,667	1,046	919	290	282	280
Region 3	4,627	3,513	3,078	523	572	585
Delaware	346	200	159	—	—	—
District of Columbia	599	452	532	157	172	169
Maryland	1,043	1,088	756	150	160	146
Pennsylvania [a]	1,393	780	720	122	124	125
Virginia	949	779	727	94	116	145
West Virginia	297	214	184	—	—	—
Region 4	7,006	5,953	5,720	466	330	437
Alabama	434	356	373	65	35	—
Florida	1,536	1,316	1,144	—	—	106
Georgia	971	1,040	994	291	234	241
Kentucky	207	96	69	—	—	—
Mississippi	491	565	546	—	—	—
North Carolina	1,734	1,266	1,012	—	—	—
South Carolina	627	358	629	110	96	90
Tennessee	1,006	956	953	—	—	—

Region 5	6,547	4,878	5,435	1,062	615	688
Illinois	1,371	944	897	345	191	148
Indiana	774	573	599	62	45	49
Michigan	791	446	523	149	114	150
Minnesota	505	551	566	79	34	40
Ohio	2,123	1,724	2,304	371	216	213
Wisconsin	983	640	546	56	15	88
Region 6	4,850	3,891	3,060	—	—	—
Arkansas	468	444	413	—	—	—
Louisiana	1,210	1,026	977	—	—	—
New Mexico [b]	324	286	281	—	—	—
Oklahoma	340	396	350	—	—	—
Texas	2,508	1,739	1,039	—	—	—
Region 7	1,417	1,176	1,269	250	268	270
Iowa	258	195	253	92	92	65
Kansas	291	258	344	—	—	—
Missouri	638	533	510	158	176	205
Nebraska	230	190	162	—	—	—
Region 8	1,051	801	868	124	146	167
Colorado	223	190	236	72	93	99
Montana	178	178	184	27	30	47
North Dakota [c]	118	69	65	—	—	—
South Dakota	142	78	71	25	23	21
Utah	245	159	180	—	—	—
Wyoming	145	127	132	—	—	—
Region 9	3,417	2,853	2,974	2,298	2,365	2,390
Arizona	367	421	258	49	77	77
California [a]	2,590	2,135	2,401	2,197	2,247	2,258
Hawaii	85	81	72	—	—	—
Nevada	375	216	243	52	41	55
Region 10	1,013	956	983	433	320	314
Alaska	103	76	101	34	—	—
Idaho	134	134	135	—	—	—
Oregon	311	336	296	49	56	59
Washington	465	410	451	350	264	255

[c] In North Dakota, three State group homes were reported combined with a State training school as one facility in 1973 and 1974. In 1971, two of these group homes were nonexistent, and data for the remaining facilities were reported separately.

Source: U.S. Department of Justice, Law Enforcement Assistance Administration, Children in Custody: Advance Report on the Juvenile Detention and Correctional Facility Census of 1974 (Washington, D.C.: U.S. Government Printing Office, 1977), pp. 26-31.

Table 25 (continued)

Region and State	Long-term facilities Halfway houses and group homes		
	1971	1973	1974
United States, total	973	1,602	1,727
Region 1			
Connecticut	—	61	41
Maine	—	—	—
Massachusetts	—	56	41
New Hampshire	—	5	—
Rhode Island	—	—	—
Vermont	—	—	—
Region 2	346	404	465
New Jersey [a]	63	100	106
New York	283	304	359
Region 3	96	139	182
Delaware	—	8	7
District of Columbia	15	20	13
Maryland	28	67	67
Pennsylvania [a]	19	—	—
Virginia	34	44	95
West Virginia	—	—	—
Region 4	153	382	370
Alabama	—	—	5
Florida	107	279	265
Georgia	20	28	23
Kentucky	—	24	23
Mississippi	—	11	18
North Carolina	—	5	—
South Carolina	—	5	7
Tennessee	26	30	29

Region 5	132	220	243
Illinois	42	20	22
Indiana	—	14	11
Michigan	90	154	149
Minnesota	—	20	25
Ohio	—	12	32
Wisconsin	—	—	4
Region 6	57	69	46
Arkansas	5	4	5
Louisiana	—	11	9
New Mexico [b]	—	—	—
Oklahoma	—	—	—
Texas	52	54	32
Region 7	63	152	177
Iowa	—	22	13
Kansas	—	6	7
Missouri	63	124	157
Nebraska	—	—	—
Region 8	7	45	50
Colorado	—	6	6
Montana	—	—	—
North Dakota [c]	7	17	22
South Dakota	—	—	—
Utah	—	22	22
Wyoming	—	—	—
Region 9	54	79	95
Arizona	—	34	44
California [a]	54	45	51
Hawaii	—	—	—
Nevada	—	—	—
Region 10	65	51	58
Alaska	—	—	—
Idaho	—	—	—
Oregon	—	—	—
Washington	65	51	58

Table 26 Adjudicated delinquents in public juvenile detention and correctional facilities, by offense, sex, region, and State, on June 30, 1974

[— represents zero]

Region and State	Total adjudicated delinquents	Offense										Offense data not available
		Total		Felonies except drugs		Misdemeanors except drugs		Drug offenses		Status offenses		
		Male	Female	Male	Female	Male	Female	Male	Female	Male	Female	
United States, total	31,270	13,891	3,058	8,022	568	3,423	755	909	252	1,537	1,483	14,321
Region 1	552	174	54	146	5	23	33	4	3	1	13	324
Connecticut	116	5	4	1	—	2	1	1	2	1	3	107
Maine	161	135	26	127	2	6	14	2	2	—	8	—
Massachusetts	37	16	11	9	2	7	7	—	—	—	2	10
New Hampshire	152	—	—	—	—	—	—	—	—	—	—	152
Rhode Island	55	—	—	—	—	—	—	—	—	—	—	55
Vermont	31	18	13	9	1	8	11	1	1	—	—	—
Region 2	1,085	266	10	194	8	24	2	8	—	40	—	809
New Jersey	550	262	10	191	8	23	2	8	—	40	—	278
New York	535	4	—	3	—	1	—	—	—	—	—	531
Region 3	3,684	1,531	274	778	28	424	23	108	2	221	221	1,879
Delaware	166	25	32	—	—	—	—	—	—	25	32	109
District of Columbia	306	110	—	104	—	—	—	6	—	—	—	196
Maryland	699	—	—	—	—	—	—	—	—	—	—	699
Pennsylvania	962	676	117	384	19	210	5	55	—	27	93	169
Virginia	1,198	548	57	215	8	154	9	28	2	151	38	593
West Virginia	353	172	68	75	1	60	9	19	—	18	58	113
Region 4	6,512	2,200	656	1,084	50	704	176	132	33	280	397	3,656
Alabama	435	305	116	182	13	51	1	8	2	64	100	14
Florida	1,330	77	10	24	2	45	6	—	2	8	—	1,243
Georgia	1,158	872	185	417	13	315	38	87	14	53	120	101
Kentucky	290	275	15	241	14	14	1	18	—	2	—	—
Mississippi	560	9	—	9	—	—	—	—	—	—	—	551
North Carolina	1,052	360	174	98	3	223	126	11	15	28	30	518
South Carolina	778	125	147	—	—	—	—	—	—	125	147	506
Tennessee	909	177	9	113	5	56	4	8	—	—	—	723

Region 5	6,640	2,399	815	1,441	152	499	204	129	34	330	425	3,426
Illinois	985	329	59	150	4	147	40	12	7	20	8	597
Indiana	666	72	1	63	—	5	—	1	—	3	1	593
Michigan	1,151	391	136	227	5	64	23	17	—	83	108	624
Minnesota	604	167	49	93	27	3	—	—	—	71	22	388
Ohio	2,638	949	476	580	59	145	114	72	19	152	284	1,213
Wisconsin	596	491	94	328	57	135	27	27	8	1	2	11
Region 6	2,832	1,481	332	1,113	94	242	113	89	23	37	102	1,019
Arkansas	444	297	112	195	21	79	1	18	4	5	86	35
Louisiana	1,026	112	116	33	11	68	79	3	10	8	16	798
New Mexico	197	163	—	112	—	14	—	14	—	23	—	34
Oklahoma	206	171	33	170	33	—	—	—	—	1	—	2
Texas	959	738	71	603	29	81	33	54	9	—	—	150
Region 7	1,635	559	129	299	28	154	36	27	2	79	63	947
Iowa	286	198	3	98	—	50	—	19	—	31	3	85
Kansas	319	233	42	159	16	66	26	2	—	6	—	44
Missouri	915	128	65	42	1	38	8	6	—	42	56	722
Nebraska	115	—	19	—	11	—	2	—	2	—	4	96
Region 8	999	576	87	425	15	83	8	19	23	49	41	336
Colorado	285	255	8	231	5	23	3	1	—	—	—	22
Montana	221	165	56	105	6	24	—	7	19	29	31	—
North Dakota	77	10	2	7	1	—	1	1	—	2	—	65
South Dakota	86	75	11	53	2	10	3	3	—	9	6	—
Utah	220	3	10	2	1	—	1	—	4	1	4	207
Wyoming	110	68	—	27	—	26	—	7	—	8	—	42
Region 9	5,922	3,938	539	2,048	117	1,158	139	308	75	424	208	1,445
Arizona	272	168	30	125	14	12	4	23	5	8	7	74
California [a]	5,249	3,485	404	1,729	81	1,101	131	268	65	387	127	1,360
Hawaii	84	58	15	58	14	—	—	—	—	—	1	11
Nevada	317	227	90	136	8	45	4	17	5	29	73	—
Region 10	1,409	767	162	494	71	112	21	85	57	76	13	480
Alaska	68	46	22	32	8	9	13	4	—	1	1	—
Idaho	135	—	—	—	—	—	—	—	—	—	—	135
Oregon	360	261	—	193	—	17	—	19	—	32	—	99
Washington	846	460	140	269	63	86	8	62	57	43	12	246

[a] California statistics were estimated on the basis of June 30, 1973 data. The 1974 statistics were originally based on juveniles and youthful offenders combined; the 1973 statistics were based on juveniles only. The percent distributions of persons among the kinds of offenses for adjudicated delinquents were quite similar for the two reference dates.

Source: U.S. Department of Justice, Law Enforcement Assistance Administration, *Children in Custody: Advance Report on the Juvenile Detention and Correctional Facility Census of 1974* (Washington, D.C.: U.S. Government Printing Office, 1977), pp. 48–51.

Table 27 Prisoners in State correctional facilities, by age and jurisdiction, on June 30, 1973

NOTE: *These data were collected from a census of prisoners in correctional facilities in each State and the District of Columbia. An inmate was defined as an adult or youthful offender sentenced to a maximum term of at least 1 year and 1 day. Juvenile offenders were excluded from the census.*

State	Total	Age										Not reported
		Under 18	18	19	20 to 24	25 to 29	30 to 34	35 to 39	40 to 44	45 to 49	50 and over	
United States	178,835	1,970	4,050	6,932	48,842	39,078	23,843	14,996	10,710	7,505	9,670	11,239
Alabama	3,873	143	137	213	1,138	834	444	320	217	140	273	14
Alaska	175	0	0	8	55	31	21	17	20	10	12	1
Arizona	1,736	8	16	57	451	394	252	188	133	84	142	11
Arkansas	1,744	31	61	75	519	379	230	134	97	75	124	19
California	18,534	1	8	79	3,374	5,152	3,615	2,384	1,621	1,085	1,200	15
Colorado	1,863	5	35	98	566	458	259	141	128	73	79	21
Connecticut	1,860	1	6	9	161	193	145	89	50	38	75	1,093
Delaware	276	0	8	19	108	78	26	19	10	4	4	0
District of Columbia	2,072	9	23	69	497	584	349	195	146	89	81	30
Florida	10,347	54	255	459	2,866	2,022	1,085	708	534	351	490	1,523
Georgia	8,266	90	258	449	2,567	1,872	1,059	649	466	343	484	29
Hawaii	311	0	2	3	108	80	51	27	14	11	12	3
Idaho	420	0	8	21	148	88	57	41	22	15	20	0
Illinois	5,611	26	108	222	1,782	1,340	728	473	378	241	271	42
Indiana	3,443	26	70	104	1,026	799	478	289	221	158	243	29
Iowa	1,409	4	11	43	500	335	174	117	79	64	79	3
Kansas	1,548	21	39	83	456	333	218	126	101	74	88	9
Kentucky	2,906	31	89	119	804	592	373	248	205	151	230	64
Louisiana	3,617	18	101	143	1,029	889	578	295	200	126	175	63
Maine	505	11	26	31	150	116	50	43	38	19	18	3
Maryland	5,231	105	181	285	1,807	1,241	669	365	232	148	195	3
Massachusetts	2,072	28	64	84	660	500	346	153	100	65	64	8
Michigan	8,115	73	263	447	2,841	1,889	1,017	550	406	288	328	13
Minnesota	1,416	9	49	104	503	311	172	93	62	51	62	0
Mississippi	1,985	16	50	77	648	400	234	160	121	89	143	47

State												
Missouri	3,779	58	98	191	976	691	460	298	197	148	184	478
Montana	310	0	1	13	85	62	47	44	22	10	25	1
Nebraska	928	15	20	45	287	176	117	71	70	53	63	11
Nevada	669	1	4	19	182	144	82	79	52	39	62	5
New Hampshire	243	2	5	13	74	57	30	25	13	10	14	0
New Jersey	5,671	8	66	113	997	1,080	787	457	343	265	330	1,225
New Mexico	699	2	14	31	230	165	106	56	41	22	28	4
New York	12,573	258	426	578	3,461	2,956	1,929	1,153	769	510	530	3
North Carolina	9,895	453	511	587	2,806	1,909	1,062	818	593	495	631	30
North Dakota	162	0	2	4	46	20	15	13	7	4	13	38
Ohio	7,999	21	97	284	2,178	1,476	882	575	451	314	354	1,367
Oklahoma	3,304	18	67	155	935	737	435	281	231	173	262	10
Oregon	1,593	5	37	89	441	349	221	141	82	68	101	59
Pennsylvania	6,153	136	148	230	1,791	1,355	743	449	327	246	271	457
Rhode Island	394	0	3	10	143	82	68	36	22	11	16	3
South Carolina	3,369	148	230	214	1,112	711	315	198	127	119	179	16
South Dakota	256	0	9	8	43	62	41	26	15	20	22	10
Tennessee	3,289	7	29	105	913	617	360	225	168	128	158	579
Texas	16,289	20	138	384	3,454	2,916	1,957	1,240	904	622	809	3,845
Utah	512	2	3	11	138	113	109	51	27	22	25	11
Vermont	185	6	15	10	53	44	20	12	18	3	4	0
Virginia	5,041	80	158	229	1,573	1,090	660	451	309	178	312	1
Washington	2,875	6	35	131	1,009	615	363	231	144	111	200	30
West Virginia	982	3	11	36	283	213	130	75	70	60	89	12
Wisconsin	2,046	10	48	129	795	454	248	143	88	63	68	0
Wyoming	284	1	7	12	73	74	26	24	19	19	28	1

Source: U.S. Department of Justice, Law Enforcement Assistance Administration, *Census of Prisoners in State Correctional Facilities 1973, National Prisoner Statistics Special Report No. SD-NPS-SR-3* (Washington, D.C.: U.S. Government Printing Office, 1976), pp. 12, 13.

Table 28 Estimated number of inmates of State correctional facilities, by selected demographic characteristics, United States, 1974

NOTE: These data are estimates derived from a stratified probability sample of adult and youthful offenders held in the custody of State correctional authorities. The survey included not only those inmates detained in facilities directly administered by State correctional authorities, but also those in any public or private institution charged with the custody of persons under the jurisdiction of State correctional authorities. Examples of the latter arrangement are inmates committed to State mental hospitals and inmates housed in YMCA's while assigned to work-release programs. For discussion of the survey sampling procedures, standard error tables, and definitions, see Appendix 14. Juvenile offenders were excluded from the survey.

Characteristic	Number of inmates	Percent of inmates
Sex:		
Total a	191,400	100
Male	185,000	97
Female	6,300	3
Race:		
Total a	191,400	100
White	97,700	51
Black	89,700	47
Other	3,400	2
Not reported	600	(b)
Age:		
Total a	191,400	100
Under 18	1,800	1
18	5,500	3
19	7,900	4
20 to 24	57,100	30
25 to 29	44,900	23
30 to 34	27,300	14
35 to 39	16,300	9
40 to 49	19,600	10
50 and over	10,300	5
Not reported	600	(b)

Characteristic	Number of inmates	Percent of inmates
Armed forces service:		
Total a,c	187,500	100
Served	51,200	27
Never served	136,400	73
Personal income (year prior to arrest):		
Total a,d	168,300	100
No income	7,600	5
Less than $2,000	32,400	19
$2,000 to $3,999	30,700	18
$4,000 to $5,999	30,400	18
$6,000 to $9,999	29,900	18
$10,000 or more	23,000	14
Amount not known	12,600	8
Not reported	1,800	1
Length of time on last job:		
Total a,d	168,300	100
Less than 5 weeks	16,900	10
5 to 26 weeks	61,100	36
27 to 104 weeks	55,100	33
105 to 260 weeks	21,500	13
261 or more weeks	13,700	8

Level of educational attainment:

Total [a,c]	187,500	100
Eighth grade or less	49,000	26
1 to 3 years of high school	65,900	35
4 years of high school	52,200	28
1 to 3 years of college	14,300	8
4 years or more of college	1,500	1
Not reported	4,700	2

Employment status (month prior to arrest):

Total [a]	191,400	100
Employed	131,000	68
Full-time	117,100	61
Part-time	13,800	7
Unemployed	59,000	31
Looking for work	23,800	12
Not looking for work	35,200	18
Wanting work	9,100	5
Not wanting work	26,100	14
Not reported	1,400	1

Marital status:

Total [a,c]	187,500	100
Married	44,300	24
Widowed	5,800	3
Divorced	31,900	17
Separated	15,200	8
Never married	89,900	48
Not reported	300	[b]

Occupation at time of arrest:

Total [a,d]	168,300	100
Professional and technical workers	4,900	3
Managers and administrators	9,500	6
Salesworkers	3,900	2
Clerical workers	7,000	4
Craftsmen and kindred workers	39,300	23
Carpenters	4,400	3
Auto mechanics	4,100	2
Painters	4,300	3
Other craftsmen	26,500	16
Operatives	48,100	29
Welders	3,700	2
Machine operators	3,800	2
Truck drivers	9,200	5
Other operatives	31,400	19
Nonfarm laborers	29,200	17
Construction laborers	8,200	5
Freight and material handlers	7,100	4
Other nonfarm laborers	13,800	8
Farmers and farm managers	400	[b]
Farm laborers and supervisors	4,000	2
Service workers	19,200	11
Others	500	[b]
Not reported	2,500	1

[a] Detail may not add to totals because of rounding. Percent distribution based on unrounded figures.
[b] Less than 0.5 percent.
[c] Includes sentenced inmates only.
[d] Includes only those inmates who had held a full-time job after December 1968 or who had been employed during most of the month prior to their arrest.

Source: U.S. Department of Justice, Law Enforcement Assistance Administration, *Survey of Inmates of State Correctional Facilities 1974—Advance Report*, National Prisoner Statistics Special Report No. SD–NPS–SR–2 (Washington, D.C.: U.S. Government Printing Office, 1976), pp. 24, 25.

Table 29 Estimated number of sentenced inmates in State correctional facilities, by offense, United States, 1974

Offense	Number of inmates	Percent of inmates
Total [a]	187,500	100
Homicide [a]	34,000	18
Murder	21,400	11
Attempted murder	4,400	2
Manslaughter	8,200	4
Kidnaping	2,200	1
Sexual assault [a]	9,600	5
Rape	8,500	5
Statutory rape	600	[b]
Lewd act with a child	500	[b]
Other	[b,c]	[b,c]
Major drug offense (except possession) [a]	8,000	4
Involving heroin	2,800	1
Involving other specified drugs (except marijuana)	2,100	1
Involving unspecified drugs	3,200	2
Robbery [a]	42,400	23
Armed	28,800	15
Unarmed	5,900	3
Undetermined	7,700	4
Assault [a]	9,000	5
Aggravated	5,700	3
Simple	1,700	1
Undetermined	1,700	1
Burglary	33,800	18
Larceny	12,200	6
Motor vehicle theft	3,200	2
Forgery, fraud, or embezzlement	8,100	4
Minor drug offense [a]	10,700	6
Involving marihuana (except possession)	1,800	1
Possession of heroin	2,600	1
Possession of marihuana	1,100	1
Possession of other specified drugs	1,200	1
Possession of other unspecified drugs	2,100	1
Activity unspecified	1,800	1
Weapons offense	1,900	1
Arson	1,000	1
Stolen property offense	1,900	1
Other sex offense	2,100	1
Drunk or drugged driving	1,100	1
Escape or flight	1,000	1
Habitual criminal	100 [c]	[b,c]
Jail offense	2,800	2
Other	2,000	1
Not reported	[b,c]	[b,c]

[a] Detail may not add to totals because of rounding. Percent distribution based on unrounded figures.
[b] Less than 100 inmates or 0.5 percent.
[c] Estimate, based on about 17 or fewer sample cases, is statistically unrealiable.

Source: U.S. Department of Justice, Law Enforcement Assistance Administration, *Survey of Inmates of State Correctional Facilities 1974—Advance Report*, National Prisoner Statistics Special Report No. SD–NPS–SR–2 (Washington, D.C.: U.S. Government Printing Office, 1976), p. 28.

Table 30 Estimated number of inmates of State correctional facilities, by alcohol consumption at the time of "present" offense or subsequent offense resulting in imprisonment, United States, 1974

These data were derived on the basis of responses to the following questions: "At the time of any offense that caused your imprisonment now, had you been drinking?" "How much had you been drinking?" "What had you been drinking?"

Item	Number of inmates	Percent of inmates
Total [a]	191,400	100
Drinking at time of offense [a]	81,700	43
Beer only [a]	19,400	10
Light	10,300	5
Moderate	3,800	2
Heavy	5,300	3
Wine only [a]	7,900	4
Light	2,300	1
Moderate	1,900	1
Heavy	3,700	2
Liquor only [a]	32,400	17
Light	7,600	4
Moderate	7,300	4
Heavy	17,400	9
Beer and wine [a]	2,900	2
Light	600	([b])
Moderate	800	([b])
Heavy	1,500	1
Beer and liquor [a]	11,100	6
Light	1,400	1
Moderate	1,700	1
Heavy	8,000	4
Wine and liquor [a]	1,400	1
Light	100 [c]	([b,c])
Moderate	300	([b])
Heavy	1,000	1
Beer, wine, and liquor [a]	6,600	3
Light	400	([b])
Moderate	800	([b])
Heavy	5,400	3
Not drinking at time of offense	107,600	56
Don't know and not reported	2,100	1

[a] Detail may not add to totals because of rounding. Percent distribution based on unrounded figure.

[b] Less than 0.5 percent.

[c] Estimate, based on about 17 or fewer sample cases, is statistically unreliable.

Source: U.S. Department of Justice, Law Enforcement Assistance Administration, *Survey of Inmates of State Correctional Facilities* 1974—*Advance Report*, National Prisoner Statistics Special Report No. SD–NPS–SR–2 (Washington, D.C.: U.S. Government Printing Office, 1976), p. 26.

Table 31 Estimated number of inmates of State correctional facilities, by extent, nature, and circumstances of drug use, United States, 1974

Item	Number of inmates	Percent of inmates
Whether drugs ever used		
Total [a]	191,400	100
Used drugs	116,500	61
Never used drugs	74,500	39
Not reported	300	([b])
Number of drugs ever used		
Total [a,c]	116,500	100
1 drug	30,900	26
2 drugs	17,900	15
3 drugs	19,000	16
4 drugs	14,800	13
5 or more drugs	34,000	29
Type of drug ever used		
Total [a,c,d]	116,500	100
Heroin	58,200	50
Methadone	17,700	15
Cocaine	52,800	45
Marijuana	107,600	92
Amphetamines	56,400	48
Barbiturates	53,000	46
Others	31,200	27
Frequency of use		
Total [a,c]	116,500	100
Daily	71,200	61
Less than daily	45,300	39
Type of drug used daily		
Total [a,e]	71,200	100
Heroin	40,600	57
Methadone	5,400	8
Cocaine	11,500	16
Marijuana	45,100	63
Amphetamines	21,000	29
Barbiturates	15,200	21
Others	7,500	11
Whether under influence of drugs at time of "present" or subsequent offense resulting in imprisonment		
Total [a,c]	116,500	100
Under influence	50,600	43
Not under influence	65,100	56
Don't know and not reported	800	1
Number of drugs under influence of at time of "present" or subsequent offense resulting in imprisonment		
Total [a,f]	50,600	100
1 drug	36,800	73
2 drugs	10,600	21
3 or more drugs	3,200	6

[a] Detail may not add to totals because of rounding. Percent distribution based on unrounded figures.
[b] Less than 0.5 percent.
[c] Includes only those inmates who reported ever using drugs.
[d] Detail exceeds total shown because inmates may have used more than one drug.
[e] Includes only those inmates who reported using drugs daily. Detail exceeds total shown because inmates may have used more than one type of drug daily.
[f] Includes only those inmates who reported being under the influence of drugs at the time of the "present" or subsequent offense resulting in imprisonment.

Source: U.S. Department of Justice, Law Enforcement Assistance Administration, Survey of Inmates of State Correctional Facilities 1974—Advance Report, National Prisoner Statistics Special Report No. SD-NPS-SR-2 (Washington, D.C.: U.S. Government Printing Office, 1976), p. 27.

Table 32 Estimated number of sentenced inmates in State correctional facilities, by detention experience between arrest and admission for "present" offense, United States, 1974

Item	Number of inmates	Percent of inmates
Whether detained between arrest and admission to prison		
Total [a]	187,500	100
Detained	175,000	93
Not detained	10,300	5
Not reported	2,300	1
Length of time detained		
Total [a,b]	175,000	100
Less than 31 days	41,800	24
31 to 90 days	45,800	26
91 to 120 days	19,100	11
121 to 180 days	27,700	16
181 to 365 days	29,000	17
366 or more days	11,500	7
Whether detention time credited toward sentence		
Total [a,b]	175,000	100
Credited	113,800	65
Not credited	47,700	27
Don't know and not reported	13,400	8

[a] Detail may not add to totals because of rounding. Percent distribution based on unrounded figures.

[b] Includes only those sentenced inmates who had served time before admission to prison.

Source: U.S. Department of Justice, Law Enforcement Assistance Administration, *Survey of Inmates of State Correctional Facilities 1974—Advance Report*, National Prisoner Statistics Special Report No. SD–NPS–SR–2 (Washington, D.C.: U.S. Government Printing Office, 1976), p. 30.

Table 33 Estimated number of sentenced inmates in State correctional facilities, by bail experience, United States, 1974

Bail experience	Number of inmates	Percent of inmates
Whether bail was set		
Total [a]	187,500	100
Bail set	140,800	75
No bail set	44,100	24
Don't know and not reported	2,600	1
Amount of bail		
Total [a,b]	140,800	100
Less than $2,000	24,700	18
$2,000 to $4,999	25,200	18
$5,000 to $7,499	23,500	17
$7,500 to $19,999	27,900	20
$20,000 or more	32,700	23
Amount not known	6,800	5
Whether released on bail		
Total [a,b]	140,800	100
Released	53,900	38
Not released	86,200	61
Not reported	800	1
To whom bail was paid		
Total [a,c]	53,900	100
Bondsman	38,400	71
Court	10,200	19
Not reported	5,300	10
Reason bail not set		
Total [a,d]	44,100	100
Released on own recognizance	3,100	7
Offense not bailable	19,100	43
Other reason	13,100	30
Reason not known	8,800	20

[a] Detail may not add to totals because of rounding. Percent distribution based on unrounded figures.
[b] Includes only those sentenced inmates for whom bail had been set.
[c] Includes only those sentenced inmates who had been released on bail.
[d] Includes only those sentenced inmates for whom bail had not been set.

Source: U.S. Department of Justice, Law Enforcement Assistance Administration, *Survey of Inmates of State Correctional Facilities 1974—Advance Report*, National Prisoner Statistics Special Report No. SD-NPS-SR-2 (Washington, D.C.: U.S. Government Printing Office, 1976), p. 29.

Table 34 Estimated number of sentenced inmates in State correctional facilities, by maximum length of sentence, United States, 1974

Maximum sentence length	Number of inmates	Percent of inmates
Total [a]	187,500	100
Less than 1 year	3,200	2
1 to 1.99 years	7,000	4
2 to 2.99 years	8,700	5
3 to 3.99 years	16,000	9
4 to 4.99 years	11,000	6
5 to 5.99 years	25,900	14
6 to 9.99 years	20,200	11
10 to 10.99 years	22,700	12
11 to 15.99 years	19,400	10
16 to 20.99 years	12,500	7
21 or more years	15,800	8
Life	21,900	12
Death	700	([b])
Don't know and not reported	2,500	1

[a] Detail may not add to totals because of rounding. Percent distribution based on unrounded figures.

[b] Less than 0.5 percent.

Source: U.S. Department of Justice, Law Enforcement Assistance Administration, *Survey of Inmates of State Correctional Facilities 1974—Advance Report*, National Prisoner Statistics Special Report No. SD–NPS–SR–2 (Washington, D.C.: U.S. Government Printing Office, 1976), p. 31.

Table 35 Estimated number of sentenced inmates in State
correctional facilities, by hours worked per week and
remuneration per hour, United States, 1974

Item	Number of inmates	Percent of inmates
Hours per week spent on work assignment		
Total [a,b]	137,900	100
Less than 21 hours	16,700	12
21 to 35 hours	35,300	26
36 to 40 hours	44,200	32
41 or more hours	35,000	25
Not reported	6,700	5
Remuneration per hour for work assignment		
Total [a,b]	137,900	100
Less than 6 cents	45,600	33
6 to 20 cents	34,200	25
21 cents or more	7,300	5
Payment in kind	6,000	4
Not paid	40,500	29
Not reported	4,400	3

[a] Detail may not add to totals because of rounding. Percent distribution based on unrounded figures.

[b] Includes only those sentenced inmates having work assignments within the facility.

Source: U.S. Department of Justice, Law Enforcement Assistance Administration, *Survey of Inmates of State Correctional Facilities 1974—Advance Report*, National Prisoner Statistics Special Report No. SD–NPS–SR–2 (Washington, D.C.: U.S. Government Printing Office, 1976), p. 33.

Table 36 Estimated number of inmates of State correctional facilities, by prior correctional experience, United States, 1974

Item	Number of inmates	Percent of inmates
Number of sentences ever served:		
Total a	191,400	100
None	500	(b)
1	55,700	29
2	43,900	23
3	36,000	19
4	23,800	12
5 or more	31,400	16
Whether sentenced more than once for the same offense:		
Total a	191,400	100
Never received any sentence	500	(b)
Received only one sentence	55,700	29
Received more than one sentence	135,200	71
Never sentenced more than once for the same offense	35,500	18
1 time	42,500	22
2 times	28,200	15
3 times	16,400	9
4 or more times	12,600	7
Time served on all sentences:		
Total a	191,400	100
No time served	500	(b)
Less than 13 months	33,000	17
13 to 24 months	30,100	16
25 to 48 months	42,100	22
49 to 120 months	52,900	28
121 or more months	26,400	14
Not reported	6,300	3

Item	Number of inmates	Percent of inmates
Number of times on probation as juvenile, adult, or youthful offender:		
Total a	191,400	100
Never on probation	82,600	43
On probation	108,300	57
1 time	41,000	21
2 times	47,100	25
3 or more times	20,200	11
Not reported	500	(b)
Number of times on probation as adult or youthful offender:		
Total a	191,400	100
Never on probation	83,100	43
On probation	107,800	56
1 time	106,900	56
2 or more times	900	(b)
Not reported	500	(b)
Number of times on probation as juvenile offender:		
Total a	191,400	100
Never on probation	123,600	65
On probation	67,300	35
1 time	47,300	25
2 times	11,500	6
3 or more times	8,500	4
Not reported	500	(b)
Time spent on probation:		
Total a,d	108,300	100
Less than 13 months	54,000	50
13 to 24 months	24,100	22

Number of past juvenile sentences:		
Total [a]	191,400	100
With past juvenile sentence(s)	63,000	33
One past juvenile sentence	40,200	21
Two or more past juvenile sentences	22,900	12
Without past juvenile sentence	128,300	67
Time served on past juvenile sentence(s):		
Total [a,c]	63,000	100
Less than 2 months	6,700	11
2 to 6 months	9,400	15
7 to 12 months	14,000	22
13 to 24 months	17,000	27
25 or more months	15,900	25

25 or more months	30,300	28
Not reported	(b,e)	(b,e)
Number of times paroled:		
Total [a]	191,400	100
Never paroled	119,500	62
Paroled	71,800	38
1 time	45,000	24
2 times	16,800	9
3 or more times	10,000	5

[a] Detail may not add to totals because of rounding. Percent distribution based on unrounded figures.
[b] Less than 100 inmates or 0.5 percent.
[c] Includes only those inmates who, prior to their "present" sentence, had also been sentenced as juveniles.
[d] Includes only those inmates who had been on probation.
[e] Estimate, based on 17 or fewer sample cases, is statistically unreliable.

Source: U.S. Department of Justice, Law Enforcement Assistance Administration, *Survey of Inmates of State Correctional Facilities 1974—Advance Report*, National Prisoner Statistics Special Report No. SD-NPS-SR-2 (Washington, D.C.: U.S. Government Printing Office, 1976), pp. 35, 36.

Table 37 Estimated number of sentenced inmates in State correctional facilities, by process of adjudication for "present" offense, United States, 1974

Means	Number of inmates	Percent of inmates
Total	187,500	100
Judged guilty	63,200	34
Pleaded guilty	120,600	64
Not reported	3,700	2

Source: U.S. Department of Justice, Law Enforcement Assistance Administration, *Survey of Inmates of State Correctional Facilities 1974—Advance Report*, National Prisoner Statistics Special Report No. SD–NPS–SR–2 (Washington, D.C.: U.S. Government Printing Office, 1976), p. 8.

Table 38 Estimated number of sentenced inmates in State correctional facilities, by type of representation, United States, 1974

Item	Number of inmates	Percent of inmates
Total	187,500	100
With legal counsel	179,400	96
Court-appointed lawyer, public defender, or legal aid attorney	127,000	68
Other lawyer	51,900	28
Type of lawyer not reported	500	([a])
Without legal counsel	7,900	4
Not reported	200	([a])

[a] Less than 0.5 percent.

Source: U.S. Department of Justice, Law Enforcement Assistance Administration, *Survey of Inmates of State Correctional Facilities 1974—Advance Report*, National Prisoner Statistics Special Report No. SD–NPS–SR–2 (Washington, D.C.: U.S. Government Printing Office, 1976), p. 9.

Figure 1 Prisoners in State and Federal institutions on December 31, United States, 1925–75

NOTE: Data for this figure were compiled by a year-end census of prisoners in the United States. Prior to Dec. 31, 1971, the prison population was defined as all adult felons serving a sentence in a Federal or State correctional institution. Beginning on Dec. 31, 1971, all jurisdictions were asked to disregard the difference between felons and misdemeanants and to count as their prison population only those inmates who had been sentenced as adult or youthful offenders to a maximum term of at least 1 year and 1 day.

[In thousands]

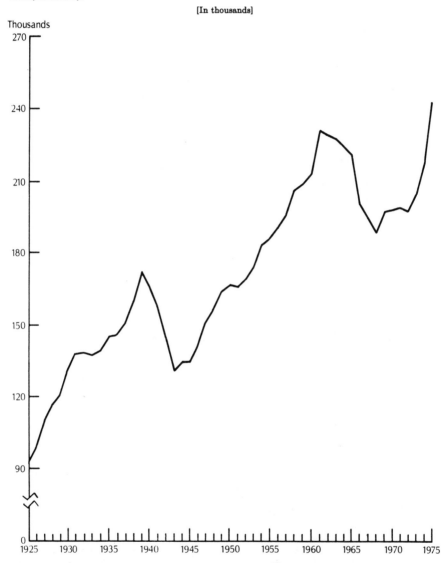

Source: U.S. Department of Justice, Law Enforcement Assistance Administration, *Prisoners in State and Federal Institutions on December 31, 1975,* **National Prisoner Statistics Bulletin No. SD-NPS-PSF-3 (Washington, D.C.: U.S. Government Printing Office, 1977), p. 13.**

Table 39 Prisoners in State and Federal institutions, by sex, region, and jurisdiction, on Dec. 31, 1974 and 1975

Region and jurisdiction	Dec. 31, 1974			Dec. 31, 1975		
	Total	Male	Female	Total	Male	Female
United States, total	218,466	211,077	7,389	242,750	233,900	8,850
Federal institutions, total	22,361	21,367	994	24,131	23,026	1,105
State institutions, total	196,105	189,710	6,395	218,619	210,874	7,745
Northeast	31,393	30,541	852	34,699	33,695	1,004
Maine	527	509	18	643	628	15
New Hampshire	219	219	0	250	250	0
Vermont	242	238	4	244	239	5
Massachusetts	2,226	2,171	55	2,416	2,336	80
Rhode Island	435	427	8	381	371	10
Connecticut	1,464	1,401	63	1,849	1,786	63
New York	14,329	13,949	380	16,071	15,642	429
New Jersey	5,219	5,067	152	5,682	5,501	181
Pennsylvania	6,732	6,560	172	7,163	6,942	221
North Central	39,713	38,450	1,263	48,731	47,214	1,517
Ohio	9,326	8,978	348	11,421	10,985	436
Indiana	3,051	2,990	61	3,897	3,784	113
Illinois	6,667	6,454	213	8,209	8,038	171
Michigan	8,630	8,410	220	10,852	10,534	318
Wisconsin	2,587	2,501	86	2,992	2,867	125
Minnesota	1,372	1,331	41	1,675	1,625	50
Iowa	1,476	1,414	62	1,819	1,747	72
Missouri	3,764	3,660	104	4,371	4,275	96
North Dakota	129	129	0	173	173	0
South Dakota	250	245	5	338	320	18
Nebraska	1,040	989	51	1,246	1,184	62
Kansas	1,421	1,349	72	1,738	1,682	56

South	90,186	86,992	3,194	102,967	99,016	3,951
Delaware	436	427	9	582	565	17
Maryland	6,247	6,084	163	6,965	6,754	211
District of Columbia	2,072	2,055	17	2,302	2,276	26
Virginia	5,032	4,869	163	5,497	5,291	206
West Virginia	989	953	36	1,176	1,134	42
North Carolina	10,932	10,546	386	11,449	10,997	452
South Carolina	4,318	4,168	150	5,600	5,391	209
Georgia	9,289	8,941	348	10,102	9,718	384
Florida	11,217	10,742	475	15,315	14,643	672
Kentucky	3,051	2,939	112	3,393	3,269	124
Tennessee	3,771	3,631	140	4,561	4,371	190
Alabama	4,259	4,074	185	4,420	4,226	194
Mississippi	2,127	2,056	71	2,422	2,346	76
Arkansas	1,938	1,871	67	2,162	2,079	83
Louisiana	4,779	4,612	167	4,835	4,628	207
Oklahoma	2,896	2,813	83	3,133	2,983	150
Texas	16,833	16,211	622	19,053	18,345	708
West	34,813	33,727	1,086	32,222	30,949	1,273
Montana	336	336	0	375	375	0
Idaho	525	514	11	580	580	0
Wyoming	269	269	0	307	307	0
Colorado	1,968	1,899	69	2,039	1,969	70
New Mexico	902	873	29	999	967	32
Arizona	2,101	2,027	74	2,647	2,538	109
Utah	548	532	16	657	634	23
Nevada	801	766	35	814	768	46
Washington	2,989	2,841	148	3,452	3,273	179
Oregon	1,993	1,913	80	2,480	2,385	95
California	21,897	21,283	614	17,296	16,598	698
Alaska	175	167	8	209	194	15
Hawaii	309	307	2	367	361	6

Source: U.S. Department of Justice, Law Enforcement Assistance Administration, *Prisoners in State and Federal Institutions on December 31, 1975*, National Prisoner Statistics Bulletin No. SD-NPS-PSF-3 (Washington, D.C.: U.S. Government Printing Office, 1977), pp. 16–21. Table adapted by SOURCEBOOK staff.

Table 40 Rate (per 100,000 general population) of incarceration in State and Federal institutions on December 31, by region and jurisdiction, 1971-75

Figures used for civilian population are based on U.S. Bureau of the Census estimates.

Region and jurisdiction	Number per 100,000 population				
	Dec. 31, 1971	Dec. 31, 1972	Dec. 31, 1973	Dec. 31, 1974	Dec. 31, 1975
United States, total	96.4	94.6	97.8	103.6	113
Federal institutions, total	10.2	10.5	10.9	10.6	11
State institutions, total	86.2	84.1	86.8	93.0	102
Northeast	56.4	56.8	60.4	63.4	70
Maine	45.1	46.3	43.8	50.4	60
New Hampshire	28.0	30.8	34.8	27.1	31
Vermont	46.5	30.0	40.3	51.5	51
Massachusetts	38.3	32.1	34.3	38.4	42
Rhode Island	40.5	36.1	43.2	48.7	41
Connecticut	63.3	59.3	54.2	47.6	59
New York	65.0	64.0	71.4	78.5	89
New Jersey	72.5	72.4	73.5	71.6	77
Pennsylvania	44.7	52.6	55.0	56.9	60
North Central	72.9	65.6	62.8	69.0	84
Ohio	84.7	77.2	71.9	86.9	107
Indiana	82.9	72.8	63.4	57.5	73
Illinois	52.4	50.4	50.3	55.9	73
Michigan	106.4	93.9	86.8	94.6	119
Wisconsin	55.4	44.9	47.2	56.4	65
Minnesota	40.2	34.5	36.0	35.1	42
Iowa	53.6	45.5	49.0	51.6	63
Missouri	76.8	74.7	79.4	88.0	92
North Dakota	21.3	28.8	24.9	20.7	27
South Dakota	57.8	51.0	34.9	37.0	49
Nebraska	69.1	62.8	66.0	67.9	80
Kansas	90.5	73.5	60.6	63.5	76

South	123.9	124.5	128.3	135.0	150
Delaware	33.2	49.3	57.1	76.1	100
Maryland	124.9	139.3	144.0	155.0	169
District of Columbia	349.2	340.8	324.2	289.2	326
Virginia	108.9	106.3	107.9	105.1	110
West Virginia	59.6	59.1	60.8	57.3	65
North Carolina	153.0	159.9	183.9	207.2	210
South Carolina	118.4	121.2	130.1	158.4	198
Georgia	146.1	174.3	173.3	191.4	204
Florida	135.8	139.3	132.5	137.9	183
Kentucky	94.1	89.5	89.4	91.7	100
Tennessee	86.1	81.9	84.2	90.9	109
Alabama	110.0	103.5	104.5	110.3	121
Mississippi	82.7	83.1	75.5	91.8	103
Arkansas	83.9	80.4	82.2	99.6	102
Louisiana	113.0	92.2	108.3	127.7	126
Oklahoma	144.2	139.7	120.4	108.5	114
Texas	140.9	136.0	146.6	140.6	154
West	81.9	78.6	85.6	93.9	84
Montana	35.4	39.5	43.5	45.6	50
Idaho	48.9	49.6	54.6	65.5	71
Wyoming	77.5	75.7	78.6	73.9	80
Colorado	85.9	81.3	77.5	79.4	80
New Mexico	61.3	55.7	66.4	80.7	86
Arizona	74.3	76.9	81.0	97.0	118
Utah	53.3	51.2	44.7	46.1	54
Nevada	124.0	121.2	134.9	130.3	136
Washington	82.4	77.1	77.1	86.2	96
Oregon	93.5	84.4	74.7	88.3	108
California	87.4	83.9	96.7	105.6	81
Alaska	65.6	61.0	56.3	57.1	56
Hawaii	33.7	38.8	37.3	38.6	42

Source: U.S. Department of Justice, Law Enforcement Assistance Administration, *Prisoners in State and Federal Institutions*, National Prisoner Statistics Bulletin No. SD–NPS–PSF–3, pp. 16, 17; National Prisoner Statistics Bulletin No. SD–NPS–PSF–2, pp. 20, 21 (Washington, D.C.: U.S. Government Printing Office). Table adapted by SOURCEBOOK staff.

Figure 2 Rate (per 100,000 general population) of incarceration in State and Federal institutions, by jurisdiction, on Dec. 31, 1975

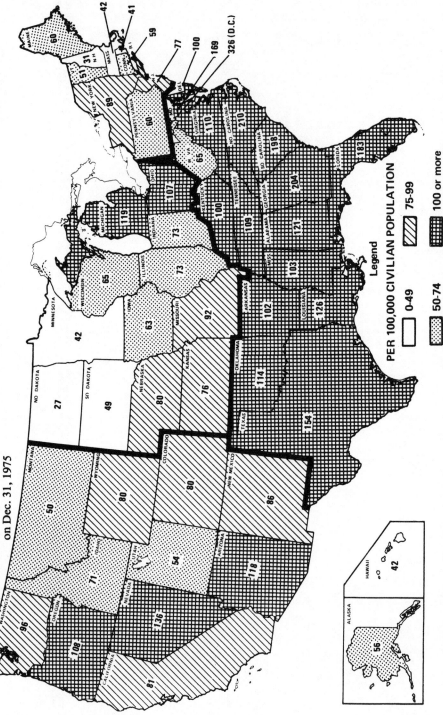

Legend

PER 100,000 CIVILIAN POPULATION

0-49 50-74 75-99 100 or more

Source: U.S. Department of Justice, Law Enforcement Assistance Administration, *Prisoners in State and Federal Institutions on December 31, 1975*, National Prisoner Statistics Bulletin No. SD-NPS-PSF-3 (Washington, D.C.: U.S. Government Printing Office, 1977), p. 12.

Figure 3 Prisoners in State and Federal institutions on December 31, by sex, United States, 1971-75

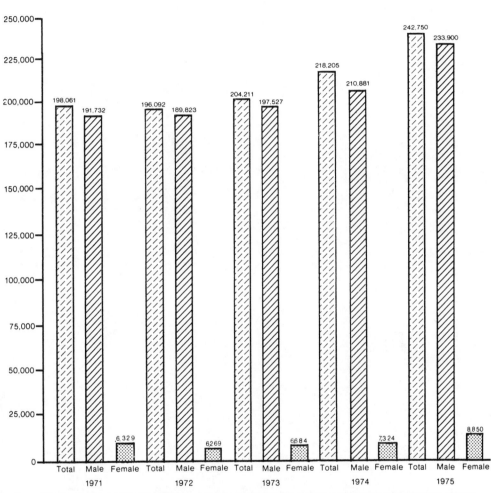

Source: U.S. Department of Justice, Law Enforcement Assistance Administration, *Prisoners in State and Federal Institutions*, National Prisoner Statistics Bulletin No. SD-NPS-PSF-3, pp. 16-21; National Prisoner Statistics Bulletin No. SD-NPS-PSF-2, pp. 14-19 (Washington, D.C.: U.S. Government Printing Office). Figure constructed by SOURCEBOOK staff.

Table 41 Sentenced and unsentenced prisoners in State and Federal institutions, by sex, region, and jurisdiction, on Dec. 31, 1975

quired to provide a year-end count of all prisoners, regardless of length of sentence. Beginning in 1974, all reporting jurisdictions were re-This table includes inmates sentenced to a maximum term of at least 1 year and 1 day and also those with lesser terms and those without sentences. The inclusion of these short-term and unsentenced prisoners results in the figures for this table being larger than those in Table 36.

Region and jurisdiction	Dec. 31, 1975		
	Both sexes	Male	Female
United States, total	253,816	244,149	9,667
Federal institutions, total	24,131	23,026	1,105
State institutions, total	229,685	221,123	8,562
Northeast	36,806	35,708	1,098
Maine	643	628	15
New Hampshire	252	252	0
Vermont	394	376	18
Massachusetts	2,443	2,351	92
Rhode Island	594	580	14
Connecticut	3,079	2,951	128
New York	16,074	15,645	429
New Jersey	6,164	5,983	181
Pennsylvania	7,163	6,942	221
North Central	49,894	48,325	1,569
Ohio	11,421	10,985	436
Indiana	4,547	4,429	118
Illinois	8,501	8,324	177
Michigan	10,852	10,534	318
Wisconsin	2,992	2,867	125
Minnesota	1,675	1,625	50
Iowa	1,868	1,796	72
Missouri	4,371	4,275	96
North Dakota	209	209	0
South Dakota	403	381	22
Nebraska	1,301	1,213	88
Kansas	1,754	1,687	67

South	107,392	103,116	4,276
Delaware	897	865	32
Maryland	6,965	6,754	211
District of Columbia	3,327	3,211	116
Virginia	6,092	5,844	248
West Virginia	1,176	1,134	42
North Carolina	12,374	11,878	496
South Carolina	6,100	5,867	233
Georgia	10,746	10,266	480
Florida	15,315	14,643	672
Kentucky	3,393	3,269	124
Tennessee	4,575	4,383	192
Alabama	4,420	4,226	194
Mississippi	2,422	2,346	76
Arkansas	2,254	2,166	88
Louisiana	4,835	4,628	207
Oklahoma	3,448	3,291	157
Texas	19,053	18,345	708
West	35,593	33,974	1,619
Montana	376	376	0
Idaho	580	580	0
Wyoming	307	307	0
Colorado	2,047	1,977	70
New Mexico	1,118	1,082	36
Arizona	2,647	2,538	109
Utah	723	694	29
Nevada	827	781	46
Washington	3,467	3,288	179
Oregon	2,484	2,389	95
California	20,028	19,008	1,020
Alaska	480	459	21
Hawaii	509	495	14

Source: U.S. Department of Justice, Law Enforcement Assistance Administration, Prisoners in State and Federal Institutions on December 31, 1975, National Prisoner Statistics Bulletin No. SD-NPS-PSF-3 (Washington, D.C.: U.S. Government Printing Office, 1977), pp. 36, 37.

Table 42 Sentenced and unsentenced prisoners in State and Federal institutions, by region and jurisdiction, on Dec. 31, 1975 and 1976

Figures for 1975 are revised, and in some cases will differ from the figures in Tables 6.39 and 6.41. Figures for 1976 are preliminary, and subject to revision.

Region and jurisdiction	Total prisoner population			Prisoners with a sentence of more than a year			Other prisoners[a]		
	1976	1975	Percent change	1976	1975	Percent change	1976	1975	Percent change
United States, total	283,145	253,816	+12	265,674	238,858	+11	17,471	14,958	+17
Federal institutions, total	28,184	24,131	+17	24,812	22,080	+12	3,372	2,051	+64
State institutions, total	254,961	229,685	+11	240,862	216,778	+11	14,099	12,907	+9
Northeast	39,414	36,806	+7	36,520	33,518	+9	2,894	3,288	−12
Maine	615	643	−4	610	643	−5	5	0	X
New Hampshire	254	252	+1	248	250	−1	6	2	+200
Vermont	419	394	+6	312	244	+28	107	150	−29
Massachusetts	2,695	2,443	+10	2,651	2,416	+10	44	27	+63
Rhode Island b	652	594	+10	492	381	+29	160	213	−25
Connecticut b	3,239	3,079	+5	1,923	1,849	+4	1,316	1,230	+7
New York	17,749	16,074	+10	17,746	16,071	+10	3	3	0
New Jersey c	6,201	6,164	+1	5,882	5,682	+4	319	482	−34
Pennsylvania d	7,590	7,163	+6	6,656	5,982	+11	934	1,181	−21
North Central	55,447	49,894	+11	54,350	48,731	+12	1,097	1,163	−6
Ohio	12,625	11,421	+11	12,625	11,421	+11	0	0	X
Indiana	4,593	4,547	+1	4,043	3,897	+4	550	650	−15
Illinois	9,643	8,501	+13	9,249	8,209	+13	394	292	+35
Michigan	12,462	10,852	+15	12,462	10,852	+15	0	0	X
Wisconsin	3,268	2,992	+9	3,268	2,992	+9	0	0	X
Minnesota	1,624	1,675	−3	1,624	1,675	−3	0	0	X
Iowa	1,941	1,868	+4	1,898	1,819	+4	43	49	−12
Missouri	5,005	4,371	+15	5,005	4,371	+15	0	0	X
North Dakota	205	209	−2	188	173	+9	17	36	−53
South Dakota	523	403	+30	480	338	+42	43	65	−34
Nebraska	1,474	1,301	+13	1,435	1,246	+15	39	55	−29
Kansas	2,084	1,754	+19	2,073	1,738	+19	11	16	−31
South	121,436	107,392	+13	114,991	102,307	+12	6,445	5,085	+27
Delaware b	953	897	+6	684	582	+18	269	315	−15

State									
Maryland [d,e]	7,912	6,965	+14	7,438	6,547	+14	474	418	+13
District of Columbia [b]	3,086	3,327	(b)	2,299	2,302	(b)	787	1,025	(b)
Virginia [c]	7,805	6,092	+28	6,947	5,497	+26	858	595	+44
West Virginia	1,299	1,176	+10	1,299	1,176	+10	0	0	X
North Carolina	13,261	12,374	+7	11,320	11,449	−1	1,941	925	+110
South Carolina [e]	6,972	6,100	+14	6,059	5,600	+8	913	500	+83
Georgia [c]	12,106	10,746	+13	11,524	10,102	+14	582	644	−10
Florida [c]	18,093	15,315	+18	18,093	15,315	+18	0	0	X
Kentucky	3,662	3,393	+8	3,662	3,393	+8	0	0	X
Tennessee	4,837	4,575	+6	4,817	4,561	+6	20	14	+43
Alabama [c,d]	5,256	4,420	+19	5,235	4,420	+18	21	0	X
Mississippi [c,d]	2,237	2,422	−8	2,015	2,180	−8	222	242	−8
Arkansas [e]	2,664	2,254	+18	2,592	2,162	+20	72	92	−22
Louisiana [c]	6,347	4,835	+31	6,347	4,835	+31	0	0	X
Oklahoma [c]	4,229	3,448	+23	3,943	3,133	+26	286	315	−9
Texas	20,717	19,053	+9	20,717	19,053	+9	0	0	X
West	38,664	35,593	+9	35,001	32,222	+9	3,663	3,371	+9
Montana	485	376	+29	478	375	+27	7	1	+600
Idaho	695	580	+20	682	580	+18	13	0	X
Wyoming	340	307	+11	340	307	+11	0	0	X
Colorado	2,249	2,047	+10	2,244	2,039	+10	5	8	−38
New Mexico	1,353	1,118	+21	1,221	999	+22	132	119	+11
Arizona	2,850	2,647	+8	2,850	2,647	+8	0	0	X
Utah	810	723	+12	738	657	+12	72	66	+9
Nevada	951	827	+15	951	814	+17	0	13	−100
Washington	3,887	3,467	+12	3,865	3,452	+12	22	15	+47
Oregon	2,859	2,484	+15	2,859	2,480	+15	0	4	−100
California	21,088	20,028	+5	18,115	17,296	+5	2,973	2,732	+9
Alaska	528	480	+10	260	209	+24	268	271	−1
Hawaii	569	509	+12	398	367	+8	171	142	+20

a Includes prisoners with sentences of a year or less, as well as unsentenced persons. The latter include, among others, those held for safekeeping, those undergoing court-ordered evaluation, civil narcotics addicts, and in States operating an integrated jail-prison system, those held awaiting trial or sentencing.
b Both 1975 and 1976 figures include jail and prison inmates, as jails and prisons in these jurisdictions form an integrated system. For the District of Columbia, figures for 1976 exclude, but those for 1975 include, inmates held in District of Columbia jail and detention center who had a maximum sentence of less than a year and a day or no sentence.
c Figures for Dec. 31, 1976 include inmates held in local jails because of overcrowding in State institutions, although such inmates are not considered by these jurisdictions to be in the custody of the State correctional system. The number held in local jails as of Dec. 31, 1976 was as follows: New Jersey (200), Virginia (790), Georgia (550), Florida (300), Alabama (2,160), Mississippi (102), and Louisiana (1,756).
d Distribution of Dec. 31, 1975, and Dec. 31, 1976, inmate populations in Maryland and Mississippi between prisoners with a maximum sentence of more than a year and those with shorter or no sentences was estimated on the basis of information provided by the jurisdiction. Distribution of the Dec. 31, 1975, inmate population in Pennsylvania was similarly estimated.
e Figures for Dec. 31, 1976 include inmates held in local jails because of overcrowding in State institutions. Such inmates are considered by these jurisdictions to be in the custody of the State correctional system. The number of inmates held in local jails as of Dec. 31, 1976 was as follows: Maryland (1,081), South Carolina (786), and Arkansas (13).

Source: U.S. Department of Justice, Law Enforcement Assistance Administration, *Prisoners in State and Federal Institutions on December 31, 1976—Advance Report*, National Prisoner Statistics Bulletin No. SD-NPS-PSF-6a (Washington, D.C.: U.S. Government Printing Office, 1977), pp. 2, 3.

Table 43 Movement of prisoners in State and Federal institutions, by region and jurisdiction, 1975

Some inmates were involved in more than one transaction; all figures on admissions and departures represent number of transactions and not the actual number of individual prisoners who were involved in such movements. Unconditional releases include expiration of sentence, commutation of sentence, and other such unqualified discharges, while conditional releases, i.e., those involving some form of supervision over the offender upon return to the community, included parole, probation, supervised mandatory release (early release because of good behavior), and other forms of conditional discharge. Generally, these figures refer to inmates sentenced to a maximum term of more than a year.

Region and jurisdiction	Number of prisoners on Dec. 31, 1974	Admissions					
		Total	Commitments from court	Parole or conditional-release violators returned	Escapees returned	Transfers from others jurisdictions	Other admissions
United States, total	218,466	190,014	129,573	18,956	8,263	16,761	16,461
Federal institutions, total	22,361	33,460	16,770	1,281	840	12,618	1,951
State institutions, total	196,105	156,554	112,803	17,675	7,423	4,143	14,510
Northeast	31,393	29,800	17,107	4,687	1,137	998	5,871
Maine	527	810	651	137	2	20	0
New Hampshire	219	322	195	36	9	82	0
Vermont	242	206	155	15	30	4	2
Massachusetts	2,226	2,020	1,028	313	235	189	255
Rhode Island	435	229	220	5	1	0	3
Connecticut	1,464	1,921	1,492	251	29	149	0
New York	14,329	9,067	6,908	1,772	387	0	0
New Jersey	5,219	4,406	2,630	1,271	261	203	41
Pennsylvania	6,732	10,819	3,828	887	183	351	5,570
North Central	39,713	33,658	26,358	3,686	1,102	437	2,075
Ohio	9,326	7,962	7,456	350	60	96	0
Indiana	3,051	2,686	2,359	232	95	0	0
Illinois	6,667	6,572	3,937	710	0	0	1,925
Michigan	8,630	6,590	4,769	1,154	655	12	0
Wisconsin	2,587	1,821	1,443	251	33	94	0
Minnesota	1,372	1,189	794	271	48	36	40
Iowa	1,476	1,130	860	136	94	16	27
Missouri	3,764	2,548	2,227	208	50	63	0
North Dakota	129	174	144	25	0	5	0
South Dakota	250	375	296	25	16	22	16
Nebraska	1,040	961	722	177	22	20	20
Kansas	1,421	1,650	1,351	150	29	73	47

South	90,186	70,652	55,565	6,073	4,347	2,202	2,465

Region / State							
South	90,186	70,652	55,565	6,073	4,347	2,202	2,465
Delaware	436	444	354	17	30	7	36
Maryland	6,247	5,554	4,745	245	412	152	0
District of Columbia	2,072	4,082	2,521	362	189	1,010	0
Virginia	5,032	3,281	2,407	391	257	164	62
West Virginia	989	1,153	479	50	83	355	186
North Carolina	10,932	8,342	6,219	539	1,584	0	0
South Carolina	4,318	4,543	3,792	110	25	315	301
Georgia	9,289	6,031	5,227	380	384	0	40
Florida	11,217	10,755	7,415	1,060	578	18	1,684
Kentucky	3,051	2,657	2,129	369	82	77	0
Tennessee	3,771	3,033	2,494	214	282	43	0
Alabama	4,259	2,716	1,954	549	186	0	27
Mississippi	2,127	1,454	1,195	116	14	0	129
Arkansas	1,938	2,088	1,692	331	19	46	0
Louisiana	4,779	1,814	1,490	260	52	12	0
Oklahoma	2,896	2,625	2,252	225	148	0	0
Texas	16,833	10,080	9,200	855	22	3	0
West	34,813	22,444	13,773	3,229	837	506	4,099
Montana	336	448	291	58	23	76	0
Idaho	525	638	519	63	12	33	11
Wyoming	269	191	175	5	6	5	0
Colorado	1,968	1,744	1,394	184	142	24	0
New Mexico	902	761	516	172	37	10	26
Arizona	2,101	1,569	1,363	117	74	15	0
Utah	548	352	239	77	25	9	2
Nevada	801	513	408	65	1	39	0
Washington	2,989	2,101	1,413	554	126	8	0
Oregon	1,993	1,745	1,337	220	157	31	0
California	21,897	11,922	5,765	1,649	201	248	4,059
Alaska	175	240	201	16	23	0	0
Hawaii	309	220	152	49	10	8	1

Source: U.S. Department of Justice, Law Enforcement Assistance Administration, *Prisoners in State and Federal Institutions on December 31, 1975*, National Prisoner Statistics Bulletin No. SD-NPS-PSF-3 (Washington, D.C.: U.S. Government Printing Office, 1977), pp. 22, 23.

Table 43 (continued)

Region and jurisdiction	Total	Departures						Number of prisoners on Dec. 31, 1975
		Conditional releases	Unconditional releases	Deaths	Escapes	Transfers to other jurisdictions	Other departures	
United States, total	165,730	89,808	30,694	766	8,582	20,316	15,564	242,750
Federal institutions, total	31,690	7,485	6,275	61	655	15,185	2,029	24,131
State institutions, total	134,040	82,323	24,419	705	7,927	5,131	13,535	218,619
Northeast	26,494	15,990	2,384	75	1,278	948	5,819	34,699
Maine	694	595	54	1	4	40	0	643
New Hampshire	291	192	16	1	12	70	0	250
Vermont	204	120	2	0	51	27	4	244
Massachusetts	1,830	705	235	8	258	332	292	2,416
Rhode Island	283	226	51	0	1	5	0	381
Connecticut	1,536	926	485	3	28	94	0	1,849
New York	7,325	6,151	669	37	468	0	0	16,071
New Jersey	3,943	3,087	208	6	270	247	125	5,682
Pennsylvania	10,388	3,988	664	19	186	133	5,398	7,163
North Central	24,640	19,106	2,563	206	1,210	559	996	48,731
Ohio	5,867	5,608	71	26	65	97	0	11,421
Indiana	1,840	1,381	336	9	60	54	0	3,897
Illinois	5,030	3,782	251	69	6	13	909	8,209
Michigan	4,368	3,279	344	22	709	14	0	10,852
Wisconsin	1,416	1,129	58	6	105	118	0	2,992
Minnesota	886	625	133	24	45	59	0	1,675
Iowa	787	429	231	8	66	10	43	1,819
Missouri	1,941	908	839	23	82	89	0	4,371
North Dakota	130	89	39	0	1	1	0	173
South Dakota	287	178	73	1	18	12	5	338
Nebraska	755	493	188	4	29	2	39	1,246
Kansas	1,333	1,205	0	14	24	90	0	1,738

South	57,871	30,200	17,347	295	4,524	3,100	2,405	102,967
Delaware	298	204	47	0	28	0	19	582
Maryland	4,836	3,267	957	12	391	209	0	6,965
District of Columbia	3,852	1,151	385	17	206	2,091	2	2,302
Virginia	2,816	1,435	899	12	291	179	0	5,497
West Virginia	966	258	40	4	95	345	224	1,176
North Carolina	7,825	4,391	1,912	28	1,494	0	0	11,449
South Carolina	3,261	665	2,539	17	36	4	0	5,600
Georgia	5,218	2,368	2,137	29	424	98	162	10,102
Florida	6,657	2,749	1,275	34	621	19	1,959	15,315
Kentucky	2,315	1,970	208	10	73	54	0	3,393
Tennessee	2,243	1,592	274	10	325	42	0	4,561
Alabama	2,555	1,418	908	17	188	0	24	4,420
Mississippi	1,159	710	411	12	11	0	15	2,422
Arkansas	1,864	1,536	244	4	25	55	0	2,162
Louisiana	1,758	778	849	29	102	0	0	4,835
Oklahoma	2,388	1,034	1,157	5	192	0	0	3,133
Texas	7,860	4,674	3,105	55	22	4	0	19,053
West	25,035	17,027	2,125	129	915	524	4,315	32,222
Montana	409	276	25	3	23	82	0	375
Idaho	583	474	36	4	10	48	11	580
Wyoming	153	51	85	1	6	10	0	307
Colorado	1,673	1,353	104	12	188	16	0	2,039
New Mexico	664	535	40	5	32	3	49	999
Arizona	1,023	550	326	11	75	5	56	2,647
Utah	243	207	12	1	21	2	0	657
Nevada	500	392	92	1	3	11	1	814
Washington	1,638	1,411	7	13	176	7	24	3,452
Oregon	1,258	713	335	7	155	34	14	2,480
California	16,523	10,864	943	70	192	298	4,156	17,296
Alaska	206	98	82	0	26	0	0	209
Hawaii	162	103	38	1	8	8	4	367

Table 44 Prisoners in Navy and Marine Corps correctional centers, by branch of service and month, 1975-76

NOTE: Inmates in the Navy—Marine Corps correctional system are of 3 types: "detained," those individuals who are confined awaiting trial; "adjudged," individuals who have been found guilty by courts-martial, but whose sentences are in the review process awaiting final approval; and "sentenced," individuals whose sentences have received final review and approval. Data in the table below are for all three types.

Month	Navy		Marine Corps	
	1975	1976	1975	1976
January	1,262	1,024	1,670	1,523
February	1,277	1,030	1,437	1,522
March	1,184	1,091	1,473	1,261
April	1,208	907	1,358	968
May	1,144	859	1,326	842
June	1,198	903	1,306	837
July	1,057	880	1,215	752
August	1,095	983	1,170	781
September	1,123	1,026	1,214	772
October	1,037	948	1,328	707
November	1,012	973	1,377	748
December	842	723	1,236	655

Source: Table constructed by SOURCEBOOK staff from unpublished data supplied by the U.S. Department of the Navy, Bureau of Naval Personnel and from the U.S. Department of the Navy, Bureau of Naval Personnel, *Navy-Marine Corps Prisoners, Semi-annual Statistical Report 1 July-31 December 1975* (Washington, D.C.: U.S. Department of the Navy, 1976), Chart I.

Figure 4 Rate of incarceration (per 1,000 enlisted personnel on active duty) in Navy and Marine Corps correctional facilities by month, 1975

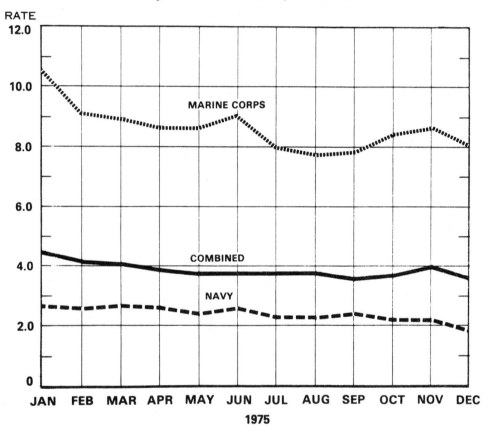

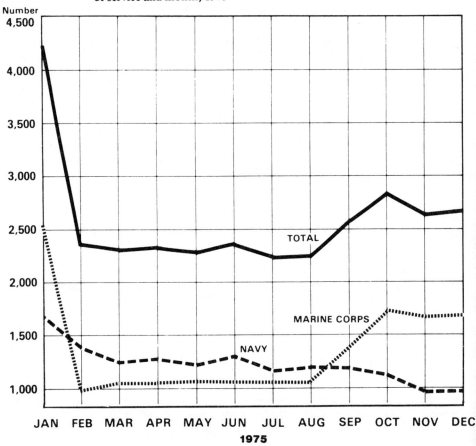

Figure 5 Admissions to Navy and Marine Corps correctional facilities, by branch of service and month, 1975

Source: U.S. Department of the Navy, Bureau of Naval Personnel, *Navy–Marine Corps Prisoners, Semi-annual Statistical Report 1 July–31 December 1975* (Washington, D.C.: U.S. Department of the Navy, 1976), Chart VIII.

Table 45 Releases and transfers of Navy prisoners from Navy and Marine Corps correctional centers, by type of offense, July 1–Dec. 31, 1975

These data include transfers to the Norfolk Correctional Center and the Federal Bureau of Prisons. For definition of offenses, see the Uniform Code of Military Justice, 10 U.S.C.A. 801–940.

Type of offense	
Military offenses:	
Desertion	11
Unauthorized absence	1,583
Missing movement	11
Disrespect, superior officer	12
Strike, or disobey order of superior officer	10
Strike, or disobey order of warrant officer, petty officer	42
Fail to obey lawful order	230
Malingering	2
Sell, dispose, damage government property	26
Wasting other property	5
Provoking words, gestures	9
General article	72
Civil-type offenses:	
Resist apprehension, break arrest	9
False official statement, sign false record	4
Operate vehicle while drunk	1
Drunk	1
Riot, breach of peace	2
Murder	1
Larceny, wrongful appropriation	132
Robbery	5
Forgery	15
Sodomy	3
Arson	3
Extortion	1
Assault	103
Burglary	1
Housebreaking	22
Perjury	2
Narcotics involvement	44
Total military offenses	2,020
Total civil-type offenses	349
Grand total	2,369

Source: U.S. Department of the Navy, Bureau of Naval Personnel, *Navy-Marine Corps Prisoners, Semi-annual Statistical Report 1 July–31 December 1975* (Washington, D.C.: U.S. Department of the Navy, 1976), Table I.

Table 46 Releases and transfers of Marine Corps prisoners from Navy and Marine Corps correctional centers, by type of offense, July 1–Dec. 31, 1975

Included are prisoners transferred to the United States Disciplinary Barracks at Fort Leavenworth, Kansas, and to the Federal Bureau of Prisons. For definition of offenses, see the Uniform Code of Military Justice, 10 U.S.C.A. 801–940.

Type of offense	
Military offenses:	
Desertion	1
Unauthorized absence	919
Disrespect, superior officer	21
Strike, or disobey order of superior officer	11
Strike, or disobey order of warrant officer, noncommissioned officer	71
Failure to obey lawful order	110
Sell, dispose, damage government property	10
Waste other property	3
Misbehavior of sentinel	12
Use provoking words, gestures	8
General article	53
Civil-type offenses:	
Resist apprehension, break arrest	7
Unlawful detention	1
False official statement, sign false record	4
Drunk	1
Riot, breach of peace	5
Murder	1
Manslaughter	1
Larceny	140
Robbery	6
Forgery	7
Sodomy	1
Arson	4
Assault	153
Burglary	1
Housebreaking	8
Perjury	1
Narcotics involvement	39
Total military offenses	1,219
Total civil-type offenses	380
Grand total	1,599

Source: U.S. Department of the Navy, Bureau of Naval Personnel, *Navy-Marine Corps Prisoners, Semi-annual Statistical Report 1 July–31 December 1975* (Washington, D.C.: U.S. Department of the Navy, 1976), Table II.

Table 47 Releases and transfers from Navy and Marine Corps correctional centers, by type of offense, Jan. 1–June 30, 1972 and July 1–Dec. 31, 1975

NOTE: See NOTES, Tables 45 and 46.

Type of offense	Number of prison releasees	
	1972	1975
Military offenses:		
Fraudulent enlistment	3	0
Desertion	35	12
Unauthorized absence	4,387	2,502
Miss movement	9	11
Contempt, disrespect	69	33
Disobey superior officer	0	21
Disobey warrant officer, petty officer	222	113
Failure to obey	213	340
Sell, damage, government property	29	36
Waste property	0	8
Misbehavior of sentinel	32	19
Malingering	0	2
Provoking words, gestures	0	17
General article	361	125
Civil-type offenses:		
Escape, resist apprehension	12	16
False official statement, sign false document	0	8
Drunk	7	2
Riot, breach of peace	18	7
Murder	0	2
Manslaughter	0	1
Larceny, wrongful appropriation	211	272
Forgery	10	22
Sodomy	4	4
Arson, extortion	7	8
Assault	142	256
Rape	2	0
Robbery	0	11
Burglary, housebreaking	2	33
Perjury, fraud	5	3
Narcotics involvement	117	83
Total military offenses	5,360	3,239
Total civil-type offenses	537	728
Grand total	5,897	3,967

Source: U.S. Department of the Navy, Bureau of Naval Personnel, *Navy-Marine Corps Prisoners, Semi-annual Statistical Report 1 July–31 December 1975* (Washington, D.C.: U.S. Department of the Navy, 1976), Table III.

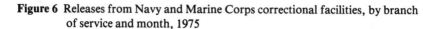

Figure 6 Releases from Navy and Marine Corps correctional facilities, by branch of service and month, 1975

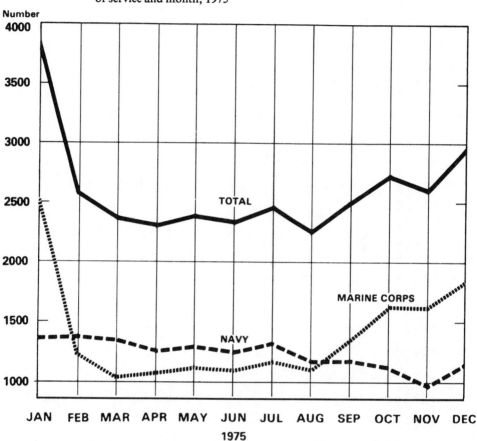

Source: U.S. Department of the Navy, Bureau of Naval Personnel, *Navy–Marine Corps Prisoners, Semi-annual Statistical Report 1 July–31 December 1975* (Washington, D.C.: U.S. Department of the Navy, 1976), Chart IX.

Table 48 Population and movement of prisoners in Federal institutions, fiscal years 1939-75[a]

NOTE: The Federal Prison System is responsible for two distinct Federal offender populations: (1) individuals who are housed in, escape from, or are in transit between the 52 Federal institutions and community treatment centers; (2) individuals who are housed in, awaiting trial in, or enroute to State, local, or private facilities that are under contract with the Federal Prison System for the housing of Federal offenders. Data in the Source only present statistics on Federal institution populations. Approximately 20 percent of the total Federal prisoner population is housed in contract facilities (Source, pp. 6, 7). Data in this report are broken down into two sets of mutually exclusive categories: (1) court commitments and other-than-court commitments; and (2) prisoners under sentence and prisoners not under sentence. The figure below presents the breakdowns within these categories. In fiscal years 1974 and 1975, persons committed for mental competency determination and mental incompetency (18 U.S.C. 4244, 4246) were included in "study and observation."

OTHER-THAN-COURT COMMITMENTS
(1) Parole violation
(2) Mandatory release violation
(3) Study and observation cases
(4) State commitments

UNDER SENTENCE
(1) Regular Adult
(2) Federal Juvenile Delinquency Act
(3) Youth Corrections Act
(4) 18 U.S.C. 4208(a)(1) and (a)(2)
(5) Narcotic Addict Rehabilitation Act
(6) Split sentence

Fiscal year ended June 30[b]	Population beginning of year	From courts	Received (transfers excluded)			Escaped prisoners returned	Other[c]
			Violators returned		Study and observation		
			Parole	Mandatory release			
1939	18,781	15,813	144	652	X	46	373
1940	20,198	15,292	184	700	X	132	10
1941	20,345	15,800	211	727	X	94	11
1942	19,956	14,994	222	730	X	115	25
1943	18,896	12,567	186	568	X	108	11
1944	16,539	13,938	226	450	X	106	9
1945	18,392	14,982	338	363	X	144	0
1946	19,987	14,832	321	367	X	174	0
1947	19,183	14,812	466	471	X	195	0
1948	18,450	12,845	499	476	X		0
1949	17,981	12,738	751	694	X	147	0
1950	17,463	14,403	710	789	X	122	0
1951	17,930	14,676	662	787	X	127	0
1952	18,417	14,823	577	547	X	134	0
1953	18,557	16,166	576	410	X	181	0
1954	19,733	17,448	657	349	X	169	0

Year							
1955	20,877	16,699	620	332	X	157	0
1956	21,606	13,971	678	364	X	113	0
1957	20,956	14,112	666	363	X	146	0
1958	21,182	13,907	732	510	X	140	0
1959	21,899	14,324	782	517	98	179	0
1960	22,838	14,210	852	555	229	196	0
1961	23,974	14,185	965	594	361	226	0
1962	24,925	13,624	1,041	597	468	324	0
1963	24,613	13,536	1,071	615	459	419	0
1964	24,248	13,220	1,031	579	429	379	0
1965	22,974	12,982	1,180	648	442	239	0
1966	22,346	12,370	1,174	595	386	256	0
1967	21,040	11,691	1,264	497	397	416	0
1968	19,815	11,653	1,408	490	396	423	0
1969	20,170	11,162	1,366	475	425	374	0
1970	20,208	11,060	1,234	399	476	493	0
1971	20,686	12,633	1,028	415	492	547	17,405
1972	20,820	13,622	1,021	326	530	565	20,441
1973	21,280	15,430	787	194	508	644	23,571
1974	23,336	15,181	774	189	1,890	561	32,556
1975	23,691	16,528	994	182	1,938	795	51,935

a Data prior to 1974 reflect sentenced prisoners only.
b From fiscal year 1970, figures include only Bureau of Prisons institutions.
c Other includes other temporary movement such as furloughs, writs, etc.
d Beginning in 1958 the term mandatory release replaces the term conditional release.

413

Table 48 (continued)

NOT UNDER
SENTENCE

(1) 18 U.S.C.
    4244 mental observation
    4246 mental incompetence
(2) Juvenile observation and study
(3) Youth observation and study
(4) Narcotic Addict Rehabilitation Act study cases

Transferred from other institutions	Discharged (transfers excluded)							Transferred to other institutions	Population end of year
	Sentence expired	Mandatorily released^d	Paroled *	Died	Study and observation	Escaped	Other^c		
3,930	5,211	7,377	2,568	104	X	65	240	3,976	20,198
3,621	4,965	7,754	2,908	99	X	138	642	3,286	20,345
4,667	5,986	8,045	2,888	121	X	109	167	4,583	19,956
3,206	6,300	7,554	2,758	106	X	84	193	3,337	18,896
2,301	4,874	6,618	3,883	69	X	106	221	2,334	16,539
2,588	4,176	5,153	3,202	73	X	101	188	2,573	18,392
3,837	4,856	4,990	3,697	66	X	102	358	3,966	19,987
3,842	4,974	5,347	4,496	69	X	152	290	4,982	19,183
3,702	5,552	4,855	5,445	54	X	193	356	3,903	18,450
3,565	4,816	5,147	3,985	47	X	218	291	3,545	17,981
2,775	5,258	5,146	3,868	50	X	137	394	2,770	17,463
3,442	5,616	5,744	3,493	37	X	138	460	3,511	17,930
3,472	5,598	6,000	3,717	52	X	152	427	3,291	18,417
4,010	9,655	2,005	3,687	42	X	160	267	4,135	18,557
4,666	9,287	2,230	4,204	60	X	223	182	4,637	19,733
5,004	10,272	2,413	4,243	55	X	185	150	5,165	20,877
4,501	9,599	2,598	4,411	47	X	170	125	4,630	21,606
4,736	8,373	2,791	4,295	33	X	134	117	4,769	20,956
5,128	6,983	3,282	4,357	49	X	155	138	5,225	21,182
5,766	6,929	3,313	4,087	50	X	176	102	5,682	18,992

6,148	7,085	3,263	4,209	54	160	201	0	6,137	22,838
8,062	6,651	3,194	4,432	54	372	197	0	8,058	23,974
6,873	6,301	3,555	4,599	49	533	242	0	6,974	24,925
7,254	6,359	3,757	5,195	45	699	346	0	7,219	24,613
7,811	6,376	3,740	5,083	57	721	490	0	7,809	24,248
7,518	6,283	3,788	5,590	68	196	383	0	7,522	22,974
7,230	6,232	3,652	5,131	64	886	229	0	7,155	22,346
7,617	5,962	3,368	5,575	57	792	343	0	7,587	21,040
7,804	4,970	3,080	6,181	60	673	527	0	7,796	19,822
7,859	4,490	2,739	5,151	44	667	480	0	8,272	20,170
8,168	4,237	2,398	4,758	44	629	406	0	9,460	20,208
9,342	4,167	2,625	4,106	35	729	640	0	10,224	20,686
10,720	5,184	2,649	4,757	56	577	652	17,561	11,670	20,820
11,868	5,336	2,562	4,802	65	636	648	20,733	13,131	21,280
11,929	5,416	2,204	4,999	51	503	711	23,960	14,063	22,436
11,933	5,184	2,089	4,908	64	1,915	725	33,184	14,657	23,691
12,228	6,002	1,910	6,142	55	1,908	655	51,510	16,643	23,566

* Includes discharges of Selective Service Act violators paroled under the provisions of Executive Order No. 8641 as follows: 1941–11; 1942–32; 1943–266; 1944–493; 1945–719; 1946–126; 1947–151.

Source: U.S. Department of Justice, Federal Prison System, *Statistical Report, Fiscal Year 1975* (Washington, D.C.: Federal Prison System, 1977), p. 25.

415

Figure 7 Admissions, releases, and end-of-year population of sentenced prisoners in Federal institutions, fiscal years 1965–75

NOTE: "Admissions" include commitments from Federal courts, offenders returned from study and observation, probation violators, District of Columbia Code violators, and commitments from military courts. "Releases" refer to parole, mandatory, and expiration releases, including both first releases and rereleases. "First release" represents the first discharge (parole, mandatory release, expiration, etc.) from confinement. "Rerelease" includes a discharge (parole, mandatory release, expiration, etc.) of one who has previously been released on this sentence and returned for violation of parole or mandatory release.

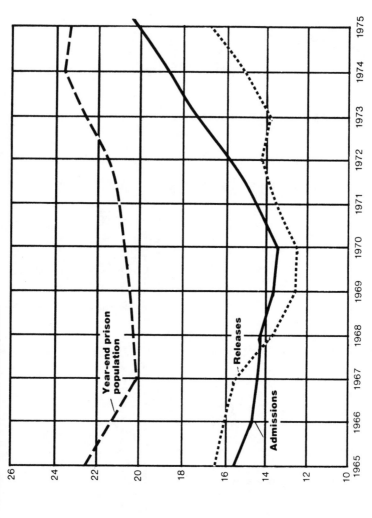

Fiscal years

Number (in Thousands)

Source: U.S. Department of Justice, Federal Prison System, *Statistical Report, Fiscal Year 1975* (Washington, D.C.: Federal Prison System, 1977), p. 11.

Figure 8 Types of releases from Federal institutions (percent of total releases), fiscal years 1965–75

[Transfers excluded]

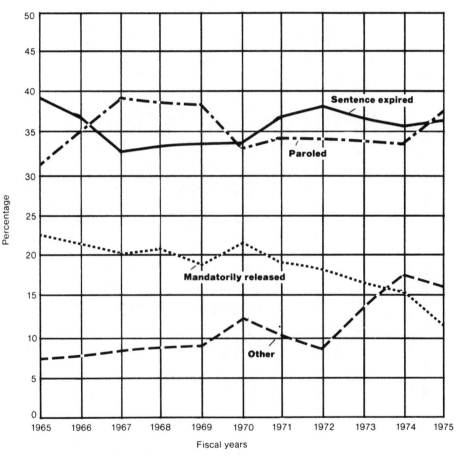

Source: U.S. Department of Justice, Federal Prison System, *Statistical Report, Fiscal Year 1975* (Washington, D.C.: Federal Prison System, 1977), p. 14.

417

Table 49 Number of, and average sentence for, sentence prisoners received by Federal institutions, by offense, race, and sex, fiscal year 1975

Offense	All prisoners			Sentenced prisoners								Youth Corrections Act	
				White				All other					
	Total	Male	Female	Number	Average sentence	Male	Female	Number	Average sentence	Male	Female	Male	Female
Total	16,910	15,828	1,082	11,756	43.9	11,216	540	5,154	67.8	4,612	542	1,797	185
Total excluding immigration and violent crimes [a]	12,402	11,449	953	8,534	42.4	8,065	469	3,868	46.2	3,384	484	1,361	160
Assault	54	53	1	25	53.3	25	0	29	65.6	28	1	7	0
Bankruptcy	4	4	0	4	25.5	4	0	0	X	0	0	0	0
Burglary	151	148	3	75	68.3	74	1	76	59.2	74	2	35	3
Counterfeiting	347	332	15	288	45.9	276	12	59	36.4	56	3	29	3
Drug laws, total	4,242	3,963	279	3,268	48.1	3,079	189	974	63.8	884	90	529	41
Non-narcotics	1,243	1,161	82	1,174	34.7	1,105	69	69	49.8	56	13	158	16
Narcotics	2,460	2,313	147	1,667	62.7	1,585	82	793	69.5	728	65	301	18
Controlled substances	539	489	50	427	28.0	389	38	112	32.5	100	12	70	7
Embezzlement	249	207	42	179	27.3	152	27	70	29.3	55	15	18	7
Escape, flight or harboring a fugitive	115	105	10	94	31.6	87	7	21	43.2	18	3	7	2
Extortion	105	97	8	89	74.5	81	8	16	51.8	16	0	11	3
Firearms	981	962	19	638	35.7	628	10	343	33.3	334	9	104	3
Forgery	779	634	145	322	39.8	275	47	457	38.4	359	98	83	34
Fraud	464	431	33	367	30.0	347	20	97	31.6	84	13	18	4
Immigration	2,313	2,279	34	2,285	7.2	2,251	34	28	12.6	28	0	6	1
Income tax	225	220	5	184	13.4	179	5	41	28.1	41	0	0	0
Juvenile delinquency	249	228	21	157	33.1	144	13	92	37.5	84	8	0	0
Kidnaping	115	109	6	89	242.0	84	5	26	254.3	25	1	13	3
Larceny/theft, total	2,752	2,515	237	1,753	42.9	1,694	59	999	36.3	821	178	361	35
Motor vehicle, interstate	1,169	1,158	11	941	44.5	931	10	228	45.1	227	1	202	2
Postal	779	581	198	263	31.0	225	38	516	31.6	356	160	78	27
Theft, interstate	304	303	1	223	50.2	222	1	81	34.5	81	0	25	0
Other	500	473	27	326	43.2	316	10	174	39.5	157	17	56	6

Liquor laws	159	157	2	113	19.4	112	1	46	16.1	45	1	3	0
National security laws	7	7	0	6	21.0	6	0	1	36.0	1	0	0	0
Robbery	1,603	1,548	55	718	132.7	691	27	885	134.6	857	28	310	13
Selective Service Acts	33	31	2	26	20.4	24	2	7	32.6	7	0	3	0
Securities, transporting false or forged	437	386	51	294	50.7	266	28	143	48.0	120	23	39	7
White slave traffic	46	39	7	15	46.7	13	2	31	47.2	26	5	1	4
Other and unclassifiable	647	607	40	528	30.2	503	25	119	40.9	104	15	35	8
Government reservation, high seas, territorial, and District of Columbia	812	747	65	235	116.2	217	18	577	102.4	530	47	184	14
Assault	113	100	13	27	69.1	25	2	86	54.8	75	11	22	4
Auto theft	17	17	0	8	36.4	8	0	9	55.1	9	0	6	0
Burglary	88	85	3	20	88.5	20	0	68	66.1	65	3	29	1
Forgery	23	15	8	5	48.0	4	1	18	80.3	11	7	2	1
Homicide	112	103	9	35	320.1	35	0	77	236.9	68	9	12	1
Larceny/theft	127	119	8	46	67.5	43	3	81	60.2	76	5	31	1
Robbery	156	145	11	30	127.4	27	3	126	131.7	118	8	58	3
Rape	42	42	0	13	215.8	13	0	29	111.9	29	0	8	0
Sex offenses, except rape	9	9	0	3	132.0	3	0	6	78.0	6	0	3	0
Other and unclassifiable	125	112	13	48	37.5	39	9	77	58.8	73	4	13	3
Military court-martial cases	21	19	2	4	37.5	4	0	17	156.2	15	2	1	0

a This total line excludes the immigration law and violent crime offenses whose unusual sentence lengths distort the average sentence length statistics.

Source: U.S. Department of Justice, Federal Prison System, *Statistical Report, Fiscal Year 1975* (Washington, D.C.: Federal Prison System, 1977), pp. 51, 52.

Table 50 Number of, and average sentence for, Federal prisoners received from court into Federal institutions, by offense, race, and sex, fiscal year 1975

"Average sentence" is in months.

[Population 16,555. Data complete on 92.9 percent of the population.]

Offense	All prisoners			Sentenced prisoners								Youth Corrections Act	
				White				All other					
	Total	Male	Female	Number	Average sentence	Male	Female	Number	Average sentence	Male	Female	Male	Female
Total	15,372	14,415	957	10,753	42.1	10,277	476	4,619	67.6	4,138	481	1,567	163
Total excluding immigration and violent crimes [a]	11,196	10,356	840	7,707	41.7	7,297	410	3,489	45.1	3,059	430	1,168	139
Assault	46	45	1	19	60.7	19	0	27	70.4	26	1	5	0
Bankruptcy	4	4	0	4	25.5	4	0	0	X	0	0	0	0
Burglary	128	125	3	61	66.6	60	1	67	63.0	65	2	30	3
Counterfeiting	306	294	12	255	46.0	245	10	51	34.0	49	2	25	3
Drug laws, total	3,989	3,733	256	3,073	47.9	2,901	172	916	63.8	832	84	501	39
Non-narcotics	1,176	1,099	77	1,109	34.1	1,045	64	67	44.8	54	13	148	15
Narcotics	2,299	2,168	131	1,557	63.0	1,486	71	742	70.0	682	60	286	17
Controlled substances	514	466	48	407	27.4	370	37	107	32.6	96	11	67	7
Embezzlement	232	197	35	167	27.9	144	23	65	29.6	53	12	15	7
Escape, flight or harboring a fugitive	98	89	9	80	21.3	73	7	18	41.6	16	2	6	2
Extortion	98	90	8	83	79.9	75	8	15	55.2	15	0	11	3
Firearms	909	893	16	585	38.0	576	9	324	33.2	317	7	96	2
Forgery	679	556	123	284	38.9	243	41	395	35.0	313	82	68	26
Fraud	429	401	28	339	30.9	323	16	90	32.1	78	12	16	3
Immigration	2,306	2,273	33	2,279	7.1	2,246	33	27	13.0	27	0	6	1
Income tax	224	220	4	183	13.4	179	4	41	28.1	41	0	0	0
Juvenile delinquency	216	197	19	137	31.3	124	13	79	35.8	73	6	0	0
Kidnaping	98	93	5	74	258.2	69	5	24	275.5	24	0	13	3
Larceny/theft, total	2,352	2,139	213	1,466	42.0	1,413	53	886	34.8	726	160	265	30
Motor vehicle, interstate	935	924	11	749	41.9	739	10	186	43.9	185	1	127	2
Postal	699	522	177	226	30.5	193	33	473	30.7	329	144	66	23
Theft, interstate	278	277	1	206	51.8	205	1	72	34.4	72	0	23	0
Other	440	416	24	285	44.2	276	9	155	36.4	140	15	49	5

Offense													
Liquor laws	153	151	2	109	18.4	108	1	44	13.9	43	1	1	0
National security laws	6	6	0	6	21.0	6	0	0	X	0	0	0	0
Robbery	1,384	1,337	47	599	139.1	576	23	785	140.8	761	24	288	13
Selective Service Acts	29	27	2	23	21.5	21	2	6	26.0	6	0	2	0
Securities, transporting false or forged	363	323	40	238	48.1	218	20	125	47.7	105	20	34	6
White slave traffic	41	35	6	12	47.3	11	1	29	48.4	24	5	0	4
Other and unclassifiable	613	577	36	497	28.8	475	22	116	41.3	102	14	31	7
Government reservation, high seas, territorial, and District of Columbia	652	595	57	178	90.5	166	12	474	100.1	429	45	154	11
Assault	91	79	12	19	32.5	17	2	72	52.6	62	10	17	3
Auto theft	15	15	0	6	36.5	6	0	9	55.1	9	0	5	0
Burglary	76	73	3	16	64.1	16	0	60	63.0	57	3	26	1
Forgery	20	12	8	4	42.0	3	1	16	79.1	9	7	1	1
Homicide	89	80	9	22	264.3	22	0	67	230.1	58	9	12	1
Larceny/theft	105	99	6	37	43.6	36	1	68	57.4	63	5	24	1
Robbery	128	118	10	24	118.5	21	3	104	132.1	97	7	50	3
Rape	34	34	0	10	248.1	10	0	24	115.3	24	0	8	0
Sex offenses, except rape	8	8	0	2	138.0	2	0	6	78.0	6	0	3	0
Other and unclassifiable	86	77	9	38	27.5	33	5	48	38.0	44	4	8	1
Military court-martial cases	17	15	2	2	39.0	2	0	15	169.5	13	2	0	0

a This total line excludes the immigration law and violent crime offenses whose unusual sentence lengths distort the average sentence length statistic.

Source: U.S. Department of Justice, Federal Prison System, *Statistical Report, Fiscal Year 1975* (Washington D.C.: Federal Prison System, 1977), pp. 49, 50.

421

Table 51 Number of, and average sentence for, Federal prisoners received from court into Federal institutions, by offense, sex, and sentencing procedure, fiscal year 1975

Offense	All court commitments				Sentencing procedure							
	Total	Male	Female	Average sentence (months)	Regular	Federal Juvenile Delinquency Act	Youth Corrections Act	Title 18, U.S. Code, 4208(a)		Split sentence	Narcotic Addict Rehabilitation Act
								(a)(1)	(a)(2)		
Total	15,397	14,438	959	49.9	8,590	217	1,731	166	2,925	1,584	184
Assault	46	45	1	66.4	28	0	5	1	5	7	0
Bankruptcy	4	4	0	25.5	4	0	0	0	0	0	0
Burglary	134	131	3	63.3	43	6	33	0	42	7	3
Counterfeiting	308	296	12	44.0	150	3	28	4	88	33	2
Drug laws, total	4,052	3,789	263	51.3	2,062	41	541	36	767	526	79
Non-narcotics	1,209	1,132	77	34.5	540	22	163	8	185	283	8
Narcotics	2,323	2,185	138	65.1	1,248	15	304	24	524	142	66
Controlled substances	520	472	48	28.5	274	4	74	4	58	101	5
Embezzlement	232	197	35	28.5	86	0	22	6	54	64	0
Escape, flight or harboring a fugitive	100	91	9	24.9	67	2	8	1	13	9	0
Extortion	98	90	8	76.1	51	0	14	1	26	6	0
Firearms	908	892	16	36.5	492	4	98	6	217	86	5
Forgery	689	562	127	36.7	385	9	94	3	124	66	8
Fraud	428	400	28	31.5	200	0	19	4	109	95	1
Immigration	2,336	2,303	33	7.2	2,147	15	7	0	63	104	0
Income tax	221	217	4	16.3	123	0	0	1	22	75	0
Kidnaping	99	94	5	260.5	50	2	16	2	29	0	0
Larceny/theft, total	2,404	2,186	218	39.2	1,287	51	295	16	498	233	24
Motor vehicle, interstate	963	951	12	42.1	525	30	129	7	205	60	3
Postal	712	531	181	30.7	393	11	89	7	132	66	14
Theft, interstate	283	282	1	47.1	143	5	23	0	66	46	0
Other	446	422	24	41.5	222	5	54	2	95	61	7

Offense										
Liquor laws	155	153	2	17.4	99	1	1	0	18	36	0
National security laws	6	6	0	21.0	3	0	0	0	2	1	0
Robbery	1,405	1,356	49	138.8	478	20	301	20	547	22	17
Selective Service Acts	29	27	2	22.4	15	0	2	0	3	9	0
Securities, transporting false or forged	368	326	42	48.5	199	2	40	6	94	23	4
White slave traffic	41	35	6	48.1	24	0	4	0	11	1	1
Other and unclassifiable	620	583	37	31.3	273	9	38	9	127	160	4
Government reservation, high seas, territorial, and District of Columbia	697	640	57	94.0	308	52	165	50	65	21	36
Assault	101	89	12	46.8	52	10	20	4	11	2	2
Auto theft	16	16	0	45.4	7	1	5	2	0	1	0
Burglary	89	86	3	60.4	21	13	27	5	4	3	16
Forgery	21	13	8	70.5	6	1	2	2	2	0	8
Homicide	88	79	9	241.3	46	0	13	10	16	2	1
Larceny/theft	112	106	6	51.9	56	7	25	7	7	6	4
Robbery	135	125	10	125.2	47	9	53	11	13	0	2
Rape	39	39	0	141.4	15	6	8	2	5	3	0
Sex offenses, except rape	7	7	0	106.3	2	0	3	0	2	0	0
Other and unclassifiable	89	80	9	33.8	56	5	9	7	5	4	3
Military court-martial cases	17	15	2	154.1	16	0	0	0	1	0	0

Source: U.S. Department of Justice, Federal Prison System, Statistical Report, Fiscal Year 1975 (Washington, D.C.: Federal Prison System, 1977), pp. 85, 86.

Table 52 Number of, and average sentence for, Federal prisoners received from court into Federal institutions, by offense and number of prior commitments, fiscal year 1975

"Average sentence" is in months.

[Population 16,555. Data complete on 93.2 percent of the population.]

| Offense | Grand total | | With known prior commitments | | | | | | | | Without known prior commitments | | Not reported |
| | | | Total | | With one | | With two | | With three or more | | None | | |
	Number	Average sentence	Number	Average sentence	Number	Average sentence	Number	Average sentence	Number	Average sentence	Number	Average sentence	
Total	15,431	49.8	5,459	63.5	2,086	59.7	1,207	63.0	2,166	67.4	6,490	48.6	3,482
Assault	46	66.4	21	81.5	7	82.3	3	128.0	11	68.3	18	40.6	7
Bankruptcy	4	25.5	1	24.0	1	24.0	0	X	0	X	2	36.0	1
Burglary	128	64.7	69	61.5	21	63.6	18	51.7	30	65.9	38	75.6	21
Counterfeiting	306	44.0	132	47.8	48	41.0	26	44.2	58	55.0	120	42.6	54
Drug laws, total	4,012	51.5	952	62.4	464	60.9	206	58.5	282	67.7	2,265	52.9	795
Non-narcotics	1,187	34.5	192	44.9	114	41.8	36	51.1	42	48.2	718	37.1	277
Narcotics	2,309	65.3	641	72.7	293	73.4	141	62.7	207	78.5	1,311	65.1	357
Controlled substances	516	28.7	119	35.2	57	34.8	29	47.7	33	24.9	236	33.2	161
Embezzlement	233	28.4	34	31.3	18	30.9	9	24.0	7	41.9	143	29.7	56
Escape, flight or harboring a fugitive	98	25.0	47	24.6	13	25.2	13	31.4	21	20.0	31	26.1	20
Extortion	98	76.1	32	81.8	16	82.9	6	117.0	10	58.8	53	77.7	13
Firearms	909	36.3	527	35.5	169	34.5	126	36.9	232	35.6	247	42.4	135
Forgery	681	36.5	363	37.7	146	36.6	72	34.9	145	40.1	196	38.7	122
Fraud	431	31.3	107	37.8	36	44.3	31	36.2	40	33.2	211	31.7	113
Immigration	2,321	7.2	294	15.8	160	13.2	48	16.8	86	20.1	926	7.6	1,101
Income tax	224	16.1	26	27.0	12	20.6	7	29.3	7	35.7	126	13.7	72
Juvenile delinquency	217	32.9	49	35.4	34	36.8	7	34.9	8	30.0	142	32.4	26
Kidnaping	98	262.4	47	281.4	17	230.1	9	300.0	21	314.0	42	221.7	9
Larceny/theft, total	2,356	39.2	1,268	42.1	376	38.5	280	45.0	612	43.0	690	39.2	398
Motor vehicle, interstate	936	42.3	574	46.1	130	45.0	127	49.6	317	45.1	229	37.6	133
Postal	701	30.6	370	32.3	133	31.0	77	32.7	160	33.2	193	32.8	138
Theft, interstate	278	47.3	117	50.3	41	44.2	25	50.4	51	55.1	101	52.0	60
Other	441	41.5	207	44.3	72	37.6	51	49.5	84	46.8	167	41.3	67

424

Liquor laws	154	17.4	85	20.6	33	16.4	23	21.3	29	24.8	58	12.8	11
National security laws	6	21.0	4	15.0	0	X	0	X	4	15.0	2	33.0	0
Robbery	1,387	140.1	720	154.1	250	150.3	164	145.6	306	161.7	501	123.9	166
Selective Service Acts	29	22.4	2	54.0	1	36.0	1	72.0	0	X	15	21.5	12
Securities, transporting false or forged	367	48.4	201	49.7	64	48.2	48	49.7	89	50.7	104	46.6	62
White slave traffic	41	48.1	16	50.6	7	58.3	4	49.5	5	40.8	20	50.4	5
Other and unclassifiable	613	31.2	187	41.1	74	36.9	46	41.9	67	45.2	278	28.7	148
Government reservation, high seas, territorial, and District of Columbia	655	97.1	270	103.4	116	90.9	60	107.0	94	116.7	251	97.4	134
Assault	91	48.4	34	54.8	13	56.9	8	64.5	13	46.6	35	48.4	22
Auto theft	15	47.7	6	35.7	4	32.5	2	42.0	0	X	6	41.5	3
Burglary	77	62.9	34	64.2	13	54.5	11	78.5	10	61.2	26	65.4	17
Forgery	20	71.7	8	78.0	5	91.2	1	36.0	2	66.0	7	55.6	5
Homicide	89	238.6	34	261.7	14	228.0	10	222.6	10	348.0	40	217.2	15
Larceny/theft	106	52.2	45	61.3	19	69.2	5	51.0	21	56.7	43	58.4	18
Robbery	128	129.5	56	130.1	25	117.7	15	124.8	16	154.5	50	118.0	22
Rape	34	154.3	9	226.7	3	72.0	2	120.0	4	396.0	18	141.0	7
Sex offenses, except rape	8	93.0	4	114.0	2	90.0	1	36.0	1	240.0	4	72.0	0
Other and unclassifiable	87	33.0	40	40.2	18	36.8	5	58.2	17	38.4	22	22.4	25
Military court-martial cases	17	154.1	5	157.2	3	194.0	0	X	2	102.0	11	159.6	1

Source: U.S. Department of Justice, Federal Prison System, *Statistical Report, Fiscal Year 1975* (Washington, D.C.: Federal Prison System, 1977), pp. 59, 60.

Table 53 Federal prisoners received from court into Federal institutions, by age and offense, fiscal year 1975

[Population 16,555. Data complete on 93.2 percent of population.]

Age at commitment	All offenses		Drug laws				Controlled substance	
			Non-narcotics		Narcotics			
	Number	Percent	Number	Percent	Number	Percent	Number	Percent
Median age	28.1	X	26.2	X	28.5	X	26.2	X
Total	15,431	100.0	1,187	100.0	2,309	100.0	516	100.0
Age 21 and under	2,641	17.1	220	18.5	212	9.2	84	16.3
17 and under	292	1.9	13	1.1	12	.5	1	.2
18	305	2.0	23	1.9	2	.1	6	1.2
19	575	3.7	53	4.5	43	1.9	24	4.7
20	680	4.4	56	4.7	55	2.4	26	5.0
21	789	5.1	75	6.3	100	4.3	27	5.2
Age 22 through 25	3,474	22.5	356	30.0	583	25.2	166	32.2
22	804	5.2	87	7.3	122	5.3	31	6.0
23	910	5.9	80	6.7	141	6.1	55	10.7
24	935	6.1	97	8.2	166	7.2	44	8.5
25	825	5.3	92	7.8	154	6.7	36	7.0
Age 26 and over	9,316	60.4	611	51.5	1,514	65.6	266	51.6
26 through 29	2,962	19.2	263	22.2	565	24.5	109	21.1
30 through 34	2,324	15.1	152	12.8	388	16.8	76	14.7
35 through 39	1,385	9.0	99	8.3	219	9.5	29	5.6
40 through 44	1,067	6.9	50	4.2	160	6.9	26	5.0
45 through 49	693	4.5	18	1.5	89	3.9	12	2.3
50 through 54	454	2.9	20	1.7	53	2.3	11	2.1
55 through 59	227	1.5	7	.6	20	.9	2	.4
60 through 64	141	.9	2	.2	16	.7	0	X
65 through 69	48	.3	0	X	3	.1	1	.2
70 and over	15	.1	0	X	1	X	0	X

Table 53 (continued)

Age at commitment	Forgery		Immigration		Transportation of stolen motor vehicle		Other larceny		Federal Juvenile Delinquency Act	
	Number	Percent	Number	Percent	Number	Percent	Number	Percent	Number	Percent
Median age	27.9	X	26.9	X	29.1	X	28.2	X	17.0	X
Total	681	100.0	2,475	100.0	936	100.0	1,420	100.0	217	100.0
Age 21 and under	98	14.4	574	23.2	156	16.7	232	16.3	213	98.2
17 and under	5	.7	53	2.1	6	.6	12	.8	141	65.0
18	3	.4	90	3.6	13	1.4	21	1.5	57	26.3
19	19	2.8	131	5.3	43	4.6	44	3.1	12	5.5
20	28	4.1	150	6.1	45	4.8	81	5.7	3	1.4
21	43	6.3	150	6.1	49	5.2	74	5.2	0	X
Age 22 through 25	162	23.8	557	22.5	180	19.2	329	23.2	2	.9
22	36	5.3	141	5.7	43	4.6	86	6.1	0	X
23	47	6.9	152	6.1	62	6.6	74	5.2	0	X
24	41	8.0	153	6.2	33	3.5	82	5.8	1	.5
25	38	5.6	111	4.5	42	4.5	87	6.1	1	.5
Age 26 and over	421	61.8	1,344	54.3	600	64.1	859	60.5	2	.9
26 through 29	164	24.1	430	17.4	166	17.7	268	18.9	1	.5
30 through 34	89	13.1	364	14.7	165	17.6	192	13.5	1	.5
35 through 39	67	9.8	223	9.0	95	10.1	134	9.4	0	X
40 through 44	28	4.1	152	6.1	85	9.1	122	8.6	0	X
45 through 49	40	5.9	90	3.6	46	4.9	77	5.4	0	X
50 through 54	16	2.3	40	1.6	34	3.6	39	2.7	0	X
55 through 59	10	1.5	25	1.0	4	.4	18	1.3	0	X
60 through 64	3	.4	16	.6	3	.3	5	.4	0	X
65 through 69	2	.3	4	.2	1	.1	3	.2	0	X
70 and over	2	.3	0	X	1	.1	1	.1	0	X

427

Table 54 Federal prisoners received from court into Federal institutions, by age and offense, fiscal year 1974

[Population 16,555. Data complete on 93.2 percent of population.]

Age at commitment	Selective Service violators		Robbery		Securities interstate		Government reservations		All other offenses	
	Number	Percent	Number	Percent	Number	Percent	Number	Percent	Number	Percent
Median age	26.2	X	26.3	X	30.6	X	24.8	X	32.5	X
Total	29	100.0	1,387	100.0	367	100.0	655	100.0	3,252	100.0
Age 21 and under	2	6.9	276	19.9	30	8.2	210	32.1	334	10.3
17 and under	0	X	12	.9	6	1.6	11	1.7	20	.6
18	0	X	26	1.9	2	.5	33	5.0	29	.9
19	1	3.4	57	4.1	6	1.6	61	9.3	81	2.5
20	0	X	89	6.4	9	2.5	56	8.5	82	2.5
21	1	3.4	92	6.6	7	1.9	49	7.5	122	3.8
Age 22 through 25	12	41.4	391	28.2	72	19.6	168	25.6	496	15.3
22	3	10.3	81	5.8	18	4.9	38	5.8	118	3.6
23	2	6.9	107	7.7	19	5.2	38	5.8	133	4.1
24	7	24.1	122	8.8	18	4.9	50	7.6	121	3.7
25	0	X	81	5.8	17	4.6	42	6.4	124	3.8
Age 26 and over	15	51.7	720	51.9	265	72.2	277	42.3	2,422	74.5
26 through 29	9	31.0	283	20.4	73	19.9	118	18.0	513	15.8
30 through 34	4	13.8	197	14.2	69	18.8	78	11.9	549	16.9
35 through 39	0	X	95	6.8	32	8.7	24	3.7	368	11.3
40 through 44	1	3.4	69	5.0	36	9.8	19	2.9	319	9.8
45 through 49	1	3.4	33	2.4	19	5.2	15	2.3	253	7.8
50 through 54	0	X	26	1.9	19	5.2	12	1.8	184	5.7
55 through 59	0	X	9	.6	13	3.5	6	.9	113	3.5
60 through 64	0	X	4	.3	3	.8	1	.2	88	2.7
65 through 69	0	X	2	.1	1	.3	3	.5	28	.9
70 and over	0	X	2	.1	0	X	1	.2	7	.2

Source: U.S. Department of Justice, Federal Prison System, *Statistical Report, Fiscal Year 1975* (Washington, D.C.: Federal Prison System, 1977), pp. 55, 56.

429

Table 55 Number of, and average sentence for, Federal prisoners received from court into Federal institutions, by age, race, and number of prior commitments, fiscal year 1975

Average sentence" is in months.

[Population 16,555. Data complete on 92.6 percent of the population.]

Age and race	Grand total		With known prior commitments								Without known prior commitments		
			Total		With one		With two		With three or more		None		Not reported
	Number	Average sentence	Number	Average sentence	Number	Average sentence	Number	Average sentence	Number	Average sentence	Number	Average sentence	
All prisoners	15,336	49.9	5,429	63.7	2,077	60.2	1,198	63.3	2,154	67.4	6,470	48.7	3,437
Native born	13,592	53.5	5,058	66.5	1,867	64.1	1,129	65.5	2,062	69.1	5,097	56.2	3,437
Foreign born	1,744	22.0	371	26.3	210	25.2	69	27.1	92	28.3	1,373	20.9	0
White	10,715	42.2	3,148	57.9	1,199	51.9	686	57.6	1,263	63.8	4,817	42.2	2,750
Negro	4,413	68.3	2,203	71.9	845	72.1	493	71.3	865	72.1	1,558	68.5	652
American Indian	174	54.2	74	64.4	31	53.5	18	62.7	25	79.0	71	53.7	29
Other	34	74.2	4	118.5	2	120.0	1	54.0	1	180.0	24	70.7	6
Age 17 and under	169	45.0	39	45.3	31	46.2	5	51.6	3	28.3	102	50.3	28
White	107	32.3	23	39.1	20	40.8	2	30.0	1	24.0	65	34.7	19
Negro	43	72.8	11	57.4	7	61.9	3	66.0	1	X	25	86.0	7
American Indian	19	53.4	5	47.4	4	45.5	0	X	1	55.0	12	60.1	2
Other	0	X	0	X	0	X	0	X	0	X	0	X	0
Age 18 through 21	2,346	50.8	549	63.3	311	62.5	130	62.6	108	66.4	1,290	55.6	507
White	1,639	41.2	295	52.4	161	49.1	72	59.8	62	52.3	918	48.0	426
Negro	655	75.0	246	76.6	148	76.9	55	67.5	43	87.4	334	76.8	75
American Indian	48	47.4	8	54.0	2	72.0	3	40.0	3	56.0	34	48.6	6
Other	4	66.0	0	X	0	X	0	X	0	X	4	66.0	0
Age 22 through 25	3,484	53.8	1,066	70.3	512	66.7	269	69.9	285	77.1	1,695	54.0	723
White	2,293	42.1	535	57.9	275	53.6	125	59.5	135	65.1	1,192	45.3	571
Negro	1,138	77.2	513	83.4	230	83.6	136	81.0	147	85.4	482	75.2	143
American Indian	41	56.5	18	67.2	7	32.3	8	43.5	3	212.0	14	70.5	9
Other	7	49.0	0	X	0	X	0	X	0	X	7	49.0	0

Age 26 through 29	2,966	49.7	1,140	61.5	455	56.6	279	67.0	406	63.1	1,167	48.1	659
White	1,923	40.8	574	54.2	221	46.1	160	55.6	193	62.2	844	41.4	505
Negro	1,014	66.6	549	69.2	226	66.2	115	83.2	208	64.7	315	66.2	150
American Indian	22	44.6	14	49.3	6	57.0	3	60.0	5	33.6	4	18.8	4
Other	7	87.0	3	98.0	2	120.0	1	54.0	0	X	4	78.6	0
Age 30 through 39	3,724	49.7	1,529	65.3	471	61.0	335	58.4	723	71.3	1,293	43.1	902
White	2,663	43.1	939	60.7	294	55.1	199	54.8	446	67.0	1,011	38.5	713
Negro	1,023	66.0	569	71.8	167	70.7	132	61.8	270	77.3	272	60.1	182
American Indian	31	77.5	21	94.0	10	72.6	4	120.0	7	109.7	6	43.0	4
Other	7	64.3	0	X	0	X	0	X	0	X	4	36.0	3
Age 40 and over	2,647	44.9	1,106	58.4	297	52.2	180	57.9	629	61.5	923	38.1	618
White	2,085	43.9	782	60.0	228	54.3	128	62.0	426	62.5	787	36.7	516
Negro	540	48.3	315	54.9	67	46.1	52	47.8	196	59.8	130	42.2	95
American Indian	13	34.0	8	27.5	2	20.0	0	X	6	30.0	1	120.0	4
Other	9	95.3	1	180.0	0	X	0	X	1	180.0	5	126.0	3

Source: U.S. Department of Justice, Federal Prison System, Statistical Report, Fiscal Year 1975 (Washington, D.C.: Federal Prison System, 1977), pp. 57, 58.

Table 56 Federal prisoners received from court into Federal institutions, by age, length of sentence, sentencing procedure, and race, fiscal year 1975

[Population 16,555. Data complete on 91.8 percent of the population.]

Age and length of sentence	Total	Sentencing procedure							
		Regular				Federal Juvenile Delinquency Act			
		White	Negro	American Indian	Other	White	Negro	American Indian	Other
Total	15,196	7,373	2,526	89	14	136	55	23	0
Under 18	168	15	1	0	0	90	33	16	0
1 year and under	29	14	0	0	0	12	2	1	0
Over 1 year under 2 years	8	0	0	0	0	7	0	1	0
2 years to 2.5 years	23	0	0	0	0	17	3	3	0
Over 2.5 years under 5 years	83	0	0	0	0	49	24	10	0
5 years under 10 years	16	0	0	0	0	5	4	1	0
10 years under 15 years	5	1	0	0	0	0	0	0	0
15 years under 20 years	1	0	0	0	0	0	0	0	0
20 and over	2	0	1	0	0	0	0	0	0
Life	1	0	0	0	0	0	0	0	0
18 to 21	2,334	932	214	17	1	43	21	7	0
1 year and under	854	738	91	8	0	8	1	2	0
Over 1 year under 2 years	66	35	10	1	0	8	3	1	0
2 years to 2.5 years	122	50	24	3	0	10	7	2	0
Over 2.5 years under 5 years	146	46	28	3	0	17	10	2	0
5 years under 10 years	944	35	19	1	1	0	0	0	0
10 years under 15 years	96	14	10	1	0	0	0	0	0
15 years under 20 years	71	12	17	0	0	0	0	0	0
20 and over	33	2	14	0	0	0	0	0	0
Life	2	0	1	0	0	0	0	0	0
22 to 25	3,462	1,486	570	25	2	1	1	0	0
1 year and under	1,152	907	195	13	1	1	1	0	0
Over 1 year under 2 years	141	69	40	2	1	0	0	0	0
2 years to 2.5 years	302	154	63	2	0	0	0	0	0
Over 2.5 years under 5 years	404	175	94	6	0	0	0	0	0
5 years under 10 years	1,075	134	71	0	0	0	0	0	0
10 years under 15 years	167	19	28	1	0	0	0	0	0
15 years under 20 years	112	12	41	0	0	0	0	0	0
20 and over	93	10	33	0	0	0	0	0	0
Life	16	6	5	1	0	0	0	0	0

26 to 29	2,936	1,424	668	14	2	1	0	0	0
1 year and under	991	746	210	3	1	0	0	0	0
Over 1 year under 2 years	142	63	47	3	0	0	0	0	0
2 years to 2.5 years	366	182	78	4	1	1	0	0	0
Over 2.5 years under 5 years	589	222	131	1	0	0	0	0	0
5 years under 10 years	468	135	93	0	0	0	0	0	0
10 years under 15 years	181	43	36	0	0	0	0	0	0
15 years under 20 years	100	14	37	0	0	0	0	0	0
20 and over	84	15	29	0	0	0	0	0	0
Life	15	4	7	0	0	0	0	0	0
30 to 39	3,688	1,987	667	23	3	1	0	0	0
1 year and under	1,169	948	183	4	1	0	0	0	0
Over 1 year under 2 years	182	83	49	1	0	0	0	0	0
2 years to 2.5 years	466	241	79	7	0	1	0	0	0
Over 2.5 years under 5 years	742	308	141	4	1	0	0	0	0
5 years under 10 years	658	249	120	1	1	0	0	0	0
10 years under 15 years	242	86	38	4	0	0	0	0	0
15 years under 20 years	106	33	28	0	0	0	0	0	0
20 and over	111	35	21	2	0	0	0	0	0
Life	12	4	8	0	0	0	0	0	0
40 and over	2,608	1,529	406	10	6	0	0	0	0
1 year and under	941	757	149	2	0	0	0	0	0
Over 1 year under 2 years	151	91	26	0	0	0	0	0	0
2 years to 2.5 years	307	170	47	3	3	0	0	0	0
Over 2.5 years under 5 years	500	222	74	4	0	0	0	0	0
5 years under 10 years	433	167	68	0	2	0	0	0	0
10 years under 15 years	146	62	21	1	0	0	0	0	0
15 years under 20 years	65	29	10	0	0	0	0	0	0
20 and over	55	24	10	0	1	0	0	0	0
Life	10	7	1	0	0	0	0	0	0

Source: U.S. Department of Justice, Federal Prison System, *Statistical Report, Fiscal Year 1975* (Washington, D.C.: Federal Prison System, 1977), pp. 76, 77.

433

Table 56 (continued)

| | Sentencing procedure | | | | | | | |
| Age and length of sentence | Youth Corrections Act | | | | 4208(a)(1) 4208(a)(2) | | | |
	White	Negro	American Indian	Other	White	Negro	American Indian	Other
Total	059	636	38	4	1,985	1,036	23	15
Under 18	2	6	3	0	0	2	0	0
1 year and under	0	0	0	0	0	0	0	0
Over 1 year under 2 years	0	0	0	0	0	0	0	0
2 years to 2.5 years	0	0	0	0	0	0	0	0
Over 2.5 years under 5 years	0	0	0	0	0	0	0	0
5 years under 10 years	2	3	1	0	0	0	0	0
10 years under 15 years	0	3	1	0	0	0	0	0
15 years under 20 years	0	0	1	0	0	0	0	0
20 and over	0	0	0	0	0	1	0	0
Life	0	0	0	0	0	1	0	0
18 to 21	551	342	23	2	93	68	1	1
1 year and under	2	0	0	0	3	1	0	0
Over 1 year under 2 years	0	0	0	0	6	2	0	0
2 years to 2.5 years	0	0	1	0	12	13	0	0
Over 2.5 years under 5 years	1	2	0	0	24	6	1	0
5 years under 10 years	518	295	22	2	27	18	0	1
10 years under 15 years	20	32	0	0	3	9	0	0
15 years under 20 years	7	10	0	0	10	15	0	0
20 and over	3	3	0	0	7	4	0	0
Life	0	0	0	0	1	0	0	0
22 to 25	484	274	12	2	282	257	4	3
1 year and under	7	3	0	0	15	8	0	1
Over 1 year under 2 years	0	0	0	0	24	5	0	0
2 years to 2.5 years	0	0	0	0	50	32	1	0
Over 2.5 years under 5 years	0	0	0	0	65	55	2	1
5 years under 10 years	457	235	10	2	73	65	1	0
10 years under 15 years	17	23	1	0	18	33	0	1
15 years under 20 years	2	7	0	0	20	30	0	0
20 and over	1	6	1	0	16	26	0	0
Life	0	0	0	0	1	3	0	0

26 to 29	21	13	0	0	444	278	8	5
1 year and under	1	0	0	0	24	6	0	0
Over 1 year under 2 years	0	0	0	0	21	7	0	0
2 years to 2.5 years	0	0	0	0	58	43	1	0
Over 2.5 years under 5 years	19	13	0	0	143	78	5	1
5 years under 10 years	1	0	0	0	114	70	2	2
10 years under 15 years	0	0	0	0	34	33	0	0
15 years under 20 years	0	0	0	0	23	24	0	2
20 and over	0	0	0	0	23	17	0	0
Life	0	0	0	0	4	0	0	0
30 to 39	0	1	0	0	636	312	8	4
1 year and under	0	0	0	0	25	7	0	0
Over 1 year under 2 years	0	0	0	0	37	10	2	0
2 years to 2.5 years	0	0	0	0	107	28	1	2
Over 2.5 years under 5 years	0	1	0	0	194	89	1	0
5 years under 10 years	0	0	0	0	169	98	0	0
10 years under 15 years	0	0	0	0	47	40	4	1
15 years under 20 years	0	0	0	0	22	22	0	1
20 and over	0	0	0	0	35	18	0	0
Life	0	0	0	0	0	0	0	0
40 and over	1	0	0	0	530	119	2	2
1 year and under	0	0	0	0	29	4	0	0
Over 1 year under 2 years	0	0	0	0	25	9	0	0
2 years to 2.5 years	0	0	0	0	67	17	1	0
Over 2.5 years under 5 years	1	0	0	0	163	35	1	1
5 years under 10 years	0	0	0	0	153	40	1	0
10 years under 15 years	0	0	0	0	51	9	0	1
15 years under 20 years	0	0	0	0	21	4	0	1
20 and over	0	0	0	0	19	1	0	0
Life	0	0	0	0	2	0	0	0

Table 56 (continued)

Age and length of sentence	Sentencing procedure			
	Narcotic Addict Rehabilitation Act			
	White	Negro	American Indian	Other
Total	75	109	0	0
Under 18				
1 year and under	0	0	0	0
Over 1 year under 2 years	0	0	0	0
2 years to 2.5 years	0	0	0	0
Over 2.5 years under 5 years	0	0	0	0
5 years under 10 years	0	0	0	0
10 years under 15 years	0	0	0	0
15 years under 20 years	0	0	0	0
20 and over	0	0	0	0
Life	0	0	0	0
18 to 21	12	6	0	0
1 year and under	0	0	0	0
Over 1 year under 2 years	0	0	0	0
2 years to 2.5 years	0	0	0	0
Over 2.5 years under 5 years	4	2	0	0
5 years under 10 years	3	2	0	0
10 years under 15 years	5	2	0	0
15 years under 20 years	0	0	0	0
20 and over	0	0	0	0
Life	0	0	0	0
22 to 25	30	29	0	0
1 year and under	0	0	0	0
Over 1 year under 2 years	0	0	0	0
2 years to 2.5 years	0	6	0	0
Over 2.5 years under 5 years	12	15	0	0
5 years under 10 years	18	8	0	0
10 years under 15 years	0	0	0	0
15 years under 20 years	0	0	0	0
20 and over	0	0	0	0
Life	0	0	0	0

26 to 29	20	38	0	0
1 year and under	0	0	0	0
Over 1 year under 2 years	1	0	0	0
2 years to 2.5 years	0	2	0	0
Over 2.5 years under 5 years	1	6	0	0
5 years under 10 years	5	11	0	0
10 years under 15 years	13	19	0	0
15 years under 20 years	0	0	0	0
20 and over	0	0	0	0
Life	0	0	0	0
30 to 39	13	33	0	0
1 year and under	0	1	0	0
Over 1 year under 2 years	0	0	0	0
2 years to 2.5 years	0	0	0	0
Over 2.5 years under 5 years	1	3	0	0
5 years under 10 years	3	16	0	0
10 years under 15 years	9	13	0	0
15 years under 20 years	0	0	0	0
20 and over	0	0	0	0
Life	0	0	0	0
40 and over	0	3	0	0
1 year and under	0	0	0	0
Over 1 year under 2 years	0	0	0	0
2 years to 2.5 years	0	0	0	0
Over 2.5 years under 5 years	0	1	0	0
5 years under 10 years	0	1	0	0
10 years under 15 years	0	1	0	0
15 years under 20 years	0	0	0	0
20 and over	0	0	0	0
Life	0	0	0	0

Table 57 Number of, and average sentence for, Federal prisoners received from court into Federal institutions, by circuit, district, and offense, fiscal year 1975

"*Average sentence*" *is in months.*

[Population 16,555. Data complete on 91.6 percent of the population.]

Circuit and district	All offenses		Drug laws					
			Non-narcotics		Narcotics		Controlled substance	
	Number	Average sentence	Number	Average sentence	Number	Average sentence	Number	Average sentence
Total	15,164	50.1	1,171	34.8	2,286	65.5	511	29.0
Military, total	9	247.1	0	X	0	X	0	X
Army	8	269.0	0	X	0	X	0	X
Navy	1	72.0	0	X	0	X	0	X
District of Columbia	511	100.9	11	45.3	59	58.3	27	30.5
Circuit total	14,644	48.2	1,160	34.7	2,227	65.7	484	28.9
First Circuit	145	48.5	10	58.0	40	49.5	8	31.5
Maine	7	59.6	1	4.0	1	72.0	0	X
Massachusetts	76	50.6	3	64.0	25	52.3	2	21.0
New Hampshire	6	43.0	0	X	0	X	0	X
Rhode Island	14	28.4	0	X	0	X	1	60.0
Puerto Rico	42	50.4	6	64.0	14	42.9	5	30.0
Second Circuit	980	42.6	29	34.2	285	52.2	33	19.8
Connecticut	70	54.9	0	X	13	65.5	2	24.0
New York:								
Northern	26	40.5	1	24.0	3	40.0	1	24.0
Eastern	328	47.6	16	30.8	97	53.2	19	27.0
Southern	498	36.9	12	39.8	155	51.4	9	5.8
Western	38	32.2	0	X	5	28.8	2	9.0
Vermont	20	80.0	0	X	12	51.5	0	X
Third Circuit	637	69.1	22	58.1	119	75.4	19	40.4
Delaware	36	73.1	0	X	4	81.0	0	X
New Jersey	189	57.6	4	57.0	24	91.3	4	22.5
Pennsylvania:								
Eastern	246	65.3	16	55.1	71	66.8	8	43.5
Middle	36	36.3	0	X	0	X	1	12.0
Western	126	100.4	2	84.0	20	85.5	6	53.0
Virgin Islands	4	111.0	0	X	0	X	0	X

Fourth Circuit	1,342	73.8	43	49.1	106	83.7	21	46.0
Maryland	272	74.5	7	49.4	34	72.7	3	62.0
North Carolina:								
Eastern	130	64.0	5	38.4	10	92.0	5	19.2
Middle	165	57.3	1	72.0	5	57.6	0	X
Western	115	70.4	0	X	4	150.0	0	X
South Carolina	186	82.0	4	31.5	1	36.0	1	24.0
Virginia:								
Eastern	328	85.8	5	85.2	24	77.5	7	62.6
Western	59	62.0	14	44.6	10	63.6	1	60.0
West Virginia:								
Northern	12	79.5	0	X	1	36.0	1	48.0
Southern	75	66.1	7	46.3	17	119.2	3	38.0
Fifth Circuit	4,456	38.8	413	44.4	602	79.6	93	42.0
Alabama:								
Northern	203	50.3	6	16.0	28	116.1	5	31.8
Middle	113	36.7	3	27.0	5	91.2	0	X
Southern	63	63.8	2	5.0	3	56.0	0	X
Florida:								
Northern	99	45.9	14	45.6	1	6.0	10	28.8
Middle	256	48.6	22	41.9	45	61.0	7	28.3
Southern	304	30.8	38	31.4	127	33.7	3	3.7
Georgia:								
Northern	249	52.7	1	24.0	16	75.8	5	48.0
Middle	88	46.3	2	30.0	6	48.0	0	X
Southern	67	51.1	0	X	1	58.0	0	X
Louisiana:								
Eastern	177	53.1	21	40.4	41	71.3	16	84.4
Western	85	48.1	2	42.0	2	96.0	2	9.0
Middle	26	66.1	1	60.0	3	160.0	1	72.0
Mississippi:								
Northern	34	57.9	0	X	0	X	0	X
Southern	50	39.0	0	X	5	88.8	1	6.0
Texas:								
Northern	274	47.0	20	27.5	41	102.7	5	26.4
Eastern	55	90.3	1	60.0	1	60.0	0	X
Southern	528	46.9	161	38.2	131	77.6	9	30.7
Western	1,778	25.3	118	63.9	143	118.4	29	39.8
Canal Zone	7	74.6	1	24.0	3	26.0	0	X

Table 57 (continued)

Circuit and district	All offenses		Drug laws				Controlled substance	
			Non-narcotics		Narcotics			
	Number	Average sentence	Number	Average sentence	Number	Average sentence	Number	Average sentence
Sixth Circuit	1,531	59.8	24	34.9	190	60.4	61	36.6
Kentucky:								
Eastern	176	55.7	1	12.0	5	38.4	1	12.0
Western	151	77.6	5	52.8	1	24.0	3	60.0
Michigan:								
Eastern	490	58.5	11	24.1	140	59.8	45	33.2
Western	56	97.8	0	X	2	72.0	1	36.0
Ohio:								
Northern	215	54.9	0	X	21	74.6	7	33.7
Southern	118	56.1	2	21.0	9	55.8	2	54.0
Tennessee:								
Eastern	144	49.9	1	72.0	0	X	1	144.0
Middle	85	44.8	2	37.5	5	39.0	0	X
Western	96	67.6	2	54.0	7	66.9	1	18.0
Seventh Circuit	833	58.4	30	43.2	190	64.4	26	46.0
Illinois:								
Northern	325	42.2	9	22.0	93	45.5	3	34.0
Eastern	73	77.3	1	6.0	11	38.7	3	29.0
Southern	62	81.3	1	72.0	4	72.0	4	49.5
Indiana:								
Northern	192	70.6	14	48.0	64	103.4	13	53.1
Southern	125	62.2	5	69.6	8	47.3	1	72.0
Wisconsin:								
Eastern	38	63.8	0	X	10	29.7	2	24.0
Western	18	27.5	0	X	0	X	0	X
Eighth Circuit	715	54.8	18	33.7	96	63.6	15	22.3
Arkansas:								
Eastern	90	35.0	3	26.0	2	27.0	0	X
Western	37	66.2	1	6.0	0	X	0	X

District							
Iowa:							
Northern	29	51.5	0	X	0	X	0	X
Southern	34	54.0	0	X	3	84.0	1	48.0
Minnesota	108	46.8	8	28.5	26	34.6	9	22.6
Missouri:							
Eastern	166	67.7	1	60.0	36	84.7	1	6.0
Western	114	56.7	1	6.0	25	61.4	4	19.5
Nebraska	55	58.1	2	66.0	4	78.0	0	X
North Dakota	26	66.0	0	X	0	X	0	X
South Dakota	56	45.5	2	48.0	0	X	0	X
Ninth Circuit	3,347	35.6	548	23.7	483	54.7	184	17.8
Alaska	21	114.5	0	X	5	309.6	2	42.0
Arizona	914	21.8	208	26.1	89	46.3	82	14.9
California:							
Northern	187	51.0	8	19.1	25	64.0	5	13.2
Eastern	183	45.9	14	16.1	14	70.9	5	38.4
Central	419	57.6	23	48.7	90	49.0	8	29.0
Southern	1,146	20.8	274	19.3	140	57.8	69	17.0
Hawaii	21	59.4	4	19.5	4	57.0	0	X
Idaho	30	95.5	0	X	1	18.0	1	6.0
Montana	26	73.0	0	X	0	X	1	30.0
Nevada	79	52.2	4	12.0	25	46.8	1	2.0
Oregon	92	75.9	1	60.0	18	43.2	1	72.0
Washington:							
Eastern	42	47.6	3	34.0	15	34.7	1	24.0
Western	185	63.1	8	53.3	56	49.4	8	22.1
Guam	2	126.0	1	72.0	1	180.0	0	X
Tenth Circuit	658	65.1	23	50.0	116	63.8	24	16.1
Colorado	139	52.8	3	41.7	36	42.9	5	9.0
Kansas	173	74.9	4	52.0	43	61.4	1	6.0
New Mexico	137	55.4	8	32.3	14	62.6	12	12.5
Oklahoma:							
Northern	56	80.9	5	78.0	11	97.1	1	24.0
Eastern	23	63.9	0	X	1	60.0	1	72.0
Western	94	77.9	2	66.0	9	126.7	3	28.0
Utah	12	43.8	0	X	1	36.0	0	X
Wyoming	24	44.1	1	36.0	1	36.0	1	6.0

Table 58 Number of, and average sentence for, Federal prisoners received from court into Federal institutions, by circuit, district, and offense, fiscal year 1975

[Population 16,555. Data complete on 91.6 percent of the population.]

Circuit and district	Forgery Number	Forgery Average sentence	Immigration Number	Immigration Average sentence	Transportation etc. of stolen motor vehicle Number	Transportation etc. of stolen motor vehicle Average sentence	Other larceny Number	Other larceny Average sentence	Federal Juvenile Delinquency Act Number	Federal Juvenile Delinquency Act Average sentence
Total	665	37.1	2,447	7.9	917	42.7	1,397	37.6	215	33.0
Military, total	0	X	0	X	0	X	0	X	0	X
Army	0	X	0	X	0	X	0	X	0	X
Navy	0	X	0	X	0	X	0	X	0	X
District of Columbia	14	66.0	0	X	6	60.0	21	39.0	0	X
Circuit total	651	36.5	2,447	7.9	911	42.6	1,376	37.6	215	33.0
First Circuit	5	23.8	4	25.5	4	33.0	12	28.0	3	20.0
Maine	0	X	0	X	0	X	0	X	1	11.0
Massachusetts	4	22.3	0	X	3	32.0	8	30.8	1	25.0
New Hampshire	0	X	0	X	1	36.0	3	X	0	X
Rhode Island	1	30.0	0	X	0	X	3	18.0	0	X
Puerto Rico	0	X	4	25.5	0	X	1	36.0	1	24.0
Second Circuit	45	26.3	20	14.2	17	27.2	121	35.5	9	23.4
Connecticut	2	48.0	0	X	2	30.0	13	41.1	0	X
New York:										
Northern	2	15.0	2	6.0	0	X	5	44.4	0	X
Eastern	12	21.8	8	14.3	1	36.0	54	29.5	5	34.4
Southern	25	25.6	9	10.4	12	24.5	42	31.9	4	9.8
Western	4	39.0	0	X	2	36.0	5	10.4	0	X
Vermont	0	X	1	64.0	0	X	2	282.0	0	X
Third Circuit	32	30.0	6	12.7	33	51.7	80	34.5	1	24.0
Delaware	2	60.0	0	X	2	66.0	4	93.0	0	X
New Jersey	8	13.9	2	5.0	11	49.4	35	20.4	1	24.0
Pennsylvania:										
Eastern	10	21.4	2	15.0	6	43.0	26	33.2	0	X
Middle	2	36.0	0	X	4	45.0	7	49.3	0	X
Western	10	44.2	0	X	10	59.4	8	57.8	0	X
Virgin Islands	0	X	2	18.0	0	X	0	X	0	X

Fourth Circuit	94	37.7	48	14.5	93	43.2	177	40.2	26	37.0
Maryland	15	50.0	0	X	9	49.7	43	41.1	1	36.0
North Carolina:										
Eastern	10	51.6	20	10.5	15	30.9	6	31.7	2	31.5
Middle	17	14.0	20	17.8	15	26.9	23	24.1	5	38.2
Western	14	36.4	2	14.0	7	43.7	24	30.7	1	12.0
South Carolina	10	32.0	3	22.0	20	49.2	31	46.0	3	21.7
Virginia:										
Eastern	18	55.0	0	X	16	58.9	46	50.8	11	42.9
Western	3	14.0	2	6.0	2	39.0	2	39.0	1	56.0
West Virginia:										
Northern	2	18.0	0	X	0	X	1	24.0	0	X
Southern	5	27.6	1	24.0	9	43.3	1	6.0	2	33.5
Fifth Circuit	183	37.1	1,410	8.4	302	40.5	343	36.4	57	34.8
Alabama:										
Northern	18	36.2	8	19.8	48	39.9	29	26.9	2	30.5
Middle	10	30.0	1	2.0	37	39.2	14	26.1	6	31.0
Southern	10	44.8	4	12.0	14	45.4	6	27.7	0	X
Florida:										
Northern	10	43.2	7	14.6	20	37.5	8	46.3	0	X
Middle	27	30.9	4	9.8	21	35.9	31	40.3	8	41.3
Southern	12	14.0	15	12.3	15	27.9	19	18.2	0	X
Georgia:										
Northern	12	32.0	15	18.1	44	49.0	28	29.7	1	42.0
Middle	8	22.5	8	18.4	13	42.9	7	36.9	3	23.7
Southern	6	23.0	12	14.7	9	37.4	7	40.9	2	16.5
Louisiana:										
Eastern	8	41.3	4	14.5	3	44.0	26	47.3	3	55.0
Western	3	70.0	0	X	14	34.3	16	38.3	0	X
Middle	5	62.4	2	42.0	2	66.0	3	34.0	1	36.0
Mississippi:										
Northern	4	63.0	6	20.2	4	27.0	6	128.0	0	X
Southern	6	13.5	9	25.3	8	39.0	5	6.0	0	X
Texas:										
Northern	21	43.6	4	25.5	17	33.5	37	36.1	0	X
Eastern	3	26.0	0	X	7	42.0	12	28.5	2	31.0
Southern	9	60.7	50	17.2	16	45.4	46	25.0	3	45.0
Western	11	48.0	1,261	7.3	10	51.0	43	53.0	26	33.3
Canal Zone	0	X	0	X	0	X	0	X	0	X

Table 58 (continued)

Circuit and district	Forgery		Immigration		Transportation etc. of stolen motor vehicle		Other larceny		Federal Juvenile Delinquency Act	
	Number	Average sentence	Number	Average sentence	Number	Average sentence	Number	Average sentence	Number	Average sentence
Sixth Circuit	99	38.3	31	24.4	131	43.6	242	35.9	27	37.0
Kentucky:										
Eastern	10	41.1	2	30.0	36	38.4	19	41.2	12	34.3
Western	7	29.1	0	X	25	65.5	16	39.8	11	35.5
Michigan:										
Eastern	20	38.7	4	16.0	9	40.2	65	40.2	1	49.0
Western	5	55.2	0	X	3	38.0	8	66.8	1	36.0
Ohio:										
Northern	8	27.8	0	X	22	42.3	43	23.7	0	X
Southern	12	39.0	0	X	6	26.0	15	35.0	0	X
Tennessee:										
Eastern	21	44.3	16	30.2	14	45.7	34	40.1	1	70.0
Middle	10	35.4	4	22.5	11	40.4	24	30.8	1	42.0
Western	6	25.5	5	12.0	5	9.6	18	26.3	0	X
Seventh Circuit	43	42.9	7	20.6	42	41.0	114	48.6	11	40.5
Illinois:										
Northern	15	30.1	4	13.5	9	23.3	48	33.8	1	28.0
Eastern	5	72.0	1	48.0	8	63.0	7	29.1	0	X
Southern	6	74.0	2	21.0	3	62.0	16	135.8	0	X
Indiana:										
Northern	6	31.0	0	X	9	36.0	26	37.4	8	43.8
Southern	11	36.5	0	X	10	41.8	12	38.5	2	34.0
Wisconsin:										
Eastern	0	X	0	X	1	24.0	3	31.0	0	X
Western	0	X	0	X	2	27.0	2	9.0	0	X
Eighth Circuit	48	31.9	4	7.0	77	43.4	97	41.9	15	36.3
Arkansas:										
Eastern	16	32.0	2	8.0	13	46.9	9	22.7	2	30.5
Western	3	18.0	1	6.0	7	29.1	0	X	2	48.0

Iowa:										
Northern	4	57.0	0	X	2	42.0	7	50.6	0	X
Southern	1	12.0	0	X	2	42.0	12	36.5	0	X
Minnesota	7	18.0	0	X	2	32.0	9	30.1	1	47.0
Missouri:										
Eastern	8	35.3	0	X	13	49.8	33	50.7	1	41.0
Western	4	27.0	0	X	17	37.8	16	41.6	0	X
Nebraska	4	48.0	1	6.0	18	50.0	6	60.0	3	47.0
North Dakota	0	X	0	X	1	24.0	3	30.0	3	20.7
South Dakota	1	18.0	0	X	2	42.0	2	6.0	3	32.3
Ninth Circuit	77	36.2	904	5.7	99	38.9	129	30.9	52	27.8
Alaska	3	44.0	0	X	0	X	0	X	3	40.3
Arizona	2	48.0	348	3.8	22	42.5	13	40.2	28	27.4
California:										
Northern	12	30.5	7	5.0	7	28.3	13	23.1	2	42.0
Eastern	16	33.4	23	10.4	18	36.0	19	21.2	0	X
Central	19	45.9	18	23.1	23	35.4	41	33.0	2	26.5
Southern	4	31.5	487	5.9	7	35.1	17	25.0	11	19.4
Hawaii	0	X	0	X	0	X	1	18.0	0	X
Idaho	2	39.0	3	6.0	5	56.4	1	24.0	2	39.0
Montana	3	64.0	0	X	2	60.0	2	69.0	4	33.3
Nevada	3	28.0	1	24.0	9	50.7	4	63.0	0	X
Oregon	4	27.0	5	24.0	2	36.0	7	45.4	0	X
Washington:										
Eastern	0	X	4	9.0	0	X	0	X	0	X
Western	9	22.3	8	11.8	4	19.0	11	21.3	0	X
Guam	0	X	0	X	0	X	0	X	0	X
Tenth Circuit	25	49.0	13	12.0	113	49.7	61	39.5	14	29.6
Colorado	7	42.0	2	12.0	19	41.5	8	20.5	4	36.3
Kansas	4	54.0	1	24.0	29	59.0	15	35.6	2	21.0
New Mexico	1	36.0	8	11.0	30	54.4	12	38.5	7	29.1
Oklahoma:										
Northern	3	96.0	1	6.0	10	48.0	4	51.0	0	X
Eastern	3	24.0	0	X	2	30.0	2	18.0	0	X
Western	6	33.0	0	X	13	40.2	14	59.6	1	24.0
Utah	1	120.0	1	14.0	1	24.0	3	26.7	0	X
Wyoming	0	X	0	X	9	44.0	3	31.0	0	X

Table 58 (continued)

Circuit and district	Selective Service violators		Robbery		Securities interstate		Government reservations		All other offenses	
	Number	Average sentence	Number	Average sentence	Number	Average sentence	Number	Average sentence	Number	Average sentence
Total	29	22.4	1,366	140.6	356	49.1	639	97.6	3,165	44.0
Military, total	0	X	0	X	0	X	0	X	9	247.1
Army	0	X	0	X	0	X	0	X	8	269.0
Navy	0	X	0	X	0	X	0	X	1	72.0
District of Columbia	0	X	18	136.0	5	76.8	288	129.8	62	72.0
Circuit total	29	22.4	1,348	140.7	351	48.7	351	71.2	3,094	42.8
First Circuit	0	X	21	95.7	5	34.6	3	144.0	30	28.7
Maine	0	X	1	240.0	0	X	0	X	3	30.0
Massachusetts	0	X	9	100.0	2	48.0	2	126.0	17	35.3
New Hampshire	0	X	3	58.0	1	36.0	0	X	1	12.0
Rhode Island	0	X	1	120.0	1	36.0	0	X	7	14.0
Puerto Rico	0	X	7	82.3	1	5.0	1	180.0	2	30.0
Second Circuit	7	23.9	103	88.7	24	35.9	7	93.4	280	28.4
Connecticut	0	X	7	105.3	2	42.0	0	X	29	49.4
New York:										
Northern	0	X	6	74.0	2	21.0	0	X	4	33.5
Eastern	3	27.0	47	106.3	1	120.0	2	36.0	63	31.6
Southern	4	21.5	34	70.1	15	22.3	4	142.5	173	23.8
Western	0	X	7	54.9	3	58.0	1	12.0	9	23.7
Vermont	0	X	2	96.0	1	108.0	0	X	2	27.0
Third Circuit	0	X	138	131.4	24	44.6	6	78.5	157	49.5
Delaware	0	X	8	111.0	4	58.5	0	X	12	46.8
New Jersey	0	X	25	152.2	9	47.3	3	11.0	63	43.0
Pennsylvania:										
Eastern	0	X	59	99.6	8	26.6	1	30.0	39	67.1
Middle	0	X	5	86.4	0	X	0	X	17	15.5
Western	0	X	41	174.1	3	66.0	0	X	26	62.2
Virgin Islands	0	X	0	X	0	X	2	204.0	0	X

Fourth Circuit	1	48.0	240	186.2	43	46.8	68	89.2	382	47.1
Maryland	0	X	49	174.4	11	45.4	17	62.5	83	50.0
North Carolina:										
Eastern	1	48.0	18	191.3	4	72.0	6	61.0	28	54.5
Middle	0	X	28	175.4	4	31.5	4	189.0	43	36.1
Western	0	X	29	162.0	2	33.0	9	58.2	23	26.6
South Carolina	0	X	35	217.7	8	45.0	5	120.0	65	55.6
Virginia:										
Eastern	0	X	70	190.2	11	51.3	27	102.1	93	.3.6
Western	0	X	3	260.0	0	X	0	X	21	61.4
West Virginia:										
Northern	0	X	5	146.4	0	X	0	X	2	39.0
Southern	0	X	3	212.0	3	36.0	0	X	24	46.8
Fifth Circuit	6	14.0	142	137.3	88	50.7	59	46.0	758	40.2
Alabama:										
Northern	0	X	9	149.3	5	52.8	1	4.0	44	34.9
Middle	0	X	10	50.4	9	32.7	1	3.0	17	29.8
Southern	0	X	3	340.0	1	18.0	0	X	20	75.2
Florida:										
Northern	0	X	6	124.0	1	18.0	6	43.5	16	58.2
Middle	2	6.0	10	112.8	6	41.0	2	20.5	71	55.6
Southern	3	12.0	9	118.7	9	42.0	1	12.0	53	24.0
Georgia:										
Northern	0	X	21	161.4	7	55.4	3	100.0	96	40.4
Middle	0	X	15	113.2	1	24.0	2	51.0	23	29.9
Southern	0	X	10	196.8	5	20.4	2	39.0	13	19.0
Louisiana:										
Eastern	0	X	5	129.6	5	60.0	2	39.0	43	31.2
Western	0	X	9	148.0	5	40.8	2	60.0	30	27.9
Middle	0	X	3	105.0	0	X	0	X	5	25.2
Mississippi:										
Northern	0	X	3	76.0	2	96.0	0	X	9	33.1
Southern	0	X	1	180.0	3	76.0	3	74.0	9	24.3
Texas:										
Northern	0	X	9	138.7	12	55.0	1	12.0	107	29.4
Eastern	0	X	9	164.7	2	42.0	1	36.0	17	145.1
Southern	0	X	6	146.0	9	54.7	7	21.4	81	40.2
Western	1	36.0	4	79.5	6	95.0	22	39.8	104	40.8
Canal Zone	0	X	0	X	0	X	3	140.0	0	X

Table 58 (continued)

Circuit and district	Selective Service violators Number	Selective Service violators Average sentence	Robbery Number	Robbery Average sentence	Securities interstate Number	Securities interstate Average sentence	Government reservations Number	Government reservations Average sentence	All other offenses Number	All other offenses Average sentence
Sixth Circuit	3	22.0	227	141.7	41	62.0	25	85.2	430	47.0
Kentucky:										
Eastern	0	X	12	270.0	8	44.0	1	12.0	69	42.6
Western	0	X	25	162.2	1	60.0	9	130.7	48	64.5
Michigan:										
Eastern	3	22.0	68	124.6	4	46.0	1	48.0	119	49.7
Western	0	X	27	142.2	1	120.0	0	X	8	47.3
Ohio:										
Northern	0	X	36	127.6	6	33.3	2	156.0	70	38.8
Southern	0	X	21	115.6	13	58.2	2	54.0	36	42.5
Tennessee:										
Eastern	0	X	10	140.4	4	52.0	6	60.0	36	42.0
Middle	0	X	7	92.6	3	188.0	1	36.0	17	36.6
Western	0	X	21	165.4	1	96.0	3	26.0	27	56.1
Seventh Circuit	4	24.0	77	144.5	30	48.1	4	333.0	255	40.1
Illinois:										
Northern	1	6.0	20	139.2	12	33.3	2	540.0	108	23.7
Eastern	0	X	10	230.4	2	60.0	1	72.0	24	63.1
Southern	0	X	4	96.0	4	73.5	0	X	18	53.3
Indiana:										
Northern	1	6.0	11	105.8	2	96.0	0	X	38	62.6
Southern	2	42.0	22	127.1	8	47.3	1	180.0	43	50.9
Wisconsin:										
Eastern	0	X	9	174.7	0	X	0	X	13	30.2
Western	0	X	1	120.0	2	30.0	0	X	11	22.1
Eighth Circuit	2	12.0	62	140.5	23	39.4	61	58.5	197	47.6
Arkansas:										
Eastern	0	X	8	85.5	6	45.0	1	6.0	28	23.4
Western	0	X	11	168.0	1	36.0	1	24.0	10	17.4

District										
Iowa:										
Northern	1	12.0	1	36.0	2	51.0	0	X	12	56.5
Southern	0	X	5	129.6	1	48.0	0	X	9	34.0
Minnesota	1	12.0	10	139.2	1	24.0	2	42.0	32	53.2
Missouri:										
Eastern	0	X	13	179.1	6	30.0	1	72.0	53	54.7
Western	0	X	6	200.0	4	43.5	2	72.0	35	54.7
Nebraska	0	X	7	80.6	2	36.0	1	96.0	7	60.0
North Dakota	0	X	0	X	0	X	11	97.1	8	59.0
South Dakota	0	X	1	12.0	0	X	42	49.4	3	52.0
Ninth Circuit	3	25.0	281	118.2	37	44.1	90	63.4	460	40.5
Alaska	0	X	3	81.3	0	X	0	X	5	55.2
Arizona	0	X	18	97.6	3	18.0	36	38.0	65	36.3
California:										
Northern	1	6.0	41	96.7	5	32.4	7	130.7	54	31.3
Eastern	2	34.5	21	137.7	4	33.0	10	35.6	37	44.2
Central	0	X	93	116.9	5	39.6	6	27.3	91	40.0
Southern	0	X	23	106.8	1	6.0	9	35.0	104	24.9
Hawaii	0	X	5	84.0	0	X	0	X	7	72.0
Idaho	0	X	0	X	2	84.0	6	172.0	7	166.0
Montana	0	X	4	120.0	1	72.0	4	72.0	5	88.8
Nevada	0	X	9	129.3	8	55.5	0	X	15	31.7
Oregon	0	X	24	147.5	5	60.0	0	X	25	64.8
Washington:										
Eastern	0	X	6	142.0	2	33.0	4	46.5	7	30.4
Western	0	X	34	134.6	1	30.0	8	135.1	38	52.8
Guam	0	X	0	X	0	X	0	X	0	X
Tenth Circuit	3	30.0	57	192.5	36	55.8	28	68.5	145	62.6
Colorado	2	15.0	9	147.0	9	54.7	3	110.0	32	63.8
Kansas	0	X	16	248.3	16	56.1	3	68.0	39	64.1
New Mexico	0	X	6	168.0	1	120.0	17	69.5	21	75.1
Oklahoma:										
Northern	0	X	5	194.4	1	72.0	0	X	15	68.6
Eastern	0	X	5	192.0	1	6.0	0	X	8	25.5
Western	1	60.0	15	174.4	8	52.5	2	21.0	20	62.7
Utah	0	X	1	120.0	0	X	0	X	4	33.0
Wyoming	0	X	0	X	0	X	3	53.0	6	55.5

Source: U.S. Department of Justice, Federal Prison System, *Statistical Report, Fiscal Year 1975* (Washington, D.C.: Federal Prison System, 1977), pp. 67-72.

Table 59 Federal prisoners received from court into Federal institutions, by district and sentencing procedure, fiscal year 1975

[Population 16,555. Data complete on 92.8 percent of the population.]

Judicial district	Regular	Federal Juvenile Delinquency Act	Youth Corrections Act	Sentencing procedure Title 18, U.S. Code 4208 (a)(1)	Sentencing procedure Title 18, U.S. Code 4208 (a)(2)	Split sentence	Narcotic Addict Rehabilitation Act
Total	8,561	216	1,735	165	2,915	1,581	182
Alabama:							
Northern	122	2	18	3	33	25	0
Middle	74	6	17	0	8	8	0
Southern	31	0	10	0	10	12	0
Alaska	14	3	3	0	1	0	0
Arizona	673	28	71	0	77	74	4
Arkansas:							
Eastern	53	2	8	0	11	19	0
Western	21	2	2	0	5	7	0
California:							
Northern	100	2	27	3	27	28	3
Eastern	91	0	22	0	34	32	5
Central	133	2	44	0	189	40	17
Southern	582	11	68	0	216	277	4
Colorado	85	4	18	0	12	17	4
Connecticut	45	0	2	1	15	3	4
Delaware	11	0	14	0	6	3	2
Florida:							
Northern	44	0	15	0	36	4	0
Middle	130	8	36	6	43	22	12
Southern	198	0	15	1	36	58	1
Georgia:							
Northern	159	1	23	1	35	44	0
Middle	69	3	5	0	6	5	0
Southern	44	2	6	0	10	5	0
Hawaii	1	0	4	0	13	3	0
Idaho	4	2	7	1	10	6	0

Illinois:							
Northern	249	1	10	5	31	35	0
Eastern	47	0	3	0	15	7	1
Southern	30	0	13	0	17	2	0
Indiana:							
Northern	90	8	46	1	32	17	2
Southern	80	2	19	0	16	9	1
Iowa:							
Northern	16	0	6	0	8	0	0
Southern	22	0	1	1	9	1	0
Kansas	27	2	36	0	93	12	5
Kentucky:							
Eastern	126	12	8	0	28	3	0
Western	86	11	25	0	24	8	0
Louisiana:							
Eastern	85	3	32	0	40	20	0
Western	66	0	2	0	5	14	0
Middle	10	1	7	2	0	3	3
Maine	2	1	1	0	1	2	0
Maryland	126	2	53	0	80	15	4
Massachusetts	53	1	15	0	7	1	0
Michigan:							
Eastern	167	1	60	1	250	21	0
Western	17	1	16	0	19	2	1
Minnesota	82	1	5	0	13	10	0
Mississippi:							
Northern	16	0	7	0	5	6	0
Southern	33	0	0	0	3	14	0
Missouri:							
Eastern	98	1	24	3	29	7	4
Western	51	0	16	0	34	17	3
Montana	6	4	10	0	6	0	0
Nebraska	15	3	16	0	21	0	0
Nevada	43	0	9	0	17	10	0

Table 59 (continued)

Judicial district	Regular	Federal Juvenile Delinquency Act	Youth Corrections Act	Title 18, U.S. Code 4208 (a)(1)	(a)(2)	Split sentence	Narcotic Addict Rehabilitation Act
					Sentencing procedure		
New Hampshire	2	0	0	0	4	0	0
New Jersey	107	1	13	3	37	36	0
New Mexico	56	7	26	1	27	21	0
New York:							
Northern	16	0	4	0	2	4	0
Eastern	115	5	30	8	87	80	5
Southern	285	4	25	5	46	131	2
Western	26	0	3	0	6	3	0
North Carolina:							
Eastern	53	2	27	0	26	23	0
Middle	115	5	19	3	13	15	0
Western	90	1	9	0	16	0	0
North Dakota	14	3	5	0	2	2	0
Ohio:							
Northern	85	0	25	4	82	21	0
Southern	76	0	5	1	30	7	1
Oklahoma:							
Northern	23	0	15	0	18	3	0
Eastern	19	0	1	0	1	2	0
Western	53	1	21	0	18	2	0
Oregon	27	0	20	0	37	9	0
Pennsylvania:							
Eastern	118	0	42	8	72	11	0
Middle	14	0	7	2	3	10	0
Western	42	0	28	4	49	5	1
Rhode Island	5	0	0	0	5	4	1
South Carolina	114	3	21	2	35	12	0
South Dakota	36	3	9	0	7	2	0
Tennessee:							
Eastern	38	1	29	1	70	6	1
Middle	53	1	9	1	16	3	2
Western	39	0	6	0	44	8	0

Texas:							
Northern	122	0	24	0	90	45	3
Eastern	24	2	0	4	20	6	0
Southern	402	3	39	2	24	59	3
Western	1,448	26	113	3	135	47	17
Utah	8	0	0	0	3	0	1
Vermont	12	0	3	0	4	1	1
Virginia:							
Eastern	130	11	82	3	87	16	2
Western	23	1	18	2	7	8	0
Washington:							
Eastern	19	0	8	0	9	6	0
Western	78	0	26	0	60	22	1
West Virginia:							
Northern	10	0	2	0	0	0	0
Southern	27	2	17	2	20	8	0
Wisconsin:							
Eastern	28	0	3	0	7	0	0
Western	14	0	0	0	3	1	0
Wyoming	17	0	5	0	2	1	0
District of Columbia	194	0	116	77	50	12	61
Guam	1	0	1	0	0	0	0
Puerto Rico	31	1	4	0	5	1	0
Virgin Islands	4	0	0	0	0	0	0
Canal Zone	7	0	0	0	0	0	0
Army	9	0	0	0	0	0	0
Navy	1	0	0	0	0	0	0
Air Force	4	0	0	0	0	0	0

Source: U.S. Department of Justice, Federal Prison System, *Statistical Report, Fiscal Year 1975* (Washington, D.C.: Federal Prison System, 1977), pp. 81, 82.

Table 60 Prisoners received into Federal institutions, excluding court commitments, by offense and type of commitment, fiscal year 1975

[Population 3,130. Data complete on 78.0 percent of the population.]

Offense	All other admissions	Prisoners under sentence						Prisoners not under sentence				
		Total	Violators returned			Title 18 U.S. Code 4208(b)	State boarded	Title 18, U.S. Code		Observation juvenile	Study youth	Narcotic Addict Rehabilitation Act
			Parole		Mandatory release			(4244) Mental observation	(4246) Mentally incompetent			
			Youth Corrections Act	Other								
Total	2,441	1,499	245	592	164	436	62	276	74	33	375	184
Assault	14	8	2	0	1	5	0	2	1	0	3	0
Burglary	30	24	5	5	6	7	1	1	0	1	1	3
Counterfeiting	48	41	4	16	6	15	0	1	0	0	5	1
Drug laws, total	463	250	30	115	25	75	5	17	3	11	113	69
Non-narcotics	128	68	11	26	6	21	4	5	1	6	36	12
Narcotics	284	158	16	78	18	45	1	11	2	1	59	53
Controlled substances	51	24	3	11	1	9	0	1	0	4	18	4
Embezzlement	33	16	3	2	0	11	0	3	0	0	13	1
Escape, flight or harboring a fugitive	22	17	1	8	4	1	3	1	0	0	3	1
Extortion	23	7	0	0	0	7	0	10	5	0	1	0
Firearms	131	71	9	10	1	51	0	34	6	0	18	2
Forgery	148	97	22	41	13	21	0	14	7	1	15	14
Fraud	55	35	3	5	2	25	0	9	3	1	7	14
Immigration	10	6	0	3	0	3	0	2	0	0	1	1
Income tax	2	1	0	0	0	1	0	1	0	0	0	1
Kidnaping	35	17	0	8	3	6	0	17	1	0	0	0
Larceny/theft, total	537	402	96	157	63	82	4	33	13	3	57	29
Motor vehicle, interstate	299	240	74	84	49	30	3	19	7	0	28	5
Postal	124	78	14	34	8	21	1	7	3	1	18	17
Theft, interstate	35	27	2	12	3	10	0	2	1	2	3	0
Other	79	57	6	27	3	21	0	5	2	0	8	7

Offense											
Liquor laws	6	6	2	3	0	1	0	0	0	0	0	0
National security laws	1	1	0	1	0	0	0	0	0	0	0	0
Robbery	367	214	22	97	18	74	3	74	19	1	49	10
Selective Service Acts	5	4	1	0	1	2	0	1	0	0	0	0
Securities, transporting false or forged	95	72	6	44	8	14	0	3	1	0	14	5
White slave traffic	5	5	1	2	0	2	0	0	0	0	0	0
Other and unclassifiable	102	35	5	12	2	16	0	34	11	5	14	3
Government reservation, High seas, territorial, and District of Columbia	304	166	32	62	10	16	46	18	4	10	61	45
Assault	39	25	6	6	2	5	6	3	0	0	9	2
Auto theft	6	2	1	0	0	1	0	1	0	0	3	0
Burglary	39	14	3	5	2	0	4	0	0	5	5	15
Forgery	10	5	1	3	1	0	0	0	0	0	1	4
Homicide	38	23	0	4	2	1	16	4	1	1	8	1
Larceny/theft	42	21	7	7	1	0	6	2	2	0	8	9
Robbery	53	27	7	9	2	0	9	1	0	1	21	3
Rape	15	8	0	1	0	4	3	3	1	2	1	0
Sex offenses, except rape	6	2	0	2	0	0	0	3	0	0	1	0
Other and unclassifiable	56	39	7	25	0	5	2	1	0	1	4	11
Military court-martial cases	5	4	1	1	1	1	0	1	0	0	0	0

Source: U.S. Department of Justice, Federal Prison System, Statistical Report, Fiscal Year 1975 (Washington, D.C.: Federal Prison System, 1977), pp. 87, 88.

Table 61 Sentenced Federal prisoners confined in Federal institutions on June 30, by offense, 1965-75

This table presents data on the population of sentenced inmates in Federal institutions on a particular day. This table should be distinguished from tables reflecting admissions to Federal institutions. Tables describing admissions deal with the flow into Federal institutions during the fiscal year, whereas tables describing populations reflect the composition of Federal institutions on a given day during the year.

Offense	1965	1966	1967	1968	1969	1970	1971	1972	1973	1974	1975
All offenses	22,346	21,040	19,822	20,170	20,208	20,686	20,820	21,280	22,436	23,048	20,949
Assault	49	54	41	53	69	126	100	94	106	104	97
Burglary	325	303	247	262	300	260	243	212	156	150	203
Counterfeiting	355	362	317	403	544	596	628	737	663	482	395
Drug laws	3,998	3,908	3,390	3,538	3,591	3,384	3,647	4,024	5,559	6,212	5,570
Non-narcotics	493	577	517	730	890	830	976	1,000	1,433	1,432	1,117
Narcotics	3,505	3,331	2,873	2,808	2,701	2,554	2,671	3,024	4,126	4,235	3,980
Controlled substances	0	0	0	0	0	0	0	0	0	545	473
Embezzlement, and fraud	404	410	341	374	377	458	541	521	536	510	527
Escape, flight or harboring fugitive	47	32	44	49	78	172	229	170	127	138	132
Firearms laws	120	107	108	97	107	226	393	545	697	920	1,022
Forgery	1,708	1,518	1,242	1,148	1,179	1,070	1,067	1,019	861	805	832
Homicide (killing federal officer)	7	7	5	8	9	19	15	12	9	10	13
Immigration	707	546	546	413	511	620	819	825	814	946	929
Income Tax	88	88	95	87	92	63	93	78	120	137	111
Juvenile delinquency (except District of Columbia)	1,050	893	853	772	655	596	492	449	432	435	337
Kidnaping	184	189	194	201	188	216	218	222	261	291	360
Larceny-theft	7,091	6,689	6,280	6,378	6,188	6,074	5,121	4,591	4,010	3,600	3,303
Transportation, etc., of stolen motor vehicle	5,653	5,441	5,124	5,094	4,825	4,524	3,512	2,900	2,401	2,089	1,706
Other	1,438	1,248	1,156	1,284	1,363	1,550	1,609	1,691	1,609	1,511	1,597
Liquor laws	1,337	1,092	762	722	618	541	486	407	312	222	111
National security laws [a]	36	36	24	26	24	18	19	17	11	7	7
Robbery	1,696	2,044	2,086	2,428	2,688	3,144	3,567	3,963	4,319	4,205	4,242
Securities, transport	791	735	711	764	791	756	760	720	640	564	582
Selective Service Acts	156	249	658	729	576	493	354	311	194	117	7
White slave traffic	163	137	119	97	74	67	64	66	58	54	64
Other and unclassifiable	495	423	689	644	572	775	646	668	602	550	585

Government reservation, District of Columbia, high seas and territorial cases										
1,156	1,120	983	863	865	902	885	889	1,029	1,106	1,296
Assault	122	119	115	113	127	151	127	129	146	145	140
Homicide	266	266	243	236	236	225	236	237	293	337	385
Rape	92	84	74	63	91	86	70	70	74	78	89
Robbery	168	146	118	117	111	117	104	143	203	219	283
Other and unclassifiable	508	505	433	314	300	323	348	310	313	327	399
Military court-martial cases	110	98	87	114	112	110	98	95	78	73	69
Assault	2	3	7	51	17	17	13	13	2	3	3
Homicide	76	61	49	15	48	54	57	56	56	49	49
Rape	25	17	24	31	30	16	9	12	8	5	4
Robbery	2	4	2	6	7	4	7	8	4	6	8
Other and unclassifiable	5	13	5	11	10	19	12	6	8	10	5
Not reported	0	0	0	0	0	0	335	645	842	1,410	155

a Except Selective Service Act.

Source: U.S. Department of Justice, Federal Prison System, *Statistical Report, Fiscal Year 1975* (Washington, D.C.: Federal Prison System, 1977), p. 43.

457

Table 62 Number of, and average sentence for, Federal prisoners confined in Federal institutions, by offense, type of commitment, race, and sex, on June 30, 1975

Offense	All prisoners			White	
	Total	Male	Female	Number	Average sentence
Total	20,948	19,997	951	12,956	87.6
Total excluding immigration and violent crimes [a]	14,423	13,619	804	9,494	65.0
Assault	97	96	1	50	90.6
Bankruptcy	5	5	0	5	32.4
Burglary	203	201	2	112	81.1
Counterfeiting	395	380	15	323	70.8
Drug laws, total	5,569	5,285	284	3,786	73.3
Non-narcotics	1,117	1,055	62	1,042	50.1
Narcotics	3,979	3,790	189	2,404	86.2
Controlled substances	473	440	33	340	53.0
Embezzlement	159	142	17	109	43.9
Escape, flight or harboring a fugitive	132	127	5	106	40.2
Extortion	163	157	6	136	111.0
Firearms	1,022	1,007	15	642	54.5
Forgery	832	706	126	336	53.1
Fraud	368	350	18	283	50.3
Immigration	929	916	13	920	15.3
Income tax	111	110	1	83	36.1
Juvenile delinquency	337	319	18	208	39.0
Kidnaping	360	350	10	263	300.3
Larceny/theft, total	3,303	3,106	197	2,262	55.3
Motor vehicle, interstate	1,706	1,695	11	1,404	52.3
Postal	733	575	158	247	46.1
Theft, interstate	329	328	1	249	69.1
Other	535	508	27	362	63.5
Liquor laws	111	109	2	78	33.7
National security laws	7	6	1	6	298.0
Robbery	4,242	4,172	70	2,013	176.6
Selective Service Acts	7	5	2	6	36.0
Securities, transporting false or forged	582	540	42	390	70.5
White slave traffic	64	61	3	29	57.4
Other and unclassifiable	585	561	24	450	70.5
Government reservation, high seas, territorial, and District of Columbia	1,296	1,219	77	342	214.7
Assault	140	129	11	35	155.2
Auto theft	14	13	1	6	57.0
Burglary	115	113	2	22	83.0
Forgery	21	17	4	4	57.0
Homicide	385	357	28	118	386.8
Larceny/theft	119	111	8	45	67.4
Robbery	283	270	13	39	187.1
Rape	89	88	1	24	262.4
Sex offenses, except rape	17	17	0	5	175.2
Other and unclassifiable	113	104	9	44	55.4
Military court-martial cases	69	67	2	18	328.3

"*Average sentence*" is in months.

[Population 23,556. Data complete on 88.9 percent of the population.]

| Prisoners under sentence | | | | | | Prisoners not under sentence | | Narcotic Addict Rehabilitation Act commitments included in total | |
| White | | All other | | | | | | | |
Male	Female	Number	Average sentence	Male	Female	Male	Female	Under sentence	Not under sentence
12.534	422	7,732	109.0	7,217	515	246	14	316	55
9,132	362	4,743	69.3	4,312	431	175	11	281	49
50	0	43	106.9	42	1	4	0	0	0
5	0	0	X	0	0	0	0	0	0
112	0	89	73.7	87	2	2	0	1	1
312	11	70	51.9	66	4	2	0	5	0
3,613	173	1,739	89.9	1,630	109	42	2	152	19
989	53	67	65.7	59	8	7	1	14	3
2,306	98	1,542	92.2	1,452	90	32	1	133	15
318	22	130	74.3	119	11	3	0	5	1
97	12	46	41.2	41	5	4	0	1	0
104	2	25	74.7	22	3	1	0	1	0
130	6	21	69.1	21	0	6	0	0	0
633	9	363	48.0	357	6	17	0	3	1
298	38	486	52.1	400	86	8	2	18	3
275	8	78	38.0	68	10	7	0	1	0
907	13	9	23.3	9	0	0	0	0	0
82	1	28	51.1	28	0	0	0	0	0
199	9	123	42.2	115	8	5	1	0	0
255	8	90	321.3	88	2	7	0	0	0
2,217	45	1,003	47.6	856	147	33	5	44	8
1,394	10	284	54.0	283	1	18	0	6	0
218	29	474	42.2	348	126	9	3	29	4
249	0	78	49.7	77	1	2	0	2	1
356	6	167	51.1	148	19	4	2	7	3
77	1	33	24.6	32	1	0	0	0	0
5	1	1	240.0	1	0	0	0	0	0
1,985	28	2,180	161.2	2,139	41	48	1	30	4
4	2	1	18.0	1	0	0	0	0	0
371	19	186	58.4	163	23	6	0	10	0
29	0	35	72.5	32	3	0	0	0	0
434	16	117	86.5	109	8	18	0	4	0
322	20	915	162.4	861	54	36	3	46	19
33	2	102	91.9	94	8	2	1	1	1
6	0	7	64.9	6	1	1	0	0	0
22	0	81	83.9	79	2	12	0	15	10
4	0	14	83.1	10	4	3	0	4	3
111	7	261	274.1	241	20	5	1	0	0
42	3	69	70.9	64	5	5	0	7	3
37	2	239	150.2	228	11	5	0	4	1
24	0	65	187.7	64	1	0	0	0	0
5	0	11	89.5	11	0	1	0	0	0
38	6	66	79.8	64	2	2	1	15	1
18	0	51	254.5	49	2	0	0	0	0

[a] This total line excludes the immigration law and violent crime offenses whose unusual sentence lengths distort the average sentence length statistic.

Source: U.S. Department of Justice, Federal Prison System, *Statistical Report, Fiscal Year 1975* (Washington, D.C.: Federal Prison System, 1977), pp. 28, 29.

459

Table 63 Federal prisoners confined in Federal institutions, by type and capacity of institution, on June 30, 1974 and 1975

Change in capacity refers to the difference between the population figures for June 30, 1975 and the planned capacity for the institution.

Institution	Population		Planned capacity	Present versus planned capacity	
	June 30, 1975	June 30, 1974ᵃ		Change	Percent
Total, all institutions	23,566	23,690	22,133	+1,433	+6.5
Juveniles and youths	1,255	1,186	1,130	+125	+11.1
Ashland	516	559	425	+91	+21.4
Englewood	348	403	325	+23	+7.1
Morgantown	214	224	190	+24	+12.6
Pleasanton	177	0	190	-13	-6.8
Young adults	4,613	4,576	4,343	+270	+6.2
El Reno	961	988	900	+61	+6.8
Lompoc	876	1,133	1,000	-124	-12.4
Milan	584	617	535	+49	+9.2
Oxford	491	211	500	-9	-1.8
Petersburg	670	612	528	+142	+26.9
Seagoville	427	443	400	+27	+6.8
Tallahassee	604	571	480	+124	+25.8
Long term adults	7,792	8,032	6,855	+937	+13.7
Atlanta	2,065	2,092	1,900	+165	+8.7
Leavenworth	1,726	1,988	1,680	+46	+2.7
Lewisburg	1,509	1,544	1,150	+359	+31.2
Marion	483	442	525	-42	-8.0
McNeil Island	838	815	750	+88	+11.7
Terre Haute	1,171	1,151	850	+321	+37.8
Intermediate term adults	3,962	4,089	3,600	+362	+10.1
Danbury	681	811	600	+81	+13.5
Fort Worth	332	384	400	-68	-17.0
La Tuna	701	727	550	+151	+27.5
Lexington	468	231	525	-57	-10.9
Sandstone	425	559	450	-25	-5.6
Terminal Island	710	791	600	+110	+18.3
Texarkana	645	586	475	+170	+35.8

Short term adults	3,823	3,713	3,822	+1	+.0
Allenwood (camp)	410	384	410	+0	+.0
Eglin (camp)	379	459	450	-71	-15.8
El Paso Detention Center	153	164	155	-2	-1.3
Florence Detention Center	94	166	130	-36	-27.7
Leavenworth (camp)	137	215	220	-83	-37.7
Lompoc (camp)	277	354	350	-73	-20.9
Marion (camp)	95	96	95	+0	+.0
McNeil (camp)	210	244	250	-40	-16.0
Montgomery (camp)	284	274	250	+34	+13.6
New York Detention Center	385	370	225	+160	+71.1
Safford (camp)	271	326	250	+21	+8.4
San Diego Metropolitan Correctional Center	485	0	456	+29	+6.4
Springfield (camp)	366	378	356	+10	+2.8
Terre Haute (camp)	277	283	225	+52	+23.1
Female offenders	1,039	965	1,208	-169	-14.0
Alderson	472	480	475	-3	-.6
Fort Worth	90	103	100	-10	-10.0
Lexington	240	96	275	-35	-12.7
Morgantown	0	103	120	-120	-100.0
Pleasanton	58	0	60	-2	-3.3
San Diego	50	0	48	+2	+4.2
Terminal Island	129	183	160	-31	-19.4
Intensive medical treatment	614	682	600	+14	+2.3
Springfield Hospital	614	682	600	+14	+2.3
Community treatment centers	468	448	575	-107	-18.6
Atlanta	44	31	50	-6	-12.0
Chicago	70	55	55	+15	+27.3
Dallas	23	34	30	-7	-23.3
Detroit	52	44	54	-2	-3.7
Houston	20	28	36	-16	-44.4
Kansas City	39	28	40	-1	-2.5
Long Beach	15	0	30	-15	-50.0
Los Angeles	46	55	50	-4	-8.0
Miami	15	0	34	-19	-55.9
New York	108	149	130	-22	-16.9
Oakland	16	24	26	-10	-38.5
Phoenix	20	0	40	-20	-50.0

a Zero in this column indicates no previous year data.

Source: U.S. Department of Justice, Federal Prison System, *Statistical Report, Fiscal Year 1975* (Washington, D.C.: Federal Prison System, 1977), p. 44.

Figure 9 Average sentence for, and average time served by, first releases from Federal institutions, fiscal years 1965–75

[Excludes Youth Corrections Act releases]

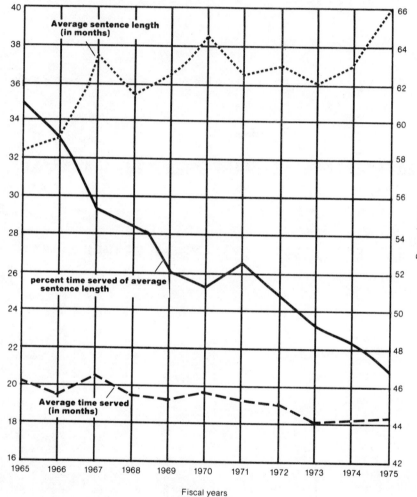

Source: U.S. Department of Justice, Federal Prison System, *Statistical Report, Fiscal Year 1975* (Washington, D.C.: Federal Prison System, 1977), p. 15.

Figure 10 Prisoners under sentence of death, by jurisdiction, on Dec. 31, 1975

NOTE: For the period covered, there were no statutory provisions for capital punishment in Alaska, Hawaii, Iowa, Maine, Michigan, Minnesota, Oregon, West Virginia, and Wisconsin.

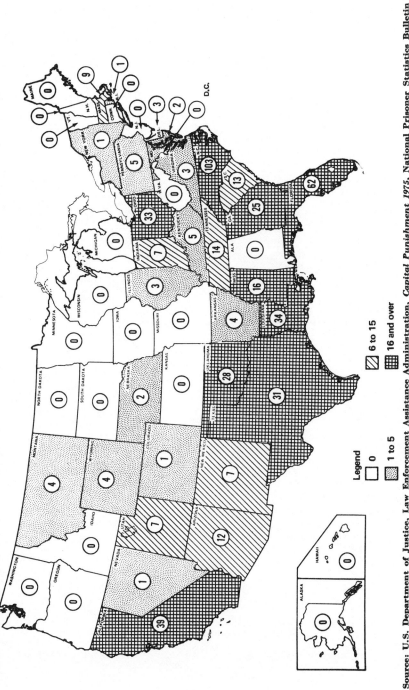

Legend

☐ 0

▨ 1 to 5

▨ 6 to 15

▨ 16 and over

Source: U.S. Department of Justice, Law Enforcement Assistance Administration, *Capital Punishment 1975*, National Prisoner Statistics Bulletin No. SD-NPS-CP-4 (Washington, D.C.: U.S. Government Printing Office, 1976), p. 10.

Table 64 Number of, average sentence for, and average time served by, first releases from Federal institutions, by offense and type of release, fiscal year 1975

Offense	All prisoners			
			Average time served	
	Number	Average sentence	Months	Percent of average sentence
Total	11,313	39.8	18.5	46.4
Assault	34	47.5	25.4	53.6
Bankruptcy	2	24.0	13.0	54.2
Burglary	51	61.3	31.2	50.8
Counterfeiting	282	48.0	21.7	45.3
Drug laws, total	2,898	45.3	20.9	46.2
Non-narcotics	926	30.8	14.2	46.0
Narcotics	1,578	58.8	26.9	45.9
Controlled substances	394	25.2	12.7	50.3
Embezzlement	177	22.0	11.0	50.0
Escape, flight or harboring a fugitive	92	36.5	21.4	58.5
Extortion	70	48.3	22.8	47.2
Firearms	558	30.4	15.4	50.7
Forgery	452	33.9	18.9	55.8
Fraud	347	26.6	12.0	45.0
Immigration	2,073	8.1	5.5	68.5
Income tax	217	14.6	7.6	52.1
Juvenile delinquency	244	34.5	17.9	52.0
Kidnaping	26	178.7	58.1	32.5
Larceny/theft, total	1,737	34.7	18.9	54.4
Motor vehicle, interstate	795	38.6	22.0	57.1
Postal	429	26.2	14.9	56.9
Theft, interstate	232	37.6	18.5	49.1
Other	281	34.5	16.5	47.8
Liquor laws	236	19.7	11.0	55.7
National security laws	4	21.0	15.8	75.0
Robbery	807	135.5	48.1	35.5
Selective Service Acts	54	17.7	10.0	56.7
Securities, transporting false or forged	250	45.0	21.3	47.3
White slave traffic	20	38.3	20.5	53.5
Other and unclassifiable	418	27.6	13.8	50.0
Government reservation, high seas, territorial, and District of Columbia	250	59.6	26.9	45.2
Assault	56	32.5	15.5	47.7
Auto theft	6	32.5	19.7	60.5
Burglary	28	28.1	15.8	56.0
Forgery	8	52.8	19.6	37.2
Homicide	30	203.2	94.8	46.7
Larceny/theft	47	24.0	12.1	50.5
Robbery	22	87.7	32.9	37.5
Rape	12	129.0	43.3	33.6
Sex offenses, except rape	3	41.3	17.0	41.1
Other and unclassifiable	38	22.2	11.5	51.8
Military court-martial cases	14	134.9	52.0	38.5

"Average sentence" is in months.

[Population 13,732. Data complete on 82.4 percent of the population.]

Releases except of prisoners sentenced under the Youth Corrections Act								Youth Corrections Act releases	
By parole				By expiration of sentence and mandatory release					
Number	Average sentence	Average time served		Number	Average sentence	Average time served		Number	Average time served
		Months	Percent of average sentence			Months	Percent of average sentence		
4,367	73.7	27.8	37.8	6,946	18.5	12.6	67.8	1,136	21.6
8	102.9	44.3	43.0	26	30.5	19.7	64.5	2	28.0
1	36.0	19.0	52.8	1	12.0	7.0	58.3	0	X
24	85.0	37.8	44.4	27	40.2	25.3	62.9	8	18.3
156	65.7	25.7	39.0	126	26.1	16.9	64.7	15	19.9
1,380	68.2	26.7	39.2	1,518	24.4	15.7	64.0	410	18.0
431	49.4	19.4	39.3	495	14.6	9.6	65.6	169	17.5
838	79.0	31.0	39.2	740	35.8	22.4	62.4	187	18.2
111	59.2	22.8	38.5	283	11.9	8.7	73.2	54	18.9
65	43.9	17.4	39.6	112	9.3	7.3	78.3	7	13.4
28	69.4	31.4	45.3	64	22.2	17.0	76.5	6	14.2
34	72.5	28.4	39.2	36	25.4	17.4	68.6	10	22.8
196	52.4	20.0	38.1	362	18.5	13.0	69.9	59	18.5
183	53.1	21.6	40.7	269	20.8	17.1	82.0	48	19.9
148	44.2	16.8	38.0	199	13.6	8.4	62.0	17	15.1
142	37.7	14.2	37.6	1,931	5.9	4.9	83.0	14	20.9
51	36.4	13.3	36.5	166	8.0	5.9	73.9	1	56.0
148	39.6	17.2	43.5	96	26.5	19.0	71.7	0	X
23	192.3	59.5	31.0	3	74.3	47.3	63.7	5	38.8
683	50.6	22.3	44.0	1,054	24.5	16.7	68.3	238	22.1
304	49.4	22.5	45.6	491	31.9	21.7	68.1	128	24.2
150	42.9	19.4	45.1	279	17.2	12.5	72.6	67	20.1
111	55.2	24.5	44.3	121	21.5	13.0	60.3	10	19.7
118	59.3	23.3	39.2	163	16.5	11.6	70.2	33	18.6
71	34.9	14.2	40.8	165	13.2	9.6	72.6	5	17.8
0	X	0	X	4	21.0	15.8	75.0	0	X
640	151.1	49.5	32.7	167	75.7	43.1	56.9	163	30.0
19	29.1	14.1	48.4	35	11.5	7.8	68.2	10	24.7
131	62.7	24.9	39.7	119	25.4	17.3	68.1	20	19.3
8	51.0	20.4	40.0	12	29.8	20.6	69.0	1	34.0
136	53.0	20.8	39.3	282	15.4	10.4	67.7	22	22.1
84	137.7	54.8	39.8	166	20.1	12.8	63.9	75	25.7
9	82.7	25.3	30.6	47	22.9	13.6	59.4	13	30.2
2	48.0	20.0	41.7	4	24.8	19.5	78.8	2	22.5
4	49.5	20.0	40.4	24	24.5	15.0	61.3	7	23.3
4	87.3	25.8	29.5	4	18.3	13.5	74.0	0	X
19	299.4	137.4	45.9	11	37.1	21.2	57.1	8	38.9
12	53.5	19.9	37.2	35	13.9	9.5	68.0	20	19.3
16	101.9	33.5	32.9	6	49.8	31.3	62.9	13	28.5
7	209.1	65.9	31.5	5	16.8	11.8	70.2	1	20.0
2	60.0	24.5	40.8	1	4.0	2.0	50.0	0	X
9	70.2	28.4	40.5	29	7.3	6.2	85.8	11	21.5
8	182.3	61.8	33.9	6	71.8	39.0	54.3	0	X

Source: U.S. Department of Justice, Federal Prison System, *Statistical Report, Fiscal Year 1975* (Washington, D.C.: Federal Prison System, 1977), pp. 95, 96.

Table 65 Number of, average sentence for, and average time served by, first releases from Federal institutions, by sentencing procedure, race, and type of release, fiscal year 1975

Sentencing procedure and race	All prisoners			
			Average time served	
	Number	Average sentence	Months	Percent of average sentence
Total	11,356	39.9	18.5	46.4
Regular	6,786	35.1	18.0	51.2
Federal Juvenile Delinquency Act	81	22.6	14.0	61.9
Youth Corrections Act (b)	0	×	0	×
Youth Corrections Act (c)	0	×	0	×
4208 (a) (1)	77	76.4	25.8	33.7
4208 (a) (2)	2,742	66.8	26.9	40.3
Split Sentence	1,400	5.4	4.1	77.2
Minority	164	40.5	19.9	49.2
Narcotic Addict Rehabilitation Act	102	95.5	21.2	22.2
Other	4	2.8	5.0	181.8
White	8,517	36.0	17.0	47.2
Regular	5,209	31.8	16.4	51.7
Federal Juvenile Delinquency Act	60	21.0	12.7	60.7
Youth Corrections Act (b)	0	×	0	×
Youth Corrections Act (c)	0	×	0	×
4208 (a) (1)	39	81.3	25.6	31.5
4208 (a) (2)	1,947	62.8	25.8	41.0
Split Sentence	1,111	5.2	4.0	78.5
Minority	96	40.4	18.0	44.4
Narcotic Addict Rehabilitation Act	52	96.4	19.3	20.0
Other	3	2.7	5.7	212.5
Other	2,839	51.5	23.1	44.8
Regular	1,577	46.1	23.2	50.2
Federal Juvenile Delinquency Act	21	27.2	17.6	64.6
Youth Corrections Act (b)	0	×	0	×
Youth Corrections Act (c)	0	×	0	×
4208 (a) (1)	38	71.5	26.0	36.3
4208 (a) (2)	795	76.5	29.7	38.8
Split Sentence	289	6.2	4.5	73.0
Minority	68	40.5	22.7	55.9
Narcotic Addict Rehabilitation Act	50	94.6	23.1	24.5
Other	1	3.0	3.0	100.0

"Average sentence" is in months.

[Population 13,732. Data complete on 82.7 percent of the population.]

Releases except of prisoners sentenced under the Youth Corrections Act								Youth Corrections Act releases	
By parole				By expiration of sentence and mandatory release					
		Average time served				Average time served			
Number	Average sentence	Months	Percent of average sentence	Number	Average sentence	Months	Percent of average sentence	Number	Average time served
4,394	73.6	27.8	37.8	6,962	18.6	12.6	67.7	1,144	21.6
2,211	69.4	29.0	41.8	4,575	18.5	12.7	68.4	0	X
37	27.9	13.9	49.7	44	18.1	14.1	77.9	0	X
0	X	0	X	0	X	0	X	1,055	20.7
0	X	0	X	0	X	0	X	89	32.3
58	92.6	29.8	32.2	19	27.1	13.5	50.0	0	X
1,873	79.5	27.7	34.8	869	39.3	25.2	64.2	0	X
7	9.9	6.1	62.3	1,393	5.3	4.1	77.3	0	X
112	43.6	18.4	42.1	52	33.7	23.2	68.9	0	X
96	99.3	21.3	21.4	6	35.5	19.7	55.4	0	X
0	X	0	X	4	2.8	5.0	181.8	0	X
3,075	69.7	26.7	38.3	5,442	17.0	11.5	67.6	757	20.0
1,598	66.2	28.0	42.3	3,611	16.5	11.3	68.3	0	X
29	27.2	13.4	49.4	31	15.2	12.1	79.8	0	X
0	X	0	X	0	X	0	X	726	19.7
0	X	0	X	0	X	0	X	31	27.2
24	116.3	34.1	29.4	15	25.3	11.9	47.2	0	X
1,299	74.5	26.1	35.0	648	39.3	25.2	64.0	0	X
4	5.8	4.3	73.9	1,107	5.2	4.0	78.5	0	X
71	43.1	17.3	40.0	25	32.9	20.0	60.7	0	X
50	99.8	19.7	19.7	2	10.5	8.0	76.2	0	X
0	X	0	X	3	2.7	5.7	212.5	0	X
1,319	82.7	30.5	36.9	1,520	24.4	16.6	68.0	387	24.6
613	77.7	31.5	40.5	964	26.0	17.8	68.6	0	X
8	30.8	15.6	50.8	13	25.0	18.8	75.1	0	X
0	X	0	X	0	X	0	X	329	22.8
0	X	0	X	0	X	0	X	58	35.0
34	75.9	26.7	35.2	4	33.8	19.5	57.8	0	X
574	90.9	31.3	34.5	221	39.3	25.4	64.7	0	X
3	15.3	8.7	56.5	286	6.1	4.5	73.5	0	X
41	44.5	20.3	45.6	27	34.5	26.2	76.0	0	X
46	98.6	22.9	23.3	4	48.0	25.5	53.1	0	X
0	X	0	X	1	3.0	3.0	100.0	0	X

Source: U.S. Department of Justice, Federal Prison System, *Statistical Report, Fiscal Year 1975* (Washington, D.C.: Federal Prison System, 1977), p. 103.

467

Table 66 Escape and apprehension activity involving escapes from Federal institutions, by institution from which escape occurred, fiscal year 1975

Institution[a]	Escape and apprehension activity fiscal year 1975 escapes only			Apprehensions in fiscal year 1975 of escapees of previous fiscal years
	Escapes	Apprehensions	Still at large	
Bureau of Prisons institutions	853	538	315	7
Percent	100.0	63.0	36.9	X
Juvenile and youths	92	75	17	3
Ashland	17	15	2	2
Englewood	40	33	7	0
Morgantown (Male)	25	20	5	1
Pleasanton (Male)	7	4	3	0
Pleasanton (Female)	3	3	0	0
Young adults	111	91	20	0
El Reno	14	10	4	0
Lompoc	7	4	3	0
Milan	14	10	4	0
Petersburg	21	19	2	0
Seagoville	33	27	6	0
Tallahassee	22	21	1	0
Long term adults	43	29	14	1
Atlanta	9	7	2	0
Leavenworth	7	5	2	0
Lewisburg	16	12	4	0
Marion Penitentiary	1	0	1	0
McNeil Island Penitentiary	6	3	3	1
Terre Haute	4	2	2	0
Intermediate term adults	162	111	51	0
Danbury	12	7	5	0
Fort Worth (Male)	35	28	7	0
La Tuna	33	14	19	0
Lexington Kentucky (Male)	27	24	3	0
Sandstone	4	4	0	0
Terminal Island (Male)	32	21	11	0
Texarkana	19	13	6	0

468

Short term adults	260	112	148	2
Allenwood	12	7	5	1
Eglin	27	20	7	0
El Paso Detention Center	6	5	1	1
Florence Detention Center	9	1	8	0
Leavenworth Camp	7	5	2	0
Lompoc Camp	105	25	80	0
Marion Camp	4	4	0	0
McNeil Island Camp	5	2	3	0
Montgomery	14	12	2	0
New York Metropolitan Correctional Center (Male)	17	1	16	0
Safford	28	10	18	0
San Diego Metropolitan Correctional Center (Male)	1	0	1	0
Springfield Camp	6	5	1	0
Terre Haute Federal Prison Camp	19	15	4	0
Female offenders	22	18	4	1
Alderson	2	2	0	0
Fort Worth (Female)	7	5	2	1
Lexington Kentucky (Female)	5	4	1	0
Morgantown (Female)	5	5	0	0
Terminal Island (Female)	3	2	1	0
Intensive medical treatment	6	4	2	0
Springfield Hospital	6	4	2	0
Community treatment centers	157	98	59	0
Atlanta Community Treatment Center	9	8	1	0
Chicago Community Treatment Center	22	10	12	0
Dallas Community Treatment Center	11	7	4	0
Detroit Community Treatment Center	13	11	2	0
Houston Community Treatment Center	15	9	6	0
Kansas City Community Treatment Center	9	7	2	0
Los Angeles Community Treatment Center	30	18	12	0
Miami Community Treatment Center	1	0	1	0
New York Community Treatment Center	38	25	13	0
Oakland Community Treatment Center	6	3	3	0
Phoenix Community Treatment Center	3	0	3	0

[a] Institution from which escape occurred. Report includes escapes while on furlough or enroute.

Source: U.S. Department of Justice, Federal Prison System, *Statistical Report, Fiscal Year 1975* (Washington, D.C.: Federal Prison System, 1977), pp. 111, 112.

Table 67 Conditional and unconditional releases of prisoners from State and Federal institutions, by type of release, region, and jurisdiction, 1975

Region and jurisdiction	Conditional release					Unconditional release			
	Total	Parole	Probation	Supervised mandatory release	Other	Total	Expiration of sentence	Commutation of sentence	Other
United States, total	89,808	78,724	3,121	7,149	814	30,694	26,640	2,234	1,820
Federal institutions, total	7,485	5,783	0	1,702	0	6,275	6,275	0	0
State institutions, total	82,323	72,941	3,121	5,447	814	24,419	20,365	2,234	1,820
Northeast	15,990	13,382	82	1,914	612	2,384	1,636	694	54
Maine	595	519	76	0	0	54	53	1	0
New Hampshire	192	191	0	0	1	16	5	11	0
Vermont	120	120	0	0	0	2	2	0	0
Massachusetts	705	705	0	0	0	235	218	0	17
Rhode Island	226	220	6	0	0	51	51	0	0
Connecticut	926	926	0	0	0	485	442	43	0
New York	6,151	4,237	0	1,914	0	669	456	213	0
New Jersey	3,087	3,087	0	0	0	208	208	0	0
Pennsylvania	3,988	3,377	0	0	611	664	201	426	37
North Central	19,106	16,179	2,184	667	76	2,563	2,343	161	59
Ohio	5,608	4,081	1,527	0	0	71	27	44	0
Indiana	1,381	1,125	256	0	0	336	336	0	0
Illinois	3,782	3,646	0	136	0	251	186	6	59
Michigan	3,279	3,267	12	0	0	344	293	51	0
Wisconsin	1,129	845	0	284	0	58	39	19	0
Minnesota	625	611	14	0	0	133	117	16	0
Iowa	429	429	0	0	0	231	219	12	0
Missouri	908	879	0	0	29	839	839	0	0
North Dakota	89	89	0	0	0	39	26	13	0
South Dakota	178	148	0	30	0	73	73	0	0
Nebraska	493	275	3	215	0	188	188	0	0
Kansas	1,205	784	372	2	47	0	0	0	0

South	30,200	26,805	452	2,841	102	17,347	14,661	1,355	1,331
Delaware	204	204	0	0	0	47	22	0	25
Maryland	3,267	2,652	0	613	2	957	129	159	669
District of Columbia	1,151	812	0	339	0	385	385	0	0
Virginia	1,435	1,435	0	0	0	899	894	0	5
West Virginia	258	241	0	0	17	40	25	0	15
North Carolina	4,391	4,391	0	0	0	1,912	1,803	109	0
South Carolina	665	665	0	0	0	2,539	2,304	235	0
Georgia	2,368	1,740	79	549	0	2,137	1,045	542	550
Florida	2,749	1,794	0	872	83	1,275	1,256	19	0
Kentucky	1,970	1,345	327	298	0	208	158	50	0
Tennessee	1,592	1,422	0	170	0	274	244	30	0
Alabama	1,418	1,418	0	0	0	908	861	0	47
Mississippi	710	710	0	0	0	411	411	0	0
Arkansas	1,536	1,536	0	0	0	244	188	37	19
Louisiana	778	778	0	0	0	849	842	6	1
Oklahoma	1,034	988	46	0	0	1,157	989	168	0
Texas	4,674	4,674	0	0	0	3,105	3,105	0	0
West	17,027	16,575	403	25	24	2,125	1,725	24	376
Montana	276	243	33	0	0	25	18	0	7
Idaho	474	232	242	0	0	36	36	0	0
Wyoming	51	30	21	0	0	85	85	0	0
Colorado	1,353	1,280	53	0	20	104	86	18	0
New Mexico	535	534	0	0	1	40	40	0	0
Arizona	550	475	50	25	0	326	294	0	32
Utah	207	207	0	0	0	12	8	3	1
Nevada	392	392	0	0	0	92	82	0	10
Washington	1,411	1,408	0	0	3	7	4	3	0
Oregon	713	713	0	0	0	335	335	0	0
California	10,864	10,864	0	0	0	943	617	0	326
Alaska	98	98	0	0	0	82	82	0	0
Hawaii	103	99	4	0	0	38	38	0	0

Source: U.S. Department of Justice, Law Enforcement Assistance Administration, *Prisoners in State and Federal Institutions on December 31, 1975*, National Prisoner Statistics Bulletin No. SD–NPS–PSF–3 (Washington, D.C.: U.S. Government Printing Office, 1977), pp. 28, 29.

Table 68 Prisoners executed under civil authority, by region and jurisdiction, 1930–75

[xx signifies that the death penalty was illegal]

Region and jurisdiction	Total	1975	1974	1973	1972	1971	1970	1965 to 1969	1960 to 1964	1955 to 1959	1950 to 1954	1945 to 1949	1940 to 1944	1935 to 1939	1930 to 1934
United States, total	3,859	0	0	0	0	0	0	10	181	304	413	639	645	891	776
Federal	33	0	0	0	0	0	0	0	1	3	6	6	7	9	1
State, total	3,826	0	0	0	0	0	0	10	180	301	407	633	638	882	775
Northeast	608	0	0	0	0	0	0	0	17	51	56	74	110	145	155
Maine	xx	xx	xx	xx	xx	xx	xx	xx	xx	xx	xx	xx	xx	xx	xx
New Hampshire	1	0	0	0	0	0	0	0	0	0	0	0	0	1	0
Vermont	4	0	0	0	0	0	0	0	0	0	2	1	0	0	1
Massachusetts	27	0	0	0	0	0	0	0	0	0	0	3	6	11	7
Rhode Island	0	0	0	0	0	0	0	0	0	0	0	0	0	0	0
Connecticut	21	0	0	0	0	0	0	0	1	5	0	5	5	3	2
New York	329	0	0	0	0	0	0	0	10	25	27	36	78	73	80
New Jersey	74	0	0	0	0	0	0	0	3	9	8	8	6	16	24
Pennsylvania	152	0	0	0	0	0	0	0	3	12	19	21	15	41	41
North Central	403	0	0	0	0	0	0	5	16	16	42	64	42	113	105
Ohio	172	0	0	0	0	0	0	0	7	12	20	36	15	39	43
Indiana	41	0	0	0	0	0	0	0	1	0	2	5	2	20	11
Illinois	90	0	0	0	0	0	0	0	2	1	8	5	13	27	34
Michigan	0	0	0	0	0	0	0	0	0	0	0	0	0	0	0
Wisconsin	xx	xx	xx	xx	xx	xx	xx	xx	xx	xx	xx	xx	xx	xx	xx
Minnesota	xx	xx	xx	xx	xx	xx	xx	xx	xx	xx	xx	xx	xx	xx	xx
Iowa	18	0	0	0	0	0	0	0	2	0	1	4	3	7	1
Missouri	62	0	0	0	0	0	0	1	3	2	5	9	6	20	16
North Dakota	0	0	0	0	0	0	0	0	0	0	0	0	0	0	0
South Dakota	1	0	0	0	0	0	0	0	0	0	0	1	0	0	0
Nebraska	4	0	0	0	0	0	0	0	0	1	1	2	0	0	0
Kansas	15	0	0	0	0	0	0	4	1	0	5	2	3	0	xx

South	2,306	0	0	0	0	0	0	2	102	183	244	419	413	524	419
Delaware	12	0	0	0	0	0	0	0	0	0	0	2	2	6	2
Maryland	68	0	0	0	0	0	0	0	1	4	2	19	26	10	6
District of Columbia	40	0	0	0	0	0	0	0	0	1	3	13	3	5	15
Virginia	92	0	0	0	0	0	0	0	6	8	15	22	13	20	8
West Virginia	40	xx	xx	xx	xx	xx	xx	xx	0	4	5	9	2	10	10
North Carolina	263	0	0	0	0	0	0	0	1	5	14	62	50	80	51
South Carolina	162	0	0	0	0	0	0	0	8	10	16	29	32	30	37
Georgia	366	0	0	0	0	0	0	0	14	34	51	72	58	73	64
Florida	170	0	0	0	0	0	0	0	12	27	22	27	38	29	15
Kentucky	103	0	0	0	0	0	0	0	1	8	8	15	19	34	18
Tennessee	93	0	0	0	0	0	0	0	1	7	1	18	19	31	16
Alabama	135	0	0	0	0	0	0	1	4	6	14	21	29	41	19
Mississippi	154	0	0	0	0	0	0	0	10	21	15	26	34	22	26
Arkansas	118	0	0	0	0	0	0	0	9	7	11	18	20	33	20
Louisiana	133	0	0	0	0	0	0	0	1	13	14	23	24	19	39
Oklahoma	60	0	0	0	0	0	0	1	5	3	4	7	6	9	25
Texas	297	0	0	0	0	0	0	0	29	25	49	36	38	72	48
West	509	0	0	0	0	0	0	3	45	51	65	76	73	100	96
Montana	6	0	0	0	0	0	0	0	0	0	0	0	1	4	1
Idaho	3	0	0	0	0	0	0	0	0	1	2	0	0	0	0
Wyoming	7	0	0	0	0	0	0	1	0	0	0	0	2	1	3
Colorado	47	0	0	0	0	0	0	1	5	2	1	7	6	9	16
New Mexico	8	0	0	0	0	0	0	0	1	1	2	2	0	0	2
Arizona	38	0	0	0	0	0	0	0	4	6	2	3	6	10	7
Utah	13	0	0	0	0	0	0	0	1	4	2	1	3	2	0
Nevada	29	0	0	0	0	0	0	0	2	0	9	5	5	3	5
Washington	47	0	0	0	0	0	0	0	2	2	4	7	9	13	10
Oregon	19	xx	xx	xx	xx	xx	xx	xx	1	0	4	6	6	1	1
California	292	0	0	xx	xx	0	0	1	29	35	39	45	35	57	51
Alaska[a]	xx	xx	xx	xx	xx	xx	xx	xx	xx	0	0	0	0	0	0
Hawaii [a]	xx	xx	xx	xx	xx	xx	xx	xx	xx	0	0	0	0	0	0

[a] Alaska and Hawaii are included in the series beginning Jan. 1, 1960, except for three federal executions in Alaska.

Source: U.S. Department of Justice, Law Enforcement Assistance Administration, *Capital Punishment 1975*, National Prisoner Statistics Bulletin No. SD-NPS-CP-4 (Washington, D.C.: U.S. Government Printing Office, 1976), pp. 16, 17.

Table 69 Prisoners executed under civil authority, by offense, race, region, and jurisdiction, 1930–75 (aggregate)

[xx signifies that the death penalty was illegal]

Region and jurisdiction	All offenses				Murder			
	Total	White	Black	Other	Total	White	Black	Other
United States, total	3,859	1,751	2,066	42	3,334	1,664	1,630	40
Percent	100.0	—	—	—	86.4	—	—	—
Federal	33	28	3	2	15	10	3	2
State, total	3,826	1,723	2,063	40	3,319	1,654	1,627	38
Northeast	608	424	177	7	606	422	177	7
Maine	xx	xx	xx	xx	xx	xx	xx	xx
New Hampshire	1	1	0	0	1	1	0	0
Vermont	4	4	0	0	4	4	0	0
Massachusetts	27	25	2	0	27	25	2	0
Rhode Island	0	0	0	0	0	0	0	0
Connecticut	21	18	3	0	21	18	3	0
New York	329	234	90	5	327	232	90	5
New Jersey	74	47	25	2	74	47	25	2
Pennsylvania	152	95	57	0	152	95	57	0
North Central	403	257	144	2	393	254	137	2
Ohio	172	104	67	1	172	104	67	1
Indiana	41	31	10	0	41	31	10	0
Illinois	90	59	31	0	90	59	31	0
Michigan[b]	0	0	0	0	0	0	0	0
Wisconsin[c]	0	0	0	0	0	0	0	0
Minnesota	xx	xx	xx	xx	xx	xx	xx	xx
Iowa[d]	18	18	0	0	18	18	0	0
Missouri	62	29	33	0	52	26	26	0
North Dakota	0	0	0	0	0	0	0	0
South Dakota[e]	1	1	0	0	1	1	0	0
Nebraska	4	3	0	1	4	3	0	1
Kansas[f]	15	12	3	0	15	12	3	0

South	2,306	637	1,659	10	1,824	585	1,231	8
Delaware[g]	12	5	7	0	8	4	4	0
Maryland	68	13	55	0	44	7	37	0
District of Columbia	40	3	37	0	37	3	34	0
Virginia	92	17	75	0	71	17	54	0
West Virginia[h]	40	31	9	0	36	28	8	0
North Carolina	263	59	199	5	207	55	149	3
South Carolina	162	35	127	0	120	30	90	0
Georgia	366	68	298	0	299	65	234	0
Florida	170	57	113	0	133	55	78	0
Kentucky	103	51	52	0	88	47	41	0
Tennessee	93	27	66	0	66	22	44	0
Alabama	135	28	107	0	106	26	80	0
Mississippi	154	30	124	0	130	30	100	0
Arkansas	118	27	90	1	99	25	73	1
Louisiana	133	30	103	0	116	30	86	0
Oklahoma	60	42	15	3	54	40	11	3
Texas	297	114	182	1	210	101	108	1
West	509	405	83	21	496	393	82	21
Montana	6	4	2	0	6	4	2	0
Idaho	3	3	0	0	3	3	0	0
Wyoming	7	6	1	0	7	6	1	0
Colorado	47	41	5	1	47	41	5	1
New Mexico	8	6	2	0	8	6	2	0
Arizona	38	28	10	0	38	28	10	0
Utah	13	13	0	0	13	13	0	0
Nevada	29	27	2	0	29	27	2	0
Washington	47	40	5	2	46	39	5	2
Oregon[i]	19	16	3	0	19	16	3	0
California	292	221	53	18	280	210	52	18
Alaska[j]	0	0	0	0	0	0	0	0
Hawaii[j]	0	0	0	0	0	0	0	0

a In this category, the 8 federal executions were for sabotage (6) and espionage (2). The 9 executions in North Carolina and the 2 in Alabama were for burglary. In California, the 6 executions were for aggravated assault committed by prisoners under a life sentence.

b The death penalty was abolished for all crimes except treason in 1847. It was totally abolished in Michigan in 1963.

c Wisconsin's death penalty was abolished in 1853.

d Iowa's death penalty was abolished in 1963.

e South Dakota's death penalty was abolished in 1915 and restored in 1939.

f Kansas's death penalty was abolished in 1907 and restored in 1935.

Table 69 (continued)

Region and jurisdiction	Rape				Other offenses Total		
	Total	White	Black	Other	Total	White	Black
United States, total	455	48	405	2	70	39	31
Percent	11.8	—	—	—	1.8	—	—
Federal	2	2	0	0	16	16	0
State, total	453	46	405	2	54	23	31
Northeast							
Maine	0	0	0	0	2	2	0
New Hampshire	xx	xx	xx	xx	xx	xx	xx
Vermont	0	0	0	0	0	0	0
Massachusetts	0	0	0	0	0	0	0
Rhode Island	0	0	0	0	0	0	0
Connecticut	0	0	0	0	0	0	0
New York	0	0	0	0	0	2	0
New Jersey	0	0	0	0	2	2	0
Pennsylvania	0	0	0	0	0	0	0
North Central							
Ohio	10	3	7	0	0	0	0
Indiana	0	0	0	0	0	0	0
Illinois	0	0	0	0	0	0	0
Michigan [b]	0	0	0	0	0	0	0
Wisconsin [c]	0	0	0	0	0	0	0
Minnesota	0	0	0	0	0	0	0
Iowa [d]	xx	xx	xx	xx	xx	xx	xx
Missouri	0	0	0	0	0	0	0
North Dakota	10	3	7	0	0	0	0
South Dakota [e]	0	0	0	0	0	0	0
Nebraska	0	0	0	0	0	0	0
Kansas [f]	0	0	0	0	0	0	0

Region / State						
South	443	43	398	2	39	9	30
Delaware[g]	4	1	3	0	0	0	0
Maryland	24	6	18	0	0	0	0
District of Columbia	3	0	3	0	0	0	0
Virginia	21	0	21	0	3	3	0
West Virginia[h]	1	0	1	0	9	0	9
North Carolina	47	4	41	2	0	0	0
South Carolina	42	5	37	0	6	0	6
Georgia	61	3	58	0	1	1	0
Florida	36	1	35	0	5	0	5
Kentucky	10	1	9	0	0	0	0
Tennessee	27	5	22	0	7	0	7
Alabama	22	2	20	0	3	3	0
Mississippi	21	0	21	0	0	0	0
Arkansas	19	2	17	0	0	0	0
Louisiana	17	0	17	0	2	2	0
Oklahoma	4	0	4	0	3	0	3
Texas	84	13	71	0	0	0	0
West	0	0	0	0	13	12	1
Montana	0	0	0	0	0	0	0
Idaho	0	0	0	0	0	0	0
Wyoming	0	0	0	0	0	0	0
Colorado	0	0	0	0	0	0	0
New Mexico	0	0	0	0	0	0	0
Arizona	0	0	0	0	0	0	0
Utah	0	0	0	0	0	0	0
Nevada	0	0	0	0	0	0	0
Washington	0	0	0	0	1	1	0
Oregon[i]	0	0	0	0	0	0	0
California[j]	0	0	0	0	12	11	1
Alaska[j]	0	0	0	0	0	0	0
Hawaii[j]	0	0	0	0	0	0	0

[g] Delaware's death penalty was abolished in 1958 and restored in 1961. Discretionary provisions of the 1961 legislation were struck down by the State Supreme Court Nov. 1, 1972, and remaining provisions were declared constitutional. Statutes were revised Mar. 29, 1974.
[h] West Virginia's death penalty was abolished in 1965.
[i] Oregon's death penalty was abolished in 1964.
[j] Alaska and Hawaii abolished capital punishment in 1957, when territories. As States, Alaska and Hawaii are included in the series beginning Jan. 1, 1960.

Source: U.S. Department of Justice, Law Enforcement Assistance Administration, *Capital Punishment 1975*, National Prisoner Statistics Bulletin No. SD-NPS-CP-4 (Washington, D.C.: U.S. Government Printing Office, 1976), pp. 18, 19.

Table 69 (continued)

Region and jurisdiction	Other offenses				
	Armed robbery		Kidnaping	Other[a]	
	White	Black	White	White	Black
United States, total	6	19	20	13	12
Percent	—	—	—	—	—
Federal	2	0	6	8	0
State, total	4	19	14	5	12
Northeast	0	0	2	0	0
Maine	xx	xx	xx	xx	xx
New Hampshire	0	0	0	0	0
Vermont	0	0	0	0	0
Massachusetts	0	0	0	0	0
Rhode Island	0	0	0	0	0
Connecticut	0	0	0	0	0
New York	0	0	2	0	0
New Jersey	0	0	0	0	0
Pennsylvania	0	0	0	0	0
North Central	0	0	0	0	0
Ohio	0	0	0	0	0
Indiana	0	0	0	0	0
Illinois	0	0	0	0	0
Michigan[b]	0	0	0	0	0
Wisconsin[c]	0	0	0	0	0
Minnesota	0	0	0	0	0
Iowa[d]	xx	xx	xx	xx	xx
Missouri	0	0	0	0	0
North Dakota	0	0	0	0	0
South Dakota[e]	0	0	0	0	0
Nebraska	0	0	0	0	0
Kansas[f]	0	0	0	0	0

South	4	19	5	0	11
Delaware [g]	0	0	0	0	0
Maryland	0	0	0	0	0
District of Columbia	0	0	3	0	0
Virginia	0	6	0	0	0
West Virginia [h]	0	2	0	0	0
North Carolina	3	5	1	0	9
South Carolina	0	3	0	0	0
Georgia	0	0	0	0	0
Florida	0	0	0	0	0
Kentucky	1	3	0	0	0
Tennessee	0	0	0	0	0
Alabama	0	0	1	0	2
Mississippi	0	0	0	0	0
Arkansas	0	0	0	0	0
Louisiana	0	0	0	0	0
Oklahoma	0	0	0	0	0
Texas	0	0	0	0	0
West	0	0	7	5	1
Montana	0	0	0	0	0
Idaho	0	0	0	0	0
Wyoming	0	0	0	0	0
Colorado	0	0	0	0	0
New Mexico	0	0	0	0	0
Arizona	0	0	0	0	0
Utah	0	0	0	0	0
Nevada	0	0	1	0	0
Washington	0	0	0	0	0
Oregon [i]	0	0	0	0	0
California	0	0	6	5	1
Alaska [j]	0	0	0	0	0
Hawaii [j]	0	0	0	0	0

Table 70 Prisoners executed under civil authority, by offense and race, United States, 1930–75

[The years 1930–59 exclude Alaska and Hawaii except for three Federal executions in Alaska: 1939, 1948, 1950]

Year	All offenses				Murder				Rape				Other offenses[a]		
	Total	White	Black	Other	Total	White	Black	Other	Total	White	Black	Other	Total	White	Black
All years	3,859	1,751	2,066	42	3,334	1,664	1,630	40	455	48	405	2	70	39	31
Percent	100.0	45.4	53.5	1.1	100.0	49.9	48.9	1.2	100.0	10.6	89.0	0.4	100.0	55.7	44.3
1975	0	0	0	0	0	0	0	0	0	0	0	0	0	0	0
1974	0	0	0	0	0	0	0	0	0	0	0	0	0	0	0
1973	0	0	0	0	0	0	0	0	0	0	0	0	0	0	0
1972	0	0	0	0	0	0	0	0	0	0	0	0	0	0	0
1971	0	0	0	0	0	0	0	0	0	0	0	0	0	0	0
1970	0	0	0	0	0	0	0	0	0	0	0	0	0	0	0
1969	0	0	0	0	0	0	0	0	0	0	0	0	0	0	0
1968	0	0	0	0	0	0	0	0	0	0	0	0	0	0	0
1967	2	1	1	0	2	1	1	0	0	0	0	0	0	0	0
1966	1	1	0	0	1	1	0	0	0	0	0	0	0	0	0
1965	7	6	1	0	7	6	1	0	0	0	0	0	0	0	0
1964	15	8	7	0	9	5	4	0	6	3	3	0	0	0	0
1963	21	13	8	0	18	12	6	0	2	0	2	0	1	1	0
1962	47	28	19	0	41	26	15	0	4	2	2	0	2	0	2
1961	42	20	22	0	33	18	15	0	8	1	7	0	1	1	0
1960	56	21	35	0	44	18	26	0	8	0	8	0	4	3	1
1959	49	16	33	0	41	15	26	0	8	1	7	0	0	0	0
1958	49	20	28	1	41	20	20	1	7	0	7	0	1	0	1
1957	65	34	31	0	54	32	22	0	10	2	8	0	1	0	1
1956	65	21	43	1	52	20	31	1	12	0	12	0	1	1	0
1955	76	44	32	0	65	41	24	0	7	1	6	0	4	2	2
1954	81	38	42	1	71	37	33	1	9	1	8	0	1	0	1
1953	62	30	31	1	51	25	25	1	7	1	6	0	4	4	0
1952	83	36	47	0	71	35	36	0	12	1	11	0	0	0	0
1951	105	57	47	1	87	55	31	1	17	2	15	0	1	0	1
1950	82	40	42	0	68	36	32	0	13	4	9	0	1	0	1

Year															
1949	119	50	67	2	107	49	56	2	10	0	10	0	2	1	1
1948	119	35	82	2	95	32	61	2	22	1	21	0	2	2	0
1947	153	42	111	0	129	40	89	0	23	2	21	0	1	0	1
1946	131	46	84	1	107	45	61	1	22	0	22	0	2	1	1
1945	117	41	75	1	90	37	52	1	26	4	22	0	1	0	1
1944	120	47	70	3	96	45	48	3	24	2	22	2	0	0	0
1943	131	54	74	3	118	54	63	1	13	0	11	0	0	0	0
1942	147	67	80	0	115	57	58	0	25	4	21	0	7	6	1
1941	123	59	63	1	102	55	46	1	20	4	16	0	1	0	1
1940	124	49	75	0	105	44	61	0	15	2	13	0	4	3	1
1939	160	80	77	3	145	79	63	3	12	0	12	0	3	1	2
1938	190	96	92	2	154	89	63	2	25	1	24	0	11	6	5
1937	147	69	74	4	133	67	62	4	13	2	11	0	1	0	1
1936	195	92	101	2	181	86	93	2	10	2	8	0	4	4	0
1935	199	119	77	3	184	115	66	3	13	2	11	0	2	2	0
1934	168	65	102	1	154	64	89	1	14	1	13	0	0	0	0
1933	160	77	81	2	151	75	74	2	7	1	6	0	2	1	1
1932	140	62	75	3	128	62	63	3	10	0	10	0	2	0	2
1931	153	77	72	4	137	76	57	4	15	1	14	0	1	0	1
1930	155	90	65	0	147	90	57	0	6	0	6	0	2	0	2

a Includes 25 armed robbery, 20 kidnaping, 11 burglary, 6 sabotage, 6 aggravated assault, and 2 espionage.

Source: U.S. Department of Justice, Law Enforcement Assistance Administration, *Capital Punishment 1975*, National Prisoner Statistics Bulletin No. SD-NPS-CP-4 (Washington, D.C.: U.S. Government Printing Office, 1976), pp. 14, 15.

Table 71 Female prisoners executed under civil authority, by offense, race, and jurisdiction, United States, 1930–75

NOTE: No executions of females occurred in 1952–53, 1959–40, 1948–60, 1952, 1956, 1958–61, and 1965–75.

[Includes State and Federal executions]

Year	Total	Offense		Race		Jurisdiction in which executed
		Murder	Other^a	White	Black	
All years	32	30	2	20	12	X
1962	1	1	0	1	0	California
1957	1	1	0	1	0	Alabama
1955	1	1	0	1	0	California
1954	2	2	0	1	1	Ohio
1953	3	1	2	3	0	Alabama, Federal (Missouri and New York)
1951	1	1	0	1	0	New York
1947	2	2	0	1	1	California, South Carolina
1946	1	1	0	0	1	Pennsylvania
1945	1	1	0	0	1	Georgia
1944	3	3	0	0	3	Mississippi, New York, North Carolina
1943	3	3	0	1	2	South Carolina, Mississippi, North Carolina
1942	1	1	0	1	0	Louisiana
1941	1	1	0	1	0	California
1938	2	2	0	2	0	Illinois, Ohio
1937	1	1	0	0	1	Mississippi
1936	1	1	0	1	0	New York
1935	3	3	0	2	1	Delaware
1934	1	1	0	1	0	New York
1931	1	1	0	1	0	Pennsylvania
1930	2	2	0	1	1	Arizona, Alabama

^a Includes one kidnaping and one espionage case (both Federal).

Source: U.S. Department of Justice, Law Enforcement Assistance Administration, *Capital Punishment 1975*, National Prisoner Statistics Bulletin No. SD-NPS-CP-4 (Washington, D.C.: U.S. Government Printing Office, 1976), p. 54.

Table 72 Prisoners under sentence of death, United States, 1966–75

Number of prisoners	1975	1974	1973	1972	1971	1970	1969	1968	1967	1966
Under sentence of death, January 1	261[a]	158[b]	329[c]	620	607[d]	524	479	434	415	351
Received death sentence during year	285	151	42	75	104	127	97	102	85	118
Other admissions[e]	0	0	30	0	11	33	33	20	5	0
Executed during year	0	0	0	0	0	0	0	0	2	1
Median time elapsed from sentencing to execution (in months)	X	X	X	X	X	X	X	X	X	X
Other dispositions[f]	67	55	239	365	102	76	85	77	69	53
Median time elapsed from sentencing to disposition (in months)[g]	40	55	44	47	52	54	36	33	41	32
Under sentence of death, December 31	479	254	162	330	620	608	524	479	434	415
Median time elapsed from sentencing to December 31 (in months)	9	10	38	37	40	37	39	33	28.9	29.5

[a] Total for Jan. 1, 1975, was revised from that reported in *Capital Punishment 1974*, NPS Bulletin SD–NPS–CP–3, November 1975, to include two prisoners in Florida, two in Georgia, one in Louisiana, one in Massachusetts, one in North Carolina, and three in Texas who were not reported by these jurisdictions in their counts of those awaiting execution on Dec. 31, 1974. In addition, the figure excludes one prisoner in Georgia, one in Pennsylvania who were incorrectly reported as awaiting execution on Dec. 31, 1974.

[b] Total for Jan. 1, 1974, was revised from that reported in *Capital Punishment 1973*, NPS Bulletin SD–NPS–CP–2, March 1975, to include one prisoner in Alabama, two in Arizona, and one in Florida who were incorrectly reported as awaiting execution on Dec. 31, 1973. In addition, the figure includes one prisoner in Massachusetts who was incorrectly excluded from the count of those awaiting execution on Dec. 31, 1973, but it excludes another Massachusetts prisoner who was incorrectly reported as awaiting execution on Dec. 31, 1973, but had actually been relieved of the death sentence in September 1972.

[c] Total for Jan. 1, 1973, was revised from that reported in *Capital Punishment 1971–72*, NPS Bulletin SD–NPS–CP–1, December 1974, to include one prisoner in California who was incorrectly reported as awaiting execution on Dec. 31, 1972.

[d] Total for Jan. 1, 1971, was revised from that reported in NPS Bulletin No. 46, August 1971, to exclude two prisoners in Florida, one in Louisiana, and one in Georgia who were incorrectly reported as awaiting execution on Dec. 30, 1970, and to include one prisoner in Louisiana and two in Pennsylvania who were incorrectly excluded from the count of those awaiting execution on Dec. 30, 1970.

[e] Prior to 1974, includes prisoners sentenced in previous years but reported late to the NPS program, as well as prisoners returned to death row after previously being reported as either escaped or transferred to a mental hospital.

[f] Includes commutations, resentencing, reversals, grants for new trials, other forms of release from the death sentence, and deaths other than executions.

[g] Prior to 1968, includes those prisoners who were not reported to the NPS program until the following year.

Source: U.S. Department of Justice, Law Enforcement Assistance Administration, *Capital Punishment 1975*, National Prisoner Statistics Bulletin No. SD–NPS–CP–4 (Washington, D.C.: U.S. Government Printing Office, 1976), p. 20.

483

Table 73 Movement of prisoners under sentence of death, by offense and race, United States, 1975

Offense and race	Reported under sentence of death on Jan. 1, 1975[a]	Received from court	Dispositions Total	Removed from under sentence of death[b]	Died	Reported under sentence of death on Dec. 31, 1975 Total[c]	Received in 1975	Received in prior years
Total United States	261[d]	285	67	65	2	479	283	196
White	118	127	31	30	1	214	125	89
Black	136	155	35	34	1	256	155	101
Other	7	3	1	1	0	9	3	6
Murder	226[e,f,g]	264[h]	54	52[i]	2	436[f,i,k]	262[h]	174[f,g,k]
White	108[f,h]	121	26	25	1	203[f,h]	119	84[f,h]
Black	112[e,h]	140[h]	27	26[i]	1	225[g,k]	140[h]	85[h,k]
Other	6	3	1	1	0	8	3	5
Rape	32[l,m]	17	10	10	0	39[l,m]	17	22[l,m]
White	8[m]	3	3	3	0	8[m]	3	5[m]
Black	23[l]	14	7	7	0	30[l]	14	16[l]
Other	1	0	0	0	0	1	0	1
Kidnaping	0	4	0	0	0	4	4	0
White	0	3	0	0	0	3	3	0
Black	0	1	0	0	0	1	1	0
Robbery	0	0	0	0	0	0	0	0
White	0	0	0	0	0	0	0	0
Black	0	0	0	0	0	0	0	0
Assault by life prisoner	1	0	1	1	0	0	0	0
White	1	0	1	1	0	0	0	0
Black	0	0	0	0	0	0	0	0
Burglary	1	0	1	1	0	0	0	0
White	0	0	0	0	0	0	0	0
Black	1	0	1	1	0	0	0	0
Arson	1	0	1	1	0	0	0	0
White	1	0	1	1	0	0	0	0
Black	0	0	0	0	0	0	0	0

[a] Prior to 1974 all prisoners sentenced in previous years but reported late to the NPS program, as well as prisoners returned to death row after previously being reported as either escaped or transferred to a mental hospital, were enumerated under the category "other admissions." Beginning in 1974, however, such prisoners were included in the count of those reported under sentence of death on January 1. This change has thus resulted in the elimination of the category "other admissions."

[b] Includes commutations, resentencings, grants for new trials, and other forms of release from the death sentence.

[c] The number of prisoners under sentence of death as of Dec. 31, 1975, included eight females sentenced to death for murder. Of this total, four were white, three black, and one an American Indian. Refer to Prisoners under Sentence of Death Section of the General Findings in the Source for additional details on female prisoners.

[d] See Table 6.104, footnote a.

[e] Includes three prisoners sentenced for murder and arson.

[f] Includes one prisoner sentenced for murder, kidnaping, and armed robbery.

[g] Includes two prisoners sentenced for murder and rape.

[h] Includes one prisoner sentenced for murder and rape.

[i] Includes one prisoner sentenced for murder and arson.

[j] Includes three prisoners sentenced for murder and rape.

[k] Includes two prisoners sentenced for murder and arson.

[l] Includes one prisoner sentenced for rape and kidnaping.

[m] Includes one prisoner sentenced for rape and burglary.

Source: U.S. Department of Justice, Law Enforcement Assistance Administration, *Capital Punishment 1975*, National Prisoner Statistics Bulletin No. SD-NPS-CP-4 (Washington, D.C.: U.S. Government Printing Office, 1976), p. 21.

Table 74 Prisoners received from court under sentence of death, by race, age at sentencing, offense, region, and jurisdiction, 1975

[xx signifies that the death penalty was illegal]

Region and jurisdiction	Total	Race							Age at sentencing					
		White			Black			Other	Under 20	20 to 24	25 to 29	30 to 34	35 to 39	40 and older
		Murder	Rape	Aggravated kidnaping	Murder[a]	Rape	Aggravated kidnaping	Murder						
United States	285	121	3	3	140	14	1	3	39	92	65	44	14	31
Northeast	4	2	0	0	2	0	0	0	0	2	0	0	1	1
Maine	xx	xx	xx	xx	xx	xx	xx	xx	xx	xx	xx	xx	xx	xx
New Hampshire	0	0	0	0	0	0	0	0	0	0	0	0	0	0
Vermont	0	0	0	0	0	0	0	0	0	0	0	0	0	0
Massachusetts	1	1	0	0	0	0	0	0	0	1	0	0	0	0
Rhode Island	1	0	0	0	1	0	0	0	0	1	0	0	0	0
Connecticut	0	0	0	0	0	0	0	0	0	0	0	0	0	0
New York	1	0	0	0	1	0	0	0	0	0	0	0	1	0
New Jersey	0	0	0	0	0	0	0	0	0	0	0	0	0	0
Pennsylvania	1	1	0	0	0	0	0	0	0	0	0	0	0	1
North Central	38	16	0	0	22	0	0	0	6	14	4	8	3	3
Ohio	28	11	0	0	17	0	0	0	5	11	4	4	2	2
Indiana	6	4	0	0	2	0	0	0	0	0	0	4	1	1
Illinois	2	0	0	0	2	0	0	0	0	2	0	0	0	0
Michigan	xx	xx	xx	xx	xx	xx	xx	xx	xx	xx	xx	xx	xx	xx
Wisconsin	xx	xx	xx	xx	xx	xx	xx	xx	xx	xx	xx	xx	xx	xx
Minnesota	xx	xx	xx	xx	xx	xx	xx	xx	xx	xx	xx	xx	xx	xx
Iowa	xx	xx	xx	xx	xx	xx	xx	xx	xx	xx	xx	xx	xx	xx
Missouri	0	0	0	0	0	0	0	0	0	0	0	0	0	0
North Dakota	0	0	0	0	0	0	0	0	0	0	0	0	0	0
South Dakota	0	0	0	0	0	0	0	0	0	0	0	0	0	0
Nebraska	2	1	0	0	1	0	0	0	1	1	0	0	0	0
Kansas	0	0	0	0	0	0	0	0	0	0	0	0	0	0

South	197	76	3	0	102	14	0	2	32	64	47	26	8	20
Delaware	3	2	0	0	1	0	0	0	1	0	0	1	1	0
Maryland	0	0	0	0	0	0	0	0	0	0	0	0	0	0
District of Columbia	0	0	0	0	0	0	0	0	0	0	0	0	0	0
Virginia	0	0	0	0	0	0	0	0	0	0	0	0	0	0
West Virginia	xx	xx	xx	xx	xx	xx	xx	xx	xx	xx	xx	xx	xx	xx
North Carolina	51	12	1	0	33	4	0	1	6	14	17	6	1	7
South Carolina	13	8	0	0	5	0	0	0	3	3	2	5	0	3
Georgia	9	1	0	0	8	0	0	0	3	2	3	2	0	1
Florida	30	12	2	0	16	0	0	0	4	8	10	2	3	3
Kentucky	3	3	0	0	0	0	0	0	0	1	1	0	0	1
Tennessee	13	7	0	0	6	0	0	0	2	3	4	3	1	0
Alabama	0	0	0	0	0	0	0	0	0	0	0	0	0	0
Mississippi	14	3	0	0	11	0	0	0	4	8	1	1	0	0
Arkansas	3	2	0	0	1	0	0	0	1	2	0	0	1	0
Louisiana	18	3	0	0	5	10	0	0	4	7	4	1	1	1
Oklahoma	21	10	0	0	10	0	0	1	6	9	1	3	0	2
Texas	19	13	0	0	6	0	0	0	1	7	4	4	1	2
West	46	27	0	3	14	0	1	1	1	12	14	10	2	7
Montana	4	0	0	3	0	0	1	0	0	1	1	2	0	0
Idaho	0	0	0	0	0	0	0	0	0	0	0	0	0	0
Wyoming	0	0	0	0	0	0	0	0	0	0	0	0	0	0
Colorado	1	1	0	0	0	0	0	0	0	1	0	0	0	0
New Mexico	4	3	0	0	0	0	0	1	0	1	2	1	0	0
Arizona	5	4	0	0	1	0	0	0	0	1	1	1	1	1
Utah	3	3	0	0	0	0	0	0	0	1	1	1	0	0
Nevada	1	1	0	0	0	0	0	0	0	0	0	0	0	1
Washington	0	0	0	0	0	0	0	0	0	0	0	0	0	0
Oregon	xx	xx	xx	xx	xx	xx	xx	xx	xx	xx	xx	xx	xx	xx
California	28	15	0	0	13	0	0	0	1	7	9	5	1	5
Alaska	xx	xx	xx	xx	xx	xx	xx	xx	xx	xx	xx	xx	xx	xx
Hawaii	xx	xx	xx	xx	xx	xx	xx	xx	xx	xx	xx	xx	xx	xx

a Includes one prisoner sentenced for murder and rape in Georgia.

Source: U.S. Department of Justice, Law Enforcement Assistance Administration, *Capital Punishment 1975*, National Prisoners Statistics Bulletin No. SD-NPS-CP-4 (Washington, D.C.: U.S. Government Printing Office, 1976), pp. 24, 25.

Table 75 Prisoners under sentence of death, disposed of by means other than execution, by race, method of disposition, offense, region, and jurisdiction, 1975

Region and jurisdiction	Total	Total			Race White			
		Murder[b]	Rape	Other[c]	Total	Murder	Rape	Other
United States	67	54	10	3	31	26	3	2
Northeast	11	11	0	0	4	4	0	0
Maine	xx	xx	xx	xx	xx	xx	xx	xx
New Hampshire	0	0	0	0	0	0	0	0
Vermont	0	0	0	0	0	0	0	0
Massachusetts	10	10	0	0	3	3	0	0
Rhode Island	0	0	0	0	0	0	0	0
Connecticut	0	0	0	0	0	0	0	0
New York	0	0	0	0	0	0	0	0
New Jersey	0	0	0	0	0	0	0	0
Pennsylvania	1	1	0	0	1	1	0	0
North Central	5	5	0	0	3	3	0	0
Ohio	0	0	0	0	0	0	0	0
Indiana	1	1	0	0	1	1	0	0
Illinois	3	3	0	0	2	2	0	0
Michigan	xx	xx	xx	xx	xx	xx	xx	xx
Wisconsin	xx	xx	xx	xx	xx	xx	xx	xx
Minnesota	xx	xx	xx	xx	xx	xx	xx	xx
Iowa	xx	xx	xx	xx	xx	xx	xx	xx
Missouri	1	1	0	0	0	0	0	0
North Dakota	0	0	0	0	0	0	0	0
South Dakota	0	0	0	0	0	0	0	0
Nebraska	0	0	0	0	0	0	0	0
Kansas	0	0	0	0	0	0	0	0

	1	2	3	4	5	6	7	8
South	34	22	10	2	11	7	3	1
Delaware	0	0	0	0	0	0	0	0
Maryland	1	1	0	0	0	0	0	0
District of Columbia	0	0	0	0	0	0	0	0
Virginia	1	1	0	0	1	1	0	0
West Virginia	xx	xx	xx	xx	xx	xx	xx	xx
North Carolina	14	6	6	2	4	1	2	1
South Carolina	0	0	0	0	0	0	0	0
Georgia	5	4	1	0	3	2	1	0
Florida	6	2	2	0	1	1	0	0
Kentucky	2	0	0	0	1	1	0	0
Tennessee	0	0	0	0	0	0	0	0
Alabama	0	0	0	0	0	0	0	0
Mississippi	1	1	0	0	0	0	0	0
Arkansas	0	0	0	0	0	0	0	0
Louisiana	3	2	1	0	0	0	0	0
Oklahoma	1	1	0	0	1	1	0	0
Texas	0	0	0	0	0	0	0	0
West	17	16	0	1	13	12	0	1
Montana	0	0	0	0	0	0	0	0
Idaho	0	0	0	0	0	0	0	0
Wyoming	0	0	0	0	0	0	0	0
Colorado	0	0	0	0	0	0	0	0
New Mexico	4	4	0	0	4	4	0	0
Arizona	1	1	0	0	1	1	0	0
Utah	1	1	0	0	1	1	0	0
Nevada	0	0	0	0	0	0	0	0
Washington	0	0	0	0	0	0	0	0
Oregon	xx	xx	xx	xx	xx	xx	xx	xx
California	11	10	0	1	7	6	0	1
Alaska	xx	xx	xx	xx	xx	xx	xx	xx
Hawaii	xx	xx	xx	xx	xx	xx	xx	xx

a Includes commutations, resentencings, reversals, grants for new trials, and other forms of release from the death sentence.
b Includes one prisoner sentenced for murder and arson in North Carolina.
c Includes one assault by life prisoner in California, one arson in North Carolina, and one burglary in North Carolina.

489

Table 75 (continued)

[xx signifies that the death penalty was illegal]

Region and jurisdiction	Race						Removed from under sentence of death[a]	
	Black				Other		Murder[b]	Rape
	Total	Murder	Rape	Other	Total	Murder		
United States	35	27	7	1	1	1	52	10
Northeast	7	7	0	0	0	0	11	0
Maine	xx	xx	xx	xx	xx	xx	xx	xx
New Hampshire	0	0	0	0	0	0	0	0
Vermont	0	0	0	0	0	0	0	0
Massachusetts	7	7	0	0	0	0	10	0
Rhode Island	0	0	0	0	0	0	0	0
Connecticut	0	0	0	0	0	0	0	0
New York	0	0	0	0	0	0	0	0
New Jersey	0	0	0	0	0	0	0	0
Pennsylvania	0	0	0	0	0	0	1	0
North Central	2	2	0	0	0	0	5	0
Ohio	0	0	0	0	0	0	0	0
Indiana	0	0	0	0	0	0	1	0
Illinois	1	1	0	0	0	0	3	0
Michigan	xx	xx	xx	xx	xx	xx	xx	xx
Wisconsin	xx	xx	xx	xx	xx	xx	xx	xx
Minnesota	xx	xx	xx	xx	xx	xx	xx	xx
Iowa	1	1	0	0	0	0	1	0
Missouri	0	0	0	0	0	0	0	0
North Dakota	0	0	0	0	0	0	0	0
Nebraska	0	0	0	0	0	0	0	0
Kansas	0	0	0	0	0	0	0	0

South	22	14	7	1	1	1	21	10
Delaware	0	0	0	0	0	0	0	0
Maryland	1	1	0	0	0	0	1	0
District of Columbia	0	0	0	0	0	0	0	0
Virginia	0	0	0	0	0	0	1	0
West Virginia	xx	xx	xx	xx	xx	xx	xx	xx
North Carolina	9	4	4	1	1	1	6	6
South Carolina	0	0	0	0	0	0	0	0
Georgia	2	2	2	0	0	0	4	1
Florida	5	3	0	0	0	0	4	1
Kentucky	1	1	0	0	0	0	2	0
Tennessee	0	0	0	0	0	0	0	0
Alabama	0	0	0	0	0	0	0	0
Mississippi	1	1	0	0	0	0	1	0
Arkansas	0	0	0	0	0	0	0	0
Louisiana	3	2	1	0	0	0	2	1
Oklahoma	0	0	0	0	0	0	1	0
Texas	0	0	0	0	0	0	0	0
West	4	4	0	0	0	0	15	0
Montana	0	0	0	0	0	0	0	0
Idaho	0	0	0	0	0	0	0	0
Wyoming	0	0	0	0	0	0	0	0
Colorado	0	0	0	0	0	0	0	0
New Mexico	0	0	0	0	0	0	4	0
Arizona	0	0	0	0	0	0	1	0
Utah	0	0	0	0	0	0	1	0
Nevada	0	0	0	0	0	0	0	0
Washington	0	0	0	0	0	0	0	0
Oregon	xx	xx	xx	xx	xx	xx	xx	xx
California	4	4	0	0	0	0	9	0
Alaska	xx	xx	xx	xx	xx	xx	xx	xx
Hawaii	xx	xx	xx	xx	xx	xx	xx	xx

Source: U.S. Department of Justice, Law Enforcement Assistance Administration, *Capital Punishment 1975*, National Prisoner Statistics Bulletin No. SD-NPS-CP-4 (Washington, D.C.: U.S. Government Printing Office, 1976), pp. 32, 33.

Table 75 (continued)

Region and jurisdiction	Method of disposition			
	Other[c]	Died		
		Murder	Rape	
United States	3	2	0	
Northeast	0	0	0	
Maine	xx	xx	xx	
New Hampshire	0	0	0	
Vermont	0	0	0	
Massachusetts	0	0	0	
Rhode Island	0	0	0	
Connecticut	0	0	0	
New York	0	0	0	
New Jersey	0	0	0	
Pennsylvania	0	0	0	
North Central	0	0	0	
Ohio	0	0	0	
Indiana	0	0	0	
Illinois	0	0	0	
Michigan	xx	xx	xx	
Wisconsin	xx	xx	xx	
Minnesota	xx	xx	xx	
Iowa	xx	xx	xx	
Missouri	0	0	0	
North Dakota	0	0	0	
South Dakota	0	0	0	
Nebraska	0	0	0	
Kansas	0	0	0	

	(1)	(2)	(3)	(4)
South	2	1	2	0
Delaware	0	0	0	0
Maryland	0	0	0	0
District of Columbia	0	0	0	0
Virginia	xx	xx	xx	xx
West Virginia	2	0	2	0
North Carolina	0	0	0	0
South Carolina	0	0	0	0
Georgia	0	0	0	0
Florida	0	0	0	0
Kentucky	0	0	0	0
Tennessee	0	0	0	0
Alabama	0	0	0	0
Mississippi	0	0	0	0
Arkansas	0	0	0	0
Louisiana	0	0	0	0
Oklahoma	0	0	0	0
Texas	0	0	0	0
West	1	1	1	0
Montana	0	0	0	0
Idaho	0	0	0	0
Wyoming	0	0	0	0
Colorado	0	0	0	0
New Mexico	0	0	0	0
Arizona	0	0	0	0
Utah	0	0	0	0
Nevada	0	0	0	0
Washington	0	0	0	0
Oregon	xx	xx	xx	xx
California	1	1	1	0
Alaska	xx	xx	xx	xx
Hawaii	xx	xx	xx	xx

Table 76 Prisoners received from court under sentence of death, by legal status at time of arrest, race, region, and jurisdiction, 1975

[xx signifies that the death penalty was illegal]

Region and jurisdiction	Total				Not under sentence				On probation			On parole		
	Total	White	Black	Other	Total	White	Black	Other	Total	White	Black	Total	White	Black
United States	285	127	155	3	173	68	104	1	0	0	0	25	13	12
Northeast	4	2	2	0	3	2	1	0	0	0	0	0	0	0
Maine	xx	xx	xx	xx	xx	xx	xx	xx	xx	xx	xx	xx	xx	xx
New Hampshire	0	0	0	0	0	0	0	0	0	0	0	0	0	0
Vermont	0	0	0	0	0	0	0	0	0	0	0	0	0	0
Massachusetts	1	1	0	0	1	1	0	0	0	0	0	0	0	0
Rhode Island	1	0	1	0	0	0	0	0	0	0	0	0	0	0
Connecticut	0	0	0	0	0	0	0	0	0	0	0	0	0	0
New York	1	0	1	0	1	0	1	0	0	0	0	0	0	0
New Jersey	0	0	0	0	0	0	0	0	0	0	0	0	0	0
Pennsylvania	1	1	0	0	1	1	0	0	0	0	0	0	0	0
North Central	38	16	22	0	26	9	17	0	0	0	0	10	6	4
Ohio	28	11	17	0	20	7	13	0	0	0	0	7	4	3
Indiana	6	4	2	0	2	1	1	0	0	0	0	3	2	1
Illinois	2	0	2	0	2	0	2	0	0	0	0	0	0	0
Michigan	xx	xx	xx	xx	xx	xx	xx	xx	xx	xx	xx	xx	xx	xx
Wisconsin	xx	xx	xx	xx	xx	xx	xx	xx	xx	xx	xx	xx	xx	xx
Minnesota	xx	xx	xx	xx	xx	xx	xx	xx	xx	xx	xx	xx	xx	xx
Iowa	xx	xx	xx	xx	xx	xx	xx	xx	xx	xx	xx	xx	xx	xx
Missouri	0	0	0	0	0	0	0	0	0	0	0	0	0	0
North Dakota	0	0	0	0	0	0	0	0	0	0	0	0	0	0
South Dakota	0	1	0	0	0	0	0	0	0	0	0	0	0	0
Nebraska	2	1	1	0	2	1	1	0	0	0	0	0	0	0
Kansas	0	0	0	0	0	0	0	0	0	0	0	0	0	0

Region and State	1	2	3	4	5	6	7	8	9	10	11	12	13	14
South	197	79	116	2	127	43	84	0	0	0	0	15	7	8
Delaware	3	2	1	0	3	2	1	0	0	0	0	0	0	0
Maryland	0	0	0	0	0	0	0	0	0	0	0	0	0	0
District of Columbia	0	0	0	0	0	0	0	0	0	0	0	0	0	0
Virginia	0	0	0	0	0	0	0	0	0	0	0	0	0	0
West Virginia	xx	xx	xx	xx	xx	xx	xx	xx	xx	xx	xx	xx	xx	xx
North Carolina	51	13	37	1	44	12	32	0	0	0	0	4	0	4
South Carolina	13	8	5	0	1	0	1	0	0	0	0	2	2	0
Georgia	9	1	8	0	5	1	4	0	0	0	0	2	0	2
Florida	30	14	16	0	28	13	15	0	0	0	0	2	1	1
Kentucky	3	3	0	0	0	0	0	0	0	0	0	2	2	0
Tennessee	13	7	6	0	12	6	6	0	0	0	0	1	1	0
Alabama	0	0	0	0	0	0	0	0	0	0	0	0	0	0
Mississippi	14	3	11	0	14	3	11	0	0	0	0	1	0	1
Arkansas	3	2	1	0	2	2	0	0	0	0	0	0	0	0
Louisiana	18	3	15	0	17	3	14	0	0	0	0	0	0	0
Oklahoma	21	10	10	1	1	1	0	0	0	0	0	0	0	0
Texas	19	13	6	0	0	0	0	0	0	0	0	1	1	0
West	46	30	15	1	17	14	3	0	0	0	0	0	0	0
Montana	4	3	1	0	4	3	1	0	0	0	0	0	0	0
Idaho	0	0	0	0	0	0	0	0	0	0	0	0	0	0
Wyoming	0	0	0	0	0	0	0	0	0	0	0	0	0	0
Colorado	1	1	0	0	1	1	0	0	0	0	0	0	0	0
New Mexico	5	3	1	1	4	3	1	0	0	0	0	0	0	0
Arizona	4	4	0	0	5	4	1	0	0	0	0	0	0	0
Utah	3	3	0	0	3	3	0	0	0	0	0	0	0	0
Nevada	1	1	0	0	0	0	0	0	0	0	0	0	0	0
Washington	0	0	0	0	0	0	0	0	0	0	0	0	0	0
Oregon	xx	xx	xx	xx	xx	xx	xx	xx	xx	xx	xx	xx	xx	xx
California	28	15	13	0	0	0	0	0	0	0	0	0	0	0
Alaska	xx	xx	xx	xx	xx	xx	xx	xx	xx	xx	xx	xx	xx	xx
Hawaii	xx	xx	xx	xx	xx	xx	xx	xx	xx	xx	xx	xx	xx	xx

Table 76 (continued)

[xx signifies that the death penalty was illegal]

Region and jurisdiction	In prison			Escaped from prison			On appeal[a]				Not reported			
	Total	White	Black	Total	White	Black	Total	White	Black	Other	Total	White	Black	Other
United States	7	4	3	3	0	3	1	0	0	1	76	42	33	1
Northeast	0	0	0	1	0	1	0	0	0	0	0	0	0	0
Maine	xx	xx	xx	xx	xx	xx	xx	xx	xx	xx	xx	xx	xx	xx
New Hampshire	0	0	0	0	0	0	0	0	0	0	0	0	0	0
Vermont	0	0	0	0	0	0	0	0	0	0	0	0	0	0
Massachusetts	0	0	0	1	0	1	0	0	0	0	0	0	0	0
Rhode Island	0	0	0	0	0	0	0	0	0	0	0	0	0	0
Connecticut	0	0	0	0	0	0	0	0	0	0	0	0	0	0
New York	0	0	0	0	0	0	0	0	0	0	0	0	0	0
New Jersey	0	0	0	0	0	0	0	0	0	0	0	0	0	0
Pennsylvania	0	0	0	0	0	0	0	0	0	0	0	0	0	0
North Central	0	0	0	1	0	1	0	0	0	0	1	1	0	0
Ohio	0	0	0	1	0	1	0	0	0	0	1	1	0	0
Indiana	0	0	0	0	0	0	0	0	0	0	0	0	0	0
Illinois	0	0	0	0	0	0	0	0	0	0	0	0	0	0
Michigan	xx	xx	xx	xx	xx	xx	xx	xx	xx	xx	xx	xx	xx	xx
Wisconsin	xx	xx	xx	xx	xx	xx	xx	xx	xx	xx	xx	xx	xx	xx
Minnesota	xx	xx	xx	xx	xx	xx	xx	xx	xx	xx	xx	xx	xx	xx
Iowa	0	0	0	0	0	0	0	0	0	0	0	0	0	0
Missouri	0	0	0	0	0	0	0	0	0	0	0	0	0	0
North Dakota	0	0	0	0	0	0	0	0	0	0	0	0	0	0
South Dakota	0	0	0	0	0	0	0	0	0	0	0	0	0	0
Nebraska	0	0	0	0	0	0	0	0	0	0	0	0	0	0
Kansas	0	0	0	0	0	0	0	0	0	0	0	0	0	0

State																
South	6	3	3	1	0	0	1	1	1	0	0	1	47	26	20	1
Delaware	0	0	0	0	0	0	0	0	0	0	0	0	0	0	0	0
Maryland	0	0	0	0	0	0	0	0	0	0	0	0	0	0	0	0
District of Columbia	0	0	0	0	0	0	0	0	0	0	0	0	0	0	0	0
Virginia	0	0	0	0	0	0	0	0	0	0	0	0	0	0	0	0
West Virginia	xx	xx	xx	xx	xx	xx	xx	xx	xx	xx	xx	xx	xx	xx	xx	xx
North Carolina	2	1	1	0	0	0	0	0	1	1	1	1	10	6	4	0
South Carolina	0	0	0	0	0	0	0	0	0	0	0	0	6	0	0	0
Georgia	1	0	1	1	0	0	1	1	1	0	0	0	0	0	0	0
Florida	0	0	0	0	0	0	0	0	0	0	0	0	0	0	0	0
Kentucky	0	0	0	0	0	0	1	0	0	0	0	0	0	0	0	0
Tennessee	0	0	0	0	0	0	0	0	0	0	0	0	0	0	0	0
Alabama	0	0	0	0	0	0	0	0	0	0	0	0	0	0	0	0
Mississippi	0	0	0	0	0	0	0	0	0	0	0	0	0	0	0	0
Arkansas	0	0	0	0	0	0	0	0	0	0	0	0	0	0	0	0
Louisiana	1	0	1	0	0	0	0	0	0	0	0	0	0	0	0	0
Oklahoma	0	0	0	0	0	0	0	0	0	0	0	0	20	9	10	1
Texas	2	2	0	0	0	0	0	0	0	0	0	0	16	10	6	0
West	1	1	0	0	0	0	0	0	0	0	0	0	28	15	13	0
Montana	0	0	0	0	0	0	0	0	0	0	0	0	0	0	0	0
Idaho	0	0	0	0	0	0	0	0	0	0	0	0	0	0	0	0
Wyoming	0	0	0	0	0	0	0	0	0	0	0	0	0	0	0	0
Colorado	0	0	0	0	0	0	0	0	0	0	0	0	0	0	0	0
New Mexico	0	0	0	0	0	0	0	0	0	0	0	0	0	0	0	0
Arizona	0	0	0	0	0	0	0	0	0	0	0	0	0	0	0	0
Utah	0	0	0	0	0	0	0	0	0	0	0	0	0	0	0	0
Nevada	1	1	0	0	0	0	0	0	0	0	0	0	0	0	0	0
Washington	0	0	0	0	0	0	0	0	0	0	0	0	0	0	0	0
Oregon	xx	xx	xx	xx	xx	xx	xx	xx	xx	xx	xx	xx	xx	xx	xx	xx
California	0	0	0	0	0	0	0	0	0	0	0	0	28	15	13	0
Alaska	xx	xx	xx	xx	xx	xx	xx	xx	xx	xx	xx	xx	xx	xx	xx	xx
Hawaii	xx	xx	xx	xx	xx	xx	xx	xx	xx	xx	xx	xx	xx	xx	xx	xx

a One prisoner arrested on a murder charge in North Carolina was appealing his conviction for manslaughter at the time he was arrested.

Source: U.S. Department of Justice, Law Enforcement Assistance Administration, *Capital Punishment 1975*, National Prisoner Statistics Bulletin No. SD-NPS-CP-4 (Washington, D.C.: U.S. Government Printing Office, 1976), pp. 30, 31.

Table 77 Prisoners under sentence of death, by offense, year received, race, region, and jurisdiction, 1975

[xx signifies that the death penalty was illegal]

Region and jurisdiction	Total	All offenses			Murder[a,b,c]			Rape[d,e]		
		White	Black	Other	White	Black	Other	White	Black	Other
United States	479	214	256	9	203	225	8	8	30	1
Northeast	16	8	8	0	8	8	0	0	0	0
Maine	xx	xx	xx	xx	xx	xx	xx	xx	xx	xx
New Hampshire	0	0	0	0	0	0	0	0	0	0
Vermont	0	0	0	0	0	0	0	0	0	0
Massachusetts	9	4	5	0	4	5	0	0	0	0
Rhode Island	1	0	1	0	0	1	0	0	0	0
Connecticut	0	0	0	0	0	0	0	0	0	0
New York	1	0	1	0	0	1	0	0	0	0
New Jersey	0	0	0	0	0	0	0	0	0	0
Pennsylvania	5	4	1	0	4	1	0	0	0	0
North Central	45	17	28	0	17	28	0	0	0	0
Ohio	33	11	22	0	11	22	0	0	0	0
Indiana	7	4	3	0	4	3	0	0	0	0
Illinois	3	1	2	0	1	2	0	0	0	0
Michigan	xx	xx	xx	xx	xx	xx	xx	xx	xx	xx
Wisconsin	xx	xx	xx	xx	xx	xx	xx	xx	xx	xx
Minnesota	xx	xx	xx	xx	xx	xx	xx	xx	xx	xx
Iowa	xx	xx	xx	xx	xx	xx	xx	xx	xx	xx
Missouri	0	0	0	0	0	0	0	0	0	0
North Dakota	0	0	0	0	0	0	0	0	0	0
South Dakota	0	0	0	0	0	0	0	0	0	0
Nebraska	2	1	1	0	1	1	0	0	0	0
Kansas	0	0	0	0	0	0	0	0	0	0

State									
South	343	141	195	7	133	165	6	8	30	1
Delaware	3	2	1	0	2	1	0	0	0	0
Maryland	2	0	2	0	0	2	0	0	0	0
District of Columbia	0	0	0	0	0	0	0	0	0	0
Virginia	3	1	2	0	1	2	0	0	0	0
West Virginia	xx	xx	xx	xx	xx	xx	xx	xx	xx	xx
North Carolina	103	30	68	5	26	56	4	4	12	1
South Carolina	13	8	5	0	8	5	0	0	0	0
Georgia	25	10	15	0	9	12	0	1	3	0
Florida	62	32	30	0	30	30	0	2	0	0
Kentucky	5	5	0	0	5	0	0	0	0	0
Tennessee	14	8	6	0	8	6	0	0	0	0
Alabama	0	0	0	0	0	0	0	0	0	0
Mississippi	16	3	13	0	3	13	0	0	0	0
Arkansas	4	3	1	0	3	1	0	0	0	0
Louisiana	34	5	29	0	4	14	0	1	15	0
Oklahoma	28	14	12	2	14	12	2	0	0	0
Texas	31	20	11	0	20	11	0	0	0	0
West	75	48	25	2	45	24	2	0	0	0
Montana	4	3	1	0	0	0	0	0	0	0
Idaho	0	0	0	0	0	0	0	0	0	0
Wyoming	4	2	2	0	2	2	0	0	0	0
Colorado	1	1	0	0	1	0	0	0	0	0
New Mexico	7	6	0	1	6	0	1	0	0	0
Arizona	12	8	4	0	8	4	0	0	0	0
Utah	7	5	2	0	5	2	0	0	0	0
Nevada	1	1	0	0	1	0	0	0	0	0
Washington	0	0	0	0	0	0	0	0	0	0
Oregon	xx	xx	xx	xx	xx	xx	xx	xx	xx	xx
California	39	22	16	1	22	16	1	0	0	0
Alaska	xx	xx	xx	xx	xx	xx	xx	xx	xx	xx
Hawaii	xx	xx	xx	xx	xx	xx	xx	xx	xx	xx

[a] Includes two prisoners (one black and one white) sentenced for murder and rape in North Carolina and one prisoner (black) sentenced to murder and rape in Georgia.

[b] Includes two prisoners (both black) sentenced for murder and arson in North Carolina.

[c] Includes one prisoner (white) sentenced for murder, kidnaping, and armed robbery in Georgia.

[d] Includes one prisoner (white) sentenced for rape and burglary in North Carolina.

[e] Includes one prisoner (black) sentenced for rape and kidnaping in Georgia.

Table 77 (continued)

Region and jurisdiction	Offense					Year received 1975	
	Kidnaping		Robbery	Arson	Burglary	1975	
	White	Black	White	Black	White	White	Black
United States	3	1	0	0	0	125	155
Northeast	0	0	0	0	0	2	2
Maine	xx	xx	xx	xx	xx	xx	xx
New Hampshire	0	0	0	0	0	0	0
Vermont	0	0	0	0	0	0	0
Massachusetts	0	0	0	0	0	1	1
Rhode Island	0	0	0	0	0	0	1
Connecticut	0	0	0	0	0	0	0
New York	0	0	0	0	0	0	1
New Jersey	0	0	0	0	0	0	0
Pennsylvania	0	0	0	0	0	1	0
North Central	0	0	0	0	0	16	22
Ohio	0	0	0	0	0	11	17
Indiana	0	0	0	0	0	4	2
Illinois	0	0	0	0	0	0	2
Michigan	xx	xx	xx	xx	xx	xx	xx
Wisconsin	xx	xx	xx	xx	xx	xx	xx
Minnesota	xx	xx	xx	xx	xx	xx	xx
Iowa	0	0	0	0	0	0	0
Missouri	0	0	0	0	0	0	0
North Dakota	0	0	0	0	0	0	0
South Dakota	0	0	0	0	0	1	1
Nebraska	0	0	0	0	0	1	1
Kansas	0	0	0	0	0	0	0

State							
South	0	0	0	0	0	78	116
Delaware	0	0	0	0	0	2	1
Maryland	0	0	0	0	0	0	0
District of Columbia	0	0	0	0	0	0	0
Virginia	xx	xx	xx	xx	xx	xx	xx
West Virginia	0	0	0	0	0	13	37
North Carolina	0	0	0	0	0	8	5
South Carolina	0	0	0	0	0	1	8
Georgia	0	0	0	0	0	14	16
Florida	0	0	0	0	0	3	6
Kentucky	0	0	0	0	0	7	0
Tennessee	0	0	0	0	0	0	6
Alabama	0	0	0	0	0	3	0
Mississippi	0	0	0	0	0	2	11
Arkansas	0	0	0	0	0	3	1
Louisiana	0	0	0	0	0	9	15
Oklahoma	0	0	0	0	0	13	10
Texas	0	0	0	0	0	13	6
West	3	1	0	0	0	29	15
Montana	3	1	0	0	0	3	1
Idaho	0	0	0	0	0	0	0
Wyoming	0	0	0	0	0	0	0
Colorado	0	0	0	0	0	1	0
New Mexico	0	0	0	0	0	3	0
Arizona	0	0	0	0	0	4	1
Utah	0	0	0	0	0	3	0
Nevada	0	0	0	0	0	1	0
Washington	0	0	0	0	0	0	0
Oregon	xx	xx	xx	xx	xx	xx	xx
California	0	0	0	0	0	14	13
Alaska	xx	xx	xx	xx	xx	xx	xx
Hawaii	xx	xx	xx	xx	xx	xx	xx

Source: U.S. Department of Justice, Law Enforcement Assistance Administration, *Capital Punishment 1975*, National Prisoner Statistics Bulletin No. SD-NPS-CP-4 (Washington, D.C.: U.S. Government Printing Office, 1976), pp. 42, 43.

Table 77 (continued)

Region and jurisdiction	Year received				
	Other	Prior years			
		White	Black	Other	
United States	3	89	101	6	
Northeast	0	6	6	0	
Maine	xx	xx	xx	xx	
New Hampshire	0	0	0	0	
Vermont	0	0	0	0	
Massachusetts	0	3	5	0	
Rhode Island	0	0	0	0	
Connecticut	0	0	0	0	
New York	0	0	0	0	
New Jersey	0	0	0	0	
Pennsylvania	0	3	1	0	
North Central	0	1	6	0	
Ohio	0	0	5	0	
Indiana	0	0	1	0	
Illinois	0	1	0	0	
Michigan	xx	xx	xx	xx	
Wisconsin	xx	xx	xx	xx	
Minnesota	xx	xx	xx	xx	
Iowa	xx	xx	xx	xx	
Missouri	0	0	0	0	
North Dakota	0	0	0	0	
South Dakota	0	0	0	0	
Nebraska	0	0	0	0	
Kansas	0	0	0	0	

South	2	63	79	5
Delaware	0	0	0	0
Maryland	0	0	2	0
District of Columbia	0	0	0	0
Virginia	0	1	2	2
West Virginia	xx	xx	xx	xx
North Carolina	1	17	31	4
South Carolina	0	0	0	0
Georgia	0	9	7	0
Florida	0	18	14	0
Kentucky	0	2	0	0
Tennessee	0	1	0	0
Alabama	0	0	2	0
Mississippi	0	0	0	0
Arkansas	0	1	0	0
Louisiana	0	2	14	0
Oklahoma	1	5	2	1
Texas	0	7	5	0
West	1	19	13	1
Montana	0	0	0	0
Idaho	0	0	0	0
Wyoming	0	2	2	0
Colorado	0	0	0	0
New Mexico	1	3	0	0
Arizona	0	4	3	0
Utah	0	2	2	0
Nevada	0	0	0	0
Washington	0	0	0	0
Oregon	xx	xx	xx	xx
California	0	8	3	1
Alaska	xx	xx	xx	xx
Hawaii	xx	xx	xx	xx

BIBLIOGRAPHY

Adams, Stuart, and Connolly, John J. "Role of Junior Colleges in the Prison Community." *Junior College Journal* (March 1971), 92–98.

Adler, Freda. *Sisters in Crime: The Rise of the New Female Criminal.* New York: McGraw-Hill, 1975.

Alper, Benedict. *Prisons Inside-Out: Alternatives in Correctional Reform.* Cambridge, Mass.: Ballinger Publishing, 1974.

American Bar Association, Commission on Correctional Facilities and Services and Council of State Governments. *Compendium of Model Correctional Legislation and Standards.* 2d ed. Washington, D.C., June 1975.

———, Female Offender Resource Center. *Female Offenders: Problems and Programs.* Washington, D.C., 1976.

American Correctional Association. *Correctional Classification and Treatment.* Cincinnati, Ohio: W. H. Anderson, 1975.

———. *Directory of Correctional Departments, Institutions, Agencies and Paroling Authorities in United States and Canada.* 1975–1976 Edition. College Park, Md., November 26, 1975.

———. *An Evaluative Summary of Research: MAP Program Outcomes in the Initial Demonstration States.* College Park, Md., 1975.

———. *Manual of Correctional Standards.* 3d ed., College Park, Md., 1966.

———. *The Mutual Agreement Program. A Planned Change in Correctional Service Delivery.* College Park, Md., November 1973.

American Friends Service Committee. *Struggle for Justice.* New York: Hill and Wang, 1971.

Arnold, David O. (ed.). *The Sociology of Subcultures.* Berkeley, Calif.: Glendessary Press, 1970.

Astrachan, Anthony. "Close-up/George Camp of Missouri." *Corrections Magazine* 1, No. 4 (March–April 1975), 33–36.

———. "Louisiana's Orleans Parish Prison." *Corrections Magazine* 2, No. 1 (September–October 1975), 25–32.

———. "Profile/Louisiana." *Corrections Magazine* 2, No. 1 (September–October 1975), 9 ff.

———. "Profile/Pennsylvania." *Corrections Magazine* 1, No. 5 (May–June 1975), 37–60.

Atkins, Burton M., and Glick, Henry R. *Prisons, Protest and Politics.* Englewood Cliffs, N.J.: Prentice-Hall, 1972.

Auerbach, Stephanie. "Common Myths About Capital Criminals and Their Victims." *Georgia Journal of Corrections* 3, No. 2 (1974), 41–54.

Badillo, Herman, and Haynes, Milton. *A Bill of No Rights: Attica and the American Prison System.* New York: Outerbridge and Lazard, 1972.

Bailey, Ronald H. "Profile/Florida." *Corrections Magazine* 1, No. 1 (September 1974), 65 ff.

Bakal, Yitzhak (ed.). *Closing Correctional Institutions: New Strategies for Youth Services.* Lexington, Mass.: D. C. Heath, 1973.

Baker, J. E. *The Right to Participate: Inmate Involvement in Prison Administration.* Metuchen, N.J.: Scarecrow Press, 1974.

"Bargaining in Correctional Institutions: Restructuring the Relation Between the Inmate and the Prison Authority." *Yale Law Journal* 81, No. 4 (1972), 726–757.

Barnes, Harry Elmer. *The Evolution of Penology in Pennsylvania: A Study in American Social History.* Montclair, N.J.: Patterson Smith, 1968 (1927).

Baunach, Phyllis Jo, and Murton, Thomas O. "Women in Prison: An Awakening Minority." *Crime and Correction* 1, No. 2 (1973), 4–12.

Becker, Howard S. (ed.). *The Other Side.* London: Free Press, 1964.

"Behavior Mod Behind the Walls," *Time,* March 11, 1974, p. 74.

Berk, Bernard B. "Organizational Goals and Inmate Organization." *American Journal of Sociology* 71, No. 2 (March 1966), 522–534.

Berne, Eric. *Games People Play.* New York: Grove Press, 1964.

———. *Principles of Group Treatment.* New York: Oxford University Press, 1966.

———. *Transactional Analysis in Psychotherapy.* New York: Grove Press, 1961.

Blake, James. *The Joint.* Garden City, N.Y.: Doubleday, 1971.

Bloomberg, Seth Allan. "Participatory Management: Toward a Science of Correctional Management." *Criminology* 15, No. 2 (August 1977), 149–163.

Blumstein, Alfred, and Cohen, Jacqueline. *An Evaluation of a College-Level Program in a Maximum Security Prison.* Pittsburgh: Urban Systems Institute, Carnegie-Mellon University, 1974.

Bohlander, Edward William. *Shock Probation: The Use and Effectiveness of an Early Release Program as a Sentencing Alternative.* Ann Arbor, Mich.: University Microfilms, 1973.

Borkin, Joseph. Review of *The Criminal Personality: Volume I* in *Federal Bar Journal* 35 (Summer-Fall 1976), 237–241.

Bowers, William J. *Executions in America.* Lexington, Mass.: D.C. Heath, 1974.

Braswell, Michael, and DeFrancis, Paul. "Conjugal Visitation: A Feasibility Study." *Georgia Journal of Corrections* 1, No. 4 (1972), 171–180.

Brautigam, Richard K. "Work Release: A Case Study and Comment." *Prison Journal* 52, No. 2 (1973), 20–35.

Brodsky, Annette M. (ed.). *The Female Offender.* Beverly Hills, Calif.: Sage, 1975.

Brody, Stuart A. "The Political Prisoner Syndrome: Latest Problem of the American Penal System." *Crime and Delinquency* 20, No. 2 (April 1974), 97–106.

Brown, Barry S., and Spevacek, John D. "Work Release in Community and Institutional Settings." *Corrective Psychiatry and Journal of Social Therapy* 17, No. 3 (1971), 35–42.

Buffum, Peter C. *Homosexuality in Prisons*. Washington, D.C.: National Institute of Law Enforcement and Criminal Justice, February 1972.

Bundy, Mary Lee, and Harmon, Kenneth R. (eds.). *The National Prison Directory*. College Park, Md.: Urban Information Interpreters Inc., April 1975.

Burns, Henry, Jr. *Corrections: Organization and Administration*. St. Paul, Minn.: West Publishing Co., 1975.

Burstein, Jules Quentin. *Conjugal Visits in Prison: Psychological and Social Consequences*. Lexington, Mass.: D. C. Heath, 1977.

Busher, Walter H. *Ordering Time to Serve Prisoners: A Manual for the Planning and Administering of Work Release*. Washington, D.C.: U.S. Department of Justice, Law Enforcement Assistance Administration, Technical Assistance Division, June 1973.

Carlson, Norman A. "The Federal Prison System: Forty-five Years of Change." *Federal Probation* 39, No. 2 (June 1975), 37–42.

Carroll, Leo. *Hacks, Blacks and Cons: Race Relations in a Maximum Security Prison*. Lexington, Mass.: D. C. Heath, 1974.

Carter, Robert; Glaser, Daniel; and Wilkins, Leslie (eds.). *Correctional Institutions*. Philadelphia: J. B. Lippincott, 1972.

Chandler, Edna Walker. *Women in Prison*. Indianapolis: Bobbs-Merrill, 1973.

Ciba Foundation. *Medical Care of Prisoners and Detainees*. Amsterdam: Elsevier, 1973.

Clearinghouse for Offender Literacy Programs. *Literacy Problems and Solutions: A Resource Handbook for Correctional Educators*. Washington, D.C.: American Bar Association, 1975.

Clemmer, Donald. *The Prison Community*. 2d revised ed. New York: Holt, Rinehart and Winston, 1958.

Cloward, Richard A., and others. *Theoretical Studies in Social Organization of the Prison*. New York: Social Science Research Council, 1960.

Cockerham, William E. "Connecticut's 'Just Community.' " *Corrections Magazine* 1, No. 3 (January-February 1975), 73–76.

Cole, George F. (ed.). *Criminal Justice: Law and Politics*. 2d ed. North Scituate, Mass.: Duxbury Press, 1976.

Connolly, Paul K. "The Possibility of a Prison Sentence Is a Necessity." *Crime and Delinquency* 21, No. 4 (1975), 356–359.

Conrad, Roan. "Profile/Connecticut." *Corrections Magazine* 1, No. 3 (January-February 1975), 63–72.

Coons, William R. *Attica Diary*. New York: Stein and Day, 1972.

Cressey, Donald R. (ed.). *The Prison: Studies in Institutional Organization and Change*. New York: Holt, Rinehart and Winston, 1966.

Crites, Laura (ed.). *The Female Offender*. Lexington, Mass.: D. C. Heath, 1976.

"Critique of Martinson by Ted Palmer Says Abandonment of 'Treatment' Not Justified." *Criminal Justice Newsletter* 7, No. 2 (January 19, 1976), 1–2.

Davidson, R. Theodore. *Chicano Prisoners: The Key to San Quentin*. New York: Holt, Rinehart and Winston, 1974.

Deming, Richard. *Women: The New Criminals*. Nashville, Tenn.: Thomas Nelson, 1977.

Denenberg, R. V. "Alaska." *Corrections Magazine* 1, No. 1 (September 1974), 53–62.

———. "Profile/Washington State." *Corrections Magazine* 1, No. 2 (November-December 1974), 31–44.

———, and Denenberg, Tia. "Prison Grievance Procedures: A National Survey of Programs Underway." *Corrections Magazine* 1, No. 3 (January-February 1975), 29 ff.

DeNevi, Don. *Alcatraz '46: The Anatomy of a Classic Prison Tragedy*. San Rafael, Calif.: Leswing Press, 1974.

Dershowitz, Alan M. "Criminal Sentencing in the United States: An Historical and Conceptual Overview." *Annals of the American Academy of Political and Social Science* 423 (1976), 117–132.

———. "Let the Punishment Fit the Crime." *New York Times Magazine* (December 28, 1975), 7 ff.

Dodge, Calvert R. (ed.). *A Nation Without Prisons: Alternatives to Incarceration*. Lexington, Mass.: D. C. Heath, 1975.

Dunbar, Ellen R. *Organizational Change and the Politics of Bureaucracy: Illustrations from the Initiation of Mutual Agreement Programming in Three State Correctional Agencies*. College Park, Md.: American Correctional Association, 1976.

Ecclestone, C. E. J.; Gendreau, P.; and Knox, C. "Solitary Confinement of Prisoners: An Assessment of Its Effects on Inmates' Personal Constructs and Adrenocortical Activity." *Canadian Journal of Behavioral Sciences* 6, No. 2 (1974), 178–191.

Education Commission of the States. *Preliminary First Year Findings: Correctional Education in the States*. Denver, Colo., 1975.

Eptein, Robin, and others. *The Legal Aspects of Contract Parole*. College Park, Md.: American Correctional Association, 1976.

Eriksson, Torsten. *The Reformers: An Historical Survey of Pioneer Experiments in the Treatment of Criminals*. New York: Elsevier, 1976.

Eyman, Joy S. *Prisons for Women: A Practical Guide to Administration Problems*. Springfield, Ill.: Charles C. Thomas, 1971.

Fitzharris, Timothy L. *The Desirability of a Correctional Ombudsman*. Berkeley, Calif.: Institute of Governmental Studies, 1973.

Fogel, David. "The Case for Determinacy in Sentencing and the Justice Model in Corrections." *American Journal of Correction* 38, No. 4 (July-August 1976), 25 ff.

———. "For 'Flat Time.' " *Christian Science Monitor,* February 11, 1976, p. 27.

———."... *We Are the Living Proof* ...": *The Justice Model for Corrections.* Cincinnati: W. H. Anderson, 1975.

"Follow-Up." *Corrections Magazine* 2, No. 2 (November-December 1975), 55–56.

Foster, Thomas W. "Make-Believe Families: A Response of Women and Girls to the Deprivations of Imprisonment." *International Journal of Criminology and Penology* 3, No. 1 (1975), 71–78.

Frankel, Marvin E. *Criminal Sentences: Law Without Order.* New York: Hill and Wang, 1973.

Frazier, Thomas L. "Transactional Analysis Training and Treatment of Staff in a Correctional School." *Federal Probation* 36, No. 3 (1973), 41–46.

Friday, Paul C., and Petersen, David M. "Shock of Imprisonment: Short-Term Incarceration As a Treatment Technique." *Probation and Parole,* No. 5 (1973), 33–41.

Fry Consulting Group. *Employment Problems of Ex-Offenders.* New York, 1973.

Gagon, John H., and Simon, William. "The Social Meaning of Prison Homosexuality." *Federal Probation* 32, No. 1 (1968), 23–29.

Galaway, Burt, and Hudson, Joe. "Restitution and Rehabilitation: Some Central Issues." *Crime and Delinquency* 18 (October 1972).

Georgetown University Law Center. *The Role of Prison Industries Now and in the Future.* Washington, D.C.: Institute of Criminal Law and Procedure, 1974.

Gettinger, Steve. "Alabama Under Strict Court Order to Upgrade Entire Prison System." *Corrections Magazine* 2, No. 3 (March 1976), 18–19.

———. "Close-Up/OAR." *Corrections Magazine* 2, No. 4 (June 1976), 41–44.

———. "Dr. Martin Groder: An Angry Resignation." *Corrections Magazine* 2, No. 6 (July-August 1975), 27–36.

———. "Parole Contracts: A New Way Out." *Corrections Magazine* 2, No. 1 (September-October 1975), 3 ff.

———. "Prison Media: Getting the News Inside." *Corrections Magazine* 2, No. 3 (March 1976), 37–44.

———. "Profile/Maine." *Corrections Magazine* 1, No. 6 (July-August 1975), 13–26.

———. "Profile/New York City's Adult Corrections System." *Corrections Magazine* 2, No. 4 (June 1976), 30 ff.

———. "U.S. Prison Population Hits All-Time High." *Corrections Magazine* 2, No. 3 (March 1976), 9–20.

Giallombardo, Rose. *The Social World of Imprisoned Girls: A Comparative Study of Institutions for Juvenile Delinquents.* New York: John Wiley and Sons, 1974.

———. *Society of Women: A Study of a Women's Prison.* New York: John Wiley and Sons, 1966.

Gibbons, Don C. *Changing the Lawbreaker: The Treatment of Delinquents and Criminals.* Englewood Cliffs, N.J.: Prentice-Hall, 1965.

Gill, Howard B. "Correctional Philosophy and Architecture." In Robert M. Carter and others (eds.), *Correctional Institutions.* Philadelphia: J. B. Lippincott, 1972.

Glaser, Daniel. *The Effectiveness of a Prison and Parole System.* Indianapolis: Bobbs-Merrill, 1969.

——— (ed.). *Handbook of Criminology.* New York: Rand McNally and Co., 1974.

———, and Zeigler, Max S. "Use of Death Penalty v. Outrage at Murder." *Crime and Delinquency* 20, No. 4 (1974), 333–338.

Griswold, H. Jack, and others. *An Eye for an Eye.* New York: Pocket Books, 1971.

Halleck, Seymour L., and Hersko, Marvin. "Homosexual Behavior in a Correctional Institution for Adolescent Girls." *American Journal of Orthopsychiatry* 32 (October 1962), 911–927.

Harris, Carl M. *Statistical Analysis of Recidivism Data.* Washington, D.C.: George Washington University, 1973.

Harris, Thomas A. *I'm OK—You're OK.* New York: Harper and Row, 1969.

Hart, William. "Profile/Michigan." *Corrections Magazine* 2, No. 5 (September 1976), 55–66.

———. "Profile/New Mexico." *Corrections Magazine* 2, No. 3 (March 1976), 27 ff.

Hawkins, Gordon. *The Prison: Policy and Practice.* Chicago: University of Chicago Press, 1976.

Haynes, F. E. "The Sociological Study of the Prison Community." *Journal of Criminal Law and Criminology* 39 (November-December 1948), 432–440.

Heffernan, Esther. *Making It in Prison: The Square, the Cool, and the Life.* New York: Wiley-Interscience, 1972.

Herron, Rex. *Project NewGate—Past, Present and Future: Issues of the Change-Agent Role in the Replication of a Demonstration Program.* Albany: State University of New York, 1973.

Hogarth, John. *Sentencing As a Human Process.* Toronto: University of Toronto Press, 1971.

Holden, Constance. "Butner: Experimental U.S. Prison Holds Promise, Stirs Trepidation." *Science* 185 (1974), 423–426.

Hopper, Columbus B. *Sex in Prisons: The Mississippi Experiment in Conjugal Visiting.* Baton Rouge, La.: Louisiana State University Press, 1969.

Hudson, Joe, and Galaway, Burt. "Undoing the Wrong." *Social Work* 19, No. 3 (1974), 313–318.

Huff, C. Ronald. "Unionization Behind the Walls." *Criminology* 12, No. 2 (August 1974), 175–194.

Ibrahim, Azmy Ishak. "Deviant Sexual Behavior in Men's Prisons." *Crime and Delinquency* 20, No. 1 (1974), 38–44.

Irwin, John. *The Felon.* Englewood Cliffs, N.J.: Prentice-Hall, 1970.

———. "Replaying Attica." *Human Behavior* (May 1973), 64–68.

Jacques, Larry L. *A National Survey of the Correctional Education Programs Available to Inmates of Penal Institutions for Adults.* Ann Arbor, Mich: University Microfilms, 1973.

James, Reverend J. T. L. "The Halfway House Movement." In Gary R. Perlstein and Thomas R. Phelps (eds.), *Alternatives to Prison: Community-Based Corrections.* Pacific Palisades, Calif.: Goodyear Publishing Co., 1975.

Johnson, Elmer H. *Crime, Correction, and Society.* 3d ed. Homewood, Ill.: Dorsey Press, 1974.

———. *Social Problems of Urban Man.* Homewood, Ill.: Dorsey Press, 1974.

———. "Sociology of Confinement: Assimilation and the Prison 'Rat.' " *Journal of Criminal Law, Criminology and Police Science* 51 (January-February 1961), 528–533.

———. *Work Release: Factors in Selection and Results.* Carbondale, Ill.: Center for the Study of Crime, Delinquency and Corrections, 1969.

Johnston, Norman. *The Human Cage: A Brief History of Prison Architecture.* New York: Walker and Co., 1973.

Jones, David A. *The Health Risks of Imprisonment.* Lexington, Mass.: D. C. Heath, 1976.

Joselson, M. "Prison Education: A Major Reason for Its Impotence." *Corrective Psychiatry and Journal of Social Therapy* 17, No. 2 (1971), 48–56.

Kassirer, Lynn Bergman. "The Right to Treatment and the Right to Refuse Treatment—Recent Case Law." *Journal of Psychiatry and Law* 2, No. 4 (1974), 455–470.

Katzowitz, Lauren. "Profile/Kentucky." *Corrections Magazine* 1, No. 4 (March-April 1975), 17–32.

Keating, J. Michael, and others. *Grievance Mechanisms in Correctional Institutions.* Washington, D.C.: Law Enforcement Assistance Administration, 1975.

Keve, Paul M. *Prison Life and Human Worth.* Minneapolis: University of Minnesota Press, 1974.

Kiernan, Michael. "Profile/Vermont." *Corrections Magazine* 2, No. 1 (September-October 1975), 33–44.

Killinger, George G., and Cromwell, Paul F., Jr. (eds.) *Penology: The Evolution of Corrections in America.* St. Paul, Minn.: West Publishing Co., 1973.

Klapmuts, Nora. "Community Alternatives to Prison." *Crime and Delinquency Literature* 5, No. 2 (1973), 305–337.

Kohlberg, Lawrence. "The Cognitive-Developmental Approach to Moral Education." In *Readings in Human Development: Annual Editions: 1976–1977.* Guilford, Conn.: Dushkin Publishing Group, 1976.

Kosofsky, Sidney, and Ellis, Albert. "Illegal Communication Among Institutionalized Female Delinquents." *Journal of Social Psychology* 48 (August 1958), 155–160.

Kurtzberg, Richard, and others. "Plastic Surgery in Corrections." *Federal Probation* 33 (1969), 44–47.

Lansing, Douglas; Bogan, Joseph B.; and Karacki, Loren. "Unit Management: Implementing a Different Correctional Approach." *Federal Probation* 41, No. 1 (March 1977), 43–49.

Leenhouts, Keith J. *A Father . . . A Son . . . And A Three Mile Run.* New York: Zondervan, 1975.

Lehman, Paul E. "The Medical Model of Treatment: Historical Development of an Archaic Standard." In Edward E. Peoples (ed.), *Readings in Correctional Casework and Counseling.* Pacific Palisades, Calif.: Goodyear Publishing Co., 1975.

Leiberg, Leon, and Parker, William. "Mutual Agreement Programs with Vouchers: An Alternative for Institutionalized Female Offenders." *American Journal of Correction* 37, No. 1 (1975), 10–13, 38.

Levinson, Robert B., and Gerard, Roy E. "Functional Units: A Different Correctional Approach." *Federal Probation* 37, No. 4 (December 1973), 8–16.

Lipton, Douglas; Martinson, Robert; and Wilks, Judith. *The Effectiveness of Correctional Treatment: A Survey of Treatment Evaluation Studies.* New York: Praeger Publishers, 1975.

Luger, Milton. "Reaction to Robert Martinson." *American Journal of Correction* (November-December 1975), 19 ff.

Mannheim, Hermann. *The Dilemma of Penal Reform.* London: George Allen and Unwin, 1939.

Markley, Carson W. "Furlough Programs and Conjugal Visiting in Adult Correctional Institutions." *Federal Probation* 37, No. 1 (March 1973), 19–26.

Marsh, John J. "Higher Education in American Prisons." *Crime and Delinquency Literature* 5, No. 1 (1973), 139–155.

Martin, J. P., and Webster, D. *The Social Consequences of Conviction.* London: Heinemann, 1971.

Martin, Lawrence H., and Snyder, Phyllis R. "Jurisdiction over Status Offenses Should *Not* Be Removed from the Juvenile Court." *Crime and Delinquency* 22, No. 1 (January 1976), 44–47.

Martinson, Robert M. "Restraint in the Community: A Modest Proposal." *Criminal Justice Newsletter* 6, No. 24 (December 8, 1975), 4–5.

————; Palmer, Ted; and Adams, Stuart. *Rehabilitation, Recidivism, and Research.* Hackensack, N.J.: National Council on Crime and Delinquency, 1976.

May, Edgar. "Prison Ombudsmen in America." *Corrections Magazine* 1, No. 3 (January-February 1975), 45–60.

————. "Profile/Arizona." *Corrections Magazine* 1, No. 6 (July-August 1975), 37–52.

————. "Profile/Missouri." *Corrections Magazine* 2, No. 3 (March 1976), 61–62.

McArthur, Virginia. "Inmate Grievance Mechanisms: A Survey of 209 American Prisons." *Federal Probation* 38, No. 4 (1974), 41–47.

McKelvey, Blake. *American Prisons: A Study in American Social History Prior to 1915.* Montclair, N.J.: Patterson Smith, 1968.

McNulty, Jill K. "The Right to Be Left Alone." *American Criminal Law Review* 11, No. 1 (1972), 141–164.

Melville, Samuel. *Letters from Attica.* New York: William Morrow and Co., 1972.

Miller, Michael J. "Vocational Training in Prisons: Some Social Policy Implications." *Federal Probation* 36, No. 3 (1973), 19–21.

Miller, Walter B. "The Molls." *Society* 11, No. 1 (1973), 32–35.

Mitford, Jessica. *Kind and Usual Punishment: The Prison Business.* New York: Alfred A. Knopf, 1973.

Morris, Joe Alex. *First Offender.* New York: Funk and Wagnalls, 1970.

Morris, Norval. *The Future of Imprisonment.* Chicago: University of Chicago Press, 1974.

Murton, Thomas O. *The Dilemma of Prison Reform.* New York: Holt, Rinehart and Winston, 1976.

————, and Hyams, Joe. *Accomplices to the Crime: The Arkansas Prison Scandal.* New York: Grove Press, 1969.

Nagel, William G. *An American Archipelago: The Federal Bureau of Prisons.* Philadelphia: American Foundation, 1974. (mimeo)

————. "On Behalf of a Moratorium on Prison Construction." *Crime and Delinquency* 23, No. 2 (April 1977), 154–172.

————. *The New Red Barn: A Critical Look at the Modern American Prison.* New York: Walker and Co., 1973.

National Council on Crime and Delinquency. *Four Thousand Lifetimes: A Study of Time Served and Parole Outcomes.* Davis, Calif.: NCCD Research Center, 1973.

————. *Guided Group Interaction.* Hackensack, N.J.: NCCD Training Center, 1972.

————. "NewGate: New Hope Through Education." In Gary R. Perlstein and Thomas R. Phelps (eds.), *Alternatives to Prison: Community-Based Corrections.* Pacific Palisades, Calif.: Goodyear Publishing Co., 1975.

————. *Residential Corrections: Alternatives to Incarceration.* Davis, Calif.: NCCD Research Center, 1973.

National Council on Crime and Delinquency. Board of Directors. "Jurisdiction over Status Offenses Should Be Removed from the Juvenile Court: A Policy Statement." *Crime and Delinquency* 21, No. 2 (April 1975), 97–99.

National Institute of Law Enforcement and Criminal Justice. *Controlled Confrontation: The Ward Grievance Procedure of the California Youth Authority: An Exemplary Project.* February 1976.

Needham, Ted, and Needham, Howard. *Alcatraz.* Millbrae, Calif.: Celestial Arts, 1976.

Newton, Anne. "Aid to the Victim: Part I: Compensation and Restitution." *Crime and Delinquency Literature* 8, No. 3 (September 1976), 368–390.

New York State Special Commission on Attica. *Attica: The Official Report.* New York: Praeger Publishers, 1972.

Nicholson, Richard C. "Transactional Analysis: A New Method for Helping Offenders." *Federal Probation* 34, No. 3 (September 1970), 29–38.

North, David S. "Women Offenders: Breaking the Training Model." *Manpower* (February 1975), 13–19.

O'Donnell, Pierce; Churgin, Michael J.; and Curtis, Dennis E. *Toward a Just and Effective Sentencing System: Agenda for Legislative Reform.* New York: Praeger Publishers, 1977.

Oswald, Russell G. *Attica: My Story.* Garden City, N.Y.: Doubleday, 1972.

Park, James W. L. "What Is a Political Prisoner? The Politics of Predators." *American Journal of Correction* 34, No. 6 (1972), 22–23.

Pell, Eve (ed.). *Maximum Security: Letters from Prison.* New York: E. P. Dutton, 1972.

Pennsylvania. Governor's Study Commission on Capital Punishment. *Report.* Harrisburg, Penn., 1973.

Perl, Kathleen Yaskiw. "Policy Statements and Model Acts." *Crime and Delinquency Literature* 8, No. 2 (June 1976), 237–253.

Pierce, Lawrence W. "Rehabilitation in Corrections: A Reassessment." *Federal Probation* 38, No. 2 (1974), 14–19.

Powell, Lewis E., and Serrill, Michael S. "Profile/Georgia." *Corrections Magazine* 1, No. 2 (November-December 1974), 65–76.

Prigmore, Charles S., and Watkins, John Cumming, Jr. "Correctional Manpower: Are We 'The Society of Captives'?" *Federal Probation* 36 (December 1972), 12–19.

"Procunier: A Candid Conversation." *Corrections Magazine* 1, No. 4 (March-April 1975), 3–8.

Reagen, Michael V., and Stoughton, Donald M. *School Behind Bars: A Descriptive Overview of Correctional Education in the American Prison System.* Metuchen, N.J.: Scarecrow Press, 1976.

Reasons, Charles E. "The Politicizing of Crime, the Criminal and the Criminologist." *Journal of Criminal Law and Criminology* 64, No. 4 (1973), 471–477.

Rector, Milton G. "The Extravagance of Imprisonment." *Crime and Delinquency* 21, No. 4 (1975), 323–330.

Roberts, Albert R. (ed.). *Readings in Prison Education.* Springfield, Ill.: Charles C. Thomas, 1973.

Rogovin, Charles. "The Genesis of the Law Enforcement Assistance Administration: A Personal Account." *Columbia Human Rights Law Review* 5, No. 1 (1973), 9–25.

Root, Lawrence S. "Work Release Legislation." *Federal Probation* 36, No. 1 (1972), 38–42.

Rose, Susan. "The Fallacy of the Medical Model as Applied to Corrections." In Edward E. Peoples (ed.), *Readings in Correctional Casework and Counseling.* Pacific Palisades, Calif.: Goodyear Publishing Co., 1975.

Rubington, Earl, and Weinberg, Martin (eds.). *Deviance: Interactionist Perspective.* 2d ed. New York: Macmillan Co., 1973.

Rushing, William (ed.). *Deviant Behavior and Social Process.* Chicago: Rand McNally and Co., 1969.

"Santarelli Bans Funding for Modifying Behavior." *LEAA Newsletter* 3, No. 11 (March 1974), 2.

Schafer, Stephen. *The Political Prisoner: The Problem of Morality and Crime.* New York: Free Press, 1974.

——. *The Victim and His Criminal.* New York: Random House, 1968.

Scull, Andrew T. *Decarceration: Community Treatment and the Deviant—A Radical View.* Englewood Cliffs, N.J.: Prentice-Hall, 1977.

Sedgeman, Judy. Review of *The Criminal Personality: Volume II* in *Psychotherapy and Social Science Review* 11, No. 4 (April 1977), 4–10.

Sellin, Thorsten. "The Origin of the 'Pennsylvania System of Prison Discipline.' " *Prison Journal* 50, No. 1 (Spring-Summer 1970), 13–20.

Sepsi, Victor J. "Girl Recidivists." *Journal of Research in Crime and Delinquency* 11, No. 1 (1974), 70–79.

Serrill, Michael S. "Critics of Corrections Speak Out." *Corrections Magazine* 2, No. 3 (March 1976), 3 ff.

——. "The Fortune Society: Championing the Ex-Offender." *Corrections Magazine* 1, No. 5 (May-June 1975), 13–20.

——. "Juvenile Corrections in Massachusetts." *Corrections Magazine* 2, No. 2 (November-December 1975), 3 ff.

——. "LEAA." *Corrections Magazine* 2, No. 4 (June 1976), 3 ff.

——. "LEAA's National Clearinghouse for Criminal Justice Planning and Architecture." *Corrections Magazine* 2, No. 4 (June 1976), 18–19.

——. "Massachusetts Adult Corrections System." *Corrections Magazine* 2, No. 2 (November-December 1975), 41–48.

——. "The Minnesota Restitution Center." *Corrections Magazine* 1, No. 3 (January-February 1975), 13–20.

——. "Prison Furloughs in America." *Corrections Magazine* 1, No. 6 (July-August 1975), 3 ff.

——. "Prison Population Rises Again, But at a Slower Rate." *Corrections Magazine,* No. 2 (June 1978), 20–24.

———. "Profile/California." *Corrections Magazine* 1, No. 1 (September 1974), 3–52.

———. "Profile/District of Columbia." *Corrections Magazine* 1, No. 4 (March-April 1975), 37–52.

———. "Profile/Minnesota." *Corrections Magazine* 1, No. 3 (January-February 1975), 3 ff.

———. "Profile/New Jersey." *Corrections Magazine* 1, No. 2 (November-December 1974), 3 ff.

———. "Treating Sex Offenders in New Jersey." *Corrections Magazine* 1, No. 2 (November-December 1974), 13–24.

———. "Walpole Prison: After the Storm." *Corrections Magazine* 2, No. 2 (November-December 1975), 49–54.

Sigler, Robert T., and others. *Furlough Programs for Inmates: Single Site Evaluation Model.* Washington, D.C.: National Institute of Law Enforcement and Criminal Justice, Law Enforcement Assistance Administration, June 1976.

———. *Furlough Programs for Inmates: Final Report.* Washington, D.C.: National Institute of Law Enforcement and Criminal Justice, Law Enforcement Assistance Administration, June 1976.

Simon, Rita. "American Women and Crime." *Annals of the American Academy of Political Science* 423 (1976), 31–46.

Singer, Linda R., and Keating, J. Michael. *Grievance Mechanisms in American Corrections: The State of the Art.* Washington, D.C.: Center for Correctional Justice, 1975. (mimeo)

Smart, Carol. *Women, Crime and Criminology: A Feminist Critique.* London: Routledge and Kegan Paul, 1977.

Smith, Robert R. "A Survey of Good-Time Policies and Practices in American Correctional Agencies." *Journal of Criminal Justice* 3, No. 3 (1975), 237–241.

Sommer, Robert. *The End of Imprisonment.* New York: Oxford University Press, 1976.

Stephenson, Richard M., and Scarpitti, Frank R. *Group Interaction As Theory: The Use of the Small Group in Corrections.* Westport, Conn.: Greenwood Press, 1974.

Suval, Elizabeth M., and Brisson, Robert C. "Neither Beauty Nor Beast: Female Criminal Homicide Offenders." *International Journal of Criminology and Penology* 2, No. 1 (1974), 23–34.

Sykes, Gresham M. *The Society of Captives.* Princeton, N.J.: Princeton University Press, 1971.

Taylor, A. J. W. "The Significance of 'Darls' or 'Special Relationships' for Borstal Girls." *British Journal of Criminology* 5 (October 1965), 406–419.

Teeters, Negley K. "The Passing of Cherry Hill: Most Famous Prison in the World." *Prison Journal* 50, No. 1 (Spring-Summer 1970), 3–12.

Texas Corrections Department. Research and Development Division. *A National Survey of Good Time Laws and Administrative Procedures.* Huntsville, Tex., 1973.

Thomas, Charles W., and Peterson, David M. *Prison Organization and Inmate Subcultures.* Indianapolis: Bobbs-Merrill, 1977.

Tittle, Charles R. "Inmate Organization: Sex Differentiation and the Influence of Criminal Subcultures." *American Sociological Review* 34 (August 1969), 429–505.

———, and Tittle, Drollene P. "Social Organization of Prisoners: An Empirical Test." *Social Forces* 43 (December 1964), 216–221.

Twentieth Century Fund. *Fair and Certain Punishment.* New York: McGraw-Hill, 1976.

United Nations. Economic and Social Council. *Capital Punishment: Report of the Secretary-General.* New York, 1973.

U.S. Bureau of Prisons. *Breaking with the Past: The Changing View of Correctional Facilities.* (No date).

———. *The Residential Center: Corrections in the Community.* (No date).

———. *Success and Failure of Federal Offenders Released in 1970.* Washington, D.C., 1974. (mimeo)

U.S. Department of Justice. *The Law Enforcement Assistance Administration: A Partnership For Crime Control.* Law Enforcement Assistance Administration, 1976.

U.S. Federal Prisons Industries, Inc. *1975 Annual Report.* Printing Plant, U.S. Penitentiary, Marion, Illinois, 1976.

U.S. House of Representatives. Internal Security Committee. *Revolutionary Target: The American Penal System.* Washington, D.C.: U.S. Government Printing Office, 1973.

U.S. Law Enforcement Assistance Administration. *Guidelines and Standards for Halfway Houses and Community Treatment Centers.* Washington, D.C.: U.S. Government Printing Office, 1973.

U.S. National Advisory Commission on Criminal Justice Standards and Goals. *Corrections.* Washington, D.C.: U.S. Government Printing Office, 1973.

U.S. Public Health Service. *Graduated Release.* Public Health Service Publication No. 2128. Washington, D.C.: U.S. Government Printing Office, 1971.

Vedder, Clyde B., and Somerville, Dora B. *The Delinquent Girl.* 2d ed. Springfield, Ill.: Charles C. Thomas, 1975.

Velimesis, Margery L. "The Female Offender." *Crime and Delinquency Literature* 7, No. 1 (March 1975), 94–112.

Waller, Irvin. *Men Released from Prison.* Toronto: University of Toronto Press, 1974.

Ward, David A., and Kassebaum, Gene G. *Women's Prison: Sex and Social Structure.* Chicago: Aldine, 1965.

Weiss, Karel (ed.). *The Prison Experience: An Anthology.* New York: Delacorte Press, 1976.

Wenk, Ernst A.; Halatyn, Thomas V.; and Harlow, Nora. *An Analysis of Classification Factors for Young Adult Offenders: Volume I: Background of the Study and Statistical Description of the Total Study*

Population. Davis, Calif.: Research Center, National Council on Crime and Delinquency, October 1974.

Wheeler, Stanton. "Socialization in Correctional Communities." *American Sociological Review* 26 (October 1961), 697–712.

Whinery, Leo H., and others. *Predictive Sentencing: An Empirical Evaluation.* Lexington, Mass.: D. C. Heath, 1976.

Wicker, Tom. *A Time to Die.* New York: Quadrangle, 1975.

Wilkins, Barbara. "Bio." *People* 6, No. 15 (October 11, 1976), 86 ff.

Wilks, Judith, and Martinson, Robert. "Is the Treatment of Criminal Offenders Really Necessary?" *Federal Probation* 40, No. 1 (March 1976), 3–9.

Williams, Vergil L. "Administration of Justice: A Bibliographical Selection." *Choice* 9 (July-August 1972), 611–618.

———. "Designing Games to Teach Correctional Skills." *Crime and Delinquency* 16, No. 4 (October 1970), 434–439.

———,and Fish, Mary. *Convicts, Codes and Contraband: The Prison Life of Men and Women.* Cambridge, Mass.: Ballinger Publishing Co., 1974.

———. "Optimum Prison Size: Cost Behavior vs. Rehabilitation Goals." *American Journal of Correction* 34 (March-April 1972), 14–19.

———. "A Proposed Model for Individualized Offender Restitution Through State Victim Compensation." In Israel Drapkin and Emilio Viano (eds.), *Victimology: A New Focus: Volume II: Society's Reaction to Victimization.* Lexington, Mass.: Lexington Books, 1974.

———. "Rehabilitation and Economic Self-Interest." *Crime and Delinquency* 17, No. 4 (October 1971), 406–413.

———. "The Token Economy in Prison: Rehabilitation or Motivation?" *Journal of Correctional Education* 24 (Fall 1972), 4–7.

Yablonsky, Lewis. *Synanon: The Tunnel Back.* New York: Macmillan Co., 1965.

Yochelson, Samuel, and Samenow, Stanton E. *The Criminal Personality: Volume I: A Profile for Change.* New York: Jason Aronson, 1976.

———. *The Criminal Personality: Volume II: The Change Process.* New York: Jason Aronson, 1977.

Zalman, Marvin. *Indeterminate Sentence Laws: Present, Past and Future.* Dallas, Tex.: Academy of Criminal Justice Sciences, 1976.

Ziegler, Jerry. "America's Largest Prison." *Corrections Magazine* 1, No. 4 (March-April 1975), 9–16.

INDEX